ANTIOCHOS III AND THE CITIES OF WESTERN ASIA MINOR

Antiochos III and the Cities of Western Asia Minor

JOHN MA

OXFORD

UNIVERSITY PRESS

OXFORD

UNIVERSITY PRESS

Great Clarendon Street, Oxford OX2 6DP

Oxford University Press is a department of the University of Oxford.
It furthers the University's objective of excellence in research, scholarship,
and education by publishing worldwide in

Oxford New York

Auckland Bangkok Buenos Aires Cape Town Chennai
Dar es Salaam Delhi Hong Kong Istanbul Karachi Kolkata
Kuala Lumpur Madrid Melbourne Mexico City Mumbai Nairobi
São Paulo Shanghai Singapore Taipei Tokyo Toronto

and an associated company in Berlin

Oxford is a registered trade mark of Oxford University Press
in the UK and in certain other countries

Published in the United States
by Oxford University Press Inc., New York

British Library Cataloguing in Publication Data

Data available

Library of Congress Cataloging in Publication Data
Ma, John.
Antiochos III and the cities of Western Asia Minor / John Ma.
p. cm.
Includes bibliographical references (p.   ).
ISBN 0-19-815219-1 hb
1. Cities and towns, Ancient—Turkey.
2. Greeks—Turkey—History—To 1500.
3. Antiochos III, King of Syria, ca. 242-187 B.C.
4. Syria—History—355 B.C.-284 A.D.   I. Title.
DS155.M293   1999
939'.2—dc21   99-23236
ISBN 0-19-815219-1 (cased)
ISBN 0-19-925051-0 (paperback)

1 3 5 7 9 10 8 6 4 2

Typeset by Regent Typesetting, London
Printed in Great Britain on acid-free paper by
Biddles Ltd., Guildford and King's Lynn

PREFACE

This work (the revised and expanded version of a D.Phil. thesis) is not a biography of Antiochos III and does not cover all of this interesting figure's reign. Rather, it concentrates on a particular region, Asia Minor, and on a particular theme, the relation between the Hellenistic empire and its structures of control and exploitation, and the Hellenistic *polis*. Both aspects can be studied thanks to a body of epigraphical material; for convenience, the relevant inscriptions are reproduced and translated in a separate annexe to the main text, where these inscriptions are referred to by their number in the annexe (in the form 'document 4, 1', meaning no. 4 in the dossier at line 1). To treat the theme through this particular test-case, I drew on a number of historiographical approaches in Hellenistic studies: political narrative, analysis of power structures, and, to my mind the most exciting development, close attention to language, rhetoric, and self-presentation. The issues surrounding presentation (analytical essay rather than biography) and sources (principally the epigraphy of the Hellenistic kings and that of the Hellenistic *poleis*) are explored in the introduction and (indirectly) the conclusion, where I try to justify my historiographical choices. I attempted to make the material and its treatment accessible to Classicists and historians who were not specialists of the third century BC. More specifically, in its present form, the work is addressed to two communities within Classics: epigraphist–historians of the Hellenistic period (in the hope of showing that a little bit of theory or at least an attempt at conceptual and abstract approaches to the material cannot harm), but also interpreters of texts (in the hope of drawing attention to material which is gripping in its details and its directness, 'good to read' and underexploited). Whether I will have succeeded in reaching any of these audiences is not for me to say.

During the elaboration of the work, I incurred many debts: it is a pleasure to list some of them, with expressions of my thanks and my gratitude, which of course do not imply agreement, or responsibility for remaining mistakes in content.

First, I take great pleasure in thanking some of my teachers. To my supervisor, F. Millar, I owe thanks for guidance during and beyond the conception and the writing of the thesis, and for

encouragement throughout the process. A number of methodological traits were developed under his advice: attention to detail
and concrete processes, coupled with awareness of the very real,
'performative', force of language as preserved in our documents,
written both in 'king-speak' and in 'city-speak' (the association of
the two approaches is paradoxical only in appearance). At least,
these were the most basic principles I attempted to follow in the
present work. I am also glad to thank S. Hornblower, my college
academic adviser, for comment and criticism on every chapter and
assistance at every stage; in addition, as my undergraduate tutor, he
first introduced me to the work of L. Robert and urged me to
conduct research on the Greek East. N. Purcell also was my college
academic adviser for a term, and taught me how to bear geography
and resources in mind when writing political history (and even
non-political history). Furthermore, I wish to thank J. Ober for
showing, both in his written work and in discussion, that it was
possible to conceive of analyses which would take into account both
the realities of power and the importance of language in shaping
these realities. On another front, I have been very fortunate to learn
something about epigraphy and Hellenistic history, in more or less
formal ways, from the scholarship and the standards of three
historians: Ph. Gauthier (who assisted me in crucial ways at the
beginning of the thesis, and whose seminar I was lucky to attend
for a few weeks); Chr. Habicht (who gave a lecture course and a
graduate seminar I attended in Hamburg in 1995, and read the
thesis at various stages); P. Herrmann (who helped me very greatly
early on, and who kindly advised me often and on many matters
during the writing of the thesis). They may not always approve of
what I say in this work or of the ways I say it, but I could not have
said it without having learnt very much from them, and I am deeply
grateful for their teaching and their advice. Finally, I would like to
thank P. Derow and M. Austin, the examiners of my thesis, for
many considerate and helpful comments on substance and on style;
and the anonymous committee which saw fit to award the thesis the
Conington Prize for 1997.

   Likewise, it is a pleasure to acknowledge my great debt to the
following, for assistance, advice, criticism, or simply discussion:
A. Bertrand, W. Blümel, G. Bowersock, A. Chaniotis, C. Crowther
(especially for his help with the epigraphical dossier), P. Derow, Ph.
Gauthier, Chr. Habicht, Kl. Hallof, D. Heimann, P. Herrmann, L.
Holford-Strevens, R. Lane Fox, J. Lightfoot (for reading through
an earlier version of this text), H. Malay and his assistant C.
Tanrıver, A. Meadows (for discussing written work, sharing ideas,

and helping me on the Ptolemaic side of things), S. Price,
N. Purcell, G. Rehrenböck, G. Rogers, M. Sayar, E. Vassilika and
P. Wilson at the Fitzwilliam Museum (for help with the Ilion
decree, *OGIS* 219, or rather the physical object itself, the monumental text *qua* carved stone). Individual remarks in the text make
clear the magnitude of my debt.

Finally, to All Souls College I owe thanks for material support
and help with travel abroad, to look at inscriptions, sites, and
landscapes of Asia Minor in September 1995 and April 1997; and to
H. O'Shea and G. Godwin at OUP for the making of this book.

J.M.

September 1998
All Souls College and Princeton

PREFACE TO THE PAPERBACK EDITION

Enough work has appeared on Hellenistic history and, specifically, on the years of Antiochos III, to make it interesting to add some texts and pointers towards new work: these appear in the sections Afterthoughts and Addenda. The pace of work also makes it clear that it is impossible to have the last word on the various topics treated in this book—this has not prevented me from writing some further observations. In addition, I have corrected some misprints, updated some references, and added a concordance to earlier places of publication. M. Nafissi has recently revised the letter of Laodike III to Iasos and the Iasian decree; I have tried to take his findings into account.

This book received the Hellenic Foundation's 2000 Award, for which I am delighted to thank the Hellenic Foundation. I would further like to thank the following people, for help the first time round, or since the book was first published: J.-M. Bertrand for many illuminating conversations, A. Bowman, A. Bresson, P. Brown (εὐνοίας ἕνεκεν), A. Erskine, A. Grafton, J. Katz, F. Lefèvre, J. Masters (for hospitality on the surprisingly rough Ionian coast), R. Parker, G. Shipley, and R. van Bremen.

J.M.

February 2002
Corpus Christi College, Oxford

CONTENTS

LIST OF DOCUMENTS

I. 216–209 BC

II. 203–201 BC

III. 197–190 BC

IV. Date Undetermined, but Certainly under Antiochos III

IV. Aftermath

ABBREVIATIONS

INSCRIPTIONS

All abbreviations of the form *I. Iasos* (to be expanded into *Die Inschriften von Iasos*) refer to volumes in the series *Inschriften griechischer Städte aus Kleinasien* (*IK*), Bonn, 1972– . Other abbreviations, starting e.g. with *Inschr.*, are earlier publications, which do not belong to the *IK* series.

I. Alexandreia Troas	(*IK* 43). *Die Inschriften von Alexandreia Troas*. Ricl, M. (1997).
I. Erythrai	(*IK* 1) *Die Inschriften von Erythrai und Klazomenai*. Engelmann, H., Merkelbach, R. 2 vols. (1972, 1973).
I. Iasos	(*IK* 28.1–28.2) *Die Inschriften von Iasos*. Blümel, W. 2 vols. (1985).
I. Ilion	(*IK* 3) *Die Inschriften von Ilion*. Frisch, P. (1975).
I. Laodikeia am Lykos	(*IK* 49) *Die Inschriften von Laodikeia am Lykos*. Corsten, Th. Teil 1: Die Inschriften (1997).
I. Mylasa	(*IK* 34–5) *Die Inschriften von Mylasa*. Blümel, W. 2 vols. (1987, 1988).
I. Stratonikeia	(*IK* 21, 22.1, 22.2) *Die Inschriften von Stratonikeia*. Şahin, M. Ç. 3 vols. (1981, 1982, 1990).
I. Tralleis	(*IK* 36.1) *Die Inschriften von Tralleis*. Poljakov, F. B. vol. 1 (1989).
Inschr. Asklepieion	Habicht, Chr., *Die Inschriften des Asklepieions* (Altertümer von Pergamon 8.3), Berlin, 1969.
Iscr. Cos	Segre, M., *Iscrizioni di Cos* (Monografie della Scuola archeologica di Atene et delle missioni italiane in Oriente 6), 2 vols., Rome, 1993.
Iscr. Cret.	Guarducci, M., *Inscriptiones Creticae*, 4 vols., Rome, 1935–50.
Inschr. Delphinion	Rehm, A., in G. Kawerau and A. Rehm, *Das Delphinion in Milet* (Milet. Ergebnisse der Ausgrabungen und Untersuchungen seit dem Jahre 1899, ed. Th. Wiegand, vol. 1, fasc. 3), Berlin, 1914: 162–442.
Inschr. Didyma	Rehm, A., *Didyma* II: *Die Inschriften*, Berlin, 1958.
Inscr. Lindos	Blinkenberg, Chr., *Lindos. Fouilles de l'acropole 1902–1914*. II. *Inscriptions*. 2 vols., Berlin and Copenhagen, 1941.

Inschr. Magnesia	Kern, O., *Die Inschriften von Magnesia am Mäander*, Berlin, 1900.
Inschr. Pergamon	Fränkel, M. (with E. Fabricius and C. Schuchhardt), *Die Inschriften von Pergamon* (Altertümer von Pergamon 8), 2 vols., Berlin, 1890, 1895.
Inschr. Priene	Hiller von Gaertringen, F., *Die Inschriften von Priene*, Berlin, 1906.
BE	*Bulletin Épigraphique* (referred to by year and rubric number).
CIG	Böckh, A., Franz, J., Curtius, E., and Kirchhoff, A. (eds.), *Corpus Inscriptionum Graecarum*, 4 vols., Berlin, 1828–77.
FD 3	Colin, G., Bourguet, E., Daux, D., and Salaç, A. (eds.), *Fouilles de Delphes* 3. *Epigraphie*, Paris, 1929– .
GHI	Tod, M. N., *A Selection of Greek Historical Inscriptions*, vol. 2., Oxford, 1948.
GIBM	Newton, C., Hicks, E. L., Hirschfeld, G., and Marshall, F. M., *The Collection of Ancient Greek Inscriptions in the British Museum*, 4 vols., Oxford, 1874–1916.
GVI	Peek, W., *Grieschische Vers-Inschriften*, Berlin, 1955.
ISE	Moretti, L., *Iscrizioni storiche ellenistiche*, 2 vols., Florence, 1967–75.
LBW	Le Bas, Ph., and Waddington, W.-H., *Voyage archéologique en Grèce et en Asie Mineure*, 3 vols., Paris, 1851–70.
ML	Meiggs, R., and Lewis, D., *A Selection of Greek Historical Inscriptions to the End of the Fifth Century* BC (rev. edn.), Oxford, 1988.
OGIS	Dittenberger, W., *Orientis Graeci inscriptiones selectae. Supplementum sylloges inscriptionum Graecarum*, 2 vols., Leipzig, 1903–5 (orig.; unchanged reprint, Hildesheim, 1960).
RC	Welles, C. B., *Royal Correspondence in the Hellenistic Period. A Study in Greek Epigraphy*, London, 1934 (orig.; unchanged reprint, Chicago, 1974).
Sardis	Buckler, W. H., and Robinson, D. M., *Sardis* VII. *Greek and Latin inscriptions*, Part I, Leyden, 1932.
SEG	*Supplementum Epigraphicum Graecum.*
Syll.	Dittenberger, W., *Sylloge inscriptionum Graecarum*, 4 vols. (3rd edn.), Leipzig, 1915–24 (orig.; unchanged reprint, Hildesheim 1960).
TAM	*Tituli Asiae Minoris*, Vienna, 1901– .
Tit. Cal.	Segre, M., *Tituli Calymnii*, Bergamo, 1952.

PAPYRI AND COINS

PCZ   Edgar, C. C. (ed.), *Catalogue général des antiquités égyptiennes du Musée du Caire: Zenon Papyri*, 4 vols., Cairo, 1925–31.

P. Haun.   Larsen, T. (ed.), *Papyri Graecae Haunienses*, vol. 1, Copenhagen, 1942.

C. Ord Ptol   Lenger, M.-Th., *Corpus des ordonnances des Ptolémées*. (2nd edn.), Brussels, 1980.

BMC   *A Catalog of the Greek Coins in the British Museum*, London, 1873– .

WSM   Newell, E. T., *The Coinage of the Western Seleucid Mints from Seleucus I to Antiochos III* (American Numismatic Society. Numismatic Studies 4), New York, 1941.

PRIMARY LITERATURE

Bosworth, *HCA*   Bosworth, A. B., *A Historical Commentary on Arrian's* History of Alexander, 2 vols., Oxford, 1980–95.

FGrHist   Jacoby, F. (ed.), *Die Fragmente der griechischen Historiker*, Berlin and Leiden, 1923–62.

ORF   Malcovati, E. (ed.), *Oratorum Romanorum fragmenta liberae rei publicae* (4th edn.) 2 vols., Turin, 1976–9.

Staatsvertr.   Bengtson, H., and Schmitt, H. H., *Die Staatsverträge des Altertums*, 2 vols., Munich, 1962–9.

Walbank, *HCP*   Walbank, F. W., *A Historical Commentary on Polybius*, 3 vols., Oxford, 1957–79.

SECONDARY LITERATURE

CAH   *Cambridge Ancient History*.

Preisigke, *Wörterbuch*   Preisigke, F., *Wörterbuch der griechischen Papyrusurkunden mit Einschluss der griechischen Inschriften, Aufschriften, Ostraka, Mumienschilder usw. aus Aegypten*, 3 vols., Berlin, 1925–31.

Robert, *OMS*   Robert, L., *Opera Minora Selecta. Epigraphie et antiquités grecques*, 7 vols., Amsterdam, 1969–90.

Wilhelm, *Akademieschriften*   Wilhelm, Ad., *Akademieschriften zur griechischen Inschriftenkunde* (Opuscula. Sammelausgaben seltener und bisher nicht selbständig erschienener wissenschaftlicher Abhandlungen 8), 3 vols., Leipzig, 1974.

ESAR	Frank, T. (ed.), *An Economic Survey of Ancient Rome*, Baltimore, 1933–40.
MRR	Broughton, T. R. S., *The Magistrates of the Roman Republic*, 2 vols. and supplement, New York, 1951–60.

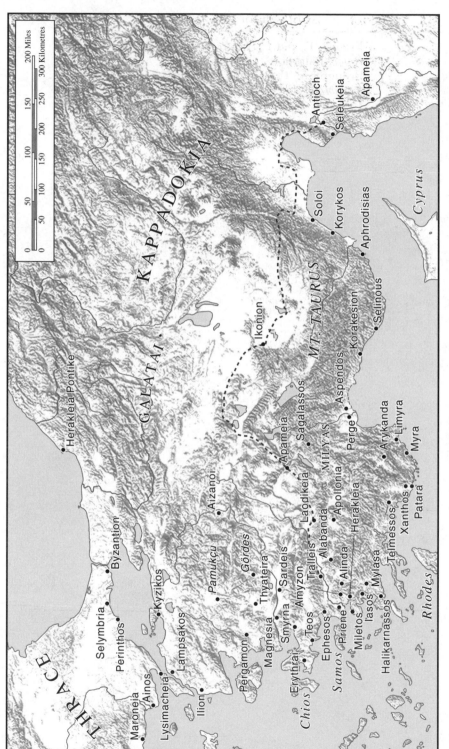

Map 1. Anatolia and the Seleukid road from Antioch to the 'land on the other side of the Taurus'. Achaios took this road on his unsuccessful attempt on the Seleukid throne in 220; Antiochos III or his armies travelled on this road in 216, c.203, in 197, and one last time in winter 190/189, after Magnesia.

Map 2. Lydia, Ionia, Karia: the better documented regions of Asia Minor. Relevant cities are indicated, as well as mountains, rivers, and some important regions or plains.

INTRODUCTION

The Great King and the Cities

How to talk about the Hellenistic world? The topic is well agreed on (if not always defined with rigour), the scholarship plentiful, so that the diversity of this world and of possible approaches can be illustrated by some recent (or not so recent) works, without any claim at comprehensiveness. There have been synoptic treatments of the period, textbooks or essays rather than intensive scholarly studies (the exception still being M. Rostovtzeff's *Social and Economic History of the Hellenistic World*); other large-scale works have examined its political history, and the coming of Rome. Works have been devoted to regions or single cities, for instance Athens, the best-documented case. Individual Hellenistic kings have been treated in biographies or studies of their foreign policies; another approach has been to study dynasties or kingdoms (like the Seleukid realm, which S. Sherwin-White and A. Kuhrt have studied in *From Samarkhand to Sardis*, insisting on its Eastern dimension). Among countless thematic studies, a fertile development is the increasing number of 'dossiers par thème', along a model preconized by L. Robert: the gathering of all the evidence (predominantly documentary) for a phenomenon, followed by a critical edition and a commentary. This method allows for the clarification of issues and focused discussion. Most topics handled have been institutional: *asylia* (the recognition of a community's immunity from plunder and reprisals); international arbitration; treaties between the Cretan *poleis*; the financial institutions of the Hellenistic city.[1]

[1] This is not the place for a full bibliographical essay (see for instance the recent introduction by P. Cartledge, in Cartledge, Garnsey, and Gruen 1997: 1–19); a sense of the recent research can be gained from the series 'Hellenistic culture and society' brought out by the University of California Press or the 'Studies in Hellenistic civilization' from Aarhus University Press. Works alluded or referred to include Green 1990, Walbank 1992, Rostovtzeff 1941 (synoptic treatments); Will 1982, Gruen 1986 (political histories); Habicht 1997 (Athens); Mehl 1986, Billows 1990, Grainger 1990, Lund 1992, Franco 1993, Le Bohec 1993 (biographies); Schmitt 1964, Huss 1976 (foreign policies of individual kings); Sherwin-White and Kuhrt 1993 (Seleukids). Documentary-dossiers-cum-studies: Rigsby 1996, Ager 1996, Chaniotis 1996, Migeotte 1984 and 1992.

The present study superficially resembles the latter class, in that it gathers in an annexe a dossier of epigraphical documents, edited and briefly commented. But the focus is not quite a single, narrowly defined theme; rather, its origins lie in a page of Livy (33.38.1–7), reproducing the language and concepts of his source Polybios,[2] the great historian of the Hellenistic world. The passage describes a moment which is vivid, complex, and immensely evocative for the modern scholar of this period. Through the actors and the relations it portrays, it embodies cardinal themes or areas of interest, which make it a meaningful topic, beyond its immediate political and chronological context (the campaign of conquest, or, from the Seleukid viewpoint, reconquest, undertaken by Antiochos III in 197 and 196).[3]

Eodem anno Antiochus rex, cum hibernasset Ephesi, omnes Asiae civitates in antiquam imperii formulam redigere est conatus. Et ceteras quidem, aut quia locis planis positae erant aut quia parum moenibus armisque ac iuventuti fidebant, haud difficulter videbat iugum accepturas; Zmyrna et Lampsacus libertatem usurpabant, periculumque erat ne, si concessum iis foret quod intenderent, Zmyrnam in Aeolide Ioniaque, Lampsacum in Hellesponto aliae urbes sequerentur. Igitur et ipse ab Epheso ad Zmyrnam obsidendam misit et quae Abydi copiae erant praesidio tantum modico relicto duci ad Lampsacum oppugnandam iussit. Nec vi tantum terrebat, sed per legatos leniter adloquendo castigandoque temeritatem ac pertinaciam spem conabatur facere, brevi quod peterent habituros, sed cum satis et ipsis et omnibus aliis appareret, ab rege impetratam eos libertatem, non per occasionem raptam habere. Adversus quae respondebantur, nihil neque mirari neque suscensere Antiochum debere, si spem libertatis diferri non satis aequo animo paterentur.

In the same year, King Antiochos, after wintering at Ephesos, attempted to reduce all the cities of Asia into the ancient structure of sovereignty. And he saw that the others, because they were located on open sites, or did not readily trust their walls, their arms, and their men, would accept the yoke without difficulty; but Smyrna and Lampsakos were claiming their freedom, and there was a danger that if they got away with what they wanted, other cities would follow the example of Smyrna in Aiolis and Ionia, of Lampsakos in the Hellespont. Therefore, he sent troops from Ephesos to besiege Smyrna, and ordered the troops at Abydos to be led out to besiege Lampsakos, after leaving only a small garrison. Nor did he only try to frighten them with force, but, by addressing them gently through ambassadors and by reproaching them for their rashness and their stubbornness, he also tried to create the hope that they would soon have what they sought, but only when it was sufficiently clear both to them and

[2] For parallels, see Pol. 5.62.6: cities resisting or not resisting Antiochos III in Koile-Syria, depending on their strength; also 5.66.6; 5.77.3; 7.15.2; 35.3.9.
[3] On date (winter 197/6 rather than spring 196), Ch. 2 § 4.

to all the others that they had obtained their liberty from the king, and did not enjoy it as the result of grasping at opportunity. To these words, their answer was that Antiochos should be in no way surprised nor angry, if they did not suffer with an even spirit the prospect that their hope of liberty be deferred.

The passage gives us the perspective of one of the central figures in Hellenistic history: a king, in that age of kings, presented as he levels an imperialist gaze on future subjects. Yet all the elements involved immediately call for further commentary. In the first place, it is important not to adopt the same generalizing perspective as Antiochos, simply to speak of *omnes civitates Asiae* as if that bald expression, evoking the map of royal strategic interests, could substitute for historical analysis. 'All the cities of Asia Minor': the first topic that the Livian passage introduces is the landscape itself, in danger of being forgotten because of its very ubiquity in the plot which it helps to shape.[4] Significant facts about this region are its magnitude, its lushness and variety, and the way in which size, resources, and diversity collaborate even nowadays to create a very large number and range of environments for human habitation, such as great harbour towns, impressive agricultural cities in the river plains, scattered villages in the highlands which are such a noticeable feature even in the Western part of the country. The same features characterized this region in ancient times, and explains the profusion of ancient communities in Asia Minor.

'All the cities of Asia'—the expression regroups communities of widely differing sizes: at one end of the scale, large, ancient, wealthy cities like Miletos or Mylasa, with their great territories and their expansionist urge to annex their neighbours; and at the other end of the scale, smaller, remote communities, like the Aiolian cities of Aigai and its neighbour Temnos, or recently discovered Piginda in the Morsynos valley.[5] Another way of looking at the diversity of this world is to examine the origins of the communities. 'All the cities': the phrase immediately evokes the old Greek cities—to name the most prominent, Lampsakos, Ilion, Phokaia, Smyrna, Erythrai, Teos, Kolophon (in reality two communities, Old Kolophon and Notion, living as a single *polis*), Ephesos, Magnesia on Maeander,

---

[4] For a sense of Asia Minor as landscape, physical and human, and the history that took place there, see Magie 1950: chs. 1–5 and 11, the more striking a feat of historical writing for the fact that Magie apparently never went to Turkey. The work also covers most of the cities, with a very full and still useful roster of references.

[5] On Aigai and Temnos, Robert 1937: 74–110. Piginda is mentioned provisionally by F. Ölmez, *Arkeoloji Dergisi* 3 (1995), 165–6, editing an inscription from the site, mentioning Zeus Pigindenos: this document substantiates a notation of Steph. Byz. s.v. Piginda. But see now Addenda.

Priene, Miletos, Iasos, Halikarnassos. But the category must also be extended to include the communities which had adopted Greek political forms (decision-making assembly, council, magistrates) along with the language: in the third century, they considered themselves, and, as far as we can tell, were considered by others as *poleis*.[6] Such communities include Sardeis in Lydia; in western Karia, Mylasa, Herakleia under Latmos, Euromos, Pedasa, Bargylia, Kaunos; in Eastern Karia, the hilltop fortress of Tabai; in Lykia, Xanthos, Limyra, Arykanda; also smaller communities such as Kildara or Amyzon, hill communities of western Karia (like Piginda, mentioned above). Another category yet is that of the communities founded or renamed by the kings (Cohen 1995): military settlements such as Thyateira in Lydia, great cities such as Stratonikeia in western Karia or Apameia in Phrygia, humbler affairs such as Apollonia under Salbake on the east Karian plateau near Tabai. Finally, this profusion of *poleis*, each with its own particular physical setting and identity, should not obscure other forms of settlement in Asia Minor, beyond the cities: the villages (two of which, Kiddioukome and Neonteichos in Phrygia, produced a remarkable joint decree honouring the agents of their landlord), the 'royal land' and the estates of the royal favourites, and, most importantly, the great shrines (the best documented of which is the Karian shrine of Labraunda, on a pass north of Mylasa).[7]

The Livian passage quoted earlier concerns a historical landscape which is fascinating because of its diversity, but also because of the richness of the documentation, mainly epigraphical, which is already very large and increases yearly (see below). In addition, much of this material has been treated by the peculiarly concrete and appealing genius of the epigraphist–historian, Louis Robert, whose lifetime's work focused on Asia Minor and explored its historical geography. For the purposes of the present study, the area concerned will be the 'Seleukid' portion of Asia Minor: much of the coastal strip with its maritime cities, ἐπιθαλάσσιοι πόλεις (the western end of the Propontis, the Straits and the Troad, Aiolis, Ionia, Karia, Lykia, Pamphylia, Rough Kilikia, Smooth Kilikia), and the western third of the Anatolian landmass. This includes the river valleys

---

[6] See further Ch. 3 § 3. Robert 1987, 526–32, illustrates how integrated Hellenistic Kaunos was in the world of Greek *poleis*. Document **16** shows how Alabanda, in 202/1, was fully accepted on a diplomatic level of interaction by the Delphic Amphiktions (though admittedly they referred to the Alabandans as 'kinsmen of the Greeks' rather than simply fellow-Greeks).

[7] The village decree is in Wörrle 1975 (*I. Laodikeia am Lykos* 1). On the royal land, see Ch. 3. Labraunda: the material is published by Crampa 1969. The topic of Anatolian shrines is treated in Debord 1982, Boffo 1985; see also Sartre 1995: 104–5.

which descend from the higher inland: the Kaikos valley (the heartland of the Attalid kingdom), the Hermos valley (which helps define
the 'Hyrkanian plain', the western, fertile triangle in western Lydia,
between Magnesia under Sipylos, Thyateira, and Sardeis), the
Kaikos corridor, and, most importantly, the Maeander plain and its
tributaries, which completed the great valley with secondary, but
important lines of communication (Marsyas, Harpasos, Morsynos).
Other areas fall within this definition and will be mentioned often,
though lack of precise evidence for our period prevents new or
concrete treatment: the hills of Mysia, the Hellespontic plains, the
plateau of Phrygia and Lykaonia, at the end of the 'Seleukid road'
which starts with the Maeander valley and connects with northern
Syria. Off this road lie two important and increasingly well-known
regions: the highlands of Pisidia with its cities, and the Pamphylian
plain. Finally, other areas in the region will be mentioned only as
they impinge on the narrative outline: cities in or near northern Asia
Minor, such as Kyzikos, Byzantion, and Perinthos (not strictly in
Asia Minor, but involved in its history), Herakleia Pontike; the kingdom of Bithynia; the principalities of the Galatians; the kingdom of
Kappadokia; and, most importantly, Rhodes, which was a naval
power, but also possessed a continental territory (the Rhodian
Peraia) and harboured further territorial ambitions on the mainland.

The narrative outline which determines the limits of the geographical context is part of the second theme the Livian passage
brings in: the high political history of the Hellenistic age. The
decision by Antiochos III to impose 'the yoke' on 'all the cities of
Asia' manifests the vitality of the high political history of the period
(the late third and early second centuries BC), even at the time of
imminent collision with Rome: from this point of view, these years
were as vital (or unstable) as the earlier age of the Diadochs. It is a
mistake to speak of the Hellenistic world's 'weakening', 'exhaus-
tion', or 'decay' merely because the period in question was immediately followed by the Romans' success, military and political, and
their subsequent hegemony. The Livian passage, which temporarily
assumes the viewpoint of Hellenistic actors in a Hellenistic world,
invites us to do the same, only at greater length: we can examine the
period without the hindsight that makes it into the prelude to
Roman conquest, but from a Seleukid, or Hellenocentric viewpoint,
to produce a chapter in the political history of the Hellenistic
world, which was never marked by stagnation or equilibrium
(Rostovtzeff's 'balance of power'), but always in constant flux, as M.
Austin has pointed out.[8]

[8] Decline: Walbank 1992: 227; Rostovtzeff 1941: 71, 72. Instability: Austin 1986.

In specific terms, the narrative history which Livy evokes, and which determines the geographical limits of the present study, is that of the Seleukid interests in Asia Minor, 'the land on the other side of the Taurus'. Antiochos III repeatedly campaigned in the region through his viceroy Achaios in 223–220 BC, in person in 216–213, c.203 (probably), 197–196 (as described in the Livian passage discussed here), 193 (in Pisidia), and finally during the Roman–Seleukid War, in 190, a campaign which ended with his defeat at Magnesia under Sipylos and the dismantling, the following year, of the Seleukid dominion in Asia Minor. These events are analysed and reconstructed in Chapter 2 of the present volume, and referred to in the Conclusion. For all the energy and tenacity displayed, the activity of this one king, Antiochos III, the sixth in the Seleukid dynasty, was not untypical, but belonged to a past of relations between the Seleukids and Asia Minor. Antiochos' project was framed in terms of this Seleukid past in Asia Minor: 'to reduce all the cities of Asia into the former structure of subjection', *in antiquam imperii formulam redigere*, as Livy writes. The Seleukids had indeed controlled much of Asia Minor, in addition to the cities of Ionia and Aiolis which Antiochos III took over in 197–196; the Seleukid dominion was founded by the victory of Seleukos I over Lysimachos in 281. However, from 246 onwards, Seleukid authority in Asia Minor had gradually collapsed, to the point of nearly total loss at the accession of Antiochos III. Hence the latter's repeated campaigning in the region, and, most importantly, the description of his actions, both by contemporaries and by himself, in terms of legitimacy and historical claims: he was not conquering, but reconquering (literally 'reacquiring', ἀνακτᾶσθαι) areas lost by his ancestors. This usage can be traced both in the literary sources and the documentary material (Ch. 1 § 1). Antiochos III thought that the Seleukid past justified present conquest; in (re)establishing control, he looked back to the past, to inscribe his actions within his own Seleukid narrative. The fact that this Great Idea was largely a trick of selective memory, imposed on a complex political history where the Seleukids took severe territorial losses, only makes it the more intriguing (Ch. 1).

The Seleukid past in Asia Minor, actual or proclaimed, as well as the narrative of Antiochos' military activities, justified by this Seleukid past: these will be important themes of the present study. Nonetheless, we must be aware that it belongs to a wider context: apart from Asia Minor (and Thrace), Antiochos III lay similar claims, based on historical rights, to Koile-Syria, Armenia, Baktria, and 'India' (in fact he dealt with a local ruler, one Sophagasenos).

He acted on these claims in his eastern campaign, or 'expedition to the Upper Regions' of 210–205 (see, briefly, Ch. 2 § 2). This draws attention to an important characteristic of the Seleukid empire: its extension and diversity, and the multiple contexts in which the Seleukid ruler behaved. Antiochos III appears not only in western Asia Minor, where he waged war, wrote letters to cities and bestowed benefactions on them, receiving honours in return; his actions are also documented in Babylon, where he is seen to perform ritual duties in the various shrines of the city, in 204 and, with great pomp, in 188/7. In Babylon, Antiochos III, like his ancestors, fulfilled the role of traditional Babylonian kingship, and could be described in traditional Babylonian terminology.[9]

That the eastern parts of the empire, and Babylonia in particular, were important to the Seleukids is clear enough, and the present work in no way challenges this point, which the reign of Antiochos III illustrates forcefully. However, the main promoters of this view, S. Sherwin-White and A. Kuhrt, have gone further, reinterpreting the Seleukid empire to claim that its geographical heart lay in Babylonia, Asia Minor and Central Asia alike being frontier zones and hence peripheral concerns (Sherwin-White and Kuhrt 1993). The long reign of Antiochos III does not support this view: out of the thirty-nine years he ruled (223–187 BC), most seem to have been spent in non-Babylonian locations, such as Asia Minor (see above: a total of nine years), the further eastern regions (210–205), or Koile-Syria (221–217; 201–199); in Babylon, he made only punctual appearances, in 220 in the aftermath of a revolt, in 204 on the way from the Upper Regions, and in 188/7 on his way to these same Upper Regions. The picture of polycentric empire and wandering ruler seems closer to the reality of Seleukid rule than the Babylon-centred picture defended by Sherwin-White and Kuhrt.[10] If we must speak of a centre, it can be more justifiably placed in northern Syria. Polybios has the physician of Antiochos III, Apollophanes, speak of Seleukeia in Pieria as 'the hearth, so to speak, of the dynasty'. This is the view of a Greek, repeated in a Greek source, to

---

[9] Sherwin-White and Kuhrt 1993: 216 (Antiochos III in Babylon in 188/7), to which add Sachs and Hunger 1989, no. -204, C, rev., lines 14–18 (Antiochos in Babylon in 204); 36–7 (discussion of Antiochos I as portrayed in a Babylonian building inscription, the 'Borsippa cylinder'), 130–1 (general discussion).

[10] For whereabouts of Antiochos III during his reign, Schmitt 1964: 85. Antiochos' longest stay in Babylon was probably before his accession: FGrHist 260 F 32.10. Reactions to Sherwin-White and Kuhrt 1993 are gathered in Topoi 4.2 (1994). The political role of wandering kingship has been studied for the Achaimenid period by P. Briant, Iranica Antiqua 23 (1988), 253–73; the notion was evoked by Sherwin-White— as a corrective to an aegeocentric view of the Seleukids (Sherwin-White and Kuhrt 1987: 16).

be sure; but Antiochos' actions, as recorded in Polybios, seem to bear out the importance of northern Syria (the so-called 'Seleukis'): Antiochos was proclaimed king, and Laodike III was later proclaimed queen, in Antioch. The expression 'kings of Syria', 'kingship of Syria', which Polybios applies to the Seleukids, reflects his awareness of the central role played by northern Syria in the actions and the self-definition of the dynasty.

Furthermore, the Seleukids never forgot their ethnic origins and identity as Macedonians, a fact reflected even in the Babylonian sources; the Aegean world remained the arena for their competition with their peers, other Macedonian kings.[11] In the superpower competition between the dynasties, Asia Minor lay in the front line, a fact reflected by its complicated political geography and history for much of the third century (see Ch. 1). Hence, at the very least, Asia Minor, even if it was a frontier zone, mattered to the Seleukids—if only for the reason that they laid historical claims to it, that these claims were contested in the realm of international high politics, and that the region was the scene for competition with the other dynasties, Ptolemaic (especially) and Antigonid: the scene where the ambitions the Seleukids harboured and the figure they cut could be measured against other Hellenistic kings. Kingly honour, the belief in inherited historical claims conceived as property rights, and the duty to look over the state as patrimony: these were not ideological superstructures, but necessities of the exercise of kingship and its perpetuation by the projection of strength in a fluid world of superpower rivalry. To maintain kingly honour by claiming, recovering, or preserving territory was to ward off the perception of weakness, fatal for the large, unwieldy Hellenistic empire (see Ch. 2 § 5). This, in itself, is a sufficient reason to explain the Seleukids' constant involvement with and concern for Asia Minor.

Other factors make clear the practical value they derived from the region (these are explored at length in Ch. 3). It supplied the Seleukid empire with personnel, most importantly military manpower from the 'military colonies' installed in the countryside (on which see Ch. 1 § 2; Ch. 3 § 1).[12] The Seleukids also raised revenue

---

[11] Briant 1994 (though Briant's remarks on Antiochos III must be qualified: the rebuilding of Lysimacheia as a residence for one of his sons does not imply his own desire to 'govern from a Near-eastern base' (467)—at the time, Antiochos was mostly in Sardeis or Ephesos, or busy with his Thracian and Anatolian campaigns). Bertrand 1992: 150–2 for the lure of the Aegean ('tropisme maritime').

[12] Asia Minor was more important as a source of military manpower from the countryside than as a source of administrators and courtiers from the cities (as sometimes claimed, e.g. Billows 1995: 78–80). Greeks could work for a king without their city being subject to him: Hegesianax of Alexandreia Troas was a Friend and diplomat for

from their Anatolian dominions, in the form of agricultural rent, tribute, and a complex, but far-reaching, network of indirect taxation (Ch. 3 § 2): even though no exact figures are known, the size and richness of the region hint at its economic importance as source of income for the Seleukids, and one need only remember the 1760 silver talents which it supplied to the Seleukids' Achaimenid predecessors (Hdt. 3.90).

Military colonies and imperial revenue evoke another theme in the Livian passage: the Hellenistic kingdom as an imperial state-formation, its nature and its workings. Livy's expression is *imperii formula*: whatever that translates,[13] it presents Antiochos' conquests as a state-building activity, and the resulting dominion as a structure of power. This theme presents another way to comment on Liv. 33.38: an essay on the workings of the Seleukid empire, drawing on wider parallels in the hope of attaining general insights on Hellenistic empires (see Ch. 3). Such an essay should aim at presenting the evidence for the structures of power, then attempt to extrapolate and explore realities, processes, and ideology. This topic was already handled in classic treatments by Bickerman (Bikerman 1938) and Musti (1966); nonetheless, it has been renewed by recent, sophisticated, research by P. Briant, S. Sherwin-White, and A. Kuhrt on the Hellenistic empires, and specifically on the Seleukid realm and its Achaimenid forebear.[14] But an awareness of the nuanced realities of empire is urged on us by the Livian passage itself, which hints at two important truths: at first sight, empire is based on the components of conquest—violence and military compulsion, as made clear by Antiochos' confidence that most cities will give in to these means; but at the same time, also requires consent or at least quiescence, and the illusion or representation of power—in other words, ideological means. The latter point appears clearly from Antiochos' determination not to allow the recalcitrant cities, Lampsakos and Smyrna, to get away with a state of freedom that did not depend on his own decision, because this would endanger the whole balancing act.

Antiochos III threatened, but also attempted to negotiate with the recalcitrant cities: his behaviour shows that empire cannot be

Antiochos III (Olshausen 1974: 191–3), at a time when his native city was resisting that king; Milesians served Antiochos IV at a time when Miletos was free, and had long been independent of the Seleukids (Herrmann 1987). Many Seleukid officials, officers, and Friends came, not from the cities of Asia Minor, but the new Seleukid foundations of northern Syria: Gauthier 1985: 169–75. On the importance of the region, Rostovtzeff 1941: 524–5.

[13] It conflates *formula provinciae* and *in formam imperii redigere* (I owe this observation to M. Crawford). [14] Briant 1982, Sherwin-White and Kuhrt 1993.

studied purely as structures. His imperial projects took place at the
expense of the *poleis*, themselves complex, touchy, and articulate
social organizations. They offer a test-case for the old, yet cardinal
issue of Hellenistic history: the relation between the Hellenistic
kingdom and the *polis*.[15] The test-case is worth studying, not only
because it presents this relation as confrontation (conquest and
resistance/accommodation) and within a defined period of time
(216–190 BC), but also because it is based on a remarkable series of
epigraphical documents, illustrating a variety of situations and
viewpoints (see below).

The theme of the relations between empire and city is interesting,
because it entails a nuanced appreciation of the condition of the
Hellenistic *polis*.[16] Pursuing this theme is one of the crucial tasks of
recent Hellenistic historiography: the revision of clichés about the
post-Classical *polis*' decadence, irrelevance, and powerlessness
before the Hellenistic kingdoms. It is clear that Antiochos' empire,
and Hellenistic empires in general, affected the *poleis*, through
direct control and legal–ideological structures (such as Antiochos'
determination that the cities' liberty should exist exclusively
through his grant, *ab rege impetratam*). The evidence proves the
existence and explicit functioning of such structures, disproving an
attempt by A. Heuss (1937) at denying any formal subordination of
the *polis*. In reaction to Heuss, some have championed or furthered
the view that the *polis* was abject and defenceless before the
might of the Hellenistic kingdoms (e.g. Orth 1977). The story of
Antiochos III and the cities challenges this view. The general instability of the political situation and the competition between the
super-powers meant that any Hellenistic king's control over cities
was fragile; the necessity for local collaboration, and the realities of
interaction and negotiation between rulers and ruled should alert us
against any straightforward model of direct control and passive
subjects. The *poleis* were capable of resistance, whether physical or
ideological—as proved by the case of Smyrna and Lampsakos. *Polis*
autonomy appeared in forms such as the will of subordinate cities to
constrain rulers through a formal language expressing reciprocity
rather than power, or to protect their civic pride and identity
through local representations. The *poleis*' strategies aimed at converting straight domination into interaction, and their workings will

---

[15] Will 1988: 335, on centrality of this issue.
[16] For recent, balanced treatments, J. K. Davies, in *CAH*² vii. 304–20; Gruen 1993;
A. Giovannini in Bulloch *et al.* 1993: 265–86; Billows 1995: ch. 3; Rhodes with Lewis
1997: 542–9. Habicht 1997 presents the test-case of Athens in the Hellenistic age.
Rostovtzeff unabashedly called the history of some communities 'thrilling to follow'
(Roztovtzeff 1941: 35–6).

be analysed in Chapter 4. In offering a thematic study on the cities' relation with their ruler, I hope not simply to move away from the simplistic clichés about the Hellenistic *polis*, but also to illustrate and explore L. Robert's oft-repeated dictum, 'la cité grecque n'est pas morte à Chéronée': such detailed studies are necessary if Robert's words are to be meaningful.

The actual treatment all these themes receive is shaped by the sources; their state and the consequent issues of presentation can be reviewed in the remaining part of this introduction. The timespan I am considering (226–188 BC) is well documented in comparison with other, earlier, periods in Hellenistic history. The reign of Antiochos III falls within the ambit of Polybios, who was interested in, and quite well-informed about, the Seleukid kingdom and Seleukid activities in Asia Minor, no doubt thanks to a variety of sources, many being oral informants from the Seleukid court or the Asian cities.[17] Antiochos' accession and early years are so well documented in the early, fully preserved books of Polybios that a Seleukid courtier has been suggested as a source (*Hofquelle*: Schmitt 1964: 175–85). Polybios provides detailed information about administrative dispositions at the king's accession, and the reorganization of the governorships in the Upper Satrapies after a revolt; about the king's movements and strategic dilemmas; about his long-term plans and vision. As for Asia Minor specifically, Polybios tells us about the circumstances and actors involved in the usurper Achaios' attempt on the Seleukid throne, and also about the topography in which this attempt took place (royal proclamation at Laodikeia on Lykos, disaffection of troops on the borders of Lykaonia, and consolatory expedition into Pisidia). Likewise, Achaios' expedition of 218 against the Pisidian city of Selge, and the opportunistic campaign Attalos I mounted in Achaios' absence, are minutely and admirably documented, especially as concerns the topography of military movements and the reactions of the local communities. From Books 4 and 5, it is clear that Polybios was aware (as many modern historians of the period are sometimes not) of the importance of the local communities, because the high political history of the superpowers was causally linked with local politics, and because

[17] On Polybios' sources, Walbank *HCP* i. 26–35; Walbank 1972: 74–84, emphasizing the difficulty of precisely tracking down any individual source, and insisting on the personal contacts Polybios, himself a detainee in Rome after 168, must have had with hostages (for instance the Seleukid hostages held on the terms dictated to Antiochos III after Magnesia) or ambassadors from all over the Greek world, especially since appeals to Rome from the Greek cities and kingdoms became increasingly frequent after Pydna.

the description of the experience of empire involves close attention
to local conditions. Polybios would have provided the sort of
detailed narrative record which could have meshed in with the
epigraphical documents to produce a closely textured history of the
cities for the years 226–188 BC sensitive to broad political developments, to the interests of the local communities, and to the complicated factors, external and internal, influencing their behaviour
towards the conquering Seleukid.

As it is, the situation is more complicated and less satisfactory,
because of the fragmentary state of Polybios after Book 5. Useful
or intriguing snippets of evidence survive in the collections of
excerpts: a description of the capture of Sardeis, the capital of the
rebel Achaios (7.15–18, completed by the fate of Achaios himself at
8.15–21); an assessment of the impact of Antiochos' eastern expedition (11.34.14); some details on the expedition of Philip V in Asia
Minor (16.1; 16.2–9; 16.10–12), tiny narrative fragments for
Antiochos' great campaign of 197–6, and a complete account for the
negotiations between the king and the Roman envoys at
Lysimacheia in 196; finally, some incidents in the Roman–Seleukid
War, and a problematic description of the aftermath of the Roman
victory, including the final settlement of Asia Minor in 188 (see
Appendix 7). The context for these fragments is supplied by Livy
and Appian, who depended on Polybios. Livy, who quotes Polybios
at length, also used non-Polybian, annalistic material, sometimes
useful for the present purpose (as for the excellent information
he provides on the settlement of Asia Minor), sometimes quite
puzzling (as for the purported invasion of Pergamene dominions
by Antiochos III in 198: Appendix 6). Appian's *Syriake* is more
concise, but seems to have relied exclusively on Polybios.[18]

The combination of the three literary sources (Polybian excerpts,
Livy, Appian) is not entirely helpful when it comes to reconstructing the narrative for Seleukid activity in Asia Minor. We are left in
the dark as to the exact events of Antiochos' campaign against
Achaios in 216–213; we know nothing of the situation after the king
left for the Upper Satrapies, after appointing Zeuxis to the governorship of 'the regions on the other side of the Taurus' (for instance,
it is difficult to understand how the invasion of Attalid territory by
Prousias I of Bithynia, in 209, fits in the political situation between
Attalids and Seleukids); finally, a major Seleukid campaign in Karia
and probably in Ionia on the king's return from the Upper Satrapies

---

[18] Brodersen 1991 provides a detailed, and in its broad outlines convincing, attempt
to prove that Appian relied solely on Polybios, and transmitted Polybian details quite
faithfully.

is barely alluded to. Even Antiochos' greatest expedition to Asia Minor, the joint campaign by land and by sea of 197–196, is scantily recorded in its latter parts, and there is no direct literary evidence for many of the king's movements with his fleet (between Lykia and Ephesos, and between Ephesos and Thrace) and for the activity of the land army after its departure from northern Syria in spring 197. Much of the Polybian detail that would have filled in the picture has been lost, too devoid of moralizing or didactic force for inclusion in the collections of Polybian excerpts, and too remote from the dramatic theme of the conflict between Rome and the Seleukids to interest Livy and Appian. These two authors handled Polybios to suit their own interests. Appian, though sometimes more faithful than Livy in preserving details unfavourable to Rome, compressed Polybios, often to the point of being misleading or inaccurate; Livy varies between carefully written episodes drawn from Polybios (*Einzelerzählungen*), and wider segments of oblique, concentrated, and sometimes inaccurate summary.[19] When Polybios did touch on the theme relevant to both Livy and Appian, the conflict between Seleukids and Rome, he was quoted extensively by these authors. They transmit informative accounts, taken from the totally lost Book 19 of Polybios, for the diplomatic confrontation between the two powers (196–192), culminating in the Roman–Seleukid War; these accounts illuminate Seleukid conceptions and anxieties about the Anatolian dominion (see Ch. 2 § 5). Livy and Appian also preserve the outline and many details from Polybios' account of the Roman–Seleukid War; these details illustrate the condition of the *poleis* and the choices they faced at a time of super-power conflict (see Conclusion, for the analysis of a few instances).

   The amount of detail that Livy and Appian did not see fit to record points out the extent to which Polybios was a Greek historian, closely interested in the Hellenistic Greek world.[20] In contrast, Livy explicitly declares that he finds this level of detail tiresome, as he notes after giving information on the beginning of Antiochos' campaign of 197 and Rhodian resistance to it: 'non operae est persequi ut quaeque acta in his locis sint, cum ad ea quae propria Romani belli sunt vix sufficiam', 'there is no need to go into the detail of every action in this region, since my efforts are hardly adequate to the events of the Roman war' (33.20.13).[21] Nonetheless,

---

[19] Brodersen 1991; Luce 1977: 205–13, though elsewhere Luce points out that Livy used Polybios extensively, conscientiously, and mostly accurately (Luce 1977: 181 and n. 99, 221).   [20] Millar 1987.
[21] Luce 1977: 43–4, points out that the function of the passage is in fact to provide an apology for including any of these details at all.

Livy often preserves interesting evidence, within the *Einzelerzäh-lungen*. For instance, his account of the Rhodian campaign waged in 197 against the Macedonian troops left in Karia by Philip V mentions Rhodian levies from various parts of the Rhodian Peraia, including *Laudiceni ex Asia* (33.18): not, as had long been supposed, mercenaries from Laodikeia on Lykos, but almost certainly members of a community in south-western Karia under Rhodian control, the Λαοδικεῖς (or τὸ κοινὸν τῶν Λαοδικέων), now attested epigraphically on an honorary decree erected at Stratonikeia (Ma 1997); this is a good example of the locally embedded and informative details which Livy on occasion transmits from Polybios. Another example is the paragraph describing the confrontation between Antiochos III and the recalcitrant cities (Liv. 33.38.1–7)—the passage on which I have been offering a commentary through-out this introduction.

Though Polybios does not allow any straightforward and integral narrative reconstruction of Antiochos' campaigns, he is nonetheless invaluable as a source of parallels which indirectly illuminate the broad historical context and the issues which I outlined earlier: the workings of the Hellenistic kingdoms as power structures, the relation between city and ruler, and the condition of the *polis* in the Hellenistic age. Polybios provides extended passages of political analysis, such as an analysis of royal euergetism and civic εὔνοια (5.90.5–8) or a crucial (but difficult) passage assessing royal behaviour towards cities, as it evolves from συμμαχικῶς to δεσποτικῶς according to expediency and circumstances (15.24a). Further insights can be gained from the narrative: Antiochos' eastern expedition, even though it does not directly concern the cities of western Asia Minor, shows us a ruler and potential subjects deploy-ing strategies for interaction and submission, ranging from straight-forward violence to symbolical acts like gifts or royal grants of local privileges; one example is the interaction between Antiochos III and the Gerrhaians (Pol. 13.9). Other passages illustrate royal conquest and its aftermath, the processes involved, the diplomacy, the politi-cal role of ruler cult (at 5.86.8–11, the cities of Koile-Syria offer 'crowns, sacrifices, altars and all this sort of thing' to Ptolemy IV after his victory at Raphia). In this respect, Polybios as indirect source for the world in which the Great King and the cities inter-acted can be completed by other literary texts, among which figure the accounts of the Maccabaean revolt from the Seleukids, as pre-served in Josephus' *Jewish Antiquities* and 1–2 Macc., because of the portrayal of the Seleukid empire as a military–imperial organization and because of the numerous royal documents quoted in these sources and which are (in the main) authentic. Bickerman's classic treatment of the 'Seleukid institutions' (Bikerman 1938) drew on the Maccabaean material, for instance, to describe the army, structures of control, or imperial finances.

Besides the literary sources, direct or indirect, other types of evidence are helpful. A number of these can be enumerated, with some examples. First, numismatics: the coins struck by Antiochos III, plentiful across his long reign, and by the cities can be used to talk about a variety of themes, such as the image of the ruler in royal portraiture, the narrative of royal campaigns and conquests, and, most importantly for the issues I wish to treat in this book, about city privileges and royal domination.[22]

Second, archaeological remains—though this evidence is disappointing: it provides a visual and material context (rather than new information) for the story and the themes of this book. Admittedly, there is a small amount of art historical evidence: ancient sculptural groups representing Marsyas flayed before Apollo may reproduce a Seleukid original, alluding to the reduction of the usurper Achaios by Antiochos III (Fleischer 1972–5). Likewise, it is true that some sites provide material evidence: the ruins of Priene even now present the striking picture of a city which kept its general Hellenistic shape, and thus helps us imagine other cities, their setting articulated by monuments, public spaces, and shrines. Another example is Aigai, which shows the deep impact of Attalid architectural patronage in the second century, after the Seleukid presence in Asia Minor had been removed. The site of Amyzon presents another physical model for the *polis*: a territory with villages or forts, and a monumental and sacral centre, where the religious and political institutions were located.[23] Nonetheless, there are too many cities for whose material forms in the Hellenistic period we have only vague ideas, because they await full excavation (Alabanda, Euromos, Teos), or because later building activity radically altered their shape. The latter is the case for cities such as Smyrna, Ephesos, Miletos, even Iasos; and also important Seleukid centres such as Sardeis, Laodikeia on Lykos, or Apameia.[24] Because

[22] Generally, Mørkholm 1991; on Antiochos III, Newell *WSM* 395–401. Royal portraiture: Mørkholm 1969: 15 (portraiture of Achaios). Royal movements: Le Rider 1990 (Antiochos II at Mylasa); Mørkholm 1969: 14–15 (movements of Seleukos III). City privileges and royal domination: the whole issue still needs clarification, but the principles I have followed in this work are those traditionally accepted (silver coinage means civic autonomy) and underlying e.g. the summaries in Le Rider 1972/3, 1973/4, 1975/6; see Ch. 3 § 3.

[23] Aigai: Robert 1937: 74–89. Amyzon: Robert 1983.

[24] See the pages by Robert, *OMS* iv. 310–16. The situation may improve with the continuing excavation and surveying work at and around Ephesos and Miletos.

of this situation, we cannot relate in detail the textual evidence with the relevant material remains. To understand how heavy a handicap this is, we need only look to second-century AD Ephesos, where G. Rogers has studied the foundation of Vibius Salutaris in its contemporary urban context: by studying the actual inscription and the ceremonies in their monumental context, Rogers interprets the ceremonies' social and ideological meaning, and the way in which they express the city's identity, especially in relation to the Roman empire. In contrast, we have a long text describing how the Teians reordered their ceremonial life around a new sacral centre (a statue of Antiochos III and an altar to the king and the Charites in the *bouleuterion*), but we cannot relate the detailed information to a specific urban layout, let alone to a meaningful symbolical geography of Teos.[25] Finally, there is very scant archaeological information for the countryside in this period, so that we have little idea what a rural shrine, a Seleukid fort, or a 'military colony' looked like, let alone how rural population was distributed in the 'royal land', or simply how it lived in, say, Hellenistic Phrygia or Lydia.

One exception to the thinness of archaeological material is the series of well-preserved city walls from the Hellenistic period. These fall into two categories: on one hand, the extensive and sophisticated defence works erected by the Hellenistic kings, exemplified by Ephesos and Herakleia under Latmos; on the other hand, the more modest walls put up by the cities to defend their urban nucleus, as can be seen at Priene, Erythrai, Notion/Kolophon by sea, or Kolophon—the latter was defended by a late fourth-century, ambitious, *Geländemauer* reminiscent of the great royal walls, which prompts us not to underestimate civic resources and determination.[26] The cities' fortifications matter, because they created the possibility of resisting conquest by a king, at least for a while, if the broader political context was right: Notion/Kolophon by sea successfully withstood a siege by Antiochos III during the Roman–Seleukid War (Liv. 37.26.5–8; 37.31.3). This is an important characteristic of the condition enjoyed by the cities of western Asia Minor, in contrast with the Classical period, where many of

---

[25] Ephesos: Rogers 1991. Teos: document **18** and Ch. 4 § 3*b*. It would be even more depressing to compare the situation for Hellenistic Teos and the case-studies offered for more recent periods: see Ozouf 1976: 225–42, for the routing of processions in Caen during the French Revolution, and 242–59 on the geography of revolutionary festivals in Paris. Generally, Ozouf is able to analyse both the intentions of festival-organizing authorities and the ambiguous realizations of these intentions; both perspectives are impossible (at least at that level of detail) for the modern historian of the Hellenistic world.

[26] Most of the evidence is catalogued and studied by McNicoll 1997.

these cities were unwalled (ἀτείχιστος) and hence enjoyed a far smaller margin of manoeuvre, as can be seen in Thucydides' narrative of the Ionian War. Admittedly, Antiochos III in winter 197/6 felt confident that he would conquer 'all the cities', because of their lack of trust in their walls and their fighting men; but this opinion reflected royal ideology and confidence, rather than any necessary outcome determined by material conditions.

A third non-literary source is the array of Anatolian landscapes: much more instructive for our purposes than 'ancient ruins', the land still allows us to study ancient *sites*—specific places in their relation with the geography. Western Asia Minor (as I defined it earlier in this introduction) still survives as a physical entity, which can be studied on maps and in the accounts of earlier travellers,[27] or by travel to modern Turkey, as long as attention is given not just to the cities, but also to routes, plains, mountains and the ways through them. I twice had the chance of travelling through this region, going along many of the historically important routes, by train, bus or minibus, car, tractor, bicycle, or on foot. Travel in Asia Minor gives a sense of its wealth and size, both explaining why an imperial power would covet it and problematizing the realities of controlling such a vast area. It also creates a sense of the relation between places and hence promotes the concrete understanding of military movements. Seeing the mass of Mt Latmos, separating Amyzon and Herakleia under Latmos, which lie close on the map, helps to understand why the Seleukids took the former but not the latter place in *c*.203. Likewise, going along the Menderes (Cumaovası)–Kavakdere corridor, one of the crossing points from the Smyrna plain to the coast (now the road between the coastal resorts and Izmir airport), illustrates its importance and possibly illuminates the movements of Antiochos III in the region in the same years (Ch. 2 § 3).[28] The awareness of geography as a source of understanding about the past is nothing new; for the Hellenistic world, it was particularly developed, by exhortation and by example, in the work of L. Robert.

The most significant non-literary source is the body of epigraphical documents, and it is worth reflecting on the nature of these documents, the limitations they impose, and the ways in which these limitations can be qualified. This source of evidence, already

---

[27] For instance Fellows 1839, 1841; Cuinet 1894; de Planhol 1958. But see Strobel 1996: 10–11, for qualifications about the practice of exclusively, and selectively, quoting early travellers as a substitute for serious historical geography.

[28] Apart from the work of L. Robert, the approach is exemplified by Syme 1995: 177–215 for Pisidia and Pamphylia; for parallels, see also Millar 1994, and van Berchem 1982, for Roman Switzerland.

respectable in quantity at the time of H. Schmitt's monograph on
Antiochos III (1964), has been spectacularly increased by recently
published texts, most of the first importance (notably—in order of
publication—the finds from Iasos, Teos, Amyzon, Herakleia under
Latmos, and Sardeis). It now counts forty-nine items relevant to the
king's activity in Asia Minor alone; to these can be added important
documents concerning Antiochos III from Koile-Syria (the
'Skythopolis dossier' concerning the estate of Ptolemaios, governor
of the region) and Media.[29] They mostly are royal letters (administrative or diplomatic), and civic decrees, usually honorific, along
with a few records of dedications, statue bases, etc. Nor are these
documents isolated: they can be read in a context provided by the
rest of Hellenistic epigraphy, which offers many parallels with
which to expand or qualify conclusions drawn from the inscriptions
concerning Antiochos III and the cities. A sense of the material's
abundance and fascination emerges even from older corpora, like
the *Sylloge Inscriptionum Graecarum*, *Orientis Graecae Inscriptiones
Selectae* (volume 1 concentrates on Hellenistic kings), or C. B.
Welles's *Royal Correspondence*; many cities of Asia Minor have their
inscriptions gathered in convenient working collections, published
in the Cologne series, *Inschriften griechischer Städte aus Kleinasien*.
As the case of Antiochos III illustrates, one great advantage to this
material is the way in which it is constantly increased, and the issues
it raises modified, by new publications, as reviewed in the *Bulletin
Epigraphique* and republished in the *Supplementum Epigraphicum
Graecum*: a glance at the bibliography to the present work will
show how the epigraphical material steadily increases, with new discoveries which make adjustments to our political narrative of the
Hellenistic world, and enrich the analyses we can elaborate.[30]

The epigraphical material provides important information for
the topic of Antiochos III and his relations with the cities. As
mentioned above, inscriptions correct the narrative written from the

---

[29] For documents from Asia Minor, see the list at the introduction to the epigraphical dossier presented as an annexe. During the three or four years taken by the research
and the writing of the thesis on which this book is based, several new documents
appeared. Other regions: for the Skythopolis dossier, the text was published by V. H.
Landau, *IEJ* 16 (1966), 54–70, republished by Th. Fischer, *ZPE* 33 (1979), 131–8,
revised by J.-M. Bertrand, *ZPE* 46 (1982), 167–74 and Fr. Piejko, *Ant Class* 60, (1991),
245–7, though Piejko's restorations for lines 5–7 and his construction of the syntax in
lines 21–4 are not convincing; I will quote the text as *SEG* 29.1613. Media: Robert
1949, Robert 1967.

[30] The earliest epigraphical works quoted are Chishull 1728, Hessel 1731, followed by
traveller–epigraphists like Leake (1824), Fellows (1839, 1841), Hamilton (1842). Among
modern examples of discoveries making important contributions, Gauthier 1989,
Herrmann 1965a, Malay 1987.

fragmentary literary sources. A single Seleukid document coming from northern Mysia and published by H. Malay in 1987 disproved a reconstruction of Seleukid territorial concessions to the Attalids in 216 and of the subsequent political history of the region.[31] In the case of the Seleukid campaigns of c.203, the record is almost exclusively epigraphical, from Amyzon and (probably) Teos:[32] the documents picture the aftermath of conquest, thus enabling us to reconstruct or deduce military narrative. In the case of the crucial campaign of 197/6, the epigraphical evidence unfortunately does not fully complete the lacunas in Livy, so that the documents mostly show the effect of the campaign at the local level. This point illustrates one strength of the epigraphical evidence: it reveals a diversity of situations and viewpoints—the campaigns of a Hellenistic king, the institutions of imperial control and their workings, the local experience of war and empire, as lived by the *poleis*. All these aspects combine to help write an essay on empire, which I proposed earlier as one of the themes raised by the seminal passage of Livy. The increase in documentation has sharpened our perception of this theme: we now have some idea of the activities of Zeuxis, the 'official in charge of the regions on the other side of the Taurus', or the high-priest and official in charge of sacred matters, Nikanor.

The other important feature is the nature of the inscriptions as immediate historical documents, rather than an author's elaboration of events. The consequence is not that inscriptions are unimpeachably real and objective; on the contrary, their value lies in the fact that they are actual instances of official languages in action, as spoken by historical agents and embodying ideologies and images as well as representing, in themselves, historical events. Some texts document the language of empire, which is not only practically oriented, but is constitutive of empire (Ch. 3 § 3); other texts, the civic decrees, express the identity of the *polis*, and its efforts to come to terms with its rulers through the medium of honorific language (Ch. 4). Concerning the latter topic, the texts which the inscriptions record (royal letters, civic decrees) do not merely mirror the interaction between ruler and city: they *are* this interaction.

An important part of this book is devoted to applying what might be called, in a broad sense, a 'text-aware' approach to the documentary material: taking the inscriptions seriously as texts, whose language matters to us as interpreters, because it mattered to the power actors who uttered them. This approach seeks out meanings, implications, and ideology, to be explored and teased out by close

---

[31] Document 4, and Ch. 2 § 1.   [32] Ch. 2 § 2; Teos: Appendix 2.

readings. Such an approach complements the more traditional positivist mode, whereby documents merely document historical facts, which lie beyond the documents themselves and whose reality is assumed to be readily reconstructible. For instance, a royal letter might speak of the subjects' loyalty, the king's benevolence, and his benefactions. We do not know if the subjects were truly loyal, nor whether the king was truly benevolent; nor do we have enough evidence to correct the affirmations of the king (to say what he *really* thought when he made his benefactions); in most cases, because of the dearth of continuous documentation, we do not even know if promised benefactions actually took place. What we can say, in all such cases, is that the letter was written and received, that the king did say these things to the recipients of his missive, that the recipients, the citizens of that supremely articulate body, a Hellenistic *polis*, inscribed the missive and perhaps produced a document of their own: all these things in themselves are very real historical facts which deserve attention. That utterances are in themselves acts is crucial to the study of the documentary evidence, and also explains their unique value. This approach is inspired by 'speech-act theory', pioneered by J. L. Austin, and developing Austin's insight that certain utterances ('I grant you freedom', 'we decide to praise you') are acts with practical consequences, and that, in a sense, all utterances are actions, performed in a certain context which influences them and is influenced by them (Millar 1992: 637).

The importance of the epigraphical material only makes it more important to underscore the difficulties inherent in its exploitation. An obvious problem is the patchy nature of the evidence for writing continuous narrative: the inscriptions somewhat palliate the fragmentary record, but are still far from allowing any complete account for the more obscure sections in the history of Antiochos' campaigns; nor do they provide any direct indication of motives or the surrounding military context. But the incompleteness of the epigraphical material has far more significant consequences than just hindering the writing of political narrative. This is especially true for the evidence concerning the *polis*. The majority of the documents arc honorific decrees, often for the ruler or his officials: a crucial dimension of dissent or resistance, by its nature, cannot ever impinge on the smooth, bland discourse of honours.[33] Furthermore,

[33] A salutary experience is to read Cic. *Verr.* 2.4.140–4, where Cicero describes a Syracusan honorific decree (*laudatio*) as issuing veiled criticism of Verres, by praising him in areas where he had precisely failed to perform his duty (or so Cicero claims). The story, whatever its reality, at least raises the possibility of insincerity and reluctance behind the institutionalized enthusiasm of the honorific decrees surviving in our evi-

the set forms in the decrees present a picture of politics as consensus, rather than as differences: ἔδοξε τῆι βουλῆι καὶ τῶι δήμωι: ἐπειδή . . ., 'it seemed good to the city: since . . .', leading to unitary decisions and actions. Yet we know that both the Classical and post-Classical *polis* experienced divisions: between rich and poor, between individuals or groups within the élite. These divisions often became apparent in the stress of wartime: Thucydides documents the process not just in his set-pieces on *stasis*, but in his detailed narrative of the end of the Mytilenean revolt, or of the Thracian cities' reactions to Brasidas' overtures; likewise, the rapid changes in allegiance which Phokaia underwent during the Roman–Seleukid war mirrored internal tensions and shifts.[34] The case of Phokaia (preserved through literary accounts, and not documentary material) illustrates how the Hellenistic kings had supporters in the cities, in the form of well-disposed 'family friends' (e.g. *RC* 17, 22), and possibly of wider groups of supporters. The picture in the epigraphical sources is of a monolithic, totally mobilised, *polis*: there is no hint of internal debate, let alone conflict, shifts in policy, tensions, changes, indifference, or of the role played by individuals, or of the attitude of the citizenry (or groups of citizens) over a period of time concerning the changes brought about by royal conquest and its aftermath.[35] The inscriptions simply talk of (e.g.) the Amyzonians, the Teians taking a decision and reacting to events *en masse*, as a unified community with a single voice and purpose.

These difficulties must be borne in mind, when trying to interpret the results of close readings to the epigraphical material. However, their severity should not be exaggerated. The concern about the picture of the Hellenistic city, as derived from inscriptions, being too 'monolithic', may rather reflect our appetite to know more about the conditions in which the decrees were produced than condemn

dence. For an example illustrating how to read stereotypical archival documents, Ozouf 1976: 198–9.

[34] Mytilene: Thuc. 3.27–8, with D. Gillis, *AJP* 92 (1971), 38–47; Brasidas: Thuc. 4.84, 103, 104, 110–14. Phokaia: Pol. 21.6, Liv. 37.9.1–4, 11.15. On the omission of debate in the epigraphical evidence, Loraux 1997: 18: 'les décrets . . . loin de rendre compte du déroulement effectif d'une assemblée, construisent et limitent le souvenir qu'il convient d'en garder.' I also am grateful to R. Osborne for showing me a paper on this issue.

[35] P. M. Fraser, reviewing Orth 1977 in *CR* 30 (1980), 158, argues that a study of the interaction between the Seleukids and cities should take the role of individual élite families into account; but it seems to me that the evidence is still insufficient for this sort of research (though note Carsana 1996, with reservations expressed by Gauthier, *BE* 97, 151 and a critical review by I. Savalli-Lestrade in *REG* 111 (1998), 308–22; Savalli-Lestrade 1996, for Attalid courtiers and their cities).

the picture of unified, consensual *polis* behaviour as unusable for the historian. The *polis* was a place where divisions and differences existed, but also where (ideally and, often, in reality) they were overcome through politics, common decision-making, and shared ideology; in normal times, class differences, political opposition, support for divergent foreign policies, all these sources of conflict were compatible with a democratic model of decision-making and a shared communal existence.[36] Forging consensus, or at least reaching the appearance of consensus for the pragmatic purpose of getting on with the life in common, was precisely the point of democratic decision-making. The inscribed decrees do not allow us to study conflict and disagreement: what they present is the normal outcome of internal processes—the decision attained, and firmly imposed on the community as authoritative by the canonical forms of the decree, implemented by the city's authorities, and presented to the world and to posterity by publication and inscription. The fact that the inscribed decrees present us with a limited worldview (their information is restricted to the outcome) and a particular, civic, ideology does not detract from the status of the decisions reached and acted on by the community as a whole. These decisions represent the public face of the *polis*: as long as that fact is never forgotten, the decrees can be considered as a legitimate and fascinating object of study, especially since it is difficult to see beyond them (so that, all too often, they are all we have), and since the communal language of the decrees is the medium which creates the *polis*' public face. The way to study this language and these documents without believing that they are the whole story is to bear in mind the pervasive violence and structures of exploitation that the Hellenistic empires lived off, and which form the general context in which the civic decrees were produced.

With these remarks on the way in which the sources, especially epigraphical, shape our perceptions and the forms we use to talk about the past, we are back at our starting-point: what form to adopt to talk about the Hellenistic world. In the present study, I have avoided the increasingly popular form of the royal biography: partly because I think that the ancient evidence is insufficient for this sort of exercise (one needs only think of later periods, for instance the Middle Ages already or the early modern period, to realize this), and partly because the focus on the figure of the king leaves out the experience and viewpoint of the local communities.

[36] As a well-documented example, see Ober 1989 for 4th-cent. Athens.

The starting-point I chose, as embodied in a passage of Livy (or his source, Polybios), was a moment in Hellenistic history which dramatized an important issue, the relation between king and city, in a particular context; a test-case with a particular narrative origin and outcome.

For the actual treatment of this issue, I avoided the full 'dossier par thème' model, where the main text is subordinate to the presentation of epigraphical documents, and, indeed, subsumed in the commentary to these documents. Another format I did not want to adopt to study the relation between a specific king, Antiochos III, and the cities of Asia Minor, is the catalogue of evidence, city by city. In this model, entries are devoted to the evidence for each individual city along with a thumbnail sketch of narrative history as experienced locally: these entries are followed by attempts at inter-pretation for (e.g.) 'royal policy' towards any *polis*, hopefully as a basis for more general interpretations. But such attempts are hindered by the lack of a full record for any single city, so that the advantages of the approach (antiquarian delight, philological rigour, attention to specifics) dissolve into uncertainty and speculation.

The present work is structured as a series of thematic studies, all written around the confrontation between Antiochos III and the cities of western Asia Minor. The themes treated have already been sketched out above: the setting, both geographical and political, of Seleukid Asia Minor (Ch. 1); the narrative history of Antiochos' (re)conquest of Asia Minor (Ch. 2); the structures, actual and ideological, of imperial power (Ch. 3); the existence of power as interaction between rulers and ruled (Ch. 4). These studies run through the material and the broadly defined topic at different angles, and each uses the sources in different ways, appealing to various techniques and approaches: reconstructing and piecing together disparate, fragmentary information to produce *histoire événementielle*; teasing out the practical implications and the ideo-logical assumptions of administrative documents; reading the imperfect dialogue between royal letters and civic decrees, by taking seriously and analysing the language of interaction.

The results of these different modes of enquiry are predictably varied in tone and feel, between the traditional political narrative, with the uncertainties entailed by the lacunary evidence, and the synchronic analytical chapters, which can palliate evidence problems by drawing on parallels in the documentary material. Yet these approaches do not lead to divergent, or contradictory, inter-pretations: they rather reflect different understandings of the same material and different ways to talk about it. Furthermore, the

studies are not, or not only, parallel *exercices de style* in the field of
Hellenistic historiography, but (as I hope to make clear in the body
of the argument and in the transitional sections) closely linked
thematically: together, they present an embedded test case, which
helps us approach the issue of the relation between Hellenistic king
and city. The first way in which these studies are linked is that each
leads to the following one, through the realization that its own
results are only part of the historical reality that the whole book
seeks to describe and understand. The narrative of Antiochos'
conquests leads to an awareness that military narrative and its concepts are, in themselves, inadequate to describe the exercise of
imperial power; hence a chapter on the structures of empire, which
itself ends with the awareness of the role played by ideology and
language, and therefore is continued by a chapter on political
language.

Conversely, the narrative establishes the precise context, the
movements and vicissitudes of the historical actors: it thus grounds
the more thematic sections, and hence helps determine the exact
methodological status of the parallels adduced in those sections. I
am not using them to talk about idealized entities, the King and the
City; for lack of a complete documentary record, the test-case of
Antiochos III has to be expanded by parallels, which establish
its typicality, and hence enable generalizations about the diverse
spectrum of possibilities but also the unity of language and institutions which characterized the Hellenistic world. These generalizations in turn can be qualified by the specific aspects of the test-case
I examine, and also further tested against other individual cases,
another function of the parallels in the thematic chapters. More
generally, the work is structured as a succession of interlocking
studies, which illuminate each other by providing background and
context for individual series of insights. The narrative, by establishing the characteristics of continual violence and the problematic,
precarious nature of the Seleukids' domination over Asia Minor,
provides a significant context to understand the workings of empire,
practical and, especially, ideological (the imperial power's claims to
ubiquitous efficacy and the monopoly of definitions are part of the
illusion of inevitability, and hence as important an instrument of
domination as armies or taxation). In turn, the study of the structures of power, physical and ideological, provides the background
for the interaction between rulers and ruled through a formalized
language of benefactions, honours, and obligation: in order to avoid
taking statements made in this language for the whole story, we
must keep awareness of the role played by violence in constituting a

Hellenistic empire and of the structures of compulsion or exploitation.

Finally, the structure of the work attempts to mirror the movement in the passage from Livy. The latter opens with a statement of imperialist vision and imperial institutions, but ends with local civic pride and values, embodied in the reply given to Antiochos III by the recalcitrant cities: they proclaimed their determination to preserve freedom even in the face of a starkly threatening imperial power and its offer of accommodation within the framework of its institutions and its ideology. Likewise, this work starts with two chapters driven by the Seleukid viewpoint, either in the form of the Seleukids' imagined past in Asia Minor or of the narrative of Antiochos' conquests, naturally shaped by the movements and projects of the king; but the book ends with a chapter which seeks to show the resilience and potency of civic language and ideals, which transformed straightforward relations of power-as-possession into a complicated interaction; the conclusion and envoi tries to characterize the Hellenistic age as one where the cities matter, because of their local persistence, whereas any individual supra-poliad empire is oddly precarious and labile. When approaching the Hellenistic world, it is crucial to pay attention to this phenomenon and to find a historiographical mode that can accommodate the imperial and the local. This is one last implication, worth exploring in depth, which we can draw from the confrontation between the Great King and 'all the cities of Asia Minor'. The whole of the present work is structured around this insight.

CHAPTER 1

The Seleukid past in Asia Minor
(281–223 BC)

1. *In All the Land beyond the Taurus, Just as under our Grandfather*

On 23 Dystros, year 103 SE (210/9), Antiochos III, on the eve of his eastern expedition, sent a πρόσταγμα to Zeuxis, the governor of cis-Tauric Asia. The king appointed his chamberlain, Nikanor, 'high-priest of all the shrines in all the land beyond the Taurus', at Nikanor's own request. In addition, 'we thought necessary that Nikanor should be in charge of the sanctuaries, and that their revenues and the other matters should be administered by him, just as under our grandfather by Dion'; furthermore, Nikanor was to be mentioned 'in the contracts and the other documents for which it is usual'.[1] Zeuxis duly passed on the instructions: a copy was found in northern Mysia; Nikanor is named as 'high-priest' in documents from Amyzon and Xanthos.[2] The *prostagma* apparently belongs to 'the continuing administrative work . . . that the king routinely dealt with, while on major campaigns, to keep the empire ticking over'.[3] But in spite of its mundane appearance, the *prostagma* on Nikanor deserves closer attention, for it is based on arresting Seleukid assumptions about the geography and history of Asia Minor.

The ἀρχιερεὺς τῶν ἱερῶν πάντων appointed over all the land beyond the Taurus has been interpreted as a high-priest of the ruler cult organized by the Seleukid state. But the document nowhere mentions ruler cult, unlike the enactment of 193 which (in instituting cult for Laodike III) explicitly refers to high-priests of Antiochos III and his πρόγονοι; furthermore, the state cult for Antiochos III was probably founded only in c.204, on the king's

---

[1] Document **4**, 29–41; 44–5.
[2] Documents **9**, **10**, **23**.
[3] Sherwin-White and Kuhrt 1993: 198.

return from his eastern expedition.[4] It is unlikely that the document abbreviates the title of Nikanor, since it is the official act of appointment. The consequence is that in the document found at Pamukçu, Antiochos III simply appoints a high-priest: the immediate parallel is *RC* 44, where he appoints a Friend high-priest of Apollo and Artemis Daittai at Daphne, in almost identical terms to the inscription concerning Nikanor. The parallel brings out the character of Nikanor's appointment: he is to be high-priest of every shrine in cis-Tauric Asia, with authority over the local priests of these shrines; furthermore, in virtue of his functions as ὁ ἐπὶ τῶν ἱερῶν, he will administrate the shrines' income. This interpretation is confirmed by the activity of Nikanor's successor as 'high priest' in Attalid Asia Minor, Euthydemos, whose authorization a local shrine (the sanctuary of Apollo Pleurenos, north of Sardeis, not linked with state ruler cult) needed before setting up a stele listing initiates of the god.[5]

The prostagma of 209 is not about royal cult, but about imperial practice and language. The geographical sphere of Nikanor's competence was patterned on the cis-Tauric command held by Zeuxis (Ch. 3 § 2); the royal enactment created a unified space, where individual difference and geographical expanse could be integrated under a single, centrally appointed official. The size and diversity of the region underline the forcefulness of Antiochos' imperial vision. Instructions to include Nikanor in the heading of documents imposed the signs of an unified Seleukid dominion, akin to the dating in local documents by the Seleukid era and by the reign of Antiochos III. The same symbolic effect of 'imperial' chronological markers appears in the 'Ptolemaic' city of Xanthos, in a document dated by the regnal year of Ptolemy III and by the tenure of various priesthoods at Alexandria.[6] In addition to the content of the *pros-*

---

[4] Nikanor priest in ruler cult; Malay 1987: 13–15. Enactment of 193: document **37**. State cult for Antiochos III only after 205: J. and L. Robert 1983: 168 n. 40.

[5] Ptolemaios, the 'strategos and archiereus' of Koile-Syria who appears in the Skythopolis inscription (*SEG* 29.1613, lines 10, 11, 21–2, 29) and at Soloi (document **21**, 2), perhaps occupied a similar function for his province, rather than a priesthood within the state-organized ruler cult? See Welles *RC*, 159 n. 7, 'he, as representative of the state, had supervision and control over particularly the finances of the temples in his satrapy', Bengtson 1944: 130 n. 1; for parallels, Bengtson 1952: 141–3: the Ptolemaic governor of Cyprus was also 'high-priest of the shrines in the island' (as well as, admittedly, a priest of the cult of the Ptolemies). Also Welles, *RC* 319, s.v. ἀρχιερωσύνη for the imperial overseer of local religion in Roman Egypt. Euthydemos: document **49**.

[6] *SEG* 36.1218—a Xanthian legal document dated to the fourth year of Ptolemy IV (202/1), and to the time when 'those in Alexandria' were priests of Alexander and of the deified Ptolemies: the formula clearly indicates that the preamble performs a symbolical function as well as a practical one (see L. Koenen, in Bulloch *et al.* 1993: 46–8).

tagma, its very production assumes that Antiochos III has the authority to name Nikanor to a position of control over all the shrines in cis-Tauric Asia Minor, both in the symbolic form of the high priesthood and the actual administrative power over temple finances. Less grand than the high priesthood, this overseership of local shrine finances also assumes—cloaked in the language of euergetical solicitude—authority and control, exemplified in non-Anatolian examples such as Heliodoros' interest in the wealth of the Temple at Jerusalem (probably accumulated surplus from subsidies).[7]

Antiochos' decision was made in reference to 'our grandfather', Antiochos II,[8] combining imperial discourse about geography and power with awareness of the past. By framing present action in reference to an earlier member of the dynasty, simply referred to as 'our grandfather', Antiochos III claims to be acting within a history of Seleukid control, in all of cis-Tauric Asia Minor, manifest in continuity of administrative practice and of dynastic rule.

The appointment of Nikanor contains a dialogue between perceived past and present actions; to be appreciated, this attitude must be located within the context of Seleukid memory about the geography and the history of Asia Minor. A parallel is the language in which Polybios describes the vicissitudes of Seleukid power in 'the region on this side of the Taurus'. Upon his accession, Seleukos III hears that Attalos I 'had already subjected all of the land on this side of the Taurus' (Pol. 4.48.7) and hastens to defend his πράγματα. After the murder of Seleukos III, Achaios undertook to recover all of the land on this side Taurus (Pol. 4.48.10): the verb used is ἀνεκτᾶτο, 'to acquire back'. Polybios writes of Achaios' successes unambiguously: he shut Attalos I into Pergamon, and took control of all the rest, τῶν δὲ λοιπῶν πάντων ἦν ἐγκρατής (Pol. 4.48.11). After his usurpation, Achaios is regularly referred to as the master of cis-Tauric Asia Minor (Pol. 4.2.6; 4.48.3; 8.20.11). Though the form used is consistently ἐπίταδε τοῦ Ταύρου ('on this side of Taurus') instead of the expression ἐπέκεινα ('on that side') preferred by Antiochos III in his *prostagma*,[9] Polybios' references to Achaios assume that all of Asia Minor was part of the Seleukid πράγματα, and that, before the usurpation of this region by Attalos I

---

[7] The office was later held by one Demetrios: document **44** (unless this is a local subordinate). Seleukids and shrines: Bickerman 1938: 121–2; Rostovtzeff 1941: 504–7; *SEG* 35.1170 for Antiochos I and his co-regent Seleukos 'giving back' incomes to the shrine of Apollo Toumoundos (perhaps adjudication over land-dispute?). Heliodoros: Bickerman 1980: 159–91. Briant 1982: 327, for Achaimenid control of shrines.

[8] Document **4**, 40–1.

[9] Document **4**, 29–30.

and Achaios, it had entirely and unproblematically been under Seleukid control.

In super-power diplomacy, the Seleukid claims could be brought forth more explicitly.[10] Antiochos III asserted ancestral claims to ownership in his diplomatic exchanges with the Romans: at the conference of 196 at Lysimacheia,[11] the king stated that he had crossed into Europe 'to recover (ἀνακτησόμενος) the Chersonesos and the cities of Thrace, since rule (ἀρχή) over these places was rightly his more than that of anyone else' (Pol. 18.51.3). Antiochos appealed to history: victory over Lysimachos had made Seleukos I master of all of his adversary's former kingdom, as δορίκτητος, spear-won territory; this implicitly justified Antiochos' rights to the cities of Asia Minor as well. Now, after some opportunistic inroads by Ptolemy III,[12] then by Philip V, Antiochos was not taking possession (κτᾶσθαι) of these places, but 're-taking possession, in virtue of his own rights': ἀνακτᾶσθαι τοῖς ἰδίοις δικαίοις συγχρώμενος (Pol. 18.51.6). In 193, Antiochos' envoy Hegesianax of Alexandreia Troas protested against the injunction that Antiochos should evacuate 'Europe' (his conquests in Thrace) if he wished the Romans to keep out of Asia: Hegesianax rehearsed the Seleukid rights to Lysimachos' former possessions of Thrace and Chersonesos, conquered by Seleukos I; he contrasted Antiochos' ancestral rights to these regions with the lack of any Roman claim to Asia (Liv. 34.58.4–6; App. *Syr.* 6). At a conference held at Ephesos later the same year, the Seleukid ambassador Minnion would appeal to historical claims in order to justify Antiochos' right to levy tribute from the cities of Ionia and Aiolis: *bello superatas a maioribus, stipendarias ac vectigales factas in antiquum ius repetit*, '[these cities,] which were conquered in war by his ancestors and made to pay tribute, [Antiochos] has recovered within their ancient status' (Liv. 35.16.6). Livy's *repetit* must translate the verb ἀνακτᾶσθαι, which appears twice in the speech of Antiochos III at Lysimacheia as well as in the description of Achaios' campaign against Attalos I. The consistency of the vocabulary corresponds to the unity of Seleukid conceptions about their history in Asia Minor, and the claims which this history enabled in the present.[13]

The verb ἀνακτᾶσθαι also appears in direct address to a city.

[10] Literary evidence: Schmitt 1964: 86.

[11] Pol. 18.51 (Liv. 33.40 rearranges the order of the arguments; App. *Syr.* 3).

[12] Presumably Ptolemy III, since the area under dispute is Thrace and the Chersonesos.

[13] In Appian (*Syr.* 1; 12), Antiochos claims Ionia and Aiolis because they used to belong to the 'former kings of Asia', presumably the Achaimenids; which is similar, but not quite the same as appeal to ancestral rights.

Laodike III refers to the benevolence of Antiochos III to the Iasians after 're-acquiring your city', τὴν ὑμέτεραν πόλιν . . . ἀνακτησάμενος. A related expression (with the same ἀνα- prefix) is found in Zeuxis' letter to Herakleia under Latmos: ἀνακεκομισμένων ἡμῶν τῶι βασιλεῖ τὴν πόλιν ἐξ ἀρχῆς ὑπάρχουσαν τοῖς προγόνοις αὐτοῦ, 'as we had recovered for the king the city, which originally belonged to his ancestors', an even more explicit statement than Laodike's.[14] These documents show that Polybios' and Livy's accounts preserve the vocabulary of Seleukid memory. It is therefore an accident of preservation that we only have these two cases of historical claims to authority and ownership in direct interaction with the cities: such references to rights based on past ownership must have been common in royal discourse addressed to the cities.

Asia Minor was not the only area where claims were justified by appeal to inherited rights. In the conflict over Koile-Syria (Pol. 5.67.2), Antiochos III, determined to prevail in the field of armed conflict (τοῖς ὅπλοις) and of legal rights (τοῖς δικαίοις), claimed not to have acted unjustly in invading Koile-Syria, since he could lay historical claims to 'the most powerful and just titles of property', κυριωτάτας καὶ δικαιοτάτας κτήσεις, based on the victory won by Lysimachos, Kassandros, and Seleukos I over Antigonos Monophthalmos (the original ruler of Koile-Syria) and on the victors' agreement to concede Koile-Syria to Seleukos I (Pol. 5.67.6–8). Likewise, just as Antiochos III (and Polybios) could speak about cis-Tauric Asia Minor as if Seleukid authority in that region were absolute, Atropatene, Parthyene, and Baktria, independent principalities, were still mentioned by the Seleukids as 'satrapies'.[15] Just as cities of Asia Minor were addressed as historically subjects of the Seleukids, Antiochos III during the eastern expedition asserted his position in respect to the Baktrian kingdom by accusing the Baktrian king Euthydemos of being a rebel (ἀποστάτης) seceding from the Seleukid empire, to which Baktria rightfully belonged (Pol. 11.34.1–2). In the following century, Antiochos IV, during the Sixth Syrian War (168), justified himself before an audience of ambassadors from pro-Ptolemaic cities

---

[14] Documents 26 A, I 6–8; 31 B, II 8–10.

[15] Schmitt 1964: 123, on Pol. 5.43.6 (the rebel Molon secures his relations with 'the neighbouring satrapies'); since the actual Seleukid provinces that neighboured Molon's province resisted him later, these 'satrapies' must be the former Seleukid provinces which had seceded earlier in the third century. Walbank 1965: 264, bases his disagreement with Schmitt's view on a discussion of Pol. 11.34.14, where the expression 'the upper satraps' is taken by Schmitt also to designate independent princelings. Walbank's criticism of the latter point is justified, but does not disprove Schmitt's interpretation of Pol. 5.43.6.

bent upon brokering a peace. He referred to τὰ ἐξ ἀρχῆς δίκαια, his original rights to ownership (κτῆσις) over Koile-Syria, originating in the history of the Diadochs (Pol. 28.20.1–9). As Polybios observes, Antiochos IV, with these arguments, 'convinced not only himself, but also his audience that he was right' (Pol. 28.20.10).

The parallels provide a context for any interpretation of the claims formulated in regard to Asia Minor. Obviously, they perform a legal function, by asserting titles to property[16] founded on two principles which E. Bickerman regarded as the legal underpinnings of the Seleukid empire: the right of conquest, and the right of inheritance. An epigraphical document, mentioning the establishment of Seleukid power in Asia Minor, succinctly mentions both principles: 'Seleukos having gained power (ἐπικρατήσαντος) in the battle against Lysimachos, Antiochos, his son, having succeeded to the kingship (διαδεξάμενος τὴν βασιλείαν)'.[17] How could these two apparently contradictory principles coexist? Bickerman argued that rights to ownership were not established by mere takeover, but by the utter defeat of an opponent, resulting in his extinction (as in the case of Antigonos at Ipsos or of Lysimachos at Kouroupedion) or in the formal surrender of his title to ownership.[18] Therefore, according to Bickerman, aggression followed by occupation, even for a length of time, did not create rights to ownership (in contrast, Roman law acknowledged occupation (usucapio) as a source for legitimate ownership).[19] What mattered was not length or continuity of occupation, but the antiquity of the claim: for Bickerman, the claims of Antiochos III to the cities of Asia Minor and Thrace were justified within the framework of Greek legal thought,[20] because the rights established by the victory over Lysimachos still held true; diplomatic difficulties between Antiochos III and the Romans thus resulted from a misunderstanding between different legal conceptions in matters of property.

[16] On past narratives (in the poets and historians) as legal justification (μαρτύρια) of titles to ownership, see Holleaux 1938a: 404 n. 3; Chaniotis 1988: 114 n. 237; Curty 1989.

[17] OGIS 335, lines 132–3; Bikerman 1938: 14–17; further references in Mehl 1980/1: 175–6.

[18] Mehl 1980/1 neglects the distinction between debellatio (Bickermann 1932a: 51–2) and mere forcible occupation: this leads him to misunderstand the rights of conquest as interpreted by Bickerman.

[19] Bickermann 1932a: 51–2; Bikerman 1950: 123: mere occupation by force does not create 'droit de propriété'. Parallels for 'reacquiring': Bikerman 1950: 123–4. A gymnasiarch on Athenian-ruled Delos inscribed the list of gymnasiarchs ἀφ' οὗ ὁ δῆμος διὰ Ῥωμαίων ἀνεκτήσατο τὴν νῆσον, commemorating the recovery of Delos by Athens in 167 (Robert 1983: 249 quoting A. Plassart, BCH 36 (1912), 395, no. 9).

[20] Bickermann 1932a: 53. The envoys of Ptolemy IV, in the negotiations during the Fourth Syrian War, whilst proclaiming their rights to Koile-Syria, admitted the Seleukids claim to 'all of Asia', abetted by Ptolemy I himself (Pol. 5.67.10).

This view might be too simple. Though there existed accepted norms of international behaviour, there was no universally acknowledged, written, code of international law or *Kriegesrecht* (Mehl 1980/1: 177); when A. Mastrocinque speaks of a 'conflitto di diritto internazionale' and of the views held by the 'giurisprudenti seleucidici', this description strikes the wrong note (Mastrocinque 1983: 91–5). The legalistic approach passes over the fact that the language of property disputes is applied to acts of conquest and warfare. The insistence of Antiochos III on his inherited rights to regions which in his view were rightfully Seleukid can be interpreted as a programme of reconquest, the Great Idea to which Antiochos devoted his life.[21] The theme of Seleukid 'ancestors' of Seleukid kings, important in royal ideology,[22] reached a new level of intensity under Antiochos III, who inaugurated a joint state cult to himself and his ancestors.[23] Schmitt speaks of Antiochos' policy of restoring his ancestors' empire ('*Restitutor orbis*'), by a plan of conquest (*Eroberungsplan*), though Schmitt is careful to point out that within this master-plan, specific contingencies and opportunism played their role.[24]

Most importantly, a legalistic approach overlooks the political nature of the claims to 'ownership'. The Seleukids spoke about the past, in terms of ownership rights, not simply in reference to accepted legal principles, but in order to cover up or legitimize aggression against other kingdoms, the violent takeover of cities and the imposition of control in oppressive manifestations such as tribute or garrisons (Pol. 21.41.2). The problematic nature of conquest, and of royal power, is clear in the passage of Livy describing the resistance of Smyrna and Lampsakos to Antiochos III (above, Introduction). The same passage also shows how conquest is deproblematized by being grounded in the past: Antiochos decided to reduce all the cities of Asia *in antiquam imperii formulam* (Liv. 33.38).[25] Other examples, mostly in the epigraphical documentation, bring out the legitimizing role of allusion to the past, to the point that πάτριος χώρα is often used for territory which was pre-

[21] Bikermann 1932a: 51; Schmitt 1964: 85; Gruen 1986: 612–19 for a short account of Antiochos' actions and long term plans.
[22] *RC* 15, line 23 (under Antiochos II?); *RC* 22, line 2 (under Seleukos II) with Welles's comments, p. 109.
[23] Rostovtzeff 1935, Bikerman 1938: 247–50. Mastrocinque 1983: 114–16 for celebration of the ancestors under Antiochos III, notably in Seleukid literature.
[24] Schmitt 1964: ch. 2; policy: 85–8 (*Eroberungsplan*); 86–90, for nuances. Doubts on a master plan of reconquest: Badian 1966b: 711–12; Will 1982: 52–3.
[25] H. White has argued that historical narratives impose moralizing agendas and authoritative meanings that enable social control (White 1992: 1–25). Debatable in general, this view is appropriate for the Seleukid version of the past.

cisely contested between two states.[26] The functions performed by the Seleukid version of the past call for an exploration of what we know about Asia Minor before Antiochos III, to confront the Seleukid version with our own narratives; these produce a picture of fluctuating powers and local responses, at variance with the Seleukid claims but providing insights into their meaning.

2. Seleukid Asia Minor

The starting point is obvious enough: the founding act of violence, the victory of Seleukos I over Lysimachos at Kouroupedion in the Lydian plain (Feb. 281 BC), when 'all of Lysimachos' kingdom became spear-won to Seleukos'; this moment (and its aftermath in the years down to 279) marked the resolution of the complicated, fluid history of the Diadochoi into a more recognizably stable system, the Hellenistic world, which was still riven by super-power warfare, but saw far less radical changes in the political make up.'[27] There is no surviving continuous account of Seleukid activities in Asia Minor, but only fragments of literary evidence, so we must rely heavily on the epigraphical documentation. The latter requires patience and ingenuity, when used to piece together political–military narrative relations; its great advantage is that it provides direct evidence for the relations between the Seleukids and the local communities.[28]

It is possible to offer a summary narrative by reign. In the seven months between Kouroupedion and an ill-fated expedition to Europe to claim the rest of Lysimachos' kingdom, Seleukos I started reorganizing his new Anatolian province.[29] Upon his

[26] J. and L. Robert 1989: 75–6; 1 Macc. 15.33–4, used against the Seleukids. *CIL* I² 725 speaks of the Lykians' ancestral liberty, 'recovered' after 167; *OGIS* 337 speaks of the 'paternal democracy' (in the sense of independence) of Pergamon—both of which are pious inventions.

[27] Pol. 18.51.4; Will 1979: 10. The events are covered in the recent biographies of Seleukos (Mehl 1986: 290–9; Grainger 1990: 173–91) and Lysimachos (Lund 1992: 184–206; Franco 1993: 58–64). For a detailed, up-to-date narrative of the last years of the Diadochoi, Strobel 1996: 186–205. Rough Kilikia is a special case: it had already come under Seleukid control in 295 (Plut. *Dem.* 32 and 47), so that the two items we can ascribe to Seleukos I probably date before 281 (the foundation of Seleukeia on Kalykadnos, the benefaction of Seleukos I to the temple at Olba: Magie 1950: 268, 269, Cohen 1995: 369–71, Bringmann and von Steuben 1995: 517, no. 460). There is some evidence for cities that did not come to terms with Seleukos I: apart from Herakleia Pontike (Memnon *FGrHist* 434 F 7), see Le Rider 1971/2: 238 on cities that went on striking lysimachuses after 281.

[28] Most of the evidence is gathered in Orth 1977 (in 'decreasing order of amount of evidence available').

[29] Expedition to Europe: Memnon *FGrHist* 434 F 8.1–3; Justin 17.2.4 (seven

assassination (by his protégé Ptolemy Keraunos, a son of Ptolemy I) in 281, he was succeeded by his son and co-regent, Antiochos I (281–261), whose reign is marked by wars.[30] Early on, he fought a war against the 'Northern League' of recalcitrant cities on the Black Sea allied with the kingdom of Bithynia; he also fought against the king of the Macedonians, Antigonos Gonatas. More serious was the arrival of Celtic invaders, in a mass migration, part of the Celtic population movements which disrupted the high politics of the Hellenistic world in the years 280–c.275. The Galatians crossed into Asia Minor (some brought over by Nikomedes I of Bithynia during his fight against Antiochos, some crossing the Hellespont of their own volition). They wrought great havoc, vividly attested in inscriptions, in Lydia and Ionia in the 270s and in Phrygia in 268/7; but Antiochos I defeated them in the 'Elephant Battle', of unknown location and uncertain date (c.269?); the Galatians remained in possession of a vast territory in central Anatolia.[31] The evidence illustrates the violence of their onslaught and the permanent threat of depredations, but also the survival of the Seleukid state and the continued operation of its forms, as implied by documents such as the village decree found near Denizli (*I. Laodikeia am Lykos* 1, from Wörrle 1975) or the Lydian documents with their Seleukid dating formulas (*TAM* 5.2.881). Antiochos I also had to face a superpower rival, Ptolemy II, in the First Syrian War, fought in Asia Minor and Syria; finally, he was confronted with a recalcitrant local power, Eumenes (I), the dynast of Pergamon, who defeated him and asserted the independence of his principality. The wars of Antiochos II are even less well documented, though he seems to have been successful in them. His activity can be traced on the Straits (Memnon *FGrHist* 434 F 15 mentions a war against Byzantion), and possibly in Thrace (Polyain. 4.16).[32] The well-

months). On Seleukos after Kouroupedion and before his western expedition, Grainger 1990: 183–7; Mehl 1986: 299–315.

[30] On Antiochos I, Will 1979: 135–52; Sherwin-White and Kuhrt 1993: 21–37; Strobel 1996: 206–14.

[31] Will 1979: 143–4; Wörrle 1975: 61–71, proposing the date of c.269 or even later for the Elephant Battle; Robert, *OMS* vii. 538–9; Mitchell 1993: 13–19; and now especially Strobel 1991 and Strobel 1996 (reconstructing two main conflicts between Antiochos I and the Galatians: 278–c.275, when the Galatians supported Nikomedes I of Bithynia; c.269, when, on this view, they invaded the Seleukid dominion before being defeated at the Elephant Battle).

[32] On Antiochos II, Will 1979: 234–48, 293–4; collection of documents with discrete analyses of them in Orth 1977: 149–72. *Bella quam plurima* of Antiochos II: Porphyry, *FGrHist* 260 F 43 (= Jer. *Comm. in Dan.* 11.6). Thrace: the alliance between a king Antiochos and Lysimacheia is perhaps to be attributed to Antiochos II rather than Antiochos I (but certainly not Antiochos III: Appendix 3). Straits: the alliance between

known Samian decree honouring Boulagoras (*SEG* 1.366, lines 5–20) reveals that Antiochos II annexed parts of the Samian Anaitis—and that a number of his Friends helped themselves to estates on Samian territory.

Within this time-span, one area of early Seleukid activity which left its mark on the landscape of Asia Minor was royal 'colonization', the foundation of new cities, the refounding or renaming of previously existing cities, and the settlement of soldiers (often Macedonians) in 'military colonies'; the latter are well attested in Lydia, for instance at Thyateira (*OGIS* 211). Some of these foundations reflect the involvement of a particular king, such as Antiocheia in the Troad (founded out of Kebren and Birytis, detached from Alexandreia Troas), established by Antiochos I or II, both of whom were active in north-west Anatolia and Thrace; or Stratonikeia, in south-western Karia, probably founded by Antiochos II as part of his campaigns west of the Marsyas (next section). Others were located along the routes, especially the 'southern route' from Tralleis to northern Syria, via the Kilikian gates[33] in the Maeander valley (Tralleis, renamed Seleukeia; Nysa, the product of a Seleukid synoikism; Antiocheia on Maeander; Laodikeia on Lykos, Hierapolis, Apameia/Kelainai), and at the start of the central Anatolian segment (Antiocheia near Pisidia; perhaps Apollonia in Pisidia; Seleukeia 'Sidera'; Laodikeia Kekaumene). Routes branching off this main road also received Seleukid foundations: Apollonia under Salbake on the Tabai plateau, on the short-cut off the Maeander valley, up the Geyre valley, and to the Acıpayam plain; Alabanda, renamed or refounded as Antiocheia, at the north end of the Marsyas valley; Seleukeia on Kalykadnos, on the road from the coast through Rough Kilikia to central Anatolia.[34] Exact attribution to whichever of the first three Seleukids is often difficult, in the state of the evidence (because of the brevity of his stay in Anatolia, Seleukos I is unlikely to have been the most active). What is striking is the large number of foundations, and their presence in the Anatolian *lieux de passage*: they constituted visible signs of Seleukid power, expressed though dynastic names, and wrote the Seleukids into the landscape.

Lysimacheia and a king Antiochos must be attributed to the time of Antiochos II (or perhaps I) rather than Antiochos III: Gauthier and Ferrary 1981.

[33] Syme 1995: 3–23 on 'the Royal Road', from the Maeander valley to the east, via the crucial crossroad in Phrygia, near modern Afyon. This is the route taken by the Ten Thousand: Xen. *Anab.* 1.2.7–21.

[34] The evidence and the bibliography are gathered and discussed in Cohen 1995; Billows 1995: 145–82 for a general survey.

Other manifestations of Seleukid presence were the structures of state power, which I will discuss later, drawing on both the earlier evidence and the documents from the time of Antiochos III (Ch. 3). For the present purposes of filling in the background to the *prostagma* issued by Antiochos III in 209, it might be enough to evoke an impression of the structures in Seleukid Asia Minor: the governors and their subordinates, the financial officials, the 'bureaucracy' through which royal orders flowed both vertically to reach subject communities and horizontally between officials,[35] the armies, the fortresses and their commanders; the 'provincial capital' of Sardeis, the world of the ancient Hellenic cities (mostly near the sea), the sanctuaries, the tributary lands stretching from the Hellespont to the Taurus,[36] the villages, the cities in the royal land, usually royal foundations; and finally the routes[37] such as the southern highway mentioned above. The picture can be capped by the figure of Antiochos II as he appears in the Boulagoras inscription, moving up country from the royal residence at Ephesos, on his way to the 'provincial capital' of Sardeis, followed by a Samian embassy intent upon reclaiming estates seized by the king's Friends and finally restored to the Samians after a hearing before the king.

The evidence suggests an increase in intensity and sophistication of these structures under Antiochos II. His northern activity is reflected in the coinage of some cities in the Troad, whose issues of alexanders were replaced by royal Seleukid coinage, in an assertion of royal authority; likewise, Lysimacheia, allied to Antiochos I, seems to have been taken over by Antiochos II, under whom the city minted Seleukid tetradrachms.[38] The same intensification of royal control can be seen in documents recording a sale of royal land to Laodike I (*Inschr. Didyma* 492, cf. *RC* 18–20), and attesting to complex forms of Seleukid land-administration (a similar transaction under Antiochos I, documented in *RC* 10–13, allows us to measure the difference). At Aigai, a boundary-stone records a survey marking out civic territory under Antiochos II (Herrmann 1959), perhaps implying the same desire to record and clarify the Seleukids' cadastral knowledge of the immense Anatolian province.

---

[35] For instance, *RC* 19; royal archives, *RC* 18, lines 27–8 and *RC* 19, lines 15–16.

[36] Laffi 1971: pl. 10.2, gives a photograph (June 1970) of the plain near the temple of Zeus at Aizanoi, in Phrygia: the rolling agricultural plain just after the harvest, a wagon heaped high with corn, the small figures of peasants in the landscape, help imagine (without any pretension at rigorous historical ecology) the inland swathe of Seleukid Asia Minor.

[37] *RC* 20, lines 10–11, proves that there was a distinct category of 'royal roads', ὁδὸς βασιλική.

[38] Seleukid coinage replacing alexanders at Lampsakos, Abydos, and Alexandreia Troas: Le Rider 1971/2: 234–9. Lysimacheia: Ferrary and Gauthier 1981.

In the context of increasingly active and complex royal control, it comes as no surprise to hear of Dion, the official in charge of the shrines and their income, appointed under Antiochos II; nor is it surprising that Antiochos III should seek precedent from the time of his active and successful grandfather (see § 1)

Another aspect of Seleukid Asia Minor was the relation between king and city. Most of the documentary evidence comes from the cities, which are at pains to present a positive image. Cities paid honours to the Seleukid king, from physical objects such as the crown and the golden 'hospitality gifts' offered by the Erythraians (*RC* 15), to more impressive forms—for instance, honorific statues (εἰκόνες), attested at Priene for Seleukos I and Antiochos I, and at Ilion for (probably) Antiochos I, in a lavish version: a gilt equestrian image set up in the most visible spot of the temple of Athena Ilias.[39] The erection of statues belongs to the idiom of civic honours for benefactors; more intriguing are the quasi-cultic and cultic honours which acknowledged royal power: the naming of civic subdivisions or of months in the civic calendar after kings, the celebration of festivals in honour of a king or named after him (such as the Antiocheia of Kolophon) and the offering of sacrifices to the king (for instance Teos for Antiochos I).[40] A good example is Smyrna, which multiplied cultic honours for the Seleukids. Months received Seleukid names: Antiocheon, Stratonikeon, and Laodikeon, implying festivals for their namesakes (attested in the case of the Antiocheia). Cults are specifically documented for Antiochos I ('god and saviour'), Antiochos II, Stratonike (under the title 'Aphrodite Stratonikis': the main civic shrine of Aphrodite now associated a Seleukid queen to the goddess), and Seleukos II.[41] As in the case of the inscriptions which record them, these 'honours worth mentioning' (τιμαὶ ἀξιόλογοι: *OGIS* 229, line 10) were intended as permanent additions to the civic landscape: the Seleukid months of Smyrna survived into the imperial period (Robert 1966*b*: 15).

Honours for the king were part of a dialogue, where the king heard petitions and granted benefactions (as in *RC* 15), in an atmosphere of mutual goodwill (εὔνοια: e.g. *OGIS* 229, lines 5–10)[42]

---

[39] Priene: *Inschr. Priene* 18, line 86; Ilion: *OGIS* 219, lines 35–8 (for attribution see Appendix 1).

[40] On honours for kings, Gauthier 1985 and Price 1984: 25–40. The evidence for cultic honours to the Seleukids (after Seleukos I) is discussed by Habicht 1970: 83–5 for Antiochos I at Ilion, and 91–105 for the Ionian League (*OGIS* 222), Erythrai (probably), Teos (*CIG* 3075) and Miletos (honours for Antiochos II).

[41] Habicht 1970: 99–102 (but see Rigsby 1996: 97–9, arguing that the title was a pre-existing epithet and not invented to honour the Seleukid queen).

[42] On this theme, in the context of Antiochos III, see Ch. 4.

This picture of the relations between city and ruler as diplomacy and cordial reciprocity is of course exactly the image which the rituals and the documents of the cities sought to publicize in permanent form. This is not a reliable source to evaluate the place of the cities within the Seleukid empire and their relation with the kings; Heuss's excessive reliance on the discourse produced by the cities resulted in his much-criticized view of royal *de iure* respect for city autonomy (Heuss 1937). At the other extreme, W. Orth has approached the documents with suspicion, and endeavoured to show how the cordial language of honours and reciprocity dissimulated a tense relationship of authoritarianism and subjection (Orth 1977). Orth's treatment is occasionally simplistic and overstated,[43] though his refusal to take the city documents at face value is a methodologically sound starting point, and he has managed to dispel the picture of the early Seleukids as disinterested friends of the cities in Asia Minor.

But the fact that the image of cordiality and benevolence presented by the cities is a construct does not mean that it should be condemned as non-factual and devoid of interest. We can still observe how the Seleukid past was refracted and preserved in multiple local histories and traces of royal activity. These substantiated the Seleukid claims to authority and legitimacy: the cities offered the visible forms of monuments and memorial rituals, which a royal interlocutor could pick out, to resume a dialogue located in continuity with the past. The letter of Seleukos II to the Milesians (*RC* 22) shows how the dynastic past could be used in communication between city and ruler, by linking themes of royal ideology with local memories, and even local human agents, the πατρικοὶ φίλοι to whom Seleukos II refers (line 9); conversely, a city such as Ilion could evoke its honours for Seleukos I in a decree for his son, Antiochos I (*OGIS* 219, lines 46–7). So this, too, was Seleukid Asia Minor: traces of the Seleukid past, local histories which presented an image of royal benevolence and civic gratitude in the form of τιμαὶ ἀξιόλογοι, an image which in turn could substantiate present claims and define the parameters for further rounds of interaction.

---

[43] For instance Orth overinterprets when he reads *Inschr. Priene* 18 between the lines to produce a story of Prienian discontent manifested through slow implementation of an honorific decree for a Seleukid official (Gauthier 1980).

3. A Seleukid Past?

The preceding section was written from the point of view of Seleukid memory, in search of a Seleukid Asia Minor—a deliberate over-simplification, leaving out the complexities of political history.[44] If one does not write solely within the Seleukid claims, it is possible to sketch out a narrative history which would have been unpalatable to the Seleukids, since it was essentially a story of their losses.

The most serious omission is the Ptolemaic presence, which is also absent from the Polybian descriptions of Achaios' activities: Achaios takes back, then rules over 'all of the land on this side of Taurus'—with no mention of the Ptolemaic empire in Asia Minor.[45] How and when the Ptolemies gained this dominion is obscure— perhaps in 281, immediately after Seleukos I was murdered—the so-called 'War of Syrian succession',[46] but possibly earlier, during the war between Seleukos I and Lysimachos, as suggested by epigraphical evidence from Lykia.[47] This intriguingly implies that Seleukid presence in Lykia and Karia was never actualized, but remained virtual, Lysimachan control being immediately succeeded by Ptolemaic presence; this certainly was the case for Samos.[48] Another possibility is that Ptolemaic conquest took place in several stages. Lykia may have become Ptolemaic early on, and Kilikia conquered later, during the First Syrian War: a recently published inscription indicates that the Nagidians participated in the foundation of a city named [Antio]cheia, perhaps under Antiochos I. This dating (on palaeographical grounds) is compatible with the earliest extant evidence for the Ptolemaic presence in Kilikia, the foundation of Arsinoe in the 260s.[49]

Two things are established. The first is the earliness of the

[44] Orth 1977 does not integrate the non-Seleukid elements of the period (for instance, never mentioning the Ptolemies), a serious problem with his final picture.

[45] Bagnall 1976: 80–116, 168–75 for Asia Minor; Huss 1976: 188–209, completing Magie 1950: 929 n. 25. This section is heavily indebted to A. Meadows.

[46] For a standard account of the 'War of Syrian succession' or 'crise successorale', Will 1979: 139–41, with sources and further references.

[47] It is possible that Lykia was already taken over by Ptolemy I in c.295, if Wörrle's dating of a Limyran inscription to 288 ('year 36' of Ptolemy I) is correct (Wörrle 1977, cf. SEG 27.929); but Meadows has pointed out to me that one could date this inscription to 247 (year 36 of Ptolemy II), and also reject the dating to Ptolemy I of an Amyzonian inscription (J. and L. Robert 1983: no. 6)—in which case the earliest evidence is a Telmessian decree dated to 282 (Wörrle 1978).

[48] Seleukid authority remaining purely virtual at Samos between Lysimachan control and Ptolemaic presence: Habicht 1957: 209–11. I. Stratonikeia 1001 should be dated to Seleukos II rather than Seleukos I (Cohen 1995: 271).

[49] Nagidos: Jones and Russell 1993: no. 2; Arsinoe: Jones and Habicht 1989.

Ptolemaic presence in Asia Minor, from the late 280s—at the same time as the earliest Seleukid documents. The second fact, equally incontrovertible and impressive, is the extent of the Ptolemaic dominions. Theocritus could write that Ptolemy II 'gives orders to all the Pamphylians, the Kilikian spearmen, the Lykians, and the warlike Karians' (17.88–9): the encomiastic vision rests on the reality of a majestic overseas empire.

It is now clear that the Ptolemaic holdings, far from simply being a string of harbours controlled by sea, stretched inland on all fronts. Ptolemaic Karia included maritime cities such as Iasos, Halikarnassos, Myndos, and Kaunos (and perhaps the Milesian peninsula as well), but also cities further east, such as Amyzon, Euromos, Mylasa, and whatever community there was on the site of the future Stratonikeia; it is likely that the province of Karia, under its own governor (*strategos*), comprised all of Karia west of the river Marsyas (the former Hekatomnid satrapy).[50] In Lykia, Ptolemaic control, starting from the coastal cities (such as Lissa, Telmessos, Patara, and Andriake), reached inland to the communities located along the river valleys, for instance along the Xanthos (Xanthos, Tlos, Araxa), or the Arykandos (Limyra, Arykanda). An epigram from Tlos shows a Ptolemaic general and courtier, Neoptolemos, beating off an invasion of the Xanthos valley.[51] The one piece of evidence for Pamphylia shows that the authority of the Ptolemaic Παμφυλιάρχης included the city of Termessos, some way inland (Robert 1966a: 53–8). For Kilikia, the evidence for Ptolemaic cities on the coast (taken over by Antiochos III in 197: Mallos, Zephyrion, Soloi, Aphrodisias of Kilikia, Korykos, Anemourion, and finally Korakesion, and other nameless *castella*, Liv. 33.20.4) has been supplemented by two discoveries: an inscription recording an episode in the vicissitudes of a Ptolemaic foundation named Arsinoe, on the coast near Nagidos, and a Ptolemaic-held site at Meydancık Kalesi (about 15 kilometres from the coast)—controlling the shortest way from Kelenderis even further inland, to

---

[50] Karia: the evidence is gathered by Magie 1950: 926 n. 21 and 929 n. 25; Bagnall 1976: 89–102; Huss 1976: 193–200; Euromos: Errington 1993: no. 3. The *strategos* of Karia is honoured by the Amyzonians (J. and L. Robert 1983: no. 3) and by the Samians under Ptolemy II (Habicht 1957: 218, no. 57). I owe the observation that Ptolemaic Karia was equivalent to the Hekatomnid satrapy to A. Meadows.

[51] The evidence is gathered in Bagnall 1976: 105–10 and Huss 1976: 191–3, with Bousquet 1986 providing freshly discovered evidence for Xanthos. Tlos: Robert *OMS* vii. 531–48, on Neoptolemos, honoured at Tlos for defeating a force of Agrianians, Pisidians, and Galatians; since the Agrianians were traditionally crack Macedonian troops, the people defeated by Neoptolemos must have been a mixed force of mercenaries under Seleukid command (Strobel 1991: 125–6) rather than roving Galatians with allies.

the Kalykadnos valley.[52] The latter case shows that 'Euergetes' dominion in Rough Cilicia constituted a network of places and routes, not merely a string of defensible sites along the coast' (Jones and Habicht 1989: 335): this remark applies to the Ptolemaic empire in Asia Minor generally. Theocritus spoke of the fleet of Ptolemy II as well as his 'many horsemen and many shield-bearing soldiers, girt in shining bronze' (17.90–4); prosaically, Polybios mentions the mercenaries stationed in αἱ ἔξω πόλεις, 'the cities abroad' (5.63.8). The overseas dominions formed a defensive system protecting Egypt: the Ptolemies 'stretched out their arm afar' (μακρὰν ἐκτε-ταχότες τὰς χεῖρας, Pol. 5.34.9). The holdings in Asia Minor clearly show how deep inland, from an early date onwards, the long arm of the Ptolemies could reach.

It is against this background of extended and durable Ptolemaic rule in Asia Minor that we should evaluate the Seleukid claims to authority over Asia Minor, starting with Antiochos II and his achievements as conqueror and organizer.[53] Ptolemy II reacted to the death of Antiochos I in 261 BC by attacking the Seleukid empire, as he (possibly) did at the death of Seleukos I. The details of the 'Second Syrian War' fought by Antiochos II between 261 and c.254, in Syria as well as in Asia Minor, are heavily disputed. What is clear is the consequent 'fine Seleukid resurgence'.[54] Antiochos II cut deep into the Ptolemaic possessions, favoured by the revolt of 'Ptolemy the son', the co-regent of Ptolemy II and in high command in Asia Minor.[55] Miletos, Ptolemaic since c.280, was 'liberated', after the interlude of an Aitolian adventurer's tyranny, by Antiochos II, who received divine honours from the Milesians. At the same occasion,

---

[52] Arsinoe: Jones and Habicht 1989: 328–35; Meydancık Kalesi: references at Jones and Habicht 1989: 335 n. 44 (admittedly the evidence is only for occupation under Ptolemy III; the general point of Ptolemaic control reaching inland still holds).

[53] Rather than reconstruct an earlier inroad under Antiochos I, on the basis of *I. Stratonikeia* 1030, a decree from an unnamed community, found at Turgut (Lagina) and dated to 268 by Seleukid kings and era, I prefer to assume that the stone is a *pierre errante* from Seleukid-held eastern Karia (Appendix 5, n. 1).

[54] Antiochos II and the 'Second Syrian War': Will 1979: 234–43.

[55] The co-regent, Ptolemy the son, appears in *RC* 14, line 9 (letter of Ptolemy II to the Milesians); his revolt (Trog. *Prol.* 26) must have taken place after the last known mention of him as co-regent, in April/May 259 (*PCZ* 3) (following Meadows *per litt.*, I would date 'Ptolemy of Ephesos' (Athen. 13.593b) to the period of Ptolemy III). Ptolemy the son is also mentioned in a subsequent inscription from Mylasa (Crampa 1969: no. 3; the document does not prove, as Crampa believed, that Ptolemy the son was still alive and active—in Seleukid service—c.240). Gauthier, in *BE* 95, 523, suggests a mention to Ptolemy the son in an Euromian inscription (Errington 1993: no. 3); *contra*, Blümel 1996 (arguing that the space is too short for Gauthier's restoration). The evidence is summarized, and re-evaluated (somewhat speculatively) in Huss 1998.

he took the Ptolemaic base of Samos; in the south, he must have taken Pamphylia and Kilikia.[56]

Better documented is the advance into the inland Karian province of the Ptolemies, a large portion of which passed to Seleukid control (as is attested under the successor of Antiochos II, Seleukos II, for Mylasa, once a Ptolemaic city). The Seleukid governor of the region, Olympichos, whose long career is documented later on, was perhaps appointed at this time. Alabanda was probably renamed Antiocheia as a result of the Karian campaign of Antiochos II; at the other end of the Marsyas valley, the king founded Stratonikeia, on a site distinguished by its great shrines and its strategic position on important routes (the Marsyas valley, leading from the Maeander plain southwards, and the route leading eastwards from Mylasa past Mobolla to the Tabai plateau). He took Alinda and Mylasa; further west, Bargylia, and, perhaps even Iasos and Herakleia (if mentions, made under Antiochos III, of earlier Seleukid dominion do not refer to the blanket claims to Asia Minor: above, section 1).[57]

But the extent of the Seleukid success does not diminish the fact that it was a reaction to Ptolemaic power: a reaction to the Ptolemaic aggression which started the Second Syrian War, but also, generally, a reaction to the presence in Asia Minor of the Ptolemaic empire, contiguous to the Seleukid dominions, on territory which may have been taken over by Seleukos I and which could be construed as legally belonging to the Seleukids. Antiochos II was a reconqueror: his activities in northern Asia Minor and in Thrace perhaps show his intention to recover territory once ruled over by Seleukos I.

That the activities of Antiochos II were a reaction to the Ptolemies is in itself significant. The Seleukid viewpoint was expressed in terms of rights over 'all of the land beyond the Taurus',

[56] Samos: *SEG* 1.366. Rough Kilikia and Pamphylia were lost to Ptolemy II, since they are mentioned in Theocritus (17.88), but no longer in the list of lands which Ptolemy III inherited from his father (*OGIS* 54).

[57] On Olympichos, see Crampa 1969: nos. 1, 3, 4; J. and L. Robert 1983: 149–50: since Olympichos was based in the city of Alinda, he must also have controlled Amyzon (though it then becomes odd that Zeuxis, in his letter to the Amyzonians in 203 did not mention a Seleukid past: document 5). The evidence for attributing to Antiochos II the partial conquest of Western Karia is circumstantial rather than direct (though Le Rider 1990 proposes numismatic evidence for Mylasa; also *BCH* 120 (1996), 773–5). Alabanda: Robert 1973. Stratonikeia: Debord 1994, and Appendix 5 of the present work; the narrative context suggests Antiochos II as founder rather than Antiochos I (Steph. Byz.): see further Appendix 5, n. 1. A Laodikeia, near Stratonikeia (Ma 1997), the 'Laudiceni ex Asia' of Liv. 33.18.3, seems like a further Seleukid implantation in the region. Bargylia: *Syll.* 426 should be dated to Antiochos II rather than Antiochos I (the official Alexandros mentioned there later appears under Seleukos II: Bengtson 1944: 94–110). Iasos, Herakleia: documents **26** A, **31** B.

shading into a belief in continuity of control. It is true that the greater part of cis-Tauric Asia Minor was in Seleukid hands, and that traces of Seleukid presence could be found in various forms. But the Ptolemies controlled a sizeable portion, taken simultaneously with the Seleukid conquest of Lysimachos' empire. The history of the Ptolemaic overseas holdings runs parallel, from the start, to the history of the Seleukid Anatolian dominion; Seleukid claims about geography, power, and history were confronted by the continuous challenge of the Ptolemaic possessions, which, as the epigraphical material amply shows, took the same forms as the Seleukid empire (administration and exaction)[58] and left the same traces of dynastic euergetism.

4. Seleukid Collapse in Anatolia

Perhaps Antiochos III drew general inspiration from Antiochos II, his grandfather, (re)conqueror and administrator; hence the reference to precedent from the time of Antiochos II, in the appointment of Nikanor. But there was another, much simpler reason. The years between the death of Antiochos II (246 BC) and the accession of Antiochos III (223 BC) saw the collapse of Seleukid power in Asia Minor, through a combination of intra-dynastic conflict and external wars. The need, obvious in the appointment of Nikanor, to refer back to a past of strong rule located before this confused period of losses, is in itself significant: either there was no clear trace of Seleukid practice in those intervening years, or the losses deprived the cis-Tauric office of any meaning, or perhaps Antiochos III chose not to acknowledge or mention the arrangements taken by the usurper, Antiochos Hierax. At any rate, the *prostagma*, through its attempt at denial, is an admission of the Seleukid losses. The events themselves are badly documented, so that it is difficult to produce a sequence for the major developments (chronology is especially insecure): the Laodikeian War, the Third Syrian War, the Brothers' War, and the successes of Attalos I.

The first Seleukid reverses took place between 246 and 241. The Laodikeian War was, at least initially, a dynastic conflict within the Seleukid empire, between two claimants to the succession of Antiochos II, on his death in 246: his baby son (named Antiochos, we now know) by a Ptolemaic princess, Berenike, and Seleukos, his son by an earlier wife, later divorced, Laodike I. Seleukos (II) prevailed; but the dynastic conflict provided the opportunity for inter-

[58] Bagnall 1976; Jones and Habicht 1989.

vention by Ptolemy III—the 'Third Syrian War', which took place in Syria, Mesopotamia, and the Aegean.[59]

Two features are important. First, the war affected the local communities—two cities on opposing sides (Smyrna in the Seleukid camp and Telmessos on the Ptolemaic) could mention, in decrees, the ravages of the same war[60]—yet also brings out, to the modern observer, the importance of the local communities' collaboration with the Hellenistic empires, and the latter's need for local loyalty.[61] The documentary record shows Seleukos' willingness to ensure the cities' loyalty by benefactions. Smyrna received recognition of *asylia*, a grant of *autonomia*, exemption from tribute and the restoration of 'ancestral' land (*OGIS* 228 and 229, lines 10–12); Mylasa also received liberty at this time (Crampa 1969: 82–3); a letter of Seleukos II to Miletos (*RC* 22), though the actual decision is lost (leaving only the dynastic rhetoric), probably concerned an analogous grant. Similarly, Kildara was rewarded for good behaviour by the Ptolemaic official Tlepolemos (Blümel 1992, with Gauthier in *BE* 94, 528). In many of these cases, the actual rewards were the result of petitions by the local community, acting on its awareness of its master's need for its collaboration.

The second feature is the vast Ptolemaic gain by the end of the war. Ptolemy III made inroads into the Syrian and Mesopotamian heartland of the Seleukid empire (a fragment of his report survives).[62] Not all of his gains in this region were short-lived: Seleukeia in Pieria was kept by the Ptolemies down to 218 (Pol. 5.58.10). Even more spectacular were the conquests in Asia Minor, of which Ptolemy III boasted (*OGIS* 54, lines 14–15).[63] Ptolemy III cancelled out the (re)conquests of Antiochos II in Kilikia and Pamphylia (though probably not in Karia);[64] in Ionia, he retook Miletos, Ephesos, and Samos, and extended Ptolemaic control into Seleukid territory, taking over Magnesia on Maeander, Priene

---

[59] Sources in Magie 1950: 736 n. 22. An inscription from Kildara in Karia (Blümel 1992, reproduced as *SEG* 42.994) reveals that Berenike's son was named (unsurprisingly) Antiochos. Divorce: Jer. *In Dan.* 11.6 = *FGrHist* 260 F 43. The land sale recorded in *RC* 18–20 is probably part of a divorce settlement.

[60] Smyrna: *OGIS* 229, lines 3–5 ; Telmessos: *OGIS* 55, line 10. *OGIS* 229 does not mention a 'siege of Smyrna' (Elwyn 1990: 179), but merely the ravaging of the city territory (as common an occurrence in Hellenistic as in Classical warfare).

[61] An echo of this fact is preserved in Justin 27, who describes 'all the cities of Asia' supporting first Berenike, then Seleukos II; even if this account is too schematic, Justin's attention to the cities' behaviour shows the importance of local support.

[62] Justin 27 for the course of the war; the report of Ptolemy III (the famous Gourob papyrus) in *FGrHist* 160, with Holleaux 1942: 281–310.

[63] Magie 1950: 936 n. 31; Will 1979: 259–61.

[64] For Rough Kilikia, the most important evidence comes from the recently published inscription from Arsinoe (Jones and Habicht 1989), and the Meydancik Kalesi site.

(perhaps), Kolophon, Lebedos (renamed Ptolemais), and perhaps Teos.[65] The Troad, the Hellespont, and Thrace show clear evidence for Ptolemaic structures of control, Larisa (refounded as Ptolemais), at Maroneia and Ainos, and possibly even at Priapos, on the south coast of Propontis, and hence implying Ptolemaic control not just at the Straits, but beyond them.[66]

The next phase of Anatolian warfare brought even graver reverses for the Seleukids. The younger brother (and co-regent?) of Seleukos II, Antiochos (nicknamed Hierax, the Hawk), after being appointed over cis-Tauric Asia Minor, seceded from Seleukid authority and, with the help of Galatian mercenaries, resisted attempts to subdue him, defeating Seleukos II before Ankyra; as a result of his victory in the Brothers' War, Antiochos Hierax ruled in Asia Minor as an independent king, striking his own coinage.[67] At some point, Hierax and his Galatian allies attacked Attalos I—with disastrous results. Attalos I defeated Hierax repeatedly, celebrating his victories in a triumphal monument (the famous 'long base', with its inscriptions and the sculpture it once supported), which give us the locations of these battles: at the Aphrodision near Pergamon, in Hellespontine Phrygia, at a place called Koloe in Lydia, and finally in Karia (*OGIS* 275, 278, 279, 280). Eusebius (preserving Porphyry: *FGrHist* 260 F 32.8) gives the date of 229/8 for Koloe and 228/7 for the battle in Karia. Hierax turned against Seleukos II; worsted in

---

[65] Magnesia on Maeander: *FGrHist* 260 F 32.8; Priene: *Inschr. Priene* 37, line 153 mentions a Ptolemaic official. Ephesos was in Ptolemaic hands during the Brothers' War (*FGrHist* 260 F 32.8). Samos: *SEG* 1.366. Kolophon: an unpublished decree for a Ptolemaic official, found at Klaros, attests 'une occupation lagide à Colophon, comme à Lebedos, et à Ephèse, et aussi, à notre avis, à Téos' (Robert, *OMS* iv. 183–4); J. and L. Robert 1989: 53 n. 267 (correct 'Philadelphe' to 'Evergète'). Lebedos: *Inschr. Magnesia* 53, line 79: Πτολεμαιεῖς οἱ πρότερον καλούμενοι Λεβέδιοι. Teos: apart from the Kolophonian decree mentioned above, an unpublished Teian inscription found by the Roberts mentions Ptolemaic queens: *OMS* iv. 149.

[66] Larisa: Robert 1987: 281–95, Cohen 1995: 157–9 (with bibliography). Ainos: a decree professes concern for the well-being of Ptolemy III and his family, which implies Ptolemaic occupation (Herzog and Klaffenbach 1952, no. 8). Maroneia: the decrees for Hippomedon, *strategos* of Thrace and Epinikos, the governor of Maroneia, republished by Gauthier 1979. Priapos: *SEG* 34.1256 (both Şahin, the first scholarly editor of the inscription, and Gauthier in *BE* 87, 280, are cautious about identifying the Hippomedon honoured at Priapos with the Ptolemaic governor, and hence about the dating to Ptolemy III). Some of these territorial gains were perhaps made during the troubled period of the Brothers' War or the conflict with Attalos I; certainly, the dispatch of Magas, son of Ptolemy III, to Asia Minor against Seleukos II or III (Huss 1977) indicates close attention to Asia Minor after the truce of 241/0.

[67] Will 1979: 294–6 (based on the chronology of Bickerman 1943/4). Ankyra: Trog. *Prol.* 27, Galatian mercenaries in Justin 27.2. The battle at Ankyra perhaps implies an invasion of Galatia by Seleukos II. Hierax's coinage is documented in the Troad, at Ilion, Alexandreia Troas, Abydos, Lampsakos, Parion (Le Rider 1971/2: 232–8); at Lysimacheia (Ferrary and Gauthier 1981: 343) and at Sardeis (Le Rider 1972/3: 251–2, based on Mørkholm 1969).

Mesopotamia, he took to flight, before meeting a violent end at the hands of bandits (Justin 27.3) or Galatians (Trogus, *Prol*. 27).

Both the Brothers' War and Attalos' victories are badly documented, and not yet elucidated by new epigraphical discoveries. The absolute chronology and the relation between the two sets of events remain obscure: one solution is to locate the Brothers' War *c*.239 BC, followed by several years of calm, until Hierax attacked the Attalid kingdom *c*.230, though it is also possible that Hierax's attack took place earlier, soon after the end of the Brothers' War; alternatively, it has been argued that the Brothers' War broke out later, in the late 230s, in parallel to the war between Hierax and Attalos I.[68]

For the present purpose, it is better to focus on the suggestive location of the battles between Attalos I and Hierax: Attalos I drove Hierax southwards, in a geographical progression which took over the inland masses of Seleukid Asia Minor. An inscription from the city of Aizanoi, in Phrygia, records a land donation by Attalos I to the city and to its shrine of Zeus: rather than reflecting Attalid advances around 216, this document preserves a trace of Attalos' conquest of the Seleukid hinterland.[69] The outcome is described by Polybios (4.48.7): 'Attalos had subjected to himself all of the *dynasteia* of the land on this side of the Taurus'; the Pergamene victory monuments celebrate achievement and completion. However, the picture in Polybios is certainly exaggerated, even though Attalos I did take over the vast majority of Seleukid possessions in Asia Minor. The cities of the Troad probably became 'allies' of Attalos I; more direct rule was imposed on the cities of Aiolis, and on Teos and Kolophon; Smyrna presumably became a free 'ally'.[70]

---

[68] Different solutions in Bickerman 1943/4 (high dating for Brothers' War, immediately followed by attack on Attalos I); Allen 1983: 195–9, following Beloch 1927: 541–3 for a low dating of the Brothers' War. Allen 1983: 35, believes that the battle in Hellespontine Phrygia occurred after the others, as Hierax was on his way to Thrace; but at that stage Hierax was probably already an adventurer without a kingdom.

[69] The inscription (a letter of Hadrian reconfirming a Hellenistic donation by 'Attalos', then Prousias I—presumably Attalos I, though Schwertheim 1988: 73 suggests Attalos II), first published (*non vidi*) in *Bolletino del Museo dell'Impero Romano* 9 (1938), 44 (*AE* 1940, no. 44); also republished, with the related epigraphical dossier from the temple of Zeus itself, in Laffi 1971. We now know that the date of Attalos' control of the site of Aizanoi is not *c*.216 (as had been suggested by Habicht 1956: 93–4): see Ch. 2 § 1.

[70] Pol. 5.77–8: in 218, Attalos I exploited the absence of Achaios to embark in a campaign of reconquest: Kyme, Phokaia, Aigai, Temnos are named, as well as Teos and Kolophon, which were taken over 'on the same agreements (συνθῆκαι) as formerly', a clear statement that these cities had been Attalid previously, i.e. since *c*.228; the same assumption must be made for the other cities. Smyrna, Lampsakos, Alexandreia Troas, and Ilion are mentioned as faithful allies. Since Teos and Kolophon had been taken over by Ptolemy III in the aftermath of the Laodikeian War, it seems that Attalos I took these cities from the Ptolemies (unless they had in the meantime fallen to Seleukos II or Hierax, or regained their independence).

In contrast, there are no traces of Attalid presence in Karia, and it even seems that Seleukos II managed to recover some measure of control, since the Sardeis mint struck coins of Seleukos II. The battles which Attalos I fought against 'Seleukos' and his generals (*OGIS* 277, *Inschr. Pergamon* 36) might have taken place against Seleukos II rather than Seleukos III (as usually asserted), reflecting Seleukid efforts late in the reign of Seleukos II.

But the Seleukid hold over Asia Minor was shattered. Sardeis soon escaped Seleukid authority (at the beginning of the reign of Seleukos III): the former Seleukid capital may even have struck its own coinage after 226, as 'autonomous' city under the Attalids.[71] Other cities asserted and preserved genuine independence: Magnesia on Maeander and Miletos were possibly independent (under nominal Ptolemaic authority?); Iasos seems to have been free from Ptolemaic control around 215: when faced with incursions from a local dynast, the Iasians did not appeal to a Ptolemy for help, but to Rhodes (*I. Iasos* 150).[72]

The Iasian document illustrates two further developments in the years after the fall of Hierax. The dynast who invaded the Iasians' territory was Olympichos, the former Seleukid governor over parts of western Karia under Seleukos II. By the time of his conflict with Iasos (*c.*215), he had become a subordinate official of Philip V, king of Macedon, who had inherited authority over parts of Karia from his predecessor, Antigonos Doson. The latter mounted a seaborne expedition to Karia, in the early years of Doson's reign (probably a single campaigning season by the king himself, in 227 or 226 or 225). Its rationale, execution, and outcome remain a mystery. Nonetheless, such a development was made possible by the disintegration of Seleukid power (or more accurately of Hierax's kingdom) in Asia Minor and the subsequent confusion. One possibility is that local powers (such as individual cities, or even Olympichos) appealed to Antigonos Doson for assistance against Attalos I.[73] The

---

[71] Seyrig 1986: 39–42, disputed by Price 1991: 321, who assigns the coinage to the 180s, because of the presence of a Sardian alexander in mint condition in a hoard of Larisa dated to the 160s (but Price admits difficulties with this dating, since after 188, Sardeis was an Attalid city and a cistophoric mint).

[72] Haussoullier 1902: 137–49, argues that Miletos stayed under the Ptolemies, though with considerable autonomy. Magnesia on Maeander: none of the royal letters acknowledging the *asylia* of the temple of Artemis Leukophryene (*RC* 31–4) implies control over the city. Iasos: *I. Iasos* 150, also Meadows 1996 for a new edition and historical considerations.

[73] On Olympichos as Antigonid official, Robert 1983: 147–9, for detailed argument. On Doson's Karian expedition, Will 1979: 366–71 with attempts at interpretation; Le Bohec 1993: 327–49 (dating, motivation: anti-Attalid position of Olympichos), 361 (assessment).

other feature which the Iasian inscription illustrates is the Rhodian influence in Karia. Rhodes already owned territory on the mainland (the 'Integrated Peraia') as well as a subject dominion on the mainland (the 'Subject Peraia'). *I. Iasos* 150 is the earliest evidence for wider Rhodian involvement in the rest of Karia. These interests would become more prominent by the time of Antiochos III; and, after the Treaty of Apameia (188), they culminated in twenty years of rule over Karia (along with Lykia).[74]

By the accession of Antiochos III, the result was clear: the dissolution of the Seleukid cis-Tauric dominion. Gone were the inland provinces and all of the coastal holdings with their cities, from the Troad to Karia. The signs of the Seleukid presence could be erased with ease. Erythrai, at some point in the very late third century, ceased to celebrate a cultic festival commemorating Seleukos I, the Seleukeia in parallel with the Dionysia (Habicht 1970: 85); though the exact circumstances are unclear, this must reflect the disappearance of Seleukid overlordship. The citizens of Seleukeia/Tralleis may have reverted to calling themselves Τραλλιανοί, if a recently published Milesian citizenship grant to a Trallian dates from the 220s (Günther 1988).

The case of the Trallians is instructive. Frustrated by the deficiency of the narrative sources, we turn to the documentary evidence from the subject communities, and use this material to write the history of super-power conflict. From this perspective, the local communities of Asia Minor are passive objects of conquest: *ut quisque fortior fuisset, Asiam velut praedam occupabat* (Just. 27.3). That the wars of the years 246–226 BC inflicted sufferings on the cities is obvious: apart from the cases of Smyrna and Telmessos, referred to earlier, a striking example is the plight of the Teians, powerless to resist an attack by pirates, who exacted a tithe on all the citizens' property: in my opinion, the incident should be dated in the period of confusion caused by the war between Hierax and Attalos I (*SEG* 44.949). But the period also saw local vitality. The citizens of Seleukeia, in rejecting the dynastic name to become 'Trallians' again, whatever the circumstances, were committing a political act which affected their own history and identity. Against the narrative background, we can reconsider the documents produced by the local communities in the context of their own history. The Boulagoras inscription (*SEG* 1.366) provides evidence for Antiochos II and Seleukid rule in Asia Minor, or for Ptolemaic

---

[74] See Meadows 1996, for *I. Iasos* 150 as evidence for early, yet persistent, Rhodian interest in Karia. Document **48** illustrates the reactions of one Karian community, Apollonia under Salbake, at the beginning of Rhodian rule.

reconquests in the Laodikeian War—a reading which looks away from Samos to superpower conflict. But we can also shift our viewpoint, to look at the Boulagoras inscription in its local context: this inscription documents the experience of one city, its troubles and its relations with different masters (and also, importantly, the continuity of its own concerns and activities, such as public trials, education, religion, and corn supply). Even more striking is the case of Arsinoe in Kilikia (Jones and Habicht 1989), a city founded by a general of Ptolemy II, reabsorbed by Nagidos when Kilikia fell to Antiochos II, then recreated under Ptolemy III—by the son of the original founder, a generation later. The behaviour of the Nagidians deserves attention: despoiled of part of their territory for the Ptolemaic foundation, they promptly reannexed the latter as soon as Ptolemaic control disappeared, and had to be placated when Arsinoe was refounded, by the face-saving solution of having the new foundation designated as a 'colony' of Nagidos.[75]

In the vicissitudes of the conflicts between the superpowers, and in spite of the varying degrees of royal control, the cities preserved their identities, and might assert themselves as actors in their own history. Miletos alternated between Seleukid and Ptolemaic control; shortly after the cordial dealings documented in *RC* 22 (Seleukos II responded warmly to an embassy and probably granted a petition for the *asylia* of the Didymeion), the Milesians defected from the Seleukid cause to Ptolemy III. Welles commented wryly on the lack of gratitude of the Milesians; beyond condemnation, we must be aware of the resilience of the cities. Civic resilience and identity are embodied in the exceptional issue of gold staters which Lampsakos and Alexandreia Troas struck to celebrate their newly found independence, around 226, when Seleukid power collapsed in the North-West: a solid golden bit of city-state pride.[76]

Smyrna is particularly interesting. It had a past under Seleukid control, when it functioned as a mint for Antiochos I and Antiochos II, and offered cultic honours to the early Seleukids (above, § 2). In the crisis of the Laodikeian War, Smyrna seized the opportunity to demand privileges from Seleukos II, in exchange for εὔνοια during the war (*OGIS* 228, 229). The city received autonomy, exemption from taxes, and royal sponsorship of its main temple's *asylia*. Soon afterwards, the Smyrnians struck an 'agreement' with the military colonists at Magnesia under Sipylos (*OGIS* 229). The transaction is suffused with the language of loyalty towards the interests of

---

[75] See further Chaniotis 1993, analysing the Ptolemaic power's attempts at saving face for all parties involved.

[76] Lampsakos, Alexandreia Troas: Le Rider 1971/2: 234, 238–9.

Seleukos II, especially as a medium of communication with the soldiers and colonists; but the agenda was the local interests of Smyrna. In effect, the Smyrnians try to carry out the take-over of a royal military colony, to extend the city's territory into Lydia: the Seleukid colonists are to become Smyrnian citizens, admit a Smyrnian magistrate, and hand over a royal fort to the Smyrnians.[77] It is likely that the attempt ultimately did not work; nonetheless, the resourcefulness of the Smyrnians in exploiting the language of loyalty to the royal power to pursue local interests shows that in the Hellenistic *polis* utterances of loyalty need not imply 'internal surrender' or the loss of civic values through 'toadying'. Indeed, Smyrna, which paid such handsome honours to the early Seleukids, by 197 could resist Antiochos III, in the name of a civic ideology of true independence (Liv. 33.38).

The cases of Smyrna, Lampsakos, and Alexandreia Troas are important, because they illustrate two related features: the local survival of civic identity and values, which reappeared after half a century of Seleukid domination; the possibility of rapid 'deprovincialisation', even after decades of provincial control by the Seleukids. These individual stories form the prehistory to the difficulties which Antiochos III had with these particular cities, when they resisted his attempts at reconquest in 196 (see Introduction and Ch. 2 § 5); the resistance of these cities would play an important part in Antiochos' worsening relations with Rome, and Smyrna would fight on the side of the Romans and Rhodians against Antiochos III—on the winning side.

5. *P. Sulpicius Galba's History Lesson*

In 193, at what would turn out to be the last conference between the Romans and the Seleukids before war, Minnion restated Antiochos' claims over the cities of Ionia and Aiolis, 'conquered by his ancestors and made to pay tribute and taxes', which Antiochos had simply restored to their former status. One of the Roman envoys, the brutally frank P. Sulpicius Galba (consul in 211 and 200), challenged this claim, by pointing out that the Seleukids had not enjoyed continuous power over the cities of Asia, some of which had been under the Ptolemies, some under Philip V, and some of which had become independent (*alias earum in Philippi, alias in Ptolomaei fuisse potestate, alias per multos annos nullo ambigente libertatem*

---

[77] On the date of *OGIS* 229, Elwyn 1990. Austin 1981: 302 n. 10: 'under a profession of loyalty to Seleucus II the city is in effect extending its influence'.

usurpasse). Galba then introduced embassies from the cities themselves: 'a very great number was admitted, and as each bought forth
complaints alongside requests, and mingled the just with the unjust,
they turned the debate into a quarrel' (*ex disceptatione altercationem
fecerunt*). The unitary Seleukid claim to historical rights over all of
Asia Minor broke down, confronted with the assertive, multiple
voices issuing from the cities as independent actors—a direct
reflection of the palimpsestic history of the region, with its competing super-powers and its latter phase of Seleukid collapse. This
was the result which Antiochos III himself, more skilful or more
arrogant, had prevented at the conference at Lysimacheia, by
cutting down on the speeches of the envoys from Lampsakos and
Smyrna, with a curt 'No long speeches', Παῦσαι τῶν πολλῶν.[78]

Sulpicius Galba's history lesson might be challenged on particulars. For instance, his view that to admit the validity of Seleukid
claims would be to allow Philip V to reclaim Corinth, Chalkis,
Demetrias, and Thessaly is debatable, since Philip had expressly
given up these places by treaty, whereas the Seleukids never
renounced their claims to Asia Minor (Bickermann 1932a: 53).
Nonetheless, Sulpicius' general argument is right. The grand
Seleukid claims to Asia Minor, which underlay ways of referring to
the region, should be confronted with other narratives—the history
of the Ptolemaic empire in Asia Minor, or the roster of Seleukid
setbacks from 246 to 223. The legal validity of the Seleukid claims
does not cancel out this history; in addition, the legal situation is
ambiguous, since there are examples where length of occupation
constituted grounds for ownership[79]—the Seleukids themselves
sometimes considered mere armed takeover as creating rights to
property.[80]

It is hard not to detect a note of aggressive anxiety in the
insistence on ancestral rights and the unique status of the Seleukids

---

[78] P. Sulpicius: 34.59.1–2 for outspokenness; generally, *MRR* 272, 323. Conference at
Ephesos in 193: Liv. 35.16–17. 'No long speeches': Pol. 18.52.4.

[79] Mehl 1980/1: 205–6 on *RC* 7: the Prienians do not get the Batinetis, in spite of their
original *ktesis*: the arbitration of Lysimachos seems to have favoured length of occupation; also Mehl 1980/1: 212, *Nachtrag* 2. On the other hand, Mehl minimizes the
importance of *Speererwerb*, especially for the Ptolemies (197–205, 208–9): in the Fourth
Syrian War, the Ptolemaic envoys did not contest the principle of 'victors' rights', but
disputed over the contents of the convention between the victors of Ipsos. (Also
Hornblower 1985: 317 n. 8 for disagreement with Mehl 1980/1).

[80] Liv. 34.58.4–6: the Seleukid envoy Hegesianax of Alexandreia Troas describes the
conquests of Antiochos III under a variety of headings, and overdetermines Antiochos'
right to them, as *parta* (acquired, taken over) as well as *recuperata*.; Pol. 28.1.4: concerning Koile-Syria, Antiochos IV reflects that *ktesis* through war is the safest and the
finest, and hence (Pol. 28.20.7–8) refers both to historical rights and to the forcible
ἔγκτησις by Antiochos III.

as possessors of such rights. At Lysimacheia, Antiochos III contrasted his activities in Thrace, natural and just (recovering—ἀνακτᾶσθαι—what was rightfully his) with the opportunistic grasping of Ptolemy III or Philip V, exploiting the distractions (περισπασμοί) of his ancestors. He was not taking advantage of Philip's troubles to take over his Thracian possessions, since he was recovering his own (Pol. 18.51). Antiochos rewrote the past, representing his actions within a history which reinterpreted the humiliating events of the third century. Of course, the figure who casually refers to the Seleukid losses as the result of 'distractions' is a Polybian creation. But the attitude found in Polybios' Antiochos can be matched with the documentary evidence; furthermore, the same logic informs Antiochos' reclaiming of tribute arrears from the cities of Asia Minor (Diod. 28.15.2)—as he did with Xerxes of Armenia (Pol. 8.23.4). This action asserts continuity of authority in spite of interruptions, and also abolishes any interruption, in order to reclaim the past; in other words, the exaction of arrears symbolically establishes the crucial element of continuity whose absence Sulpicius Galba so priggishly denounced.[81]

Belief in ancestral rights since Kouroupedion allowed the Seleukids to ignore the intervening events, and to speak as if Seleukid authority pertained, by virtue of selective memory and skewed geographical perspectives: Achaios could be described as holding authority over all of cis-Tauric Asia Minor, and Nikanor could be appointed to a supreme priestly dignity over the whole region. Conversely, the historical claims could legitimize the process of conquest; once Antiochos III had re-established Seleukid power, he could look back on the troubled past as an accident, and abolish it by demanding tribute arrears. The Seleukid past played a crucial role in the definition of present successes and past humiliations; it acted as a 'myth', not in that it was a total fabrication, but in that it presented an authoritative discourse that enabled forms of power. The Seleukid version is a selective arrangement of facts into a meaningful relationship, a 'story-line' or *intrigue* (Veyne 1978: 35–42), built around the premiss of the historical rights enjoyed by Antiochos III in Asia Minor, and the *telos*, or happy ending, of his success in reasserting these rights. Whether this story-line, rather than the history lesson given by P. Sulpicius Galba at Ephesos in 193, would turn out to be valid, would be determined by the balance of power and the outcome of warfare.

[81] Parallels can be found in Thuc. 8.5.5, with Lewis 1977: 97; Fowden 1993: 29–30, for the Sassanian dream of 'reimposing' tribute on the lands which had once paid it to the Achaimenids.

CHAPTER 2

The Reconquest of Asia Minor:
A Narrative (226–192)

A stele found at modern Gördes, in ancient north-eastern Lydia, preserves the dedication of a Seleukid ἡγεμών, Arkesilaos, 'in gratitude for the safety of Apollophanes, son of Apollophanes, of Seleukeia in Pieria', the well-documented physician of Antiochos III.[1] The inference is that Apollophanes, no doubt at Antiochos' side, passed though north-eastern Lydia or close enough to concern an officer stationed there—but when did this take place? Perhaps during Antiochos' campaign in 216–213 BC to subdue the usurper Achaios; or the activity in 204–203, on his return from his eastern expedition; or the campaign of 197–196, which swept from Syria to the Straits; or a march to Thrace; or even the Seleukid–Roman War.[2] By its very chronological incertitude, the stele directs attention to the history of Antiochos III as one of military movements across the Seleukid empire: Asia Minor 'on the other side' of the Taurus, the eastern satrapies, Syria and Koile-Syria (tabulated in Schmitt 1964: 85). Antiochos' movements, over a fantastic distance, from the Hindu Kush to Thrace, were dedicated to the violent reimposition of control—and the stele from Gördes, erected by a Seleukid officer, belongs to this geography of war.[3]

The king constructed the empire in the wake of his campaigning. The full title of Zeuxis, the governor of cis-Tauric Asia, was ὁ ἀπολελειμμένος ὑπὸ τοῦ βασιλέως Ἀντιόχου ἐπὶ τῶν ἐπιτάδε τοῦ Ταύρου πραγμάτων, 'the official left in charge of affairs on this side of the Taurus' (see Ch. 3 § 2). A Babylonian diary records, for the year 274, that Antiochos I 'left his . . ., his wife and a famous official in the land Sardeis, to strengthen the guard'; much later, a 'First

---

[1] Document **39**. Pol. 5.56, 5.58; Brown 1961.
[2] On dating, Herrmann 1970: 95–7. However, Apollophanes was already physician to Seleukos II (*regn.* 246–226 BC): *SEG* 33.673, line 2; this makes a lower date difficult.
[3] For a parallel for restless campaigning as a demonstration of royal success (*baraka*) in traditional Moroccan kingship: Geertz 1993: 134–42.

Friend' of Antiochos VII was ἀπολελειμμένος δὲ καὶ ἐπὶ τῶν τόπων, 'also left as governor of the area', as he is described in a dedication found at Acre.[4] The king, in his movements, appointed governors and left them at their posts: the participle ἀπολελειμμένος represents the king's absent authority and his having-been-there.[5] The officer Arkesilaos, who dedicated the Gördes inscription, was also 'left behind' at his post (a garrison? a 'military colony'?) by the king, no doubt during one of his campaigns.

Antiochos III moved from one zone of his empire to another, alternating his focus of attention; his last campaign took him away from his defeat in Asia Minor, back to the eastern provinces (where he met a violent death). But Asia Minor was the focus for repeated efforts to assert control, over twenty-six years (223–197). It is worth laying out what we know of Antiochos' campaigns, for several reasons. First, new epigraphical discoveries have modified the standard picture (Schmitt 1964, Will 1982). Even though our knowledge is lacunose,[6] we can now rewrite some areas, or define more sharply the schedule of events. Second, the narrative of these campaigns brings the historical geography of Asia Minor to the forefront; within this framework, the narrative portrays the consti-tution of an imperial space through administrative and ideological structures (§ 4). The process is the more interesting for the difficulties and the resistance it met with, locally and internationally (§ 5). Finally, the narrative provides the necessary context for the documents produced by the cities—namely, the processes of con-quest and imperial control which the cities experienced at their expense.

1. Achaios (223–213 BC)

The first stage in the reconquest of Asia Minor took place under Achaios, cousin of Antiochos III, from a family closely linked to the Seleukids and with a past of imperial service.[7] Achaios first acted as governor for cis-Tauric Asia Minor, then seceded from the Seleukid

[4] Zeuxis: document 29, 3–5; Babylonian calendar: Sachs and Hunger 1988: no. -273, B, rev., line 29; Acre: Landau 1961.

[5] Bengtson 1937: 19 n. 2 for comment and further examples; Bengtson 1944: 102 on provincial office as representation of an absent ruler.

[6] J. and L. Robert 1983: 53 n. 93, 56: gaps in the epigraphical record at Amyzon, one of the better-documented sites.

[7] Family ties with Antiochos III: Schmitt 1964: 30–1; Meloni 1949: 536–7. Cousin of Antiochos III: Pol. 4.51.4 and 8.20.11. Beloch 1927: 205–6, held that Achaios must have been uncle and not cousin to Antiochos III (followed by Billows 1995: 96–9), but Schmitt and Meloni argued convincingly against Beloch's view.

empire to create his own, short-lived kingdom. In spite of the recently published inscriptions from Sardeis, the episode is still poorly documented. Achaios had accompanied an expedition by Seleukos III, in 223, 'to see to his interests' and recover cis-Tauric Asia Minor (Pol. 4.48.7); the personal intervention of the king followed the defeat of his generals at the hands of Attalos I, and the subsequent loss of Sardeis.[8] Seleukos III reached Phrygia (*FGrHist* 260 F 32.9), where coinage in his name was struck under the supervision of courtiers;[9] he was faced with insubordination from his army, and murdered in summer 223. Achaios punished the murderers, and, refusing the diadem offered by the troops, saved the βασιλεία for Antiochos, the younger brother of the king (Pol. 4.48.9–10). Antiochos III, on his accession, appointed Achaios governor of cis-Tauric Asia Minor, and Achaios set out to 'recover all the land of this side of the Taurus' (Pol. 4.48.10, with Schmitt 1964: 109–11).

In late summer 223, according to Polybios (4.48.2, 4.48.11), he had already established control over all of cis-Tauric Asia Minor, driving Attalos I back into the original Pergamene dominion. Polybios' statement is exaggerated, though Achaios did achieve substantial results. Sardeis became the Seleukid 'provincial capital' once more, and struck coins where the portrait of Antiochos III exhibits features recalling Achaios' own, a reflection, conscious or not, of Achaios' king-like powers.[10] He retook the cities of Teos and Kolophon (but not Smyrna), Kyme, Myrina, Phokaia, Aigai, Temnos, and the region of Mysia, with places on the border with the Troad. Achaios' advance deep into Aiolis explains Polybios' description of Attalos I shut in his ancestral kingdom; his presence in Mysia implies that he had re-established Seleukid authority over the regions further east (Lykaonia, Phrygia, Lydia, eastern and central Karia).[11] It is possible that Achaios' successes motivated the

---

[8] Pergamene victory: *OGIS* 277; *Inschr. Pergamon* 36. Loss of Sardeis: Ch. 1 § 4. Clashes between Seleukid and Attalid forces may have prompted Ptolemy III to send his son Magas to Asia Minor: Huss 1977; a high-ranking Seleukid officer, Andromachos (Achaios' father) was captured and sent to Alexandria (Pol. 4.51.1).

[9] Mørkholm 1969: 14–15. These issues bear monograms also found in coins struck at Antioch. Mørkholm suggests that this coinage was struck under the authority of the mint of Antioch; more likely it was struck under the supervision of some of Seleukos' Friends, who had previously exercised similar functions at Antioch, and now accompanied the king on his expedition.

[10] For the chronology, Schmitt 1964: 161. Coinage: Mørkholm 1969: 15.

[11] For the cities of Aiolis, Teos, Kolophon, and Myrina, our evidence is the fact that in 218, Attalos I had to take these cities back, and marched into Mysia: Pol. 5.77–8; the places of Karseai and Didyma Teiche, taken by Attalos, have been located by Robert on the border between Mysia and the Troad: Robert 1937: 194–6. Attalos I treated the Smyrnians well, because they had 'preserved to the greatest extent their faith towards

dispatch of Magas, the son of Ptolemy III, to Asia Minor.[12] However, Achaios probably did not achieve such results in the Troad, where Lampsakos, Alexandreia Troas, and Ilion resisted him.[13] Polybios mentions that the cities of Aiolis and near Aiolis had 'gone over to Achaios out of fear' (Ἀχαίῳ προσεκεχωρήκεισαν διὰ τὸν φόβον: 5.77.2); specific information on Achaios' reconquest would greatly contribute to our knowledge of Seleukid Asia Minor, Attalid rule between c.227 and 223, the problems of reimposing Seleukid authority, and the local communities caught in the alternation between Seleukids and Attalids.

Achaios is referred to, but not active, during the entwined events of the years 222–219: first, the revolt of Molon, the governor of the eastern provinces, who declared himself king before being crushed by Antiochos; secondly, the Fourth Syrian War, fought over Koile-Syria (219–217).[14] In 220 Achaios attempted to usurp the Seleukid kingship (Pol. 5.57.3–8): assuming the diadem and the royal title at Laodikeia in Phrygia, he marched on Syria, but was thwarted when the troops mutinied, on the frontiers of Lykaonia (perhaps on the approaches to Ikonion, the last important stopping-point before the road headed towards the Kilikian Gates),[15] on realizing that they were marching against 'their original and natural king'; Achaios was forced to return, with a detour to regain the troops' goodwill by allowing them to plunder Pisidia. The sequence of events is difficult to explain.[16] The breakaway kingdom of Hierax perhaps offered inspiration (Will 1982: 26). Achaios may have thought of himself

---

him' (Pol 5.77.6). For Mysia, also Holleaux 1938b: 33–4 (Mysians in Achaios' army, though these could simply be mercenaries).

[12] Huss 1977 prefers this context for the presence of Magas in Asia Minor: 'Seleukos having just died' in P. Haun 6 being Seleukos III rather than Seleukos II; Habicht 1980.

[13] Meloni (1949: 536 n. 2 and 1950: 175 n. 2) believes that Pol. 5.78.6 (διὰ τὸ τετηρηκέναι τὴν πρὸς αὐτὸν [sc. Attalos I] πίστιν) means the three cities of the Troad surrendered to Achaios after resistance (also Schmitt 1964: 165 and n. 3); a parallel for this usage is found in RDGE 18, line 5. Piejko 1991b: 33, holds that Achaios took over Ilion, and that this was the occasion when the Ilians offered sacrifices and prayers at the accession of a king Antiochos—on this interpretation, Antiochos III (OGIS 219, lines 16–18). However, Pol. 5.78. and especially 5.78.6 imply that in 218, Attalos I did not need to reconquer the cities of the Troad (as has been written), but went through the Troad only because of the revolt of his Aigosagian auxiliaries; the latter 'crossed to Asia', upon Attalos' invitation—into the Troad, held by or sympathetic to the Attalids: Pol. 5.78.5–6. It is unlikely that Achaios took over cities in the Troad c.223, and that Attalos recovered them soon afterwards, since Attalos' expedition of 218 seems the first time he took the military initiative, when Achaios' forces were diverted to Pisidia.

[14] On both, Will 1982: 17–23; detailed treatment of Molon in Schmitt 1964: 116–50; Gera 1998: 3–20 on Fourth Syrian War.

[15] Leake 1824: 44–5, for the ridge before the plain of Konya.

[16] Against the 'conspiracy theory' in Will 1982: 23–6 and Will 1962 (Achaios' usurpation directed against Hermeias), Schmitt 1964: 185–8.

within Seleukid legitimacy, as is suggested by the coinage he issued at Sardeis, repeating Seleukid symbols (especially the anchor, on the shield of the admittedly un-Seleukid Athena Alkis: *WSM* no. 1440) and by the fact that Achaios never again tried to attack the Syrian heartland of the dynasty, even when Antiochos III was at war in Koile-Syria.[17]

Achaios' rule lasted about six years, from the usurpation in summer 220 to his capture and the surrender of the citadel at Sardeis in autumn 214 or winter 214/13. The kingdom of Achaios, seen from the inside, could provide parallels for the history of Antiochos III in western Asia Minor, especially for the mechanisms of control, and the negotiations with the subject communities. But none of the letters written by 'king Achaios' to the cities (Pol. 4.2.6; 5.57.2; 5.57.5) has survived. We know of a governor of Sardeis, Aribazos (Pol. 7.17.9; 8.21.9); and, in Mysia or Hellespontic Phrygia, of a governor (στρατηγός), Themistokles (Pol 5.77.8). A Themistokles appears in the Trallian document *RC* 41, line 9, as 'ὁ στρατηγός', probably the governor of Karia (or Lydia?); it is conceivable that this inscription preserves a letter of Achaios, concerning the city of Tralleis, and referring to the decision by an earlier Seleukid king, [Antio]chos (see Appendix 3).[18] At the local level, few documents refer to events under Achaios: an unsuccessful attempt in 221/0 by Magnesia under Maeander to have a contest for Artemis Leukophryene acknowledged as panhellenic; an alliance between Miletos and Seleukeia/Tralleis, dated to 218/17 (showing that the Trallians, who seem to have dropped the Seleukid *ethnikon* in the 220s, had reverted to it—in 223, under compulsion by Achaios, when he was still the general of Antiochos III?); and possibly an honorific decree for a Trallian ambassador to 'the king' (Achaios?).[19]

---

[17] Will 1982: 26. A puzzling passage in Polybios (8.17.11) concerns Achaios' plan, in winter 214/13 to go to Syria and seize power thanks to a movement in his favour in Antioch, Koile-Syria, and Phoenicia (but the last two regions were not Seleukid).

[18] Bengtson 1944: 116–17, argues that Themistokles was appointed by Achaios when he was governor of Asia Minor rather than independent king.

[19] Magnesia: *Inschr. Magnesia* 16, Rigsby 1996: 180, 188–9. Alliance: *Inschr. Delphinion* 143, same document *I. Tralleis* 20 (stephanephoria of Epikrates in Miletos, which Rehm dated to 212/11, but should be dated earlier, to 218/17, on account of Wörrle's redating of the Milesian *stephanephoroi* list, *Inschr. Delphinion* 124: Wörrle 1988: 428–37). Embassy: the alliance between Miletos and Tralleis/Seleukeia mentions Menodoros Timeou (*Inschr. Delphinion* 143, line 5), who also is named as *stephanephoros* in a Trallian inscription (*I. Tralleis* 26, line 1) in honour of a citizen who went on embassy 'to the king', conceivably king Achaios, if we posit, on the grounds of Menodoros' eminence, a close connection in time between Menodoros' *stephanephoria* and the alliance between Tralleis and Miletos (for which Menodoros represented Tralleis).

It is difficult to relate any of these documents or these events to the reign of 'king Achaios'.

The absence of documentation is the more regrettable because Achaios' activity and military might[20] were centred on Anatolia. Achaios avoided entanglements with the great powers, by keeping away from the dominions of Ptolemy IV (who supported him with aid)[21] and the Antigonid holdings of Karia; his main target was Attalos I, on whom he waged war throughout his reign[22]—in a continuance of the mission assigned to him in 223. He also intervened in local conflict, such as the war between Byzantion and Rhodes in 220 (Pol. 4.48.1–4, though Ptolemaic pressure soon forced Achaios out), and, in 218, the war between Pednelissos and Selge, an episode well documented through Polybios (5.72–6); though an attempt to capture Selge failed, Achaios 'subjected to the yoke the Milyas and most of Pamphylia' (Pol. 5.77.1)—Termessos and Sagalassos may have fallen to him, as well as the smaller cities of the Milyas (Komama, Olbasa, Pogla).[23] Achaios' intervention in Pisidia illustrates the meshing of local dynamics and high politics characteristic of the Hellenistic period.

Apart from the Pisidian episode, the other documented event is the campaign undertaken by Attalos I, when Achaios was occupied in Pamphylia.[24] Attalos started out with a force of Galatians, the Aigosages, specially ferried from Europe to Asia Minor, and recovered Kyme, Myrina, Phokaia, Aigai, and Temnos; further south, the Teians and the Kolophonians sent in embassies to 'hand themselves over', upon the same terms as before (in the case of Teos, as a tribute-paying subordinate community). Attalos also received courteously the envoys of independent Smyrna.[25] He next

---

[20] Pol. 4.48.12, cf. 5.77.1; also the eagle clutching a palm branch or a wreath figured on Achaios' bronze coinage: WSM 1441, 1442, 1445, 1446, 1448, 1450.

[21] Support by the Ptolemies: Pol. 7.16.7; 8.15.10; also 5.63.8: Ptolemy IV recalls forces from 'cities of the exterior', probably including Asia Minor, without fear of aggression on Achaios' part. Schmitt 1964: 166–71 and Will 1982: 25–6, 30–1, minimize the Ptolemaic connection, largely in reaction to earlier scholarship which saw Achaios as entirely motivated by 'Alexandrian gold' (e.g. Holleaux 1942: 131–2, 134).

[22] Pol. 4.48.2: that Achaios and Attalos I were both contacted by the Byzantines in their search for allies against the Rhodians does not prove that the two kings were at peace (Schmitt 1964: 263) since Attalos was still 'shut up in his paternal kingdom'.

[23] On the region, through which Achaios necessarily passed on his way to Pamphylia, whether from Laodikeia or Apameia (Syme 1995: 204): Syme 1995: 177–203 (with Hall 1986).

[24] Holleaux 1938b: 17–42; Schmitt 1964: 262–4.

[25] Pol. 5.77.4–6. Polybios' account is silent about Erythrai; the city was probably Attalid in 201 (Pol. 16.6.5). Allen 1983: 45–57, proposes an unacceptable interpretation of the status of the Teians: pace Allen, Teos was not a vaguely 'free' city under some form of Attalid protectorate and making occasional payments to the Attalids (47, based on an excessively narrow interpretation of ἐγχειρίζειν in Pol. 5.77.5), but a subject city

moved into Mysia and the 'Mysian *katoikiai*' (probably through western Lydia, since he crossed the Lykos, and taking over Thyateira in the process, though Polybios is silent on this city), and reached the Propontis, taking over Karseai and Didymateiche (probably the westernmost places held by Achaios in the region); the latter was surrendered by Achaios' governor, Themistokles. Attalos then turned south again, ravaging the plain of Apia (the modern Balıkesir plain), and finally reached the river Mekestos. But his plans for marching into eastern Mysia were thwarted by a mutiny among the Aigosages, forcing him to withdraw to the Troad,[26] where he dealt cordially with Lampsakos, Alexandreia Troas, and Ilion, for their loyalty, but where he also settled the Aigosages (they would cause havoc in the following two years).[27] When Achaios returned from Pisidia to Sardeis, he 'warred continuously with Attalos' (Pol. 5.77.1), to recover lost territory. This second round of reconquest was less successful than the campaign of 223–222. Attalos retained control of the Aiolian cities, as well as Teos, Kolophon, and Thyateira, probably taken over in 218 on the march to Mysia.[28] The simultaneous events (Achaios' Pamphylian involvement, Attalos' north-western campaign) show the extension of Achaios' dominion (from the Aegean into inland Anatolia) and, at the same time, its vulnerability.

The final act was the campaign waged by Antiochos III across the Taurus, starting in 216, the spring after his defeat at Raphia in 217 (Pol. 5.107.4)—which freed Antiochos from the dilemma of choosing between Koile-Syria and the need to reduce his rebellious relative.[29] Antiochos had refused to acknowledge Achaios as anything else than a rebel, ἀποστάτης: in winter 219/18, he opposed attempts by Ptolemy IV to include Achaios in any treaty (Pol. 5.67.12–13). The expedition into Asia Minor of 216 came under a double heading of legitimacy: the reconquest of ancestral Seleukid holdings, and the suppression of a rebellious subordinate.

Antiochos 'came to an arrangement' with Attalos I, κοινοπραγίαν

paying tribute; this is proved by the first Teian decree for Antiochos III (document **17**) which explicitly mentions tribute to Attalos), and the fact that Attalos I took hostages from the city. See further Ch. 3 §§ 2–3.

[26] Pol. 5.77.7–78. For the topography, Robert 1937: 184–97, preferable to Meloni 1950: 166–76 (who emends Polybios to have Attalos I cross the Kaikos instead of the Lykos and reach the Karesene via Adramyttion). On the 'Mysian *katoikiai*' (Pol. 5.77.7), Robert 1937: 191–3 (villages in a region devoid of cities), Schwertheim 1988: 74 n. 33 (military colonies, since they would have presented Attalos I with a valuable objective: not compelling).

[27] Troad: Pol. 5.78.6.

[28] Pol. 16.1.7 with Robert 1962: 38.

[29] On the strategic dilemma, Schmitt 1964: 173–5.

(Pol. 5.107.4), against Achaios. The statue to Zeuxis, erected by the citizens of Pergamon (*OGIS* 236), might date to this collaboration, rather than the 190s or after the battle of Magnesia (Dittenberger). Schmitt believed that the price paid by Antiochos III was the cession of an enormous tract of territory in north-west Asia Minor, including Mysia and Hellespontine Phrygia up to Aizanoi (Schmitt 1964: 264–7, 302 for map). In fact the stele discovered near Balıkesir shows that most or all of Mysia was taken back by Antiochos III: Attalos I was simply left in control of whatever he had saved from Achaios' counter-campaign.

Far from allowing a vast amount of land to pass over to Attalos, Antiochos III recovered most of Achaios' kingdom. Most or all of Mysia was brought back under Seleukid dominion; though the fact that Prousias was active near Abydos in 216 (when he exterminated the Aigosages: Pol. 5.111.6), and that he invaded the Attalid kingdom in 208 (Liv. 28.7.10; Habicht, *RE* s.v. Prousias, 1092–3), imply that Prousias retained control of northern Mysia for several years, before Seleukid authority was re-established.[30] If *OGIS* 219 can be dated to Antiochos III, his campaign against Achaios might provide a context, implying Seleukid activity deep into the Troad (unlikely, since Attalos I was allowed to retain his other dominions outside of the Pergamene kingdom itself). Hellespontine Phrygia was recovered by Antiochos III, who also seized Achaios' conquests in Pamphylia and Pisidia; Sagalassos may have fallen into Seleukid hands at this occasion.[31] Greater Phrygia and Lykaonia must have been recovered earlier.

[30] On the *koinopragia* of 216, Allen 1983: 58–65, suggesting that the most important concession made by Antiochos III was to recognize the Attalid kingdom as a separate and sovereign state, and arguing against the view of massive territorial concessions by Antiochos III; also Gruen 1996: 16–19, discussing the introduction of the cult of Magna Mater to Rome in 205: the sacred stone came not from Pessinous (since the Attalid holdings were not so extensive at that point), but from Pergamon itself. On Mysia, see Schwertheim 1988: 73–6, who translates Liv. 38.39.15 (in 188, Eumenes II receives from the Romans *Mysiam, quam Prusia rex ademerat*) as 'Mysia, which the king (sc. Antiochos) had taken from Prousias'. But this is difficult to reconcile with Pol. 21.46.10, where the text reads Μυσούς, οὓς πρότερον αὐτοῦ παρεσπάσατο: Schwertheim would interpret the subject of this sentence as being Antiochos III, whereas ⟨Προυσίας⟩ has usually, and rightly, been inserted into the text, since Livy, translating Polybios, mentions Prousias. The solution is probably that Prousias seized parts of Mysia before 216 from Attalos I (in the aftermath of Attalos' campaign of 218?), and that Antiochos III seized the region from Prousias (since Mysia was definitely Seleukid down to the Peace of Apameia). In 188, the seizure of Mysia by Prousias was the one which Eumenes II and the Roman commissioners referred to, since it established 'the historical claim of Pergamum to possession of Mysia' (Baronowski 1991: 452 n. 4). It is not clear when Seleukid authority was established over northern Phrygia: perhaps as late as 197 (§ 4).

[31] Hellespontine Phrygia: Schwertheim 1988: 70–3 (Hellespontine Phrygia was Antiochos' since it belonged to the territories at the disposal of the Romans in 188), Wörrle 1988: 460 (Antiochos III in Hellespontine Phrygia); Pamphylia: Schmitt 1964:

The reconquest of inland Asia Minor took place with ease; by 214, Achaios was cornered in Sardeis.[32] Antiochos III must have been helped by the dynastic loyalty of (ex-)Seleukid troops and officials rallying to him, as happened when the king took to the field against the usurper Molon: 'it is difficult for rebels to risk attacking kings in daylight and face to face'.[33] Antiochos presumably was also aided by the quiescence or opportunism of the local communities.

Sardeis was captured and sacked (Pol. 7.15–18), in late 215 or early 214; Achaios was caught in late 214 (Pol. 8.15–21), while trying to smuggle himself out of the citadel of Sardeis; in Polybios' words, 'it was resolved first to cut off the unfortunate man's extremities, then to cut off his head and sew it up in an ass-skin, while impaling the body' (Pol. 8.21.2–3); the citadel surrendered shortly afterwards. The punishment undid Achaios' pretensions to royal charisma (expressed in numismatic portraiture, or the physical deference shown to Achaios by his companions: Pol 8.20.3–4). The mutilation and the impalement were taken from Near-Eastern imperial practice; they publicized Seleukid authority, after the interlude of the usurpation. The same message was perhaps expressed in a Greek visual vocabulary: the famous Hellenistic group representing Marsyas on the point of being flayed before a seated Apollo might be a Seleukid work of art dramatizing the punishment of Achaios (elderly and bearded, like Marsyas) by Antiochos III (youthful and beardless, like Apollo).[34]

The symbolical message was reflected in immediate and concrete measures of repression and reorganization.[35] The one city we know about is the 'provincial capital' of Sardeis, thanks to epigraphical documents dating to 213, in the immediate aftermath of the campaigns against Achaios.[36] The city was fined, and a new 5 per

279 (Pamphylia recovered by Antiochos III around 216: the accounts of Antiochos' progression by sea in 197 do not mention any conquests between Rough Kilikia and Lykia). Sagalassos: K. Vandorpe, in Waelkens and Poblome 1995: 299–305, for city seal with a Seleukid elephant; but perhaps the city fell under Seleukid control in Antiochos' Pisidian campaign of 193. Nothing suggests that Achaios, then Antiochos had conquered Pisidia at this time (as proposed by Waelkens, in Waelkens 1993: 42).

[32] Gauthier 1989: 15–19 (much swifter progression of Antiochos' campaign than had been believed).

[33] Quote from Pol. 5.52.9; also 5.41.9; 5.46.8; 5.54.1; for loyalist feelings in Achaios' army, 5.57.6.

[34] Van Proosdij (1934); Sherwin-White and Kuhrt 1993: 189. Marsyas: Fleischer 1972–5.

[35] The land-conveyance to Mnesimachos (*Sardis*, no. 1) should not be dated to this time (Atkinson 1972): Debord 1982: 244–7, Billows 1995: 144 n. 70.

[36] Document **36** does not concern Sardeis after Achaios (Piejko 1987): Gauthier 1989: 171–8. Piejko 1987 further attributes *Sardis*, no. 88, to Antiochos III; I see no reason for preferring Antiochos III to Eumenes II, or even Achaios.

cent tax was perhaps imposed as a punitive measure; troops were
billeted on the population, and commandeered the city's gymnasion
for their use. These conditions were alleviated upon petition to
Antiochos, who later granted benefactions: a securely funded
yearly grant of 200 *metretai*, about 8,000 litres, of oil for the young
men in the gymnasion (restored to the city), and tax-exemption for
a festival in honour of Laodikeia. This festival belonged to a set of
cultic honours for Antiochos' spouse, Laodike III, and were perhaps a response to benefactions from her as well. It also is possible
that Antiochos granted the city exemption from agricultural taxes
and gave grain, both for consumption and for sowing, thus helping
the city restart its agricultural cycle after the disruption of war.[37]
The documents suggest that Antiochos III and Laodike stayed in
Sardeis, where over several months[38] they received embassies from
the Sardians, and no doubt from other communities of the reconquered regions. This was Antiochos' first stay in Asia Minor. His
unfamiliarity is apparent in his reply to the Sardians' petition for
release from rent on ἐργαστήρια, royally owned workshops:
ἀπολύομεν δὲ ὑμᾶς καὶ τοῦ ἐνοικίου οὗ τελεῖτε ἀπὸ τῶν ἐργαστηρίων, εἴπερ
καὶ αἱ ἄλλαι πόλεις μὴ πράσσονται, 'we also exempt you from the rent
which you pay on the workshops, at least if it is true that the other
cities do not pay for it'. The Sardians had supported their petition
with appeals to parallels and precedents from other cities; the king
accepted the argument—but was unable to confirm the particulars.[39]

On departing (winter 213/12?), Antiochos III 'left behind' the
officer Zeuxis as governor of cis-Tauric Asia Minor. His responsibilities are already apparent in the first letter of Antiochos III to the
Sardians: timber for the reconstruction (συνοικισμός) of Sardeis is to
be cut and brought in 'as Zeuxis sees fit', and 'we have written to
Zeuxis and Ktesikles concerning all these matters'—the restitution
of the commandeered gymnasion, the cancellation of the additional
tax, and perhaps the terms for the payment of a fine.[40] The recon-

[37] Fine: document 1, 2 (with Gauthier 1989: 20–2). Supplementary tax: document 1,
5–6, with Gauthier 1989: 33–6; though the additional tax which Antiochos is seen to
suppress in that document may have been imposed by Achaios. Billeting: document 1,
6–7 (gymnasion) and document 3, 6–8. Benefactions: document 3, with Gauthier 1989:
85–96; cult for Laodike: document 2. Gift of grain: 41 C (assuming it concerns the city
and not, for instance, the installation of colonists). The fragmentary letters 41 A and B
could also date to c.213, but this is not certain.
[38] The first letter of Antiochos III (document 1) was issued in March 213, Laodike's
letter (document 2) in June, and Antiochos' 'second' letter later still (document 3: after
Laodike's letter).
[39] Document 3, 8–10; Gauthier 1989: 107.
[40] Document 1, 4, 7–8. On Ktesikles (perhaps ὁ [ἐπὶ τῶν προσόδω]ν, certainly a high-
ranking financial official), Ch. 3 § 2.

struction of Sardeis (documented in the archaeological record) is the
only securely documented instance of the long-term activity of reorganizing Asia Minor. The fragmentary inscription from Tralleis
(*RC* 41) might be a letter of Zeuxis, in the aftermath of the war
against Achaios, addressed to the citizens of Seleukeia/Tralleis on
the subject of some financial obligation; in this case, the 'general
Themistokles' mentioned in line 9 could be the governor of Mysia
under Achaios, who defected to Attalos I in 218 (Pol. 5.77.8) and
who then would have defected back to Antiochos III in 216.[41] In a
letter to Zeuxis, preserved in *AJ* 12.147–153, the king ordered the
settling of 2000 Jewish families in Lydia and Phrygia, after unrest
in these regions: assuming that the document is authentic, the
context must be the continuing pacification of inland Asia Minor.[42]

By 213, Antiochos III had recovered inland Asia Minor, from the
Kilikian gates to Mysia, and even retaken Pamphylia (earlier lost to
Ptolemy III). But the resurrected Seleukid dominion lacked the
western and coastal zones, from the Troad (unless *OGIS* 219 is to
be dated to this period, implying a Seleukid presence) to western
Karia and Lykia, and, to the south, Rough Kilikia; all of which
could be construed as 'ancestral possessions' belonging to Seleukos
I, and almost all of which had been under actual Seleukid control.

2. *After the Expedition to the Upper Regions (204–202 BC)*

Between 212 and 204, Antiochos was in the east, where he
endeavoured to reimpose Seleukid authority. In 212, he reduced
Xerxes, the king of southern Armenia, to submission (Pol. 8.23);
the geography implies renewed Seleukid control over Kommagene
and northern Armenia (Sherwin-White and Kuhrt 1993: 190–7). In
211–210, Antiochos mustered his forces in Media (Justin 41.5.7). In
209, Antiochos issued to Zeuxis the *prostagma* concerning Nikanor
(Ch. 1); the context might provide a clue to Antiochos' intentions:
recreating the office of 'high-priest of all the shrines in the land
beyond the Taurus' publicized the fiction of uniform Seleukid

---

[41] For the rebuilding of Sardeis after the sack, Gauthier 1989: 32–3, with references
to the literature. On *RC* 41, Appendix 3.

[42] On the letter, Bengtson 1944: 110–12; also Appendix 3, on the hypercritical view of
Gauger 1977. Document **41** C could concern the settlement of military colonists near
Sardeis, though it would be more likely addressed to Zeuxis than to the Sardians.
Gauthier 1989: 41 n. 89, is cautious on the theory that partisans of Achaios caused the
unrest. The boundary stone *MAMA* 4.75 has been dated by its editors to 211/10, but in
fact is much later (unpublished paper by Th. Drew-Bear: see Appendix 3), and tells us
nothing about Seleukid reorganization.

authority in western Asia Minor, during an absence in the east. Antiochos further designated co-regent his eldest son, Antiochos.[43]

Antiochos III then set out on his 'expedition to the Upper Regions', directed against Arsakes II, king of the Parthians (209), Euthydemos, king of Baktria, and finally Sophagasenos, 'king of the Indians'—in fact a local dynast, otherwise unknown (206). On all three, Antiochos III imposed the same form of settlement as in Armenia: the grant of the 'subject' kings' right to rule, compounded with tribute or payment of ransom-money. Antiochos withdrew to southern Iran (where he spent the winter 206/5), then to Persis, whence he sailed against the Gerrhaians in Arabia; in exchange for a 'grant' of liberty, he received a gift, or ransom, of silver and spices.[44] Antiochos' dealings with the 'rebel' states in the eastern regions offer parallels and contrasts with the negotiations between the king and the cities of western Asia Minor (Ch. 3). At this time (205), envoys from Magnesia on Maeander, seeking acknowledgement of their contest for Artemis Leukophryene as isopythian (and of their city as *asylos*, inviolate), met Antiochos III in Antiocheia in Persis (*RC* 31, 32; *OGIS* 233): the first time we see the king concerned with the west since the *prostagma* about Nikanor. After the winter, he continued his westward march, and in spring 204 (month I, day 8), he sacrificed at the Esagil in Babylon (Sachs and Hunger 1989: no. -204, C, rev., lines 14–18). Less easy to date as precisely as the king's movements, an increase in coinage, in all metals, must reflect the results of the eastern expedition; the representation of elephants on several issues may allude to the 150 elephants Antiochos extracted from Sophagasenos.[45]

Appian describes Antiochos as 'having invaded Media and Parthia and other peoples which had already revolted before his time, and having performed many great things, and receiving the name Antiochos the Great' (καὶ μέγας Ἀντίοχος ἀπὸ τοῦδε κληθείς: App. *Syr* 1). The earliest evidence for the epithet appears in 202, confirming Appian.[46] This epithet may reflect the creation by Antiochos of the state cult for himself and his ancestors, to celebrate his exploits and the reimposition of Seleukid authority over the possessions in the East.[47]

---

[43] Nikanor the high-priest: document **4**. Antiochos the son: J. and L. Robert 1983: 163 n. 1; Schmitt 1964: 13 and n. 1, generally 13–20.

[44] Parthians: Pol. 10.28–31 and Justin 41.5.7. Baktria: Pol. 10.49 and 11.34.1–11. 'India' and the return to southern Iran: Pol. 11.34.12–14. Gerrhaians and Persian Gulf: Pol. 13.9. On Seleukids in the Persian Gulf, J.-F. Salles in Sherwin-White and Kuhrt 1987, 75–109.   [45] *WSM*, 397; Rostovtzeff 1941: pl. 7.1.

[46] But the title 'Great King' (βασιλεὺς μέγας) was not taken on at this time: Appendix 4.

[47] State cult founded in *c*.205: J. and L. Robert 1983: 168 n. 40. The only evidence is a reference in the *prostagma* on cult for Laodike: document **37**. Sherwin-White and

Polybios appraises the 'expedition into the Upper regions' in a well-known passage:

οὐ μόνον τοὺς ἄνω σατράπας ὑπηκόους ἐποιήσατο τῆς ἰδίας ἀρχῆς, ἀλλὰ καὶ τὰς ἐπιθαλαττίους πόλεις καὶ τοὺς ἐπὶ τάδε τοῦ Ταύρου δυνάστας, καὶ συλλήβδην ἠσφαλίσατο τὴν βασιλείαν, καταπληξάμενος τῇ τόλμῃ καὶ φιλοπονίᾳ πάντας τοὺς ὑποταττομένους· διὰ γὰρ ταύτης τῆς στρατείας ἄξιος ἐφάνη τῆς βασιλείας οὐ μόνον τοῖς κατὰ τὴν Ἀσίαν, ἀλλὰ καὶ τοῖς κατὰ τὴν Εὐρώπην.   (Pol. 11.34.14–16)

he made not only the upper satraps subject to his own rule, but also the cities by the sea and the dynasts on this side of Taurus, and, in short, he secured the kingdom, having intimidated all his subjects by his daring and industry: for it was through this expedition that he seemed worthy of the kingship not only to the inhabitants of Asia, but also to the inhabitants of Europe.

Leaving aside the problems connected with Antiochos' eastern achievements,[48] what exactly does Polybios mean? He implies that the expedition to the Upper Territories reduced to subjection the communities of Asia Minor, the latter being included in the ὑποταττόμενοι which Antiochos impressed with his daring and industry. Polybios' statement should not be watered down to speak of the 'propaganda effect' in Asia Minor: the passage is informed by the claim that Asia Minor had rightfully been a Seleukid possession ever since the victory of Seleukos I at Kouroupedion in 281 (Ch. 1). The 'upper satraps', and the maritime cities and dynasts of Asia Minor, are equated as two groups within the Seleukid empire, their vacillating loyalties secured by the demonstration of Antiochos' energy: Polybios perhaps echoes the official Seleukid presentation. Another possibility is that this passage preserves a garbled trace of Seleukid military and diplomatic activity in Asia Minor, during the eastern expedition and in its immediate wake.[49]

At any rate, Polybios links the end of the eastern expedition with cis-Tauric Asia Minor—Antiochos' destination, after his activity in the Persian Gulf. The king probably spent part of 204 in north Syria, whence he made initial contacts with the ἐπιθαλάσσιοι πόλεις of Asia Minor, in the form of benefactions, for instance at Teos (if the

Kuhrt 1993: 209–10, suggest that the cult was created in 193, if the present tense in the *prostagma* on cult for Laodike is to be taken narrowly: 'just as high-priests of us are appointed throughout the kingdom, so there should be established, in the same places, high-priestesses of her also' (document **37**, 21–4); but I prefer to interpret the present tense as describing general practice, rather than implying that priests of Antiochos III were being appointed at that very moment (193).

[48] Positive reassessment in Sherwin-White and Kuhrt 1993: 197–201.

[49] 'Propagandistische Wirkung': Schmitt 1964: 90–2. 'Eau bénite de cour': Will 1982: 65–6. Gruen 1986: 613 and n. 6 (interprets Pol. 11.34.14 as directly describing the Seleukid activity of c.203 in Asia Minor, which is not what the text says).

Teian decrees date from c.203: Appendix 2).[50] In late 204 or in spring 203, Antiochos crossed the Taurus. Around this time, after the death of Ptolemy IV (204), the Ptolemaic minister Agathokles sent an ambassador to Antiochos 'in Asia', requesting that he keep to the truce struck with Ptolemy IV in 217 (Pol. 15.25.13); another envoy was sent to ask for assistance from Philip V, 'in case Antiochos should try to break the treaties with them more completely' (ἐὰν ὁλοσχερέστερον αὐτοὺς Ἀντίοχος ἐπιβάληται παρασπονδεῖν). The formulation might imply that the Seleukids had started aggressions against Ptolemaic dominions, by the time of Philopator's death.[51]

The activities of Antiochos are partially documented through contemporary inscriptions, from western Karia, with (probably) another series of documents for the Ionian city of Teos. Apart from locating at least some of the movements and (re)conquests of c.203 on the map, they also provide a picture of local responses in the aftermath of takeover by the Seleukids.

The most complete evidence comes from Amyzon, on the northern flank of Mt. Latmos. The earliest inscription is a letter dated to 15 Daisios in the year 109 SE (May 203 BC), the moment of the takeover by the Seleukids: the author tries to reassure the Amyzonians of his good intentions towards 'all those who have handed themselves over to us'. This document, long attributed to Antiochos III, is rather the work of the governor of cis-Tauric Asia Minor, Zeuxis.[52] An inscription on the architrave of the temple of Artemis states that Zeuxis dedicated land to the shrine while in Amyzon.[53] In contrast, letters by Antiochos to the army at Amyzon and Labraunda (below) do not entail his presence in western Karia; the implication is rather to the contrary, especially since at Labraunda, the king's instructions were passed on by Zeuxis.[54] It is

---

[50] Document **17**, 6–10 ('the other side of the Taurus' in this case designates the city's point of view, unlike document **4**, 29–30).

[51] On the death of Ptolemy IV, Schmitt 1964: 189–237. Against the thesis of Seleukid aggression, Walbank (*HCP* ii. 484, *ad* 15.25.13) points out that ὁλοσχερέστερον might mean 'in any significant way' rather than 'in any more significant way', and hence not attest Seleukid aggression c.204. The case usually adduced for aggression against the Ptolemies, the takeover of Amyzon, has been reinterpreted by Meadows (below). 'In Asia' must mean Asia Minor rather than Asia in the broadest sense (including northern Syria): document **14** shows an Amyzonian ambassador reaching the king, in or soon after 203, without any hint at a long journey to northern Syria.

[52] Letter to the Amyzonians: document **5**. Attribution: Ma, Derow, and Meadows 1995 and commentary to document **5**. J. and L. Robert 1983: 144, no. 13, is perhaps a letter of Antiochos III, confirming and expanding Zeuxis' arrangements; cf. document **31** A, I 9.

[53] Dedication: document **7**.

[54] Letter to the army at Amyzon: document **6**; at Labraunda: referred to in document

important to grasp that what took place was an act of conquest, and not a voluntary alliance between Amyzon and the Seleukid state. The letter of Antiochos to his army at Amyzon (above) is eloquent enough about the military operations forming the background of such lenifying utterances, and there is clear evidence of the violence and spoliations (see Ch. 3 § 1). These were followed by a declaration of the shrine's *asylia*, which protected it from spoliation, but also was a reflection of royal authority over local statuses.

The Amyzonian material documents a single community in the aftermath of conquest, and the imposition of various forms of Seleukid state power (Ch. 3 § 2), concrete (such as the plethora of officials attested) and symbolical, such as the 'regnal formula'— the city's decrees now started with a fixed Seleukid formula: Βασιλευόντων Ἀντιόχου Μεγάλου καὶ Ἀντιόχ[ου τοῦ υἱοῦ, ἔτους] ἐν[δ]εκά- του καὶ ἑκατο[σ]τοῦ, μηνὸς Δίου, ἐπὶ ἀρχιε[ρέως Νικάνορος, τοῦ] δὲ Διὸς τοῦ Κρηταγενέτα καὶ Δικτύννης Τιμαί[ου], (kings, Seleukid era, Macedonian month, imperial eponymous officials such as the high-priest Nikanor or the mysterious priest of Zeus Kretagenetes and Diktynna).[55]

Amyzon is the best documented of a series of cities which Zeuxis took over (referred to by Zeuxis), and the brevity of the letter to the Amyzonians may indicate how busy the viceroy was. From the Maeander plain, Zeuxis marched up the Marsyas valley, recovering Alabanda/Antiocheia for the Seleukid empire. When an Antiocheian ambassador to Delphi asked for acknowledgement of his city's *asylia* in 202/1, he also praised Antiochos III, 'the benefactor of the Antiocheians, thanking him for preserving the democracy and the peace for the Antiocheians, according to the disposition of his ancestors'—a clear sign of Seleukid takeover, and the general phrasing of the Delphian decree might veil a mention of a grant of *asylia* by Antiochos to the city.[56] Furthermore, it has been

15. J. and L. Robert 1983: 204–6, no. 23, line 16, mentions 'the king's presence', but need not refer to this time, or could simply mean 'in cis-Tauric Asia Minor'.

[55] Preambles of Amyzonian decrees: documents **9** (quoted here) and **10**. Nikanor: **4**. Priesthood of Zeus Kretagenetas and Diktynna: also **30**, where he seems to be a locally elected official (but still imposed by the Seleukids?). The priesthood might be related to contemporary Seleukid involvement on Crete (next section).

[56] Other cities: document **5**, 2. Alabandan *asylia*: document **16**. The Alabandan embassy also went through Athens: Pounder 1978. Pounder 1978: 56, writes that the campaign for *asylia* was a reaction to protect the city against Antiochos' aggressive attentions; but *OGIS* 234 clearly implies that the city was 'Seleukid' at this point (Wörrle 1988: 441 n. 69; but Alabanda had not been continuously Seleukid since Antiochos II, as Wörrle seems to say). Piejko 1991a: 20, believes that the *OGIS* 234 shows that Antiocheia/Alabanda was declared inviolate by an oracle; in fact, the inscription refers to Pausimachos consulting the oracle at Delphi, but not previously to the inception of the campaign for Antiocheian/Alabandan *asylia*. See Appendix 2.

recently shown that the coinage of Antiocheia/Alabanda, certainly struck under Seleukid control, is to be attributed to the time of Antiochos III (rather than Antiochos II).[57] Further west, Alinda fell to Zeuxis;[58] from there, he took over Amyzon, and, to the south, Mylasa: Zeuxis ordered troops to respect the Mylasan shrine at Labraunda, and a fragmentary letter found in the sanctuary of Sinuri, in the territory of Mylasa, is perhaps from Antiochos III.[59] Zeuxis, and Antiochos III, presumably respected the formal 'autonomy' of Mylasa, the result of a grant by Seleukos II. It is also possible that Antiochos III granted *asylia* to the city, or acknowledged such a status.[60]

How far did the Seleukid advance into Karia reach in 203? It did not affect the Karian coast: cities such as Herakleia under Latmos, Iasos, and Bargylia were available for Philip V to take over in 201 (see § 3). To the south-west of Mylasa, the city of Kildara probably did not fall to the Seleukids, since Philip V controlled it later. To the east of Mylasa lay the territory of Stratonikeia, a former Seleukid foundation; the Rhodians had been given the city by Seleukos II (the most likely interpretation of Pol. 30.31.6), and they had kept control of it continuously until Philip V captured it in 201 (Appendix 4). Most puzzlingly, Euromos was not taken by Zeuxis— it too was available for (re)capture by Philip V in 201—though the city lies close to Mylasa. The explanation for the incompleteness of the Seleukid conquests in the region probably lies in the 'pact' with Philip V (§ 3). Fulfilment of the Seleukid ambitions in the region would have to await the campaign of 197.

Nonetheless, the Seleukid gains amounted to a sizeable portion of the Karian 'interior' (μεσόγαια: Strabo 14.22), with important cities such as Mylasa, Alabanda, and Alinda. The advance into Karia

[57] Waggoner 1989; Antiochos II argued for by Robert 1973.
[58] Alinda: document **9**; J. and L. Robert 1983: 147 (Alinda controls Amyzon and must have been taken over first).
[59] Mylasa: document **15**. Sinuri: Robert 1945: 12 (the reconstruction offered by Piejko and noted in *SEG* 39.1122, is not convincing). However, it is possible that both these documents pertain to Antiochos II, who was active in the region (Ch. 1 § 3). *I. Mylasa* 126, honouring an ἀρχιδικαστής in the δικαστήριον of Karia, who was also 'a Friend of the king', is usually dated to the time of Antiochos III, but is more likely Ptolemaic: Appendix 3 (at any rate, the expression 'Friend of the king', contrasting with 'the kings' (plural) found in Amyzonian documents after 202, goes against a dating before the death of Antiochos the son in 193).
[60] Autonomy: Crampa 1969: no. 5. *Asylia*: documents dating to the last years of the third century show the Mylasans asking Cretan cities for acknowledgement of their *asylia* and *aphorologesia*, perhaps in relation to grants by Antiochos III (*I. Mylasa* 643, lines 8–13; 644, 7–10; 660, 2–3; 661, 5–7—the last two published in *EA* 19 (1992), 12–13, now *SEG* 42.1003, 1004; Rigsby 1996: nos. 187–209, gives the whole series of Cretan documents found at Mylasa).

recovered substantially the same territory which Antiochos II and Seleukos II had once controlled. It is tempting to call this region 'Chrysaorian Karia', from the name of the religious league regrouping communities such as Antiocheia/Alabanda, Mylasa, Alinda, and Amyzon, and active in this period.[61]

Zeuxis' military operations of 203,[62] including the takeover of Amyzon, have been interpreted as aggression against the Ptolemaic empire; which explained the dispatch of an ambassador from Alexandria to Asia Minor with a warning for Antiochos to refrain from infringing the truce struck in 217 after Raphia (above). This version (Schmitt 1964: 227; Will 1982: 109, 112–13) is no longer the obvious one. Amyzon certainly was a 'Ptolemaic' city under Ptolemy II, as proved by the material published in J. and L. Robert 1983: 118–32. However, we know that the inland portion of Western Karia was taken from the Ptolemies by the Seleukids (under Antiochos II, before 254: see Ch. 1 § 3); under Seleukos II, the region was governed by Olympichos. When Antigonos Doson took over parts of Western Karia around 227, the Seleukid governor passed into his service. From his base in Alinda, Olympichos must have controlled Amyzon (though probably not Herakleia under Latmos),[63] in addition to Mylasa, where his presence is well attested. Between 221 and 214,[64] he undertook incursions against the territory of Iasos (*I. Iasos* 150; above Ch. 1, § 4), before being warned off by the Rhodians. This activity implies that Olympichos controlled Euromos, whose territory his troops crossed on their way to attack Iasos; a subsequent Euromian decree of *c*.201, in speaking

---

[61] On the Chrysaorians, Oppermann 1924; J. and L. Robert 1983: 223–5; a Mylasan inscription (Crampa 1969: no. 5, lines 15–16) distinguishes between Chrysaorians and 'the other Karians'. Documents **11**, **16**, *IG* 2² 2313, line 54, for existence in this period. However, several Chrysaorian communities were under Rhodian control, including Stratonikeia, with the federal shrine of Zeus Chrysaoreus; so that the Chrysaorian League straddled two major Hellenistic states.

[62] Document **9**, 13, speaks of a war (τὸν περιεστηκότα π[όλεμον]). The soldiers sent by Zeuxis under Ophelandros and the siege of the χωρίον mentioned in document **13** are probably related.

[63] Wörrle 1988: 442: Herakleia under Latmos was 'Ptolemaic' continuously down to 201, when Philip V conquered the city. This is likely: Herakleia is never named alongside Iasos, Bargylia, Euromos, and Pedasa in the negotiations between Philip V and the Romans during the Second Macedonian War (Pol. 18.1–2), and therefore belonged to the Ptolemaic cities Philip was summoned to restore to Ptolemy V (Pol. 18.1.14). Furthermore, a Herakleian Menekrates appears both in *IG* 9² 1, 173, on embassy to request Aitolian intercession with the Herakleians' ruler, a Ptolemy, and in the letter of Zeuxis to Herakleia of 196 (document **31** B) as an envoy to the Seleukid viceroy. If both documents refer to the same Menekrates, Herakleia was probably Ptolemaic close to 196.

[64] The dating is assured because *I. Iasos* 150 mentions a Rhodian ambassador (lines 38, 95), who died, at Alexandria, in 213 (Cook 1966: 24 no. 9).

of the city being 'restored' to Philip V, alludes to this period of Antigonid control, under the local governorship of Olympichos.[65]

By 201, the Antigonid zone under Olympichos had broken up; the city of Euromos was probably independent for a few years, before being (re)conquered by Philip V (see below).[66] It is possible that a Ptolemaic resurgence, in the last years of Ptolemy IV, destroyed Olympichos' dominions, and reasserted control over north-west Karia. This would explain why Zeuxis, in his letter to the Amyzonians, seems to promise the *status quo* which had prevailed under Ptolemy (ἃ καὶ ἐν τῆι Πτολεμαίου [. . .], *RC* 38, line 5). Such a reaction might seem strange under Ptolemy IV, who apparently neglected the overseas empire; the reference in Zeuxis' letter might simply designate some precise privileges once granted by a Ptolemy.[67] Another possibility is that Zeuxis is not referring to a king of the Ptolemaic dynasty, but (for instance) is confirming a decision taken by a subordinate named Ptolemaios (or even by one of Olympichos' subordinates bearing that name?).

It is equally possible that many of the cities in north-western Karia were genuinely independent, though perhaps under some degree of Rhodian influence. This is suggested by the formulary of an Amyzonian inscription recording the decision to impose a special tax (εἰσφορά) on all citizens, to reimburse a loan taken by the city towards contributions to the Chrysaorian League, a feature suggesting possible autonomy and the concomitant absence of royal subsidies (J. and L. Robert 1983: 217–27, no. 28). The decree is dated by the *stephanephoros* and by the Ionian month Heraion (rather than by a Macedonian month, as under the Ptolemies or Seleukids): the decree shows no sign of subjection to a royal state, unlike the Seleukid documents of 202 and 201 (above). But the *eisphora* decree cannot date to the years after 188, under Rhodian domination, since it does not have the compulsory 'Rhodian' preamble mentioning the priest of Helios at Rhodes and the Rhodian calendar (see J. and L.

---

[65] Ma, Derow, and Meadows 1995. On Alinda controlling Amyzon, J. and L. Robert 1983: 17 and 147. Euromos under Olympichos: J. and L. Robert 1983: 150; subsequent Euromian decree: Errington 1993: 21, no. 4, line 3.

[66] Disappearance of the Antigonid province of Olympichos: Wörrle 1988: 440. The inscription referring to depredations by some person or community (Errington 1993: 27, no. 6), might date to a period of independence after the disappearance of Olympichos.

[67] Letter of Zeuxis: document 5. Ptolemy IV neglecting empire: Pol. 5.34.4. On the other hand, the capacity for reaction of the local Ptolemaic forces should not be underestimated: Samos, captured by Philip V, was recovered for Ptolemy V, after a siege of the akropolis by Ptolemaic forces (Habicht 1957: no. 64: ἐν τε τῆι ἀποκαταστάσει τῆς πόλεως εἰς τὰ τοῦ βασιλέως Πτολεμαίου πράγματα).

Robert 1983: 250–1). This document was likely produced after the disappearance of Olympichos' authority over this part of Karia, at a time when Amyzon was independent, but part of the Chrysaorian League, at some time between 213 and 203.[68]

Rather than aggression against the Ptolemaic dominion, Zeuxis' Karian campaign intervened in a complex situation created by the interaction of super-power politics and local players. Upon this landscape, Zeuxis imposed the 'simplification through conquest' of Seleukid takeover, and his activities are typical of the Seleukid project in the region (Ch. 1), in spite of their incompleteness (imposed by external factors: see § 3).

Apart from western Karia, the Ionian city of Teos provides evidence for Seleukid activity in Asia Minor in the last years of the third century—if the two important Teian decrees are to be dated to this context (which I prefer) rather than 197 (see Appendix 2). The Teian documents give a vivid picture of the king's passage through Teos, with his Friends and contingents of his army; it is possible that Laodike accompanied him, since the Teians also respond to her benefactions (Herrmann 1965a, 110). Antiochos III went before the assembled Teians, and 'released the city as holy, inviolate, and free from tribute', specifically from the heavy contributions (συντάξεις) which the city had been paying to Attalos I. The impression from the Teian documents is of a more peaceful takeover than at Amyzon: the Teians thanked the king for the πίστις he showed when staying in the city with troops, and there is no mention of garrisons or governors. However, this might be misleading, since the first Teian decree elides the specific events by which Antiochos was allowed, or gained, entry into the city: 'he restored the affairs (or his affairs) to a satisfactory conclusion', ἀποκατέστησε τὰ πράγματα εἰς συμφέρουσαν κατάστασιν.[69]

---

[68] An objection is that the list of citizens who paid the *eisphora* is headed by Pankrates and Menippos, sons of Melaineus, honoured in another Amyzonian inscription, J. and L. Robert 1983: 204–9, no. 23: this inscription refers to the activity of the two brothers in the time of the Great King (line 15), and how the brothers had something to do with a king, presumably Antiochos (line 6), when they were still young, νεώτεροι. The *eisphora* decree starts by listing important citizens (J. and L. Robert 1983: 226), who held office in the Seleukid period: would Pankrates and Menippos, young men under Antiochos III, have been important enough (or old enough) to figure at the beginning of a list of citizens drawn up before 203? However, it is possible that the king in question is not Antiochos III: this would explain why the expression βασιλεῖ μεγάλῳ appears in line 15, in the middle of the inscription, to distinguish him from the king referred to earlier at line 6; the activity of Pankrates and Menippos would then have started earlier than under Antiochos III.

[69] Teian inscriptions: documents **17, 18, 19**. 'Holy, inviolate, and free from tribute': document **17**, 18–20; 33–4; 47–8. Peaceful takeover: J. and L. Robert 1983: 137; but note Herrmann 1965a: 110: 'Der Anschein eines ruhigen, gewaltlosen Übergangs braucht

A likely context is a foray by Antiochos from Sardeis, with only a brief stay at Teos.[70] The route might have taken Antiochos towards Smyrna, then southwards on the highway towards Ephesos (Pritchett 1982: 272) into the plain south of Smyrna; from this plain it would be easy to reach Teos, over the Ionian mountains, by the Menderes/Kavakdere corridor. If Teos was taken over in 204 or 203, then the same probably happened to neighbouring Kolophon ('Seleukid' in the 190s); on this geographical argument, it is likely that Lebedos also fell to Antiochos then. There is thus no need to see Teos as an isolated Seleukid outpost or enclave (as Herrmann had proposed, tentatively).[71] Both Teos and Kolophon had been 'Attalid' cities, taken back by Attalos I in 218 (above, § 1); Attalos I, weakened by his efforts in the First Macedonian War, then by a conflict with Prousias I, may have accepted the *fait accompli* of Antiochos' foray, or surrendered them against compensation—perhaps the 400 talents owed by Antiochos III in 189? (Pol. 21.17.5, Liv. 37.45.15, with Herrmann 1965a: 110–13). Activity in the region might have been directed at the Ptolemaic base at Ephesos, at the end of the plain south of Smyrna—perhaps the aggression about which the Ptolemaic minister Agathokles complained (above).

The Karian activities of Zeuxis constituted a sustained campaign of conquest, followed by consolidation and further fighting; the presence of Antiochos III at Teos, if it is to be dated to 203, implies a different rhythm. When Antiochos crossed the Taurus, it is likely that he visited the 'provincial capital', Sardeis, whence he dispatched Zeuxis to Karia. The king himself may have embarked on an armed tour of Seleukid cis-Tauric Asia Minor, to make his presence felt again after an absence of over nine years, conduct a reconnaissance in force, make a probe at Ptolemaic Ephesos, and exploit local disaffection with the Attalids.[72] If the Ilian decree for a

natürlich nicht unbedingt der Wahrheit zu entsprechen'. 'Satisfactory conclusion': document 17, 10–11.

[70] Document 17, 29–36: that Antiochos instructed the Teians to send him an embassy suggests that he had already left.

[71] Herrmann 1965a: 114–16. Kolophon: document 42, a statue base for Antiochos the son, points to the city being 'Seleukid'; though that statue is probably to be dated after 197, since Antiochos III is 'the great king'. A decree for the Attalid prince Athenaios, which Holleaux dated around 197 (Holleaux 1938b: 51–60), has been redated by Habicht to the 150s (Habicht in *Inschr. Asklepieion*, 27–8 nn. 1–5) and hence does not support Attalid possession of Kolophon c.200. Lebedos: Herrmann 1965a: 114 and n. 141, 116, arguing that the dynastic name Ptolemais, attested c.205 and in the 190s, would hardly have persisted under Seleukid domination; on this line of reasoning, Ptolemais/Lebedos did not fall to Antiochos III in 197 either. I think it possible that the name Ptolemais persisted under Seleukid domination.

[72] Herrmann 1965a: 118, proposes a campaign aimed at reconquering Asia Minor, interrupted because of events in Egypt, in favour of the offensive in Koile-Syria.

king Antiochos (*OGIS* 219) should be attributed to Antiochos III
(see Appendix 1), the closing years of the third century might
provide a satisfactory context: the king, moving into Mysia, would
have made contact with Ilion, and won the city over (Mastrocinque
1983: 67–9).

Antiochos' armed tour, like Zeuxis' campaign of conquest in
Karia, was interrupted, for reasons which belong to international
high politics (§ 3). Antiochos turned from Asia Minor to Koile-
Syria, around 202. This enterprise (the Fifth Syrian War) ended
with the defeat of the Ptolemaic forces, at Panion (200).[73] The
process of conquest is illustrated by documents such as a letter of
Antiochos III to the governor Ptolemaios concerning the status of
Jerusalem (*AJ* 13.138–44), a parallel to the Amyzonian documents;
or the dossier of petitions and enactments concerning Ptolemaios'
private estates at Skythopolis, his reward for defecting to the
Seleukid side.[74] By the time a Roman embassy came to broker a
settlement between Antiochos III and Ptolemy V (Pol. 16.27.5), in
200,[75] the Seleukid conquest of Koile-Syria was complete. It was at
this time that Antiochos III took the title of βασιλεὺς μέγας, 'Great
King' (Appendix 4), embodying claims to be 'king of Asia'.

Livy writes that, in 198, while still in Koile-Syria, Antiochos
organized an invasion of the Attalid kingdom (literally, that he
invaded it himself), before withdrawing after an intervention from
Rome (Liv. 32.8.9–16, and 32.27.1). It is certain that the king did
not travel from a major war in Syria back to Asia Minor for the sake
of a minor expedition and quickly relinquished territorial gains.
Some scholars have suggested that Livy records some anti-Attalid
activity by local Seleukid forces; however, I incline to reject the
account as an annalistic invention (Appendix 6). At any rate, if some
local Seleukid aggression took place in 198, it was dwarfed by the
third expedition into western Asia Minor launched in 197.

[73] Fifth Syrian War: Will 1982: 118–21; Gera 1987, Gera 1998: 20–34.
[74] Estates: *SEG* 29.1613. On Ptolemaios, see Habicht's comments in Jones and
Habicht 1989: 335–46: Ptolemaios belonged to an Aspendian family of long-standing
tradition of service to the Ptolemies; his father and grandfather had served as governors
of Kilikia, and both founded (in successive generations) the Ptolemaic colony of Arsinoe
(Habicht and Jones 1989); Ptolemaios' father, and Ptolemaios himself, had been
governors of Koile-Syria for the Ptolemies, until Ptolemaios deserted to Antiochos III
(Gera 1987).
[75] On this embassy, Walbank, *HCP* ii. 533–4; Will 1982: 119–21; Holleaux 1957: 159
with further references, 345, 350–1; Warrior 1996; it is also catalogued, with comments
and bibliography, as no. 60 in Ager 1996.

3. *Philip V, the Rhodians, Attalos I, and the Romans (201–200 BC)*

The second occurrence of Seleukid activity in cis-Tauric Asia Minor cannot be viewed in isolation from the context of international politics, especially the ambitions which Philip V entertained in the eastern Aegean and in Asia Minor.[76] After the peace of Phoinike (205) which ended the inconclusive war fought against the Aitolians and the Romans (the 'First Macedonian War'), Philip V sponsored a privateer to operate in the Kyklades and along the coasts of Asia Minor, supported the Cretans in their war against the Rhodians, and sent an agent on a mission to damage the Rhodian fleet. It is difficult not to see Philip's actions in *c.*204 as motivated, at least in part, by competition with the Rhodians in the eastern Aegean, for instance over Kos and the Kyklades, and by the desire to weaken the great naval power of the region as a prelude to invasion. Around this time, Antiochos III attempted to broker a peace between the Cretans and the Rhodians, perhaps to reduce the disruption in the coastal region of Asia Minor, since he now had re-established control over parts of Ionia, around Teos (above, § 2).[77]

It was Philip's ambitions in the eastern Aegean which led to an agreement with Antiochos III, in the winter 203/2.[78] The existence of this agreement is stated by Polybios (16.1.8–9): Philip, during his expedition in the kingdom of Pergamon, asked Zeuxis for supplies κατὰ τὰς συνθήκας, with Zeuxis' reluctant agreement; later, he complied with a similar request (Pol. 16.24.6).

But what were these συνθῆκαι? Literary sources[79] mention a pact struck between Philip V and Antiochos III, stipulating nothing less than the partition of the Ptolemaic empire. Polybios states that 'when king Ptolemy [IV] died, Antiochos and Philip agreed on the partition of the empire of the child he had left behind [Ptolemy V], and initiated evil deeds, Philip laying hands on Egypt, Karia, and Samos, Antiochos on Koile-Syria and Phoenicia' (3.2.8)— to Polybios' indignation (15.20.3). Livy (31.14.5) seems to follow Polybios; Appian (*Mak.* 4), however, describes the pact as a rumour

---

[76] Walbank 1940: 108–37; Holleaux 1952: 211–335.

[77] Privateer: Pol. 18.54.8, Diod. 28.1 (Dikaiarchos sent to collect tribute in the islands). Cretan War: Diod. 27.3; Diod. 28.1; Pol. 13.4.2, 13.5.1. Rhodes: Pol. 13.4–5 and Polyainos, 5.17. Generally, Holleaux 1952: 124–45 and 163–77, who argues that this activity was destined to raise money for an Antigonid fleet (139–42). Antiochos III in Crete: Holleaux 1952: 191–9 (peace between some Cretan cities and the Rhodians directed against Philip V); on Crete, Philip V, Antiochos III, and the Teian request for *asylia*, Kreuter 1992: 57–61.

[78] Chronology: Schmitt 1964: 229–37; *HCP* ii. 472–3.

[79] Commented list of sources, Schmitt 1964: 237–9; also *Staatsvertr.* no. 547.

(λόγος, δόξα), brought to Rome by a Rhodian embassy in autumn 201, and the terms of the pact are different from those in Polybios (3.2.8): Philip would help Antiochos to campaign in Egypt and Cyprus, while Antiochos would assist Philip in the conquest of Kyrene (!), the Kyklades and Ionia.[80]

The 'Syro-Macedonian pact' has a historiography of its own.[81] Some have accepted the Polybian version wholesale (for instance Holleaux and Schmitt).[82] In reaction, D. Magie denounced the pact as a Rhodian fabrication designed to provoke the Senate's alarm. For Magie, the events of the years 202–200 fell into two unrelated sets: Philip's activity in the eastern Aegean, and Antiochos' campaign in Koile-Syria; the existence of a pact between Philip V and Antiochos III was thus unnecessary to explain the events. Furthermore, Errington convincingly argued against the importance Holleaux lent to the 'Syro-Macedonian pact', and suggested that a local agreement between Philip V and Zeuxis provided Polybios with the basis for a deduction concerning a broader pact.[83]

However, the argument that an agreement between Antiochos III and Philip is historically superfluous cannot hold. The Seleukid advance into western Karia came to a halt (see above, § 2), and the Seleukid forces in Asia Minor did not act against Philip V by collaborating with Attalos I and the Rhodians, even when Philip was at his weakest, and even after Philip V had departed from Asia Minor in winter 201 (see below) and left scanty forces behind (in fact, not until his defeat by the Romans at Kynoskephalai in 197). In addition, Philip V, returning from Pergamon, crossed parts of Seleukid-held Lydia, starting with the 'Seleukid' city of Hierakome (Pol. 16.2.8–9).[84] Conversely, Philip V did not attack Seleukid territory proper, until compelled by lack of supplies during the winter 201/0 (Pol. 16.24). The pattern supports the existence of, at the least, an agreement of non-interference between the two kings, as mentioned by Polybios.

Pressure from Philip V, whatever the exact terms, might explain

[80] Schmitt 1964: 250–6 tries to conciliate Polybios and Appian, but his arguments are unconvincing, e.g. on the different attribution of Egypt in Polybios and Appian: Errington 1971: esp. 345–7.

[81] Schmitt 1964: 239–41; Will 1982: 114–18; Gruen 1986: 387–8.

[82] Holleaux 1935: 320–2, 328–30; Schmitt 1964: 235–61 and 301, map 4. Criticism of Schmitt 1964: Berthold 1975–6: 101 n. 22.

[83] Magie 1939, followed by Errington 1971: 348–9 (pact unnecessary); Errington 1971 for Polybios as inventor of the pact.

[84] Schmitt 1964: 246–8. But Schmitt 1964: 246, is mistaken to write that the plundering of Alabandian territory by Philip in winter 201/0 and the honours voted to Philip by Hierakome (*TAM* 5.2 1261 A) are proof of Seleukid 'tolerance', since the first was a measure taken out of a need for supplies, and the second was a local initiative.

why the Seleukid advance broke off,[85] and why Antiochos' attention shifted from Asia Minor to Koile-Syria. The possibility of any collaboration on a wider scale remains mysterious, and even more so whether it was primarily, or at all, directed against the Ptolemaic empire. The fact remains that Philip V acted in the eastern Aegean, free from Seleukid opposition. The year 202 was occupied by operations in the north Aegean and the Propontis (Lysimacheia and Chalkedon were taken over, Kios sacked, Thasos 'enslaved' on the way back to Macedonia);[86] Philip then spent 201 in operations across western Asia Minor, ranging from the plain of Thebe north of Pergamon, to Knidos in southern Karia: the year 'when Philip was overrunning Asia', Φίλιππος . . . ὅτε τὴν Ἀσίαν κατέτρεχεν (Pol. 16.24.9).

Philip started by working through the Kyklades, forcibly taking over a number of the islands and installing garrisons.[87] The island route across the Aegean ends at Samos, where Philip seized the Ptolemaic naval base and fleet, incorporating the ships and crews into his own force.[88] Philip then besieged Chios (Pol. 16.2.1–3); off Chios, he was defeated by the joint fleet of the Rhodians and Attalos I (Pol. 16.2–8). Another naval battle took place off Miletos, near the island of Lade, where Philip drove off the Rhodian fleet (Pol. 16.15). Probably between the battle of Chios and the battle of Lade, Philip invaded the kingdom of Pergamon (Pol. 16.1); repulsed by the defences of the city, he marched and counter-marched his force across the whole length of the kingdom in search of provisions. It was after this foray that he sent to Zeuxis, asking for supplies 'according to the agreement' (Pol. 16.1.9). Holleaux believed that Philip reached Pergamon by an inland march from Miletos; more likely, the expedition was at least in part seaborne, landing near the mouth of the Kaikos, and embarking again near Ephesos.[89]

[85] Initiative by Philip, concessions by Seleukids: Schmitt 1964: 248–50. Walbank argued that Philip V could not put an embargo on Antiochos' Syrian campaign (Walbank 1965: 264), but this does not take into account the powerful fleet Philip was raising.

[86] Lysimacheia and Chalkedon: Pol. 15.23.8; 18.3.11 and 18.4.5; *Staatsvertr.* no. 549 (with Robert 1955: 268–70, for correct dating); Robert 1955: 266–71. Kios: Pol. 15.23.6. Thasos: Pol. 15.24.

[87] Island route through the Aegean: Hdt. 6.95.2; Ormerod 1924: 19–20 and 20 n. 1. Violence at Paros: Liv. 31.31.4. Garrisons at Andros, Paros, and Kythnos (only): Liv. 31.15.8.

[88] Seizure of Samos, Holleaux 1952: 223–34, and 239–43 for 'Egyptians' in the fleet of Philip; the takeover was an act of war, in spite of Holleaux 1952: 310–12: Liv. 31.1.4, Habicht 1957: 237–8, Shipley 1987: 192.

[89] The order followed here is that proposed by Holleaux in a number of studies assembled in Holleaux 1952: 211–98, esp. at 213–33; except that the situation of the expedition into Pergamon between the battles of Chios and Lade is taken from

The latter phase of Philip's expedition, in south-western Asia Minor, met with greater success. He attacked the independent states of Knidos and Kos (which briefly lost the island of Kalymna),[90] then the Rhodian dominions. The island of Nisyros was perhaps taken over;[91] on the continent, Philip conquered all or most of the Rhodian Peraia, then, following the Tralleis–Physkos road into the Marsyas valley, Stratonikeia (a Rhodian city since the time of Seleukos II: see Appendix 4).[92] Philip then took Iasos, Bargylia, and Kildara; he may have taken Theangela, and given it to Halikarnassos, just as he would hand the territory of Myous over to Magnesia on Maeander (below). At the end of the Latmic Gulf, he took Herakleia under Latmos, over which Philip appointed two *epistatai* from Kalymnos; inland, Euromos and Pedasa.[93] Philip's achievement in South-west Asia Minor was substantial (though ragged on the ground): a Karian 'province', with its own governor

Walbank, *HCP* ii. 499–500, and 502–3 for the suggestion that the expedition was partly seaborne, against Holleaux 1952: 253–5 (land-march from Miletos and back); also Magie 1950: 747–9 n. 39. Berthold 1975 argues that the battle of Lade took place before the battle of Chios, based on a reading of Pol. 16.9, the eulogy for the Rhodian navarch Theophiliskos, who died after the battle of Chios; however, many of Berthold's arguments are already answered by Holleaux.

[90] Knidos: *FD* 3.1, no. 308, with Homolle's commentary, 171 n. 2; *I. Iasos* 606 (Bargylietan decree, probably acknowledging *asylia* for Knidos); an epiphany of the Koan goddess Artemis Hyakinthotrophos is mentioned in *I. Knidos* 220. Kos: Holleaux 1952: 273–6; Sherwin-White 1978: 120–4, and 124–8: Kalymnos was detached from Kos by Philip V—perhaps confirmed by the presence of Kalymnians governing Herakleia under Latmos for Philip: Wörrle 1988: 433–4.

[91] *Syll.* 572 (cf. *IG* 12.3.91), with Thompson 1971: 618–19: Philip V took over Nisyros, and allowed it 'to use its ancestral and present laws', i.e. undid the incorporation of Nisyros into the Rhodian state.

[92] Rhodian Peraia: Pol. 16.11.2–6, cf. 18.2.3; 18.6.3; 18.8.9 and App. *Mac.* 4.1; *Inscr. Lindos* 151 makes it clear that Philip had taken over Pisye, Idyma, and Kyllandos. Liv. 33.18.4 mentions Macedonian troops at Thera and 'Alabanda' in 197. The reading 'Alabanda' is defended by Briscoe 1973 who argues that Alabanda was Antigonid, but more likely the city remained Seleukid down to 190, so that the text should be emended to some other Karian place-name (Robert 1954: 378–9 n. 4, suggested Lobolda). Stratonikeia: cf. Liv. 33.18.4–7; 33.18.19; 33.18.21–2; *I. Stratonikeia* 3 (201) and 4 (198), attesting Antigonid control at Panamara, near Stratonikeia (Debord 1994 argues that Panamara was not yet part of Stratonikeia).

[93] Iasos, Bargylia: cf. Pol. 16.12; 18.8.9; Liv. 34.32.5 and 33.18.19 (Bargylia). Iasos, Bargylia, Euromos, and Pedasa are referred to in Pol. 18.2.3 (Pedasa should be added) and Pol. 18.44.4 (in the SC of 196). Euromos: Errington 1993: no. 4. Kildara: J. and L. Robert 1983: 187: 'étant situé tout près de Bargylia, fut sûrement occupé par Philippe V'; the city was framed by Antigonid conquests of 201 (Bargylia, Stratonikeia, Pisye, and Idyma). Theangela: Descat 1997 (a 'Philippeus', i.e. a Euromian between 201 and 196, appears in a document attesting the incorporation of Theangela into the *polis* of Halikarnassos—assuming the stone is from Theangela and not from Halikarnassos, as argued by Bean and Cook 1955: 115). Herakleia under Latmos; Wörrle 1988: 433–4. Pugliese-Carratelli 1987: 122–3, suggests that the apparition of Artemis Kindyas at Bargylia (*I. Iasos* 613) dates to the invasion of Philip V, but the text does not countenance this.

and local officials,[94] stretching from the mouth of the Maeander to the Keramic Gulf, arching inland, around Seleukid-held Mylasa, up to and including most of the Rhodian Peraia, and to the upper Marsyas valley at Stratonikeia. But Philip allowed the Rhodians and Attalos I to trap him in the Gulf of Bargylia; in the winter, reduced to 'the life of a wolf' (Pol. 16.24.4), he cajoled or bullied Mylasa, Alabanda, and Magnesia on Maeander for supplies. Magnesia, in return for supplying figs, received the town of Myous, detached from Miletos[95] (Pol. 16.24.9). Philip even carried out acts of aggression against Seleukid territory, unsuccessfully trying to capture Mylasa by a botched *coup de main* and plundering the territory of Alabanda (the latter no doubt operating from Stratonikeia).

In early 200, Philip V slipped past the blockade (Holleaux 1952: 287–92). In Greece, after getting involved in hostilities against Athens (Liv. 31.14.6–10), Philip undertook a campaign in Thrace (Liv. 31.16), besieging Maroneia, which soon fell, followed by many places in Thrace and the Chersonesos (up to Sestos: *HCP* ii. 539, *ad* Pol. 16.29.3). Abydos fell after a horrendous siege (Pol. 16.29–35; Liv. 31.16.6–18.9). The north Aegean expedition, with its swift progression through a string of coastal cities, is reminiscent of the advance of Antiochos III in 197 (see § 4). Another similarity is that most of the places taken over were Ptolemaic.

The thinness of the evidence hinders general interpretation. Were the campaigns directed against the Ptolemaic empire? Philip assailed Ptolemaic possessions—Samos, perhaps Halikarnassos and Myndos[96]—but these were hardly the exclusive target of his campaign. Was Philip motivated by 'ancestral claims', analogous to those of Antiochos III? In Karia, he could consider his activity as the reconquest of 'ancestral possessions', the holdings of Antigonos Doson. The failed attempt on Mylasa might be interpreted as aimed at recovering a city which had once been 'Antigonid' (see § 2);[97] but Polybios does not mention any claim by Philip V to ancestral rights during the negotiations at Nikaia with the Romans and their allies

[94] Wörrle 1988: 443 for appraisal of Philip's Asian holdings. Governor of Antigonid Karia: Liv. 33.18.6. *Epistates* at Panamara: *I. Stratonikeia* 4; Herakleia under Latmos: previous note.
[95] Supplies: Pol. 16.24.6; attempt on Mylasa, territory of Alabanda ravaged: Pol. 16.24.7. On Myous' absorption into Miletos, Herrmann 1965*b*: 90–103, esp. 93–6, 101–2. Holleaux 1952: 230–2, 255, held that Myous was given to Magnesia when Philip was marching to Pergamon or back from Pergamon, but it is unlikely that the expedition took place entirely by land (above). The situation of Magnesia is unclear.
[96] Schmitt 1964: 259–60 (against Holleaux 1952: 306–13). 'Ptolemaic' cities may be referred to in Pol. 18.2.4. In 197, the Rhodians protected the Ptolemaic cities (Liv. 33.12–23), and the same may have happened in 201–200.
[97] Schmitt 1964: 243–5: 'ererbte Rechte auf Karien'.

(18.1–10), for instance as a reply to the Rhodian insistence that Philip evacuate Euromos. In any event, inherited claims would concern a small part of Karia, and not the Rhodian Peraia, the Knidian peninsula, Samos, or Chios; nor would they concern Thrace, Abydos, or the Propontis; besides, the Karian activity of Philip came only after a naval phase in areas where Philip had no ancestral rights whatsoever. The most likely explanation is still an attempt at Aegean power. To speak in terms of the individual ambition of Philip V (and a spirit of rivalry with Antiochos III?) at least reflects the viewpoint of one contemporary, Alkaios of Messene, who spoke of Philip's Zeus-like greatness.[98]

The impact on the local communities is the most interesting feature: if there were more evidence, especially epigraphical, the single year taken up by Philip's war of conquest in Asia Minor would offer a subject-matter as rich as Antiochos' activities in the region. The material available illustrates the variety of local responses: the military resistance of Kos (*Syll*. 568, 569, with Holleaux 1952: 274–5); revolt after Antigonid conquest, as in the case of Samos (Habicht 1957: no. 64); the rhetorical strategies of subject communities such as Euromos, which honoured the Antigonid general who had conquered the city 'in accordance with our prayers' and took on the name 'Philippeis'.[99] The same sort of euergetic dialogue can be seen in the Panamarian decree on public prayers for the safety of Philip, his queen, and his children (*I. Stratonikeia* 3), or in the Panamarian decree for an Antigonid official (*I. Stratonikeia* 4). These documents show us the rulers in the guise of benefactors: Philip making dedications at a local temple, an Antigonid governor restoring the walls of a local town after the earthquake of 199. Just as illuminating is the decree passed after the battle of Lade by the Milesians (Pol. 16.15.6): καταπλαγέντας τὸ γεγονός, οὐ μόνον τὸν Φίλιππον, ἀλλὰ καὶ τὸν Ἡρακλείδην στεφανῶσαι διὰ τὸν ἔφοδον, '[according to Zenon and Antisthenes], terrified by what had taken place, they voted a crown not only for Philip, but also for Herakleides on account of the attack' (or 'through fear that he might attack', preferred by Walbank, *HCP*). The course of action taken by the Milesians, once it was clear that Philip had been victorious at Lade, gives a stark example of the function of civic honours for a king (or his officials): to provide a medium for communicating and for influencing behaviour (see Ch. 4 § 2*b*).

---

[98] I still agree with Walbank 1942: 134–7, on *Anth. Pal.* 9.518 (the epigram, celebrating Philip's Zeus-like greatness, is encomiastic, not ironical).

[99] Philippeis: document **29**, 5. Errington 1993: no. 4, lines 1–4: decree for Alexandros Admetou, who 'restored the city to King Philip, in accordance with our prayers'.

The alienation of civic territory and its conveyance to another city by royal *fiat* exemplifies the impact of Philip's presence. This may have happened in the case of Theangela, possibly given wholesale to Halikarnassos;[100] the best attested case is that of the conveyance of Myous and its territory (annexed by Miletos some time in the late third century) to Magnesia on Maeander. The royal gift increased Magnesia's territory south of the Maeander, down to the Gulf of Miletos, but deprived Miletos of the *Μυησία,* its territory in the Maeander valley.[101] Nearby, Herakleia under Latmos, in addition to suffering the flight of its agricultural serfs, lost parts of its territory[102]—as a supplementary gift to the Magnesians, or as compensation to the Milesians for the loss of Myous? In the latter case, the tract in question would have been taken from the only point of contact after Miletos lost the *Myesia*: the Bucak plain, south of Herakleia, the latter's agricultural territory.[103] The zero-sum game of territory-redistribution by royal *fiat* caused long-lasting disruption in the tight network of small, competing cities in western Karia; the three communities concerned would fight territorial wars in the 180s.[104] A measure of the disruption is given by the peace treaty between Magnesia on Maeander and Miletos: a clause precludes either party from ever again accepting a part of the other's territory, with an emphatic profusion of negatives, μὴ εἶναι μήτε Μάγνησιν τὴν Μιλησίων χώραν μ[ή | τ]ε τὴν περαίαν μήτε ἄλλην μηδεμίαν μηδὲ φρούριον, μήτε Μιλησίο[ις | τὴ]ν Μαγνήτων χώραν μήτε τὴν περαίαν μήτε ἄλλην μηδεμίαν μηδ[ὲ | φρ]ούριον παρὰ μηθένος λαβεῖν μήτε δι' αὑτῶν μήτε δι' ἑτέρων μητ' ἐγ κτ[ήσει | μή]τε ἐν δόσει μήτε ἐν ἀναθέσει μήτε καθιερώσει μήτε κατ' ἄλλον τρόπ[ον | μηθέ]να μηδὲ κατὰ παρεύρεσιν μηδεμίαν, 'let it not be possible neither for the Magnesians to take the territory of the Milesians or their coastal territory or any other

---

[100] Descat 1997 (arguing that Theangela belonged to Halikarnassos at some time between 201 and 196, but not that Philip V was responsible: a local takeover, of a type well attested in Hellenistic history, is another possibility).

[101] The *Myesia* may have been the ἱερὰ χώρα which the Milesians lost in wars but the Romans restored to them in 188 (Pol. 21.46.5).

[102] Serfs: document **31** B, III 10; and I. 12–14 on general στενοχωρία, no doubt caused by Philip V (with Gauthier, *BE* 89. 277, p. 404 on the meaning: 'want, poverty' and not 'land-shortage'). Loss of land: document **31** B, II 9–10, Wörrle 1988: 469–70.

[103] Robert 1987, 177–84, 198–214. *Syll.* 633, lines 82–3, shows that the Milesians did lay claim to parts of the Bucak plain, adjacent to the *Ionopolitis* (Robert 1987: 204–10). In fact, *Syll.* 633, 78–87, shows that the Milesians and Herakleians fought over ownership both of a tract near the *Myesia*, on the north side of the Gulf of Herakleia, and of land on the south of the Gulf, near Ionopolis, in the Bucak plain. Either, or both, may reflect a redistribution of territory effected by Philip V.

[104] Robert 1987: 210–14, on the close links between these cities. Errington 1989a for date of Miletos' wars against Herakleia and later Magnesia (the peace between Miletos and Magnesia is preserved in *Syll.* 588). As a parallel, Hornblower 1982: 142–3, observing that Achaimenid gifts of land were only possible through dispossession of subjects.

territory of theirs whatsoever or a fort, nor let it be possible for the Milesians to take the territory of the Magnesians or their coastal territory or any other territory of theirs whatsoever or a fort, not through their own agency or through other parties, nor as a possession, nor as a gift, nor as a dedication, nor as a consecration, nor in any other way or according to any pretext whatsoever' (*Syll.* 588, lines 40–6).

Generally, the activities of Philip V in the Aegean had the effect of complicating the political mosaic in Asia Minor, where four major powers competed (Antiochos III, Attalos I, the Rhodians, and now Philip V). The Rhodians started immediately their own war of reconquest in the Peraia, from 201 onwards: a dedication by Nikagoras, a Rhodian general, mentions his 'reacquiring the territories of Pisye, Idyma, and Kyllandos, and the forts in these territories', ἀνακτησάμενος τάν τε Πισυῆτιν χώραν καὶ τὰν Ἰδυμίαν καὶ τὰν Κυλλανδίαν καὶ τὰ ἐν αὐταῖς φρούρια (*Inscr. Lindos* 151, lines 4–5; second copy found on Karpathos, *Syll.* 586), in the years 201–198. The verb is exactly the same as that used by Antiochos III to describe his ancestral claims; the parallel is reinforced by the expression Livy uses for the Rhodian campaign of 197: *ad vindicandam a Philippo continentis regionem—Peraeam vocant—possessam maioribus suis*, 'to recover from Philip the region on the mainland— they call it Peraia—which had been owned by their ancestors' (Liv. 33.18.1)—more precisely, Stratonikeia. The Rhodian eagerness to 'reacquire' ancestral possessions illustrates how Philip's Asian campaign further embroiled the palimpsestic history of western Asia Minor.

Attalos I and the Rhodians appealed to Rome (Pol. 16.24.3; Liv. 31.2.1–2; App. *Mak.* 4). The Senate, then the *comitia* decided on a confrontation with Philip (Liv. 31.6–8.1),[105] and, in 200, delivered an ultimatum to Philip V before Abydos, where he was handed a *senatus consultum* requesting him not to make war on any of the Greeks, nor to attack the possessions of Ptolemy; and to accept arbitration for compensation to Attalos and to the Rhodians (Pol. 16.34.3–4.). Philip's response was to ignore the Roman requests, and accept war with Rome. The Second Macedonian War ended with a crushing victory for the Roman army, led by T. Quinctius Flamininus, at Kynoskephalai in 197.

It was the same Roman delegation of 200 which, after delivering the ultimatum to Philip V, ended up before Antiochos III and unsuccessfully tried to broker a settlement between him and

---

[105] On chronology: Warrior 1996. In general, Berthold 1975–6; Will 1982: 131–49; Gruen 1986: 382–98, 534–6.

Ptolemy V, after the Seleukid victory in the Fifth Syrian War, and perhaps ensure Seleukid neutrality in the war with Philip V (Pol. 16.27.5, and see § 2). The trajectory of this delegation shows the beginning of Roman involvement in the Eastern Aegean. One consequence of Philip's expedition was to bring Asia Minor, and Antiochos III, within the horizons of the Romans; conversely, the concept of Greek freedom publicized in the ultimatum of 200 and in the *SC* of 196, and Roman willingness to intervene as interlocutors of the various powers in Asia Minor, would play an increasingly important part during the next years.

4. *Constructing a Seleukid Space (197–192 BC)*

In spring of 197 BC, Antiochos sailed from Syria with 100 cataphract ships and 200 'undecked', lighter vessels—a fleet raised on the resources and the naval know-how of his recent conquest, the Phoenician seaboard.[106] A land army set out for Sardeis under two of his sons and two senior officers, Ardys and Mithridates.[107] The aim, according to Livy, was the subjection of the Ptolemaic cities in Kilikia, Lykia, and Karia (Liv. 33.19.8–11). Other Seleukid officers perhaps participated in the expedition, or were perhaps active in its wake, such as Ptolemaios, son of Thraseas (below), and Themison, a Seleukid officer who commanded cavalry at Raphia, and is now attested at Aigeai, making a dedication to Zeus Kasios for the safety of the Great King Antiochos, Antiochos the son, queen Laodike, and the royal children (παιδίων). The dedication perhaps implies the presence on the expedition of all, or most of, the royal family, including Laodike.[108] The active participation of Ptolemaios and

[106] Compare Braudel 1966: 147: in the 7th and again the 16th cent., it was the conquest of Syria that enabled the Islamic world to break into 'la grande histoire méditerranéenne'. Phoenician crews: Liv. 35.48.6; *SEG* 41.1556.

[107] On the commanders of land army, Wörrle 1988: 451–4: Antiochos did not have two sons called 'Ardys and Mithridates', as Livy 33.19.9–10 seems to imply, so that these must have been the senior officers known from Polybios, sent to assist Antiochos' two sons—unless Polybios, Livy's source, was confused by the fact that one of Antiochos' sons, the future Antiochos IV, was also called Mithridates: document **31** A, I 3 (at Pol. 16.18.6 and 16.19.10, Antiochos [IV] is 'Antiochos the youngest of the sons' and not 'Mithridates', but this does not preclude a mistake of Polybios in describing the campaign of 197; in which case, the commanders of the land army were one unnamed son, Mithridates/Antiochos, and the officer Ardys). Wörrle suggests that Seleukos and Mithridates/Antiochos went with the land army, their youth explaining the supervision of two experienced officers.

[108] Ptolemaios at Soloi: document **21**. Themison at Aigeai: document **20**. Sayar (forthcoming) suggests that Aigeai played an important role in the naval preparations and movements in the early stages of the expedition.

Themison is no more than a suggestion, since none of the documents attesting their presence in Smooth Kilikia can be precisely dated to 197 or the immediate aftermath of the expedition of 197. Nonetheless, the presence of two important Seleukid officials in Smooth Kilikia, the area where the expedition started off, does suggest activity on the rear of Antiochos' advance.

In Rough Kilikia, the coastal places readily surrendered to Antiochos on his westward progression—Mallos, Soloi, Zephyrion, Aphrodisias, Korykos, Anemourion, Selinous, 'and other forts on this coast, out of fear or voluntarily' (Liv. 33.20.4–5; cf. *FGrHist* 260 F 46). In Soloi, the Seleukid governor of Koile-Syria, Ptolemaios, son of Thraseas, made a dedication 'to Hermes, Herakles, and the great king Antiochos'—in the city gymnasion, a frequent venue for royal euergetism and ruler cult.[109] Ptolemaios came from an Aspendian family which had produced two governors of Rough Kilikia for the Ptolemies (Jones and Habicht 1989: 335–45); he may have left his province to take part at least in the early, Kilikian, stages of the campaign because of his local connections, since the Ptolemaic presence also took the form of inland places (see Ch. 1 § 3), whose surrender would have to be negotiated.

At Korakesion, the Ptolemaic garrison put up resistance, and Antiochos lay siege to the city and its citadel (whose strong position is reflected in the κόραξ-toponym).[110] During the siege, the Rhodians warned Antiochos against sailing beyond the Chelidonian islands— 'not out of hostility, but out of the suspicion that Antiochos would help Philip and become an obstacle to the liberty of the Greeks' (Pol. 18.41a.1, cf. Liv. 33.20.1–3). The Rhodian declaration may have been patterned on the Peace of Kallias, which imposed a similar interdiction on the Persian King[111]—in reply to the title 'Great King' assumed by Antiochos III. Antiochos sent an embassy to Rhodes, offering to renew the ancestral alliance with the Rhodians, and stressing his good relations with Rome (Liv. 33.20.6–10). The news of Philip's defeat at Kynoskephalai removed the Rhodian pretext (Liv. 33.20.10).

Antiochos may have reached Korakesion in May 197; the

[109] Soloi: document 21. However, there is no reason to attribute *RC* 30 to 197: Appendix 3.

[110] Liv. 33.20.4–5; J. and L. Robert 1983: 156–61, with photographs of the site (modern Alanya).

[111] Mastrocinque, 1983: 54, asserts that the geographical limit in the Rhodian ultimatum was not the Chelidonian islands (a later invention, for Mastrocinque), but the frontiers of Karia, a 'Rhodian zone'. But operations in 190 (Liv. 37.15.6–7; 37.16) and the cession of Lykia to the Rhodians in 189 (Pol. 21.24.8), indicate Rhodian interest in that region; nor does Rhodian interest in Karia preclude the wish to keep Antiochos further away.

confrontation with the Rhodians lasted until mid-June 197, when the news of Kynoskephalai arrived (Schmitt 1964: 286). Meantime, the land army reached Sardeis, which lies approximately forty days away from Syria.[112] However, Seleukid land troops under Mithridates may have taken Arykanda in inland Lykia (Agatharchides of Knidos, *FGrHist* 86 F 16)—off the direct route from Syria to Sardeis. The land army cannot have marched parallel to the fleet, along the coast, since the coastal road along Kilikia is modern. Antiochos, held up at Korakesion, possibly ordered Mithridates to split off from the rest of the land army, march down to Pamphylia and then Lykia; from Korakesion, orders could have reached the land army by the road leading up the Kalykadnos valley.[113]

After the news of Kynoskephalai made the Rhodian ultimatum irrelevant, Antiochos progressed past Seleukid Pamphylia, over to Lykia: Andriake, Limyra, Patara, and Xanthos (*FGrHist* 260 F 46). Antiochos III consecrated Xanthos to Leto, Apollo, and Artemis, the poliad gods; the gesture is not a sign of powerlessness in the face of Xanthian resistance (as has been claimed), but a reflection of Antiochos' authority.[114] A decree of the Xanthian *neoi* mentions services (building work in the gymnasion) by a citizen ἐν τοῖς ἀναγκαιοτάτοις καιροῖς, perhaps the hardship of Seleukid takeover; religious rules debarring soldiers in equipment from the Letoon might reflect the same event.[115] At the western end of Lykia, Antiochos took Telmessos, where he reorganized the city's status and territory (below).

The Rhodians then intervened militarily: they 'did not omit their other concern of protecting the liberty of the cities allied to Ptolemy and which were threatened with war by Antiochos, for they helped some with military aid, some by warning them of the enterprises of the enemies, and were responsible for the liberty of the Kaunians, Myndians, Halikarnassians, and Samians.' (Liv. 33.20.11–13).

---

[112] The Ten Thousand took 42 stages: Xen. *Anab.* 1.2.5–21; 1.4.1–5.

[113] This assumes that the 'Mithridates' in Agatharchides is Antiochos' general (as has been agreed since first proposed by Ed. Meyer: Holleaux 1942: 184 n. 6) and not the Pontic king Mithradates VI (active in Lykia), who was proposed by Bevan 1902: ii. 295: 'the expression ταῖς Μιθριδάτου ἐλπίσιν does not appear to fit negotiations in which a Mithridates acts as a mere subordinate'. But Jerome *In Dan.* 11.14 writes *Ptolomaei partium* for Judaean pro-Seleukid notables in 200, adhering to Ptolemaios son of Thraseas, by then a Seleukid general (Gera 1987: 64–6): this example makes it possible that Agartharchides is referring to Antiochos' general.

[114] Document **22**, Schmitt 1964: 287, Herrmann 1965a: 119–20; Boffo 1985: 319–25 argues in favour of compromise, even if the exact terms are irrecoverable.

[115] Le Roy 1986: 298 for the *neoi* decree (document **24**); 279–300 for the Letoon inscription (*SEG* 36.1221). Gauthier 1996: 23–6, is cautious about the suggestion.

Operations did not extend to Lykia, probably because of the speed of Antiochos' naval advance and (possibly) the presence of Seleukid land forces in Lykia. The Rhodians' intervention aimed at denying a harbour to Antiochos' fleet beyond Telmessos; in addition, 'protecting the liberty' of the (subject) Ptolemaic cities was a convenient cover, in the language of civic liberty, for the pursuit of Rhodian interests in the region.[116] But an agreement was reached—Antiochos passed through, and the Rhodians received Stratonikeia, captured by Seleukid land forces from its Macedonian garrison.[117] Stratonikeia had earlier been ceded by Seleukos II to the Rhodians (Appendix 5), and the Rhodians may have appealed to this precedent to convince Antiochos to hand over the city: an agreement couched in the terms of the Seleukid past would have been acceptable to both parties. The conveyance of Stratonikeia fostered cordiality between the two powers (Pol. 30.31.6: ἐν μεγάλῃ χάριτι), and in 196, Antiochos would confidently propose to refer the grievances of the Smyrnians and Lampsakenes to Rhodian arbitration (Pol. 18.51.4).[118]

The next harbour reached by Antiochos was Iasos (Bargylia remained occupied by a Macedonian garrison until 196). A fragmentary Iasian decree alludes to fighting against the soldiers of the Antigonid garrison.[119] It is probable that Iasos had already been taken by Zeuxis, as active in Karia in 197 as he was in 203–201, perhaps operating out of Mylasa. In the same region as Iasos, Zeuxis took over Kildara (an inscription preserves the end of his letter to the city). North-west from Mylasa, the Philippeis/ Euromians contracted an alliance with Antiochos III, through Zeuxis, in late summer 197: their dealing with Zeuxis implies that Antiochos was still held up at Telmessos. Pedasa, in the same area as Euromos, must also have fallen under Seleukid control. Beyond the Euromos plain, Herakleia under Latmos probably was 'recovered for the king' by Zeuxis at this time (his own expression).[120]

---

[116] It is an oversimplification to write (Rawlings 1976: 9–13) that the Rhodians in 197 'freed' Kaunos, Halikarnassos, Myndos, and Samos from Ptolemaic influence.

[117] Liv. 33.18.21 (per Antiochum); Pol. 30.31.6: the Rhodians received Stratonikeia 'from Antiochos and Seleukos' (Seleukos II rather than Seleukos, the son of Antiochos III).

[118] However, the presence of Rhodians in the entourage of Antiochos (which Rawlings 1976: 14–21, makes much of) is irrelevant to the question of official collaboration between the king and Rhodes. The entente between the two powers encouraged Rhodians, in a private capacity, to serve the king.

[119] Document 26 B, I 16–17.

[120] Iasos taken over by Antiochos III: Holleaux 1952: 309 n. 2; Zeuxis at Iasos: suggested by J. and L. Robert 1983: 178 n. 127. Kildara: document 25, with J. and L. Robert 1983: 187. Euromos: document 29—alternatively: Antiochos III swept by, and

Zeuxis may have been responsible for the capture of Stratonikeia, and even the takeover of cities near Karia, such as Priene, Magnesia on Maeander, and Miletos.[121]

Zeuxis' activity explains why Jerome, after Kilikia and Lykia, passes on to Ephesos (*FGrHist* 260 F 46): the list reflects the successes of Antiochos III himself, with the fleet; the Karian cities had already fallen to Zeuxis by the time the king arrived. Beyond western Karia, Antiochos captured Ephesos,[122] Ptolemaic since the Laodikeian War (Ch. 1 § 3), in late summer 197 at the earliest (Schmitt 1964: 288).

The subsequent chronology is unclear. Livy writes that, after spending the winter 197/6 in Ephesos (*cum hibernasset Ephesi*), Antiochos decided to 'reduce all the cities of Asia into the old formula of subjection', sending troops from Ephesos to put pressure on Smyrna, and from Abydos to attack Lampsakos; these events are clearly located by Livy in early 196, *eodem anno* (33.38.1–7). The king himself (*ipse*), in spring 196, made for the Hellespont, and ordered his land troops to cross from Abydos into the Chersonesos, where he took over the cities (Madytos and Sestos are named by Livy) and started rebuilding Lysimacheia, destroyed earlier by Thracians after Philip V evacuated it (Liv. 33.38.8–14).[123] The passage seems to imply that Antiochos left mopping-up operations in Asia Minor to subordinates, while himself campaigning in the Chersonesos (Mastrocinque 1983: 74–7).

Schmitt has argued that the operations in Asia Minor northwards of Ephesos should be located at least partly in late 197 and in the winter 197/6 (Schmitt 1964: 289–95), because Antiochos' land troops were already at Abydos in spring 196 (Liv. 33.38.8) and hence must have wintered there. On this view, Livy's *eodem anno* is the translation of a Polybian κατὰ τοῦτο τὸ ἔτος designating the year ending with the campaigning season of 197, and *cum hibernasset* Livy's own observation. Teos (if the Teian decrees should be dated

the Euromians/Philippeis entered an alliance with him only some time after his passage. I see no reason to suppose that Euromos acted out of fear of the Rhodians, and with encouragement from Philip V (Errington 1986). Herakleia: document **31** B, II 8–9, with commentary; we can only be sure that conquest took place some time before summer 196.

[121] Priene: documents **32, 33**. Magnesia: Seleukid in 190 (Liv. 37.10.12). No evidence for Miletos.

[122] Rawlings 1976: 13–14, argues that Frontinus, *Strat.* 2.9, refers to the capture of Ephesos by Antiochos III (rather than Antiochos II) with Rhodian assistance; his arguments are not convincing, and the incident must refer to an earlier Antiochos.

[123] Franco 1993: 265–70. However, I believe the treaty between an Antiochos and the Lysimacheians is not to be attributed to Antiochos III: Gauthier and Ferrary 1981, and Appendix 3. Destruction of Lysimacheia: Robert 1955: 269.

to this time), Kolophon, and Phokaia would then have been taken over in late 197, and possibly Erythrai.[124]

However, it is likely that Abydos was captured not by Antiochos' fleet, sailing up to the Troad and back to Ephesos in late 197, but by the land army. After reaching Sardeis around May 197, it probably operated northwards, taking Attalid-held Thyateira. An inscription, dating between 209 and 193, and referring to arrangements after the violent capture of an unnamed city by Seleukid troops, may reflect land operations in 197. Another unnamed city, in Hellespontic Phrygia, seems to have been deprived of autonomy and some property under Antiochos III, perhaps subsequent to capture by the land army at this time.[125] This city might be Apollonia on the Rhyndakos (proposed by Holleaux), and would then have been taken in the course of Seleukid operations to roll back the dominions of Prousias in north-west Anatolia[126] (above, § 2). From Lydia, land troops could pass into the (Seleukid) plain of Apia, and hence into the Karesene, on the borders of the Troad—the route taken by Attalos I in 218 (above, § 1). If the Ilian inscription *OGIS* 219 were dated to Antiochos III (Appendix 1), this might provide a suitable context. Assuming that the land army had already driven to the Straits in 197, the fact that Seleukid troops wintered at Abydos holds no chronological implications for the progression of Antiochos from Ephesos. Furthermore, the list of cities in Jerome suggests that Antiochos did stop at Ephesos in 197, since that city is the last named. Finally, the Lampsakene decree for Hegesias suggests that Lampsakos, though under threat in 197, came under siege by Seleukid forces only very late in 197 or early in 196.[127]

Nonetheless, it is tempting to see Livy's account as preserving some trace of Seleukid activity in the winter 197/6, because of the clear break at 33.38.8 (*initio veris*), the moment of Antiochos' spring expedition to Thrace: what preceded took place in the winter. The initial remark (Liv. 33.38.1) *eodem anno* must be a Livian suture; the chronological marker *cum hibernasset Ephesi* translates a Polybian notation locating the events described while Antiochos wintered at Ephesos. What took place was not a campaign of conquest in

---

[124] Teos documents: Appendix 2; takeover in late 197: Piejko 1991a: 22. Phokaia; Liv. 36.43.8, App. *Syr.* 22. Erythrai: Liv. 36.43.10 only mentions the presence of the Roman fleet there, without any information on the status of the city; it is unlikely that *RC* 15 should be dated to 197, as has been claimed by Piejko (Appendix 3).

[125] Thyateira: Attalid in 201 (Robert 1962: 38–9), Seleukid in 190: Liv. 37.8.7; 37.44.5. Unnamed cities: document **36**, with Gauthier 1989: 171–8; Korrhagos inscription (*SEG* 2.663, with Rostovtzeff 1941: 1472 n. 44)

[126] Holleaux 1938b: 114–16 suggesting Apollonia; above, section 2 for Prousias' activity in Mysia and the Troad in 216 and 208.

[127] Ferrary 1988: 135 n. 12.

northern Ionia and Aiolis, but demonstrations of force against Smyrna and Lampsakos, as Livy tells us; operations in northern Ionia presumably were conducted in the spring 196, while the king himself went on to Thrace.

The chronology of the latter half of the campaign must reflect the intentions of Antiochos. If he started out to take over Ptolemaic possessions from Kilikia to Karia, when did his aims extend to the (re)conquest of 'all the cities of Asia Minor' (Liv. 33.38.1)? Unlike Livy, Polybios (18.41a.2) mentions designs on Ionia and the Hellespont before the capture of Ephesos. The defeat of Philip at ·Kynoskephalai, the death of Attalos I, and the successes of Zeuxis in Karia presumably encouraged Antiochos. But the lack of chronology deprives us of any sequence of intentions and events. We can nonetheless perceive the general pattern: a coastal sweep, from Antioch to Thrace, followed by, or co-ordinated with, a series of campaigns by land.[128] In Livy's account (33.38.2), Antiochos III draws comfort from the (projected) ease of conquering 'all the cities of Asia'; this portrayal should not obscure the achievements of the campaign of 197, which reduced a great number of cities (ten places named for Antiochos alone), some formidably fortified, like Limyra or Herakleia under Latmos.[129] Part of the explanation for the military success may lie in the earthquake of 199/8 (preceded by smaller tremors). At Iasos, the damage left the city vulnerable and open to Seleukid offers of aid towards reconstruction.[130] The earthquake also hit Rhodes (Justin 30.4.3) and perhaps weakened Rhodian capacity for military operations against the Seleukids, at a time when the reconquest of the Peraia from the Antigonid garrisons was still underway (§ 3).

An important result was the permanent elimination of the remnants of the Ptolemaic empire in Asia Minor (as well as the small Antigonid 'province' in Karia). By 196 Antiochos III and Ptolemy V were negotiating, and a peace treaty must have followed (in 195?), acknowledging Antiochos' gains. In winter 194/3, Ptolemy V married Antiochos' daughter, Kleopatra: the wedding took place at Raphia, where Antiochos had lost to Ptolemy IV in

---

[128] One might compare the observations of Fellows 1839: 204, 216–18, on the superficiality of travelling past Lykia by boat: by nature, Antiochos' naval campaign was restricted to harbours and a narrow coastal strip, and the work of consolidation inland (for instance in Kilikia, or up the Xanthos valley in Lykia) must have been done by land troops.

[129] Ten cities: *FGrHist* 260 F 46. Limyra: Wurster 1974: 272. Herakleia: Krischen 1922. Generally, on fortifications, McNicoll 1997.

[130] Earthquake: sources and discussion in Holleaux 1952: 209 n. 1; also *I. Stratonikeia* 4, 16–18; Habicht 1957: no. 64 (earlier shocks); *Iscr. Cos* ED 178, 31–2 with Habicht 1996: 88; Robert 1987: 102–3. Iasos: document **26** I, A 6–8.

217.[131] It is hard not to see the choice of venue as a celebration of Seleukid *revanche* on the part of the most successful among the Hellenistic kings at that moment. Little wonder that Hannibal chose to take refuge with Antiochos in 195 (Liv. 35.49.5–7; Holleaux 1957: 180–3).

In 196, the Xanthians honoured an Ilian rhetor by sending a stele, complete with honorific decree, to his home city. The boat carrying the stone sailed past a political landscape reshaped by Seleukid conquest.[132] The southern seaboard of Anatolia, from Soloi to Telmessos, was now Seleukid; northwards—after the Rhodian Peraia and the Ptolemaic cities 'protected' against Antiochos, but soon taken under Rhodian control (Kaunos was simply bought from its Ptolemaic governors: Pol. 30.31.6)[133]—came further Seleukid dominions such as Iasos, Miletos (perhaps), Priene, Ephesos, and most or all of the coast up to the Erythrai peninsula. North of the peninsula—omitting Smyrna, which preserved the independence it had enjoyed since the 220s—parts of Aiolis had become Seleukid again, though there is no epigraphical evidence (as for Karia) to clarify the situation for the formerly Seleukid cities: Kyme, Myrina, Phokaia, Aigai, and Temnos (controlled by Achaios, but then retaken by Attalos I: Pol. 5.77.4 and above, § 1).[134] The Attalid kingdom proper was untouched (though it lost its Lydian possessions), as were the (Attalid) plain of Thebe around Adramyttion and the continental holdings of Mytilene. In the Troad, apart from Ilion, Dardanos, Rhoiteion, Gergis, Skepsis, and Priapos were Seleukid; Lampsakos resisted Antiochos, and perhaps Alexandreia Troas; away from the coastal cities, inland Troad must have become royal

[131] Negotiations in 196: Pol. 18.51.10; Liv. 33.40.3; App. *Syr.* 3. Marriage of Ptolemy V and Kleopatra negotiated: Leuze 1923: 221–9 on date; Will 1982: 192. There is no reliable evidence on the terms of the treaty; Holleaux 1942: 337–55 on the question whether Kleopatra received Koile-Syria as a dowry (unlikely). Liv. 33.41 and App. *Syr.* 4, say that Antiochos, at the news of Epiphanes' death, sailed south and later tried to conquer Cyprus in autumn 196; but he was sailing away from Cyprus, when a storm devastated his fleet off Smooth Kilikia. The story (drawn from Polybios) perhaps reflects contemporary anxieties about Antiochos' activity and aggressiveness in the years 197–196.

[132] Xanthian stele: document 23. Schmitt 1964: 278–85 on extent of reconquests of 197, with some irrelevancies.

[133] Appian, *Mithr.* 23 indicates that the Kaunians became subjects of the Rhodians ἐπὶ τῷ Ἀντιόχου πολέμῳ, which might mean 'around the time of . . .', and hence indicate a relatively late date.

[134] Phokaia is the only city where Seleukid presence is attested; Temnos may have been under Antiochos' control; Kyme perhaps escaped conquest by Antiochos in 197, as it seems to have rallied to the Seleukid side only in 190 (Liv. 37.11.15), unless it was taken over by Antiochos, then defected in winter 191/0, under Attalid pressure or encouragement (Liv. 37.8.5): I hold this the likelier solution.

land again, as under Antiochos I (*RC* 10–13).[135] Across the Straits, the Chersonesos was Seleukid, and Lysimacheia functioned as the residence for the king's son, Seleukos, and also as a Seleukid mint. Further along the Thracian coast, the Seleukids held cities once controlled by Philip V, Ainos and Maroneia, perhaps taken in the Thracian campaign of 196.[136]

Consolidation and extension followed. The speed of the campaign in 197–196 entailed bypassing many places; Antiochos' belief that 'all the cities of Asia' would fall under his control, once the recalcitrant cities of Smyrna and Lampsakos had been reduced, indicates an expectancy of gradual extension. Bargylia, 'freed' of its Macedonian garrison in 196 by Roman intervention (Pol. 18.48.2), was possibly taken over by the Seleukids afterwards.[137] Nearby Theangela perhaps fell under Seleukid control at the same time. A document dated between 201 and 196 probably shows us Theangela absorbed into Halikarnassos, whereas a decree datable to the 190s attests an autonomous *polis* of the Theangelans again: the Theangelans may have rallied to the Seleukids to escape synoikism into Halikarnassos.[138] Other cities must have followed: Polybios has Eumenes II refer to 'cities alienated from us' by Antiochos III (21.20.8): he may mean that Antiochos detached cities from him (rather than from the Attalid kingdom in general), after his accession in 197.

More spectacular were the king's campaigns. In 196, after preliminary ravaging of the Thracian land near Chersonesos, Antiochos

[135] Adramyttion and the plain of Thebe were not under Seleukid control in 190, when the Seleukid army ravaged the region (Liv. 37.19.7–8). Troad: Schmitt 1964: 283–4. Alexandreia Troas only appears alongside Smyrna and Lampsakos in 192 (Liv. 35.42.2), but may have resisted Antiochos from the start: Liv. 33.38.1–7 does not say that Smyrna and Lampsakos were the only non-Seleukid cities in 197, but the most important ones. Taşlıklıoğlu and Frisch 1975: 221 attribute a festival for an Antiochos at Skepsis to the aftermath of conquest by Antiochos III, but the date of the inscription where this festival is first documented (*c*.200?) is not necessarily equivalent to the date of foundation (the Roberts prefer Antiochos I or II: *BE* 76. 573).

[136] Chersonesos: Liv. 33.38.9; 37.9.7–8. Lysimacheia as mint: Newell, *WSM* 1615–21. Ainos, Maroneia: Liv. 37.60.7. 196 is a likely date for the capture of Ainos; Maroneia may have been taken later. Grainger 1996: 337, 341, holds that these two cities could not have been taken in 196, because the Roman commissioner L. Stertinius 'freed Ainos and Maroneia from control by garrisons of King Philip' in summer 196, (just as P. Lentulus was sent to free Bargylia). But Polybios merely says that L. Stertinius was sent to free these cities (Pol. 18.48.2), not that he actually freed them: as in the case of Iasos, he might have been pre-empted by Antiochos III.

[137] *WSM* no. 1468: coinage of Antiochos III at Bargylia. Mastrocinque, 1983: 57–9, writes that Bargylia was 'taken' from the Romans, in 192–190; but the Seleukids did not leave a garrison behind in Bargylia, so there is no reason to date the Seleukid takeover of the city to the Syrian War. However, Le Rider 1990 would attribute this coinage to Mylasa under Antiochos II.

[138] Descat 1997 (on *SEG* 29.1089).

marched deep into central Thrace, and also gained control of cities on the northern Propontis shore, such as, it now seems from a very recent publication, Perinthos.[139] In 195 came a second Thracian expedition; one Brikkon son of Ateuristos, an Apameian officer, of Galatian origin, killed near Maroneia, may have fought in this campaign.[140] A final Thracian expedition took place in 192[141] (Liv. 35.23.10; 35.35.7). Wars on the periphery publicized Antiochos' status as protector of his subjects, an important part of royal ideology (App. *Syr.* 6: 'he freed the Greeks who were subject to the Thracians'); they also proclaimed that the (re)conquest of the old Seleukid dominions was complete. Antiochos further went on campaign in southern Anatolia: in 193, he set out from Ephesos, marching up to Apameia, whence he descended on the Pisidian cities.[142] The narrative outline of these post-196 campaigns can be traced; it is more difficult to reconstruct their results. The extent of Seleukid control as imposed by Antiochos III in Thrace is yet unclear (up the Hebros valley into the 'Roumelian plain', along the north shore of the Propontis and along the western Black Sea coast (Grainger 1996)?). Incertitude also applies for southern Anatolia (though the presence of Pisidians in the Seleukid army at Magnesia, alongside Lykians and Pamphylians, suggests control of the southern regions: Liv. 37.40.14).[143]

Diplomacy further extended Seleukid influence: Kyzikos and Byzantion were the target of benefactions or diplomatic pressure, perhaps hinting at overlordship, and reflecting involvement on the north shore of the Propontis (App. *Syr.* 6; 12; Grainger 1996: 335–6,

---

[139] Grainger 1996: 336–7: in 196, the Roman commissioner Lentulus went in search of the king by sailing to Selymbria (Liv. 33.39.1). Grainger's analysis is confirmed by an inscription, published by M. Sayar, recording an alliance between Perinthos and the kings, Antiochos III and Antiochos the son: document **35**.

[140] Second Thracian expedition: Liv. 34.33.12; 34.43.4; Holleaux 1957: 180–3. This is probably the same expedition referred to in App. *Syr.* 6, rather than a third Thracian expedition in 194: Brodersen 1991: 95 (Grainger, 1996: 340–1, accepts this expedition in the absence of contrary evidence). Maroneia epigram: *SEG* 24.637, same document *ISE* 115, with Grandjean 1971 (believes in expedition of 194).

[141] Leuze 1923: 244 and n. 2; Aymard 1940: 101 and n. 3.

[142] Liv. 35.13.5; 35.15.1 (Apameia); from Apameia Pisidia can be reached by the Keçiborlu pass (de Planhol 1958: 24). Mitchell 1991 for urbanization in Pisidia.

[143] Pisidia: Sagalassos may have been taken over by Antiochos III in the 190s (for a Seleukid-inspired seal in the city, K. Vandorpe, in Waelkens and Poblome 1995: 299–305), the Rhodian speech given in Rome in 189 (Pol. 21.22.14) lists Pisidia among the spoils of the war against Antiochos III, that might be given to Eumenes II (Kearsley 1994 for new evidence of Attalid presence in Milyas and Pisidia in general: *SEG* 44.1108); Pisidia was a conquest of Antiochos III (and not recovered after a 'revolt', as written by Waelkens in Waelkens 1993: 42). On the other hand, Strabo 12.7.3 claims that the Selgians were never subject to any of the kings. Recent research has emphasized the links between Pamphylia and Pisidia (Brandt 1992; Mitchell 1991: 121; generally de Planhol 1958).

338). The Seleukid dominance on the Anatolian coast must have had some effect on the eastern Aegean islands. Antiochos III wrote to the Koans, informing them of his esteem for his physician Apollophanes, and, perhaps, requesting some privilege for him (*SEG* 33.673). The structure of the letter resembles instructions to royal officials or subordinate communities: though Kos was independent, the unchallenged proximity of Seleukid rule made itself felt.[144] To the east, the Galatians were brought into alliance, in 195 or 194, as was Ariarathes IV of Kappadokia and Pharnakes I of Pontos; these kings married daughters of Antiochos III. Earlier, Antiochos had offered a daughter to Eumenes II (App. *Syr.* 5; Pol. 21.20.8; probably the same daughter, Nysa, promised *c.*195 to Pharnakes); but Eumenes declined this attempt to integrate him into the system of Seleukid control and influence.[145] One symptom of the now firm Seleukid implantation on the western coast of Asia Minor can be seen in the Aegean contacts of Antiochos III, with Delos and Athens. These form the background to Antiochos' later involvement with Greece itself, and also contrast with the earlier Seleukids' meagre Aegean involvement, which reflected their weaker hold on the Anatolian seaboard.[146]

In the 190s, Antiochos III by a combination of military efforts on a vast scale and of diplomacy, managed substantially to impose, or (in

---

[144] Structure: cf. *RC* 45; document 4: foregrounded object of royal decision, followed by instructions (the latter are missing on the Koan letter, but likely). Similarly, Samothrake in the time of Ptolemy III was free, but had close relations with the Ptolemaic governors in Thrace: Gauthier 1979.

[145] Galatians: App. *Syr.* 6, Liv. 37.40.10 (though Grainger 1996: 335, believes the Galatians in Appian to be Galatians of Thrace). Ariarathes: App. *Syr.* 5. Pharnakes: Tracy 1992: 307–13, reconsidering *OGIS* 771 (cf. *IG* 11.1056), the Athenian decree honouring Pharnakes I and his promised bride, 'queen Nysa, daughter of king Antiochos and queen Laodike'; by redating this decree to early 195, on palaeographical and chronological grounds, Tracy establishes that this Nysa must be the daughter of Antiochos III (and not Antiochos the son or Antiochos IV, as had been supposed). The offer of (presumably) this princess to Eumenes (App. *Syr.* 5, Pol. 21.20.8) must have come before she was offered to Pharnakes, and specifically after the campaigns of 197 and 196, as Pol. 21.20.8 implies. In this case, we should disregard Appian when he writes that Eumenes 'saw that [Antiochos] was already on the point of fighting a war against the Romans', a remark which had led Leuze (1923: 211) to place the offer in 192 or 191.

[146] Lefèvre 1996, for earlier contacts between Antiochos III and Greece. Delos: Baslez and Vial 1987: 291, 303–4. Athens: Habicht 1994: 166–71 (Seleukid benefactions, and also, on the basis of *IG* 2² 785, Athenian delegations to Antioch). See also Tracy 1992: 307–13, redating to *c.*195 *OGIS* 771 (cf. *IG* 11.1056), the Athenian decree for Pharnakes I of Pontos and his queen Nysa, now shown to be the daughter of Antiochos III; this has important consequence for lines 28–30, which justify honours for Nysa 'because it is fitting that the Athenians conspicuously remember for good and honour the benefactors of the people and those born of benefactors': the reference is to benefactions by Antiochos III.

his view) reimpose control over most of cis-Tauric Asia Minor: the result was the creation of a great imperial space, whose narrative history and geographical shape I have outlined above. This Seleukid space was articulated by Antiochos' and his sons' movements along fixed points: northern Syria, Ephesos, Lysimacheia which acted as a 'provincial capital' for the Thracian dominions. While one of the king's sons, Seleukos, resided in Lysimacheia, the co-regent Antiochos appears at Antioch—where he married his sister, Laodike (IV), in winter 196/5 (App. *Syr.* 4) and received Hannibal in 195 (Liv. 33.49.6), while presiding over contests at Daphne.[147] But he also appears at Ephesos, whence his father sent him back east, to the important governorship of the Upper Regions; he died in Syria, in late summer 193, at the start of his journey (Liv. 35.13.5; 35.15.3).[148] While in Asia Minor, Antiochos the son possibly sent letters to Teos, confirming privileges granted by his father; nearby, one Dioskourides erected a statue of him before the temple of Klarian Apollo.[149] Empire was also constituted by royal discourse into a space where individual difference mattered less than the king's power to define statuses (Ch. 3). After recovering Iasos, Antiochos III 'gave back its liberty':[150] local autonomy could be tolerated because its existence was a function of royal power. In the saying attributed to Antiochos III (Plut. *Mor.* 183 F) that the cities should ignore royal orders if contrary to their laws, concern for local autonomy is combined with the assumption that he would regularly write letters bearing orders (ἄν τι γράψῃ παρὰ τοὺς νόμους κελεύων γενέσθαι).

Antiochos' behaviour was not anomalous (as Magie 1950: 107, claimed). It was the arbitrary powers of a Hellenistic king that made

---

[147] Syria: Liv. 33.19.8; 33.41.9; 35.13.4; App. *Syr.* 4. Ephesos: Liv. 33.49.7; 35.13.4; 35.15.7 (palace). Lysimacheia: Pol. 18.51.8; App. *Syr.* 3; Liv. 33.40.6; 33.41.4. Kraeling 1964, with *BE* 65. 436, for an inscription from Antioch attesting a festival in 198/7 at Antioch; perhaps the festival celebrated in 195 on a trieteric basis.

[148] Death of Antiochos the son: Schmitt 1964: 15–19. Aymard 1949 reconstructs a dynastic crisis (Laodike divorced, her sons disgraced). The contract between Ptolemaios of Telmessos and the Kardakes (Segre 1938: 190, line 22), dates to Hyperberetaios of 119 SE (September–October 193), starts Βασιλευόντος Ἀντιόχου without the co-regent: a documentary *terminus ante quem* confirming Livy and supplementing the arguments of Aymard 1940 (against 192, championed by E. Cavaignac on the grounds of a cuneiform document). Antiochos III himself, before his accession, travelled from Apameia to Seleukeia on the Tigris, to be greeted by the governor and the population: Sherwin-White and Kuhrt 1993: 140.

[149] Documents **19** B and C with commentary. Liv. 35.15.4 mentions his popularity—though the context is unreliable (rumours about Antiochos' motives for allegedly poisoning his co-regent). On the other hand, Seleukos and Mithridates/Antiochos did not write *RC* 9: Appendix 3. Klaros: **42**.

[150] Document **26** A, I 8–9 (Laodike); the process illustrates Antiochos' own general statement at Lysimacheia (Pol. 18.51.9).

possible Antiochos' reorganization of the territory of Telmessos: while leaving in place the local dynast, (Ptolemaios, whose daughter was appointed priestess of Laodike in 193), Antiochos took over the city and installed a military colony (the Kardakes) on its territory.[151] These phenomena are no different from the redefinition of the territory of Aigai by Antiochos II (Orth 1977: 169–70 on Herrmann 1959), the seizure of the Samian Anaitis by the same king (*SEG* 1.366) or the redistribution of land imposed by Philip V on Miletos and Herakleia (previous section). Specific to Antiochos III is his appeal to a Seleukid past as a deproblematizing strategy (Ch. 1; Liv. 33.38.1), to present the fact of empire as a natural object, grounded in history; a message reinforced by the removal of other superpowers from the scene, leaving Antiochos the sole interlocutor of the local communities.

However, there were other ways to describe the situation. The Telmessians struck coinage with the Seleukid motif of Apollo sitting on the omphalos; but the reverse showed the Rhodian-inspired head of Helios (*BMC Lycia*, 86, no. 1). The combination (whatever its exact motivation and meaning) illustrates the viewpoint of one 'Seleukid' community, aware of other powers than Antiochos III. Other cities would actively resist; the existence of these genuinely independent cities signalled the failure to complete the work of reconquest and create a perfect Seleukid space.

5. Contesting the Seleukid Space (197–192 BC)

Shortly before being defeated by L. Scipio before Magnesia, Antiochos III would name Smyrna, Lampsakos, and Alexandreia Troas[152] as the ἀρχαί of his conflict with Rome (Pol. 21.13.3, cf. Liv.

[151] Segre 1938; Wörrle 1978: 222 and n. 105: from Liv. 37.56.4, it is clear that the city of Telmessos and the estates of Ptolemaios are distinct, which must result from a decision of Antiochos III. Daughter of Ptolemaios: document **37**, 30. Military colony: Segre 1938; in addition, the Telmessian inscription published by Wörrle 1979 has been shown to concern a royal colony by the Roberts (*BE* 80, 484), but need not be a letter of Eumenes II (Robert) rather than Antiochos III; even if the letter were Attalid, it might still concern a second Seleukid colony installed near Telmessos. Antiochos did not deprive Ptolemaios of his estate (Segre 1938: 198): the pluperfect in Liv. 37.56.4–5, *agrum qui Ptolemaei Telmessii fuisset*, must not refer to expropriation by Antiochos III, but rather by the Romans, who gave Ptolemaios' estates to Eumenes II (Wörrle 1978: 222 n. 105, confirming Magie 1950: 762–3). Briscoe 1981 *ad loc.* argues against this view (Liv. 37.56.4 is ambiguous: Eumenes II received *Telmessum item et castra Telmessium, praeter agrum, qui Ptolemaei Telmessii fuisset*); but he does not notice that Eumenes II inherited the right to the debt owed by the Kardakes to Ptolemaios as payment for purchased land (Segre 1938: 190, lines 7–10; Wörrle, *loc. cit.*)—which implies that Eumenes had taken over Ptolemaios' property in general.

[152] Alexandreia: preceding section, n. 135.

35.17.7). The remark concerns the diplomatic preliminaries to the war, in the years 196–193.[153] The successive rounds of negotiations show how Antiochos' activity in Asia Minor could be interpreted and challenged; in turn, his reactions provide insights into the nature of Seleukid power. Antiochos' remark calls attention to a remarkable body of discourse[154] about empire and geography, and hence another viewpoint than the military narrative of conquests.

The involvement of the Romans originated in their victory over Philip V in 197, and the ensuing right to dispose of what Philip had controlled (Pol. 18.49.6). The *senatus consultum* (*SC*) of 196 (Pol. 18.44) proclaimed the liberty of all the Greeks of Asia and Europe; it specified that Philip would free Euromos, Pedasa, Bargylia, Iasos, Abydos, Thasos, Myrina, and Perinthos. The *SC* was not explicitly directed against Antiochos III: its detailed provisions aimed at undoing the results of Philip's Aegean campaigns (§ 3); the general proclamation is an extension of the demands put to Philip in 200 (not to wage war on any Greek: Pol. 16.27.2, 18.34.3) and which could now be represented as fact (Pol. 18.47.2).[155] As a performative speech-act, the *SC* created, or aimed at creating a certain state of affairs, within a geographical zone, on its own logic: the Romans acted as if they were alone, ignoring the fact that the settlement intersected with the Seleukid space created in 197 (Euromos, Pedasa, Iasos, Abydos, and even Perinthos had already been taken over by Antiochos). This attitude is more important than the question of whether the *SC* was a 'hidden warning' to Antiochos III.[156]

Smyrna and Lampsakos gained acceptance within the world of the Roman settlement. Lampsakos, in late 197, sent an embassy, under Hegesias, to Rome (via Massalia) and, on the way back, to Flamininus at Corinth in 196; their appeal was based on mythical kinship (between the Romans, descended from the Trojans, and the

---

[153] Badian 1964, Will 1982: 181–204, Mehl 1990 (narrative accounts); Bickermann 1932a (interpretative essay); Gruen 1986: 611–36 (minimalist).

[154] Apart from Polybios (transmitted through Livy (mainly), Appian, Diodoros), the issues and the way they were talked about are documented in two contemporary inscriptions, the Hegesias decree (*I. Lampsakos* 4) and the Roman letter to the Teians (document **38**).

[155] οὐδένα γὰρ ἔτι τῶν Ἑλλήνων οὔτε πολεμεῖσθαι νῦν ὑπ' οὐδενός οὔτε δουλεύειν οὐδενί: not an order (Ferrary 1988: 142—one would expect μηδένα; also mistranslated by Liv. 33.34.3!), but a statement of fact justifying the Roman order to Antiochos III (προσηγόρευον μὴ διαβαίνειν εἰς τὴν Εὐρωπήν).

[156] Interpreting the *SC* from the Roman aims in the Second Macedonian War: Gruen 1986: 620–1. Ferrary 1988: 141 n. 33, argues that the *SC* was directed against Antiochos because he reacted to it; but Antiochos' reaction does not illuminate the Senate's intentions. Perinthos: the evidence is an inscription (document **35**), published by M. Sayar, concerning an alliance between Perinthos and Antiochos III.

Lampsakenes, a community of the Troad), and supported by the Massalians, also linked to the Lampsakenes by kinship (both cities had been founded by Phokaia), and allies of Rome. The embassy is documented in the Lampsakene decree for one of the ambassadors, Hegesias (*I. Lampsakos* 4).[157] As a result, the Lampsakenes managed to secure inclusion in the Roman peace treaty with Philip V (had Lampsakos at some point been threatened by Philip, during his activity in the Propontis or the Straits?).[158] Smyrna also appealed to Rome, though the details are not known as they are for Lampsakos; cultic honours for Rome, inaugurated in 195 (Tac. *Ann.* 4.56.5), must represent the Smyrnian response to a specific 'benefaction', in defence of the city's interests.[159] Both cities were acknowledged by Rome as players in the international scene, thus confirming the independence which they had enjoyed since the 220s, and assisting, from the outside, their refusal to be integrated within the Seleukid space (Liv. 33.38.1–7). Alongside Alexandreia Troas (which only appears as a recalcitrant city in 192, but probably resisted Antiochos early on), these two cities managed ideological and military resistance to the Seleukids, from 197 to 192 (Liv. 35.42), in a local history which spans the duration of Antiochos' recreated Seleukid Asia Minor.[160]

The Smyrnians and the Lampsakenes were also directly supported by the Romans: their appeals provided the occasion for diplomatic conflict between Rome and Antiochos.[161] The outline of

[157] See also Curty 1995: 78–82, no. 39, with commentary on the mythical kinship (and 80 n. 7, for arguments against a connection between the Hegesias decree and a possible mention of Massalia in a Phokaia decree of this period, *Inschr. Priene* 65). On the identity of the Romans as descendants from the Trojans, and the political role the 'Trojan legend' played in the relations between Rome and the Greek world, Gruen 1996: 11–15; Gruen 1992: 6–51; Curty 1995: 257–8. Badian, *Entretiens Hardt* 17 (Geneva, 1972), 178–9 suggested that this embassy appears in Ennius (I think this unlikely).

[158] Hegesias: *I. Lampsakos* 4, with Ferrary 1988: 133–41 (against Bickermann 1932b, who claimed that the Lampsakenes misunderstood the Senate).

[159] The Smyrnian cult is not equivalent to *deditio* to Rome (claimed by J. A. O. Larsen, in R. Chevallier (ed.), *Mélanges d'archéologie et d'histoire offerts à André Piganiol* (Paris, 1966), 1635–8), even though Pol. 18.49.1 may imply that one of the recalcitrant cities considered surrendering to the Romans (ἐγχειριοῦσιν σφᾶς). Mellor 1975: 14–16, is unhelpful, as pointed out by Errington 1987: 100–1.

[160] Smyrna, Lampsakos, and Alexandreia Troas were still holding out from Antiochos III in 192, at the eve of the Roman–Seleukid War (Liv. 35.42, the first time we hear of Alexandreia Troas). *I. Alexandreia Troas* 4, a decree honouring a phrourarch (Robert, *OMS* i. 65–74, for attribution to Alexandreia Troas), might refer to military resistance against Antiochos III, notably by fending off a surprise attack on a fort at Chryse (lines 2–3, [πρα]ξικοπούντων, though the geography of a Seleukid *coup de main* is not obvious).

[161] App. *Syr.* 2, Diod. 29.7. Gruen 1986: 621 n. 42: the Lampsakene appeal against Antiochos was not carried out by Hegesias, but a later embassy—but lines 74–5 of the Hegesias inscription might describe such an appeal.

these diplomatic encounters is well known, with some obscure patches: in 196, Flamininus received a Seleukid embassy at Corinth in the summer, and the king received a Roman embassy at Lysimacheia in the autumn; in 195, Seleukid envoys met Flamininus at Corinth again, and were referred to Rome (where they probably did not go). After an interval of a year and a half, Antiochos reopened negotiations by sending an embassy to Rome in winter 194/3, which was followed by the dispatch of three envoys from Rome to Asia in 193, where they met with Antiochos at Apameia, in late summer, and with his courtier Minnion in the autumn, at Ephesos.[162]

What is striking about this series of negotiations is their repetitiveness and their uniformly unsatisfactory outcome. Rather than look for substantial changes and concessions,[163] we should realize that either party spoke from a position which its interlocutor was unwilling to acknowledge; utterances were issued in a loop which could have carried on indefinitely, but for precipitating events in Greece in 192. The Romans demanded that Antiochos evacuate 'Europe' and stay in Asia (Pol. 18.47.2, 18.50.8–9; Liv. 34.58.2–3); to varying degrees, they also proclaimed the liberty of the Greek cities in Asia, either directly or by sponsoring the grievances of the recalcitrant cities[164] (Roman championship of Ptolemaic interests was soon voided by the settlement between Antiochos III and Ptolemy V: see § 4). The Seleukids responded by substituting for the distinction between Europe and Asia their own geography, grounded in the Seleukid past: Antiochos III was reconquering

---

[162] Corinth: Pol. 18.47.1–4. Lysimacheia: Pol. 18.49–52. Corinth (bis): Liv. 34.25.2. Rome: Liv. 34.57.4–59, Diod. 28.15, App. *Syr.* 6. Apameia: Liv. 35.15.1–2; the conference in App. *Syr.* 12 cannot be set at Ephesos, from where the king was absent (Liv. 35.16.1), and must concern Apameia. Ephesos: Liv. 35.16.1–17.2. Holleaux 1957: 156–79, for order of negotiations; 166–75, against negotiations in 195 (which might be inferred from Liv. 34.33.12, 34.57.4 and 34.59.8).

[163] App. *Syr.* 12 has Antiochos offering to leave autonomous the Rhodians, the Byzantines, the Kyzikenes, and 'all the other Greeks which live in Asia', except for the Aiolians and the Ionians. It is unlikely that Antiochos would already have offered to withdraw from the cities of southern Asia (Badian 1964: 138 n. 78): at the eve of Magnesia, Antiochos' offer was far more restricted, and even after Magnesia the Seleukids were reluctant to give up Pamphylia (Pol. 21.45.11) and unwilling to give up Soloi (Pol. 21.24.13). 'All the other Greeks' must be a confusion by Appian. Antiochos therefore spoke of recognising the autonomy of independent states on the fringes of the Seleukid space itself, such as Rhodes or Byzantion (Bickermann 1932a: 50), cities over which he had extended the shadow of his diplomacy and influence; this amounts to a scaling back of his wider ambitions, but no concession on the substantial matter, the status of the cities of Asia Minor.

[164] Pol. 18.47.1, 18.50.5–7 (the Antigonid cities would have been declared free by the Romans, in accordance with the *SC* of 196); Pol. 18.44.2, Liv. 34.58.8–13 (extended to all the cities of Asia). Sponsoring grievances: Pol. 18.52.1–3, Liv. 35.17.1–2.

Thrace, which had belonged to Seleukos I;[165] they also denied the Romans' right to 'interfere' (πολυπραγμονεῖν) in Asia Minor, which was Antiochos' by right, and where the Romans had no ground to give orders.[166]

These utterances should not be simplified or rationalized[167] to speak of 'propaganda war', 'cold war', 'spheres of influence', 'blocks'; the debate about Antiochos crossing to Europe was not about the creation of a 'buffer zone' between the Seleukid and the Roman spheres, whether in the Balkans or in Greece.[168] By recasting the ancient terms in 'timeless' modern concepts of geopolitics, these descriptions pass over what is historically specific and intriguing about the negotiations. We should rather try to explore the logic of two competing discourses, with a view towards laying out their assumptions, the workings of their conflict, and the conceptual geography which each tried to impose.

The difficult feature is the rationale of the Roman demands— why they initiated the confrontational process, to the Seleukids' astonishment (Pol. 18.51.1; Liv. 34.57.10; Diod. 28.15.2). The proclamation of Greek liberty in 196, issued after Kynoskephalai, represented a commitment that could not be renounced without losing face (Liv. 34.57.11). But 'public consistency' (Gruen 1986: 621) cannot account for the demand that Antiochos evacuate 'Europe', which reveals Roman anxieties about security, or ignorance about the precise geography involved, as opposed to the map of their anxieties: the Senate seemed to fear that the Seleukid advance across the Straits would automatically lead him westwards to threaten Rome (Pol. 18.50.9).[169] Such fears are exemplified in the series of measures taken after the last conference with Antiochos, to ensure the security of Sicily and Italy (Liv. 35.23.1–10). This

---

[165] Pol. 18.51.4–6; Liv. 34.58.4–5; App. *Syr.* 6.

[166] Pol. 18.51.2 and 9; Liv. 34.57.10–11; Diod. 28.15.2; App. *Syr.* 12; Liv. 35.16.5–6.

[167] e.g. Briscoe 1972: 35 n. 4 on Liv. 34.58.3: '*si se ille Asiae finibus non continet et in Europam transcendit, ut et Romanis ius sit Asiae civitatium amicitias et tueri quas habeant et novas complecti* is merely a rhetorical way of saying "if Antiochus does not keep out of Europe we will drive him out of both Europe and Asia Minor"'—by trying to extract the 'real' message, Briscoe simplifies the workings of a complex statement and reduces the specifics of contemporary discourse to a brutal summary.

[168] Badian 1964: 120; Errington 1989*b*: 276, 282.

[169] Bickermann 1932*a*: 66–75; Mastrocinque 1983: 131–3; Franco 1993: 265–70. Gruen 1986: 625 dismisses the references in Livy to anxiety about Antiochos, on the grounds that the Senate proceeded with the evacuation of Greece in 194; but that action, imposed by consistency with the *SC* of 196, might explain the energy with which the evacuation of Europe was demanded from Antiochos in winter 194/3. Franco 1993: 269–70, on the imitation of Seleukos I by Antiochos III, and on the possibility of professed aims on Macedonia, once part of the realm of Lysimachos and hence theoretically belonging to the inheritance of Seleukos I.

geography of anxiety was an important motive for Roman actions; it was increased by external factors, such as the presence of Hannibal at Antiochos' court, or Attalid exaggeration (Liv. 35.23.10). Roman preoccupation with Antiochos seems to have been constant, from 197–196 onwards: the references in Polybios (18.39.3; 18.43.2; 18.48.4) are confirmed by documentary evidence on the attitude of L. Flamininus, in late 197. The legate in command of the Roman fleet promised to the Lampsakene embassy that he would include Lampsakos in any agreement he might strike up, in the course of operations—presumably directed against the advance of Antiochos III, since the war against Philip V had ended.[170]

To constrain Antiochos within this conceptual geography, the Romans exercised various forms of pressure, as is obvious from the conference which took place in the winter 194/3. If Antiochos did not evacuate Europe, Flamininus claimed the right for the Romans to maintain or strike up 'friendships' in Asia—to enjoy influence with communities in a region which the Seleukids constructed as an imperial dominion (Liv. 34.58.1–4). The Seleukid envoys responded by denying the Romans any rights in Asia (whereas Thrace was Antiochos' by right); Flamininus then appealed to the discourse of Greek freedom, again as a means of pressure, in parallel to his earlier attempt, to force the evacuation of Europe: this is clear from the debate itself, where Flamininus' threat to defend the liberty of the Greek cities of Asia was succeeded by a restatement from Sulpicius Galba of the initial demand to evacuate Europe (Liv. 34.58.8–59.2). The hierarchy of demands was made explicit by Flamininus himself, the next day (Liv. 34.59.4–5): *populum Romanum, qua virtute quaque fide libertatem eorum* [i.e. of the Greeks of Europe] *a Philippo vindicaverit, eadem ab Antiocho, nisi decedat Europa, vindicaturum*, 'the Roman people would defend the liberty [of the Greeks of Europe] against Antiochos, unless he left Europe, with the same valour and trustworthiness with which it had defended this liberty against Philip'.[171]

The Seleukids' response shows how seriously they took the challenge. Various discursive strategies aimed at denying the legitimacy of Roman claims, and keeping the Romans at distance: for instance, the analogy between Seleukid rule in Asia and Roman power in Italy justified the Seleukid empire in terms the Romans could not

[170] Ferrary 1988: 140, on *I. Lampsakos* 4, lines 32–6 (cf. Bickermann 1932*b*: 296). In fact, L. Flamininus' power to contract such agreements is highly problematical.

[171] Bickermann 1932*a*: 61: 'das Recht des Sieges parierte [Flamininus] mit dem auf die Freiheit'; Desideri 1970/1, 506, 510 (engagement for liberty is *strumentalizzato*). Badian 1964: 127 and n. 70, would excise *nisi decedat Europa*; against, Ferrary 1988, 144–6.

reject.[172] More aggressively, the Seleukids used the concepts of Greek liberty to contest the Roman control of the Greek cities in Italy (Liv. 35.16.2–4; P. Sulpicius Galba did not address the point, but shifted the debate by challenging the Seleukid historical claims in Asia Minor). Antiochos' landing at Demetrias in 192 was also partly motivated by the same urge to 'turn the tables on Rome' (Badian 1964: 130–1), by appearing to free the Greeks from Rome.[173]

It is easy to see why the Seleukids reacted to the Roman demands as to a threat to the imperial construct of 197–196. The confrontation was not about 'rival sloganeering' centred on Greek liberty: Antiochos did not present his conquests under the heading of the 'liberation of the cities', but rather appealed to dynastic legitimacy and euergetic solicitude;[174] local autonomy was a status which he could grant, within an imperial space where he held the monopoly of performative utterances (§ 4); local resistance (actual or ideological) was an anomaly, which would soon be reduced and lead to assimilation within the Seleukid space (Liv. 33.38.1–2). The Romans challenged the dynastic past of the Seleukid power in Asia Minor, by referring to a history of Seleukid weakness and absence in Asia Minor (Liv. 34.58.10–11; 35.16.7–11; Ch. 1 § 5), and undid the Seleukid claim to a legitimate, unproblematic power grounded in the past. They further challenged the Seleukid effort at appearing the sole efficient interlocutor of the local communities, by engaging Smyrna and Lampsakos in an international dialogue where these cities were acknowledged as independent powers, and by encouraging the proliferation of local claims in the face of Seleukid attempts at creating an unitary space (Liv. 35.17.1).

A contemporary document illustrates how Roman discourse could force open the Seleukid space.[175] In winter 194/3, the Seleukid envoy Menippos, in addition to his mission for Antiochos, acted

[172] Denying Roman *locus standi*: Pol. 18.52.9. Italy: Pol. 18.51.2, Liv. 34.58.6.

[173] Liv. 35.32.11–12; 35.44.6; 35.48.8; 36.9.4; Pol. 20.8.1. Antiochos' projected support for an expedition of Hannibal to Italy, if authentic, proposed to threaten Italy just as the Romans threatened his dominions in Asia (Liv. 35.42.3–4).

[174] 'Rival sloganeering': Gruen 1986: 636, cf. 619; Mastrocinque 1983: 61–4 ('liberation propaganda'). Antiochos III did not regularly present himself as the 'liberator of the cities', though Alabanda in 202 and Iasos *c*.197 chose to speak of him in those terms (document **16**, 20–21; **26** B, I 13 = 44 Blümel). The Seleukid viewpoint is clear from document **26** A, I 8–9; **31** B, II 8–9; Pol. 18.52.9. Possible exceptions are the fragmentary letter to Teos (**19** B) and Antiochos' freeing the Greeks from the Thracians (App. *Syr.* 6).

[175] Document **38**. Gruen 1986: 628–9 calls this document amicable, neglecting anomalies pointed out by Errington 1980 (though Errington's interpretation of the letter as a 'versteckte Drohung', 284, is too crude; the same applies to Errington 1989*b*: 279).

for the Teians: he asked the Senate to acknowledge the city's *asylia*. The reply addressed to the Teians by the praetor M. Valerius Messalla, the tribunes, and the Senate, observes diplomatic courtesies by praising Menippos and proclaiming the authors' piety; it also shows anomalies (apart from boastful confidence in divine favour). In lines 19–24, the Romans grant that Teos should be ἀφορολόγητον ἀπὸ τοῦ δήμου τοῦ Ῥωμαίων, literally 'tribute-exempt from the Roman people'. This formula is problematic: the direct parallel is the letter of the Athamanian kings, also for the *asylia* of Teos (*RC* 35), and the formula might be a misunderstanding in both cases.[176] Are the Roman authorities exempting the Teians from tribute, as if they had any right or claim to levy tribute from a community within the Seleukid empire—hence assuming a discursive position normally reserved for the ruling power? Or is the meaning that the Teians can be *asyloi* and free from tribute with the consent of the Roman people?—thus granting approval to an administrative status in the Seleukid empire.[177] In both cases, the Roman utterance interferes within the Seleukid space.

Discursive interference from the Romans also appears at the end of the letter, with its promise of further φιλάνθρωπα, if the Teians should observe goodwill towards the Romans (διατηρούντων ὑμῶν καὶ εἰς τὰ μετὰ ταῦτα τὴν πρὸς ἡμᾶς εὔνοιαν, 'if you should preserve in the future too your goodwill towards us'). The formula is unparalleled in royal letters on *asylia* (*RC* 26, 27, 28, 31, 32): it is patterned on the interaction between king (or royal officers) and subject communities, where relations of power are mediated through a contract of euergetism and local 'goodwill'.[178] What Menippos had expected was a favourable response to a request circulated, under Seleukid patronage, among the international community; instead, the Romans spoke the language of authority to a city located within the Seleukid empire, where Antiochos' utterances should have been the only authoritative ones. The letter to the Teians preserves a

[176] On these documents, Herrmann 1965*a*: 140–1; Appendix 2. The significance of the reference to ἀφορολογησία and sacred city and territory in a series of Cretan decrees in favour of Mylasa (*I. Mylasa* 643, lines 8–13; 644, 7–10; 660, 2–3; 661, 5–7—the last two published in *EA* 19 (1992), 12–13 and reproduced as *SEG* 42.1003, 1004) is obscure, because of the lacunose state of the documents and the absence of any clear chronological context.

[177] This interpretation is supported by a Roman letter to the Jews, agreeing to the concessions made by the Seleukid minister Lysias in 164, after Judas Maccabaeus' initial successes (ὑπὲρ ὧν Λυσίας ὁ συγγενὴς τοῦ βασιλέως συνεχώρησεν ὑμῖν, συνευδοκοῦμεν: 2 Macc. 11: 35, with Habicht 1976: 12 and nn. 22–4).

[178] Document 5, 7–9 (Amyzon); 25, 7–11 (Kildara); 26 A, I 25–29 (Iasos); 31 B, I 14–15 and IV 9–11 (Herakleia); also Ch. 4 § 1, where the notion of 'contract clause' is explored through examples.

documentary trace of the process which Flamininus, in the same winter 194/3, had called 'striking up friendships' in Asia (Liv. 34.58.3) and which the Seleukids called 'meddling' (πολυπραγμονεῖν).

Roman 'meddling' threatened Seleukid power, by contesting its bases and its logic (Bickermann 1932a: 65; Bikerman 1938: 140–1). It disrupted Seleukid authority, the illusion, essential in any power configuration, that there is nothing exterior to the dialogue between ruler and ruled, the faculty of the empire to be accepted as part of things. It challenged Seleukid ideology in its function as discursive cover for relations and realities, creating authority by suppressing alternatives: *periculum erat ne, si concessum iis foret quod intenderent, Zmyrnam in Aeolide Ioniaque, Lampsacum in Hellesponto aliae urbes sequerentur*, 'there was a danger that, if they were granted with what they wanted, Smyrna in Aiolis and Ionia, Lampsakos on the Hellespont would provide an example for other cities to follow' (Liv. 33.38.3). The normal functioning of Seleukid imperial ideology was threatened by the Roman presence within the Seleukid space, as Antiochos' council was well aware, in late 193, when it decided on war, rather than witnessing the dissolution of empire through the loss of authority and the intrusion of external agents (Liv. 35.17.3–9; Briscoe 1981: 30–3):

initium semper a parvis iniusta imperandi fieri, nisi crederent Persas, cum aquam terramque ab Lacedaemoniis petierint, gleba terrae et haustu aquae eguisse. Per similem temptationem a Romanis de duabus civitatibus agi; sed alias civitates, simul duas iugum exuisse vidissent, ad liberatorem populum defecturas.

unjust power always started from small things, unless one believed that the Persians, when they asked the Spartans for earth and water, needed a clod of earth and a gulp of water. The Romans were making a similar attempt in the case of the two cities [Smyrna and Lampsakos]; but other cities, as soon as they saw two of them shed the yoke, would defect to the people that should set them free.

6. Beyond Narrative

Throughout this chapter, the focus has been on super-power conflict, mostly in the form of Seleukid campaigns of (re)conquest in Asia Minor, from 226 down to the diplomatic confrontation between Antiochos and the Romans in the 190s. The narrative has followed the unfolding of ambition and violence across the landscape of Asia Minor: Philip V threatening the coastline with his *lemboi*, his bold marches across the Pergamene territory; most memorably, the great campaigns of 197–6, sweeping from Antioch to Thrace, conducted on sea and on land by Antiochos III, with an armada of 300 warships large and small, and a host of subordinate commanders (the king's sons, his nephews, Zeuxis in Sardeis) co-ordinating an onslaught by land, cities falling under Seleukid control by the dozen—*omnes Asiae civitates* . . . History as war-driven narrative: what could be more real, in its impact on people's lives and hence on its claim on the historian's attention, than this story of Hellenistic Big War, of royal campaigns and conquest?

Yet the rounds of negotiations of 196–193 show that conquest and empire, the materials of military narrative, are not natural objects, but constructions, with their own logic and their own mechanics. Conventional military narrative, with its ready-made formulas and lifeless metaphors, is oddly powerless to evoke the historical specifics of conduct and experience, even for as apparently elemental a phenomenon as super-power warfare. This became especially apparent to me as I was writing such an account for this chapter, especially for the Hellenistic age, where the evidence is poor and the situation highly complex, thus often leaving no alternative but speculation and common-sense guesses to support conventional narrative, especially if the goal is a reasonably smooth and coherent account.[179] It is sometimes hard to escape the feeling that military narrative history comes down to

> might-be maps of might-have-been campaigns
> showing in colour the obediences
> before and after

> (W. H. Auden, 'Makers of History')

So narrative is not an end, but a beginning; sentences such as 'Antiochus' imperialist appetite was insatiable' (Gruen 1986: 613) or 'la Caria era zone d'influenza rodia' (Mastrocinque 1983: 54) or 'pressure from Philip V, whatever the exact terms, might explain why the Seleukid advance broke off, and why Antiochos' attention shifted from Asia Minor to Koile-Syria' (§ 3), though probably factual, mean little. Narrative provides the necessary context for a series of historical operations, starting with an analytical study of the realities of empire. The relentless recounting of war and conquest, followed by the problematization of control in the diplomatic

---

[179] Lefèvre 1996, in analysing a Delphian (almost certainly Amphiktionic) inscription mentioning Antiochos III, draws attention to the complexity of the period, and the uncertainty of our knowledge, especially for the complicated ultimate years of the third century (*c*.205–200).

sparring between the Seleukids and Rome raise a series of questions: 'when a conqueror conquers, *what* does he conquer? What is the relationship between place and power?' (N. Purcell, *JRS* 80 (1990), 178). More prosaically, what does he create by conquest? How is authority enforced, and control maintained? To what purposes are authority and control put? These questions can only be answered in a study describing and analysing the structures of state power in the Seleukid empire, in its force and its limitations, the limitations which the Roman challenge highlighted (Ch. 3).

The Roman demands and the Seleukid responses also set forth a direct illustration of how power and empire are about language as much as about physical constraint: the discursive position of the masters, the flow and the form of orders, the modes of address of the subjects. Language, in its capacity to name and to define, was as 'real' a constituent of power as the violence which Chapter 2 narrates or the structures of constraint in Chapter 3; language was as important a feature of empire as the statuses of liberty or subjection which have so taxed modern scholarship on the topic of 'city and ruler'; in fact, these statuses themselves are part of the language of power, so that language must be counted among the structures of domination. An awareness of performative language as part of the exercise of power informs F. Millar's study of the Roman emperor in his world (Millar 1992: 637); for the Hellenistic period, J. M. Bertrand has examined similar issues (Bertrand 1990), drawing explicitly on the methods of discourse analysis. But it is difficult to 'own' a language, especially if it is used in a dialogue: beyond the language of power, we can also study the language of interaction, and the effect it had on the relationship between city and ruler. Here again, the case of Antiochos III and his relations to the cities of Asia Minor is ideal, because of our knowledge of the *événementiel* context and of the quantity of epigraphical material, directly recording royal utterances and civic decrees (see Introduction); this body of discourse allows us to study the Seleukid empire as interactions, the rhetorical strategies of ruler and ruled, and the workings of consent and collaboration (Ch. 4).

None of this means that the narrative is to be forgotten wholesale, or merely serves as scene-setting for the analytical exercices of the next chapters. The conclusions proposed in these chapters are, explicitly or implicitly, shaped by the general picture that emerges from the military narrative. The flux and instability of political history in the arena of Asia Minor invites us to caution about the durability and extension of control exercised by any one power in the region. That stability often is the impression emerging from the evidence may reflect the state power of the Seleukid empire and the latter's capacity to integrate local communities within its structures; or it might result from the durability and autonomy of a state apparatus, in existence from the Achaimenids onwards and independent of high politics; or it might again be an ideological effect of the structures of domination—more simply put, a pompous illusion fostered by the ruling power. The analysis offered in Chapter 3 entertains all these possibilities, and tries to approach the reality of empire from a variety of perspectives: the instability evident in the narrative does not preclude a synchronic study of empire, but should help us avoid too static a picture.[180] Likewise, the pervasive violence of the military narrative, the violence which forms the basis for imperial acquisition, is a simple, but necessary corrective to the picture of euergetical cordiality in the dialogue between ruler and ruled: it should sharpen our feeling for the balance of power that underlay the relation between city and ruler. The reality or threat of violence only makes more remarkable the complex and sophisticated discourse which the cities used to address their rulers and try to constrain them.

The present chapter, devoted to military narrative, started with the evocation of the movements of Antiochos, warrior king, across the landscape; it ends with more abstract considerations on instability and violence, and the shadow of violence. The next chapter, on the structures of power, will take the impact of violence as its starting point, to explore its concrete workings and immediate effects, and the more lasting structures which violence enabled and supported ('organized violence') as the basis of empire: the structures of Seleukid state power.

[180] For a methodological defence of the synchronic approach, Ober 1989: 36–8.

CHAPTER 3

Empire as Structures

ἅπαντες γὰρ οἱ τὴν ἐπιτάδε τοῦ Ταύρου κατοικοῦντες οὐχ οὕτως ἐχάρησαν
Ἀντιόχου λειφθέντος ἐπὶ τῷ δοκεῖν ἀπολελύσθαι, τινὲς μὲν φόρων, οἱ δὲ φρουρᾶς,
καθόλου δὲ πάντες βασιλικῶν προσταγμάτων, ὡς ἐπὶ τῷ τὸν ἀπὸ τῶν βαρβάρων
αὐτοῖς φόβον ἀφαιρῆσθαι καὶ δοκεῖν ἀπηλλάχθαι τῆς τούτων ὕβρεως καὶ παρα-
νομίας.

all the inhabitants of the land on this side of the Taurus were not so much
pleased, when Antiochos was defeated, at the prospect of being freed from
tribute for some, garrisoning for others and from royal injunctions for all,
as at the release from the terror the barbarians inflicted on them and at the
thought of being delivered from their violence and their lawlessness.

Pol. 21.41.2

Polybios invaluably records the local communities' point of view on
Seleukid rule, not long after its destruction at the battle of Magnesia
(winter 190/189). The richness and thoughtfulness of the Polybian
passage (describing reactions in the Greek cities after Manlius
Vulso's Galatian expedition of 189) are apparent when compared to
Livy's reductive paraphrase (38.37.2–3: *regia servitus*). Its particular
value is that it complements the Polybian description of Antiochos'
imperialist ambitions, found in translation at Liv. 33.38 (see
Introduction). The latter generated commentary in various forms:
an exploration of the forms taken by Seleukid imperial memory,
when projected on the landscape of Asia Minor, and a narrative of
the military action which actualized Seleukid claims and geography.
The present passage, short though it is, prompts further reflection,
beyond military narrative, on the dominion recreated by the
campaigns of Antiochos III, and more generally on the nature of
empire and on its character.

The feature that first attracts attention is the massive visibility of
Seleukid power. Military means of compulsion (rather than actual
violence) distributed among the local communities and living at
their expense; immediate extraction of surplus in the form of
tribute; and, the simplest expression of imperial domination, direct

orders (προστάγματα) telling subjects what the state wanted them to do: the exercise of power took place within a visible framework of compulsion, and the figures of Seleukid power remembered by former subjects fit theoretical descriptions of the 'empire of domination', which controlled local communities without dissolving them within the imperial state.[1] At this level, sophisticated, recently developed, approaches to power (power as 'battlefield', power-as-knowledge) are less useful than the straightforward anatomy of power-by-conquest or power-as-possession, precisely the forms which more sophisticated models find uninteresting.[2] In this respect, one traditional method of studying the Seleukid empire has been to catalogue and illustrate forms, the same forms which Polybios singled out in his description: garrisons, tribute, and finance, or the hierarchy of governors that transmitted royal orders. The classic work of this sort of scholarship is Bickerman's *Institutions des Séleucides* (Bikerman 1938), whose results can be confirmed, modified, or updated through the recent epigraphical discoveries, especially those concerning Antiochos III, but also the documents from other Hellenistic states, which provide parallels to expand or modify Bickerman's detailed analyses and general views. This is one way of studying the relationship between empire and local community: by portraying the structures of state power though which empire made itself felt, and which constituted the experience of the subjects. Much of the present chapter will be devoted to arranging and describing the available material along these lines.

Yet this approach, though at first sight mundane, is not purely antiquarian, but offers a fruitful starting point. First, it leads to a series of dynamic historical questions exploring the processes of empire: what was involved exactly, what did the Seleukid state want, what was it capable of? What was the experience of empire like? In the following sections, I will try to combine both approaches: the panoramic review of evidence, and the subsequent historical questions. The evidence allows a nuanced, yet fairly coherent picture for the Seleukid empire as state;[3] or at least for various elements of Seleukid state-power: the material often does not directly attest, but seems to imply a sophisticated and extensive apparatus. Second, administrative history should be combined with

[1] Finley 1983: 45; Weber 1968: 946; Doyle 1986: 19, 21, 30–47 and esp. 45–6; Mann 1986: 533–8.
[2] Foucault 1975: 35; Lukes 1974.
[3] On studying early empires, Mann 1986; Nicolet 1990: 7–8, for the concept of state elaborated by students of early-modern Europe (when the modern bureaucratic state was created) and its applicability to the ancient world.

an awareness that the capabilities of a state reside not only in its potential for direct violence, control, and exploitation, but also in its ideological force: for instance, its ability to be accepted as natural, or *perceived* as 'sophisticated and extensive' (to reuse the expression above); or its resort to a system of classification of the landscape into royal land, and into cities subject, subordinate, and 'free', categories created and sustained through the definitions offered by the imperial state. This awareness of the ideological force wielded by the structures of power should help deepen our interpretation of these structures, but also may compel us to move to other approaches to the study of power.

1. *Conquest and Control*

Hellenistic kingship was essentially concerned with war; we know that Antiochos III sometimes liked dancing in arms—an apt metaphor for the military narrative of Chapter 2.[4] But for Antiochos III, the only events recorded in any detail are the capture of the Kilikian cities in 197 and Antiochos' movements in the Chersonesos in 196 (Ch. 2 § 4). Royal documents bluntly, but uninformatively, speak of 'reacquiring' or 'recovering' cities; just as nondescript, though for different reasons, civic decrees (for instance, from Teos, Alabanda/Antiocheia, or Iasos) are evasive about the moment of conquest.[5] In the preceding narrative, I tried to avoid the usual metaphors of battle-and-conquest narrative, since their (would-be) vividness cannot supply the specific knowledge about historical processes; instead, I used the bland expression 'to take over' for Antiochos' campaigns, partly inspired by the Hellenistic usage (παραλαμβάνω, παράληψις) and partly because of the lack of specific evidence.

For a concrete idea of the process, we must turn to parallels— Antiochos' campaigns in Koile-Syria (219 and 218), Attalos' foray of 218, or Philip's Thracian conquests of 200, or, beyond the limits of the late third century, Alexander's route from Granikos to Issos; the march of Lysimachos and Prepelaos in 302, from the Hellespont, before the battle of Ipsos; or Mithridates' irruption into western Asia Minor in 88. What emerges is a semi-ritualized genre,

[4] Pol. 11.34.15–16; Bikerman 1938: 12–14; Austin 1986; Sherwin-White and Kuhrt 1993: 129. Dancing in arms: Athen. 4.155b.
[5] Royal letters: documents **26** A, I 8; **31** B, II 8–9; Teos: **17**, 10–11; Alabanda/ Antiocheia: **16**, 19–22; Iasos: **26** B, I 9–18. Further Ch. 4 § 3, on the functions of allusiveness in civic language.

the progress of the royal conqueror city by city, in the rhythms of pre-mechanized warfare: τὰς δὲ πόλεις ἐπιπορευόμενος ἐπειρᾶτο τὰς μὲν βίᾳ, τὰς δὲ πειθοῖ πρὸς αὐτὸν ἐπάγεσθαι (Pol. 5.62.5: Antiochos III in Koile-Syria). When we say that a Hellenistic king 'conquered' a region, we mean this process, in its different manifestations— capture by siege, conditional surrenders, voluntary rallying after 'persuasion' or for local reasons, betrayal by local officers of the rival power—and in its overall dynamics as the royal progress gathers momentum, and intimidation provokes a domino effect.[6] This model of military activity supplies the context for features baldly recorded in the narrative of Antiochos' campaigns: the sack of Sardeis and other cities; the surrender of Madytos and the domino effect in the Chersonesos in 196; the surrender of Amyzon and other neighbouring communities; the voluntary rallying of Teos in c.203 and Arykanda in 197, the first in the hope of lighter tribute than under Attalos I, the second in the expectation of debt relief for the city; the swift fall of the Kilikian and Lykian coastal places in 197, perhaps abetted by the betrayal of Ptolemaic officials.[7]

Within this model, three aspects come across as defining. They can be enumerated and studied in a chronological order which mirrors the initial stages by which an empire installed itself: first, the violence with which conquest took place; second, the negotiation of statuses that defined the subject communities' place in the empire; third, the establishment of permanent structures of control: garrisons and forts.

The first aspect, violence, is obvious enough: the formalized, repetitive character of the king's conquering progress cannot obscure the violence wrought by his δύναμεις, only briefly mentioned in the narrative sources.[8] The fate of cities sacked (Sardeis, or the unnamed city in *Sardis* 7.1, no. 2) is too obvious to deserve much comment other than Polybios' description of Sardeis' fall—the scenes of carnage and Polybios' final grim comment should be borne in mind, when reading the courteous letters written subsequently by

[6] 'City by city': J. and L. Robert 1954: 84, cf. Bikerman 1938: 133: 'le transfert de la suprématie s'effectuait ainsi par une suite de conventions tacites ou expresses entre le vainqueur et les vaincus, conclues au fur et à mesure de la conquête'. Fourth Syrian War: Pol. 5.58.2–62.6; 5.68.7–71.12; Attalos I: Pol. 5.77.2–9; Philip V: Liv. 31.16. Alexander: Arr. *Anab.* 1.17–2.6; Lysimachos: Diod. 20.107, Franco 1993: 47–52; Mithridates: App. *Mithr.* 20–7.

[7] Sack of Sardeis: Ch. 2 § 1; other cities: document **36** and the unnamed city in the Korrhagos inscription (*SEG* 2.663, with Rostovtzeff 1941: 635 and 1472 n. 44); Chersonesos: Liv. 33.38.9–10; surrender of Amyzon and other communities: document **5**, 2; Arykanda: Ch. 2 § 4; Teos: Ch. 2 § 2; Kilikia and Lykia: Ch. 2 § 4.

[8] Pol. 5.77.3, Attalos' campaign of 218 ('for some cities, violence was needed'); App. *Syr.* 1 (τὰ ἀπειθοῦντα ἐβιάζετο), 2 (δέει τῷ τῆς ἁλώσεως).

Antiochos and Laodike to the Sardians, and crisply copied on stone.

ἡ δὲ λοιπὴ δύναμις εἰσπεσοῦσα πανταχόθεν ἅμα κατειλήφει τὴν πόλιν. καὶ τὸ λοιπὸν ἤδη, τῶν μὲν φονευόντων τοὺς ἐντυγχάνοντας, τῶν δὲ τὰς οἰκήσεις ἐμπιπρώντων, ἄλλων δὲ πρὸς τὰς ἁρπαγὰς καὶ τὰς ὠφελείας ὡρμηκότων, ἐγίνετο παντελὴς ἡ τῆς πόλεως καταφθορὰ καὶ διαρπαγή. καὶ Σαρδέων μὲν τοῦτον τὸν τρόπον ἐγένετο κύριος Ἀντίοχος.

the rest of the army, attacking from all parts simultaneously, had captured the city. And from then on, as some killed those they encountered, some set the houses on fire, others rushed out to steal and to collect booty, the destruction and sack of the city was complete. Thus did Antiochos become master of Sardeis. (Pol. 7.18.9–10)

Amyzon also suffered, although it was not sacked or punished for rebellion, but 'handed itself over' to Zeuxis. His lenifying pronouncements only highlight the evidence for looting and violence: property plundered from the Amyzonians and stored in the fortress of Alinda; the flight of the citizens, in spite of Zeuxis' injunctions; the kidnapping of temple-slaves, recovered only through an embassy to Antiochos himself.[9] Royal orders constrained the army from harming the shrines at Amyzon and Labraunda, a source of protection against abuses; they can also be read as testimony to the threatening potential of the army, and the effects of military presence.[10] Nor was Karia unique: Xanthos suffered in the Seleukid takeover of 197, and the Letoon put up inscribed regulations excluding armed men around this time, perhaps in reaction to abuses by Seleukid soldiery (Ch. 3 § 4); Herakleia would complain of material losses incurred during 'the wars', conquest by Philip V, then Antiochos III.[11] A telling detail is the series of measures in favour of cities (such as Sardeis) immediately after takeover: gifts of materials for rebuilding or temporary tax relief (a similar case is the series of measures granted to Jerusalem in 200).[12]

Violence and spoliation were not an accidental by-product of warfare, but intimately connected with its purpose. Hellenistic empires were geared towards violent acquisition of property (Austin 1986);

[9] J. and L. Robert 1983: 136–7 ('l'armée séleucide est là'); Sherwin-White and Kuhrt 1993: 201–2; already Schmitt 1964: 246, postulating from the very need for 'beruhigende Briefe' that Amyzon had suffered in the Seleukid conquest. Loot in Alinda: document 10, 13; citizens fleeing to the autonomous cities: ibid. 15–17; sacred slaves carried off: document 14, 4–7.

[10] Letters to army: documents 6, 15.

[11] Xanthos: Le Roy 1986. Herakleia: document 31 B, II 12–14.

[12] Sardeis: documents 1, 3; unnamed city: 36, 12–21; Jerusalem: Jos. AJ 12.138–44, esp. 139 (destruction of city), 141 (reconstruction), 143–4 (tax exemptions, freeing of Jews carried off as slaves).

the Amyzonians' goods and slaves were seized and stored in a royal fortress openly, under the authority of the royal state. The crudest form was the application of violence and the levying of a fee or ransom, from the local communities—a recurrent theme of Antiochos' expedition to the Upper Satrapies, and also of Cn. Manlius Vulso's dealings with the Anatolian populations he encountered in his Galatian campaign.[13] The principle not only affected movable goods, but extended to landed property. Antiochos II confiscated the Samian Anaia, and some of his Friends took over Samian estates, when Samos fell under Seleukid control during the Second Syrian War (Ch. 1 § 2); anxious to avoid a similar occurrence, the Herakleians petitioned Zeuxis, c.197, for retention of τὰ ἔγγαια, thus pre-empting any possible confiscation of property by the Seleukid state. The unnamed city in the Korrhagos inscription, less fortunate, probably lost sacred estates when captured by Antiochos III.[14]

Furthermore, violence, destruction, and depredation played their part in the techniques of power used by the Seleukids, creating the atmosphere of terror, φόβος, instrumental in the conquering royal progress and essential to the image of royal might. Out of desire to be taken seriously as a king, Antiochos XII neglected the governor of Damascus who had surrendered the citadel to him, because 'he wanted to seem to have taken over the city through the fear he inspired' (τῷ παρ' αὐτοῦ φόβῳ βουληθεὶς δοκεῖν παραλαβεῖν τὴν πόλιν: Jos. AJ 13. 388). The terror inspired by royal violence forms the backdrop for the discursive interaction between ruler and subject (see Ch. 4); it informs and problematizes the royal claim to benevolence and protection (see below); it explains the Teians' praising Antiochos for 'preserving his trustworthiness', when he stayed in the city with court and troops. One need not believe that the Hellenistic *polis* was powerless and abject before the kings to understand that the reality and the threat of harm weighed heavily in the relation between king and city.[15]

The most important transaction that followed the takeover by the Seleukids was the regulation of local statuses. The practice was defined by Bickerman: conquest entailed the momentary loss of the vanquished party's political existence, to be recreated by an unilateral pronouncement (a performative speech-act *par excellence*)

[13] Antiochos in the east: Pol. 8.23.5, 11.34.10, 11.34.12, 13.9.5. Manlius Vulso: Liv. 38.13.13; 38.14 (from Pol. 21.34); 38.15.6; 38.15.10–11 (the last two from Pol. 21.35–6).
[14] Anaia: *SEG* 1.366, lines 5–20; Herakleia: document **31** B, II 16; Korrhagos inscription: *SEG* 2.663, lines 10–11.
[15] Fear: e.g. Liv. 33.38.9 (Antiochos III in 196 BC); Pol. 5.55.10 (Antiochos III intimidates Artabarzanes); Pol. 5.77.2, 5.77.4, 5.77.8 (Achaios, Attalos I).

of the conqueror, on terms of his choosing and subject to his goodwill.[16] Bickerman's 'surrender and grant' model for the legal structure constituted by conquest is supported by literary evidence for the 'droit de la victoire' in the time of Antiochos III, such as a definition of the relations *cum bello victis dicerentur leges* (Liv. 34.57.7) or Antiochos' desire to ensure that Smyrna and Lampsakos enjoyed liberty as a royal grant (Liv. 33.38.6–7), a principle he proclaimed at Lysimacheia before the Roman envoys (Pol. 18.51.9). Bickerman's model also describes accurately the early, but archetypal case of Alexander's treatment of the Greek cities in Asia Minor: statuses resulted from the conquering king's pronouncement, and their continuance depended on his goodwill.[17] Conquest further entailed the legal forfeiting of property rights—the victor's gracious pronouncement recreated the rights of the conquered to enjoy their belongings as well as their political existence (e.g. Diod. 18.18.4: after the Lamian War, Antipatros allowed the Athenians ἔχειν τήν τε πόλιν καὶ τὰς κτήσεις καὶ τἆλλα).

Bickerman's unilateral grants are preserved in the documentary material: the earliest surviving evidence is the 'Alexander edict' (*Inschr. Priene* 1, same document *OGIS* 1, *GHI* 185), establishing statuses and royal ownership of land in the region of Priene. The best evidence concerns Antiochos III. A letter from Antiochos to the governor of Syria and Phoenicia defined the privileges of Jerusalem, and allowed the Jews to live in accordance to their ancestral laws (Jos. *AJ* 12.142, with Bickerman 1980: 44–85). In Asia Minor, a series of documents, less complete than the letter concerning Jerusalem, illustrate the process. In Teos, Antiochos entered the city, then made a speech before the assembled people defining the city's privileges (he 'set free the city and the territory holy and inviolate and exempt from tribute'); the arrangements were confirmed in a later interview followed by a royal letter. Iasos was 'reacquired' by the king, who then restored its freedom and its laws to the city, as a gracious act.[18] A similar sequence of events perhaps took place at Alabanda and Xanthos, where we now only have a record of the proclamation or acknowledgement of these cities'

---

[16] Bickermann 1932: 56–61; Bikerman 1938: 133–41; Bikerman 1939: 344–5; also, in his classic treatment of the letter by Antiochos III concerning Jerusalem, Bickerman 1980: 67–72.

[17] Earlier examples of victor's rights: Xen. *Cyr.* 2.3.2. Alexander and the Greek cities of Asia Minor: Bikerman 1934; Bosworth 1988: 250–8 on Priene (*Inschr. Priene* 1) or Aspendos (Arr. *Anab.* 1.17.26–27). The criticism levelled against Bickerman by Tarn 1948: 199–227 (accepted by Badian 1966a: 62 n. 10) does not address Bickerman's 'surrender and grant' model of interaction between city and conqueror.

[18] Teos: document **17**, 17–20, 47–8; 29–36 for confirmation of grant. Iasos: **26** A, I 8–9.

asylia.[19] In Amyzon and Kildara, Zeuxis wrote to the city, promising to maintain previous arrangements. His short initial letter to the Amyzonians was followed by a more detailed letter, and probably a letter from the king, regulating local privileges, such as the *asylia* of the Artemision, which was 'given back as *asylos*' by Antiochos III and his son.[20] When Herakleia was taken by Zeuxis, the citizens obtained a few concessions on the spot, such as exemption from billeting; later, the citizens negotiated further privileges. Likewise, the unnamed city which appears in *Sardis*, no. 2, though sacked and burned by Antiochos' army, later received various grants from his commanders.[21]

The royal grant formalized force into a relation of legal authority, an important ideological tool of domination (see § 3). It also determined the forms of Seleukid presence, such as those described in the passage of Polybios commented above (21.41.2).[22] Apart from privileges (exemption from tribute or from garrisoning) the ruler's performative speech-act would decide on the degree of subordination, from 'free' to subject (§ 3). Iasos, Alabanda/Antiocheia, and even the unnamed city in *Sardis*, no. 2, seem to have been declared free; the city in the Korrhagos inscription (*SEG* 2.663) probably lost its autonomy as punishment for resistance; Amyzon remained 'subject'. The stakes explain why the Herakleians sent no less than twenty-two ambassadors to Zeuxis, each defending a particular dossier concerning the city's privileges. The letter of Antiochos III concerning Jerusalem appears a unitary product of the royal will; a chance reference reveals that the settlement was in fact negotiated by a Jewish envoy (2 Macc. 4: 11). It is likely that the royal pronouncements concerning many other communities were the object of negotiations to preserve or extend local privileges.

In addition to the pronouncement on statuses, the aftermath of conquest was defined by the stationing of detachments and garrisons. Appian (*Syr.* 2) describes Greek cities receiving Antiochos'

---

[19] Alabanda/Antiocheia: document **16**; Xanthos: **22**.

[20] Amyzon: document **5**. Kildara: **25**. Zeuxis' subsequent letter to Amyzon: **8 A**; possible letter from Antiochos III: Robert 1983: no. 13. Asylia of the Artemision: **8**.

[21] Herakleia: document **31**. The fact that the city had obtained a grant of *anepistathmeia* before a second round of negotiations with Zeuxis is shown by the phrasing ὅπως ὑπάρχῃ καὶ μετὰ ταῦτα ἥ τε ἀνεπισταθμεία (B II 15—the rest of the sentence seems to imply that the city was initially also granted authority over its τέλη, later lost in the detailed negotiations with Zeuxis, since Zeuxis' letter attests royal authority over Herakleia's harbour tax). Unnamed city in *Sardis*, no. 2: document **36**.

[22] The early Seleukid document published by Malay 1983, stipulating taxes to be exacted by someone (a royal official?) and obligations (*corvée* labour) might represent the details of a royal settlement (for a city or in the royal land?).

garrisons, around 196, out of fear—the same garrisons which would
be remembered as a hardship of Seleukid rule in winter 189/8 (Pol.
21.41.2 and above); the treaty of Apameia mentioned *castella* as a
feature of Seleukid Asia Minor (Liv. 38.38.4). The Hellenistic
world presents many parallels: the Ptolemaic overseas empire, the
Macedonian control of Greece (and the 'Fetters') or Seleukid
Judaea after 168, ringed with fortresses and dominated by the
garrison of a purpose-built fort in Jerusalem;[23] these present an
image of control through disseminated military resources. In Koile-
Syria, Antiochos III instructed that the privileges of Ptolemaios'
estates (Ch. 2 § 3) should be enforced by 'the phrourarchs and the
local governors',[24] assuming the presence of garrisoned forts in the
countryside. For Seleukid Asia Minor, the evidence, though incomplete, is at least sufficient to give an outline of the military presence,
and sometimes to pinpoint it with some specificity. Beyond the
mapping out of the militarized landscape, at issue are the workings
of compulsion and the landscape of control, beyond general statements on 'chains of fortresses'.[25]

Three places are prominent in Antiochos' campaigns: Sardeis,
Ephesos, and Lysimacheia: (re)conquered in 214, 197, and 196
respectively, they functioned as military bases, logistical depots, and
arsenals, comparable to the Ptolemaic naval base at Samos.[26]
Military presence took the form of garrisons in the citadel of Sardeis
and Ephesos under specially appointed officers; at Sardeis, soldiers
were also billeted in the town (at least in 213).[27] At Ephesos, the
garrison no doubt manned the formidable fortifications of the city;
perhaps further detachments were stationed on the coast, near
Phygela, where a fort was occupied under the early Seleukids

[23] Ptolemaic parallel: Bagnall 1976: 220–4, (now add J.and L. Robert 1983: 124 no. 4
and 124–7 for phrourarchs near Amyzon and in Xanthos). Macedonian practice: Billows
1990, index s.v. 'garrisons, Antigonos opposes use in Greece' for Kassandros; Launey
1987: 634 n. 2 for some examples; Pol. 18.11.5, 18.45.6 for the 'Fetters of Greece'.
Judaea: 1 Macc. 1: 33–5, 2: 31–7, 4: 41 (Akra), 1 Macc. 9: 50–3, 12: 45, 13: 33 (fortresses around Jerusalem). Briant 1982: 20–1, on fortresses in the hinterland of Kappadokia
under Eumenes of Kardia in 322.
[24] *SEG* 29.1613, line 16 (the actual provision is lost; this does not modify the implications).
[25] Bar-Kochva 1976: 26 (and n. 35), 36 (though the only forts he mentions are
Perge, Korakesion—because the usurper Tryphon used it as a base?—and Palai-
Magnesia).
[26] Pol. 18.40a: Ephesos coveted in 197 by Antiochos III as base for further operations.
App. *Syr.* 28–9, Liv. 37.31.1: Lysimacheia arsenal and stores. Samos: Ch. 1 § 3.
[27] Sardeis: Pol. 21.16.1, Liv. 37.44.7; the city and its citadel were already each under
their separate official under Alexander (Arr. *Anab.* 1.17.7–8). Ephesos: Liv. 37.13.9
(Diod. 20.111.3 for garrison in the acropolis in 302). Soldiers billeted at Sardeis: document 3, 7–8.

(similarly, Antiochos II had left a garrison in the coastal region opposite Samos, the Anaitis).[28]

Antiochos III also secured important coastlines: in Thrace, garrisons appear at Ainos and Maroneia; in Lykia, at Patara and perhaps at Telmessos or Kalynda, since Seleukid troops besieged the nearby Rhodian town of Daidala in 190; Antiochos may also have continued the Ptolemaic practice of garrisoning 'the forts' on the territory of Xanthos. Likewise, it is probable that Antiochos III left garrisons in the Kilikian coastal places he took, for instance at Soloi (a Seleukid stronghold in 246) and Korakesion, captured from a Ptolemaic garrison in 197.[29] In addition, military means were distributed along important routes. Alinda had a governor and probably a garrison; it controlled the route off the Marsyas valley, from Alabanda to Mylasa.[30] A likely military district ($\phi \nu \lambda \alpha \kappa \acute{\eta}$) at Eriza straddled the road from Pamphylia to Laodikeia (an important highway down the ages).[31] In the same region, a cavalry detachment occupied Apollonia under Salbake, on the route which branched off the Maeander plain into the Morsynos valley and the Geyre plain (the future site of Aphrodisias), crossing the Tabai plateau to join the Laodikeia–Perge route in the Acıpayam plain. This shortcut from the Maeander valley to the Perge road (bypassing Laodikeia) was taken by Manlius Vulso, Trajan, and Caracalla, testimony to its importance and convenience.[32] In Lydia, the officer Arkesilaos, whose dedication was found in Gördes (Ch. 2, introd.), may have commanded a detachment left to control the Phrygios valley, on a

[28] Phygela: *I. Ephesos* 1408, with Mastrocinque 1979: 53–4. Anaitis: *SEG* 1.366, lines 16–17.

[29] Ainos, Maroneia: Liv. 37.60.7. Patara: Liv. 37.16.7. Daidala besieged: Liv. 37.22.3. Ptolemaic garrisoning of 'the forts in Xanthos': *SEG* 33.1183 with J. and L. Robert 1983: 126. Soloi: *FGrHist* 160, Col. II. Korakesion: Ch. 2 § 4 on Liv. 33.20.5.

[30] Alinda governor: document **9**; road from Alabanda to Mylasa: Strabo 14.2.23. The governor and troops presumably resided in the 'second acropolis', an enclosure distinct from the acropolis itself: Bean 1971: 196–7.

[31] Perge: Pol. 21.41.1–5 (Liv. 38.37.9–11). Eriza: *OGIS* 238 is a dedication by $\phi \nu \lambda \alpha \kappa \hat{\iota} \tau \alpha \iota$, perhaps the garrison of a $\phi \nu \lambda \alpha \kappa \acute{\eta}$ like that attested at Kermanshah, a similarly strategic location (Robert 1967). *OGIS* 238 is probably not Attalid, as argued by Ramsay 1895: 256–9, since the region was not 'assigned by the Romans to Eumenes' (it went to the Rhodians). A garrison in Perge (Pol. 21.41.1–5, cf. Liv. 38.37.9–11) might have controlled the city permanently, or represent a temporary measure during the Roman–Seleukid War. Perge–Laodikeia road: Ramsay 1895: 255; J. and L. Robert 1954: 27, 29 n. 3, 81 (route of the Ottoman couriers from Antalya to Smyrna; earlier, taken by Louis VII and Ibn Battuta) and also *OMS* 5. 733–4 on the 'plaine de Karayük', or Acıpayam plain; de Planhol 1958: 25, on the 'Korkuteli road' from Pamphylia to Denizli.

[32] Apollonia: hipparch in document **44**. Route: Liv. 38.13.11–14.1 (Manlius Vulso); J. and L. Robert 1954: 33, 38–9; 150–1 and 223–4 (Trajan), 274–5 (Caracalla); 39: 'chemin commode'. In addition to the cavalry detachment at Apollonia, J. and L. Robert 1954: 289–90, suggest a Seleukid garrison at Tabai.

route from Sardeis to Mysia; this route would have been important when Attalos I controlled Thyateira (216–197?).[33] Further north, the fort of Didyma Teiche, lost by Achaios to Attalos I in 218 (Pol. 5.77.8), occupied a strategic position on the Granikos. The route from the Maeander valley to the Kilikian Gates must have been controlled by garrisons and military posts—*castella ad Maeandrum amnem* (Liv. 37.56.3). Another likely area of control is the road from Sardeis to Ephesos, along the Hermos valley, then turning south (just before Smyrna) through the Karabel pass (Pritchett 1982: 272). The Seleukid concern for controlling the axes of communication[34] can be traced earlier: Olympichos, presumably starting when still a Seleukid governor, held the fort at Petra, near Labraunda, controlling the pass on the road between Mylasa and Alinda (Crampa 1969: no. 4). That Olympichos held on to this fort after Seleukid control was succeeded by the Antigonid (and after he had become a *de facto* semi-independent local dynast) shows that control of routes is hardly a specifically Seleukid practice. It can be paralleled in the Ptolemaic fort at Meydancık Kale, on a road from the Kilikian coast to the Kalykadnos valley (Ch. 1 § 3); it also recalls the policing of Anatolian routes in Roman imperial times (Mitchell 1993: 121–4), or Ottoman *zeybek* in the Maeander valley (Hamilton 1842: i. 527).

Antiochos' order, quoted above, to phrourarchs in Koile-Syria, implies military presence distributed through the land, a practice which can be paralleled in other periods.[35] The fortresses of Mysia, which would figure in the Roman war against Aristonikos/Eumenes III, may have been garrisoned under the Seleukids already.[36] The control of the productive countryside was perhaps partly ensured by the 'strategic' garrisons: the cavalry at Apollonia controlled a route, but also a productive niche, the Tabai plateau wealthy in grain and timber; the same applies for the Maeander valley, important as a route and for its agricultural wealth.[37] Seleukid garrisons could

[33] Dedication of Arkesilaos: document **39**. The Attalids also kept troops at this site: *TAM* 5.1 690 (dedication to Zeus Porottenos by Attalid officer for the safety of Eumenes II).

[34] Debord 1985: 347–8 (north-east Lydia, but applicable generally).

[35] Achaimenid Asia Minor: Briant 1982: 20–1, 38 ('quadrillage militaire très serré'); Tuplin 1987: 209–17, esp. 213 on Xen. *Anab.* 7.8.8–15. Kappadokia under Eumenes of Kardia: Briant 1982: 20–1. The Phrygian countryside under Antigonos: Billows 1990: 206, 207, 261, 280–1. Karia under Philip V: Liv. 33.18.6 (*castella* and garrisons). A garrison in Mt. Latmos suggests Ptolemaic control of the countryside through military posts: J. and L. Robert 1983: no. 4.

[36] Mysian forts: J. and L. Robert 1989: 32–3; however, these might be fortified villages, or an Attalid development.

[37] Tabai plateau: J. and L. Robert 1954: 22–40. In the 19th and 20th cents., the Tabai plateau has played an important economic role by processing the raw wool from the low-

reside in subject communities: Karseai, in Northern Mysia, received a garrison under Achaios (Pol 5.77.7–8), just as in Jerusalem a garrison occupied the citadel (2 Macc. 4: 28 with Schürer 1973: 154 n. 39). Some of these forces were permanent 'garrison-communities', military settlers: Antiochos III settled 2000 Jewish families in Phrygia and Lydia, specifically as a pacification measure after Achaios' revolt (if the letter in Josephus is authentic: Appendix 3); earlier, under Seleukos II, the members of a garrison occupying a fort near Magnesia under Sipylos also held κλῆροι in the nearby countryside. The Kardakes settled on the territory of Telmessos may have performed similar duties.[38] Finally, a feature which made the Seleukid presence visible in the countryside was the scatter of Macedonian settlements, for manpower rather than active defence and control.[39]

Political vicissitudes influenced the landscape of control, as illustrated by the implantation of Jewish military settlers in Phrygia and Lydia (above). The immediate aftermath of conquest probably brought garrisoning and the stationing of troops (as happened in the Fourth Syrian War: Pol. 5.61.2; 5.70.6; 5.70.12; 5.71.11). Phokaia and Iasos were occupied by φυλακαί, special detachments sent in response to the immediate crisis of the Roman–Seleukid War (Liv. 37.12.5; 37.17.3): could the garrison at Patara or Abydos (see above), only attested in the untypical year 190, fall in this category? Bickerman and Robert insist on the distinction between a permanent garrison controlling a city (φρουρά) and a temporary detachment on active service in wartime (φυλακή); but the evidence is rarely detailed enough to describe the distribution of military means

lands into cloth (J. and L. Robert 1954: 52): it might have done so in the Hellenistic period, giving another reason for the Seleukids empire to control, or at least tax, the working and movement of textiles. Maeander valley: Robert 1937: 415–17.

[38] Magnesia: *OGIS* 229, 89–108, esp. 100–3; though Tuplin 1987: 227, notes that the actual defence of the fort seems to be (totally?) in the hands of a Seleukid detachment on active duty. Kardakes: Ch. 2 § 4. Bar-Kochva 1976: 216 n. 27, argues that these are not military settlers because Eumenes II, in his letter of 181 concerning 'those who live in the village of the Kardakes', mentions no military duties but only other obligations (such as poll-tax); but the original settlement may have changed in character by 181, under a different dynasty, a possibility which Bar-Kochva does not manage to argue away.

[39] List in Bikerman 1938: 80 n. 2, though it is difficult to tell if these establishments are Seleukid or Attalid (Debord 1985: 348); Bar-Kochva 1976: 21–48 on the military colonies (though his thesis that every instance of κατοικία, even in Roman inscriptions, indicates a Seleukid settlement, is dispelled by G. M. Cohen, *Anc. Soc.* 22 (1991), 41–50). I cannot see how military settlements 'acted as a barrier between the Greek cities and Galatian incursions' or 'served to curb [Pergamon's] influence' (Bar-Kochva 1976: 26); see rather J. and L. Robert 1948: 20 n. 5 on the 'caractère essentiellement rural, et non stratégique', of such settlements.

in time and space.[40] The king's campaigns also influenced the size of military resources in a region by his presence with the royal standing army, at least partly distributed in the countryside on garrison duty or while inactive: under Seleukos II, a corps 'from the phalanx', the Seleukid infantry mainstay, was detached to the fort of Palai-Magnesia; the city itself received billeted soldiers and soldiers 'under the sky'—a Seleukid camp.[41]

Finally, we know nothing concerning the size or nature—local levies, royal detachments, mercenaries?—of the troops at the disposal of the Seleukid 'provincial governors', whose title, στρατηγοί, implies military duties.[42] Since garrisons were directly responsible, under oath, to the king (as under the Achaimenids and Alexander),[43] governors and garrison commanders may have checked each others' power (next section). The governors of local communities, such as the ἐπιστάτης of the Artemision at Amyzon, may have had troops at their disposal (we know Zeuxis dispatched soldiers to Amyzon, perhaps in 202 or 201, though under their own officer), or relied on forces in forts nearby.[44]

Though the incomplete evidence makes it difficult to evaluate the density of control, it does suggest that permanent garrisoning did not often affect the cities of the western coast. There is no trace of garrisons in the cities in the Troad apart from Abydos. The Aiolian cities seem to have been left ungarrisoned: Attalos I in 218 did not encounter garrisons of Achaios, and Antiochos III found it necessary in 190 to have his son, Seleukos, hold military demonstrations in the region to keep the cities from defecting.[45] Similarly,

---

[40] Tuplin 1987: 208, 212 on the difficulty of using narratives of military operations for studying routine control. Φρουρά, φυλακή: Bikerman 1938: 53 and n. 4; J. and L. Robert 1954: 301 n. 3. The Seleukid official in *I. Ephesos* 1408 commands a φυλακή in Phygela: military district (as in Iran) or temporary detachment? Smyrna may have received a detachment in the Third Syrian War: *OGIS* 229, line 105 (the detachment sent to guard the fort at Palai-Magnesia is paid out of royal funds: royal troops?). Tuplin 1987: 209–10, 235 for *ad hoc* occupation of strategic places under the Achaimenids.

[41] *OGIS* 229, lines 103–4 (soldiers from the phalanx); 14, 21, 35 (soldiers in the city and in a camp).

[42] Bengtson 1944: 115–25. The western στρατηγοί descend from the fighting satraps appointed by Alexander in the west, such as Kalas (Berve 1926: ii. no. 397) Balakros (no. 200) or Antigonos Monophthalmos (no. 87): Bosworth 1988: 230. Liv. 33.18.6 and 9 show Deinokrates, who governed the Karian possessions of Philip V, garrisoning his *castella* with local levies.

[43] *OGIS* 229, lines 38–9, 63; Pol. 21.41.3. The garrison and its commander swore an oath to hand over intact (παραδιδόναι) what they had taken over (παραλαμβάνειν) from the king. Under Achaimenids and Alexander: Berve 1926: i. 274 and 276.

[44] Troops sent by Zeuxis: document **13**; governor at Amyzon: **10**. Bengtson 1944: 145, postulates the presence of standing contingents, drawn from the central royal army, in all the satrapies of Asia Minor.

[45] Attalos' foray: Pol. 5.77.4. Seleukos in Aiolis: Liv. 37.8.5; 37.18.1–2; 37.21.6; Pol. 21.6.2–6). Phokaia: App. *Syr.* 22, Liv. 36.43.11–12).

we may surmise that many Ionian cities were ungarrisoned from the events of 218 (when Attalos I marched unopposed) and of 190 (when many defected to the Romans or were taken over by them: Erythrai, Teos, Kolophon, and Miletos). Herakleia under Latmos was granted exemption from billeting, and surrendered to the Scipios in 190, before Magnesia. Phaselis or Aspendos freely assisted the Rhodian fleet in 190, implying the absence of a Seleukid garrison.[46] Even the unnamed city in *Sardis*, no. 2, after sack, fire, and massacre, expected to be left ungarrisoned, 'as previously'. New evidence might reveal garrisons in cities or on their territories; besides, the circumstances in 218 and 190, when Attalos I and the Romans found cities devoid of Seleukid military presence, were unusual: Achaios in 218 and Antiochos III in 190 were mounting important military operations and may have recalled garrisons from cities to concentrate them.[47] However, the Attalids or even Lysimachos showed a similar restraint in the region.[48] Furthermore, the absence of Seleukid garrisons in Ionian and Aiolian cities is matched by the lack of evidence under Antiochos III for governors or Seleukid minting in these communities, which seem to have formed a privileged group in Seleukid Asia Minor.

This 'restraint' should not be exaggerated: Greek cities on important coastlines, like Ephesos, were garrisoned; any city could receive an emergency φυλακή (see above: Iasos, Phokaia). The violence of Seleukid takeover (above) may have lingered as a deterrent reminder; furthermore, no city was far from the royal forces, wherever stationed. Alabanda, Mylasa, and Iasos were normally ungarrisoned, but a Seleukid contingent probably held the fort at Alinda, within easy reach of all three places.[49] Generally, Seleukid Asia Minor was a militarized frontier bordered by rival powers (the Ptolemaic empire, the Attalid kingdom, Rhodes) and threatening populations (Galatians, Pisidians, Thracians); the wide distribution

---

[46] Erythrai: Liv. 37.8.5; 37.11.14 (Erythraian ships assist Rhodians); 37.12.10. Teos: Pol. 5.77.5 (Attalos I); Liv. 37.27.9–28.3 (no Seleukid garrison in 190). Kolophon: Pol. 5.77.5; Liv. 37.26.5–9 (besieged by Antiochos III in 190); Miletos: Liv. 37.17.3. (on Roman side in 190). Herakleia: documents **31** B, II 15 (ἀνεπισταθμεία) and **45** (letter of Scipios). Phaselis: Liv. 37.23.1; Aspendos: Liv. 37.23.3.

[47] Likewise, Ptolemy IV summoned mercenaries from αἱ ἔξω πόλεις in the military build-up before Raphia (Pol. 5.63.8); the Antigonid governor of Karia mustered the garrisons scattered in *castella*, to face a Rhodian attack in 197 (Liv. 33.18.6–9).

[48] Lysimachos: Burstein 1986 (garrisons in Dobrudja, but not in e.g. Priene). Attalids: Allen 1983: 109.

[49] From Alinda, a horseman could reach Alabanda in four hours, Mylasa in a day and a half (J. and L. Robert 1983: 17 n. 25; Fellows 1841: 58, 64–7), and Iasos is not far from Mylasa. In April 1997, I took a day's cycling (nine to ten hours, including a long break at Labraunda) for the second of these routes, from Milâs to Karpuzlu (ancient Alinda).

and the constant proximity of important means for coercion are beyond doubt (Bengtson 1944: 91).

The disseminated forces fitted into a broader structure. The 'chain of fortresses', as practical technology of domination, was powerless in itself. Seleukid forts, including the Akra at Jerusalem, could not prevent the growth of Maccabaean power. If not backed up by a wider structure of power, the dissemination of garrisons could prove worse than useless. Ptolemy VI installed garrisons in various cities of Koile-Syria, when he intervened in the region during intra-Seleukid dynastic upheavals and hoped to extend his control; after he died of wounds sustained in battle, his garrisons were promptly slaughtered by the inhabitants of the cities the garrisons were meant to control (1 Macc. 11: 18). The ultimate instrument of control was the king, who in campaign with his standing army, going forth to meet invaders in decisive battles and to subdue rebellion, as in the case of Molon, Achaios (Ch. 2 § 1), Maccabaean Judaea, Kilikian cities in the second century (2 Macc. 4: 30–1; 1 Macc. 11.14)—or Notion-Kolophon, besieged by Antiochos III in 190 for rallying to the Romans (Liv. 37.26.5–9). The garrisons slowed the progress of an invader (as happened to Antiochos III in Koile-Syria, in 219: Pol. 5.62.6); they also made local rebellion difficult across the empire, thus enabling the standing army to be applied in concentrated operations of repression (such as the massacre carried out by Antiochos IV in Jerusalem on his return from Egypt: according to 2 Macc 5: 11–16, this resulted from the king's mistaking local, intra-Jewish armed conflict for revolt, ἀποστατεῖν). How effective were these modes of control? As argued above, the ease with which Attalos I went through Aiolis, Ionia, and Mysia, or the swift gains of the Romans in 190 along the coast, may be misleading, because they took place in the stress of war. Another impression may be gained by the Seleukid control and military presence on the Tabai plateau, surrounded by rugged mountains and bandit country: Robert commented that it took 'un pouvoir central fort, très fort', such as the Roman empire or modern Turkey, to keep the area pacified. The remark might also apply to the Seleukid state, at least as we can imagine it in certain settings, such as the important road crossing the Tabai plateau.[50]

This analysis of the modes of control shades into a description of functions—externally, warding off aggression; internally, repressing or preventing revolt: establishing the Seleukid state as primary

---

[50] J. and L. Robert 1954: 41–2; though see Shaw 1984, for evidence of endemic banditry throughout the Roman world, and for an analysis of the structural relationship between banditry, society, and state.

wielder of force within the 'Seleukid space' constituted by conquests and subsequent settlements. One crucial purpose of the system was the extortion of resources from the local communities in the form of violent seizure, as happened to the Amyzonians (above), or taxation: the garrison-commander at Jerusalem was responsible for raising tribute (2 Macc. 4: 28). The fortresses could accumulate the profit of empire: at Soloi, in 246, one such treasury contained 1500 T.[51]

The landscape of control was also a landscape of extortion through 'organized violence' (a *leitmotiv* of Briant 1982; next section). Conversely, the structures of organised violence generated their own needs; in a self-sustaining relation, these costs were met out of the income which the structures of control allowed the state to raise. The local communities also supported the Seleukid forces in kind, by providing lodging or fodder, and perhaps labour to maintain the road system which unified the structures of control across Asia Minor.[52] The language of protection[53] covered the interests of the state as organised crime, or racketeer,[54] the model of empire as exaction we find in Polybios (21.41.2). Violence and military control, impressive in themselves, participate in a broader system of administration and appropriation, which can be studied simultaneously in its nature, its realities, and its ideological workings.

[51] *FGrHist* 160, Col. II; cf. Briant 1982: 20–1, 210–11, on the forts as part of a system of exaction and as treasuries. The Hellenistic 'treasury' (γαζοφυλάκιον) is a well-documented phenomenon: Pergamon started out as a Lysimachan treasury (Strabo 13.4.1); a Ptolemaic γαζόφυλαξ resided in Halikarnassos (*PCZ* 59036); Mithridates VI kept a series of treasuries in his kingdom (Strabo 12.3.28); Franco 1993: 189–91 on the treasuries which Lysimachos must have kept in Anatolia.

[52] Lodging: document 3. Fodder: Wörrle 1979: 87–9, with *BE* 80, 484 (a continuation of Ptolemaic practice, as Wörrle observes). There also is evidence for cities providing supplies for royal troops, but usually *ad hoc* in wartime: *I. Erythrai* 24, lines 15–16; 28, lines 29–32, 41–8; Liv. 37.27.3; also *MAMA* 6.173 (Attalid Apameia). Labour: document 36 mentions exemptions from λῃτουργίαι; Malay 1983 gives an early Seleukid document from Aigai, where *corvée* labourers receive supplies from the royal treasury. For a parallel, Mitchell 1993: 124–7 on probable *corvée* labour for the Roman road system; J. and L. Robert 1983: 30–2 for Roman examples, especially the participation of the cities of Asia in the upkeep of the Trachôn, from Ephesos to the Maeander valley. Braudel 1966: i. 47–8, describes Anatolia as 'le cœur d'une incomparable histoire routière' and 49, for roads as prerequisite of effective government. On roads and landscapes, I have learnt much from van Berchem 1982.

[53] Documents 5, 6, 15. After successful campaigning in Koile-Syria (218), Antiochos III left soldiers to protect his new subjects: πᾶσι τὴν ἀσφάλειαν προκατασκευάζειν τοῖς ὑπ' αὐτὸν ταττομένοις (Pol. 5.71.11).

[54] Organized crime: Tilly 1985; already expressed in ancient times: Austin 1986: 465–6 with examples. Racket: Tilly 1985: 170–1; Mann 1986: 100 ('the gigantic protection racket of political history').

2. Officials and Administration

The Polybian word for royal orders, πρόσταγμα, is also a Seleukid
term for a royal 'edict'. The Pamukçu stele shows how a *prostagma*
was implemented. When Antiochos III appointed Nikanor 'high-
priest of all the shrines on the other side of the Taurus' and 'official
in charge of the shrines', he notified Zeuxis: σύνταξον οὖν συνεργεῖν
αὐτῶι εἰς τὰ προσήκοντα τοῖς προδεδηλωμένοις· καταχωρίζειν δὲ αὐτὸν
καὶ ἐν τοῖς χρηματισμοῖς οἷς εἴθισται· καὶ τῆς ἐπιστολῆς τὸ ἀντίγραφον
ἀναγράψαντας εἰς στήλας λιθίνας ἐχθεῖναι ἐν τοῖς ἐπιφανεστάτοις ἱεροῖς
(lines 41–9), 'Do therefore give orders for your subordinates to work
with him in the matters that are appropriate to what has been previously explained, and to mention him in the contracts for which it
is usual, and to write up the copy of the letter on stone stelai and
expose them in the most conspicuous sanctuaries'. The plural
participles in the infinitive construction imply a multitude of subordinates, beyond the direct recipient of the royal order.[55] Zeuxis
was to pass on three instructions to his subordinates: to collaborate
with Nikanor in matters concerning his duties, to see that Nikanor's
name was included in contracts, and to publicize the royal decision
through inscription on stone stelai in the most conspicuous shrines.
Zeuxis sent a copy to one Philotas, with a covering letter of his own;
Philotas sent a copy of the king's letter to one Bithys, with Zeuxis'
letter and another covering letter. All three missives—Antiochos',
Zeuxis', Philotas'—were inscribed on a large stele, surmounted by a
massive semicircular pediment. The stone was found in Mysia, no
doubt close to the site of a shrine in the Pamukçu plain, a *lieu de
passage* dominated by various landmarks[56] (the stele now lies in the
courtyard of Manisa Museum). The letters *ABΓ* on the pediment
might represent a reminder for the stone cutter of the sequence in
which to cut the letters,[57] the ultimate stage in this chain of communicated orders.

   To study the processes preserved on the stele and their implications, will lead us to explore the imperial institutions that constituted the Seleukid space: 'power as means, as organisation, as
infrastructure, as logistics' (Mann 1986: 518). When Antiochos III

---

[55] *Prostagma* as technical term: Holleaux 1942: 205–11; and *C. Ord. Ptol.* for the
collection of Ptolemaic royal ordnances (designated by the same term of *prostagma*),
gathered and commented by M.-Th. Lenger. Pamukçu stele: document 4, and n. 1 to
the translation of these lines on the plural participles.

[56] Robert 1962: 381 n. 3 (mentioning a pool with sacred fish), 385–6; Cuinet 1894: 42,
for hot springs. Further document 4 and commentary.

[57] Malay 1987: 7 and n. 5; though it is not clear exactly how these numerals would
have functioned.

passed through Teos, he stepped before the assembled citizens, and promised to free the city from taxes; later, the Teians sent an embassy to the king, who told them that he had kept his word, and that he had indeed freed (παραλέλυκε) the city from taxes. The actual 'freeing from taxes' was an administrative process:[58] the king's decision had to be passed on to the right subordinates, and communication had to be followed by practical effects (in this case, making sure officials knew not to claim taxes from the city). The process took place away from the city, in the world of royal administration, so the incident incites us, as historians, to look for those documents (such as the Pamukçu stele) about the workings of royal administration—rather than trust, as the Teians were meant to do, in its magic-like efficacy. Antiochos III, before an embassy from a subordinate community, referred to an administrative process, which executed his will, as something mysterious and quite natural at the same time: the scene should make us ponder the ideological function wielded by the apparatus of administration and by its efficiency as a display of power.

(a) The World of Zeuxis

Zeuxis, at the first stage of communication, is a well-known figure, the overall governor of Asia Minor (see below); he received the king's order, from Iran (Ch. 2 § 2), reaching him almost certainly in Sardeis (the administrative centre in Asia Minor since the Achaimenids and Alexander). The next official down the chain of command, Philotas, must be the governor (strategos) of Mysia; his subordinate, Bithys, is the hyparch, governing a sub-division of the satrapy. Under Bithys there were further subordinates (not illustrated on the Pamukçu stele), who, Bengtson speculated, were called 'toparchs' and which since Bengtson wrote, have indeed appeared under the title ἐπιμελητὴς τοῦ τόπου or προεστηκὼς τοῦ τόπου, 'the man in charge of the place', a portmanteau formula rather than an official title.[59]

In contrast to well-documented cases such as Alexander's administration or Ptolemaic Egypt (where we can study not just policies

---

[58] Document 17, 17–20, 29–36.

[59] Bengtson 1944: 12–29 for chain of command; 102–3 for Zeuxis (Bengtson's broader theory that Seleukid governors were always called satraps without military powers, except for militarized provinces like Asia Minor, need not detain us here: Bengtson 1944: 38–48). Lower echelon: Wörrle 1975: lines 3–4 and pp. 72–5 (not a village magistrate, as Sartre 1995: 101 writes); SEG 29.1613, line 14 (not Ptolemaios' private manager, pace J.-M. Bertrand, ZPE 46 (1982), 170–1—Ptolemaios' own staff are οἱ παρ' ἐμοῦ).

but personnel),[60] we still have little sense of the provincial organization these titles covered—for the reign of Antiochos III, we have evidence for exactly two provincial governors, Philotas (209) and Anaximbrotos (193); the first governed Mysia, the second either Karia or Phrygia[61]. We similarly know little about the satrapies themselves. A list of nine satrapies (by the time of Antiochos III) given by Bengtson is based on the description of Asia Minor in the settlement of 189–188, especially Liv. 38.39.15–16 and Liv. 37.56.2–7.[62] However, geographical usage does not necessarily indicate administrative organization. Did the Milyas, mentioned in these Livian passages, constitute a satrapy by itself,[63] or was the region (a *lieu de passage*, with its north–south valleys) administered as part of a neighbouring satrapy such as Pamphylia or Phrygia? Such a practice of regrouping several 'regions' into a single satrapy had been current earlier. Ionia and Lydia were administered by one satrap in the late Achaimenid period and under Alexander, who also joined Pamphylia and Lykia to Phrygia (governed by Antigonos, the future Diadoch).[64] Even if the Livian list of territories corresponded to provincial divisions in Asia Minor at the time of Magnesia, the situation may have been different under Achaios, or after the reconquest of 216, or the forays of *c*.203, or the sweep of 197. Nor do we know about the shape of satrapies: the 'Hellespontine satrapy' is usually equated with Hellespontine Phrygia, yet stretched into the Troad, at least under Antiochos I (*RC* 10–13). Indeed, the whole concept of tidy satrapies, with well-defined frontiers and 'satrapal capitals' is open to question. The hyparchies, the subdivisions of the satrapy, are equally obscure. The 'hyparchy around Eriza' (*OGIS* 238) no doubt covered part or all of the Acıpayam plain. In Karia,

---

[60] Alexander: Berve 1926: vol. i; Bosworth 1988: 229–58. On members of Seleukid personnel, we can only reflect on their Macedonian names, implying a 'colonial' background (in the sense that they came from the Macedonian ruling group, settled by the Hellenistic kings in the east): Nikanor, Philotas, Zeuxis son of Kynagos (document **7**, with Robert 1964: 11 n. 4 on the Macedonian name Kynagos); contrast the richness of a recent essay (Orrieux 1983) on the Ptolemaic agent Zenon.

[61] Anaximbrotos: document **37**; Robert 1967: 282, prefers Phrygia, 'sans y tenir'. Polybios may have given details for administrative reorganization after Achaios' usurpation as he does for the aftermath of Molon's revolt (5.54.12).

[62] Bengtson 1944: 13–16; earlier satrapies, 13–14, but only the satrapy on the Hellespont is known by a documentary source (*RC* 11, 3–4) and the existence of satrapies of Lydia and Phrygia is probable, but not yet documented. Doubts: Musti in *CAH*² vii. 1, 186–9.

[63] Bengtson 1944: 14 thinks a satrapy of Milyas probable, because Antiochos III practised the 'Aufspaltung der grossen Satrapien' (hardly compelling). For the Milyas, Hall 1986; Syme 1995: 177–92.

[64] Ionia and Lydia: Arr. 1.12.8, 1.17.7; Liv. 37.56.2, *et Lydiam Ioniamque*, perhaps implies that Ionia and Lydia were governed as the same satrapy under the Seleukids. Antigonos' satrapy: Bosworth 1988: 233.

'Karia Hydrela' might be one such subdivision, comprising the south-eastern portion of the upper Maeander valley; the area west of the Marsyas river, the old Hekatomnid, then Ptolemaic dominion, may have constituted another (administered as a unit by Olympichos, who thus seems to have started as a Seleukid hyparch).[65]

The figure for whom we have evidence is Zeuxis[66]—not the 'satrap of Lydia' (Pol. 21.16.4), but far more important: the viceroy of Asia Minor, appointed after the suppression of Achaios (Ch. 2 § 1). The title appears in the alliance he struck with the Philippeis/ Euromians in 197: ὁ ἀπολελειμμένος ὑπὸ τοῦ βασιλέως Ἀντιόχου ἐπὶ τῶν ἐπιτάδε τοῦ Ταύρου πραγμάτων, 'the man left by the king in charge of the affairs on this side of the Taurus'. This seems an official title, adapted to the geographical location; no doubt Antiochos said 'this side of the Taurus' when he was in Anatolia.[67] Bengtson recognised the importance of the office early on; he placed Zeuxis in a sequence of Asia Minor viceroys, such as Alexandros under Antiochos II (the brother of Laodike I), Antiochos Hierax as co-regent with Seleukos II, and Achaios; precedents can be found in the financial official Philoxenos, sent by Alexander 'to collect the tribute from the regions in Asia on this side of the Taurus' (Arr. 3.6.4), and in several Achaimenid generals who held emergency authority in Western Asia Minor, such as Memnon, or Cyrus the Younger.[68] Another parallel for Zeuxis' position is the high-command of the Upper Satrapies, often held by the heir to the Seleukid throne, and perhaps the governorship of the Chersonesos and Thrace held after 196 by Seleukos (the son of Antiochos III).[69] But the case of Zeuxis is uniquely valuable: this very high-ranking official is documented

[65] Karia Hydrela: Liv. 37.56.3 (Magie 1950: ii. 762). Trans-Marsyan Karia: another argument is the priesthood of Zeus Kretagenetas and Diktynna, which appears in the 'imperial heading' (regnal year, Seleukid calendar, etc.) of decrees at Amyzon in 202–201 BC (documents 9, 10), and in a decree regulating various offices at Euromos c.197 BC (document 30), but not in the 'imperial heading' of a decree of Xanthos of 196. It seems that the priesthood, and its official imposition as an element in the heading of decrees, was limited to Karia West of the Marsyas as a unit. (On this cult, J. and L. Robert 1983: 166; also below, § 3).

[66] J. and L. Robert 1983: 176–87; Gauthier 1989: 39–42.

[67] Document 29, 3–6; 4, 29–30 speaks of 'the other side of Taurus' for Anatolia; but the letter was written in Iran; Errington 1986: 2 n. 5 on the official character of Zeuxis' title in alliance with the Philippeis/Euromians. Zeuxis' title was predicted almost exactly by Bengtson 1944: 109–10.

[68] Seleukid governors of cis-Tauric Asia Minor: Bengtson 1944: 94–110, though his attempt to find such an official under Antiochos I already is not convincing (Musti 1965: 157–60). Philoxenos: Bosworth 1988: 242; Memnon: Arr. Anab. 1.20.3, 2.1.1; Diod. 17.23.6; Cyrus: Xen. Hellen. 1.4.3, Anab. 1.9.7, 1.1.2; Thuc. 8.5.4.

[69] Upper Satrapies: Bengtson 1944: 78–89; Schmitt 1964: 15–18; Robert 1950: 73–5. Seleukos: Pol. 18.50.8.

enough to allow analysis; furthermore, because he was not a royal kinsman (unlike Achaios or many of the men quoted above), he may be more typical of the 'normal' Seleukid officials.[70]

Zeuxis' full title, given in the Euromian inscription, informs us about the nature of his power: not a 'governor' (*strategos*), as in Bengtson's reconstruction, but an official ἐπὶ τῶν πραγμάτων—a viceroy or 'chief minister' with full powers, within a geographically limited area (a policy probably motivated by Antiochos' bad experiences with Hermeias, the full 'chief minister' earlier in his reign). Zeuxis' functions explain the breadth of his competence and the extent of his power—καὶ ἅπαντα τὰ ἄλλα, 'and all the other matters', in his own words.[71] A military commander, he received the surrender of Amyzon, as well as other cities; he sent troops to Amyzon under a commander he appointed, and issued orders restraining the soldiers from intruding on the shrine at Labraunda. He probably established Chionis as governor at Alinda, and Menestratos as *epistates* of the Artemision at Amyzon; on his own authority, he restored land to that shrine: in turn, the Amyzonians sent several embassies to negotiate with him.[72] In 197, Zeuxis took over Kildara, promising to maintain its privileges; he concluded an alliance with Euromos, perhaps on his own initiative, certainly through his own agency, which gives an idea of the transactions he was authorized to conduct; he also received an embassy from Herakleia, negotiating their privileges and adding an extra fiscal privilege on his own initiative.[73]

An index of Zeuxis' powers is the Amyzonians' perception of him in their decrees. They shortened the title to ὁ ἐπὶ τῶν πραγμάτων, omitting the geographical limitation on his powers; a citizen is honoured for going on embassies to Zeuxis and 'securing many great privileges' from him.[74] Most strikingly, the Amyzonians honoured Menestratos, the *epistates* of the Artemision, 'for writing

---

[70] Antiochos' kinsmen nonetheless occupied important functions in the patrimonial system of the Seleukid empire: apart from Achaios, Antiochos' sons and cousins are attested in high office (often military)—Antipatros the 'nephew', Pol. 5.79.12 (with *HCP*), 21.16.4, Liv. 37.45.5; previous note, for Seleukos; Schmitt 1964: 29–31.

[71] On the 'chief minister', Bikerman 1938: 187–8; Hermeias: Schmitt 1964: 150–8 (and generally ch. 3). 'All the other matters': document **15**, 5 and J. and L. Robert 1983: 140 n. 15.

[72] Documents **5**, **13**, **15**, **9**, **10**, **7** with J. and L. Robert 1983: 180: the donation 'n'émane pas du roi, c'est une mesure prise par le vice-roi, qui place son nom après celui d'Idrieus, le bienfaiteur ancien'. Embassies: **9**, 6–7 and **35**, 4–5.

[73] Kildara: document **25**; Euromos: **29**. Herakleia: **31**. Meadows suggests that *I. Mylasa* 24 might be a grant of Zeuxis to Mylasa (Ma, Derow, and Meadows 1995: 80 n. 23).

[74] Title: documents **9**, 7–8; **10**, 9; **13**, 4; **47**, 5. Embassy to Zeuxis: **47**, 4–6.

to Zeuxis, the official in charge of affairs, concerning the goodwill which the people has continuously towards the kings and towards Zeuxis', γράφων πρὸς Ζεῦξιν τὸν ἐπὶ τῶν πραγμάτων ὑπὲρ τῆς εὐνοίας ἣν ἔχων διατελεῖ εἴς τε τοὺς βασιλεῖς καὶ εἰς {ι} τὸν Ζεῦξιν: a reflection, from the point of view of a subject community, of Zeuxis' power and of its proximity. Another piece of evidence may give an indirect, visual statement of Zeuxis' position at Amyzon. When Zeuxis dedicated land to the Amyzonian Artemision, an inscription record-ing the dedication was carved on the architrave above the monu-mental entrance to the shrine. This was done in an archaizing style, imitating the dedicatory inscription, on the same architrave, by the powerful Hekatomnid 'satrap' Idrieus, in fact a local dynast.[75] The similarity in visual style may convey a local perception of Zeuxis' powers; it might also be a gesture of Zeuxis, showing the sort of figure he made locally. Zeuxis often acted as the king's proxy, during the latter's campaigns in the Upper Satrapies (209–205, pre-ceded by preparations in 210) or in Koile-Syria (202–200, followed by a period of consolidation in 199–198)—out of a total of 24 years that Zeuxis was in office (winter 214/213 to winter 190/189), a total of 10 years or more during which communication with the king would be impossible or very slow.[76] It was probably during one such period that Zeuxis wrote a direct, administrative reply to a Sardian embassy.[77] Zeuxis represented stability and availability in a state formation where the king, by nature, was a restless warrior.

Yet we must not exaggerate Zeuxis' powers to conceive him as a 'feudal' lord or a 'dynast' (in spite of the dedication on the same architrave and in the same style as the Hekatomnid Idrieus: above). He was no less, but no more, than the highest official in cis-Tauric Asia Minor, the direct subordinate of the king, but his subordinate nonetheless, integrated within the royal state. All of the decisions

[75] Document 7, with J. and L. Robert 1983: 93–4.

[76] The royal *prostagma* concerning Nikanor took one month and ten days to reach Zeuxis from Iran, impressive considering the distance but in absolute terms a slow process—document 4. Sherwin-White and Kuhrt 1993: 198, would date the *prostagma* a year or even two earlier; the document would then have reached Zeuxis only after a year (or two years), one month and ten days. But after autopsy, I believe that the stone reads 'year 103', not '102' or '101' (document 4, commentary). One problem is that on the more recent dating, the order, after a month and a day to cover the distance between Iran and Sardeis, required 17 days to reach the *strategos* of Mysia, a comparatively tiny distance. The only similar document is the *prostagma* of 193 (document 37), which took 7–11 weeks to reach the *strategos* of Phrygia or Karia from Pisidia, where the king was campaigning (Aymard 1949: 339–42). Nonetheless, the slowness of communications between Zeuxis and Antiochos when the latter was in Syria or in the Upper Regions is clear.

[77] For Antiochos' absences from Asia Minor, Ch. 2 §§ 2 and 3. Zeuxis and Sardeis: document 40, 8–9: ἡ περὶ τούτων ἀπόκρισις γραφεῖσ[α | ὑπὸ Ζ]εύξιδος.

taken by Zeuxis concerning Herakleia had to be confirmed by the king himself:[78] τά τε ὑπὸ Ζεύξιδος συγχωρηθέντα ὑμῖν κυροῦμεν. Likewise, Zeuxis' letter to Amyzon, confirming its previous privileges, was presumably validated by a royal letter.[79] Likewise, any change in status lay within the competence of the king. The *asylia* of the Artemision was decreed by Antiochos III (and Antiochos the son), and perhaps announced directly to the city; Zeuxis merely wrote concerning this decision (possibly a covering letter accompanying the royal announcement).[80] Zeuxis himself made clear that the surrender of local communities, and their future loyalty, were to the benefit of King Antiochos: τὴμ πᾶσαν πολυωρίαν ποησόμεθα ὑμῶν ὅσωιπερ ἂν εὐνωέστεροι καὶ προθυμότερο[ι] φαίνησθε εἰς τὰ τῶι βασιλεῖ Ἀντιόχωι συμφέροντα, 'we will take all measures of solicitude for you inasmuch as you show yourselves the better-disposed and the more eager towards the interests of king Antiochos'.[81] The Euromians accurately described the intermediary position of Zeuxis' office when they spoke of τὴν συνθήκην τὴμ περὶ τῆς συμμαχίας τῆς συντεθειμένης πρὸς βασιλέα μέγαν Ἀντίοχον διὰ Ζεύξιδος (lines 7–8). Zeuxis' position is identical to the position of the officers who granted a number of privileges and exemptions to the unnamed city of *Sardis*, no. 2, probably captured and sacked by Seleukid forces in 197: the apparent authority of the officers in the field was balanced by the necessity for subsequent royal approval. Nor is Zeuxis' case exceptional: in 164, the Seleukid viceroy Lysias, ὁ ἐπὶ τῶν πραγμάτων (the same position Zeuxis had held, but without the geographical limitation) wrote in response to a petition from the Jews under Judas Maccabaeus that 'I informed the king of whatever must be brought before him also; whatever lay within my competence (lit. whatever was possible), I granted to you:' (ὅσα μὲν οὖν ἔδει καὶ τῶι βασιλεῖ προσενεχθῆναι διεσάφησα, ἃ δὲ ἦν ἐνδεχόμενα συνεχώρησα· 2 Macc. 11: 18). Ptolemaic officials were similarly constrained: at Iasos, a Ptolemaic officer granted the city the right to levy certain local taxes, but had to refer to the king the matter of exemption from the *syntaxis*, the tribute-like 'contribution' exacted from the city on the proclaimed pretext of defending its territory (*I. Iasos* 3).

Zeuxis' activity as subordinate is evident during the king's direct

---

[78] Document 31 A, I 9.

[79] Document 5, possibly confirmed by royal letter, J. and L. Robert 1983: no. 13.

[80] *Asylia* dossier of Amyzon: documents 6, 8. A parallel is the restitution of laws and ancestral constitution to the unnamed city of the Korrhagos inscription, which can only be effected by Eumenes II and not by his governor (*SEG* 2.663, lines 9–10: ἠξίωσεν τὸν βασιλέα ἀποδοθῆναι τούς τε νόμους καὶ τὴν πάτριον πολιτείαν κτλ.).

[81] Quote from letter to Kildara, document 25, 7–11; also 31 B, IV 9–10 (Herakleia); 5, 7–9 (almost certainly Zeuxis to Amyzon).

presence in Asia Minor. At Sardeis in 213, Antiochos delegated the question of wood supply for the reconstruction of the city, καθ' ἂν συνκρίνῃ Ζεῦξις; he informed Zeuxis of his decisions in favour of the Sardians (a regular grant of oil, alleviated conditions of troop billet-ing, *ateleia* for the Laodikeia). Zeuxis himself, when ordering the troops to respect the shrine at Labraunda, would speak of the ἐπιμέλεια τῶν [ἱερ]ῶν (Robert's restoration) which the king had entrusted to him—a broad brief which justified Zeuxis' specific decision concerning Labraunda.[82] In these cases, Zeuxis' role was purely instrumental, diffusing the royal order, dividing it into sub-orders for the appropriate officials, generating instructions to implement the general terms of the royal order—the nature of Zeuxis' activity appears the same as any subordinate's. At times, Antiochos' presence could even elide Zeuxis' function. In 193, the king (then in Pisidia) issued a *prostagma* on cultic honours in favour of Laodike. But instead of sending it to Zeuxis, for the governor-general of cis-Tauric Asia Minor to diffuse (as had happened with the *prostagma* of 209), Antiochos wrote directly to the level of the satrapy, for instance to Anaximbrotos, the *strategos* of Phrygia (or Karia?): his presence in the province seems to 'deactivate' the powers of Zeuxis as viceroy, and it is likely that Antiochos simply wrote to Zeuxis as governor of Lydia, to imple-ment his *prostagma* in the region around Sardeis. In contrast, when addressing the edict to the Upper Satrapies, Antiochos wrote to Menedemos, probably the governor-general of the East, for him to diffuse the instructions at a lower level.[83]

In spite of his special competence, Zeuxis can be considered typical. First, the dual nature of Zeuxis' office, authoritative and empowered when acting 'downwards', yet answerable and subordi-nate when dealing 'upwards', is characteristic of any official belong-

---

[82] Documents 1, 3. For context, see Ch. 2 § 1. Labraunda: 15, 4–5.

[83] This is one interpretation of the fact that on the 'Dodurga stele' (document 37), containing a copy of the *prostagma* of 193, Zeuxis does not appear; but there are other solutions—for instance, Zeuxis might have been temporarily disgraced in 193 (was he perhaps demoted to the status of *strategos* of Lydia, which might explain why Polybios gives him this title in 21.16.4, in winter 190/189?), or the matter may have seemed so august to Antiochos that he wished to communicate it himself to the satrapy governors (which still illustrates the point that the king could bypass Zeuxis). I have also assumed that Menedemos was viceroy of the Upper Satrapies (Robert 1950: 73–5), though the exact date of appointment is not known, and the fact that Menedemos addressed his instructions not to the satrap of Media, but to the city of Laodikeia on Media (Robert 1949: 5–30) and to Thoas, the commander of a *phylake* (Robert 1967) raises the possi-bility that Menedemos was himself the satrap of Media. Equally problematic, the appointment of Antiochos the son as viceroy in the East falls around this time, and Schmitt has shown that in 193 he was about to set out east to take up office (Schmitt 1964: 15–18).

ing to a chain of command.[84] Second, officials deal with their
superior comparatively rarely, but very often with the populations
under their authority (Bertrand 1974: 31); in turn, the subject
population deals less often with the superior than with the subordinate, who looms mightily in their local horizon. This aspect is
important when studying the interaction between imperial state and
subject communities (Ch. 4 § 2c). For the present, what emerges is
the exemplary aspect of Zeuxis' function as most powerful local
official, whose activity (oscillating between local powers and mere
implementation) can help us to imagine his subordinates (*strategoi*,
hyparchs, local governors) and characterizes the system of governors as a coherent, unitary state apparatus, organised around the
tension of hierarchy, and not a loose feudal structure.

(b) The Royal Economy and its Officials

Nikanor, the beneficiary of the *prostagma* of 209, did not belong to
Zeuxis' subordinates, but to another set of officials, appointed, not
over 'the affairs' within a geographical region, but to specific tasks
or actions, usually in relation to the royal economy,[85] the profits
of ownership or taxation. In the first category, the most important
feature is the 'royal land'—βασιλικὴ χώρα, or, starkly, ἡ τοῦ βασιλέως,
'the (land) of the king'—comprising villages, their land and their
inhabitants, λαοὶ βασιλικοί, who can be described as 'subject' or
'tributary' populations, but also seem to be owned by the king
(Antiochos II sold an estate with its villagers).[86] The royal domain
paid tribute (or rent) to the king[87]—mostly in kind, as is suggested
by the royal wealth in grain, though some evidence suggests payment in cash.[88] This is still an aspect of Seleukid Asia Minor about

[84] Unnamed city: document **36**. Nature of subordinates: Barnes 1988: 71–81 for
theory, Bertrand 1974 for a case study (Alexander's hyparchs).
[85] The term derives from ps.-Arist., *Oec.* 2. Generally, Bikerman 1938: ch. 4;
Rostovtzeff 1941: 464–72; Briant 1982.
[86] βασιλικὴ χώρα: *RC* 11, line 17, and *RC* 12, lines 19–20 (cf. also [χώρα] βασιλεία in the
lex portorii provinciae Asiae, *SEG* 39.1180, line 27). The elliptical expression ἡ τοῦ
βασιλέως from Zeuxis' letter to the Herakleians, document **31** B, III 8 (the section gives
Zeuxis' summary of the Herakleian petition, so that it is not clear if the phrase is Zeuxis'
or the Herakleians'). Λαοὶ βασιλικοί: *RC* 11, line 22; *RC* 18, lines 8–9. The evidence does
not support Bickerman's suggestion that 'the royal land' was the expression used for the
king's private property, nor indeed his distinction between crown land and the king's
private patrimony (Bikerman 1938: 184).
[87] *Inschr. Priene* 1, lines 9–13 with Sherwin-White 1985: 80–1; *RC* 3, line 83.
[88] Cash tribute: *Sardis*, no. 1, line 6 and line 8 (the document dates to Antigonos
Monophthalmos—as shown by Debord 1982: 244–7, Billows 1995: 144 n. 70—but the
situation presumably also applied under the Seleukids). Royal grain: Liv. 38.13.8–10,
Pol. 21.40.8–12, Liv. 38.37.7–9 (Seleukids supply grain for the Roman army in
189–188); grain stores at Lysimacheia (App. *Syr.* 28); earlier, huge gift of grain of

which we are very poorly informed (unlike the situation of Egypt, where the royal land and its workings are much better documented). Besides the tributary villages, the royal land also included natural resources such as the forests of the Tmolos or Mysia.[89]

The royal territory was not confined to the inland swathe, from the Hellespont to the Kilikian Gates: it stretched into the western coastal region, flowing around the territory of the cities: where the city territory stopped, there began the royal domain, a familiar and visible reality.[90] The king also owned property within cities: a letter of Antiochos III to Sardeis shows the king waiving rent on a royally owned portico, since (the Sardians claim) this is the practice in other cities: the king rented out the portico (and its *ergasteria*, shops) *en bloc* to the city (which probably sub-leased the shops). The king waived the rent—but retained property rights. The king owned real estate, with dormant rights to rent, in several other cities, who dealt with him as their landlord as well as their political master.[91]

The other aspect of the 'royal economy' was the network of taxation which stretched across the imperial space, and played a major part in constituting it. Subject cities were taxed collectively, paying cash tribute (*phoros*) [ἐκ] πασῶν τῶν γινομένων προσόδων πα[ρ᾽ ἕκαστον] ἐνιαυτόν, 'out of all the incomes that are produced for each year'.[92] Conceptually, the city is not a tax-collector for the central power, distributing the fiscal burden among the citizenry: it is the city itself which is taxed, surrendering a cut of its income to the imperial state. Apart from regular tribute, the cities could be asked for a special contribution, σύνταξις: though formally distinct from *phoros*, this

Seleukos II to Rhodes: Pol. 5.89.9. *RC* 3, lines 80–5, cannot be used to prove either cash tribute or tribute in kind: Antigonos merely tells the Teians that the 'tributary land' is a readily accessible source of wheat, but it is unclear whether he is thinking of the Teians purchasing their grain from the tributary villages or from royal stores.

[89] Forests: document 1, line 4, with Gauthier 1989: 28; Mysian forests: Liv. 37.56.1, *Mysiae regias silvas* (text emended by McDonald 1967: 2 n. 8), Robert 1955: pls. 46–7 for views of the Mysian mountains and the forests around Sındırgı, Robert 1987: 138–48.

[90] *Inschr. Priene* 1, lines 10–13 (Priene at the time of Alexander); Herrmann 1959 (Aigai under Antiochos II); document 31 B, III 8 (Herakleia under Antiochos III).

[91] Document 3, 8–10 with Gauthier 1989: 101–7, arguing that Seleukid kings erected buildings in 'subject' cities, and retained ownership rights. Another possibility is a royal claim to intestate property in the subject cities; Millar 1992: 158–63, for late Ptolemaic and Roman practice. Equally possible is the confiscation of real estate pledged by the city as security for a royal loan: a joke preserved in Strabo 13.3.6, takes as its starting point the loss of Kyme's porticoes to creditors, when the city defaults on reimbursement.

[92] Collective tax: Bikerman 1938: 106–10. 'Out of all the incomes': document 36, 16–18. There is no evidence for Seleukid *phoros* in kind from the cities, such as the levy in horses paid by the Aspendians to the Achaimenids, then Alexander: Arr. *Anab.* 1.26.3.

could be levied on a regular basis (like the payments εἰς τὰ Γαλατικά made by the Erythraians under Antiochos I or II), and thus end up as merely an increase (earmarked for various purposes) of *phoros*: the Teians use *syntaxis* and *phoros* interchangeably.[93] Finally, the Seleukid empire extracted services, λητουργίαι, probably *corvée* labour for the needs of the imperial state, such as the upkeep of the road system (see § 1 for evidence and parallels).

The Seleukid state also made itself manifest through a multitude of indirect taxes, agricultural duties, personal dues—the system which the pseudo-Aristotelian *Oeconomica* calls the 'satrapic' economy (2.1345^b–1346^a), the income-raising network at the provincial level. The evidence concerning Maccabaean Judaea, long the only detailed source for Seleukid indirect taxation (Bikerman 1938: 115–18, 131–2), is now supplemented by a long and informative document for Asia Minor, Zeuxis' summary of the Herakleian petition for exemption from certain taxes. The Herakleians asked to be spared—and, by implication, the Seleukid state might raise—a tax on agricultural produce, an *ennomion* ('pasture rights') on herds and on beehives, a tax on the import and sale of grain within the city, a harbour tax, and dues on the movement of goods from the royal land (ἐκ τῆς τοῦ βασιλέως) into the city whether for personal use or for resale.[94]

These items are paralleled in the fragmentary evidence for the rest of Seleukid Asia Minor (apart from general mentions of *ateleia*). Agricultural levies appear in a fragmentary, early Seleukid, document from Aigai (Malay 1983): the Seleukid state is seen taking in levies on grain (probably), fruit-trees, flocks of sheep and goats, beehives, and, remarkably, even game: a leg off each boar and each deer. An agricultural tax is possibly attested at Seleukeia/Tralleis, and probably in the unnamed city of *Sardis*, no. 2;[95] at Sardeis, Antiochos III seems to have collected a tax on transactions within the city (a one-twentieth due, technically a royal tax added to, and doubling the amount of, a civic tax), no doubt some form of sales tax.[96] The taxation on the import and sale of grain within the city

---

[93] Distinction: Herrmann 1965a: 138–45; supported by the fact that an Iasian petition to an official of Ptolemy I does not mention *phoros* (the Iasians were exempt), but a reduction in the *syntaxis* they paid as a contribution towards 'the defence of the territory' (*I. Iasos* 3, lines 4–5). Erythrai: *RC* 15, 26–28 (*phoros* and contribution to the Galatian fund, presumably money for war against the Galatians). Teos and the blurring of *syntaxis* and *phoros*: document **17**, 14, 18–19, 33–4, 48 (*contra*, Allen 1983: 50–3, Sherwin-White 1985: 85).   [94] Document **31** B, III 3–9.

[95] Tralleis: *RC* 41, line 8: a tithe (δεκατήν) paid to the royal chest; unnamed city: document **36**, 23 (restoration of Piejko), [ἐκ τῶν γεν]ημάτων.

[96] Document **1**, 5–6: παραλύομεν δὲ καὶ τῆς προσεπιβληθείσης εἰκοστῆς ἐπὶ τὴν πολιτικὴν (the civic twentieth rather than the *politike ge*: Gauthier 1989: 33–6).

was the subject of a petition to Zeuxis from a Prienian ambassador, as it had been on the part of Herakleia (above). Taxation on the movement of grain and of goods is likely to have been general practice, with tolls at the entrance into city territories or at city gates, and perhaps at the frontiers between satrapies.[97] The practice of taxation on trade explains why the harbour dues at Herakleia were taken over by the Seleukid state (transforming a Herakleian civic tax into an imperial due).[98]

Apart from the widespread practice of levying a share of agricultural produce and collecting dues on the movement of goods, many features of non-tributary taxation were localized. The Herakleians specifically petitioned for the status quo ('the privileges granted by the kings') to be maintained, which hints at local solutions and precedents.[99] A poll-tax appears in the letter from Eumenes II concerning the inhabitants of the *Kardakon kome*, near Telmessos; a *cheironaxion*, or artisan tax (levied against the right to ply a craft) was mentioned in a royal letter (Attalid or Seleukid) to a similar colony, in the same region. These two taxes are unparalleled in Asia Minor; rather than Attalid innovations (as Segre believed for the poll-tax), these taxes must be a legacy from the Seleukid administration of Antiochos III and, ultimately, the Ptolemaic administration[100]—localized taxes, raised because of precedent and not by application of a standardized imperial formula. Such a practice, reminiscent of the complex system of local taxes and privileges in Ancien Régime France, may seem cumbersome and unsystematic to a modern eye. It nonetheless offered the advantage of precisely targeting local resources for exploitation. The levy on game attested at Aigai (above) seems unique to that city, and must reflect a local resource—hunting in the highlands of Aiolis, the modern Yunt Dağ—and the imperial state's intention of taking its

[97] Priene: document 33. Bikerman 1938: 116 (commenting *AJ* 12.141: Antiochos III orders wood to be brought to Jerusalem, μηδενὸς πρασσομένου τέλος); Gauthier 1989: 25–6.

[98] The case of Herakleia suggests that the Seleukids controlled most, or all harbours, in their dominion, to be able to raise tolls or custom rights on goods entering the Seleukid empire (Gauthier 1989: 26 n. 37).

[99] Document 31 B, II 14–15: παρακαλέσοντας τά τε ὑπὸ τῶν βασιλέων συγκεχωρημένα | [συνδιατηρηθῆν]αι. Wörrle 1988: 465, observes that the agriculture tax and *ennomion* are assessed in proportion to land-surface ('yokes': III 6), drawing a parallel with Achaimenid practice, on the basis of the land survey for the purpose of tax assessment carried out after the Ionian Revolt (Hdt. 6.42.1), but this might simply be the most obvious way of assessing an agricultural tax.

[100] Poll-tax: Segre 1938: 190, lines 10–11; 199–203 for the unconvincing suggestion that the poll-tax was introduced around Telmessos by the Attalids (Rostovtzeff 1941: 338: 'possibly this was a heritage from Ptolemaic times'). *Cheironaxion*: Wörrle 1979: 83 at line 7, 91–2 (Ptolemaic precedent), and Robert, *BE* 80, 484, for context of the letter.

cut. A parallel is the tithe on juniper-berries, paid by the Kaudians to their master, the city of Gortyn (Chaniotis 1996: no. 69). Finally, the Telmessian documents show that the network of indirect, or non-tributary, taxation affected the communities in the countryside and the royal domain, as well as the cities; the sanctuaries were likewise included, unless specifically exempted.[101]

The evidence is not sufficient to reconstruct local, concrete, details: for instance, the only figure we have for tribute in Seleukid Asia Minor is that of twenty *mnai* annually, one-third of a talent, untypical because it comes from the unnamed city of *Sardis*, no. 2, devastated by Seleukid capture (one would expect tribute to be rated in talents, and in two or three figures).[102] Nonetheless, the documentation illustrates the operations involved and their density. The picture can be expanded with Ptolemaic parallels (for agricultural taxes, taxation on goods, indirect taxes perceived within subject communities), or even Ottoman parallels: like the Seleukids, the sultan taxed herds and beehives.[103] These illustrate a general point about empires of domination: the condition for their existence, and one of their main activities, is the extraction of surplus, through means direct (rent, tribute) or indirect (sales taxes, dues, tolls), but all visible; the network of indirect taxation played as important a role, both practical and ideological, as the raising of tribute which Briant (1982) has emphasized in his essays on the Achaimenid and Hellenistic empires. The principles of the 'fiscal economy' could be openly expressed: a Ptolemaic governor wrote to the Arsinoeans 'you will do well to work and sow all of it (i.e. your

[101] Exemptions: *Syll.* 353 (Prepelaos, Lysimachos' general, grants *ateleia* to the Artemision at Xanthos); *RC* 9, line 3 (*ateleia* restored); *RC* 47 (ἀτέλεια προβάτων for the κάτοικοι of Apollo Tarsenos, granted by Attalids). All these examples imply that Hellenistic kings routinely taxed shrines (though were ready to exempt them from taxation).

[102] Tribute: document **36**, 16–19. Normal figures: in comparison, Jerusalem (or the whole Jewish *ethnos*?) apparently paid 300 talents (Bikerman 1938: 107–8), and the Rhodians raised 120 talents a year from Kaunos and Stratonikeia (Pol. 30.31.7), though the figure might include indirect taxes as well as tribute. The discussion of the (allegedly crushing) impact of royal taxation on the cities offered by Gallant 1989 is marred by his ignoring indirect taxation, and his imprecise use of the documents: in his first example, the Milesian inscription *Inschr. Delphinion* 138, Gallant is unaware that it is not clear whether the sum the Milesians owe to Lysimachos is regular tribute, or as preferred by many commentators, a one-off payment, perhaps as reimbursement of a loan (Rostovtzeff 1941: 1340); his second example, *Syll.* 955 (also *IG* 12.7. 67 B), from Amorgos, does not concern tribute at all.

[103] Ptolemaic parallels: general survey in Rostovtzeff 1941: 273–316 (296 for Ptolemaic taxation on bee-keeping); *OGIS* 55 for agricultural taxes at Telmessos under the dynast Ptolemaios; tolls: e.g. *PCZ* 59093; Ptolemaic taxation within the cities: Wörrle 1979: 106–11, Bagnall 1976: 85–7 on *OGIS* 41 (Samos). Ottomans: Babinger 1978: 451.

land), so that you yourselves might live in prosperity and so that the revenues which you provide to the king may be greater than those which were produced originally' (ὅπως αὐτοί τε ἐν εὐβοσίαι γίνησθε καὶ τῶι βασιλεῖ τὰς προσόδους πλείους τῶν ἐν ἀρχῆι γινομένων συντελῆτε), and conversely, the Samaritans drew the attention of Antiochos IV to the fact that, if left outside the scope of the anti-Jewish persecution, 'applying ourselves in security to our work, the revenues which we provide to you will be greater' (the phrases used are similar).[104] This is the rationale which underlies the professed solicitude of the kings for the local communities' well-being, populousness, and enjoyment of their property (τὰ ἴδια).[105]

The royal economy mattered, both for the Seleukid state, which depended on its workings, and for the subject communities, at whose expense it operated; it required its own set of officials, centralized at Sardeis or distributed in the satrapies. The most important official was Ktesikles, based in Sardeis; his exact title is unknown, but ὁ ἐπὶ τῶν προσόδων, cautiously proposed by the Roberts, is attractive. Antiochos notified the Sardians that γεγράφα-μεν περὶ πάντων πρὸς Ζεῦξιν καὶ Κτησικλῆν: the parallel expression suggests that Ktesikles, among the financial officials, held the same pre-eminent position as Zeuxis did in the hierarchy of governors.[106] Apart from Ktesikles, there were other 'central' officials, concentrated at Sardeis, whose powers were exercised at the level of the cis-Tauric province: on a mission to Sardeis, an embassy from the east Karian city of Apollonia under Salbake dealt with Ktesikles, Menandros the *dioiketes*, Demetrios the *eklogistes* (tax-collector or 'financial controller'?), who was acting on the report of Demetrios the 'official in charge of the shrines'—probably the successor to Nikanor in this function, which also entailed the control of shrine finances.[107] The relationships, formal or actual, between these officials, and their hierarchical position in relation to Ktesikles are not clear. At the 'provincial' level, financial officials—*dioiketai* and

---

[104] Arsinoe: Jones and Habicht 1989: 319, lines 6–9. Samaritans: Jos. *AJ* 12.261.

[105] Document 5, 1–7; cf. Arr. *Anab.* 1.17.1, Theocritus 17. 95–107; 2 Macc. 11: 22–33. Also Briant 1982: 175–225 and esp. 179–88; 23 n. 6; J. and L. Robert 1983: 189–91 for Seleukids rebuilding cities and gathering scattered populations.

[106] Ktesikles at Sardeis: Gauthier 1989: 42–5 (residence in Sardeis is likely because the Apollonian embassy of document 44 dealt with a whole set of central financial officials in that city). Title: J. and L. Robert 1954: 292 and n. 1 (cautious); Gauthier 1989: 4 and n. 97.

[107] Apollonian embassy: document 44, 4–24. *Eklogistes*: J. and L. Robert 1954: 292–3—either an auditor ('contrôleur financier', from ἐκλογίζεσθαι), or a tax-collector (like the Ptolemaic ἐγλογίστης; from ἐκλέγειν). A tax-receipt from second-century Baktria proves the existence of an official named ὁ ἐπὶ τῶν προσόδων and subordinates named λογευταί—inspired by Seleukid practice (Bernard and Rapin 1994: 284–9). For an official in charge of shrine finances in the Attalid period, Malay and Nalbantoğlu 1996.

oikonomoi—operated in parallel to the governors and their subordinates. These officials were clearly distributed below the satrapy: under Antiochos II, a *dioiketes* is named alongside the phrourarch in the Anaitis, and both seem to have a local competence; the Skythopolis dossier shows that Ptolemaios' estate fell within the purview of two different *dioiketai*; finally, the mention of ἡ περὶ Σάρδεις οἰκονομία shows that Lydia was divided into several *oikonomiai* no doubt each administered by its own *oikonomos*. This situation probably continued under the Attalids: an *oikonomos* appears at Pleura (not far from Sardeis), where he also seems to be dealing with matters of land and property.[108] A royal letter of Antiochos IV, quoted by Josephus (*AJ* 12.261), mentions ὁ τὰ βασιλικὰ πράττων, undoubtedly a local financial official, operating alongside a meridarch, at the level of a subdivision of Koile-Syria and Phoenicia; the Seleukid official Nikomedes, honoured by the Amyzonians as well as the *epistates* of the Artemision and the governor of Alinda, must have been a local financial official of just this sort (a *dioiketes?*), working in a sub-division of the satrapy of Karia—perhaps a hyparchy, or a specifically financial sub-division (such as the *oikonomia*).[109]

For the time being, it is impossible to document exactly what all these officials (whose names are attested) actually did. The processes involved, let alone their signficance, are still obscure, but the evidence is suggestive. The Apollonians sent an embassy to Sardeis (above), to petition Ktesikles and Menandros the *dioiketes*, and faced a complaint from Demetrios the *eklogistes*, who summoned the embassy before him (Δ[ημητρίου] τοῦ ἐγλογιστοῦ εἰσκαλεσαμένου τοὺς [πρεσ]βευτὰς (. . .) καὶ διαμ[φι]σβη[τήσαντος] πρὸς αὐτοὺς ὑπὲρ τῶν ἱερῶν κωμῶν κτλ.). It seems that the *eklogistes* contested the Apollonians' rights over a group of 'sacred villages': the issue was perhaps whether the revenues from these villages belonged to the Seleukid state or the Apollonians, and the transaction documents a financial

---

[108] *Dioiketes* near Anaitis: *SEG* 1.366, line 17. *Oikonomia* around Sardeis: document **41** D and Gauthier 1989: 131–4; the document implies some relation with landed property, since the document records a conveyance of royal land within this *oikonomia*. Attalid *oikonomos*: document **49** shows an Attalid *oikonomos* receiving instructions to designate a spot for a shrine to erect a stele (was the shrine on royal land?); see further § 2c.

[109] Local financial official alongside meridarch: Bengtson 1944: 173 and n. 2. Nikomedes: document **11** and J. and L. Robert 1983: 188. The obvious parallel is Ptolemaic practice at the level of the nome. An early Seleukid inscription from Central Asia, recording an administrative note to two officials, Andragoras and Apollodoros, might be another example of a governor and a financial official working in parallel (Robert 1960: 85–91, though Robert suggests Apollodoros was an official in charge of sacred matters).

official's attentiveness to local statuses and their fiscal repercussions.[110] There is evidence for the administration of the royal domain—land-surveys, record-keeping—under the *oikonomos*, who (at least in Koile-Syria) also intervened in judicial cases involving the villages (in collaboration with the local governor).[111] Finally, the *dioiketes*, whose title simply means 'administrator', may have routinely handled many affairs relevant to the royal economy. Antiochos III promised money to the Herakleians, for the construction of an aqueduct, and passed on the instructions to a *dioiketes*: τό τε [ἐσόμενον ἀ]νήλωμα εἰς τὴν ἐπισκευὴν τοῦ ὑδραγωγίου οἰόμε[θα δεῖν δίδο]σθαι ἐκ βασιλικοῦ ἐφ' ἔτη τρία, καὶ περὶ τούτων γεγράφαμεν [*c.*8/9 τ]ῶι διοικητῆι. The *dioiketes* handled disbursement from the royal treasury (τὸ βασιλικόν): it was perhaps in this quality that a *dioiketes* received instructions (the content is now lost) from Antiochos III concerning Nysa, or that Menandros, the central *dioiketes* in Sardeis, interviewed the embassy from Apollonia.[112] A *dioiketes*, Strouthion, was instructed by Laodike to convey to the Iasians her gift of forty tons of wheat a year, for ten years;[113] under Antiochos II, a *dioiketes* is found supervising the transfer of estates, seized from Samian citizens, back to their original owners (*SEG* 1.366, lines 15–18). In Koile-Syria, under Antiochos III, Ptolemaios son of Thraseas asked for the royal rulings concerning his estates to be communicated to the local *dioiketai*, Heliodoros and Kleon, even though they were not directly affected: one ruling concerns the judicial authority of Ptolemaios (*qua* landlord), the *oikonomos* and the local governors, another the exemption of Ptolemaios' estates from billeting and the repression of abuses on the part of local soldiery;[114] the *dioiketes* may have been expected to supervise any decision affecting the royal economy. This wide range of activities is described by the expression 'to handle the king's business', πράττειν τὰ βασιλικά (Jos. *AJ* 12.261). Generally, these examples illustrate the importance of the officials, and show that local communities saw them regularly, in the practical execution of the royal economy's demands.

[110] Document **44**, 4–14.
[111] Land surveys: Herrmann 1959; *RC* 18–20. Record-keeping: land sale (to Laodike I) and survey registered εἰς τὰς βασιλικὰς γραφὰς τὰς ἐν Σάρδεσιν, *RC* 19, 15–16 (does the phrase imply royal archives outside of Sardeis?). Jurisdiction: *SEG* 29.1613, lines 13–14.
[112] Herakleia: document **31** B, II 11–14. Nysa: **43**. Apollonia: **44**, 6–10.
[113] Document **26** A, I 15–18. Laodike gave 1000 *medimnoi* a year; an Attic *medimnos* is 52.176 litres, which, at 0.772 kg./litre, entails 40.279 kg. per *medimnos*; 1000 Attic *medimnoi* weigh 40 tonnes, 279 kg. Figures: Foxhall and Forbes 1982: 84.
[114] *SEG* 29.1613, C–D, E–F, G–H.

(c) Empire at Work

Some broader remarks can be made about the administrative structures of Seleukid Asia Minor. First, the various administrative systems were separated: the hierarchy of governors, the financial officials, the military sphere of phrourarchs directly answerable to the king. In the decree from Apollonia (mentioned above), a general characteristic is the discrete authority of the financial administration to make its own decisions: Ktesikles and Menandros are sole recipients of petitions, Demetrios, the *eklogistes*, has the power to change (κινεῖν) the *status quo*, after hearing an embassy summoned on his initiative. Zeuxis is nowhere to be seen, and the cavalry commander stationed at Apollonia intervenes informally, interceding with Demetrios—an action which shows where the power of decision lay.

The *cloisonnement* of the different branches of administration is usually explained as the 'separation of powers' into departments that could check each other, to prevent the emergence of local power bases. The practice is not specifically Seleukid. The Achaimenid king took care to see that garrisons in various strategic places (for instance, Sardeis) answered directly to him. After capturing Sardeis, Alexander named a commander of the citadel, a satrap of Lydia, and a financial official; an ordinance of Philip V shows how garrison-commanders and financial officials throughout his kingdom were meant to control and report on each other.[115] Rather, the practice is inseparable from the exercise of imperial power: Antiochos' last gesture in Asia Minor, after the defeat of Magnesia, was to appoint, in scrupulous but futile respect of the rule, a governor of Lydia and a separate commander of Sardeis (Liv. 37.44.7). There are other possible explanations, not mutually exclusive: perhaps a continuously felt or passively inherited inclination for efficiency, a separation in different styles and aims of government.

In practice, the distinction should not be overemphasized. The governors intervened in the royal economy: a *strategos* transferred a royal land-donation to its beneficiary; under Antiochos III, Zeuxis managed the gift to the Sardians of timber from the royal forests of Taranza, and took decisions on landownership at Amyzon (dedicating ἀγροί, to the gods of the Artemision).[116] At Skythopolis, juris-

---

[115] Achaimenids: Lewis 1977: 53 n. 21, to which add Hdt. 1.154.3, attributing the practice at Sardeis to Cyrus the Great; Hornblower 1982: 147–52, gathering examples but warning against excessive formalism. Alexander: Arr. *Anab.* 1.17.7. Philip V: *IG* 12 suppl. 644 (same document Hatzopoulos 1996: ii. no. 13). See also Orrieux 1983: 25–6: 'separation of powers' in Ptolemaic Egypt.

[116] Land-donation (under Antiochos I): *RC* 10–13. Zeuxis: documents **1**; **7**.

diction over the villages was exercised by the *oikonomos*, the local governors, the *strategos* of Koile-Syria and Phoenicia, and the phrourarchs.[117] The implementation of a royal decision concerning the sale of royal land could weave between the hierarchy of governors and the 'financial' administration: Antiochos II ordered Metrophanes, probably the *strategos* of the Hellespontine satrapy, to see to the conveyance of a piece of royal land sold to Laodike I, and to record in the Sardeis archives the sale and concomitant land survey; Metrophanes passed the order on to an *oikonomos*, Nikomachos, who in turn gave instructions to their final recipient, a hyparch, theoretically a subordinate of Metrophanes the governor (*RC* 18–20).[118] Likewise, the investigation of the finances of the Temple at Jerusalem under Seleukos IV involved the *strategos* of Koile-Syria and Phoenicia, the king, and Heliodoros, ὁ ἐπὶ τῶν πραγμάτων, the chief minister, rather than the 'financial administration' (Bickerman 1980: 159–81).

Collaboration between officials was recognized as a necessity. When appointing Nikanor to his responsibilities as high-priest and ὁ ἐπὶ τῶν ἱερῶν, Antiochos III gave a clear order to Zeuxis: σύνταξον οὖν συνεργεῖν αὐτῶι εἰς τὰ προσήκοντα τοῖς προδεδηλωμένοις· 'pass on the instruction to work with him in the matters relevant to what has just been said [Nikanor's duties, the king's rationale and expectation]'.[119] The verb used is συνεργεῖν, and the collaboration it implies in the routine of administration was hardly a special policy of Antiochos III or a specific feature of Nikanor's office. The tribute was managed by the financial officials (under the *eklogistes?*), but a practical role must have been played by the military forces disseminated in the satrapies, and by the local governors; at Jerusalem, the garrison commander was responsible for the collection of tribute.[120] The governors and the garrisons probably collaborated in

---

[117] *SEG* 29.1613, lines 13–16.

[118] This interpretation differs from Musti 1965. I prefer Welles's sequence: Antiochos II to Metrophanes (*RC* 18), Metrophanes to the *oikonomos* (*RC* 19), letter of the *oikonomos* to the hyparch [now lost]: these documents were inscribed in reverse chronological order, but the stele ended with the report of the hyparch, the last in the administrative sequence (*RC* 20). It is possible, however, that Metrophanes, instead of a *strategos*, was a high official in the 'financial' administration

[119] Document 4, 41–3.

[120] Billows 1995: 279–84 speculates that the hyparchies were the main unit for tribute collection, just as the chiliarchies, territorial divisions in Asia Minor, had been under Antigonos Monophthalmos (but there is no evidence for the hyparchies). It is still not clear whether Seleukid indirect taxation was farmed out. *OGIS* 55, lines 16–17, proves the practice of tax-farming in Telmessos under the dynast Ptolemaios. For infrastructure assisting in the collection of indirect taxes (by tax-farmers?) under the Attalids: lex portorii provinciae Asiae (*SEG* 39.1180), lines 67–8 (ἐποίκια καὶ [σταθμοὺς] βασιλικούς, οὓς βασιλεὺς Ἄτταλος Εὐμένους υἱὸς τελωνίας χάριν ἐστήσατο).

collecting the agricultural taxation, the rights on herds and beehives, the poll-tax, and other personal taxes; military forces, such as
the cavalry stationed at Apollonia or the *phylakitai* in the hyparchy
of Eriza (both on important roads), presumably helped to raise taxes
on the movement of goods and control the movement of persons, as
well as collecting tribute from local communities, as the garrison
commander did at Jerusalem.[121] The aspects which Polybios distinguished in his subtle description of the Seleukid empire—tribute,
garrisons, royal orders (21.41.2; see above, Introduction)—merged
on the ground, in the execution of imperial administration.

The second general feature that emerges is the pattern of the surviving material: scanty information on the local officials (*strategoi*,
hyparchs), and, in comparison, the frequency of material pertaining
to central officials, concentrated at Sardeis. The pattern reflects the
centralization of cis-Tauric Asia Minor under Antiochos III (this
may have been the case under earlier Seleukid rulers as well).[122] It is
hardly surprising that the Sardians or the Prienians sent embassies
to Zeuxis: he probably resided in the first city, and Priene is part of
Ionia, traditionally governed together with Lydia (above).[123]
However, Laodikeia on Lykos also addressed itself directly to
Zeuxis, *qua* viceroy of the province, rather than to the *strategos* of
Phrygia; likewise, Apollonia under Salbake dealt with the financial
officials at Sardeis, not with any local officials or governors.[124] After
the disappearance of Seleukid control in 189, the Amyzonians
would remember sending embassies to Zeuxis, not to the *strategos* of
Karia.[125] This fact will not be changed by new evidence: even if it
turns out that Amyzon, Laodikeia on Lykos, or Apollonia under
Salbake routinely dealt with the local *strategos*, it will remain true
that widely separated cities addressed themselves to the viceroy
Zeuxis or the central financial officials. The Seleukid practice of
appointing a viceroy and financial high-officials over the whole cis-
Tauric region subordinated the satrapies and their governors to a
version of the Achaimenid satrapy of Sardeis, which had included
most of Anatolia in a single unit.[126]

[121] Jerusalem: 2 Macc. 4: 28.
[122] *RC* 18–20, with its central registration at Sardeis of a land-sale near Kyzikos, or
Syll. 426, which shows Bargylia lavishly praising Alexandros (brother of Laodike I and
probably viceroy for cis-Tauric Asia Minor) are suggestive.
[123] Sardeis: document **40**. Priene: **33**.
[124] Laodikeia: document **32**, 3–4. Apollonia: **44**.
[125] Document **47**, 4–6. The Seleukid official honoured in document **12** could be the
missing provincial governor.
[126] The Seleukid cis-Tauric province had a different shape, because of the loss of
eastern Phrygia to the Galatians, and the inclusion of the Troad and the Hellespontine
regions (the old satrapy of Daskyleion). On the satrapy of Sardeis, Lewis 1977: 52–3,

A third remark concerns method and presentation. The result of this survey of the meagre evidence is an inert panorama of 'institutions'—not substantially different from Bickerman's classic *Institutions des Séleucides* or Bengtson's kingdom-by-kingdom study, *Die Strategie in der hellenistischen Zeit*. But we can also explore the implications which the documents hold out and the questions they raise. Seen under this light, Asia Minor under Antiochos III is rich in documents which are uniquely interesting, because they illustrate experience with specific evidence.

We may start once more from the Pamukçu stele. The Seleukid state appears as an apparatus for transmitting and issuing orders, from the king at the top, to the subordinate officials who actually gave the instruction to inscribe the letters onto the stele, and who may have left a discreet trace in the three numerals carved on the stele pediment (Malay 1987). In this world, everyone says 'we'; patronymics and ethnics are dropped; the language is *koine*, not dialect: while a dedication by Ptolemaios, son of Thraseas, at Soloi, is in Doric, the series of his memoranda to Antiochos III is written in functional *koine*.[127] The participants share a language of orders: the Pamukçu stele, like other similar documents (*RC* 10–13, *RC* 18–20) is structured by the verb συντάσσω, which designates instructions, or, most often, the order to give orders;[128] it describes the process by which the apparatus of empire transmits the royal order down the hierarchy, a new sub-order being generated and passed on at each stage.

The flow of orders downwards also generated responses from below: the *oikonomos* Nikomachos asked the hyparch to report on the completion of the land-sale to Laodike I by Antiochos II, especially the archiving of the sale at Sardeis (*RC* 19, line 13: ὡς ἂν συντελεσθῆι γράψον καὶ ἡμῖν 'when it is done, write to us also'); part of the hyparch's report survives (*RC* 20). Instructions were also notified 'horizontally', on account of the parallel networks of administration: a royal edict concerning exemption from billeting for Ptolemaios' estates was sent to the military officers in the region,

Petit 1990: 180. The importance of the central financial officials shows that the phenomenon is one of administrative centralization rather than Zeuxis' personal power.

[127] No patronymics: Bikerman 1938: 193; Robert 1960: 87 n. 5; J. and L. Robert 1983: 114 and n. 140 for examples. Ptolemaios' dedication: document **21** and commentary.

[128] Under Antiochos III: document **1**, 7 and **3**, 5; **15**, 3; *SEG* 29.1613, line 2; *RC* 44, lines 33–41. Other Seleukid examples; *RC* 10, line 4, *RC* 11, lines 19 and 24, *RC* 12, line 5; *RC* 18, lines 19 and 24; *RC* 19, line 6; Robert 1945: 12, for an occurrence in a fragmentary letter of a king Antiochos (Appendix 3): [καλῶς οὖν ποιήσ]αις σύνταξας restored by Piejko (*SEG* 39.1122, though the rest of the restoration is unacceptable); Herrmann 1959: Συντάξαντος βασιλέως Ἀντιόχου ὅροι τῆς Αἰγαίδος. Ptolemaic: *RC* 14, line 14; Preisigke, *Wörterbuch* s.v.; *C. Ord. Ptol.*, no. 24, line 5. Attalid: Segre 1938: 190 line 7.

but also to the local financial officers (*SEG* 29. 1613, lines 38–9). We learn from an Amyzonian honorific decree that the *epistates* of the Artemision, Menestratos, wrote to Zeuxis, and 'often' to Nikomedes and Chionis. No doubt Menestratos did mention the Amyzonians' εὔνοια towards the Seleukid kings and Zeuxis in his letters, as the Amyzonians claim—among other matters, such as acknowledgement of orders addressed to him or to neighbouring officials, receipts, reports on orders carried out, demands to his superiors or 'colleagues'.[129] At times, communication was face-to-face, when Zeuxis was on campaign (for which there is good evidence) or on his circuit (undocumented, but probable). The hipparch stationed at Apollonia went twice, probably on official business, to Sardeis (where he helped the Apollonians in their dealings with a financial administrator); under Seleukos IV, the *strategos* of Koile-Syria and Phoenicia went to see the king and informed him of surplus accumulating in the Temple at Jerusalem.[130]

The administrative system, beside conveying orders and producing communication, generated its own actions. The case of Apollonia under Salbake is instructive. Demetrios, ὁ ἐπὶ τῶν ἱερῶν, reached a decision concerning the 'sacred villages' near the city—perhaps that, *qua* sacred communities, they should not belong to the city, but fall within the χώρα, where they would be liable to tribute. We do not know how he reached his decision (personal inspection? the denunciation of a neighbouring city? the petition of the villagers? the report of a subordinate official?); at any rate, he reported to Demetrios the *eklogistes*, who acted on the information. The *eklogistes* caught an Apollonian embassy which was at Sardeis on another business, summoning them for several hearings; he knew that Apollonian representatives were at Sardeis, that their city had been the subject of a recommendation from ὁ ἐπὶ τῶν ἱερῶν, and what action to take.[131] The Seleukid administration appears active and informed, perhaps even bureaucratic in the Weberian sense (rationally and autonomously organized).[132] It is true that an excessively modernistic interpretation should be avoided. The whole process was cumbersome, with two journeys from Apollonia to Sardeis and

---

[129] Document **10**, 7–12. These operations are well documented in the Zenon dossier (examples analysed in Orrieux 1983). Another example of horizontal communication: document **49**, where a letter from the Attalid 'high-priest' to an *oikonomos* is also transmitted to another official, probably the *dioiketes*.

[130] Apollonia: document **44**, 4–24. The hipparch probably did not go to Sardeis especially to assist the Apollonians: the second time, he arrived there only after the Apollonians. Jerusalem: 2 Macc. 3: 7.

[131] Document **44**.

[132] Weber 1968: iii. 956–1005.

back (180 km. and four or five days each way via Hierapolis and Apollonia on Maeander, the future Tripolis);[133] the city and the administration communicated not by memoranda, but through embassies, since even a subject city existed as a self-governing body (next section); finally, the main resource of the Apollonians was not appeal to bureaucratic rules, but the patronage of a local Seleukid officer. Nonetheless, the 'archaic' features do not change the implication of a powerful and active administration (J. and L. Robert 1954: 299).

The Amyzonian inscriptions further illustrate the extension of Seleukid state power. Amyzon, with its monumental shrine and its scattered villages, lay high in the foothills of Mt. Latmos, six hours away from the Maeander, and four hours from Alinda—unlike Apollonia under Salbake, Amyzon was not located on a major route.[134] Yet the Amyzonians simultaneously dealt with a Seleukid official appointed over the shrine, the governor of Alinda, a financial official (see above, on Nikomedes), the viceroy Zeuxis, an officer (with troops) sent by Zeuxis, possibly another (now obscure) official, and finally the king himself: six or seven levels of Seleukid authority.[135] Amyzon was not exceptional, as shown by the case of Aigai and Temnos, located in the mountains of Aiolis. In the 390s (admittedly a troubled time for Persian authority in Asia Minor), according to a speaker in Xenophon (Derkyllidas), these cities could plausibly be said to be outside the Great King's authority (*Hellen.* 4.8.5). In the Hellenistic period, however, they lay within reach of the Hellenistic empires: these 'Seleukid' cities were taken over by Attalos I, recaptured by Achaios, taken again by Attalos I, in 218 (Pol. 5.77.4) and probably fell back into Seleukid control in 197. The territory of Aigai was surveyed on the orders of Antiochos II; the city benefited from Attalid architectural euergetism. Just as tellingly, we learn from a chance reference in a decree of the Temnians that they celebrated a contest for Dionysos and the 'the kings'—whether Seleukid or Attalid, the fact implies royal euergetism, such as the subsidies we know the city received from the

[133] It would take a day or two to journey from Apollonia through the Tabai plateau, then over the formidable Baba Dağ (ancient Mt. Kadmos) to Laodikeia (J. and L. Robert 1954: 25–31, whence it emerges that the crossing could take five or six hours). From Laodikeia to Sardeis, the traveller might take four days (the Ten Thousand took four stages to travel from Sardeis to Kolossai: Xen. *Anab.* 1.2.6).

[134] Settlement pattern at Amyzon: J. and L. Robert 1983: 271–3. Remoteness: ibid. 17; 50–2 and 59–61.

[135] Documents **5–14, 47**. The unnamed official is honoured in **12**, but since the beginning of the decree is lost, it is unclear whether this is yet another official in addition to Menestratos, Chionis, and Nikomedes, or the successor of one of these.

Attalids.[136] If the documentation were fuller, the experience of
Aigai, Temnos, and other highland communities such as Kildara
would resemble the dealings of Amyzon with the Seleukid administration.

One of the services the Amyzonians praised Menestratos for was
his care ὑπὲρ τῶν ἄλλων ἡμῶν πολιτῶν τῶν κατοικούντων τὰς αὐτονόμους
προσκαλούμενος εἰς τὸν συνοικισμὸν τοῦ Ἀρτεμισίου, 'for the rest of our
citizens, those who live in the autonomous (cities), by inviting them
to the repopulation of the Artemision'.[137] The Amyzonians speak
of 'inviting' (through proclamations in the cities?), though one
might wonder if the *epistates* of the Artemision resorted to more
pressing means. At any rate, Menestratos was expected to know
where the other citizens (probably refugees in the aftermath of the
campaign of *c*.203) resided—the 'autonomous' cities, such as
Mylasa or Alabanda. At Herakleia, the situation did not involve
citizens, but 'villages' and 'dwellers' (probably agricultural serfs):
the Herakleians asked Zeuxis that these be 'rounded up': ὅπως καὶ οἱ
δῆμοι καὶ οἱ οἰκηταὶ συναχθῶσιν καθότι καὶ πρότερον ὑπῆρχον.[138]
Presumably they had fled to the territory of other cities, or taken
refuge in the Latmos; how Zeuxis was expected to bring them back
is unclear. Nonetheless, the Herakleians hoped that Zeuxis would
do so, which provides a subject community's perception of the
Seleukid state's capabilities. In both cases, the Seleukid state played
along: its concern was the control of the human resource (to avoid
diminution in income through the flight of producers)[139]—an operation implying strong capabilities and constant attention.

The *prostagma* concerning Nikanor raises questions about its
implementation. How was the king's performative utterance
realized? Sometimes, this was straightforward: in the execution of

---

[136] Aigai: Herrmann 1959; Robert 1937: 82–7 for buildings. Temnos: Herrmann
1979: 242–3, lines 9–10: ἀγών for Dionysos and the kings (decree found in Teos); *RC* 48,
fragmentary letter of Eumenes II to the city. The same remarks hold true for Mysia,
only loosely subjected to the Achaimenids (*Anab.* 3.2.23–26), yet firmly under Seleukid
control.

[137] Document **10**, 14–16; next section for 'the autonomous ones'. J. and L. Robert
1983: 191, remark on the implication that people can come and go from 'autonomous'
cities, and speculates that this was not the case for subject cities or the villages. But
citizens of such subject cities as Sardeis or Lysimacheia were given Milesian citizenship
in 202/3 and 197/6 (Günther 1988: nos. 3, 4).

[138] Document **31** B, III 10. Territory of Herakleia: Robert 1987: 198–214.

[139] *RC* 18, 11–13, indicates that Antiochos II sold an estate with its *laoi*, including
those which had moved to other villages, which implies some control of the human
resource. Babinger 1978: 235, describes the Ottoman prohibition of movement by the
subject populations keen to avoid taxation or *corvée*. This sort of movement is an
inevitable by-product of an imperial space with differentiated statuses and privileged
communities.

his duties, Nikanor could rely on the collaboration (συνεργεῖν, see above) of the local governors, who would enforce Nikanor's royally decreed authority. More problematic: Antiochos III had decided that Nikanor would be mentioned in legal acts; this decision was conveyed to the subjects by 'publication' on stelai in the most prominent shrines. We can assume this amounted to wide publicity; how was this item then implemented? How could Zeuxis and his subordinates check on compliance, and how could they sanction disobedience? In Amyzon, the *epistates* of the Artemision could have enforced the order, or reminded the Amyzonians of it. But Amyzon (where the eponymy of Nikanor appears in 202 and 201) and Xanthos (where the eponymy appears in 196) were taken over by the Seleukids long after the original promulgation of the *prostagma*, which shows that a body of knowledge was kept alive among the administration.[140]

Another series of processes which can be explored in some detail relates to the office of 'high-priest of the sanctuaries' in cis-Tauric Asia Minor combined with the authority of ὁ ἐπὶ τῶν ἱερῶν.[141] As high-priest, Nikanor was meant to take care (alongside 'the other things') of 'the sacrifices', the regular schedule of offerings in the local shrines, presumably by dispensing royal subsidies and actually performing sacrifice, as a representative of the king's pious zeal; the royal subsidies to the Temple at Jerusalem, to finance local sacrifices, offer a parallel (*AJ* 12.140, 13.243; 2 Macc. 3: 2–3). As 'official in charge of the sanctuaries', Nikanor's brief was to administer 'the finances and the other matters'. Again, Jerusalem might provide a parallel: the Temple was in receipt of annual subsidies from Seleukos IV, for the purpose of sacrifices; the 'προστάτης appointed over the sanctuary', a Jew appointed to act as a local Seleukid official, reported to the governor of the satrapy that surplus from the subsidies was accumulating in the Temple treasury; the

---

[140] Prostagma: document **4**. Amyzon: **9, 10**. Xanthos: **23, 24**. The actual implementation may have been loose. In the Καρδάκων κώμη near Telmessos, a contract concluded in 193 (Segre 1938: 190, B, lines 1–2) would qualify for the eponymy of Nikanor, and, in addition, of the high-priest of Antiochos and his ancestors and of the priestess of Laodike; none of these appears on the contract. Unless the eponymy of these three officials had been abrogated, the Kardakes, in spite of being a 'military colony' probably founded by Antiochos III, did not bother to observe the regulations of three royal edicts, publicized on stelai in the most prominent shrines. On the other hand, Kadoos, priest of Apollo Pleurenos, when applying to Nikanor for permission to inscribe a list of the god's initiates, duly asked 'that I be allowed to set up a stele, having inscribed his (Nikanor's) name . . .' (document **49**).

[141] Document **4**, 29–40. There is no trace of an official in charge of shrines/sacred affairs in the relations between Seleukos II and Labraunda (Crampa 1969), perhaps because the office lapsed under Seleukos II, which would explain why Antiochos III referred to precedent under Antiochos II (document **4**, 40–1).

matter was investigated by the 'chief minister', Heliodoros, who went to inspect (ἐπίσκεψις) the Temple finances (but, the story goes, was prevented by supernatural visions: 2 Macc. 3: 2–13, with Bickerman 1985: 159–72). Menestratos, the *epistates* of the Artemision, may have technically been a subordinate of Nikanor, acting in the same capacity as the *prostates* of the Temple at Jerusalem. One documented action is the report filed by Demetrios, ὁ ἐπὶ τῶν ἱερῶν, to the *eklogistes* (above), probably a recommendation on the status of 'sacred villages' near Apollonia; as the Roberts observe, Demetrios seems to have enjoyed some authority in all things sacred, including, in this case a pair of villages dependent on a city (J. and L. Robert 1954: 296–7).

A final, intriguing, document, is important, first because it provides more specific evidence for the office ἐπὶ τῶν ἱερῶν and second because it confirms our impressions of Seleukid administration in general. This is the recently published list of the *mystai* of Apollo Pleurenos, in Lydia. Dating to Eumenes II, it mentions that the erection of the stele was authorized by the Seleukid official in charge of sacred matters, Nikanor (and later confirmed by Nikanor's successor under the Attalids, one Euthydemos).[142]

Memorandum to Euthydemos the high-priest from Kadoos, the long-standing priest of Apollo in Pleura: I earlier asked Nikanor, under Antiochos the king, for permission to put up in the shrine a stele on which I should record his name, and mine and that of the initiates (*mystai*), and now I ask you, if it seems appropriate to give that order, to write to Asklepiades the *oikonomos* to give me a place in which I may set up the stele on which I may record your name and mine and that of the initiates.

The affair thus mobilized the whole apparatus of administrative communication (complete with ὑπόμνημα and the 'order-to-give-orders', expressed by συντάσσω) between subject, high official, and subordinate officials—not once, but twice, first under the Seleukids, then under the Attalids—before selected parts of the dossier were published as authorization for the inscribed list. But the whole involvement of the imperial state is all the more striking because the matter, initiated by a memorandum from the priest of Apollo Pleurenos, seems purely local: the desire of the priest to put up a list of the *mystai*, for whatever reason (perhaps as a religious-ceremonial gesture, or to help control access to certain religious activities, restricted to initiates?). But why did Kadoos, the priest, involve the Seleukid and Attalid authorities? He did not merely follow the *prostagma* of 209, and, as he was required to do, take care to

---

[142] Document **49**.

mention Nikanor's high-priesthood in the heading of his document. Why did Kadoos feel the need, or obligation, to petition (ἀξιόω) Nikanor in the first place, for permission to erect a stele, listing the initiates of a local deity, in that deity's own shrine, and why did he ask Nikanor's successor to designate a place, still within the shrine, for the stele? The exact circumstances are still unclear; proximity to Sardeis, Nikanor's residence, may have subjected the shrine at Pleura to more intense forms of Seleukid control, or close scrutiny by Seleukid officials and hence to Kadoos' prudent request for permission; the issue of property may imply that this particular shrine was built on land somehow considered the king's own. It would be uncautious to build a general picture from this single piece of evidence, extrapolating to claim that the Seleukid state exercised tight control over the internal adminstration of every local shrine in the royal land. Nonetheless, the stele from Pleura illustrates one possible case, by attesting direct and close control, detailed involvement with the affairs of a local shrine, and a subject's need to obtain permission for a local gesture; all these aspects taking shape in bureaucratic communication both vertical and horizontal. It thus belongs to the body of evidence that implies, at least for certain parts of the Seleukid empire, an active, attentive administration endowed with strong capacities for control and involvement.

(d) Institutions as Rhetoric

When Antiochos III designated a high-priest and official over all the shrines of cis-Tauric Asia Minor, in reference to precedent 'under our grandfather', asked a hierarchy of subordinates to publicize the decision epigraphically, and required that the high-priest be included in the heading of all legal acts, he was issuing a complex message about imperial power. The proclaimed intention that Nikanor take care of sacrifices as high-priest and of shrine finances as ὁ ἐπὶ τῶν ἱερῶν proclaimed authority and legitimacy, and imposed on the immense landscape of Asia Minor, fragmented geographically and historically, the uniformity of imperial administration (Ch. 1 § 1). Analogously, the compulsory eponymy of Nikanor belonged to a set of institutions which imposed the Seleukid presence on the passage of time, now measured in the subject communities by Macedonian months and Seleukid years, but also by the slower beat, in years and decades, of kings ruling or officials' occupying their function (βασιλευόντων Ἀντιόχου καὶ Ἀντιόχου τοῦ υἱοῦ . . . ἐπ' ἀρχιερέως Νικάνορος), and the even broader scale of the Seleukid era, which covered over a century of Seleukid power by the time of

Antiochos III.[143] The imposition of a Seleukid conceptual geography and a Seleukid time are acts of symbolical violence, as real as the military violence which characterized the empire (whether actual violence during conquest, or the latent underpinning of control: previous section).

The Pamukçu stele does more than just publicize the Seleukid claims. It belongs to a whole genre of documents, where a royal order is not simply put up to inform the local communities of its content ('from now one everyone is to mention the name of Nikanor in contracts')—for that purpose, the form is cumbersome and less effective than a simple proclamation, πρόγραμμα (*AJ* 12.145–6). Rather, much of the ideological effect of the document resides in the fact that it is not directly addressed to the subjects: its effect is to display the mechanism of order transmission and implementation. The administrative dossier is not converted into a direct act of communication with the ruled, but simply displayed in monumental form: king speaks to official, official speaks of official, without ever consulting or addressing the party finally concerned, the shrines whose high priest Nikanor becomes and whose finances he will oversee, the individuals and communities which will preface their documents with Nikanor's name—local compliance on the part of *les administrés* is publicly taken for granted. The technology of government was also a rhetoric of power, and hierarchical communication functioned as performance or as narrative, celebrating the efficacy of orders and the overcoming of distance and time by the empire at work. The similarity of these documents was a further significant feature. L. Robert described the effect of comparing identical copies of the *prostagma* of 193 concerning cultic honours for Laodike, one found in Phrygia, two in Iran: 'Rien ne peut mieux faire sentir ce qu'était l'empire des Séleucides.'[144] The effect is compounded by the fact that this *prostagma* sets in motion the apparatus of administration to carry out the king's will to celebrate himself and his queen through cultic honours. The king's decision is motivated by the tender feelings (φιλοστοργία) which he receives from the queen and which he has for her. To proclaim these feelings, the king's letter mobilizes the imperial administration, thus demonstrating the patrimonial nature of the empire: the official display of family feelings and of a familial style makes clear the nature of the state, organized and described as a family business (πράγματα).

---

[143] Documents **9**, **10**. On the notion of Seleukid time, Sherwin-White in Sherwin-White and Kuhrt 1987: 27.

[144] Robert 1949: 8 (the second Iranian copy of the *prostagma* was published by Robert 1967).

Both this *prostagma* and the earlier one concerning Nikanor confronted the traveller with a repeated epigraphical narrative of Seleukid administration, exhibiting the same initial royal instruction concerning Nikanor and tracing the path of its implementation down local branches of Seleukid administration; unity of purpose spoke of a central power, the diversity of local agents gave an implicit yet vivid representation of the extension of the empire. Finally, the form of the epigraphical publication of adminstrative dossiers adds to their ideological force: the monumental form, in its permanence and its visibility, ensures the iteration of the royal speech-acts, and thus gives substance to the efficiency it claims for itself. The genre of the hierarchical dossier expresses the power to command: the classification of the landscape into administrative units, the enforcement of orders, the regulation of details; its rhetorical function is to make visible, or help to imagine, the structures of power.

The rhetoric of empire played its part in constructing a Seleukid space, within which individuals and communities were aware of the state. It comes as no surprise that Antiochos II and his subordinates should have distinguished between a Seleukid financial officer, ὁ οἰκονόμος, and the private manager of Laodike I, ὁ οἰκονομῶν τὰ Λαοδίκης (*RC* 18, line 24; *RC* 20, lines 4 and 6). The same distinction is made, however, by the peasants on the estate of Achaios the elder, in 269 (*I. Laodikeia am Lykos* 1): even if they spoke of Achaios as 'lord of the place' (enjoying full private ownership of his estate), the peasants could differentiate between institutions of the central state (the official dating by reign of the Seleukid kings, the eponymy of the local Seleukid governor) and their landlord's managers (ὁ τὰ Ἀχαιοῦ οἰκονομῶν, ἐκλογιστὴς τοῦ Ἀχαιοῦ).[145]

Awareness of empire among subjects took a more articulate form than mere taking notice. The obsession, common to rulers and ruled, with φιλάνθρωπα, privileges, grants, statuses, obtained through the mechanism of 'petition and response' (Millar 1992), is summarized by Zeuxis' letter to Kildara: 'the same things are granted to you as to all the others by the [great] king Antiochos'.[146] Zeuxis' phrase is based on assumptions about the nature of empire, as patrimonial state, the ruler's personal affair (πράγματα):

---

[145] Achaios the elder is not a 'dynast', though he is called κύριος τοῦ τόπου by his peasants, but the private owner of a large estate, like Ptolemaios in Koile-Syria: I assume that τόπος here designates this estate, whereas the same word, in the expression ἐπιμελητὴς τοῦ τόπου earlier in the same document, designates an administrative subdivision of the Seleukid empire.

[146] Document **25**, 2–5. The exact phrasing and translation are now obscure, but the generalising force of the sentence is clear.

Antiochos III justified the appointment of Nikanor in an egocentric language combining references to Nikanor's disposition towards the king, the king's feelings and convictions, his dynastic awareness, and his *bon plaisir*.[147] The Teians considered that they paid their taxes (*phoros, syntaxis*) directly to Attalos I, and owed such taxes to Antiochos III, and that it was Antiochos III (and Laodike) who had personally freed the city from tribute—as indeed he had, through a speech in the assembly.[148]

The implication was the Seleukid state's pervasiveness, except in those specific locations, areas, or periods, where it agreed to hold back, as a result of petition by the ruled and the benevolence of the ruler: this is obvious in the relation of the local communities with the royal economy, as in the cases of Herakleia or Sardeis (discussed above; both cities managed to obtain *ateleia* for the period of a festival).[149] It does not matter if exemptions were frequent: 'benefactions', φιλάνθρωπα, represented a system of government, based on the assumption that the conditions of the local communities' existence are the result of their relations with the ruling power.[150] This ideology of pervasive, accepted, imperial presence was a tool of domination in itself, for naturalizing empire, for constructing empire as the closing limit of the subjects' horizon—the ideology which Roman 'meddling' in 196–193 BC challenged from outside (Ch. 2 § 5). It found its expression in a system of legal statuses and in the assumptions underlying it; these can be studied in the case of the best-documented local communities, the *poleis* of Asia Minor.

3. City Statuses: The Typology of Subordination

The *polis* was a corporate body of citizens, organized in a decision-making community, structured by norms and essentially democratic institutions whose authority regulated the common life; by nature, the *polis* was a state.[151] It was many other things: a monumental

---

[147] Document **4**. For royal conviction (πέπεισμαι) as the proclaimed motive for action, Herrmann 1965a: 54.

[148] Patrimonial state: Weber 1968: iii. 1006–69; personal monarchy: Bikerman 1938: 7–17. Nikanor: document **4**. Teos and taxation: **17**, 19–20, 33–4, 48, (Antiochos' speech was held in the *bouleuterion*, 'the place in which he executed some favours and promised others', and hallowed by a nexus of ritual: **18**, 29–38).

[149] Documents **31** B, IV 5 (Herakleia); **3**, 10–12 (Sardeis).

[150] An illuminating parallel—because the situation is a direct descendant of the Hellenistic—is provided by the Roman empire: Millar 1992: 420–2 on the 'vocabulary of gifts' modulating the relations between ruler and ruled.

[151] Arist. *Pol.* 1252ᵃ: *polis* as κοινωνία, with e.g. Manville 1990: 35–54; Sakellariou 1989: 66–77, 159–211. W. Schuller, in Hansen 1993: 106–28: institutional analysis of the

urban centre and a territory; a descent group with its myths; a system of participatory rituals; a sense of place and of past, and hence an identity; a locus of human interaction, and hence a society.[152] But all these aspects were deeply politicized, and for the present purposes, the *polis* as state is what matters, especially in such institutional forms as the military control of territory, the raising of public monies, their management by accountable officials, and the mutual acknowledgement as *polis* by other *poleis*, linked in a 'multi-power-actor civilization'.[153]

Though not necessarily enjoying independence (an aspiration rather than a coterminous characteristic), the *polis* was self-governing and politically autarkic; 'allied' cities such as Euromos, but even subject cities such as Tabai or Amyzon, under direct Seleukid control (see below), possessed decision-making bodies, finances, military means.[154] The Hellenistic *poleis* kept their distinct political existence; it is a mistake to downscale them to 'towns . . . left to run themselves', as unremarkable a phenomenon in the Hellenistic world as in 'mediaeval England, middle America or the Soviet Union' (Green 1990: 198). One may contrast Ottoman Turkey: the landscape which had harboured the life of the Hellenistic *poleis* was subjected to state-fostered segmentation (Barkey 1994: 26–7, 40), with élites segmented from common people in a world without a civil society (in contrast to the powerful common identity of the *polis*), and town segmented from town (unlike the vibrant international life of the *poleis*). The comparison between Hellenistic Asia Minor and the Ottoman province of Aydın points out how the assumption that local communities should 'run themselves' is not natural, but a legacy from the *polis* and a reflection of the latter's values.

polis as state. Murray 1990: 21 on *polis* as expression of the common will. Hahn 1978: 20–2 for analysis of the 4th-cent. decree from Xanthos (on the 'trilingual stele'), exhibiting all the traits of the decision-making *polis*. See now Jonnes and Ricl 1997, for a village, Tyriaion, receiving a charter as a *polis* from Eumenes II: it will enjoy its own constitution and laws (ἴδιοι νόμοι).

[152] Beyond the state: J. Ober, in Hansen 1993: 129–60 (*polis* as society). On civic norms and identity, Heuss 1937: 247–8. Nicolet 1990: 5–6, on the *polis* as the world of politics, *par excellence*.

[153] Politicization: Murray 1990. Recognition by other *poleis*: Robert, *OMS* 1. 331, on the list of *theorodokoi* from Delphi, the register of official hosts for Delphian *theoroi* in every *polis*. 'Multi-power-actor civilization': Mann 1986: 76.

[154] *Polis* not necessarily independent: Welles 1956: 87; Hansen 1995. *Polis* as autarkic, if not necessarily sovereign: Veyne 1976: 106–10. Military: Euromos: document **30**, 3–8, the *kosmoi* have responsibility for military activities; Tabai has an army in 189, which gives trouble to Manlius Vulso and was probably not raised overnight after Magnesia (Liv. 38.13.11–12; likewise, Liv. 38.15.4, for army at Termessos in 189); Amyzon: J. and L. Robert 1983: nos. 20 and 23 for citizen army.

How did the *poleis* fit into the Hellenistic empires? The issue was raised in winter 197/6 by the stand-off between Antiochos III and the recalcitrant cities, Smyrna and Lampsakos (see Introduction); we can investigate it through the literary and documentary evidence, much of it Seleukid and especially from the time of Antiochos III, to study the hierarchy of legal structures which integrated the *poleis* into an empire, and aimed at their provincialization.

My position is at variance with the first important attempt at a systematic theory of the relation between city and ruler, proposed by A. Heuss (followed by Tarn and Magie).[155] Heuss held that the autarkic self-governance of the *polis* (which he correctly saw as essential to its nature) amounted to full sovereignty, which in purely legal terms, was not infringed by the Hellenistic kings, because it was, by definition, untouchable. Formally, the cities were allies of a king, and nothing more; all manifestations of the royal state were informal: royal garrisons, governors, taxation, did not affect the cities' sovereignty, because they were mere adjuncts to the cities' workings, helpful activities sanctioned by the community (as illustrated by the grateful civic decrees honouring these activities). For Heuss, the relation was never one of legal subordination, but of hegemonic alliance—even if, as Heuss is aware, the kings controlled the cities *de facto*.[156]

Heuss's theory has been disproved, most tellingly by Bickerman (one need not belabour the technical flaws in Heuss's arguments),[157] who demonstrated the existence of formal, legal structures, which shaped the relation between ruler and ruled, including the *poleis*. As noted earlier (§ 1), Bickerman's 'surrender and grant' model for the legal basis of subordination is substantiated by the literary and documentary evidence. Conquest of a local community was followed by the recreation of its status by royal grant, on terms of the conqueror's choosing: Antiochos III 'reacquired' (ἀνακτησά-

---

[155] Heuss 1937; Tarn 1948: ii. 199–227; Magie 1950: 56–7, 822–34 (where the view is restricted to 'real' Greek cities).

[156] Heuss insisted in a 1963 *Nachwort* that his theory bore exclusively on the legal relation between ruler and city (misunderstood by Green 1989: 183).

[157] Bikerman 1939 (also Orth 1977: 184–5, for *Kollisionen* between royal power and formal sovereignty of the cities, though some examples are debatable, such as his interpretation of royally sponsored 'foreign judges' as interference in civic autonomy). Versnel 1990: 74 and n. 123 attempts to resurrect Heuss's theory: 'Heuss's first thesis [no explicit legal structures] has not been disproved.' But Versnel misunderstands the force of Bikerman's objections and arguments; Bikerman adduces facts which point to legal (and not just political, de facto) relations. Technical flaws: Bikerman 1939; Robert in Holleaux 1942: 325 n. 1; J. and L. Robert 1954: 300 nn. 1, 6.

μενος) Iasos, but gave back its laws and liberty.[158] The nature of the transaction between city and ruler was the same as that between Antiochos III and the vassal kings of the East, to whom he granted the right to rule (Ch. 2 § 2 on e.g. Pol. 8.23, 11.34.9); it explains royal authority over the territory and even the existence of cities, some of which were abolished by a ruler's fiat, dissolved in royal foundations, or given to other cities.[159] The possible coincidence of *polis*-existence (local political autarky, acknowledgement as a *polis*) and of subordination is further proved by cases, Classical and Hellenistic, where cities subordinated other cities: fifth-century Thasos controlled cities on the coast opposite the island, Sinope in 400/399 'owned' the neighbouring city of Kotyora and levied tribute off it, and several cities in Hellenistic Crete exercised rights of domination, openly formalized in treaties, over other communities.[160]

Many *poleis* were simultaneously self-governing (the necessary condition for their political existence)[161] and subordinate to the king—precisely the situation which Heuss denied. They were self-governing, because the king by 'giving back' their constitution[162] or their laws had granted their continuing existence as political communities;[163] they were formally subordinate to a king, as we can tell

[158] Document **26** A, I 8–9. 'Giving back' does not imply that city liberty was inalienable, as Heuss or Magie held; only that the community had enjoyed liberty earlier.
[159] Authority over civic territory: Seleukid marking out of the territory of Aigai (Herrmann 1959, with Orth 1977: 169–70). Abolition of cities' existence: Antigonos Monophthalmos founded Antigoneia (later Alexandreia Troas) out of several *poleis* of the Troad (Billows 1990: 294–5). Robert 1951: 1–36, shows that the Seleukids recreated Kebren and Skepsis by detaching them from the new city. Lysimachos suppressed Kolophon and Lebedos to increase his foundation, Arsinoeia/Ephesos: J. and L. Robert 1989: 80–4 on Paus. 1.9.7 and 7.3.4–5. Cities given to other cities: Lysimachos gave several cities to Ilion (Strabo 13.1.26); Ilion received Rhoiteion and Gergis from Rome (Liv. 38.39.10).
[160] Thasos: Hdt. 7.109.2; 7.118; *ML* 89. Sinope: Xen. *Anab.* 5.5.7 with Austin and Vidal-Naquet 1972, proposing the term 'micro-empires' for such situations. Hellenistic Crete: Chaniotis 1996: 160–8.
[161] J. and L. Robert 1954: 301 n. 2: a city is not necessarily independent because it issues decrees—so do subordinate cities, if they are to be cities/*poleis*.
[162] Bengtson 1944: 141 and n. 4; 218 and n. 4; above, § 1.
[163] Alexander granted the freedom of the Lydians, the Euergetai, and the city of Nysa, yet subjected all of them to the authority of a satrap, and, in the case of the Lydians, to tribute (Arr. *Anab.* 1.17.4–7; 3.27.5; 5.2.2; also 7.20.1: plan to conquer the Arabs and to allow them to 'live according to their customs')—these grants probably correspond to the restoration of local self-governance. Antiochos III may have granted its ancestral constitution (π[άτριος πολιτεία], a restoration proposed by J. and L. Robert) to Amyzon (1983: no. 13, line 2). A clear case is Phokaia, which surrendered to the Romans in 190, and whose ancestral constitution (πάτριον πολίτευμα) and territory were restored in the aftermath (Liv. 37.32.14, Pol. 21.45.7); this is not a grant of autonomy (as to e.g. Herakleia), but merely the consent to the continued existence of the city as political community, albeit (probably) under Attalid subjection (Mastrocinque 1994: 452). The

from open signs of the king's legal authority and rights. Subordinate cities could be bought, sold, or given (Bikerman 1939: 341–2): Aigina, captured by the Romans, was given to the Aitolians, who sold it to Attalos I (Pol. 22.8.10); Antiochos IV gave Tarsos and Mallos to his mistress (2 Macc. 4: 30). Under Ptolemy II, the Telmessians uttered curses against whoever might ask for their city, their villages, or their land ἐν δωρεᾶι, and received reassurance that this would not happen (*SEG* 28.1224): the curses, directed against whoever should ask for the city as a δωρεά, imply the royal right to give a city, as he could dispose of villages or of portions of the civic territory; Ptolemy III exercised just this right, giving Telmessos to Ptolemaios, son of Lysimachos (*OGIS* 55). The implications of 'gift' status are spelled out by the confrontation between the Rhodians and the Lykians, who had been given to the former by Rome in 188: not hegemonic alliance (as the Lykians had hoped), but subordination (Pol. 22.5). The legal rights over a subordinate community, conceived in terms of ownership, were comparable to those of earlier Near-Eastern kings (and in fact descend from them). Laodike, when she described Antiochos III as 'reacquiring' Iasos, meant nothing less.

The most obvious form of domination was royal taxation, to support the 'royal economy' (§ 2*b*). Subordinate cities paid tribute, φόρος, φόροι—an obligation imposed on the cities, and which could only be lifted by a master's gracious decision. Alexander transferred the Ephesians' tribute to the benefit of the Artemision: the local shrine benefited, but the city was still burdened by a compulsory financial obligation which the ruler decided on (Arr. *Anab.* 1.17.10). Heuss's claim that tribute did not infringe the city's autonomy is unconvincing; we should rather see the φόροι as a formal marker of subjection, in the case of the subordinate cities as much as the dependent villages of the royal domain.[164] The royal economy also penetrated the civic sphere of the subordinate *poleis* through the forms of indirect taxation (listed in the previous section). Here, too,

transaction between Antiochos VII and Hyrkanos was similar: the king gave back the Jews' πάτριος πολιτεία, but also imposed heavy terms amounting to subjection (Jos. *AJ* 13.244–8).

[164] Heuss 1937: 106–13, argued that the imposition of tribute did not matter, because it was levied from the city *en bloc* and hence did not infringe the city's autonomous internal workings; and because there were many forms of direct taxation, some formally voluntary. But the first argument is irrelevant: internal autonomy is not equivalent to external independence (J. and L. Robert 1954: 300 n. 2); as for the second, to focus on the diversity of direct taxation (and on the formally voluntary contributions) does not diminish the fact that φόρος was imposed, legitimate, regular, and that the local community had no control.

Heuss's attempt to minimize the intrusion is unacceptable.[165] The indirect taxes raised by the imperial state created a parallel fiscality within the *polis*, over which it had no authority and which benefited a foreign body: hence a formula found in decrees of subordinate cities, granting 'exemption from the taxes of which the city is mistress', ἀτέλειαν πάντων ὧν ἡ πόλις κυρία—implying there were taxes the city did not control.[166] The link between royal finances and royal authority in the subordinate city is illustrated by the tax of one-twentieth, which Antiochos III added on to the civic tax at Sardeis, in winter 214/213. After recapturing the city from Achaios (Ch. 2 § 1), the king could impose a new tax in a subject city, or cancel it (as Antiochos did soon afterwards). The same conclusion emerges from an earlier document, the convention between Theangela and the dynast Eupolemos, who took the city over on terms, including the right to raise indirect taxes within the city (the inscription records a levy on beehives, as at Herakleia under Antiochos III).[167]

Royal taxation was synonymous with royal domination, to the point that the settlement of Asia by the Romans in 188 would define free cities as those exempt from paying tribute to anyone (below and Appendix 7). There are other manifestations of direct royal power within the city.[168] Some cities received permanent royal garrisons (§ 1), military forces answerable to the central power only—such as the cavalry detachment stationed at Apollonia under Salbake. A subordinate city might find itself under a royal governor (§ 2), formally appointed by the king with authority over the city, as for the governor of Alinda, named by Antiochos III;[169] the monumental

---

[165] Heuss 1937: 115–24, argued that indirect taxes raised by the kings did not infringe city autonomy, because cities also raised their own indirect taxes, so that royal taxes were but a 'geringe Modifizierung'—but such taxes were raised by an external power unanswerable to the city, and the taxes themselves lay outside the city's authority.

[166] Apollonia: document **44**, 30–1, with J. and L. Robert 1954: 298 and n. 9. Crampa 1972: no. 42, is quite explicit: this document from Labraunda, dating to the dynast Eupolemos but confirming an act of the satrap Pixodaros, mentions that a benefactor to the Plataseis is to enjoy immunity from local taxes, but will pay τὰ βασιλικ[ὰ] τέλη (lines 16–17). Corsaro 1985 for the notion of parallel royal and civic taxation systems.

[167] Sardeis tax: document **1**, 5–6. Eupolemos: Robert 1936: no. 52 (lines 4–5 for beehive tax). Herakleia: **31** B, III 5.

[168] Ptolemaic parallels: *PCZ* 59341 with Orrieux 1983: 53–4 (authority of Ptolemaic officials at Kalynda).

[169] Heuss 1937: 17–36, claimed that the royal governors were only military commanders with a tactical brief which happened to coincide with the physical location of a *polis*, or that (in formal terms) they were only auxiliary to the autonomous workings of the city. But the latter are compatible with the governor's formal authority over the city, as proved by documentary evidence: Holleaux 1942: 217–20 (*epistates* of Seleukeia in Pieria), *OGIS* 329 (Attalid governor of Aigina).

shrine of Amyzon, the Artemision, was administered by an official, appointed by Antiochos III. Seleukid officials appear as the recipients of honorific decrees (Ch. 4 § 2c), but this should not obscure the fact that they belonged to a power structure openly imposed on the local communities and not answerable to them.[170]

Two instances are particularly significant. Antiochos III owned property in Sardeis (a portico) as well as in other cities (§ 2b), an infringement of local autarky. In the Classical *polis*, property had been owned exclusively by the citizens, and exceptions were granted only by their collective decision; in contrast, some cities in the Hellenistic period lost the monopoly of authority over property rights within their urban centre—to the advantage of the king, their political master. Second, royal pronouncements often were directly performative inside the political space of the city, dictating actions or norms. For instance, in Attalid Aigina, the king issued both laws and *ad hoc* orders (προστάγματα) with the force of legal precedent, and recorded in the city archive, [τὸ δημ]όσιον;[171] in Seleukid Kolophon, the farming of the civic taxes was regulated κατὰ τὸ τοῦ βασιλέως διάγραμμα.[172] The *prostagma* issued by Antiochos III in 209 shows the immediate effect of the royal will: the king decided that the high-priest Nikanor would henceforth be named on all legal transactions, and Nikanor duly appears in decrees from Amyzon and Xanthos. However enforced, the king's decision, taken centrally and unaccountably, applied immediately at least in some *poleis*.

Direct intrusions by the central power resulted in restrictions on various aspects of the subordinate *poleis*. In some cases, city governors may have overseen meetings of the assembly, or vetted the content of proposals; in others, city decrees were subject to approval by the royal state.[173] Though the details are now lost, a Sardian document mentions an answer (ἡ περὶ τούτων ἀπόκρισις) of Zeuxis, concerning some civic matter (possibly his approval of an honorific decree).[174] Furthermore, the diplomatic life of some cities

---

[170] Alinda: document **9**. Artemision: **10**.

[171] *OGIS* 329, lines 13–15, with new reading from Gauthier 1993a: cases judged ἐπὶ τὰ καλῶς καὶ δικαίως νενομοθετημένα ἡμῖν ὑπὸ τῶ[ν βα]σιλέων κατά τε τὰ εἰς [τὸ δημ]όσιον κεχρηματισμένα π[ροσ]τάγματα καὶ τοὺς νόμους. Gauthier's new reading shows that the king's pronouncements had permanent legal force (43 n. 14, for the implications against Heuss who believed royal pronouncements were only advisory and temporary).

[172] de la Genière, *REG* 103 (1990), 105: lines 23–4 of yet unpublished inscription.

[173] Governors: Holleaux 1942: 199–254 on Seleukeia in Pieria under Seleukos IV (the phenomenon is not yet attested in Anatolia). Approval: Kearsley 1994 (Olbasa under Attalos II; reproduced as *SEG* 44.1108); Jonnes and Ricl 1997 (laws of the new *polis* of Tyriaion subject to approval by Eumenes II). An earlier example appears in the Xanthos trilingual stele, where the satrap is named as ultimate authority (Πιξόδαρος κύριος ἔστω: *SEG* 27.942, line 35).

[174] Document **40**. Robert 1964: 14 and n. 1, understands Zeuxis' ἀπόκρισις as a

was restricted. When needing 'foreign judges' from another city, Laodikeia under Lykos did not ask the Prienians directly, but sent an embassy to ask Zeuxis to write to the Prienians; only then did the Laodikeians send an embassy to Priene. Crowther suggests the same pattern might be deduced from decrees of Antiocheia on Maeander.[175] For certain cities, the royal state thus controlled, or interfered with full participation in the intra-poliad life. A striking instance of this is the declaration of Antiochos III, concerning acceptance of the Leukophryeneia of Magnesia on Maeander: γεγρά-φαμεν δὲ καὶ τοῖς ἐπὶ τῶν πραγμάτων τεταγμένοις, ὅπως καὶ αἱ πόλεις ἀκολούθως ἀποδέξωνται (RC 31, lines 25–8): the picture is not of cities recognizing a request from another city, but of subordinate cities receiving instructions through the administrative hierarchy of empire.[176] Finally, the Seleukid state may have controlled the movements of the citizens in the subordinate cities (J. and L. Robert 1983: 191), just as it did with the villagers of the royal land (§ 2).

It is unclear how far we can generalize from individual mani-festations of subordination. Local conditions were influenced by granted privileges, such as exemptions from taxes or *corvée* ('litur-gies'), as examined above (§ 2b). Another variation in formal status must have resulted from the grant of *asylia* ('inviolateness'): a shrine, or a city which had been 'consecrated' to a god, were declared immune from violent spoliation, in war or as forcible redress; under Antiochos III, Amyzon, Teos, Antiocheia/Alabanda, Xanthos were recognised as 'sacred and inviolate' among the cities of his kingdom. However, the administrative implications of *asylia*, partly a variation of internal status inside the Seleukid state, partly a matter of international diplomacy, are still obscure (it is not at all clear whether the status was mostly a matter of religion-based honour and distinction, or if it entailed practical privileges in matters of taxation or jurisdiction).[177]

decision obtained by the honorand of the decree. He also tentatively interprets the κρίσις mentioned later as 'la décision prise par ce décret'.

[175] Document **32**, with Crowther 1993: esp. 61–7. Antiocheia on Maeander: ibid. 64–7 and his appendix 3.

[176] Giovannini, *Ancient Macedonia* 2 (1977), 471–472 on the fact that the king spoke in the name of the subject cities when acknowledging an international request for *asylia*.

[177] Exemptions at Herakleia: document **31**. Asylia: **8, 16, 17, 18, 19, 22**; Appendix 2; Schlesinger 1933; Rigsby 1996. Administrative implications: Rostovtzeff, 1941: 844–5, suggested that *asylia* entailed 'privileges in respect of royal taxation' and possibly exemption from royal jurisdiction; however, Xanthos, consecrated by Antiochos III and declared *asylos*, prefaced its decrees with an imperial preamble, as did Amyzon (**22, 9, 10**), and the shrine at Amyzon, though *asylos*, was under a Seleukid official (**10**). Rigsby 1996: 13–25, comments on the difficulty in determining what practical advantages the status entailed. But *asylia* brought fiscal advantages in the Roman period: P. Herrmann, *Chiron* 19 (1989), 155–6.

Nonetheless, in spite of local variation, some broader patterns can be discerned. There seems to exist a formal marker defining categories within the subordinate cities: the 'regnal formula', imposed on the legal acts of some cities, now dated by the ruling king, various centrally defined eponymies, the Macedonian calendar. Under the Seleukids, the regnal formula turns up at Tabai, Apollonia under Salbake, Amyzon, Xanthos, indirectly at Sardeis—but not in Herakleia under Latmos, which was subordinate, as shown by the forms of royal taxation attested there (Herakleia dates decrees by local *stephanephoria* and by local calendar). Likewise, under the Ptolemies, Methymna, Amyzon, Telmessos, Lissa, and Xanthos prefaced decrees and local acts with a regnal formula[178]—but not Samos, even if the latter did, in its own words, belong to the king's πράγματα, a fact confirmed by Ptolemaic authority over civic finances and an administrative decision concerning the right of refuge in the Heraion.[179] The regnal formula implies that certain cities were part of the royal dominion, like the villages or the 'military colonies' in Seleukid and Attalid Lydia, while others were subordinate, yet not part of the royal land. Herakleia asked for exemption from duties on private imports 'from the (land) of the king into the city', implying that the city did not belong to the royal dominion proper.[180]

It thus seems there were (at least) two groups of subordinate *poleis*. One comprised the communities integrated in the royal dominion; these were the cities directly affected by Antiochos' pronouncements on the eponymy of the high-priest Nikanor (above) or on the state cult for Laodike.[181] We might call these communities 'cities in the χώρα', 'subject cities' (*cités sujettes*) or 'provincial cities' (*villes provinciales*);[182] apart from those where the regnal formula is

---

[178] Seleukids: Tabai, J. and L. Robert 1954: no. 3; Apollonia, ibid. no. 165; Amyzon, documents **9**, **10**; Xanthos, **23**, **24**; Sardeis, **2**, **7**, **12**. Herakleia, **31** B, II 3: the epigraphical publication of Zeuxis' letter is prefaced only with the local *stephanephoria*. Ptolemies: Methymna, *OGIS* 78; Amyzon, J. and L. Robert 1983: nos. 5, 6; Telmessos, *SEG* 28.1224, *OGIS* 55; Lissa, *OGIS* 57, 58; Xanthos, *SEG* 33.1183, 36.1218, 38.1476A, 36.1220. An example from Phanagoreia, a Bosporan subject city of Mithridates VI: *SEG* 41.625.

[179] Bagnall 1976: 82, on Habicht 1957: no. 64, lines 26–8 for 'restoration to the *pragmata* of king Ptolemy', *c*.200 BC; *OGIS* 41 for control of finances; Habicht 1957: no. 59 for Heraion. But there is no trace of regnal formula in Samian decrees under Ptolemaic domination: Schede 1919: nos. 9. 11, 12, 13; Habicht 1957: nos. 49, 52, 58, 61, 64.

[180] Regnal formulas in villages and colonies: *TAM* 5.2.881; *I. Laodikeia am Lykos* 1; *SEG* 40.1062, *TAM* 5.2.1307, *TAM* 5.1.221, *TAM* 5.2.1188, *SEG* 28.902, *TAM* 5.2.1190 (Attalid); Robert 1962: 76–8, for Attalid regnal year under Attalos II in a military colony at Sındırgı, in Mysia. Herakleia: document **31**, B III 8.

[181] J. and L. Robert 1954: 302 n. 6.

[182] The expression seems implied by *RC* 11, lines 21–22 (cities ἐν τῆι χώραι τε καὶ

attested (above), this category probably included many cities of Karia, Lykia, and the 'subject hinterland', and most of the royal foundations such as Laodikeia on Lykos.[183] The other group was made up of cities formally subordinate to the king, but not integrated within the royal land: for instance, Herakleia under Latmos under Antiochos III (and, indeed, under the Ptolemies), Samos under the Ptolemies, Aigina under the Attalids, Erythrai under Lysimachos or Demetrios Poliorketes (*RC* 15). The 'cities in the χώρα' were presumably exposed to more intrusive forms of control and direct contact with royal administration. However, it is difficult to tell whether this difference in forms actually reflects a systematic, explicit difference (I do not know what the Greek expression might have been for the second category of subordinate cities lying outside the *chora*). The significance of the observable differences is difficult to determine. The exact consequences, legal and practical, of the distinction between 'subject cities' and 'subordinate cities' are yet unclear, and the experience of both may have been similar: cities 'subordinate' and 'subject' could be ruled by a royal governor (*SEG* 2.536, Herakleia under Philip V; *OGIS* 329, Attalid Aigina). Magie 1950, 56–118 (esp. 56–65) and 822–33, revising Heuss's theory, argued that the freedom of all Greek cities was formally unalienable and respected as such by the kings; subordination, on this view, was restricted to 'the subject communities of the interior', no true Greek cities. This view is mistaken. First, there are clear cases of subordinate communities among the old Greek cities (e.g. Priene under Lysimachos).[184] Second, many communities of the interior were fully Hellenized and recognized as Greek (for instance, Xanthos was a 'Dorian' city and had a mythical kinship with Ilion), and conversely, Alabanda/Antiocheia which the Delphians considered only 'related to the Greeks',[185] was recognized as free by Antiochos III. Nonetheless, a difference between old Greek cities and Hellenized communities might be reflected in the distinction between subordinate cities on the one hand, and subject 'cities in the χώρα' along with new royal foundations on the other hand.

Beyond variations, local or typological, the different manifestations illustrate ways in which the Hellenistic empire could intrude on the political life of the *poleis* or restrict it, and hence give some

συμμαχίαι), though *RC* 12 only mentions 'cities in our alliance'. 'Subject cities': J. and L. Robert 1954: 302. 'Provincial cities': Bikerman 1934: 369.

[183] Document **32**, a decree from Laodikeia, does not show the regnal formula, but this may be explained by the document being inscribed in another city, autonomous Priene, where the preamble to the Laodikeian decree may have been left out.

[184] Orth 1977: 102–5, Franco 1993: 85; *contra*, Lund 1992: 207–8.

[185] Xanthos: document **23**, Curty 1995: 183–93. Alabanda: document **16**, 12–13.

idea of the situation of subordinate *poleis*, along a spectrum of possibilities. The consequence is the opposite of Heuss's conclusion: the existence of formally subordinate cities, whose condition was determined by their legal status. The evidence, compelling at the time of Bickerman's critique of Heuss (Bickerman 1939) is now overwhelming: it establishes that the Hellenistic kingdoms had legal structures (inherited, along with the 'regnal formula', from the Achaimenids and Alexander) to subordinate the autarkic *polis*, to intervene by ordnances and taxation within the sphere of the polis, or integrate it into the imperial state; all these, openly and (on the kingdoms' own terms) legitimately.[186]

The other category of the cities is, in the expression of an Amyzonian decree, αἱ αὐτόνομοι, 'the autonomous ones'; the abbreviation implies an institutionalized status.[187] These were the cities to which the king had granted or recognized not only their autarkic existence as political communities (as for the subordinate cities), but their full liberty: when Iasos was given back its liberty and its laws, its relation to Antiochos III was simply one of 'alliance and friendship'.[188] In formal terms, these cities were 'genuinely' independent. The settlement of Asia Minor by the Romans in 188 confirmed the freedom of the cities which had been free before the Roman–Seleukid War (Liv. 37.56.3–6 and Appendix 7): this concerned not only Chios or Smyrna (which were independent from any Hellenistic empire), but also Mylasa, Antiocheia/Alabanda, and even Antiocheia in Pisidia.[189] None of these landlocked cities had been freed by the Romans during the Roman–Seleukid War, as Herakleia had been by the Scipios: they owed their freedom to a royal grant, as we know for certain in the case of Mylasa, and as is almost certain for Antiocheia/Alabanda (its freedom had been recognized by Antiochos III). Antiocheia in Pisidia was declared free in 188 no doubt because the city had received a grant of freedom from Antiochos III (perhaps for services during the war against Achaios in 216?).[190] Formally, the freedom of Mylasa (by royal grant) was identical to that of any genuinely free city. This principle can be used

---

[186] Bengtson 1944: 132–142, argued that all cities lay outside the 'provincial administration' of the Hellenistic empires; the case of Apollonia under Salbake (document **44**) and the administrative enforcement of the *prostagma* of 209 indicate otherwise.

[187] Document **10**, 15 (assuming that the stonecutter has not omitted πόλεις).

[188] Document **26** A, I 5, 8–9. *RC* 71–2 for a late Seleukid grant of freedom to Seleukeia in Pieria.

[189] Mylasa: Pol. 21.45.4; Alabanda: Pol. 30.5.15, Liv. 43.6. Antiocheia in Pisidia: Strabo 12.8.14. Generally, Bikerman 1937.

[190] Alabanda: document **16**. Mylasa had received freedom from Seleukos II, a grant recognized by Philip V (Crampa 1969: no. 5, lines 33–6); it is probable that when Antiochos III took the city over, he confirmed the grant made by his father.

to postulate statuses where direct evidence is lacking. Iasos, free under Antiochos III, was probably free after 188 as well; the same applies to Euromos, which was not taken over by Antiochos III, but contracted a full-blown alliance with him through Zeuxis (below): it is likely that this city remained free after 188, rather than being given to the Rhodians.[191] Conversely, because Pedasa was free in the 180s (when it was synoikized into Miletos: *Inschr. Delphinion* 149), it probably was left 'free' by Antiochos III in 197.

This conclusion is confirmed by the terminology used to describe the freedom granted to a city by a king: it is the same as for a genuinely free city (for instance, one which had never known or escaped royal domination). Seleukos II 'granted to the Smyrnians that their city and their territory be free and exempt from tribute (ἐλευθέραν καὶ ἀφορολόγητον)', as a Delphian decree put it (*OGIS* 228, lines 6–8); in a slightly later decree, *OGIS* 229, the Smyrnians themselves described the king as 'preserving the autonomy and democracy (τὴν αὐτονομίαν καὶ δημοκρατίαν) for the demos' (lines 10–11), but also of 'the autonomy and democracy and the other things granted to the Smyrnians by king Seleukos' (lines 65–6). Under Antiochos III, Laodike described her husband as restoring liberty to the Iasians; a slightly later Iasian decree refers to him as 'preserving the democracy and autonomy ([τὴν δημοκρ]α[τ]ίαν καὶ αὐ[τ]ονομίαν)'; the democracy of Alabanda/Antiocheia was also preserved by Antiochos III, according to an Amphiktionic decree.[192] The three words, αὐτονομία, δημοκρατία, or ἐλευθερία, used interchangeably or in combination, designate fully free government:[193] they are used by truly independent states. For instance, the Lykians, after being freed from Rhodian domination, spoke of πάτριος δημοκρατία (*CIL* 1².725); Lampsakos used αὐτονομία and δημοκρατία to describe the independence it was trying to protect from Antiochos III (*I. Lampsakos* 4, lines 33–4, 73–5). The concept of αὐτονομία was not downgraded, in the Hellenistic period, to 'self-government combined with subordination to a superior power' (e.g. Hansen 1995: 41–2). The list of instances provided by Hansen to support this definition mingles examples of autonomy granted by a

---

[191] Iasos: document **26** A for freedom grant by Antiochos III; free after 188: Crowther 1995a: 232–3. Euromos: the Rhodian intervention in 167 (Pol. 30.5.11–15) does not necessarily mean that the city was Rhodian (it may simply have been an ally).

[192] Iasos: documents **26** A, I 8–9 and B, I 15–16; **28**, 2. Alabanda: **16**, 21–2.

[193] Ferrary 1988: 186 with earlier bibliography; Ferrary 1991: 564–5; Rhodes with Lewis 1997: 531–6. Musti 1966: 138–45, proposed that δημοκρατία retained its meaning of 'democracy' in the internal sense; but this is debatable: the Smyrnian decree *OGIS* 229, at lines 67–9 distinguishes between δημοκρατία (independence?) and ἰσονομία ('democracy'?). This is not the place to review the scholarship on αὐτονομία in the Classical age (survey in Hansen 1995).

ruler (for instance to Erythrai by Antiochos I or II, to Smyrna by Seleukos II) and cases of genuine freedom, like that of Lampsakos in *Syll.* 591; a fact which demonstrates how the terminology, and the concept, were the same for both groups.

The 'autonomous ones', such as Iasos or Mylasa, were free from the manifestations of direct royal control, such as tribute (and, probably, from royal indirect taxation) or garrisoning. Such phrases as 'free and exempt from tribute' 'free and exempt from garrisons' spell privileges out, rather than imply that a city could be free, yet pay tribute.[194] It is probable that the autonomous cities enjoyed their own jurisdiction, just as free cities in Roman Asia lived outside the governor's authority.[195] They conducted their own diplomacy freely. Iasos resorted to foreign judges from Priene, Myndos, and other cities in this period, without having to apply to Zeuxis first, as the subject city of Laodikeia on Lykos did (above); even if Antiochos III sponsored the Iasian appeal to foreign judges, he only supplied advice to the city (supplemented by an oracle), and did not control its diplomacy.[196] Priene, in the 190s, asked for Rhodian arbitration on its ancient dispute with Samos (*Inschr. Priene* 37), without referring to the Seleukid state; although many documents probably date to this period, there is no clear evidence for intrusion from the Seleukids.[197] 'Free' cities could also mint their own silver coinage, in the form of tetradrachms on the Attic standard, either 'alexanders' (patterned on Alexander's coinage, but distinguished by local marks) or civic designs: again, there is no formal difference between cities which had received a grant of freedom from a king and genuinely independent cities.[198] Alabanda/Antiocheia and Mylasa, both free cities (above), struck coins (autonomous civic issues in the first case, alexanders in the second) under Antiochos

---

[194] *Iasos* 2, line 30; *RC* 15, lines 22–3; *OGIS* 228, lines 7–8. That freedom and exemption from tribute are (or should be) synonymous emerges from a comparison of the Livian and the Polybian accounts of the Roman settlement of Asia Minor in 188: Liv. 37.56.4–6 and Pol. 21.24.6–9, 21.45.2–3.

[195] Ferrary 1991 on the Klaros decrees (J. and L. Robert 1989): the judicial independence of Kolophon was protected by the action of two citizens (Polemaios decree, lines II 51–61; Menippos decree, lines I 40–8, II 4–7 and esp. I 39–40: τῆς ἐπαρχείας ἀπὸ τῆς αὐτονομίας χωρισθείσης. On *I. Mylasa* 126, where Mylasa honours a royal judge, see Appendix 3 (probably not under Antiochos III as often said, but Ptolemaic).

[196] Crowther 1995b, dating documents mentioning foreign judges at Iasos to the 190s BC and relating them to *OGIS* 237 (document **28**).

[197] Prienian documents: Hiller von Gaertringen dates many to 'um 200?'; more impressive is the fact that there is no clear indication of Seleukid presence, apart from documents **32** and **33** (Zeuxis and grain).

[198] 1 Macc. 15: 6: Antiochos VII grants the Jews their full freedom and the right to mint coinage. Seyrig 1986: 104–6, for Arados, which struck alexanders starting 259/8, probably when the city was granted freedom by Antiochos II (otherwise unattested).

III.[199] Since, in this period, Skepsis and Side minted coinage on their autonomous designs, and Kolophon, Teos, Phaselis, Perge, and Side issued alexanders, these cities must have been 'free' as well (in the case of Teos, two fragmentary royal letters mention 'democracy' and 'liberty', perhaps documents granting liberty to the city).[200] Most of Heuss's proposals about the informal nature of the Hellenistic king's power over the city, mistaken in the case of the subordinate cities, might apply to the 'free' cities, whose constitutional integrity was formally respected by the royal state.[201]

But even the 'autonomous ones' were *de facto* exposed to the demands of the ruling power. Iasos was a 'free' city under Antiochos III; nonetheless, during the Roman–Seleukid War, the king installed a garrison in the city (Liv. 37.17.3)—a temporary φυλακή rather than a permanent φρουρά, but a garrison nonetheless, imposed at the king's desire; if Perge was a free city, as suggested by its coinage, the garrison which appears there in 188 (Pol. 21.41.1–5) was probably of the same temporary nature (though Polybios calls its commander a φρούραρχος), and further illustrates Seleukid power over the 'autonomous ones'. Parallels substantiate this picture. An earlier document from Iasos (*I. Iasos* 3) seems to imply that an official of Ptolemy I had considered taking over the local πρόσοδοι, the civic taxes, including the harbour dues; that the Iasians made him swear an oath not to do so betrays their anxiety, and illustrates the threat of erosion to a free city's 'liberty'. The same document also shows how a 'free' city could be made to pay contributions, in the form of a 'contribution', σύνταξις, exacted from Iasos, at a level fixed by the king, and, it seems, as payment towards Ptolemaic protection of Iasian territory.[202] The εἰσφοραί paid by the 'free' Islanders under Ptolemy II fall in the same category (*Syll.* 390, line 16). Royal instructions to free cities, though formulated as requests, did not admit disobedience: Larisa, like all other Thessalian cities (Pol. 4.76.3), was free; yet Philip V decided (κρίνω) that the city

[199] Alabanda: Le Rider 1973/4: 256–7; Robert 1973: 448–53; Waggoner 1989. Mylasa: Akarca 1959: 13.

[200] Skepsis: Kagan 1984 for Skepsian autonomous coinage dated to Antiochos III on stylistic grounds; the conclusion is that Skepsis was free under Antiochos III. Strabo 13.1.54 mentions that Skepsis was 'under the Attalic kings' in the second century: if this means that the city was formally subordinate to the Attalids, the city was given to Eumenes II in 188 because it had earlier been subject to the Attalids (Appendix 7). Side: Seyrig 1986: 61–6. Kolophon: Le Rider 1972/3: 254–5, Price 1991: 248; Teos: Le Rider 1972/3, 255–6, Price 1991: 298; document **19** B, C. Phaselis and Perge: Seyrig 1986: 42–52, Price 1991: 349, 358. The details of civic coinage and status are not fully established (Robert 1973: 463), and the whole issue needs re-examination.

[201] Bikerman 1938: 133, 141–5 on the life of the 'villes franches' (indebted to Heuss 1937).

[202] *I. Iasos* 3, lines 4–5, 7–9, 14–15.

should admit all its metics to citizenship: he communicated his decision to Larisa in a short letter, and when the Larisans dissented, he enforced his will through a second letter (*Syll.* 543 with Bertrand 1990: 111–12). Finally, free cities may have introduced changes to their institutions under Seleukid influence or suggestion. It is likely that the constitutional changes introduced in Euromos after 197 (and somehow Cretan-inspired) took place under Seleukid influence; at least, this is suggested by the introduction of a civic priesthood of Diktynna and Zeus Kretagenetas, mirroring a centrally administered, Seleukid, priesthood (named in the 'regnal formula' in subject Amyzon): this new priesthood was attached to the *stephanephoria*, presumably a traditional magistracy in the city. Both the creation of new offices, and the addition of a new priestly office to an older form, suggest extensive reorganization of public affairs in the city of Euromos. Mylasa also had a priesthood of Zeus Kretagenes associated with the Kouretes (attested from the second century onwards): this civic priesthood could have been introduced at the time of Antiochos III under Seleukid influence or in imitation of Seleukid provincial institutions. Both Euromos and Mylasa provide suggestive (though not yet conclusive) evidence for the effect royal power, or simply the proximity of royal institutions, could have within a formally 'free' city.[203]

More significant still than the presence of *de facto* encroachments by the Seleukid state on the independence of the 'autonomous cities' is the fact that the freedom enjoyed by the latter was openly and essentially precarious. Their freedom, though nominally equivalent to the full freedom of genuinely independent cities like Smyrna or Lampsakos *c*.200, was in fact considered by the king as still dependent on his goodwill: in the 'surrender and grant' model, even full freedom is a status, a privilege allowed by the ruling power and revocable by it. Cities which had received their freedom by royal grant could lose it by royal *fiat* (Bikerman 1938: 138). There is a clear parallel in the grant of full freedom to the Jews by Antiochos VII, revoked once the king no longer needed their help (1 Macc. 15: 3–9 and 27, Jos. *AJ* 13.245–6). Though there are yet no documented instances in Hellenistic Asia Minor of 'autonomous' cities being deprived of their liberty, the possibility seems strongly implied by Antiochos' claim that the cities of Asia should receive and enjoy

---

[203] Euromos: document **30**, and introduction: the document is too fragmentary to reveal the role played by the Seleukid state in the constitutional changes. Mylasa: J. and L. Robert 1983: 166; *I. Mylasa* 102, 107, 806 (all 2nd-cent. BC). Why the Seleukids imposed or inspired institutions imitating Cretan practices is still obscure (short note by Gauthier in *BE* 95, 525).

their liberty as a gift from him, litterally 'through his grace', διὰ τῆς αὐτοῦ χάριτος (Pol. 18.51.9). The Seleukid empire, like all Hellenistic kingdoms, posited itself as a space within which even full freedom was a function of dependency on the king's power to decide and define.

The typology of statuses has obvious implications for the nature of the relations between ruler and city, and in general for the Hellenistic *polis*. However, before setting these out, we should examine problems with Bickerman's 'surrender and grant' model. First, it is clear that some cities did contract alliances with a king (a possibility Bickerman considered purely theoretical: Bikerman 1938: 140). Lysimacheia concluded an alliance with Antiochos I or II,[204] and later with Philip V, and Philippeis/Euromos with Antiochos III.[205] What survives of these alliances shows that the form was the same as any alliance between two free states. Nonetheless, Polybios has Philip admitting to taking over (προσλαμβάνειν) Lysimacheia (Pol. 18.4.5), and installing troops in the city (Pol. 18.3.11), whilst claiming that his soldiers were not a permanent garrison, but a temporary protection against the Thracians (Pol. 18.4.6). The experience of Euromos and Antiochos III was no doubt similar to that of Lysimacheia with Philip V. These cases point to an alternative legal model: a full alliance between city and ruler, followed by *de facto* encroachments on civic autonomy, because of the ruler's political power over the city (did these encroachments lead to a change in formal status?). This process is in fact described by Polybios as the shift in kings' conduct, from συμμαχικῶς to δεσποτικῶς (Pol. 15.24.4). In the end, there may have been little practical difference for cities which had entered royal control through 'surrender and grant', and those which had contracted an alliance with a king who enjoyed *de facto* control.

Second, the state and the nature of the evidence might make us uneasy with a smooth, systematic picture, such as the one I have developed in this section, based on Bickerman's 'surrender and grant' model. The better documented cases (Mylasa, Iasos, Alabanda) corroborate Bickerman, through what is explicitly known, and through what the evidence implies. In other cases, we are reduced to speculation inspired by Bickerman's model (as for Teos: above). There are anomalies in the evidence: for instance, the

[204] *Ilion* 45 with Appendix 3. The argument for attribution to Antiochos I or II rather than Antiochos III is that the provisions in the treaty are incompatible with the way Antiochos III treated the Lysimacheians (Gauthier and Ferrary 1981)—unless one assumes that such provisions were blatantly violated.

[205] Lysimacheia and Philip V: *Staatsvertr.* 549. Euromos and Antiochos III: document **29**. See also document **35**, Perinthos and Antiochos III.

Seleukid garrison at Perge (which struck its own coinage), which was perhaps a temporary φυλακή (above). Ephesos under the early Seleukids poses similar difficulties: the city struck silver coinage, yet was a royal residence under Antiochos II, and, in 246, an official ἐπὶ τῆς Ἐφέσου is attested by Phylarchos (*FGrHist* 81 F 24). One might argue that the status of the city changed under Antiochos II; that royal sojourns at Ephesos do not make the city subject; that the official attested in 246 was in charge of a temporary garrison. In any case, the Ephesians participated in a decree of the Ionians honouring Antiochos I and asking him to preserve the liberty and the democracy of the Ionian cities (*OGIS* 222), a clear indication that Ephesos was formally an 'autonomous' city, at least at that moment.[206] For now, the anomalies can still be explained away, or at any rate do not seriously impair the usefulness of Bickerman's model.

Third, the language is ambiguous. I have tried to distinguish two groups, of different status: subordinate or subject cities (enjoying local autonomy), and 'autonomous' cities (*de facto* under the control of an autocratic power): yet the language of self-government, 'own laws' and possibly even liberty could apply to both cases.[207] Conversely, the language of enslavement could be used to describe both, irrespective of legal status. Flamininus did so at Rome in the negotiations of 193 (Liv. 34.58.8–59.1); the Iasian exiles described the Seleukid control of Iasos, the 'free' city, as enslavement (Liv. 37.17.6). One wonders if the 'servitude' from which the Iasians claimed to have been freed by Antiochos III was not the *de facto* control compatible with a formal status of 'freedom' under Philip V. The language of liberation was indefinitely repeatable to describe the end of *de facto* power over a community; the 'propagandistic' use of the concept of freedom and liberation as a slogan is well documented, especially during the time of the Diadochoi (Gruen 1986: 133–42). In 197, the Rhodians claimed to be protecting the

[206] Coinage: Le Rider 1972/3: 245–6. Antiochos II at Ephesos: *SEG* 1.366, line 10. It is perverse to argue, with Orth 1977: 130, that *OGIS* 222 actually proves Ephesian subjection, because of their anxiety. Nonetheless, it is difficult to believe that Ephesos, an important naval base, endowed with powerful fortifications, was not used by Seleukid forces under Antiochos I: how was this compatible with full autonomy? Another problem is the coexistence of a royal mint (striking royal coin) and local silver coinage at Kyme (Le Rider 1975/6: 355–6), or in Attalid Ephesos (Le Rider 1972/3: 247).

[207] The inhabitants of Kaudos were integrated into Gortyn, to which they paid tribute and were liable to various obligations, yet preserved some form of self-government, described as permission to remain 'free and autonomous': *Iscr. Cret.* 4.184. *I. Erythrai* 29 honours the *strategoi* for preserving the *demokratia* and passing the city as free to their successors: if this inscription were dated before *RC* 15 (when Antiochos I or II declared the city free), it would show the terminology of liberty used internally in a subordinate city.

liberty of Ptolemaic cities (Liv. 33.20.11–12)—in fact subordinate communities, under direct control by the Ptolemaic state.[208]

The question is whether these difficulties with the concept, the evidence, and the ambiguous language seriously challenge the juridical model proposed by Bickerman. For Versnel (1990), the undoubted ambiguities in language and occasionally in practice mean that the whole situation was confused and fraught with the inconsistent 'double realities' of full autonomy and full subjection. This view must be rejected, because it is based on uncritical acceptance of Heuss's thesis, neglecting the documented cases that establish the existence of legal concepts about subordination and 'freedom' within an imperial space, even in the absence of a code of international law. Although the terms used for these concepts could be used vaguely or in reference to a number of other things, the fact remains that, in certain contexts, αὐτονομία or ἐλευθερία were as clearly defined as ἀφορολογησία or ἀνεπισταθμεία, with consequences as real—because they were concepts of the same nature, royally defined privileges within Bickerman's model which is still the most satisfactory account of the formal basis for empire.

If we accept as historically documented Bickerman's model for a typology of legally defined statuses, underpinning the relations between rulers and ruled, there still remains the question of the signficance we should lend to this phenomenon. One view on the legal statuses holds that they were unimportant, because the king could overturn them at any time, and wielded overwhelming power, only thinly veiled by propaganda such as the language of liberty (A. H. M. Jones 1940: 102). At its most extreme, this view denies any substance to legal statuses—meaningless, *ad hoc* smoke screens for the realities of power, the oppressiveness of the kings, the despairing servility and powerlessness of the cities; the historian need not bother to distinguish between statuses or explore their content, but focus on the grim facts.[209]

Orth's position, a reaction against the excessive legalism of Heuss, is problematic for several reasons. The 'harsh realist' model is based on the assumption of constant, overwhelming power on the part of the kings. This assumption is questionable because of the instability of politics in the multipolar Hellenistic world. Especially in western Asia Minor, the situation was more complicated than Orth's melodrama of royal oppression and local powerlessness (Ch. 1 § 4), which cannot accommodate the cases of Smyrna or Lampsakos: these cities, under Seleukid control for fifty-odd years,

---

[208] Bagnall 1976: 81–8, 94–9.
[209] Orth 1977: *passim* and 178–87; Piejko 1988b; Green 1990: 198.

seized their chance in the 230s or the 220s BC, and later retained their liberty. Furthermore, many of the readings Orth offers for central documents are either mishandled, as in the case of his interpretations of the (routine) implementation of Prienian honours for the Seleukid officer Larichos, or brutally reductive, as in the case of his interpretation of the early Seleukid documents from Ilion. It is impossible to follow Orth when he reads *OGIS* 219 as permeated with the city's *Unfreiheit* and fear, or *RC* 10–13 as proof of the city's servility and powerlessness, and hence of his claim that Ilion's formal status of autonomy was meaningless.[210] *OGIS* 219 is not about powerlessness, but combines various idioms in a complex discourse: diplomatic congratulation (a widespread phenomenon analysed in *RC*, p. 43), euergetic honours, moralizing praise for the king (alternating between descriptions of the king as patrimonial ruler and as protector of the cities: further Ch. 4). The transaction in *RC* 10–13 involved Ilion's interest—the attachment of a privately owned estate (taken out of the royal land) to the city's territory. The problematic nature of Orth's readings casts doubts on the validity of the 'harsh realist' model in its extreme version.[211]

Moreover, it is clear that legal statuses played an important, but complex, part in the relationship between Hellenistic ruler and Hellenistic city: first, they gave the imperial state the concrete and diverse local forms which the cities would experience, and hence were taken seriously by both sides; second, the typology of statuses, as a system of classification and a totalizing ideology, was in itself a tool for domination, which multiplied the actual force of the Hellenistic empire. By neglecting these two related effects, the 'realist' approach championed by Orth and others is far too crude when it comes to representing the experience and practice of domination by the Hellenistic imperial states.

Legal statuses were expected to have legal force, even if they were precarious grants from an autocratic master. A letter from Olympichos to Mylasa, dated *c*.220, announces that he is restoring to the city the fort of Petra near Labraunda 'which we had been forced to hold on to for no other reason than that this was useful to the city' (Crampa 1969: no. 4, lines 10–13). Mylasa had been a free city since the late 240s, and Olympichos (or the Antigonid state) had no right to garrison a fort on Mylasan territory. However, Olympichos occupied Petra for possibly two decades (we do not

---

[210] Larichos: Gauthier 1980; Orth 1977: 50–61 (approved by Versnel 1990: 78–9).

[211] See also Chaniotis 1993: after the Ptolemaic reconquest of Kilikia *c*.246 BC, the governor had to take diplomatic precautions to save face for Nagidos and Arsinoe, the Ptolemaic foundation absorbed by Nagidos under Antiochos II.

know when occupation started). Olympichos' action might be taken to prove the arbitrary power of a Hellenistic empire. But as long as the priest at Labraunda tried to obtain his independence from Mylasa, rights over the fort were moot; once it was established that Labraunda and the region belonged to Mylasa, and the legal situation became clear, blatant illegality was impossible. Olympichos had to give in to Mylasa's demands, vacating Petra. Tellingly, he even felt the need to present an apology or justification for his actions, claiming that he had occupied the fort only to defend the city, and admitting that he had no other right to be there; this constitutes a remarkable admission to the force of legal argument and hence the reality of legal forms in shaping behaviour and realities.

Statuses mattered because they shaped the forms empire took on the ground. A sign of their importance is the energy put by the cities into the process of negotiating them; Millar's remarks on the practical importance of missions from the cities to the Roman emperor are applicable to Hellenistic diplomacy.[212] The statuses and privileges embodied the local bargains, compromises, and precedents which formalised the relations between ruler and ruled; such arrangements, a standard feature of patrimonial empires, are more important than physical compulsion in creating the conditions for the cooperation of the ruled, notably the crucial consent to surplus extraction (Weber 1968: 1010–11). A striking example, though outside the world of the Greek *polis*, comes from Hyrkania, where the peasantry probably had Antiochos III acknowledge privileges dating back to the Achaimenids (Pol. 10.28 with Briant 1982: 499–500). Under Antiochos III, the Sardians successfully appealed to general practice in other cities to ask the king to waive his rent on a portico. In their petitions to Zeuxis, the Herakleians justified several demands by appeal to precedent. At Herakleia, when the Seleukid state took over the local harbour due, the Herakleians asked that the king should still pay to the city a share of the revenue, for oil in the gymnasion, as had been the custom of those who farmed out the harbour tax; they also requested that a festival be exempt from taxation, as it had been previously. Zeuxis and Antiochos agreed, inflecting the 'royal economy' to fit local tradition.[213] These examples underline the concreteness of legal status

---

[212] Millar 1992: 418, 420; Millar 1967: 81–2 for the importance of local status for 'the nature of a man's contacts with the State'; Millar 1983.

[213] Document **31** B, III 2–4; IV 6–7. The Herakleian practice, public services paid for by tax-farmers, is amply paralleled in Kos, where the tax-farmers who contracted out a variety of indirect taxes were expected to furnish a public sacrifice and tents for the subsequent feast: *Syll*. 1000.

and precedent, their importance for the local communities, and the
expectation that the ruling power would respect its commitments.[214]

This expectation—admittedly alongside the fear that the commitments might be forgotten or overturned—appears in frequent documents where the local communities attempt to bind their political
masters by the exchange of oaths or the publication of agreements
(for instance Robert 1936: no. 52, lines 27–9: Eupolemos swears to
let the Theangelians put up a stele publicizing the settlement). Iasos
exacted oaths from Ptolemy I and his officials; the liberty of the
city was included in these oaths as an essential condition for the cooperation between city and ruler; conversely, the Ptolemaic official
asked an Iasian embassy for guarantees (πίστιν δοῦναι) that their
claim concerning an earlier grant of autonomy was genuine (*I. Iasos*
2, 3). Likewise, Olympichos swore an oath to enforce the Mylasan
rights over Labraunda, which he eventually fulfilled, when the
Mylasans made Philip V remind Olympichos of his engagements
(Crampa 1969: nos. 3, 7). Beyond the procrastination in this particular case, what matters is the fact that the ruling power was
bound by its commitments and by local privileges. Admittedly, the
possibility always existed that a Hellenistic king would not keep his
commitments. In 201, the Thasians surrendered to Philip V on
terms: exemption from garrisoning, tribute, billeting, and the use of
their own laws (full autonomy or local self-government?); the conditions were seemingly accepted by Philip's general, but the city was
then 'enslaved' by Philip (Pol. 15.24.1–3). Yet this disregard for
agreements was anomalous, and perceived as scandalous; Philip's
reputation for untrustworthiness explains the difficulties he met in
his Aegean ventures, and the fragility of his Aegean dominions (Ch.
2 § 3), is an illustration of Arendt's basic insight that pure violence
does not constitute power (Arendt 1970): even if violence is a
visible and immediately effective way of making others do your will,
in the long run, violence is not enough to inaugurate lasting power,
since in itself it will not create consent or collaboration (which, in
Arendt's more controversial development of her theory, are the sole
constituents of power). The case of Philip V only shows how the
system of statuses and privileges embodied commitments on the
part of the Hellenistic ruler, and expectancies on the part of
the ruled.

Nonetheless, the fact that the legal statuses represented concrete,
widely publicized commitments on the part of the Hellenistic king
should not obscure the ideological function these statuses played

---

[214] Documents **3**, 8–10; **5**, 5.

within the structures of imperial power. The existence of a scale of statuses strengthened the hold of an empire over the local communities. By allowing itself to be constrained or petitioned into giving privileges (that is, lessening demands), the empire of domination channelled the energies of the ruled into petition rather than resistance or defection, into improving the immediate situation rather than challenging the framework of imperial authority. An early example appears in the oath the Athenians imposed on the Chalkidians c.446 BC: 'I will pay to the Athenians the tribute (to the amount) which I will convince the Athenians' (*ML* 52, lines 25–7), the Athenians' open willingness to negotiate on the tribute drawing attention away from the assumption that the tribute was permanent. Negotiated statuses and the gradation of privileges acted as a system exercising repressive tolerance: concessions strengthened the framework, by creating a dialogue based on the assumption of the ruling power's legitimacy and by making it seem benevolent. The granting of privileges and the respect of legal statuses by the ruling power made the subjects accept the broader framework of legitimacy, which assumed that the king had the right to define such privileges and statuses (see further Ch. 4 § 5). Most of the privileges granted by the Hellenistic kings exemplify this phenomenon: for instance, the extensive roster of privileges and exemptions so readily granted by Zeuxis and Antiochos III to Herakleia, and especially their willingness to follow local custom when levying a harbour-due, presumably made the Herakleians accept the exaction of such taxes as fair and legitimate.[215]

Local statuses inscribed the cities in the ideology of the patrimonial empire (§ 2*d*), since by nature they are based on the assumption that the king holds the monopoly of performative utterances within the state; statuses are defined by his pronouncements, and can be represented as his benefactions. This is the ideology which underlies the system of statuses and privileges which the Seleukids (and other Hellenistic empires) used to classify and organize their subject communities. The ancient imperial ideology is unwittingly reflected in a modern list of royal benefactions: military defence, freedom, democracy, cash, buildings, land, privileges such as *asylia* or *ateleia* (Bringmann 1993: 9)—the king's refraining from exactions is described with the same vocabulary as an actual gift. The city's political existence not only is determined by the ruler, but can be represented as the sum of the privileges which it enjoys by the ruler's grace—as reflected in the language describing this

---

[215] Document **31**; other examples: **19** (Antiochos III and Teos), *RC* 15 (Antiochos I or II and Erythrai).

situation, τὰ ὑπάρχοντα (that which a city 'has' from its ruler), τὰ προϋπάρχοντα (that which a city has enjoyed from earlier times, under the present ruler's predecessors), τὰ δίκαια, τὰ φιλάνθρωπα, τὰ συγκεχωρημένα;[216] the underlying structure was the same for a subject city (a Hellenized city or a royal foundation) or for a 'free' old Greek city, which justifies treating both categories together.

As seen above, the Hellenistic kings considered even full freedom as the result of royal benefaction. This may have been stated explicitly in a royal letter to Teos, where ἐλευθερία is mentioned alongside φιλάνθρωπα, and possibly assimilated to the latter category.[217] The typology of statuses gave meaning to the *de facto* relation of force between king and city; it closed the local community's horizons to anything outside the imperial space, where the limit was a status of 'full freedom' by grant and on the condition of the ruler's continued goodwill. This totalizing ideology, with its classification system of statuses, its assumption that the king held the right to define these statuses, its resort to repressive tolerance to achieve acceptability, assigned the local communities a place in the world, or in a world which this ideology created. A symptom of this ideology at work might be found in the treatment of *asylia* for cities inside a Hellenistic kingdom The word *asylia* designates a state of freedom from spoliation or reprisals, concomitant with the designation of a place as sacred to a deity; this state, traditionally, could only result from acknowledgement by the international community. Yet it seems that *asylia* (and not just the consecration to a god which enabled *asylia*) could also be the result of a royal grant, a privilege given by the king just like tax-exemption or freedom from billeting (even though this *status* then had to be publicized outside the kingdom by the old method of international canvassing): this was probably the case at Teos.[218] Within the imperial space of graduated statuses and granted privileges, it seems that *asylia* was considered, by a fiction or a distortion of the nature of *asylia*, as just another

---

[216] *I. Erythrai* 30, line 5; *RC* 22, lines 16–17; *RC* 38, line 5; *RC* 42, lines 3–7; document **19** C, 4–7; **25**, 2–6; **44**, 14–16; J. and L. Robert 1983: no. 22, lines 4–9; *RC* 48, lines A 5–6, B 22–3. On freedom as benefaction, Hahn 1978: 23–4. A strict parallel is the usage in Ptolemaic Egypt, where φιλάνθρωπον (act of generosity) describes grants from the king, as pointed out by Lenger 1953: 495–6: 'des allègements de charges fiscales, des amnisties, des privilèges juridictionnels, des droits d'asile, des immunités, des garanties contre les actions arbitraires, des titres de protection de la personne et des biens'.

[217] Document **19** C, 5–6 ([τἆλλα] φιλάνθρωπα proposed by Herrmann).

[218] On the institutional issues of *asylia*, Appendix 2 and Rigsby 1996. Teos: document **17** and Appendix 2. A parallel might be the royal grants of *asylia* in Ptolemaic Egypt (though the meaning seems to be different, closer to the modern 'asylum'); the material is gathered in *C. Ord. Ptol.*, with J. Bingen, in L. Criscuolo, G. Geraci (edd.), *Egitto e storia antica dall'ellenismo all'età araba* . . . (Bologna, 1989), 24–30.

royally granted privilege, because all statuses must originate with a performative speech act by the king.

This ideology, based on *de facto* power, was an instrument of domination, offering forms for the integration of the *polis* within an imperial space and mediating imperial presence over and within the *polis*: the ideological resources for the constitution of a supra-*polis* state without having to dissolve the local communities in a fully constituted territorial state. The forms (statuses, privileges) played a more important role in maintaining control than the presence of 'factions' (often proposed as the main means of control over cities, in spite of the poor evidence).[219] The typology of statuses reflects the trend towards the provincialization of the *polis*, the conversion from free state to community dependent on grants and privileges, the typology is itself a powerful tool for bringing this trend to pass. This state of affairs would become generalized under Roman domination, when a city must resort to petition as a matter of course, the emperor spoke the royal language of liberty-as-gift and annulled liberty by *fiat*.[220]

Smyrna and Lampsakos rejected this model in 196, and their resistance was ideological as well as military (Liv. 33.38.1–7). These cities refused to give in to the offer of a grant of liberty (unlike Mylasa or Alabanda, in 203, which probably did surrender to Antiochos III on condition of such a grant). Their resistance serves as a reminder that the provincialization of the *polis* in the Hellenistic period was not a foregone conclusion, but was matched by rapid deprovincialization, both before Antiochos III (Ch. 1 § 4) and afterwards, especially in Judaea and Phoenicia; the genuinely free city would long remain a reality. The Smyrnian and Lampsakene recalcitrance also points out, even as it contests, the logic underlying the Seleukid model, and its functions: classification of the ruled within the cage of imperial space, where the ultimate privilege was 'autonomy' by royal grant; the fostering of consent; the monopoly of legitimacy, grounded in a Seleukid past, the recalcitrant cities'

---

[219] Factions: Bikerman 1938: 145–7. The evidence is mostly wartime (e.g. Liv. 37.9.1–4, 37.11.15, Pol. 21.6.4–6; Liv. 37.17.5), when underlying issues were exacerbated and factions could betray the city to the power they favoured; in peacetime, the 'factions' may have been restricted to a few individuals with ancestral ties to a king (*RC* 17, line 5; 22, line 9), and it is difficult to see how a 'faction' could easily control a *polis* with its democratic institutions (though Machiavelli, *The Prince*, ch. 5, takes this process as a definite possibility for the cities of Renaissance Italy).

[220] Petition: Memnon of Herakleia observes that Herakleia Pontike, when subjected to Roman publicans which the city perceived as 'the beginning of slavery', should have petitioned to the Senate, rather than murder the publicans (*FGrHist* 434, 27.6). Liberty as gift: e.g. Reynolds 1982: no. 13, lines 2, 7; *SEG* 32.469, lines 8–10. Emperors taking away freedom: Dio Cass. 54.7.6, 57.24.6 (Kyzikos under Augustus, Tiberius).

liberty being considered insolent insubordination (Liv. 33.38.3, 5–6).

4. *Beyond Structures*

At first sight, it is difficult not to be impressed by the strength of the Seleukid state. The immediate impression is that of its material force. It conquered local communities by the threat or the application of violence: large contingents of professional troops, strategic movements by land and by sea on a vast scale. Its military means controlled, directly or indirectly, the local communities and the landscape, by garrisoning cities or by holding strategic points or routes. Its far-reaching, hierarchically organized administrative structures implemented royal orders; levied tribute, indirect taxes, services; controlled the movement of people; generated communication vertically, from high officials to subordinates, and horizontally, between different types of officials; produced its own decisions and actions; kept records, archives, a live body of administrative knowledge. Is this picture an accurate reflection? It certainly describes the situation at least in parts of Asia Minor, and even in some remote parts, as Amyzon, Kildara, Aigai, and Temnos suggest: these were highland communities, not sited on the main axes of communication, but which still had to deal with the Seleukid state on a regular basis.

Yet this picture is impossible to substantiate more generally or to nuance, for lack of precise and detailed evidence; what remains, and what I have developed in the earlier sections of this chapter, is an impression of Seleukid power, drawn from the implications of the documents. Without further evidence to trace matters on the ground, this picture is less about realities than about a rhetoric of power, and hence about ideology: the implications of the documents concern the existence of a space structured by administration, the efficiency and ubiquity of royal authority, the meticulousness of control, the successful workings of the system. These help to imagine empire; these are all about ideology, the 'implications of the implications'. It is essential continuously to bear in mind the ideological nature of 'imagined empire', as we spin out the implications of the documents. This does not condemn the picture as unreal: on the contrary, one strand of the argument presented in this chapter is that ideology played a very real role in constituting empire, and that a Hellenistic empire like the Seleukid realm depended on ideological force as much as on physical violence. The impressions of 'strong state-ness' given out by the rhetoric of our Seleukid documents are an implicit constituent of this ideology of empire. The typology of legal statuses and privileges are another, explicit feature, which assigned the local communities a place in the space of empire. It presented the existence of the cities as the sum of the grants which the ruler had agreed to; it rested on the assumption of the ruler's power to name, and of the pertinence of the categories he wielded when dealing with the cities. This ideology of empire, expressed through a practical system of definitions and statuses, was a powerful tool for domination, and is as impressive an instrument of Seleukid state power as the more obvious, material means of control. The impression and ideology of strong state-ness, by a self-fulfilling movement, could help make the Seleukid state strong.

Nonetheless, the impression of a powerful state apparatus is difficult to substantiate, and might be largely ideological—or simply an illusion. This should make us reconsider the evidence for Seleukid Asia Minor, and notice the untidy elements which do not fit an unified picture of structures and *institutions séleucides*. One instance can be found in western Karia, Seleukid since 203 (Ch. 2 § 2). Amyzon was certainly in contact with several layers of Seleukid authority, as described above. It also belonged to an organisation called the Chrysaorian League, presumably an ethnically based federation, about which we know very little. It had its own institutions (including an assembly and financial institutions) and federal citizenship (all Chrysaorians had certain rights in all Chrysaorian cities). It was centred on a shrine near Stratonikeia, a city under Rhodian control. Apart from Amyzon, important 'Seleukid' cities like Alabanda ('Antiocheia of the Chrysaorians'), Alinda, and Mylasa were Chrysaorian communities, along with Stratonikeia, Keramos, and Thera, from Rhodes' Subject Peraia.[221] It is surprising to discover the existence of an organization whose membership was drawn from both the Seleukid and the Rhodian dominions, especially if one considers that the Seleukid state restricted the external diplomacy of at least some of its subject cities. How the Chrysaorian League coexisted with the concrete territorial and administrative structures Seleukid state, and how this coexistence should modify our picture of the nature of Seleukid control is yet unclear.

Just as problematic is the existence of 'dynasts', personal rulers of small principalities, who seem to have existed in the middle of the

---

[221] Amyzon: document **11** (whence it appears that all Chrysaorians share privileges in every Chrysaorian city), and J. and L. Robert 1983: no. 28 (finances). Chrysaorians; J. and L. Robert 1983: 223–5.

Seleukid state, such as the Philomelids in Phrygia, or Moagetes in the Kibyratis; if the case of Ptolemaios of Telmessos, under the Ptolemies is typical, dynasts had full enjoyment of their principality, where they could levy indirect taxes and agricultural dues (*OGIS* 55). We do not know how these were controlled or integrated (if indeed they were integrated). Were they considered 'vassal' rulers, like those in the eastern parts of the Seleukid empire? Or were they hereditary Seleukid governors? (The 'dynast' Olympichos started off as a Seleukid governor, perhaps a hyparch, and continued as an Antigonid governor.) In the latter case, why would certain families have been allowed to retain governorships as their prerogative—as a reward, or because they were too entrenched locally to be removed? Or were they some sort of 'baron', enjoying large estates as a power base? (Ptolemaios certainly enjoyed jurisdiction on his estate at Skythopolis.) Yet another possibility is that a dynast like Moagetes was largely free from Seleukid control, tolerated because he was too difficult to reduce. The question is clouded both by problems of definition and terminology, and by the lack of any new evidence.[222] It is nonetheless clear that the presence of dynasts made the Seleukid state far less homogeneous than a general survey of administrative structures or a map presenting 'Seleukid Asia Minor' as a solid territorial block might hint. Furthermore, the relations between the state and forms of organisation in the royal land, such as the villages and the shrines, must have made a large claim, perhaps the largest, on the Seleukid officials' activity, because of the extension and economic importance of the *chora*; yet these relations are still very poorly documented. The details of control and exaction, the nature and frequency of contacts, all these matters still escape us, in spite of evocative pieces of evidence from the villages or concerning the shrines.[223] Finally, a survey of imperial structures, such as I have given in sections 1–2 of this chapter, precisely leaves out the regions where imperial power

[222] The evidence is gathered in Billows 1995: 81–110, and Kobes 1996. Philomelids: Philomelos appears as an independent power player in the confused local conflicts of 189: Pol. 21.35.2; Moagetes: Pol. 21.34. Was the Kibyratis free from Seleukid dominion, like Selge, which Strabo (12.7.3) claims was never subject to the kings (despite the activity of Antiochos III in Pisidia?). However, it is probable that the Kibyratis was Seleukid around 260: Strobel 1991: 125–6, argues persuasively that Tlos was under Seleukid attack at that time; if so, Seleukid troops assailed the Xanthos valley from the north, coming down from the Kibyratan march, which was presumably Seleukid-held (on the geography, J. and L. Robert in *BE* 50, 183, on the decree for Orthagoras of Araxa, edited by G. E. Bean, reproduced as *SEG* 18.570).

[223] Villages: Wörrle 1975. Shrines: Debord 1982; Boffo 1985; Virgilio 1987 for programmatic essay; Brandt 1992: 69; I have argued that the office and activity of Nikanor imply administrative control of the shrines (§ 2*c*).

did not obtain, since such a survey goes where the evidence leads it. It is dangerous to extrapolate from Seleukid activity in the *lieux de passage*: Debord (1985: 347–8) has observed that in Lydia at least, Seleukid control seems restricted to the plains and valleys, leaving out much of the rougher country in North-Eastern Lydia; likewise, the Rhodian 'control' of Lykia may have been far more limited than modern historians assume, and mainly centred on the Xanthos valley (Zimmermann 1993). To generalize from the patchy evidence is tempting, because it produces a more satisfying picture; but to do so would amount to taking too seriously the inclusive ideology of the Seleukid space, precisely the danger this section has tried to highlight.

If we had the evidence to confront the ideology of empire, and the implications of state power which our documents deliberately give out, with local realities, the picture might be surprising. The early and classical Ottoman state, or Revolutionary France, or Napoleonic France, hardly strike us as weak states: they show a developed centre of power, the profusion of military means for compulsion, a careful bureaucracy, and extensive administrative structures. Yet the former drew an eloquent declaration by Braudel: 'pauvre despotisme des Turcs!'; concerning France, R. Cobb described the 'hinterland of indifference', which started immediately beyond the great cities and the main avenues of communication, even in the Ile-de-France.[224] It would be fascinating to map out Seleukid power in Asia Minor, to observe where the Seleukid state was thick and where thin, to try to explain why. This would allow us to evaluate to what extent the imperial ideology was an illusion that sustained Seleukid power, or the product of a truly powerful and invasive empire of domination; we might be able to judge whether the Seleukid empire was, like the Ottoman empire, a paradoxical combination of state power and of structural weakness, and why. If the evidence were as plentiful as for more modern periods, we could even conceivably start to relate long-term patterns of settlement and social organization with the impact and the forms which an empire of domination took in the landscape, both urban and rural. For the time being, we do not know how loud we should sigh 'pauvre despotisme des Séleucides!', or whether it would be justified at all.

The firmest conclusion to emerge from this chapter is the real contribution which ideology makes towards constituting empire.

---

[224] Turks: Braudel 1966: i. 34–6. Indifference: Cobb 1975: 30–4, 38; much of Cobb's work is devoted to showing the powerlessness or the irrelevance of even strong, militant governments like the pre-Thermidorian Revolutionary state, or the Napoleonic state.

But unlike the structures of power-as-possession, this aspect cannot be studied by inert, anatomizing methods like lists of officials or of taxes. In studying how the typology of statuses strengthened Seleukid power, I have mentioned the need for consent or accept-ability; earlier on, I noted the fact that the royal pronouncements and the privileges they granted where the object of negotiations and bargaining between rulers and ruled. Both aspects point out how the experience of empire escapes mere cataloguing of structures; statuses and privileges represented bargains struck between ruling power and local community, and could be used for further negotia-tions.[225] This points to another way in which power can be approached, even within an empire of domination like the Seleukid empire: power as interaction. In other words, the models which study 'power-as-battlefield' can be reintroduced into the study of Seleukid Asia Minor, if we examine the interaction between rulers and ruled. Luckily, the very medium of this interaction is pre-served: we have the actual documents, couched in conventional forms, royal letters, civic decrees. Just as the system of statuses and privileges should not be minimized to a meaningless cover for brutal realities of power, so these conventional forms should not be reduced to hypocritical façade and servile toadying: the political language of the actors was not an epiphenomenon to the realities of power, but was very real, since it constituted the relations between ruler and ruled, through processes of exchange. It offers us ways to pursue and refine the analyses of power offered in Chapter 3: these will be taken up in the next chapter.

[225] The same process for the Roman empire: Millar 1983: 80, 'not . . . a one-sided series of pronouncements from the centre of power, but . . . a constant dialogue of petition and response'.

CHAPTER 4

Empire as Interaction

A sense of empire as a process of exchange can be gained even from documents which at first sight express the full weight of royal power, such as Zeuxis' letter to Amyzon, written immediately after taking the city over.[1] The particular case of Amyzon is framed in the wider context of 'all those who have trusted and handed themselves over to us', in the rhetoric of extension and totality essential to representations of imperial power; Zeuxis' professed solicitude speaks of the asymmetry between the royal state and the local community; the letter ends by notifying the Amyzonians that Zeuxis has ordered his subordinates to take care of them and refrain from abuses. The structures of control are already in place; local *status quo* depends on the performative utterance of the imperial state. All these features—paralleled in Zeuxis' letter to Kildara[2]—characterize the discourse of empire: the world of downward-flowing orders, with its own style and values derived from the patrimonial nature of the state, the world 'where you means it'.[3] Even so, Zeuxis' letters include a feature which is the more interesting because it follows expressions of imperial power: the promise of future benefaction, if the local community behaves well—'we will take all care for you, inasmuch as you show yourselves the better disposed and the more zealous towards the interests of king Antiochos'.[4] Such expressions are common, in the epigraphical material pertaining to Antiochos III and in the Hellenistic period generally; we may usefully call them 'contract clauses'.[5] They admit that the reality of interaction

[1] Document **5**. The analysis offered here is inspired by Marin 1978: 104, on royal discourse: the point is 'faire passer sa totalité, sa plénitude dans la 'petitesse' de l'occasion présente'. [2] Document **25**.

[3] Royal orders: Bertrand 1990: 108–9, 114–15. Style: Wörrle 1978: 204–6. Patrimonial ideology: Ch. 3 § 2. You meaning it: Pocock 1984: 34, 42.

[4] Document **25**, 7–11; Amyzon (fragmentary, but unmistakable): **5**, 7–9.

[5] Antiochos III: also documents **26** A, I 25–30 (Laodike to Iasos); **31** A, I 14–15, B IV 9–10 (Antiochos, Zeuxis to Herakleia); can be guessed in **19** D, 8–10 (Laodike to Teos). Other: *RC* 14, lines 12–14; *SEG* 42.994, lines D 14–17; 2 Macc. 11: 19; 1 Macc. 10: 27; Jos. *AJ* 13.48 (signalled by Piejko 1991a: 64); Jonnes and Ricl 1997: 3–4, lines 36–8, 47–8.

between ruler and ruled is a process of reciprocity, rather than simply a vertical relationship of control and exploitation; the terms in which the exchange is defined are not straightforward, but couched in a conventional language whose functions and effects will have to be explored.

That reciprocity was a figure used by the Seleukid state alerts us to the importance of considering a Hellenistic king in a context of interaction, rather than as the untrammelled author of actions directed at passive cities. This holds true for the most visible royal activity: material benefactions to the cities.[6] Of course, it is legitimate to consider them from above, as a structural feature of empire: gifts as manifestation of royal power, an aspect so well documented for Antiochos III, and in such a variety of recipients of benefaction, that it is worth recapitulating the evidence and pausing to reflect on it, albeit briefly. Antiochos gave grain to Priene and Herakleia; he made grants of cash to Herakleia (whose citizens baldly asked for a yearly subsidy 'as large as possible', but amounting to at least five, or perhaps nine, talents); he could make more specific gifts for institutions, for instance oil for the gymasion, as he did with Herakleia and Sardeis; he could subsidize the expense of maintaining amenities, as with a water-conduit at Herakleia; he could help with the expensive business of reconstruction, as at Sardeis and perhaps earthquake-stricken Iasos (where a gymnasion, the Antiocheion, might be attributed to him, and the *bouleuterion* and *archeion* were probably rebuilt after Seleukid takeover).[7] All these items find parallels in the general history of Hellenistic kingship, such as the Korrhagos decree which documents Attalid grants to cities, or the case of the Temple of Jerusalem, the recipient of benefaction both in the form of long-term gifts and of immediate help with building.[8]

The case of Iasos, documented in some detail, stands out because of the complexity and breadth of the arrangements, which allow us to examine the impact of royal euergetism within the recipient community. Laodike promised the city forty tons of wheat a year, for ten years, with instructions to use the income raised by selling the grain for the dowries of the poor citizens' daughters (εἰς προῖκας ταῖς τῶν ἀσθηνούντων πολιτῶν θυγατράσιν), at a maximum of '300 Antiochcian

---

[6] Veyne 1976: 340 n. 131; Bringmann 1993, summarizing the results of a survey of royal euergetism: the results are published in Bringmann and von Steuben 1995, a compendium of the available evidence; Gauthier 1985: 39–53.

[7] Documents **1**, **3**, **31**, **33**. Water-conduit: **31** A, I 11–13. Iasos: Crowther 1995*b*, Robert 1937: 450–2 (gymnasion), Hicks on *GIBM* 443, same document *I. Iasos* 252 (*bouleuterion*, *archeion*—but if these buildings had been financed by Antiochos III (Hicks), one might expect the inscription to record the fact).

[8] *SEG* 2.663 (also *SEG* 2.580, lines 16–18, *RC* 48, line D 4); Jos. *AJ* 12.138–41.

drachmai' per dowry. The gift is not only alimentary, supplementing the meagre agricultural resources of Iasos;[9] it intervenes in the
fabric of the city, facilitating marriage and citizen reproduction,
lessening social inequality and conflict in the aftermath of earthquake and warfare; Laodike describes her gift as 'a benefaction to
the poor citizens and a common service (κοινὴν εὐχρηστίαν) to the
whole people'. Laodike, as queen, allows the royal benefactions to
extend into the private sphere of marriage; the expression
'Antiocheian drachmai' in which Laodike measures the dowries
(rather than 'Attic drachmai' or 'Alexandrian drachmai', δραχμαὶ
Ἀλεξανδρεῖαι), by using an ideologically loaded standard rather than
the usual phrases for international weight standards, serves as a
reminders of royal beneficence in the transaction concerning citizen
families and their daughters.[10] Furthermore, it seems that
Antiochos III fostered social peace in the city, by sponsoring the
resort to 'foreign judges' to arbitrate conflict, under the divine
sanction of an oracle of Apollo: both the king and the god urged the
city to live its common life in harmony (πολιτεύεσθαι μεθ' ὁμονοίας).[11]
Even if the process was unobtrusive, resting on the acceptable
authority of an oracular god, this activity introduced royal
beneficence into the centre of *polis* existence, through the patronage
of local reconciliation and civic harmony; this state of affairs, rather
than more conventional gifts, may be what the Iasians designated as
τὰ μέγιστα ἀγαθά received from the king.[12]

Iasos, the recipient of euergetical attention from Antiochos and
Laodike, was formally a 'free' city (Ch. 3 § 3). Yet benefactions
allowed the Seleukid state to extend its presence into the local communities, regardless of juridical status. By intervening in areas of
need, such as the cities' precarious food supply or unsystematic
budgets,[13] and by paying for expensive building projects, the king

---

[9] Strabo 14.2.21, qualified by Crowther 1995*b*: 112 n. 120; Ph. Gauthier, *BCH* 114
(1990), 438 and nn. 61–2; for a sense of the territory of Iasos and its sub-units, see
further the studies by E. La Rocca, J. Benoit, R. Pierobon Benoit, G. Ragone, R.
Ragone, G. Traina, within the survey published in *ASNP* 3rd ser. 23 (1993), 847–998.

[10] Document **26** A. Iasos was a free city, and (on current orthodoxy) could have
minted its own coinage; it presumably chose not to do so. Attic-Alexandrine standard:
E. Will, *Gnomon* 68 (1996), 696–7.

[11] Document **28**, 1–7. Crowther 1995*b* points out that the call for *homonoia* suggests
the resort to foreign judges, and dates (on palaeographical and prosopographical
grounds) a cluster of 'foreign judges' decrees concerning Iasos to the 190s; as Crowther
(1995*b*: 120), observes, the fact that the *archeion* had to be rebuilt at this time perhaps
implies destruction in social unrest (*qua* repository for debt records).

[12] Document **28**, 9–10.

[13] Food: a later parallel in Robert 1949: 74–81, for the Roman period; Broughton, in
ESAR 4. 607–9; Garnsey 1988: 14–16 on the frequency of grain shortage (with
Hellenistic references). Budgets: Will 1988: 334 n. 11 (though see Migeotte 1984 and
1992 for a qualification of the traditional view).

could foster dependency on gifts, integrate the cities, legitimize his rule through an ideology of beneficence, create local ties of obligation, instil consent (cf. Ch. 3 § 3), and multiply the force of his often indirect administration by developing avenues of influence in addition to channels of command. Through these functions, gift-giving could act as a system of government; in Strabo's words, force and *euergesia* are the king's two resources for persuasion (9.2.40).[14]

Nonetheless, it is misleadingly one-sided to view royal euergetism solely from above. The roster of benefactions obtained by Priene or Herakleia were granted to requests from these cities: gift-giving belongs to a wider context of petition and response, and the 'system of government' must also be examined as a system of interaction.[15] Laodike's letter to Iasos invites us to do so by prolonging her complex gift with a 'contract clause' promising future benefactions if the Iasians behave 'as is appropriate' and remember the εὐεργεσίαι. We must study benefaction as part of a transaction of gift-giving, a cycle of giving and remembrance.[16] The way in which gift-giving is handled by both parties takes us back to language, the formalized, stereotypical language through which the transaction was described and conducted, and which allowed both parties to express requests for gifts and the legitimizing force of benefaction. Strabo's statement (9.2.40) that the king did not need words to persuade must be qualified. Antiochos III before Smyrna and Lampsakos (Liv. 33.38.5), uttered threats but also spoke conciliatory words (*leniter adloquendo*).

1. *The Language of Euergetism*

The interaction between king and city took place through canonical forms, the royal letter and the civic decree. The dossier of texts concerning the relations between Antiochos III and the cities is large and consistent enough for a survey of these forms, and also of the language shared by both parties. These texts also have the advantage of being typical of Hellenistic diplomatics in general, so that their examples can be expanded with parallels, and the findings they encourage apply to the Hellenistic world in general.

[14] Gauthier 1985: 41; Bringmann 1993; H. Claessen in Claessen and Skelnik 1978: 563–7 on the early state, which extracts surplus but derives legitimation by returning some of it as gifts: likewise, the wherewithal for Seleukid benefactions derived from the profit of empire.

[15] Gauthier 1993b: 213–15 for a nuanced appreciation of royal *euergesia* and local initiative.

[16] Veyne 1976: 76–81.

The kings (or their officials) communicated to the cities through letters written on a stereotypical format and, in their diplomatical nature, different from the curt messages of administration: a preamble, usually acknowledging an embassy from a city, accepting and approving honours decreed by the city; a main decision or action by the king, described in terms of his own motivation and feelings; a concluding section, with features such as a contract clause and reference to a future, oral, report by the city's ambassadors.[17] There are several letters of this type written by Antiochos III. His letters to Teos, though mutilated, exhibit the basic structure, which can also be guessed at in the largely lost letter of Antiochos to Herakleia, and which underlies the long letter of Zeuxis to the same city.[18] Parallels are easy to find, such as the letters of Ptolemy II to Miletos (*RC* 14), Seleukos II to Miletos (*RC* 22), or Ptolemy III to Xanthos (*SEG* 36.1218), all these examples, substantially preserved, showing the same uniformity of composition (which also influenced the letters of Roman officials and emperors).[19] Though there were variants in composition (for instance in the case of royal initiative, as with Laodike's benefaction to Iasos), the tone, the style, and the basic grammar of royal correspondence remained the same (motivated personal decision, notified to the city concerned). The uniformity of royal letters makes it impossible to be absolutely sure about documents whose heading is lost and where no telling details are preserved, for instance the early second-century letter to Ilion, which could be by an Attalid (or even a Roman official?) as well as Antiochos III.[20]

The canonical form developed by the city was the honorific decree: after a preamble (dating formulas, proposers, 'sanction formula' authenticating the decree), a series of 'considerations' or motivating clauses introduced by ἐπειδή and giving reasons for the decisions, a 'hortative clause' introduced by ὅπως/ἵνα and describing the aim of the decree (usually in quite general terms: the city wants it known that it rewards its benefactors), and finally the resolutions, in the form of a series of infinitive constructions explaining what the city had decided (ἔδοξε/δεδόχθαι τῆι βουλῆι καὶ τῶι δήμωι)—all in a single sentence: subordinate clauses (the motivations and the

---

[17] Welles in *RC*, pp. xliii–xlv (perhaps minimizes the difference between memoranda and letters to cities); Mourgues 1995: 120–1.

[18] Antiochos to Teos: document **19**. Herakleia: **31**. Other letters of Antiochos, Laodike, or Zeuxis : **1**, **2**, **3**, **5**, **26** A, **34** (probably), **43** (the latter probably an administrative note).

[19] The letters of the Scipios to Kolophon and Herakleia are a good example; Mourgues 1995: 120–1 for the letters of the emperors.

[20] Document **34**.

'hortative' clause) and the main ἔδοξε-clause.[21] The structure is obvious in decrees for non-royal honorands, such as the Amyzonian decree for Hermeias or the Xanthian decree for the rhetor Themistokles; it also governs, in a more complex form, the long Teian decrees honouring Antiochos and Laodike.[22] Because of the honorific nature of these decrees, they were inscribed on stone, an act which publicized and perpetuated the decisions, and thus played a self-conscious role in the honours offered by the cities. The concept was familiar enough to be used metaphorically: Antiochos declared Teos *asylos* and tax-free, ἵνα γενομένης ἐπαύξεως τῶν κατὰ τὴν πόλιν μὴ μόνον εὐεργεσίας λάβῃ τὴν ἐπιγραφὴν τῆς τοῦ δήμου, ἀλλὰ καὶ σωτηρίας, 'so that, after the increase of the matters of the city, he should receive the title (lit. 'inscription', *titulus*) not only of benefactor of the people, but also of its saviour'.[23] Inscriptions not only documented, but belonged to the honours requiting benefactions. The two parties, city and ruler, were radically different, and hence the language and medium of exchange were not totally homogeneous. The values and motives belong to different worlds: patrimonial loyalty in royal correspondence, communal values of service and good citizenship in the decrees. The royal letter and the civic decree are two different forms: the first active, performative, addressed to a recipient; the second a record of past decision narrated and displayed autarkically.[24] Nonetheless, the two forms take each other into account, and can legitimately be considered as the interlocutors in a dialogue; they also share a vocabulary for benefaction and gratitude, a vocabulary of great uniformity and durability. If the controversial Ilian decree *OGIS* 219 is indeed to be attributed to the period of Antiochos I rather than that of Antiochos III (Appendix 1), the early date combined with the similarity in phraseology to documents of the latter period (like the Teos decrees) illustrate the currency and the durability of the language of euergetism.

Both forms can be described as conducting a dialogue, because they are built around reciprocity and exchange. By their very syntax, they are structured as reactions, or motivated decisions: on the part of the king, a reaction to an embassy or to realizing a local community's good behaviour; on the part of the city, a reaction to a

---

[21] *BE* 76. 173, for a more complete exposition of the elements in a typical civic decree; Gauthier 1985: 9–10, Bertrand 1990: 101; Mourgues 1995: 107 n. 6.

[22] Documents **14, 23, 17, 18**.

[23] Epigraphical publication: e.g. documents **11**, 9–12; **27**, 5–9. Teos: **17**, 20–2, possibly the king's own expression (with Herrmann 1965a *ad loc.* for ἐπιγραφή).

[24] On the contrast, Bertrand 1990, with illuminating analyses of examples.

benefaction, real or perceived, requited through τιμαί.[25] Civic decree
and royal letter never talk about or represent an isolated moment,
but suppose a past stimulus or a future reaction—or both.
Reciprocity could be implied by as simple and delicate a feature as
a καί in the hortative clause from a Teian decree, ἵνα οὖν καὶ ἡμῖς ἐμ
| [παν]τὶ κα[ιρῶ]ι φαινώμεθα χάριτας ἀξίας ἀποδίδοντες τῶι τε βασι | [λε]ῖ
καὶ τῆ βασιλίσση, 'so that we too, may be conspicuous in returning
tokens of gratitude to the king and the queen'. More explicitly, the
hortative clauses of civic decrees professed the intention to show
εὐχαριστία or to 'return worthy signs of gratitude' (χάριτες),[26]—for
instance, in a decree from Amyzon for the official Nikomedes: ὅπως
ἦι πᾶσι φανερὸν | ὅτι ὁ δῆμος εὐεργετηθεὶς ἀποδιδῶι χάριτας ἀξία[s] | τοῖς
εὐεργετοῦσιν αὐτόν, 'so that it may be obvious to all that the people,
when done good by, returns worthy signs of gratitude to those who
are its benefactors'. The hortative clauses declare the intention of
the decrees: to create reciprocity and to maintain the euergetical
exchange. In the royal letters, the contract clause (which I have
defined above) expresses reciprocity, linking royal benefaction
and civic reaction in a self-perpetuating spiral, as in an elaborate
example from Zeuxis' letter to the Herakleians:

καὶ καθόλου καὶ ἐν τοῖς ἄλλοις φρον-
[τιοῦμεν ἵνα ἐ]μ μηθενὶ τῶν δυνατῶν καὶ καλῶς ἐχόντων ὑστερῆτε, ἀλλὰ τύ-
[χητε τῆς προ]σηκούσης ἐπιμελείας. Διὸ καὶ εὖ ποήσετε καὶ αὐτοὶ διαφυλάσ-
[σοντες τὴν εἰς] τὰ πράγματα εὔνοιαν· οὕτω γὰρ πολλῶι μᾶλλον καὶ ἡμεῖς
[οὐδὲν ἐλλείψομε]ν πρ<ο>θυμίας εἰς τὸ συγκατασκευάζειν τ[ὰ πρὸς δ]ό[ξαν]
[καὶ τιμὴν ἀνήκοντα]

and we will take complete care that you be not deprived in any matter of
the possible measures that would benefit you, but that you should receive
the suitable attention. Therefore, for your part, you will do well to preserve
your goodwill towards the (king's) affairs, for thus we will all the less leave
out anything pertaining to eagerness to carry out measures which [have to
do with the honour and the repute (of the city)]

A promise of care (ἐπιμέλεια) is followed by an injunction to keep
εὔνοια towards the king's affairs—which in turn will make Zeuxis

[25] Royal reaction: e.g. document **19** A, *RC* 22. Civic reaction to benefaction: Habicht
1970: 206–7; 163–5, commenting Arist. *Rhet.* 1 1361a (τιμαί defined as return for
εὐεργεσίαι).
[26] *Καί*: document **17**, 40–2, cf. **10**, **17**, **13**, 12–13. Εὐχαριστία: **16**, **40**; in contract clause
at end of Laodike's letter to Iasos, **26** A, I 28, possibly in **26** B, II 15; **19** A, 5 (Antiochos'
summary of a Teian decree); also *RC* 15, lines 7–8. Χάριτες: **11**, 10–12, whence the quote
in the text; also **10**, 17–18; probably **13**, 12–13; **17**, 40–2; **18**, 33, 40–1; J. and L. Robert
1983: no. 4*bis* and p. 126 (*SEG* 33.1183 with Bousquet 1986: 29–30 n. 15) for Ptolemaic
examples from Amyzon and Xanthos; document **23** for example with non-royal
honorand; further Habicht 1970: 163.

care all the more for the Herakleians.[27] I give, in order that you give, in order that I give—this continuous dialogue explains the density of diplomatic exchanges between king and city, as we can perceive it between Teos and Antiochos III, or in other cases. An Erythraian decree for Antiochos I or II (*I. Erythrai* 30) received a favourable reply from the king, which in turn provided the occasion for another Erythraian decree (*RC* 15: letter and follow-up decree).

The dynamic, open structure characteristic of the euergetical dialogue is reinforced by the very language in which the interaction was couched. The formalized vocabulary and syntax guarantee reproducibility; more importantly, the interaction is framed, or expressed, through generalizing idioms of consistency, which characterize any transaction as normal rather than exceptional. All these functions can be illustrated from the material pertaining to Antiochos III and his relation to the cities (with occasional resort to parallels, to establish the typicality of this particular test-case). These functions are interwoven within the same documents (often within the same clause), in long, complicated sentences. Nonetheless, it is worth illustrating each strand separately, and for both parties in turn: this thematic dismantling of densely packed clauses will allow us to examine the various strategies within a rhetoric of generalization, and the way they complement each other.

An obvious feature is that individual acts of euergetism or *eucharistia* are never presented as isolated in time, but located in a chronology of benefaction and gratitude. Firstly, they are presented against a background of precedent. In the civic decrees, this is achieved by the πρότερόν τε sub-clause summarizing past conduct. An example can be found in the motivating clauses of the Iasian decree for Laodike, which starts with an elaborate clause, augmented by a genitive absolute describing Antiochos' past behaviour towards all the Greeks; this clause is followed by details concerning Iasos in particular, enumerating earlier benefactions (πρότερόν τε), then specific and recent deeds (in the lost part of the text). The opening of the first Teian decree for Antiochos III, though fragmentary, is clearly constructed along the same pattern.[28] In the royal documents, this function is performed by the elements preceding the main decision. Laodike ascribes her benefaction to the Iasians to frequently (πλεονάκις) hearing from Antiochos of his solicitude for his friends and allies generally, and Iasos in particular; Antiochos III starts a letter to the Teians by noting that they have the same

---

[27] Document **31** B, IV 7–12.
[28] Iasos: document **26** B, I 9–18; Teos: **17**, 1–10. Other examples: **9**, **13**, **44**; also Habicht 1970: 162 n. 4 (e.g. *OGIS* 11).

disposition διὰ παντός, 'throughout'; Antiochos I or II in a letter to the Erythraians notes how their εὔνοια has held διὰ παντός and speaks of his own εὔνοια, which he has continually chosen to have ἐν ἀρχῆι.[29] The present moment is extended back in time by references to earlier relations; but it is also projected forward by the promise of future benefactions, requested by the cities or promised by the king or his subordinates (the future tense is typical of the contract clauses, but can occur outside them). A characteristic verb is συναύξειν, to increase the honours enjoyed by the cities. Equally typical is the adverb ἀεί, qualifying future benefactions: Laodike promises to the Sardians [καὶ πειρασό]μεθα ἀεί τι ἀγαθὸν συνκατασκευάζειν τῆι πόl[λει].[30] No wonder that the verb διατελέω, 'to do continuously', frequently appears, both as an avowed and as an imputed state.[31] These examples could be reinforced by countless parallels drawn from the epigraphical material. They establish the ubiquitous usage of time references, as the opening move in both civic decree and royal letter, and allow us to understand their function. Chronological indications drew parallels between present and (often safely generalized) past, and took the present as justification for prognosis of similar behaviour (expected or promised) in the future. They thus extended the interaction in time, beyond the immediate transaction (a royal gift, civic honours): they constructed a context of continuity for each round of the euergetical dialogue, mirroring the latter's structural openness to indefinite repetition.

In addition to 'vertical' generalization through time, specific acts could be placed in a 'horizontal' context of constant beneficence to 'all Greeks' or even 'all men'. The Teians praised Antiochos for making 'a very great demonstration of his pre-existing trustworthiness (πίστις) towards all men': in addition to describing a particular action (Antiochos' sojourn in Teos) against the background of qualities proven in the past, this particular passage made a generalization about Antiochos' relation with 'all men', generalizing beyond a specific place, Teos, as well as a particular moment.[32] Both

---

[29] Iasos: document **26** A, I 4. Teos: **19** B, 4. Erythrai: *RC* 15, lines 6, 15–16. Also in letter of Ptolemy III to Xanthos: *SEG* 36.1218, line 21.

[30] Future tenses in royal letters: documents **2**, 18–19 (Laodike to Sardeis); **19** B, 12–13 (Antiochos III to Teos); **26** A, I 28–9 (Laodike to Iasos); **31** B, IV 7–8 (Zeuxis to Herakleia); **34**, 3 (Ilion). Συναύξειν: **26** A, I 10; **31** B, III 15; also *RC* 15, line 12, *RC* 9, line 7 (for gods, as in document **4**, 36), *SEG* 2. 663, lines 5–6; discussion of later parallels in Veyne 1976: 367 n. 324. Ἀεί: **11**, 6–7; **12**, 2–6 (Amyzon), and in royal letters, quoted above, **2**, **19** B, **26** A.

[31] Self-referential, by royal speaker: documents **26** A, 6 and **37**, 9, also *RC* 15, line 16 and *RC* 62, line 3; self-referential, by *polis*: document **10**, 9; *OGIS* 219, line 18. Descriptive, by city: documents **9**, 9; **10**, 17; **13**, 5–6; **17**, 26, 37; **44**, 2, 29; concerning non-royal honorands, **14**, 4–12; **33**, 11; **48**, 32.   [32] Document **17**, 24–5.

Teos and Iasos speak of the king's behaviour towards (or before) the
pan-Hellenic community: in the Teians' words, he professed to be
the 'common [benefactor] of all the Greek cities and of ours' and 'set
before the Greeks' an example (παράδειγμα) of his character; the
Iasians described Antiochos preserving his ancestral disposition
(προγονικὴ αἵρεσις) towards all the Greeks, and following his
ancestral beneficence (εὐεργεσία) towards the Greeks. Conversely,
Laodike referred to 'the Greeks' (in the dative, τοῖς Ἕλλησι) in her
fragmentary letter to the Teians.[33] This trope was less common
than the ubiquitous references to time,[34] but performed the same
function of placing any single utterance in a generalized context of
parallels. In this case, the city receiving a benefaction was compared
to a wider human group towards which the ruler felt, or showed,
beneficence; the comparison established the typicality of any individual transaction, and also connected its specific circumstances to a
broader, publicized, space, the pan-Hellenic community or even the
entire human race. Finally, another, and analogous, generalizing
trope is the notation κοινῆι/ἰδίαι, used in civic decrees to describe
past εὐεργεσίαι, or by royal letters in future promises: benefaction
extends both to the public sphere and to individuals, each of whom
ideally benefits from the benefactions.[35]

Both the chronological references and the extension in geographical terms illustrate an underlying notion of consistency, as
made visible in any individual transaction. Against this background,
consistency is also declared openly in moralizing references to
character; these make explicit the generalizing function of the
chronological and geographical references. This moralizing vocabulary of consistency and character is a striking feature of the language
of euergetism, expanding rather perfunctory references to utility
and profit (χρείας παρέχεσθαι, τὸ συμφέρον). Action does not constitute, but reveals, character, by 'making a display' (ἀπόδειξιν
ποιεῖσθαι)[36] of a moral quality or by proving itself consistent

[33] Documents **17**, 6–8, 26–7; **26** B, I 10–11; **28**, 3–5. Laodike: **19** D, 5. J. and L.
Robert 1983: 134, give references under Antiochos III, and restore a mention of pan-
Hellenic benevolence in document **5**, 2 (Zeuxis to Amyzon).

[34] Erskine 1994: 71 6, shows that for the Hellenistic period, the concept of common
benefactor of all men is more frequent in private petitions than in the diplomatic
language of the cities.

[35] In civic decrees: documents **9**, 10; **10**, 16–17; **26** B, I 12; **44**, 1–2; also *SEG* 33.1183,
line 9, *SEG* 2.663, line 6, *OGIS* 329, lines 23–4; document **33**, 12–13, for a non-royal
honorand (Priene). Royal letters: documents **19** A, 14–15 (Antiochos to Teos), **34** (to
Ilion, probably).

[36] Documents **10**, 7–8; **13**, 11 (context mutilated); **17**, 24–5 (Teos on Antiochos); **19**
A, 6–7 and 17–18 (Antiochos on the Teians demonstrating their qualities); **31** A, I 15 (in
contract clause of Antiochos' letter to Herakleia). Holleaux 1942: 92–4, for a long roster
of parallels (supplemented by Robert).

(ἀκόλουθα πράττειν)³⁷ with a model: for instance, according to a Teian decree, Antiochos' benefactions 'set out as an example to all the Greeks what character (τρόπος) he bears towards those who are his benefactors and well-disposed towards him'.³⁸ Behaviour is described in terms of 'choice', αἵρεσις³⁹ or προαίρεσις, the latter a deliberate choice revealing essential character: the Teians used both προαίρεσις and προαιρεῖσθαι in the opening three lines (unfortunately fragmentary) of their first decree honouring Antiochos. The phrase is also used by the royal interlocutors: Antiochos expressed his desire to see the Sardians' situation improve; Laodike insisted on her 'reasoned choice' (προαιρουμένη) to follow Antiochos' favour for the Iasians.⁴⁰ This repertoire is supplemented by declarations or imputations of intention: the choices are made by responsible actors, and reflect their desires, which in turn reflect their character. The royal letters often motivate their decisions with the participle βουλόμενοι; the Iasians speak of their διάληψις (literally their 'thought') towards Antiochos and Laodike, and, more generally, the 'hortative clauses' in the civic decrees are in fact declarations of intent.⁴¹ Conversely, both parties commend their interlocutor's wish to act in a certain way, or impute action to such a wish.⁴² But the euergetical language includes more than just neutral references to consistency with character: it allows itself a whole descriptive and evaluative register to talk about character. In the letter of Antiochos I or II to Erythrai, the vocabulary is original, but the thought conventional: the king notes that εὐχαριστία is a result of the Erythraians' ἀγωγή, ('course of action', literally 'upbringing'), and, from the city's decree, can deduce the Erythraians' nobility, τὸ εὐγενὲς ὑμῶν.

By saying that the language of euergetism strives at generalization

³⁷ Documents 12 (Amyzon asks official to follow the king's character); 16, 22 (different wording but equivalent meaning); 26 A, I 11–12 (Laodike says she follows Antiochos' σπουδή); 28, 3–5 (Iasians on Antiochos following the εὐεργεσία of his ancestors). Holleaux 1938b: 114, for parallels ('formule banale').

³⁸ Document 17, 26–7.

³⁹ Documents 10, 19–20 (Amyzon on Menestratos) 26 B, I 10 (Iasos on Antiochos); 19 A, 6, B 8, C 13 (Antiochos on Teians). Parallels in royal correspondence: e.g. RC 14, line 13; 15, lines 15–16; 22, line 14; SEG 36.1218, line 20. The word is usually translated as 'policy'.

⁴⁰ Προαίρεσις: Arist. Nic. Eth. 3.1111b4–1113a14 (I thank M. Burnyeat for this reference); J. and L. Robert 1989: 22. Teian decree: document 17, 4–6. Sardeis: document 3, 1–3; Laodike and Iasos: 26 A, I 11–12, 29–30.

⁴¹ Royal letters: document 26 A, which speaks both of Laodike's intentions, and, indirectly, of Antiochos' intentions (which Laodike wishes to follow); RC 15, line 25. Iasos: document 28, 11.

⁴² Documents 19 A, 6 (admittedly in Antiochos' summary of a Teian decree), 17, 16 (Teians on Antiochos' desire to χαρίζεσθαι τῶι δήμωι), 37 (Teians on Laodike having the same γνωμή as Antiochos).

by making individual transactions into shows of character, I argue against reading too strictly the view that the cities awarded τιμαί for particular benefactions from the king, as Habicht pointed out. The latter, perfectly true observation does not mean that the transaction only concerned a particular concrete benefaction, to the exclusion of the honourer's and the honorand's personality: the open, dynamic structure converted the euergetical transaction into ongoing dialogue, the generalizing vocabularies transformed individual acts into paradigmatic manifestations of character. In Schubart's words, the dialogue was not just about 'einzelne Leistungen', but also 'dauernde Haltung'.[43] This view has to be qualified: the civic decrees or the royal letters often did not praise moral qualities in general, but character as manifested in a relationship: not (e.g.) αἵρεσις *tout court*, but αἵρεσις πρός τινα, as in fact in most of the examples quoted above.[44] The Amyzonians praised the *epistates* Menestratos for καλοκἀγαθία εἰς πάντα τὰ τῶι δήμωι συμφέροντα, 'excellence in relation to the interests of the people'. The morally loaded, and potentially abstract, notion of 'excellence' is unambiguously linked, in the context of the decree, to behaviour towards a very specific community.[45] The moralizing notations described character, but their horizons often remained those of the specific exchange between benefactor and recipient. Nonetheless, even these context-bound evaluative terms had a generalizing force. What a concept such as καλοκἀγαθία did was to make explicit the assumptions which underlay the whole dialogue: the existence of moral norms, which dictated appropriate behaviour (caring for subordinates, returning gratitude), and according to which rational choices were made and approved. These norms also appear in the short phrases built around προσήκειν or καθήκειν: Antiochos or Zeuxis promises 'appropriate care' for a city, the Teians want to be seen to offer 'appropriate honours' to Antiochos and Laodike, royal letters praise or expect appropriate behaviour (gratitude or goodwill) from the local communities.[46]

Apart from describing the context for action, character and moti-

[43] Habicht 1970: 165, 208. Quote from Schubart 1937, 21.

[44] Documents **19** A, 6–7 (Teians' policy towards Antiochos III), **26** B, I 10 (Antiochos' policy towards all the Greeks), **10**, 19–20 (Menestratos' policy towards Amyzon), **17**, 24–6, 26–7 (Antiochos' πίστις towards all men and τρόπος towards his benefactors).

[45] Document **10**, 7–8.

[46] 'Appropriate care': documents **19** A, 15, **31** B, IV 5, 9; also *RC* 14, line 3 (Ptolemy II cared for Miletos, 'as was appropriate'). Appropriate honours: **18**, 69; **40**, 12; also Crampa 1969: no. 4, line 2 (in letter of Olympichos). Appropriate behaviour, ὡς προσῆκόν ἐστι (*vel sim*), from the cities: **19**.C, 13–14; **26** A, I 26; **31** A, I 15; **31** B, IV 9; also *RC* 15, line 32.

vation, the language of euergetism also supplied a vocabulary for presiding values. The most common word in the euergetic exchange is εὔνοια, 'goodwill', imputed or avowed by both city and king.[47] It describes the appropriate feelings after receipt of benefactions: in Aristotle's words, ὁ μὲν γὰρ εὐεργετηθεὶς ἀνθ᾽ ὧν πέπονθεν ἀπονέμει τὴν εὔνοιαν, τὰ δίκαια δρῶν (Nic. Eth. 1167ᵃ14); but, according to the same Aristotelian passage, it also denotes genuine and (paradoxically for the euergetical dialogue) disinterested esteem and goodwill. The word belongs to a register which mitigates the pragmatic process of exchange, by expressing it in terms of cordiality and courtesy. Both parties claim or are said to act out of zeal and enthusiasm (ἐκτένεια, σπουδή, προθυμία) towards their interlocutors:[48] these qualities are not only the stimulus to benefaction, but characterize the atmosphere of the interaction. Action can be described in intimate terms: the Amyzonians reward Menestratos for his 'gentle behaviour' (συμπεριφερόμενος), Antiochos accepts civic honours φιλοφρόνως, φιλανθρώπως, οἰκείως[49] just as one of his ancestors received Erythraian honours οἰκείως (RC 15, line 13): with familiar kindness. Finally, the diplomatic correspondence of the kings is elaborately cultured in its syntax and its vocabulary, taking the trouble of courtesy towards recipients: a style reflecting the broader 'style' of cordiality in the transactions between city and king.[50]

The generalizing vocabularies of time, space, moral consistency, and cordiality, as illustrated in the dossier concerning Antiochos III, constitute a stable and uniform language of ready-made phrases; the pre-scripted regularity of forms is essential to the restoration of lacunary documents. The result is a langue de bois, a formalized, reproducible, diplomatic idiom, in which actions fall along a plot involving institutionalized characters, conventionally admirable motivation, and a set of cordial values to preside over the individual occasion: the benevolent king, the grateful city, εὐχαριστία, εὔνοια. Any transaction couched in this language became

---

[47] City for king, imputed: RC 6, line 10; 14, line 10; 15, line 6. City for king, avowed: documents **10**, 9–10; **17**, 27. King or royal official for city, imputed: documents **13**, 5, 8; **17**, 5; **18**, 92–3. King for city, avowed: document **19** B, 12; RC 15, line 16. Further Schubart 1937: 8–10 (from king), 16–18 (from subjects).

[48] City for king, imputed: document **19** A, 9, 17. City for king, avowed: **18**, 93–4. King or royal official for city, imputed: **9**, 9; **17**, 38–9; **44**, 7, 9; also Inschr. Delphinion 139, lines 29–30. King or royal official for city, avowed: **26** A, I 12, 30–2; **31** B, III 13; also RC 14, line 2; **15**, lines 24, 31 (Erythraians told to remember the king's 'most zealous efforts').

[49] Amyzon: document **10**, 17. Antiochos III: **19** A, 11 and C, 11; **31** A, I 7.

[50] Style: Schubart 1920; also Welles's remarks after each letter in RC; Bousquet 1986 (analysing letter of Ptolemy III, with prose rhythm); the Roberts' remarks in BE 70, 553, arguing that a royal letter is too curt and imperative to have been addressed to the city of Telmessos.

a stereotypical, stylized affair: syntax proclaimed it a continuous relation, each round open to indefinite exchange and repetition, the generalizing vocabularies located it always at the same point in time and space (present dealings mirroring the past and announcing the future, and typical of dealings with men in general), for the same reasons (the character of the participants, appraised in a shared moralizing vocabulary) and with the same outcome of εὔνοια. Even though our documentation is incomplete, and there were other ways of expressing interaction (above, for royal orders; below, § 5), it is clear that the language of euergetism as used between king and subordinate city was extremely common; even if it fell short of total hegemony, it attained currency or even orthodoxy.

How can we approach this language? The preceding paragraphs attempted to examine it internally and structurally, as working system of meaning. A full linguistic treatment of the political languages of the Hellenistic age, of their lexicon and their syntax, with quantitative and semantic analyses, lies beyond the scope of the present study.[51] But even so, the limits of a purely linguistic treatment of euergetism appear readily. It is clear that the language of euergetism was not confined to the dialogue between city and ruler, but also operated between city and individual benefactor (citizen, foreigner, or king), and between cities: the expression 'firm and true χάρις' is found in a Xanthian decree for a rhetor as well as a Seleukid letter praising Milesian behaviour; the expression 'wanting to favour the *demos* (χαρίζεσθαι τῶι δήμωι)' was applied by the Teians to the conduct of Antiochos III, but also to the city of Mylasa, when the latter sent 'foreign judges' to Teos (easily paralleled).[52] *Εὔνοια* is similarly flexible. In a Ilian decree, it designates the support shown by army and friends to the king (*OGIS* 219, lines 15–16); it was used by the Romans, to describe the behaviour of Erythrai during the Roman–Seleukid War—free adhesion to the Roman side and military assistance (Pol. 21.45.5). The expression 'to be well disposed', εὐνοικῶς, is used as a coded expression for submission (or lack thereof) in a report by an official to Seleukos I on Herakleia Pontike (μὴ εὐνοικῶς ἔχειν τοῖς τοῦ Σελεύκου πράγμασι, Memnon,

---

[51] Manifesto in Nicolet 1990: 9–10: 'établir patiemment *le* ou plutôt *les* lexiques politiques de l'antiquité'. Methodology and examples (from modern and contemporary history) in Robin 1973. For Classical Athens, the 'language of public approbation' in honorific decrees, and the 'cardinal virtues' which appear in the epigraphical material, are studied in Whitehead 1993.

[52] Χάρις: document **23**, *RC* 22, line 12. Favouring the *demos*: **17**, 16, also *I. Mylasa* 624, line 4, and parallels listed by Robert, *OMS* i. 94–5, e.g. *Inschr. Magnesia* 97, lines 23–4, 65, 70: the Teians ask the Magnesians to do a favour to the *demos* (sc. of Teos) by noticing Teian honours for a Magnesian.

FGrHist 434 F 7); it also describes the behaviour of the Xanthian rhetor (εὐνοικῶς διακεῖσθαι), honoured in the decree mentioned above. How should we interpret εὔνοια when avowed by Antiochos III for a city he controlled, or by a subordinate city (whatever its formal status) for its ruler? 'Loyalty' or 'faithfulness' (offered as a translation by Schubart 1937: 8–10, 16: 'Treue') do not exhaust the versatility of the word, its primary denotations as well as its context-specific meanings.

The consequence is that the language of euergetism is clearly a well-defined, stable, institutionalized, language, but also that we must study this language in its world, where it performs several functions, as discourse: language as a representation or a mediation of power, in conditions that influence and are influenced by this language.[53] In the present case, these conditions are the narrative of Anatolian (re)conquest by Antiochos III (Chs. 1, 2), and the imperial structures of domination and exploitation (Ch. 3)—relatively well known, these allow us to study empire as discourse. We can evaluate the stereotypical utterances against what we know or think to have been the case, and hence try to understand functions and effects.

This approach entails taking the discourse of euergetism seriously. It is easy to pass over the stereotypical elements in the ancient documents, in the search for 'real' events, or—para-doxically—dismiss these elements because of their very ubiquity. The conventional nature of euergetical discourse is often deplored, as a smoke-screen hiding historical fact. Holleaux denounced the platitudes in a decree by Cretan auxiliaries on Cyprus for the later Ptolemaic official Aglaos of Kos: 'l'art d'écrire pour ne rien dire', 'un exemplaire, accompli et lassant, de cette langue prolixe et diluée, veule et vague, toute en formules abstraites', 'cette langue . . . factice et convenue, calquée sur des modèles courants', a judgement Holleaux supported with a long roster of parallels for each conventional phrase (Holleaux 1942: 88, 92–7). Yet the fact that the decree did not tell Holleaux the things he wanted to know (what Aglaos was doing on Cyprus) should not prevent consideration of the things the Cretan soldiers wanted to tell us. The obvious fact that political language, in Orwell's words, is used to cover murder

---

[53] Robin 1973: 20–9, for difference between language and discourse, between studying 'énoncés' (utterances) and 'énonciations' (conditions, production, practice of utterance). The present approach is inspired by the 'Cambridge school' (Pocock 1987), in the belief that its methods (studying political vocabularies and grammars, exploring individual applications of linguistic competence) are at least as suitable for the Hellenistic documents, actual instances of *parole politique*, as for the great authors studied by the Cambridge school.

and theft (the organized violence and spoliation analysed in Chapter 3), does not make it less interesting to study in its workings, the more so if we are aware of the realities being covered up. Nor has anything been achieved when this language has been denigrated as 'grotesque servility', 'toadying', or rhetorical verbiage:[54] its currency and durability still remain, as a historical fact requiring interpretation. Diplomatic exchange through language was a reality, and occupied an important place in the life of the cities: Teos and Sardeis had special funds, earmarked as τιμαὶ τῶν βασιλέων, for the needs of interaction with the king.[55] The stereotypical language of euergetism was the standard medium for interaction between ruler and ruled, shaping communication and actions; as much as the legal statuses (Ch. 3 § 3), it was a very real part of the experience of empire.

2. Talking to: Instrumental Functions

Because the language of euergetism did not straightforwardly express power and subordination, it performed a number of ideological, or political functions. It is too simple to speak of 'propaganda'—a problematic concept to apply to an age without mass-media, and a description which does not adequately cover the varied realities of interaction. A first avenue of interpretation is to examine separately the instrumental workings of the language of euergetism, from the point of view of both king and city: which goals the interlocutors used language to achieve, and how they achieved them. This approach is the more interesting for the fact that the collaboration of both parties in dialogue was compatible with different intentions and results.

(a) Power as Benefaction

It was possible to talk about the empire of domination in a realistic language acknowledging the realities of control and exploitation, as in the case of Polybios' description of Seleukid imperial structures, or documents mentioning local communities left in peace to produce more income for the royal economy (Ch. 3, Introduction

---

[54] Orth 1977: *passim*; Green 1990: e.g. 198. Contrast Brown 1992: 7–8, for the importance of late-Roman culture alongside the realities of autocracy; 31–4, on the 'fine dust of ancient phrases' and the role of rhetoric.

[55] Documents **18**, 63, Teos; **40**, 19, Sardeis (probably, though Robert thinks the lacuna may be too long for the restoration [τιμὰς] required by the sense and the Teian parallel).

and § 2); the hierarchy of juridical statuses is also a language predicated on the ruler's monopoly of performative utterances (Ch. 3 § 3). Other idioms dissimulated or deproblematized the fact of domination. This is the function of Antiochos' references to the Seleukid past, which justified empire by precedent, and by the assumption that imperial domination was based on a set of well defined property rights (original conquest accompanied by formal cession of territory or the demise of the former owner, and transmission of conquered territory by legacy). This conception of power justified by history was made explicit in royal letters; it perhaps also underlies the 'ancestral ideology', exemplified by claims to ancestral beneficence and the state cult for the Seleukid ancestors (Ch. 1 § 1).

Unlike the references to the Seleukid past (programmatic statements), the euergetical register called for the involvement and the acquiescence of the ruled. Gifts, or what was represented as gifts (often simply refraining from certain forms of exploitation), were presented as tokens of a more general characteristic, the ruler's kind concern for the ruled, his desire to benefit them, and the euergetic nature of the king.[56] A simple way in which the ruler's generous nature expressed itself was the supplementary gift: after granting favours asked for by the Herakleians, Antiochos III increased the royal grant of gymnasion-oil by thirty *metretai*, and promised to finance an aqueduct; analogously, a city sacked by Seleukid troops asked for tax-exemption, and (it seems) was granted additional privileges, on the initiative of a Seleukid official rather than on the city's petition.[57] Assuming that such actions result from the ruler's initiative (rather than informal petitions not recorded), they illustrate an insight by P. Veyne, on the function of the 'joli geste symbolique' constituted by 'le cadeau supplémentaire', which proves the depth and genuineness of the benefactor's feelings, above the routine of patronage (Veyne 1976: 79). The importance of the ruler's initiative is explicitly confirmed by the documents: an important feature of the description of the beneficent ruler and his actions concerns his efforts at originality in his gifts (literally 'to think up' gifts).[58] The striving for originality added weight to the

[56] On this 'sujet passablement ressassé', Gauthier 1985: 40–2, for main references. For theoretical writing on kingship, Murray 1970, and p. 311 for the diffusion of 'ethical kingship' in documentary material; Billows 1995: 56–70.

[57] Documents **31** A, I 8–14 (the extra oil is certainly a voluntary gift, the aqueduct probably); **36**, 11–21. For a parallel, Habicht 1997: 70: Antigonos Monophthalmos adds a grant of cash to a gift of grain and timber promised to the Athenians by Demetrios Poliorketes.

[58] Document **26** A, I 28–9 with *BE* 71, 621 p. 503 (ἐπινοῶ as technical term for expected or promised behaviour from the benefactor).

constantly proclaimed concepts: royal care (πολυωρία, ἐπιμέλεια), for the cities' welfare and their repute (τιμή, δόξα); a specific form was humanitarian aid for communities in hard times, and assistance with their ἐπανόρθωσις, as in the case of Sardeis or Iasos.[59]

Laodike's letter to the Iasians illustrates this vocabulary, by speaking of Antiochos' ἀντίληψις, an expressive word for efficient help;[60] furthermore, the letter shows how the concepts of benefaction are assembled in a syntactical structure that makes power acceptable, and urges the Iasians to accept Seleukid power along with Seleukid benefaction. The decision to give grain to the Iasians is preceded by a long, complex clause, explaining Laodike's motivation through a series of participles and sub-clauses.[61] These are written in the moralizing language of motivation, described in the previous section; it is worth closely reading the whole passage, and analyzing the syntax, to study the assumptions and 'truths' which the benefaction and its description foist on the Iasians.

> Βασίλισσα Λαοδίκη Ἰασέων τῆι βουλῆι καὶ τῶι δή-
> μωι χαίρειν· ἀκούουσα πλεονάκις τοῦ ἀδελφοῦ ἥν   4
> τε ἀντίληψιν τῶν ἑαυτοῦ φίλων καὶ συμμάχων
> διατελεῖ ποιούμενος καὶ ὡς τὴν ὑμέτεραν πό-
> λιν συμπτώμασιν περιπεσοῦσαν ἀπροσδοκή-
> τοις ἀνακτησάμενος τήν τε ἐλευθερίαν ὑμῖν   8
> ἀπέδωκεν καὶ τοὺς νόμους καὶ τὰ λοιπὰ προτέθει-
> ται συναύξειν τὸ πολίτευμα καὶ εἰς βελτίονα δι-
> άθεσιν ἀγαγεῖν, προαιρουμένη δὴ καὶ ἐγὼ ἀκόλου-
> θα πράσειν τῆι σπουδῆι αὐτοῦ καὶ ἐκτενείαι καὶ διὰ   12
> τοῦτο καταθέσθαι τινὰ εὐεργεσίαμ μὲν εἰς τοὺς
> ἀσθενοῦντας τῶν πολιτῶν, εὐχρηστίαν δὲ κοι-
> νὴν τῶι σύμπαντι δήμωι, γεγράφεικα Στρουθί-
> ωνι τῶι διοικητῆι ἐφ' ἔτη δέκα κατ' ἐνιαυτὸν πυρῶν χιλί-   16
> ους μεδίμνους Ἀττικοὺς εἰς τὴν πόλιν παρακομί-
> ζοντα παραδιδόναι τοῖς παρὰ τοῦ δήμου· κτλ.

Queen Laodike to the council and the people of the Iasians, greetings. Having often heard from my brother what urgent help he continually deploys for his friends and allies, and that after recovering your city as it had fallen into unexpected calamities, he gave back to you your liberty and your laws, and in the other matters he strives to increase the citizen body

[59] Care: documents **5**, **31** A, I 8–9 and B, III 13–16, IV 2, 9; **34**. Also *RC* 14, line 3; 22, lines 15–16; generally, Habicht 1970: 230. Ἐπανόρθωσις: document **3**, 1 (Sardeis, also document **1** for the reconstruction of the city); **26** A (Laodike for Iasos); also Jos. *AJ* 12.139 for reconstruction of Jerusalem, damaged in the Seleukid conquest of 200; Robert 1960: 517–19.
[60] Document **26** A, I 5, with J. and L. Robert 1983: 135 n. 2, a short lexical essay ('le mot dit beaucoup').
[61] Document **26** A, 3–18. A full translation can be found there.

and bring it to a better condition, and making it my own intention to act in accordance with his zeal and eagerness, and, because of this, to confer some benefaction on the poor among the citizens, and a general advantage to the whole people, I have written to Strouthion the *dioiketes* for him to send along to the city one thousand Attic medimnoi of wheat a year, for ten years, and hand them over to the representatives of the people . . .

This long sentence declares that Laodike gave grain to the Iasians, and, more importantly, expands on this action (expressed by the main proposition) by two participial clauses, which tell us why Laodike acted this way: first, because she had been hearing (ἀκούουσα) from Antiochos of his disposition, and second, because of her own committed choice (προαιρουμένη) to follow Antiochos' zeal. Sub-clauses give details on the first participial clause (ἀκούουσα) concerning the king's attitude as perceived by Laodike: general care for allies and friends, and specific action for Iasos; the latter theme is expanded by a participial phrase of its own, which describes the circumstances under which Antiochos came to show care for Iasos: when he had 'reacquired' the city (ἀνακτησάμενος). Major themes of royal ideology or practice are expressed in this complex of nested clauses: royal solicitude and beneficence, ancestral rights over a local community, the king's right to 'give back' local liberty and laws. The second participial clause focuses on Laodike's desire (προαιρουμένη) to imitate the king's euergetical enthusiasm, which makes her (διὰ τοῦτο) wish to confer a benefaction on the city's poor and the city more generally. The euergetical themes stated in the first (ἀκούουσα) participial clause are repeated or alluded to in the second participial clause, this time as facts: since Laodike wishes to act in accordance with them, they must be there for her to form this wish at all.

The syntactical structure of the letter poses these themes as facts (and does so twice), in the participial clauses which accompany and depend on the action expressed in the main verb: facts which must be true, since they are materialized in the repeated gift of grain, which the long sentence finally comes to as the point of communication. Accepting the gift dissuades the Iasians from questioning both the primary statements (I did this because I heard of Antiochos' benevolence and because I wish to imitate him) and the secondary, implicit statements (since my benevolence imitates Antiochos' benevolence, Antiochos is benevolent; since he 'reacquired' your city, and since he 'gave back' your liberty as a sign of benevolence, he enjoys ancestral political rights as well as being benevolent). By accepting the present, the Iasians are supposed to accept the Seleukid version—which Laodike helpfully restates (she is imitating Antiochos' euergetical zeal, a given fact) at the end of the letter (lines 29–32). The facts, political in nature, of reconquest justified by ancestral rights and of monopoly over definitions and statuses, are not dissimulated, but referred to as conditions of beneficence: Antiochos III, after 'reacquiring' the city, gave back its liberty, and now strives 'to increase its *politeuma* and to bring it to a better situation'.[62] Seleukid (re)conquest allowed Antiochos to extend to the Iasians in particular the care which in general he showed his friends and allies. The political force of this statement would be the more remarkable if Iasos had not previously been subordinate to the Seleukids (under Antiochos II or Seleukos II), but Laodike was rewriting Iasian history into a Seleukid past, by simply alluding to previous Seleukid dominion as a background (and a condition) to the present benefaction; the Iasians, in accepting the benefaction, would also agree to the rewriting of their past. These statements on royal beneficence and its implications are reinforced by a secondary participial clause: Antiochos gave back liberty and the laws, τὴν ὑμέτεραν πόλιν <u>συμπτώμασιν περιπεσοῦσαν ἀπροσδοκήτοις</u> ἀνακτησάμενος, 'having reacquired your city <u>as it had fallen in unexpected disasters</u>' (the earthquake of 198)—this participial clause qualifying τὴν ὑμέτεραν πόλιν gives not just the circumstance of reconquest, but a motivation for Antiochos' subsequent actions. Antiochos acted as he did, because he noticed the disasters which had befallen Iasos; for the sentence to make sense, this fact (or this statement, presented as a fact by the participial clause) must be relevant, and it can only be relevant if the king feels humanitarian solicitude for his subjects. Finally, another, less logical, effect of Laodike's sentence is to marginalize the political themes: conquest and monopoly of statuses are mentioned in a subordinate clause (ὡς τὴν ὑμέτεραν πόλιν κτλ.) to a participial clause qualifying the main verb which notifies the decision to give grain: the power relation is circumstantial, mentioned as an aside to the action presented as important, the fact of giving, the εὐεργεσία.

A similar case to Laodike's letter to the Iasians is Zeuxis' dealings with the Herakleians. This example is less elaborate in its syntax, but its straightforwardness illustrates all the better the way in which language, associated with the act of giving, imposed certain truths: power presented itself as benefaction, but benefaction was also an expression and means of power. The Herakleians asked Zeuxis to preserve τὰ ὑπὸ τῶν βασιλέων συγκεχωρημένα, the *status quo* of prece-

---

[62] Lines 6–11: I construct the clause in the present tense (τὰ λοιπὰ προτέθειται συναύξειν κτλ.) as still governed by the participial clause ἀνακτησάμενος; but if the clause were paratactic, the sense would be the same.

dents and grants made by indefinite royal masters in the city's past.[63] Zeuxis replied by speaking of his desire to restore the people to its former situation, to increase the city—standard formulas in the language of royal euergetism—and to preserve τά τε ἐπὶ τῶν προγόνων τοῦ βασιλέως [συγκεχ]ωρημένα, 'the grants made by the ancestors of the king (i.e. Antiochos III)'; to an indefinite past, Zeuxis substitutes the partisan Seleukid version, by which all of cis-Tauric Asia Minor had been (rightfully, and—inexactly—in actual fact) a Seleukid dominion since 281 BC (Ch. 1). By accepting the grants and benefactions, the Herakleians accept the rewriting of their local history into an episode of the Seleukid past, as relevant to the present master.[64] Here, as in the case of Iasos, it is possible that the city actually had never been subject to the Seleukids, and that Zeuxis, like Laodike, was rewriting local contexts into a vague Seleukid past.

The nature of the link between the euergetical discourse and royal power, and its effect, can be interpreted in different ways. For instance, we could describe the euergetical discourse as a rewriting of power into benefaction, and hence a process of euphemism. The essence of kingship could be defined as benefaction, rather than power[65]—a deproblematizing image of power, which is given substance by actual benefactions presented as characteristic of the ruler's personal disposition and the nature of his rule. A related feature is the presentation of rule not only as benefaction, but as protection and active care; this is not only explicitly expressed in royal letters, but, to a certain extent, underlies phrases about conserving or preserving local privileges—this representation of power-as-protection is a traditional feature of Near-Eastern kingship.[66] The insistence on care legitimates power, since its motivation and its effect are to promote the welfare of the ruled (Murray 1970; also *CR* NS 16 (1966), 226–7). Another possible interpretation is that the benefaction elides, or camouflages, power, and institutes a fiction of free exchange between ruler and ruled (dissimulating the fact that ruled in fact have no choice).[67] Polybios (5.11.6) contrasts the tyrant

[63] Parallel: Crampa 1969: no. 5, line 11 'granted by the kings' is a local formula for *status quo*.

[64] Document **31** B, II 14, III 14–15.

[65] The theme is already analysed in Ch. 3, as an essential part of the ideological tools of power (§§ 2*d*, 3, 4). On kingship and benefaction, Gauthier 1985: 40–1, with references.

[66] Protection: document **5**; further Ch. 3 § 1, *ad finem*. Conserving; documents **19** B, 18; **34**, 5; also *RC* 15, line 26. Generally, Briant 1982: 179–80, 182–8 on the ideology of Near-Eastern kingship as protection.

[67] Holleaux 1942: 226–7, on εὔνοια, creating the illusion of 'témoignage spontané' of adhesion.

(who rules by fear) and the king, whose characteristic is 'to do good
to all and be loved on account of his beneficence and kindness, thus
ruling and presiding over people with full willingness', βασιλέως δὲ
τὸ πάντας εὖ ποιοῦντα, διά τὴν εὐεργεσίαν καὶ τὴν φιλανθρωπίαν
ἀγαπώμενον, ἑκόντων ἡγεῖσθαι καὶ προστατεῖν: in this ideal relation, the
exercise of kingship through pure benefaction seems a zone where
power is absent, replaced by influence and willing adhesion. The
contract clause in royal letters suggests that compliance, or deference, to the king, is a choice of the local community, acting out of
the moral obligation to remember and requite past benefaction: the
word εὔνοια, used in contract clauses, and generally in royal
language addressed to local communities (§ 1), also designates the
attitude of cities towards kings who are not their political masters
(*RC* 25, lines 28–9; 66, line 11);[68] Polybios speaks of kings in the
past receiving εὔνοιαν καὶ τιμήν in return for magnificent gifts—a
relationship of pure euergetism. The fact that the same language
could be used in the relationship between ruler and ruled as well as
between king and independent city[69] suggests yet another interpretation: euergetism could be described as creating a relation parallel
to the power structure—a distraction from power. Euergetism
offered a channel for interaction which did not pass through the
realities of domination, drawing away the attention of the ruled.
Veyne remarked on the difficulty of distinguishing between the
different aims of royal gifts to the cities (maintain diplomatic
cordiality with independent powers, publicize royal generosity,
symbolize 'une relation de dépendance': Veyne 1976: 228–30): the
ambiguity only made the form more versatile, and more appropriate
to obfuscate subordination.

The differences between these functions of the euergetical discourse applied from above matter less than their shared characteristic. They illustrate the effect of benefaction, and the language of
euergetism that accompanied benefaction, when applied from the
rulers to the ruled. Gifts, the evocation of past gifts, the promise of
future gifts, the ruler's proclaimed initiative in thinking up new
gifts, his beneficent character, manifested in his decisions: reference
to these themes created legitimacy for the king, represented his
power, and deproblematized it by shifting the focus of discourse

---

[68] Reference for εὔνοια, both in a free and a subordinate context, in Holleaux 1942: 226
n. 3, 227 n. 1. The contract clause, in this context, reduces a power relation to the free
exchange and reciprocity between city and benefactor, such as that proclaimed at the
end of Athenian honorific decrees (e.g. *Syll.* 535, lines 68–70; 540, lines 48–51, signalled
in Piejko 1991a: 64).

[69] On this topic, Gauthier 1993b: 214; Veyne 1976: 229.

from power to benefaction. This discourse played its role in fostering consent and making power acceptable; in this role, its aim was
to depoliticize the relation of the empire to its subjects. A specific
example is the intricate syntax of a royal utterance such as Laodike's
letter to the Iasians, as analysed above: the participial clauses,
dependent on the main action (Laodike has given grain), make the
Iasians accept royal ideology and the royal worldview, as part of the
whole package of royal euergetism. More simply, talking about
giving also allowed the rulers to mention the subjects' obligations,
not in terms of political subordination, but in moralizing terms, as
'appropriate behaviour' after receiving gifts and in the expectancy of
more gifts: Laodike, in the contract clause at the end of her letter to
the Iasians, promised further benefactions if they showed themselves οἴους καθήκει.[70] The language of euergetism, when spoken by
king or queen, expresses the whole politics of the act of giving
from ruler to ruled. The 'gentle addresses' to which Antiochos III
treated the Smyrnians and the Lampsakenes were probably
expressed in this register: power-as-benevolence, appeal to euergetical memory, promise of gifts, the whole written in complex, elaborate sentences posing themes of royal ideology as facts by shifting
them to subordinate or participial clauses which emphasized, and
were substantiated by, the main action, the royal euergetical
gesture. That these recalcitrant communities were not taken in does
not detract from the importance of this language, which reached
other communities, and aimed at imposing certain images of royal
power on them (admittedly, they had less choice than Smyrna or
Lampsakos).

(b) Diplomacy and Manipulation

The royal language of giving was matched by a civic language of
receiving, the language of τιμαί and honorific decrees in direct communication with the kings. The appropriate response to benefaction
was the dispatch of an embassy to the king, to send greetings, rejoice
over his good health, and read out an honorific decree taken by the
city;[71] honours decreed by a city (praise, the erection of a statue,
ruler cult), were publicly communicated to the king, and performed
before him, in the abstract, through the reading of the decree and
presentation by the city's envoys: the aim was expressly to bring
the city to the attention of its royal interlocutors, ἵνα δὲ ὁ βασιλεὺς
Ἀντίοχος καὶ ἡ ἀ[δ]ελφὴ αὐτοῦ | [βασί]λισσα [Λ]αοδίκη εἰδήσωσι τὴν

---

[70] Document **26** A, I 26.
[71] Documents **11**, 4–7; **18**, 107–13; **31** A, I 4–5; cf. *RC* 6, *OGIS* 11, 219, *Inschr.*
Delphinion 139.

εὐχαριστίαν τοῦ [δ]ήμου, 'in order that king Antiochos and his sister queen Laodike should know the gratitude of the people', as a Teian decree put it.[72]

A first function of communication with the king was the demonstration of goodwill, loyalism, or even submission. Civic decrees instructed the ambassadors to proclaim that the local community had the interests of the ruler at heart, that the ruler's good health and fortune was in accordance with the city's prayers, ὡς εὐχόμεθα; the formula was used in a decree of Euromians/Philippeis to describe reconquest by Philip V—an Antigonid official 'restored the city to king Philip', [καθά] Ι περ εὐχόμεθα.[73] The decrees informed the king of sacrifices or prayers for his welfare.[74] Even if the language of honours is not explicit about the power relationship involved, this elementary function of demonstrating submission emerges from the behaviour of cities towards kings who are threatening, because near and recently victorious in war—the first gesture was to issue an honorific decree and send crowns, as tokens of submission. Miletos, alarmed at Philip's success at Lade in 201, decreed crowns for the victor (Pol. 16.15.6 and above, Ch. 2 § 3); Ptolemy IV, after his victory at Raphia, marched into Koile Syria to the accompaniment of crowns, sacrifices, altars, and other honours (Pol. 5.86.8–11), a fact we need not attribute with Polybios to the natural fickleness of the inhabitants.[75]

A more sophisticated function was the mediation of requests to the ruler: honours usually introduced petition. The Amyzonian decrees for Seleukid officials were brought by ambassadors, who then exhorted them to 'always be responsible for some good for the *demos*' (παρακαλέσουσιν αὐτὸν ἀεί τινος ἀγαθοῦ παραίτιον γενέσθαι τῶι δήμωι). Laodike, in a letter to the Sardians, simply described the ambassadors as 'exhorting', in the absolute, without direct object or explanatory subordinate clause: καί οἱ πρεσβευταί παρεκάλουν

---

[72] Document **18**, 107–8; cf. **28**, 10–13. In *OGIS* 222, lines 20–4, the Ionians ask Antiochos I to choose a site for a *temenos* to him: the request demands a reply, and hence attention, from the king.

[73] City prayers: document **18**, 112; cf. the Telmessian decree in honour of Eumenes II, republished by Segre, *Riv. Fil.* 60 (1932), 446–52, lines 13–14: Eumenes has won καλῶς καὶ ἐνδόξως καὶ ὡς εὐχόμεθα τοῖς θεοῖς. Euromians/Philippeis: Errington 1993: 21–3, no. 4, lines 3–4.

[74] Documents **2** B, 13–15; **27**, 2–5 (assuming this decree of a phyle was communicated to Antiochos III); also *OGIS* 219, lines 20–5 (long description of public prayers at Ilion for the welfare of king and queen), definitely communicated to the king.

[75] The honours decreed by the cities after 'Antiochos' takes power on the death of 'Seleukos' (*P. Berol.* 21286: Brashear 1984), might concern a similar situation. Bosworth, *HCA* i. 226 for earlier parallels: golden crowns as initial acknowledgement of inferior status.

ἀκολούθως τοῖς ἐν τῶι ψηφίσματι κατακεχωρισμένοις.[76] In the latter case, Sardeis had recently been recaptured and sacked by Antiochos III. The honours decreed by the Sardians for Laodike—cultic honours in the form of a *temenos* and a festival named Laodikeia, sacrifices to Zeus Genethlios for the safety of Antiochos, Laodike, and their children—were clearly a local initiative, which allowed the Sardians to approach the ruler (or his wife) in the euergetic register, start a diplomatic exchange—Laodike would hardly turn down the cultic honours, symbolizing local goodwill—and, in the aftermath of these discursive moves, to invite the ruling power to respond in the same language of euergetism. Laodike duly acknowledged the honours, praising the Sardians' enthusiasm and promising future benefactions. After honouring Laodike, the Sardians also approached Antiochos; his reply is almost entirely lost, but it no doubt acknowledged similar honours for himself; a third letter by him speaks, in standard euergetical language, of his desire to assist with the city's ἐπανόρθωσις and his committed choice (προαιρούμενοι) to improve the situation of the city—hence a series of benefactions and the alleviation of the burden of billeting.[77] The Sardians, after the ravages of siege and sack by their ruler, still could resort to the resources of the euergetical language, to address the ruling power in a discourse that would shape its reaction along pre-scripted lines of benefaction: the evidence allows us to see euergetical discourse in action, and the incremental shifts in the attitude and language of Antiochos III, as he lets himself be drawn into the institutionalized dialogue of honours and benefaction.

Rather than being mere homilies which requested royal euergetism in general terms, honours more frequently introduced precise petitions. The Herakleians decreed honours (crowns, sacrifices to gods and kings) for Antiochos III and his family, before presenting Zeuxis with a multitude of dossiers (ὑπομνήματα) on privileges to be defended or benefactions to be requested by the twenty-two envoys: gifts in nature or in kind, various tax-exemptions, territory. Neither Zeuxis nor Antiochos seems to have refused much of the Herakleians' long and complex petition.[78] The dealings between Herakleia and the royal state give a detailed example of the instrumental function of honours in introducing specific petitions; but

[76] Amyzon: documents **11, 12**. Sardeis: **2** B, 15–16. *OGIS* 219, line 48, probably contained a general exhortation to the king requesting good disposition towards Ilion.

[77] Documents **2** B, C (that this letter answers a different embassy than B can be inferred from the different composition of the embassy); **3**.

[78] Document **31** A (crowns), B (II 10–11 for sacrifices). A parallel is found in the φιλάνθρωπα and the τιμαί offered to the Scipios by the same city (**45**, 14–15, justifying restoration [τιμάς]).

they are hardly unique. A trace of such a petition is preserved in Antiochos' replies to Teian embassies: one of the letters explicitly promises some action 'in accordance with your request', [κ]αθάπερ ἀξιοῦτε.[79] Parallels abound: a decree of the Ionians contains cultic honours for Antiochos I, and a request that the king protect the freedom of the cities; letters of Antiochos II (?) and Seleukos II summarize petitions coming after civic honours; most tersely, though not unpleasantly, Ptolemy III acknowledged the practical goals of an embassy from Xanthos, bearing a decree honouring him and Berenike II with crowns and statues: τὴν τε εὔνοιαν τῆς πόλεως ἐνεφάνισαν καὶ περὶ ὧν ἠξιοῦτε τὰ ὑπομνήματ' ἐπέδωκαν, 'they spoke of the *eunoia* of the city and handed over the dossiers concerning the things you ask for'.[80]

Why were honours addressed to the king effective in making him respond favourably to petitions? We might consider the honours as a symbolical fee (sometimes not so symbolical, as in the case of the gold ξένια offered by Erythrai to the Seleukid king, gold crowns of real value, or gifts of money called 'crowns')[81]—an offering to the king, demanding requital in some form, according to the rules of exchange; honours when offered as initiative from below started the euergetical dialogue, in which the appropriate response was (more) benefactions—the content of these benefactions being determined, or at least suggested, by the petitions which followed the honours. Finally, the actual expression of the honorific decrees played an instrumental role, by publicizing expectations and projecting norms onto the recipient. Civic honours and their messages, open or implicit, aimed at achieving a manipulative effect, as suggested by R. Billows. By echoing the royal themes of power as benefaction or ancestral attitudes, the cities could exercise 'moral pressure' on the kings to ensure the favourable reception of petitions. An early example is the famous Athenian ithyphallic hymn to Demetrios Poliorketes (291 or 290), which by speaking of the king's divine and active protection presents a not-so-hidden request for assistance, especially against the Aitolians and their Theban allies. Later civic decrees in presenting petitions refer to the precedent of royal ances-

[79] 'In accordance with your request': document **19** C, 14. **19** A almost certainly gave Antiochos' reply ([οἰό]μεθα δεῖν τὴμ πόλιν [ὑμῶν . . .], 'we believe that your city should . . .') to a Teian petition, alluded to in lines 15–16 (the Teian ambassadors speak of their instructions, whose precise tenor is now lost). **19** E could also be a response by a petition from the *koinon* of the Artists of Dionysos.

[80] *OGIS* 222, lines 14–18; *RC* 15 and 22; *SEG* 36.1218, lines 17–19. Also Crampa 1969: no. 4 (Olympichos to Mylasa).

[81] *RC* 15, line 5; Bikerman 1938: 111–12. Also Diod. 17.24.3, Arr. *Anab.* 1.26.2 (Alexander asks the Aspendians to pay a fee of 50 talents), 2.13.8; Millar 1992: 140–2 for Roman parallels.

tors, as in *OGIS* 222, line 20, or the paraphrase of ambassadors' speech in *RC* 15, lines 23–4.[82] In the case of Antiochos III, a simple but very explicit example comes from the 'first' Teian decree, which speaks about 'the great advantages through which our city has reached happiness—some of which he now is bringing about, some he will bring about': [τ]ὰ μὲν συντελεῖ τῶν ἀγαθῶν δι' ὧν εἰς εὐδαιμονίαν παραγίνεθ' ἡ πόλις ἡμ[ῶ]ν, τὰ δ' ἐ[πι]τελέσει. The explicit theme of this phrase is celebration of Antiochos' beneficence and power, in the form of power over thè city and of power to do good; nevertheless, the phrase, which was read out to the king, perhaps commented on by ambassadors, and inscribed on the main city temple, was a public reminder of royal promises and a means of pressure on the king. Other examples are indirect. It is likely that the Sardian decree on cult for Laodike, and the Herakleian decree honouring the king and his family (before detailing a long list of requests) presented the honours in the generalizing register of royal beneficence, to project expectations and shape interaction into institutionalized euergetical channels, favouring positive responses to petition. A royal letter to Teos, agreeing to a local request, promises action 'in accordance with the example [of my ancestors]', perhaps echoing the wording of the Teian decree it responds to.[83] If we had the text of any speech delivered face-to-face by civic ambassadors to the king, we would probably have many more examples of directly manipulative rhetoric and appeal to the values of royal euergetism.

The ideal case illustrating this direct instrumental function of euergetical discourse must be the behaviour of the Rhodians, described by Diodoros as using honours and skilful decrees to make the kings pay them ἑκουσίους φόρους (31.36, Gauthier 1993*b*: 214–15). We are entitled to find exaggerated this image of a city using honours to transform kings into benefactors (or even payers of 'voluntary tribute', a metaphor which reverses a more usual relation of king and city), and it is true that Rhodes was exceptional by its independence and its neutrality. Nevertheless, Diodoros documents ancient awareness of the manipulative force of the honorific language, and hence validates modern interpretations of this function.

The use of language by the ruled to act upon the rulers is essential for a nuanced appreciation of the realities and the experience of empire. Its importance can be substantiated by parallels in other

---

[82] These examples are treated in Billows 1995: 70–80, esp. 74–8. On the Athenian hymn, and its political context, Habicht 1997: 92–4.

[83] Teian decree: document **17**, 27–9. Sardeis: **2** B; Herakleia: **31**. Letter to Teos: **19** C, 14–16.

periods, for instance in Late Antiquity when the city élites constrained the representatives of an autocratic imperial state through
rhetoric and the prestige of classical culture (Brown 1992: 3–70). In
the case of the Hellenistic cities, the manipulation or pressurizing of
rulers through discourse shows how the honours, and especially the
statements and generalizations which framed the presentation of
honours, had direct political force, in actual interactions. These
statements present a specific case of the general function of language
as 'role assignment' within a binding linguistic contract; modes and
content of address shape the response, if the latter is to be expressed
within the same language (Pocock 1984). The shared, institutionalized language of euergetism, used in a dialogue where the terms
were not exclusively owned or controlled by the empire, the party
which wielded the means of physical compulsion, allowed the ruled
to convert transactions into dialogue, where they could address the
ruling power in certain ways, to cast it in well-defined roles and to
obtain what they wanted from it.

(c) 'As for the Other Euergetai': Socializing the King's Officials

A well-documented and particularly significant case of role assignment is the decree honouring a royal official, in gratitude for
services or as an initial diplomatic move (requiting general goodwill
rather than specific favours). There are many instances; Robert
recognized the type as a subgenre of the honorific decree.[84] The type
is attested at Amyzon, where the citizens honoured the governor at
Alinda, the administrator of the Artemision, a financial official (?),
another unspecified official, soldiers, and their commander; perhaps
they also honoured Zeuxis (who went through the city and dedicated lands to the gods of the Artemision) and the king with now
lost decrees.[85] Apollonia under Salbake honoured the local cavalry
commander for services; a fragmentary decree from Sardeis might
honour a Seleukid official with a statue and a share of the meat from
public sacrifices (the honorand is not a Sardian).[86] The most elaborate example comes from Teos, which offered citizenship (on a
'potential' basis, i.e. open to permanent immigrants) to the 'cities
named after the ancestors of the king', the great Seleukid cities of
north Syria, Antioch, Seleukeia in Pieria, Laodikeia by the sea:

---

[84] J. and L. Robert 1983: 194 (with further examples); also Habicht 1970: 57 n. 9
(Athens); Launey 1987: 642–50; Gauthier 1985: 45. Schubart 1937: 21–6, amalgamates
images of officials from below, and prescriptions from above. For a study of Attalid
philoi between court and *polis*, Savalli-Lestrade 1996.

[85] Documents **9, 10, 11, 12, 13**; **7** for Zeuxis at Amyzon.

[86] Apollonia: document **44**; Sardeis: **40**.

Gauthier has argued that this measure (purely honorific, rather than concretely addressed to immigrants from those cities) was directed at the Seleukid king's Friends, many of whom came from these cities, and some of whom had earlier stayed in Teos.[87]

Some honours proclaimed distance between the city and the royal official installed near or in it: the dispatch of an embassy, the insistence on publicity in the hortative clause, these are characteristic features of the decree for the royal official, and designate the latter as an outsider to the city.[88] Likewise, the title εὐεργέτης, as a formal title (equivalent to registration in an official list of a city's benefactors), which the Amyzonians gave to royal officials, might also characterize them as non-citizens, since (as Gauthier has shown) the title was never formally given by Hellenistic cities to their citizens, but only to foreign benefactors;[89] the title *proxenos* given to some officials certainly has this implication (*SEG* 29.1216; cf. *SEG* 34.1256). But mostly, the local dimension of the honours integrated the imperial official into the city: Amyzon granted citizenship to at least one Seleukid official, Menestratos, the governor of the Artemision, with the right to own land, to participate in festivals, and to hold office; Amyzon also granted him additional privileges, such as a portion of public sacrifices, a literal share of the communal life, and also an honour granted to other, citizen, benefactors: καθότι καὶ τοῖς [ἄλλοις εὐεργέταις].[90] The same privilege of Amyzonian citizenship, when granted to Nikomedes, probably a financial official with a wider area of competence than simply Amyzon, gave him rights and privileges in all the Chrysaorian cities:[91] practical advantages, linked to local identity.

Honours for royal officials socialized them, by reinscribing them into the world of the cities. In royal administration, individuals are called by name, with no patronymic or ethnikon, as abstract and interchangeable conveyors or executors of orders (J. and L. Robert 1983: 114–15): this practice reflects the practical language of empire, and the empire's awareness of itself as an ideally rational state, autonomously organized (Ch. 3 §§ 2c–d). In contrast, the Amyzonian decree honours Menestratos, son of Agathokles, of

---

[87] Document **18**, 90–104; Gauthier 1985: 169–75, developing Herrmann 1965a: 79–84. **39** for a Friend from Seleukeia in Pieria, the doctor Apollophanes.

[88] J. and L. Robert 1983: 194; documents **11**, **12**.

[89] Document **10**, and J. and L. Robert 1983: no. 3, showing the title given to the Ptolemaic governor of Karia, Margos; Gauthier 1985: 7–39: cities never formally titled citizen benefactors as εὐεργέται; 37, for the complicating fact that the Amyzonians may have started doing so in the late third century.

[90] Document **10**, cf. **14** for similar honours given to a citizen benefactor.

[91] Document **11**. J. and L. Robert 1983: 223–5 on the Chrysaorian League and its institutions.

Phokaia: the Seleukid official is given an identity in the network of *poleis*, as citizen and the son of a citizen, an individual who happened to have been appointed to a position by king Antiochos; he was praised in terms consonant with local moral values and local interests, for his καλοκἀγαθία εἰς πάντα τὰ τῶι δήμωι συμφέροντα. Both features can be paralleled in the Amyzonian decree for Chionis, the governor of Alinda, whose patronymic and *ethnikon* were named before his function in the imperial administration, and who was praised for helping the city with [πά]ντα τὰ συμφέροντα [καὶ καλῶς ἔ]χοντα.[92] The royal officials could hardly refuse these honours, couched in terms of moral approval and giving tokens of respect (and also of the very submission and cordial consent which the empire of domination sought among its subjects). The local identity offered by the civic decrees was much preferable to an alternative, critical, conception of the royal official: the 'flatterer', κόλαξ, or servant of the king (Herman 1980/1). A suitable metaphor for the transaction comes from Theangela, where the citizens presented a royal official with an honorific decree and two jars of honey (Robert 1936: 90).

But the royal officials could not accept local honours and local identity without a share of obligations; the language of honours cast them in the role of benefactors, either by starting the euergetical dialogue or by describing past actions in euergetical terms; for instance, administrative communication (probably) between Menestratos and his colleagues was rewritten by the Amyzonians as writing to Zeuxis, Nikomedes, and Chionis about the εὔνοια of Amyzon towards the kings and towards them.[93] The ascribed role as εὐεργέτης allowed the local community to address the royal official in that capacity and make demands: envoys to Nikomedes requested him to do good to the demos, 'since he is an *euergetes*', παρακαλέσουσιν ὄντα εὐεργέτην πει | ρᾶσθαι ἀεί τινος ἀγαθοῦ παραίτιον γίνεσθαι τῶι δήμωι. The Teian grant of (potential) citizenship was intended to make the citizens of Antioch, Seleukeia, and Laodikeia (and, presumably, the royal Friends who fell in this category) 'the readier towards the benefactions, being zealous in all circumstances, as is a fine thing for one's own fatherland', ἑτοιμότεροι π[ρὸς] | τὰς εὐεργεσίας, σπευδόντες διὰ παντός, καθά[π]ερ | [καλό]ν ἐστιν ὑπὲρ τῆς ἰδίας πατρίδος.[94] Even if the measure was symbolical,[95] and the

[92] Documents **10**, **9**. J. and L. Robert 1983: no. 4 (Amyzon) and 4 A (Xanthos, republished *SEG* 33.1183), show Ptolemaic officials honoured for their καλοκἀγαθία.

[93] Document **10**, 8–12.

[94] Amyzon and Nikomedes: document **11**, 6–7. Teos: **18**, 96–9.

[95] However, in our surviving decree, the grant of citizenship to these cities is only a possibility, to be proposed to the assembly in the following *archairesiai*: document **18**,

citizens of these three cities did not all instantly become 'dual citizens' of Teos as well as their own πατρίς, the grant of citizenship would perhaps have given the Teians a way of addressing Seleukid officials who were also citizens of these cities (as many were): as members of communities with which Teos had shared royal benefactions, and hence as quasi-citizens with a sense of obligation towards Teos.

The consequence was to convert the royal official into a local *euergetes*, exercising patronage and receiving honours from a city, in a constant spiral of exchange. This mechanism probably came into play at Apollonia Salbake, where a decree honours a cavalry commander (hipparch), stationed there by the Seleukid state: repeatedly and with ultimate success, he defended the interests of the city before the central authorities at Sardeis. The Seleukid hipparch was not a native of Apollonia, so that the Apollonians must have created the ties for him to decide to intercede with the Seleukid state. The city rewarded him with local citizenship with exemption from civic taxes, and yearly repeated public honours at a festival: front seating (*prohedria*) and crowning with a golden crown. These honours furthered the relation, by giving it a formal, institutional shape (the citizenship grant), and by inserting the hipparch into civic ritual, where publicity, iteration, and material rewards combined to give the euergetical contract between local community and Seleukid officer visibility (and hence a means for informal pressure to keep commitments) and continuity. It would be fascinating to know more about the case of Apollonia under Salbake and the (now nameless) Seleukid hipparch: how the local honours affected his sense of identity, his relations with his men, and his routine dealings with other Seleukid officials; what outcome the ties between the city and the officer had, especially after the extinction of the Seleukid dominion in the area in 189 BC; how experienced, cynical, or calculating the Apollonians were.[96] The questions are unanswerable, but they could be asked for many more cases; in this specific instance, they are raised sharply by the apparent effectiveness of the Apollonians in converting a Seleukid cavalry officer into a local benefactor.

A similar transaction, though on a more ambitious scale, may have happened in the case of Teos, which managed to have its request for *asylia* presented by a high-ranking Seleukid diplomat

100–4. Conceivably, the proposal regulated concrete details (it is also possible that the proposal was rejected).

[96] Document **44**. The Amyzonians honoured Seleukid soldiers along with their commander, Ophelandros: **13**.

and officer, Menippos, when he went to Rome in winter 194/3 BC as part of the diplomatic confrontation between Rome and Antiochos III (Ch. 2 § 5). It is remarkable that Teos found means to convince the Seleukid diplomat to transact this piece of local business along-side the much weightier matter of the protracted and increasingly frustrating misunderstanding between Rome and Antiochos.[97] Menippos was a Macedonian (Liv. 36.11.6): like Zeuxis (or, indeed, the Seleukid kings themselves), his primary ethnic identity was not linked to a *polis* but rather described as descent from, and member-ship of, the Macedonian group ('ethno-class') spread out across and dominant in the eastern Hellenistic world since the time of Alexander. Menippos thus cannot have been approached by the Teians *qua* citizen of the cities in the Seleukis; nonetheless, it is likely that the Teians approached Menippos (perhaps while he was stationed in the region) in the language of euergetical reciprocity, a language in which it was difficult to turn down requests because they were tied to honours.

The process should not be minimized (Launey 1987: 642–3: 'dis-tinctions honorifiques illusoires et en général peu coûteuses'): we should be aware that it represented a subtle modification in the conditions of empire, and hence generally to the balance of power in the relation, material and discursive, between the cities and the Hellenistic ruler. The exercise of empire depended on the garrison commanders and the officials installed locally; to a certain extent, these *were* the empire, in the most concrete sense, because they enabled the crucial activities of control and of exaction, or carried these activities out. Furthermore, they represented the principles and the ideology on which the empire of domination was based: the hierarchical system of a state, separation of powers, direct account-ability to the ruler, patrimonial empire, strong state-ness; the public enactment of this ideology through the working of imperial institu-tions as performance was itself an important tool of imperial power (Ch. 3 § 2*d*). Because of the important role of Seleukid officials, and because they were in constant contact with the ruled (Ch. 3 § 2*a*), the weakening of their ties with the ruling power, their 'embedding' in local contexts, posed a serious problem: this process has generally been identified as a threat to the 'empire of domination' as a social formation, and often culminated in an empire's dissolution (Mann 1986: 144, 170–1, 535–6). By socializing the royal officials through euergetical interaction and role ascription, the local communities, consciously or not, but at any rate actively, encouraged the process

---

[97] Document **38**. Even if the Teian mission was approved by Antiochos III, the Roman letter attributes the initiative and the choice of Menippos to the Teians.

that most weakened the practical exercise of empire. Their behaviour tended towards the decentralization of the means of imperial power, and hence the grounding of the 'free-floating resources' on which it depended: officers and functionaries, individuals addressed by the king and by their colleagues by bare name without patronymic or *ethnikon*, though occasionally with Seleukid aulic titles, officials who owed their loyalty to the king and hence looked to a centre of power, and who could be shifted around at the order of the Seleukid state. At the ideological level, the socialization of royal officials threatened the substitution of local horizons and relations full of local meaning to performance in a hierarchized, autonomous, self-aware system of imperial state power. A striking example of the effect of this process is the behaviour, in times of crisis, of imperial garrisons, which chose locally meaningful solutions over loyalty to the faraway centre of empire: in winter 190/189 BC, after the defeat of Antiochos III at Magnesia, the citizens of Sardeis and the garrison in the acropolis sent joint ambassadors to surrender to L. Scipio.[98] The integrating and socializing force of euergetical interaction between city and official vividly illustrates how the language of euergetism, in a particular situation, influenced the reality of empire in an effective and 'real' manner.

(d) Publicizing Norms and Expectations

In addition to the targeting of specific, nearby, embodiments of imperial power, role assignment by the cities could play a more diffuse function: publicizing perceptions of the rulers and the norms they supposedly adhered to. In the abstract, actions were considered as performances before the world; the Teians and the Iasians presented Antiochos III as acting in a beneficent way towards, or before, 'all the Greeks' (§ 1). The 'hortative clauses' of decrees for kings or royal officials make explicit the desire to publicize the euergetical transaction. The Teians, in erecting a fountain named after Laodike, intended that 'that an example of the gratitude of the people should be seen in a central location before all the foreigners who come to the city', ἵνα . . . τοῖς εἰς τὴμ πόλιν ἀφικνουμένοις τῶν ξένων [παρά] | δειγμα πᾶσιν ὑπάρχον ἐμ μέσωι φαίνηται τῆς εὐχαριστίας το[ῦ

---

[98] Liv. 37.44.7. Also *FGrHist* 160, col. II, lines 6–7 (inhabitants of Soloi and garrison pursue common (pro-Ptolemaic) policy during Third Syrian War). For a parallel, see Le Roy Ladurie 1975: 35, 95: the *châtelain* at Montaillou, theoretically an official of the Count of Foix, obeys Montalionais notables. But it is difficult to evaluate the phenomenon in the Hellenistic period, because we do not know how long royal officials were stationed in any community, before being transferred (in fact, we do not know if the Seleukids regularly practised the transferral of adminstrative personnel at all).

δή]Ιμον.⁹⁹ The monument was concretely designed to perform communication with the rest of the world, issuing in a visual and permanent form its message about royal benefaction and civic gratitude, from its site on the agora, near the harbour where many foreigners would first set foot in the city.¹⁰⁰ The monument was not isolated, but the centre for religious rituals (next section), performed publicly; likewise, these rituals honouring Antiochos III spoke openly and repeatedly of his benefactions, past or future, to the city. All the inscribed civic decrees honouring Antiochos III or his officials (indeed, all inscribed Hellenistic civic decrees honouring a king or a royal official) ideally performed the same function, by their nature as public inscription: they diffused a local perception about the Hellenistic king and proclaimed the norms governing the transaction between local community and ruler, by presenting a permanent version, exposed for anyone to read, for all times.

In addition to being publicized in the cities, in inscriptions, monuments, or rituals, for foreigners to see and talk about, images of a king's euergetical activity or character were actively diffused by diplomatic contacts. The Antiocheian/Alabandan ambassador who went round Greece asking for acknowledgement of *asylia* for the city, spoke before the Delphic Amphiktions: ὁμοίως δὲ καὶ περὶ βασιλέος | Ἀντιόχου τοῦ εὐεργέτα Ἀντιοχέων εὐλόγηκε εὐχαριστῶν | αὐτῶι διότι τὰν δημοκρατίαν καὶ τὰν εἰράναν {αν} τοῖς Ἀντιοχεῦσιν | διαφυλάσσει κὰτ τὰν τῶν προγόνων ὑφάγησιν, 'likewise, he spoke well about king Antiochos, the benefactor of the Antiocheians, giving thanks to him, because he preserves the democracy and the peace for the Antiocheians, in accordance with the example of his ancestors'. Antiochos the *euergetes*, his defence of peace and liberty following the ancestral example, the city's *eucharistia*: these notions were displayed before the prestigious audience of a pan-Hellenic shrine. The embassy does not seem to have mentioned in any other way than an allusion to the example of Seleukid ancestors the fact that the city in question had been (in some way) refounded by Antiochos II, and certainly was renamed after him. On an international, or pan-Hellenic, scene, the city spoke of civic, not dynastic identity, and cordial relations with a benevolent king. The Amphiktions collaborated, by issuing a decree of their own echoing these themes, and by further diffusing them through epigraphic publication at Delphi and large statues of Alabanda/Antiocheia and Antiochos III; the king's statue may have been located among earlier statues of

⁹⁹ Document **18**, 64–9.
¹⁰⁰ Hamilton 1842: ii. 14–15 (recognizable 'open space' with monuments near the south harbour); Béquignon and Laumonier 1925: 290.

Seleukid rulers (probably starting with his father, Seleukos II), in a gesture echoing the Antiocheian/Alabandan ambassador's speech in praise of Antiochos' adherence to ancestral example.[101] The behaviour of the Amphiktions illustrates how the community of cities could collaborate to diffuse acceptable images of kingship, and the commitments of specific kings.

'All the Greeks': the notion was not simply the horizontal dimension for generalizing language, but also a very real space of dense and vibrant inter-communal interaction, as documented by the epigraphy of the cities involved (A. Giovannini in Bulloch et al. 1993: 265–86). Within this world, local descriptions of the king's actions and motivations could be interpreted, perceived, or diffused. The statements about the king's actions and his character, the implicit messages of monuments and rituals, the performances before a pan-Hellenic audience: these were not 'performative' in the strict, Austinian sense of 'doing things with words' ('I declare you free'), but nonetheless had a significant political force, qua public descriptions of the rulers, circulated and received very widely. Austin himself, the initiator of speech-act theory, observed that statements (abstractly considered as non-performative, since predicated on truth-value), when considered as utterances in the real world, were also performative, in that their efficiency depended on their relevance to a context, and in that they had an effect on their recipients.[102] So civic statements about kings, diffused by various means, were efficient in defining actors and behaviour, promoting the euergetical discourse as the orthodox medium for interaction between ruler and ruled, publicizing moralizing norms and commitments to these norms, and hence enforcing behaviour desired by the local communities. The collaborative efforts of the system of cities in diffusing descriptions and praise of rulers in the euergetical discourse constituted the latter into an accepted political culture, in which the ruled could achieve a measure of agency, since it allowed the cities to constrain and manipulate the Hellenistic kings (as analysed in the two previous sections). A parallel (closely related chronologically and historically) is the description of the Romans as 'common benefactors' by the Greek cities of the second and first centuries: the title acknowledges Roman universal hegemony, but on certain terms, as long as power took the preferred manifestation

---

[101] Speech: document 16, esp. 19–22. Statue, possibly among earlier Seleukid portraits: Hintzen-Bohlen 1992: 104–6, 140.

[102] Pocock 1984, and generally the essays in Shapiro 1984, on the power of language to define the world and shape political relations. Austin on statements: Austin 1975: 132–47.

of benefaction. The practice expressed Roman power but also an ideology of empire and its acceptance by the Greeks.[103] Talking about rulers played its part in the wider phenomenon of 'role assignment', by which the ruled trusted in the stereotypical language of euergetism and its socializing and civilizing force[104] to constrain rulers within acceptable norms, once the network of cities had diffused the commitments of individual rulers and the norms which they (or their subjects) said they would follow.

3. *Local Meanings and the Self-Identity of the* Polis

The cities' statements, outside of direct interaction or the indirect construction of a political world favouring euergetical interaction, played an important role within the cities in making local knowledge: they defined the cities themselves as well as the ruler. For a city to approve the king's αἵρεσις is an explicit description of the king, but also an implicit description of the city, of its relation to the king, and its right to formulate a public judgement; for Iasos to praise Antiochos and Laodike implies the right to do so.[105] Analogously, an academic author might thank someone, in his acknowledgements, for 'characteristically acute criticism': this act of public praise presumes the author's capacity, and establishes his right, to pronounce such judgements. This role is a local dimension of civic discourse: statements about the self, for consumption by the producers themselves. This function is not directly practical and manipulative, as in the cases studied above; it is much closer to the civic statements about rulers, circulated internationally to achieve relevance and impact. In fact, the phenomenon I am considering here concerns the same sort of statements, and the same impact which apparently constative statements can have on people and things—but both in a local context. It is a widespread and important function of civic discourse, and it is important because it represents an act of local power.

---

[103] Ferrary 1988: 130–2. Erskine 1994: the title passed from the world of the individual petition to the king, to that of diplomatic interaction between Greek city and Rome, and hence implied an asymmetrical relationship between the two latter parties.

[104] I owe the concept to an unpublished paper by D. Gambetta; Veyne 1976: 78–81, on the reality of symbolical gestures. I have often heard J. Davis reflect that the ideal type of the 'English gentleman' must have been developed and diffused by Italian chambermaids and servants, to protect themselves against the real article, young 18th-cent. upper-class Englishmen bent on enjoying their Grand Tour.

[105] Document **26** B, II 4–5, 14–15.

(a) Talking about the Ruler

The most important place for such statements is the series of motivating clauses in the civic decrees. Even more than the participial
clauses of the royal letter (§ 2a), the motivations are a statement of
truth: ἐπειδή . . ., 'since P, then Q', formally equivalent to 'if P—and
P is the case—then Q'. In the absence of local historiography, of
which little has survived, the motivating clauses supply the cities'
narratives: by comparing these with our own narratives, we can try
to understand how the cities represented their power relation to the
empire.

The considerations of the first Teian decree for Antiochos and
Laodike are fairly preserved, and narrate the king's dealings with
the city. The general context is first indicated: on the other side of
the Taurus, Antiochos was the source of many favours for the
Teians; he then went to 'our region' (τοὺς καθ' ἡμᾶς τόπους) and
'restored the affairs to an expedient state'.[106] If the date is c.203, the
broader historical context will have been Antiochos' return from his
impressive eastern expedition (Ch. 2 § 2); but the only relevant facts,
in the local horizons of the decree, are his benefactions to Teos from
an undetermined afar. When the king arrives in the region, the
decree describes his actions—which we would dearly like to know
more about—in general terms (he restored things to an 'expedient'
state), and ambiguously: was the situation after Antiochos' actions
'expedient' (συμφέρουσαν) for the king, for the city, for both? When
the king stays in the city, the motivations for his behaviour are
described in local terms, and as strictly oriented towards Teos: concern for its plight, piety towards the city's great god Dionysos, the
wish to receive titles of honour (benefactor, saviour) from Teos[107]—
possible echoes of a royal speech in the Teian assembly, but repeated in the civic narrative, where they now become part of local
knowledge about the ruler and his esteem for the city. Antiochos
acts out of desire to do a favour to the city, θέλων χαρίζεσθαι τῶι
δήμωι: because this expression is part of a pre-existing diplomatic
language, used between cities (above), it integrates Antiochos and
his motivations within local intra-poliad cordiality. The king's
actual entrance, with troops and Friends, may have been a pageant
of royal might, of the sort so beloved by the Hellenistic monarchs
and so flattering to their power; the people may have gone out in
procession, organized by civic bodies or age groups, dressed in
white and wearing crowns, sacrificial victims at the ready, to greet
Antiochos, in the ceremony of ἀπάντησις, with its religious over-

---

[106] Document **17**, 8–11.   [107] Ibid. 11–22.

tones;[108] the city perhaps surrendered 'freely, in a festive atmosphere' (J. and L. Robert 1983: 137). But these hypotheses remain no
more than suggestions when confronted with the sober narrative in
the decree itself, which tells us simply that 'the king stayed in the
city with the Friends and the troops with him, making a very great
demonstration of his pre-existing trustworthiness towards all
men'.[109] Antiochos' entrance is mentioned matter-of-factly, and the
emphasis is on his πίστις, the king's keeping his engagements to the
city, as an occasion to give a moralizing description of the king.
Approval of the king's πίστις is a reversal of the royal language,
where kings commend officials or subjects for trustworthiness: the
local perspectives espoused by the Teian decree allowed the Teians
to appropriate the royal language of appraisal for their own uses, to
talk about royal behaviour towards the city, in a *polis*-centred
narrative.[110] The decree does not say explicitly that the city
surrendered to Antiochos III, a fact which we must read between
the lines. It neglects any celebration of the king on his own terms; it
is vague about the achievement of royal campaigns, about the
takeover of Teos, the king's entrance in the city, or it describes these
events from the point of view of local interests. A second decree
spoke of 'the goodwill (εὔνοια) of the king and his friends for the
people, and our enthusiasm (ἐκτένεια) towards the king and his
friends', as the situation which motivated the Teians' desire to grant
isopoliteia to the Seleukid cities of northern Syria:[111] the relationship
between Teos and the Seleukid king (and his friends, a crucial
element in the Seleukid state) is portrayed as one of cordial
reciprocity, rather than a power relation. This is the version which
the Teian decrees, and their epigraphical publication, offered
(where we would write high political and administrative history): a
selective, *polis*-centred narrative.

   The case of Teos is hardly unique. The motivations of the Iasian
decree on cult for Laodike are incomplete; it is still clear that, compared with the Teian decree, they are more specific about the arrival
of Antiochos. Valuably, the Iasian document comes after the letter
of Laodike, who gives her own narrative of past relations between
Antiochos III and Iasos, and we can contrast the two versions,
Seleukid and local. Laodike's letter marginalized the question
of reconquest and legal status, even as it rested on the ideology of

---

[108] Habicht 1970: 234; Robert 1987: 470–4, 523–4; cf. Brown 1992: 13–14 for the
parallel of the late-antique *adventus*.
[109] Document **17**, 22–5.
[110] Document **4**, 23–4 (restored in line 21), for royal courtier (cf. *RC* 44, line 2; also
Robert 1960: 105–6 with 106 n. 1); for city, *RC* 63, line 8.
[111] Document **18**, lines 92–4.

conquest-and-grant and royal monopoly of status definition: these were less important than (even though validated by) the main fact of royal generosity, restated and imitated by Laodike herself (§ 2a). In contrast, the Iasian decree speaks of Antiochos' pan-Hellenic euergetism, as exemplified in his striving to help the weak and to free the enslaved; in the case of Iasos, he rescued the city from slavery (τὴν δὲ ἡμέτεραν πόλιν πρότερό[ν] | [τε] ἐγ δουλείας ῥυσάμενος ἐποίησεν ἐλευθέραν—not quite how Laodike portrays the situation); Antiochos expelled the garrisoning soldiers and made the Iasians masters of their city again (ἡμᾶς κυρίους).[112] The Iasian decree brings back the political aspects (subordinated to benefaction in Laodike's letter) to the foreground, even if the decree must have gone on to commemorate royal benefactions; the Iasians echoed the theme of royal solicitude and humanitarian concern, but also chose to com-memorate, not a king 'reacquiring' a city and setting it free out of compassion, but a liberator, chasing a foreign garrison to make the city free again. Faced with the eleemosynary concerns of Laodike, which carried royal benefaction and sentiments deep into the *polis*, and drew attention to, or summoned, social divisions within the city between the poor citizens and the others, the Iasians in their responding decree reasserted the existence of the *polis* as corporate, political, autonomy-centred, and essentially unitary organism. The rephrasing of Seleukid viewpoint into local narrative and *polis* val-ues illustrates the vitality of civic ideology, and the functions of the civic imagination: narrative on terms acceptable to the *polis*.

A third example is provided by the Ilian decree *OGIS* 219, prob-ably honouring Antiochos I (as I believe: Appendix 1). The con-siderations (lines 2–16) echo royal ideology: the king and his relation to *pragmata*, army, and Friends; his patrimonial rights over an inherited empire; his military prowess (ἀρετή), looked on with favour by the gods (τὸ δαιμόνιον). Nonetheless, the central trope in this passage is the antithesis, repeated three times, between cities and kingdom: the king seeks to restore the cities of the Seleukis to peace and original happiness, and to 'reacquire his paternal empire'; this duly (διό) happens, when the king's 'fine and just enterprise' results in the restoration of the cities to peace, and the kingdom to its original situation; the king then goes to 'the region on this side of the Taurus' and brings peace to the cites, and increase to τὰ πράγ-ματα καὶ τὴν βασιλείαν. The king's successes are celebrated within a conceptual geography, insistently developed, which distinguishes between πόλεις and τὰ πράγματα/ἡ βασιλεία. Cities are not part of the

---

[112] Document **26** B, I 9–18.

king's affairs, and have a different relationship to the king from that
of the kingdom: the latter is the king's hereditary possession, while
the cities enjoy the king's care for their peace and their happiness.
The decree's motivating clauses (*considérants*) are thus structured
around a tension between royal ideology and civic worldview: they
express themes of royal ideology, yet keep their distance from this
ideology, by promoting a *polis*-centric conception (which does not
correspond to Seleukid administrative geography—there were in
fact *poleis* within the *basileia*: Ch. 3 § 3). Another way of maintaining distance is the vagueness and allusiveness of the narrative of
royal successes, comparable to the narrative in the first Teian
decree. This feature would be the more remarkable if the decree
could be proven to date from the time of Antiochos III (as some
argue): whatever the exact date, but especially if dated to *c*.197 BC,
the decree would give a bland and dramatically simplified version of
the exploits performed by Antiochos III since his accession, and
illustrate even more strikingly how civic decrees proposed narratives from a local viewpoint.

The local narratives in the civic decrees, with their reticence
about celebrating the king on any terms but their own, contrast with
other ways of representing royal power: for instance, the lavish
celebrations described by C. Geertz for Elizabethan England or
traditional Indonesian kingship, where subjects collaborate with
the rulers in producing festive images (Geertz 1993: 121–34); the
absolutist historiography or the 'ceremonies of information' broad-
casting the news of royal victories (never defeats), in the France of
Louis XIV;[113] or, within our period, the portrayal of royal wealth
and might given by an envoy of Antiochos III before the Achaians,
in 192 BC: the empire of domination materialized in its variegated
army, containing Dahai, Medes, Elymaians, Kadousians, and in its
fleet manned by Sidonians, Tyrians, Aradians, Sidetans (Liv.
35.48.4–6). Antiochos himself spoke of his power in the same way
when he wrote to the Greek cities in the preliminaries and the early
stages of the Roman–Seleukid War, a practice archly described by
the elder Cato: *litteris calamento bello gerit, calamo et atramento
militat* (*ORF* 8.20). The selective narratives of civic decrees moved
in a different world, of their own making: they viewed the king from
local perspectives; they acknowledged his might, but related it to
polis interests; they restated civic ideology: a sense of the dignity of
the local community, its autonomy or autarky, its existence outside
the king's *pragmata*, its status as a genuine interlocutor of the king.
To a certain extent, these features are self-fulfilling: the implicit

[113] Marin 1978; Fogel 1989.

lical, from the king-
ch narratives.

he king, ritual, and
onventionally called
role in helping cities
las been recognized,
which responded to
70: 160–5, 206–13).
ation to the king, by
ke power to save the
5: 42–7, 160). For S.
tion, classifying the
divine power; a way
sense of it, from the
(Price 1984: 25–40,
I had brought them
cultic images of him
in god of the city, to
ὶ σωτῆρε]s alongside
cultic image, in the
providence, whose
dministrative action
ivine power.[114] The
II and his ancestors
n gods of the city'.[115]
nterpreted from the
t 1970); this is illus-
ting ruler cult apart
vith the king (*OGIS*
al acknowledgement
e power of the king;
of cultic honours
ter than the *polis* by
), but there is room
The same applies to
ng to terms with the
se of it—but which
sulate civic identity
These questions can

ient 26 B, II 12–13.

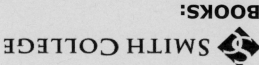
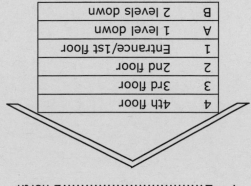
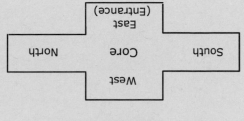

be answered, by studying the details of the creation of ruler cult, the 'honours which make memory', and not just the immediate χάρις of euergetical interaction with the benefactor: μὴ μόνον χ[άριν] | ἔχουσαι τὴμ παραυτίκα ἀλλὰ καὶ μνήμην ποιοῦσαι τὴν εἰς τὸ[ν ἅ] | παντα χρόνον.[116] This approach leads to examining the manipulation of social memory and civic identity, an active process whose contents and functions we can study, through the well-documented cases of Teos and Iasos.

One instructive case is the creation of a new festival at Teos, the Antiocheia and Laodikeia, and the way in which it was woven into civic life. The festival took place in Leukatheon, the first month of the year, a ceremonially charged moment in the ritual calendar, with the inauguration of new magistrates, the 'graduation' to citizen status of the ephebes, and the Leukathea, a festival of the civic subdivisions known as the *summoriai*. It was into this civic time that the Antiocheia and Laodikeia were introduced.[117] The festival mobilized all levels of the population: the magistrates (and their guests, the Dionysiac artists installed in Teos) held an official feast; the citizens sacrificed by *summoriai*, and the foreigners in the city performed private sacrifices in their houses; the festival reasserted the boundaries within the citizen body and between citizens and others, even as it affirmed the *polis* as a physical place and a population integrally affected by the prescribed holiday and court vacation.[118] The rituals performed by the *summoriai* were patterned on the Leukathea, with a subsidy from the central finances of the *polis*, and supervision by a priest of the city (the priest of Poseidon for the Leukathea, the priest of Antiochos for the Antiocheia and Laodikeia); they involved offerings on an altar which each *summoria* built on its property, next to its altar (παρὰ [τὸν βωμὸν τῆς συμορίας]): the juxtaposition of altars illustrates how reproduction of existing ritual allowed the integration of ruler cult within existing structures. The new festival introduced ruler cult at the level of local associative life below the level of the *polis*, yet always aware of belonging to it (through central funding and central religious supervision). The civic sub-units, by their very names, may have served as reminders

---

[116] Distinction in document **18**, 65–7 ('(honours) which not only have gratitude in the immediate present, but which also make memory for all times').

[117] Leukatheon: document **18**, 21, implies that the festival took place in this month, since the deadline for financial applications to the city *tamias* was Leukatheon 4. Ceremonial month: ibid., 37–8, 39. Leukathea and *summoriai*: Şahin 1985 for evidence.

[118] Document **18**, 3–28. The holiday, as moment of ritual celebration or simply of general pause from daily labours, and more abstractly as a time for memory and self-aware communion, must count among the mechanisms which define the 'imagined community' (Anderson 1991).

of the city's mythical history, and hence acted as important *loci* for civic identity.[119] The new festival for Antiochos and Laodike was inscribed in the 'holy book' of the city, both literally, as a new entry in the official calendar (ἀναγ[ράψαι] | [δὲ τ]αύτην τὴν ἑορτήν εἰς τὴν ἱερὰν βύβλον), but also, more generally, as inscription within the constituent structures of civic identity.

The other phenomenon documented at Teos is the creation of new centres for civic life, intended as memorial acts of homage to the benefactions and the character of Antiochos and Laodike. The Teians created a new site for ruler cult, the *bouleuterion* adorned with a sacred statue (ἄγαλμα) of Antiochos, as a memorial of his benefactions, 'some of which he realized, some he promised and subsequently realized': what had been a constraining formula in direct address to the ruler (§ 2*b*) has now turned into celebration.[120] The intention was 'to consecrate to King Antiochos the Great' the place where these events happened, the *bouleuterion* as venue for his speech before the assembled *ekklesia*:[121] the consecration itself is a cultic homage to Antiochos as recipient of divine honours, and echoes his benefaction, the consecration of the city and territory of the Teians as *asylos*. In front of this statue, on Leukatheon 1, the principal magistrates (*strategoi, timouchoi, tamiai*) sacrificed on the common hearth of the city, to the king, the *Charites*, and *Mneme,* the euergetical values of reciprocal gratitude and memory.[122] On the same day, the ephebes, upon graduation into adult status, were led by the gymnasiarch into the agora for the first time, and offered the same sacrifice; the intention was didactic, showing the citizens-to-be that gratitude towards benefactors was the most important part of political life, τὰ κοινά:[123]

ἵνα μηθὲν πρότερον ἄρξωνται πράσσειν τῶν κοινῶν πρὶν ἢ χάρ[ι]-
[τα]ς ἀποδ[ο]ῦναι τοῖς εὐεργέταις καὶ ἐθίζωμεν τοὺς ἐξ ἡαυτῶν πά[ν]-
[τα] ὕστερα καὶ ἐν ἐλλάσσοντι τίθεσθαι πρὸς ἀποκατάστασιν χάριτος

---

[119] Rogers 1991, for Roman Ephesos. The only attested *summoriai* are the Ἐχίνου συμμορία (Şahin 1985), presumably named after a local hero, and ἡ Δατύλου συμμορία, attested on a Teian gravestone recording honours paid to the deceased by various bodies. (The form Δατύλου was suggested by Wilhelm for Ἀλτύλου, proposed by H. Hauvette-Besnault and E. Pottier, the editors: the stone bears traces rendered as ΛΛΤΥΛΟΥ; Datylos might be the same as an Athenian hero Datylos/Datyllos, first identified by Wilhelm in *IG* 1³ 383, line 76; for references, see J. and L. Robert, *OMS* vii. 310 n. 58).

[120] Document **18**, 29–63.

[121] Document **17**, 17. The *bouleuterion* (perhaps the 'small theatre' which can still be seen on the site) could presumably have held many, or all, of the Teian citizen body (on the 'small theatre' or odeion at Teos, Béquignon and Laumonier 1925: 288–9).

[122] Document **18**, 33–8.

[123] Ibid. 38–44.

so that they do not start to undertake anything concerning the community
before returning gratitude to the benefactors and so that we should
accustom our progeny to value everything less than the returning of
gratitude.

Teian athletes, victorious in the prestigious pan-Hellenic
'crowned' contests were now to crown the king's *agalma* (presumably with the very wreath they had won) and offer the same sacrifice
to king, *Charites*, and *Mneme* on the common hearth, their first act
on their eiselastic entrance into the city.[124] The traditional gestures
of the city's finest, victorious in contests abroad, are now reconfigured as tribute to the king, the path of their movement in the city
rechanelled to the new centre. The message is perhaps that the
king's power to benefit the city is superior to the symbolical advantages athletic victory brought to the city, or that the athletic contests
are less important than the contest to gain a city's gratitude through
euergetism (on this notion, Gauthier 1985: 11–12, 129–30).

The *bouleuterion* was already an important location on the map of
civic life, since it was the meeting place of the council, and probably
of the assembly, and also served as the spot where public lists and
decisions were temporarily published on whitened boards, thus
making it a centre for public communication between the *polis* as
state and the citizens;[125] marked as a memorial site, it now became
the centre to which civic ritual accompanying cardinal moments was
shifted[126]—the uncertain moment when the magistracies were
renewed; the *rite de passage* by which the city admitted new
members; the triumphal entrance of the victorious athletes—to pay
homage to the *agalma* and the sacrifice to king, *Charites*, and
Mneme. Civic life was reconfigured around a particular image: King
Antiochos the Great, whose benefactions had brought prosperity.
This image was made concrete by the cult statue, to which first
fruits of 'the crops which grow on trees' were offered, and which
stood crowned with a wreath which was changed as the seasons went
by:[127] a symbol of the providential nature of the king, and the permanence of the city's gratitude, manifested by recurring patterns of
change centred around the enduring, monumental statue.

The Teians honoured Laodike with an eponymous fountain,[128]

---

[124] Document **18**, 46–50. On eiselastic entrances and customary sacrifices, J. and L.
Robert 1989: 21–2; there is an instance in document **16**, 31–2 (Pausimachos will 'introduce' into Antiocheia/Alabanda the crown he won at the Soteria).

[125] Temporary publications: see the inscription relative to the absorption of Kyrbissos
by Teos, published by J. and L. Robert, and reprinted in *OMS* vii. 299, lines 17–18.

[126] 'Umgestaltet', Herrmann 1965a: 68.

[127] Document **18**, 50–9.

[128] Ibid. 64–90.

which can be analysed in the same terms as the nexus of rituals around the *bouleuterion*. The fountain had the same memorial function, established a monument of Teian *eucharistia* in the middle of the public space of the city, ἐμ μέσωι, and paid homage to her piety. Around this new centre, the Teians rearranged public religion—priests and priestesses drew water from the fountain to use in public sacrifices πρὸ πόλεως—and private ritual: just as important moments of civic life were relocated at the statue of Antiochos, the cardinal events of death and marriage in Teos would now require the fetching of water from the fountain of Laodike, for use in the prescribed ablutions, thus integrating the presence of ruler cult and its messages into private life. The fountain and the ceremonies, public and private, were marked as sacred by religious dress worn when drawing water (white clothes, crowns, and, for the bridal bath, some vestimentary or ritual feature described in a lacuna of the text).

The processes at Teos find close parallels at Iasos. Before the altar of Antiochos III, the *strategoi* passed the keys of the city to their successors, who then offered sacrifice, on the altar, to the king and his ancestors, '[as to com]mon gods of the city':[129] a parallel with the inauguration of new magistrates at Teos; in both cases, the delicate moment in the life of the city is put under the protection of the king and a monument which makes him visible (a statue at Teos, an altar at Iasos). This piece of ceremony occurs in a decree mostly devoted to honours for Laodike: it must be an addition to a nexus of rituals decreed earlier and centred around the altar of Antiochos (already in existence when the ceremony of the keys was devised): if we knew about these, we would probably notice many points of contact with practices at Teos. It is also likely that the transferral of the keys had been a pre-existing civic ceremony, now capped with a sacrifice to the king, its civic meanings overlaid with the functions of ruler cult for Antiochos III.[130] Also parallel is the sense of metaphor: the keys, a symbol and an instrument of the state's security, are passed before the altar of the king who has proved the φύλαξ of the city: the title is unusual, and was devised by the Iasians, to articulate the metaphor in the ritual.[131] Likewise, the Iasians instituted a cult of Laodike as Aphrodite Laodike, which presided over marriage: the cult involved sacrifices by newly married couples and processions of women of marrying age. It commemorated Laodike's benefaction appropriately (the queen provided dowries for poor citizen women) and also extended ruler cult into private life, just as the fountain of Laodike

[129] Document **26** B, II 6–14; contra, Nafissi 2001, 123–7.
[130] Parallel: document **30**, 5, for the practice as purely civic ceremony at Euromos.
[131] Document **26** B, II 6.

did at Teos. Finally, the distribution of ruler cult into civic subdivisions appears in the decree of an Iasian *phyle*, honouring
Antiochos and his family; the Iasian *phyle* may also have built an
altar to the king.[132] Ruler cult at Teos and Iasos, though richly documented, fits into well-known and studied patterns, and an extensive
commentary could be easily provided by drawing on many parallels
which can be found throughout the Hellenistic world — for the
involvement of ephebes; the grafting of ruler cult onto pre-existing
forms (for instance, at Athens, images of Antigonos Monophthalmos
and Demetrios Poliorketes woven into Athena's *peplos*); the consecration of memorial sites (such as the place where Demetrios
Poliorketes set foot in Athens in 304); cultic practice at the level of
civic subdivisions (for instance the imitation in the deme of
Rhamnous of the Athenian cult for Antigonos Gonatas), often with
funding from the city; and the extension to the private sphere.[133]

These parallels ensure that the case of Teos is not unique. Its
importance lies in the richness and the concentration of details.
Robert, in the outline of an unpublished article on 'nouveaux cultes
de Téos', emphasized the elegance with which ruler cult was integrated into pre-existing religion and civic ceremony, and hence its
connection with local institutions of great vitality.[134] The creative-
ness and smoothness of the process should not obscure how
deliberately and comprehensively important constituents of social
life were reorganized around new centres, to 'create memory'. By
a conscious, open, political, process (decision-making in the
assembly), the Teians constructed and manipulated social memory,
at all levels of public and private life—in civic ceremonials such as
the magistrates' *passation de pouvoirs* or the graduation of ephebes;
in private gestures such as the washing of a corpse or the bathing of
a bride. The process demonstrates how a rational, historically-
minded society can consciously mobilize social resources (in the
present case, the institutions of the *polis*) to create and manipulate

---

[132] Documents **26** B, II 17–44 and frag.; **27**.

[133] Ephebes: *Inschr. Delphinion* 139 (ephebic oath); *I. Ilion* 31; ruler cult in the gymnasion is attested at Soloi under Antiochos III (document **20**), and was widespread:
Robert 1960: 124–55 with further references; Habicht 1970: 143–4; Robert 1987: 291
and n. 66. Demetrios: Habicht 1970: 44–5, 48–50 (on Diod. 20.46.2, Plut. *Dem* 10.5 and
Mor. 338a). Festivals grafted onto, or imitated from, pre-existing festivals: Habicht
1970: 50–5 (Demetria and Dionysia, Athens), 76–8 (Demetria and Dionysia, Euboia),
85–7 (Dionysia and Seleukeia, Erythrai), 149 (Seleukeia as extension of Panathenaia,
Ilion). Subdivisions: *SEG* 41.75 (Rhamnous); Habicht 1970: 152, on *I. Ilion* 31, which
also shows central funding for tribal cult; this practice is further documented in *OGIS*
11, lines 24–6. Private elements: Robert, *OMS* vii. 599–636.

[134] *BE* 69, 496, announcing a new document from Teos relevant to the question; also
Price 1984: 37–9 (against the conventional (or obsolete) thesis of decline in traditional
religion in conjunction with the rise of ruler cult).

pervasive, living memories of the past, for a political purpose. The consequence of this finding is that it allows us to examine the political functions and the effect of social memory as deliberately reconstructed in reaction to the coming of Antiochos III.[135]

The analysis and laying out of the workings of social memory thus leads us back to the question of its function. The memorial sites and rituals of 'ruler cult', within the community, confronted and processed a large, extra-poliadic, threatening event: the campaigns of (re)conquest waged by Antiochos III, as they worked themselves out in local contexts. This event was fast consigned to μνήμη, by the almost immediate creation of commemorative ritual.[136] Ruler cult worked as 'instant memory': it created memory and hence meaning out of the confused present; the Teians (and, likewise, the Iasians) made sense of a potentially traumatic occurrence (armed takeover by the Seleukid empire, alarmingly resurgent under Antiochos III) by classifying it into the past and choosing how to remember it. The memories would be not be those of conquest, violence, submission by local communities which had no choice, but acceptable ones, consonant with civic pride, its sense of worth, its sense of participation in a process of exchange: memories of euergetical χάρις, the king's benefactions, motivated by concern for the Teians' plight and resulting in the city's happiness, the city's desire to reciprocate by honours (which themselves, through repetition, would become memorials). This is the message carried deep into civic structures, by a new festival, and by the reconfiguration of public ceremonial and private ritual around new centres. The process was a speedy one: the Teian and the Iasian decrees document the creation of 'instant memory' soon after the Seleukid takeover; at Xanthos, a priest of the kings, Antiochos III and Antiochos the son, is in office in 196 BC, the year following Antiochos' campaign in the region.[137]

[135] See Loraux 1997, for the world of the *polis* presented as a timeless, anthropological world, where 'everything happens in the present tense', and for the deliberately depoliticizing force of this way (both ancient and modern) of conceiving the *polis*. The thoughts presented here owe much to Rogers 1991, notably at p. 139, on the rational, systematic character of the creation of civic ritual in Roman Ephesos by Vibius Salutaris.

[136] The second Teian decree, document 18, cannot come much later than Seleukid takeover; the same applies for the Iasian decree 26 B, which is not the first decree in honour of Antiochos and Laodike.

[137] Xanthos: document 23. At Amyzon, a local priest of Antiochos III and Antiochos the son is not attested in document 9 (autumn 202), but appears in document 10, in late 201, two and a half years after the Seleukid takeover, which took place in May 203 (document 5). However, document 10 only shows when the Amyzonians started to date their civic documents by the priest of the kings, not when they created the priesthood: this could have taken place earlier.

The manipulation of social memory—swiftly cast into monuments, iterated in public and private rituals to mobilize civic subdivisions and human groupings, and proclaimed by inscriptions in visible spots of the city—would ensure the uniformity of remembrance and impose consensus. The creation and perpetuation of an agreed-on version of the recent past could help to reinstate social harmony and *polis* coherence after the potentially divisive adhesion to a new power: it is likely that certain Teians had supported the Attalids, or that some Iasians had favoured the Antigonids (just as the Seleukids had long-standing partisans in Kyme or Miletos: *RC* 17; 22). Monuments and ritual thus substituted social memory to politics. So the Teians would reach consensus on consciously crafted memories of Antiochos' coming and its results. Consciously crafted memories: in preference to a narrative of conquest by Antiochos III, imperialist, restorer of the Seleukid fortunes, warrior king, mouth scarred and teeth missing from a cavalry battle in Baktria, prone to heavy drinking and after-dinner dancing in arms,[138] the Teians unanimously and repeatedly made themselves commemorate the king's beneficence, the speech in the *bouleuterion* declaring the city *asylos* and free from tribute, euergetical promises kept, all these events subsumed and fetishized in the unarguable, concrete image around which manifestations of civic life revolved—Antiochos III as benign agrarian deity, first-fruits at his feet, a changing crown of seasonal produce on his head.

(c) The Polis' Version

The motivations of the civic decrees and the selective social memory created by ruler cult worked to the same effect: they created local narratives, which we might call 'non-realistic' in contrast with the realistic way of talking about empire in the passage of Polybios analysed in Chapter 2 (21.41.2) or in documents where the exploitative nature of empire is stated without qualms. The local narratives historicize the potentially traumatic present: conquest, subordination (greater or lesser, but real) were written into the inert stuff of history,[139] in which form they could be shaped to produce acceptable versions, leaving the power relation unsaid, and focusing on

[138] Warrior: Ch. 2, introduction (the 'imperialist' tag is borrowed from Sherwin-White and Kuhrt 1993). Drinking: Bikerman 1938: 34–5 on Aelian, *VH* 2.41. Teeth: Pol. 10.49. Dancing: Athen. 4.155b.

[139] Veyne 1978: 63: 'l'histoire est un des produits les plus inoffensifs qu'ait jamais élaborés la chimie de l'intellect' (silently reworking an epigram by P. Valéry, substituting 'inoffensifs' to 'dangereux'). On civic epigraphy as local history, Boffo 1988 (e.g. 21–2, on the production of local memory and local knowledge).

memories of euergetical exchange; they neutralized the problematic realities of Hellenistic high politics, and insulated civic pride from their impact. In the aftermath of traumatic events, the Teians and the Iasians could reassure themselves that the local historiography of civic decrees and memorial rituals would pass on to their descendants carefully controlled narratives crafted out of the confused present.

Local narratives also allowed the cities to offer their own definitions of the world, if only for local consumption: they judged the king, praised him, spoke approvingly of *his* trustworthiness, gave meaning to his actions, honoured him in certain terms, remembered his actions in certain forms; through local narratives the cities could objectify, and hence exercise some form of symbolical power over, their rulers. The Teians, in their decree, proclaim confidently that the honours they offer to Antiochos and Laodike will show the world that they know how to 'decree the honours which are suitable for each person': an assertion of the capacity to judge, and the ability to reward adequately anyone, including a Seleukid royal couple.[140] Talking about the ruler was a way for the cities to talk about themselves, imagine their relation to the ruler, and by talking about the world, in the past or the present tense, to try to control it. These local versions were quite different from the administrative, legal, and ideological structures of the Seleukid empire (explored in Chapter 3): the very difference illustrates the function of 'non-realist narratives'—to offer local definitions within, and against, a broader imperial ideology where definitions were the monopoly of the king. In T. Morrison's *Beloved*, a slave-owner beats a slave (after an argument over the interpretation of the slave's eating the master's pig: theft, or improvement of the master's property, i.e. the slave himself?): the beating demonstrates that 'definitions belonged to the definers, not the defined'.[141] But the cities offered their own selective narratives about the king and his relation to them, affirming their own definitions, and their right to define; they created local forms of ideological counter-power, and took an active part in the 'struggle for the real' through their own discursive resources (Rogers 1991: 69, quoting Geertz, on the parallel case of civic ritual in Roman Ephesos).

These practices should not be scorned as pure wishful thinking or local delusions. The 'non-realistic' narratives organized the experience of empire, from the point of view of the subordinate communities, a fact that is sufficient to warrant examination; that the

[140] Document **18**, line 69.
[141] Quoted by K. Bradley, *CJ* 90 (1995), 445.

local communities responded to imperial power by offering narratives where power was omitted in the favour of beneficence and reciprocity is itself revealing of their strong self-identity, the tenacity of their values and sense of autonomy. The phenomenon had practical political consequences. By insulating local civic identity and pride, 'non-realistic' narratives allowed the *polis* to preserve a sense of purpose in the face of subordination and integration within a supra-polis empire. This could realize itself in action to seize independence from the Hellenistic empires, as the recalcitrant cities of Smyrna and Lampsakos did. Smyrna had earlier offered cultic honours to the Seleukids (Habicht 1970: 99–102); these must have been conceived in ways that preserved civic identity as well as interacted with the rulers. At the very least, this persistence of purpose allowed the local communities to develop the patience, the sense of local interests, and the opportunism[142] which characterized their behaviour in the multi-polar Hellenistic world.

4. The Successes of Royal Discourse

The interpretation offered above might seem too optimistic, and another is possible: instead of focusing on local versions preserving *polis* pride, we might notice the speed and fluency with which the ceremonies of ruler cult introduced into the heart of the city images of kingship which corresponded to the royal ideology itself, the power-as-benefaction which was the central representation in the king's discourse. The Hellenistic *polis*, for all the resilience of its ideology, was not impermeable to this discourse; its acceptance within the *polis* contributed to the creation of a cultural *koine* centred on empire, and diffusing the effects of the ideological force of empire, analysed earlier (Ch. 3 §§ 2 and 3).[143]

The case of the Teians, again, is worth pondering. I have tried to show that ruler cult performed local functions, that might have strengthened or insulated civic identity; nonetheless, it is impossible not to notice that ruler cult thoroughly reorganized civic ritual around royal images, by manipulating civic structures at a very deep level. The Teians put concrete representations (a statue of Antiochos III, a fountain named after Laodike) of the Seleukid king and queen in sites which were central to the symbolical map of the

---

[142] Rostovtzeff 1941: 35.
[143] 'Cultural *koine*': the concept is inspired by Mourgues 1995, studying the propagation of official ideology into the decrees of the Graeco-Roman cities; Price 1984, for the role of the imperial cult in Roman Asia Minor.

city: the *bouleuterion* where political processes took place (meetings of the council and assembly, publication of public acts), and the *agora*, the central space where only grown citizens could enter, and where citizen met citizen in daily interaction. Furthermore, the Teians granted their citizenship to the cities of the Seleukis, one of the administrative and symbolical centres of the Seleukid empire: in Polybios (5.58.4) Antiochos' physician, Apollophanes of Seleukeia in Pieria, called the latter city the 'foundress' (ἀρχηγέτις) and 'almost, so to speak, the hearth' of the Seleukid state's power (σχεδὸν ὡς εἰπεῖν ἑστίαν ὑπάρχουσαν τῆς αὐτῶν δυναστείας).[144] Even if the Teian grant was purely symbolical, and directed at Seleukid officials who might come from these cities (as suggested by Gauthier: above, § 2c), the decision was still represented as the result of a desire for close relations with these cities, by sharing Teian citizenship, itself represented as merely a way to share royal benefactions[145]—'to put in common, so to speak, with the cities named after the ancestors of the king the favours which were given and those which will be given by the king to the people, so that, after a grant of our citizenship to them, they should be the readier to benefactions and show eagerness in all matters, just as it is a fine thing to do with one's own father-land'. The grant of *isopoliteia* may have resulted in diplomatic contacts, and possibly in the adoption by the Teians of practices from the imperial cities of the Seleukis, namely a civic cult for Antiochos III and his ancestors. This cult is attested both at Seleukeia in Pieria—and Teos, where the privileged position given to Antiochos III probably indicates that the cult was introduced in his reign (*OGIS* 245: new text in *SEG* 35.1521; 246—both after the time of Antiochos III). Since the 'second Teian decree' tells of Teos' desire to foster links with the cities at the centre of the empire, Herrmann suggested that the Teians imitated the Seleukid practice of civic dynastic cult from these cities, where it is attested (Herrmann 1965a: 149–56; Rostovtzeff 1935). This would show an old Hellenic city, formally 'autonomous', adopting a practice from new royal foundations, 'subject' cities *par excellence*, whose identity was defined by their dynastic name ('the cities named after the ancestors of the king'). At the very least, the cultic title Μέγας in Teos was taken from central Seleukid practice both administrative (as in the 'regnal formula') and probably cultic. By adopting these

---

[144] The recent emphasis, by Sherwin-White and Kuhrt 1993, on the importance of Seleukid Babylonia does not detract from the importance of the Seleukis in the Aegean world (whose conceptual geography balances 'Asia on this side of the Taurus' and North Syria). On the cities of the Seleukis, F. Millar, in Sherwin-White and Kuhrt 1987: 110–33.

[145] Document **18**, 90–104.

forms, Teos participated in a wider culture of empire, expressed through the ubiquity of signifiers of empire imposed on geographical diversity and extension (Ch. 3 § 2d). Again, Iasos offers a parallel showing that the case of Teos is not unique: as already mentioned in the preceding section, Iasian *strategoi*, upon entering office, sacrificed on the king's altar to the king and his ancestors.[146] This goes further than usual cultic honours from subordinate cities for Hellenistic rulers: the opening gesture of the chief military magistrates of the city was a ritual which acknowledged an important theme of Seleukid ideology under Antiochos III (the 'ancestral theme' so important in his self-representation and his actions), but also echoed the practice of dynastic cult in the royal foundations.

A more widely attested feature is the assimilation of royal language into the language of civic decrees. Assimilation goes deeper than simply repeating items from the royal repertoire, such the designation of Apollo as ancestor of the Seleukid dynasty,[147] or the adoption of chancery forms, such as referring to Antiochos III as 'the Great King Antiochos', found in all 'Seleukid' cities irrespective of formal status—at Antioch (one of the 'imperial' cities of the Seleukis), Xanthos (a 'subject' city) and Iasos (a 'free' city).[148] An example of deeper assimilation is perhaps to be found in Zeuxis' paraphrase of a decree from Herakleia under Latmos: τὸ ψήφισμα καθ' ὃ ὤιεσθε δεῖν, ἀνακεκομισμέ|νων ἡμῶν τῶι βασιλεῖ τὴν πόλιν ἐξ ἀρχῆς ὑπάρχουσαν τοῖς προγόνοις αὐτοῦ, | θυσίας τε συντελεσθῆναι τοῖς θεοῖς καὶ τοῖς βασιλεῦσιν καὶ τοῖς τέκνοις αὐτῶν, 'your decree, according to which you thought it right, after we had recovered for the king the city which had originally belonged to his ancestors, to offer sacrifices to the gods, the kings, and their children'. Assuming that Zeuxis is accurately paraphrasing the civic decree, the Herakleians, in the considerations of their decree, seem to have accepted the Seleukid version of their past, according to which Zeuxis was not conquering the city, but merely recovering it, in virtue of the ancestral property rights of the Seleukids.[149] However, this might more likely be the result of Zeuxis reformulating in Seleukid terms a vaguer local narrative, like those found in Teos or Iasos (§ 2a).

More conclusively: as motivation for honours, cities can mention the honorand's services not only to themselves, but also to the king. The Amyzonians honoured Ophelandros and his soldiers, for

---

[146] Document **26**, B II 11–12.

[147] *OGIS* 219, lines 26–7; 212, lines 13–14; documents **22**, **28**; Delphian (or rather, Amphiktionic: Lefèvre 1996) document commented in *BE* 55, 122 (used by the Amphiktions).

[148] Antioch: Kraeling 1964. Xanthos: document **22**. Iasos: **26** B, I 9; **27**, 3; **28**, 12.

[149] Document **31** B, II 8–10.

services ὑπὲρ τῶν τῶν βασιλέων πραγμάτων (the phrase occurs in the considerations, and, significantly, in the 'hortative' clause: the Amyzonians made clear that they honoured those who strove for the interests of the kings, Antiochos III and Antiochos the son); the Xanthian *neoi* praised their gymnasiarch Lyson 'for *eunoia* towards the city, themselves, and the affairs of the kings'.[150] The figure is common: the Euromians/Philippeis mentioned services to the interests of Philip V in their decree for his general Alexandros Admetou; the Antiochenes praised Theophilos of Seleukeia in Pieria 'for his *philotimia* and his *eunoia* towards the Great King Antiochos, Antiochos the son, Queen Laodike and their children, and towards themselves' (i.e. the citizens of Antioch).[151]

It is natural that the king should praise individuals or communities for their attitude towards himself and his *pragmata*, as part of the patrimonial ideology of empire: Antiochos III praised Nikanor in these terms, or a courtier whom he appointed to a priesthood in Antioch; likewise, the king and Zeuxis advised the Herakleians to keep their *eunoia* towards the king's *pragmata*, and Laodike may have done the same with the Teians;[152] earlier, Antiochos I praised the *eunoia* of Aristodikides in a letter concerned with a land grant to him (*RC* 12). It is far more surprising to see this expression in the civic decrees: the city says, in effect, '*we* praise *you* for services to *him*', introducing a royal third party in the exchange between benefactor and honourer. By admitting goodwill towards the king as part of the reasons to honour an individual, the city proclaims awareness of its integration within a supra-poliad empire, whose interests (the personal interests of the king) are of relevance to the city;[153] this awareness is voiced through expressions taken from royal language, now integrated within the cardinal form for civic self-expression, the decree.

[150] Documents **13**, 9, 12–14; **24**, 32–34.

[151] Errington 1993: no. 4; Kraeling 1964. Also: *Syll*. 342, lines 12–15 (Athenian decree for Medeios of Larisa, Friend of Antigonos Monophthalmos and Demetrios Poliorketes); *Syll*. 343, lines 6–16 (Athenian decree for Oxythemis of Larisa, for his behaviour towards 'the kings' (Antigonos and Demetrios) and their *pragmata*); *Syll*. 426, lines 10–12, 41–2 (Bargylietan decree for judge from Teos); Kearsley 1994 (*SEG* 44.1108), lines 10–11 (Olbasan decree for Attalid official); Bikerman 1938: 128 n. 6 (Antiocheia on Pyramos for Seleukid financial official); *LBW* 3.1486 (same city for citizen); *IG* 11.4.114 (Laodikeia in Pieria for the chief minister Heliodoros); *MAMA* 6.173, line 14, with *BE* 39, 400 (decree of Apameia in Phrygia for citizen who showed his *eunoia* towards the *pragmata* of the Attalids).

[152] Document **4**; *RC* 44; documents **31** A, I 15 and B, IV 10; **19** D, 9–10. Parallels—for individuals, *IG* 11.3.1113; *RC* 44, 45, 58; for communities: *RC* 22, 31, 71; *OGIS* 229, lines 8–9 (in Smyrnian decree describing royal action); 2 Macc. 11, 19; Holleaux 1942: 94.

[153] Gauthier 1996: 7: 'dans une cité dépendante, le loyalisme dynastique fait partie, au même titre que le patriotisme, des qualités reconnues à ses bienfaiteurs'.

The phenomenon goes beyond the mere demonstration of loyalism, for instrumental purposes in interaction with the ruler (§ 2*b*). Two instances may illustrate the depth with which the 'cultural *koine* of empire' had entered, if not the consciousness of the *polis*, at least its public forms. At Iasos, a *phyle* carried out rituals (libations, perhaps a sacrifice) and pronounced public prayers, 'for [all] advantages to happen to the Great King Antiochos, queen Laodike, and their children, and to the city': ἐπεύχεσθαι δὲ τοὺς φυλέτας [πάντα γίν]|εσθαι τἀγαθά βασιλεῖ τε μεγάλωι Ἀ[ντιόχωι] | καὶ βασιλίσσηι Λαοδίκηι καὶ τοῖς τέκνοις | καὶ τῆι πόλει.[154] At the level of the civic subdivision, as part of civic ceremonial, the *phyle* now uttered common prayers for the welfare of the king and his family with the welfare of the *polis*. The *phyle* was one of the constituent parts of the city and hence a prime context for ceremonials of belonging to the *polis* (above, for Teian *summoriai*; Rogers 1991 for Roman Ephesos); yet the public prayers which manifested the citizens' sense of community were diverted from their primary function, now to speak of loyalism and integration within a suprapoliad empire: the welfare of the rulers was not only mentioned in the public prayers, but also named in precedence the *polis* itself—in an old, juridically 'free' city like Iasos.

The second phenomenon (though not yet uncontestably illustrated under Antiochos III) is the introduction of the king into the forms of decrees: a city (name now unknown), in a decree honouring a king Antiochos and Priene for the dispatch of a Prienian 'foreign judge', prefaced the decisions with the formula [ἀ]γαθῆι τύχηι κἀιπὶ σωτ[η]|[ρίαι τοῦ τε βασιλέως καὶ τῶν ἐκ]γόνων αὐτοῦ, in place of the more usual formulas stating that the decisions in a decree are taken for the welfare of the city, or simply ἀγαθῆι τύχηι: the local decree is taken under the wish for the welfare of the king and his descendants (*Inschr. Priene* 24, lines 19–20).[155] Nor is the practice isolated or restricted to 'subject' cities (as the city in *Inschr. Priene* 24 probably was).[156] At Samothrake, a decree (in honour of Lysimachos) prefaces the decisions with the formula ἀγαθῆι τύχηι |

---

[154] Document **27**, 1–5. **18**, 3 attests sacrifices and libations at Teos, as part of the Antiocheia and Laodikeia. Earlier, during the formative period of the Diadochs, when many of the forms of diplomacy and interaction were developed, the Ephesians responded to the news of military successes by Demetrios Poliorketes by organizing prayers 'for things to go [even better] for Demetrios the king and the people [of the Ephesians]' (*Syll.* 352, lines 6–7).

[155] Perhaps [ἀ]γαθῆι τύχηι κἀιπὶ σωτ[ηρίαι τῆς πόλεως καὶ τοῦ βασιλέως καὶ τῶν ἐκ]γόνων αὐτοῦ? For examples of the normal formula, documents **10**, 18; **16**, 11; **17**, 44; **32**, 13.

[156] It applied to the king for a foreign judge, just as Laodikeia on Lykos did with Zeuxis (document **32** and Crowther 1993; Ch. 3 § 3).

[βα]σιλέως Λυσιμάχου καὶ τῆς πόλεω[ς] (*Syll.* 372, lines 19–20): as in the Iasian prayers, the king is named before the city.

How royal ideology was diffused among the cities is unclear; local initiative may have played the major part. Seleukid governors and dignitaries perhaps performed a role; for instance, the dedication (of a statue, a room in a gymnasion, a whole gymnasion?) by Ptolemaios Thraseou at Soloi may have been part of a whole nexus of euergetism and dealings with the local community, which would have accepted royal ideology as part of the benefactions from Ptolemaios.[157] An important role was certainly performed by the details of interaction, when royal interlocutors could use their discursive position (gifts accompanied by explanations and descriptions) to impose their assumptions on the cities: I have examined the letter in which Laodike explains her gift of grain to the Iasians (§ 2*a*). Another channel may have been the local Seleukid officials, whom the cities tried to socialize by citizenship grants and honours (§ 2*c*). These honours, as argued above, may have represented local obligations and hence possible restraints on the officials' behaviour; but, conversely, the price to pay was possibly the admission of very big fishes into small ponds, the introduction of Seleukid officials into the space of the city, where these men could sit in the assembly, meet citizens on a daily basis, and 'partake of all the other things' alongside the citizens. Menestratos, the *epistates* of the Artemision at Amyzon, became an Amyzonian citizen: what did he say, when the assembly of Amyzonians met (no doubt in the theatre which belonged to Amyzon's monumental complex)? How constrained did he feel by his new co-citizens as he sat in their midst? What sort of speeches did he make? Did his mere presence inhibit discussion of issues that might have gone against Seleukid interests? Did it exercise subtle pressure, even without the need for vocalizing the 'Seleukid point of view', so that the Amyzonians felt it would be politic to make the right gestures and references, and always take the Seleukid state into account when transacting common affairs? None of these questions can be answered, but they are suggestive enough to the historical imagination. At the very least, they make it possible that Menestratos helped introduce Seleukid-influenced forms and ideology into the *polis* of Amyzon.[158]

Another possible channel for the diffusion or imposition of royal ideology is the creation of state cult for Antiochos III and his ancestors, and later for Laodike. It is true that this state-organized,

---

[157] Document **21**.

[158] Menestratos: document **10**. On the notion of power as influencing the issues, before they come to the light of decision-making, Lukes 1974.

centrally administered ruler cult should be distinguished from the local cults, decreed by the cities for local reasons (Bikerman 1938: ch. 7; Habicht 1970). At the same time, it is difficult not to see some relation between the two forms (Sherwin-White and Kuhrt 1993: 202–10, esp. 209). The one case documented in some detail is the cult for Laodike, though it hardly presents a simple picture of centrally defined practice imitated locally: civic cults at Sardeis (213 BC), Teos (probably c.203) and Iasos (c.196) in fact all preceded Antiochos' decision to honour Laodike with a state cult (193).[159] In the *prostagma* creating the state cult for Laodike, Antiochos is content to mention his personal motivation: to increase Laodike's honours, because of her love and care for him and her piety towards the divine; we are left to guess at broader functions, or effects. Did the local cults somehow 'prepare' or 'facilitate' the creation of a state cult for Laodike?[160] Another interpretation is to see the central cult, by its uniformity and mobilization of empire-wide resources, as a way for the ruling power to offer, retrospectively, a unifying model for pre-existing, local cults, and hence a means to subsume, symbolically, local manifestations within a broader, supra-poliad form: the very nature of imperial activity.[161]

At first sight, then, a register of successes for the empire of domination, in the symbolical realm: the development of an imperial culture, shared by ruler and ruled alike; the acceptance by the *polis* of practices, values, linguistic elements from royal discourse; the operation of channels for royal forms and royal ideology to enter the space of the *polis*, such as (perhaps) frequent contacts with Seleukid administrators; the creation of overarching forms such as centrally organized ruler cult, perhaps proposed, or experienced, as models for local practices. It is impossible to say how much these impinged on the thoughts or the consciousness of citizens in the local communities beyond the forms and the course of public behaviour. As concerns the latter, the example of the Teians, once more, is suggestive. The Teians, in 190, during the Roman–Seleukid War, kept their *eunoia* to Antiochos III, though they had not received a Seleukid garrison (as Iasos did) and though other cities rallied to the Romans (like neighbouring Kolophon); the Teians supplied the

---

[159] Gauthier 1989: 73–8: this series of earlier cults of Laodike does not affect the essential distinction between civic cult and state cult, but raises the issue of the relation between the two forms; documents **2**, **18**, **26** B, and **37**.

[160] Gauthier 1989: 77; Sherwin-White and Kuhrt 1993: 209.

[161] It would be interesting to know if local cults for Laodike in turn imitated features of the subsequently developed central cult for the queen, such as the golden crowns bearing her portrait, worn by the high-priestesses in the state cult.

Seleukid fleet *benigne* (for which read εὐνόως, εὐχαρίστως), and promised five thousand jars of wine (Liv. 37.27.3). The Teians' loyalist behaviour was no doubt shaped by the constant infusion into civic life of particular images—the king's past services to them, their debt of gratitude towards him—and perhaps by their imitation of practices from the 'imperial' cities of the Seleukis.

Yet the situation is more complex. Royal discourse, assimilated at a local level, could be used to further local interests. The Smyrnians conducted their annexation of a Seleukid colony at Magnesia under Sipylos in the language of loyalty towards Seleukos II and concern for his interests (*OGIS* 229). More modestly, a city could use images of royal beneficence as unanswerable arguments in petitions or homilies addressed to royal officials: the Amyzonians asked an official to behave in accordance with the 'choice' of the king (παρακαλέ[σουσιν αὐτὸν] | [ἀκό]λουθα πράσοντα τῆι τ[οῦ βασι]|[λέ]ως αἱρέσει). A parallel can be found in the considerations of a Xanthian decree for a Ptolemaic phrourarch, καλὸς κἀγαθὸς . . . καὶ ἄξιος τοῦ βασιλέως.[162] A theme of royal ideology, adopted locally, was used to manipulate or to ascribe roles to the royal officials (previous section): a warning against assuming that the diffusion of royal discourse implies the passivity or debasement of local communities, since this same royal discourse can be recontextualized by the local communities. Indeed, this example shows the limits of analysing the discursive interaction between the various actors (king, cities, officials) as discrete strands, rather than as a continuous phenomenon operating at many levels simultaneously.

5. Conclusion: Kings and Cities, Power and Language, in the Hellenistic Period

So the different effects of the diffusion of royal discourse at the local level belong to a wider diversity: the features studied above performed a variety of functions, in different contexts and for different audiences. Of course, the diversity would appear greater if other languages or voices than that used in the dialogue of euergetism had survived in any sizeable amount: the epigraphical material tells us that which the cities chose to monumentalize. We do not have any threatening letters from the kings, or letters refusing petitions.[163]

[162] Document **12**; *SEG* 33.1183, line 7. Also *Syll.* 502, lines 14–17; *I. Stratonikeia* 4.
[163] Threatening letters: Liv. 33.38.5, chastizing tone of Antiochos' ambassadors to Lampsakos and Smyrna. Refusal of petition: a later case in Reynolds 1982: no. 13 (Octavian refusing autonomy to the Samians; published, significantly, by the Aphrodisians who received a copy of the decision).

There are some cases of confrontation or subordination, such as *RC* 6, in which Lysimachos speaks bluntly of the Prienians' obedience to his general, or the stormy interview between Seleukos I and Herakleia Pontike (Memnon, *FGrHist* 434 F 7), or the dealings between the Attalids and Amlada after a revolt (*RC* 54); these remain exceptions in our material. Nor is there any large surviving body of Hellenistic political rhetoric or of Hellenistic literature from the cities (rather than the royal courts). The ideological debate between ruler and ruled may have been harsher than the deliberate blandness of the euergetical language lets on, and the general political culture much more diverse (Will 1988: 333–5). Some traces remain of realistic discourse, especially in Polybios: observations that the kings are intent on enslaving the cities, or a speech urging the Achaians to refuse a gift from Eumenes II, even if it was worthy of the Achaians, because the προαίρεσις of the benefactor and the purpose (χρεία) of the gift were bad; the gift was a mere δέλεαρ, a piece of bait, to entrap the Achaians.[164] The speech shows awareness of the language of euergetism, only to subvert and demystify it. Less sophisticatedly than Polybios' demystifying moves, but with equal forcefulness, the Panamarians, once Karia became free in 167, chiselled out the name of a Rhodian governor they had earlier honoured with a decree of the standard form for imperial officials (*I. Stratonikeia* 9).

Another area where the evidence is lacking concerns the internal workings of the *polis*. The decrees which embody deliberate, public, stylized gestures do not inform us on dissent or debates within the cities: we do not know how easily these decrees were adopted, whether there were groups opposed to these motions, whether decisions were reached with large or small majorities (as far as I know, no honorific decree for a king or royal Friend mentions the size of the assembly or the number of those who voted against the proposal), to what extent the adoption of a certain type of language and attitude mirrored internal changes in the conduct of public affairs in the assembly of any *polis*. It is difficult to picture, for instance, the assembly at Xanthos in 197–6 BC. We know that Tlepolemos Artapatou was a priest *pro poleos* in the city, a former Ptolemaic courtier (and product of a family with a distinguished tradition of Ptolemaic service), once greatly powerful in Alexandria where he acted as regent for young Ptolemy V in 203–202, now retired to his home city: if he attended the assembly where decrees were passed inaugurating ruler cult for Antiochos III, the new

---

[164] Memnon *FGrHist* 434 F 11.3, Pol. 21.22.8, 22.8; ibid. for speech of Apollonidas.

Seleukid master of the city, and reflecting Seleukid discourse, we can only wonder if he argued unsuccessfully against the Seleukid-ization of Xanthos, or if he was forced to view the process from the sidelines, with a cynical or a jaundiced eye.[165]

Nonetheless, the vast majority of the epigraphical evidence is written in the language of euergetism: the bulk of the material, the pervasiveness of its distribution, and in fact its very uniformity emphasize the currency of this language as means of communication between political actors in the Hellenistic world; this situation, though it does not tell us about things we would like to investigate in further depth (attitudes beyond the surface of euergetical cordi-ality), is in itself important and demands serious attention. The nature of the evidence (mainly epigraphical, and hence monu-mental, celebratory, and selective) entails studying a power relation mediated through the language of euergetism, a language where power is not spoken of. It is a mistake to speak of civic decrees as overt expressions of submission, as Orth does when he interprets *OGIS* 219 as imbued with *Unfreiheit*, or Gawantka in describing the 'ungewöhnliche Ergebenheitsadresse an dem König' of the second Teian decree; at a primary level, the civic decrees precisely avoid talking about power, juridical or *de facto*, and the language of euergetism is not intrinsically servile.[166] It was a close reading of royal letters and civic decrees, and a willingness to take their pri-mary meanings as the whole story, that led Heuss to describe the relationship between king and cities as purely euergetical (seen formally), with no juridical link of subordination: a remarkable homage to the power of this language to dissimulate power. Like-wise, A. Giovannini proposed, on a strict reading of the Teian decrees, that Antiochos III had not taken over Teos, but merely helped it by interceding with Attalos I to ask for tax relief.[167]

Yet power does impinge on the language of euergetism. Royal letters mention conquest, albeit obliquely. The contract clause, promising benefactions in return for εὔνοια, is absent from contexts other than the dialogue between ruler and ruled; furthermore, the cities never complete the hortative clauses of their decrees honour-ing rulers by the commonplace (found in decrees for 'normal' *euergetai*) that public honours will create emulation among other potential benefactors, an inappropriate conceit in the exclusive

[165] These thoughts are only the beginning of a reply to questions raised in an examina-tion by M. Austin. Xanthos: documents **22**, **23**, **24**. Tlepolemos: J. and L. Robert 1983: 168–71, vividly evoke the figure.

[166] Orth 1977: 50–61; Gawantka 1975: 123. On the civic style of honorific decrees expressing the city's dignity and sense of worth, Veyne 1976: 235–7.

[167] Heuss 1937; Giovannini 1983.

interaction with a political master.[168] The language of euergetism itself invites us to study how it is used to mediate the extratextual dimension of power. Thanks to the very uniformity of the medium, the diversity of the different interlocutors' behaviour can be studied within a picture which integrates the multiplicity of possible viewpoints and functions.

I hope to have shown that the language of euergetism could be used by royal interlocutors to represent, or camouflage, power as benefaction, as a means to foster local quiescence and hence multiply the indirect rule of the empire of domination, by lessening the need for actual violence (as opposed to ideological violence). Conversely, the same language, and the same contents, were used by the local communities, to interact with the rulers, introducing petitions in such way as to apply moralizing pressure on the rulers and channel reactions along the pre-scripted lines of euergetism. Whose interests did this transaction serve? The cities could obtain what they wanted; the list of benefactions and grants received by Herakleia under Latmos is particularly impressive, catalogued over four inscribed blocks. At the same time, the formulas accompanying royal acceptance of petitions defined a royal ideology which the cities received along with the gifts, the concept of power as benefaction, but also the royal principles of ancestral rights and monopoly over the right to define statuses: the transaction ends up strengthening royal power, by making the local communities agree to the legitimizing, deproblematizing discourse of the king. Furthermore, as seen in the previous chapter (§ 3), the fact that the king allowed himself to be petitioned into euergetical behaviour in itself strengthened his rule, by presenting the latter as accessible and flexible to the subjects' wishes: petition becomes a more viable solution than local revolt; the language of euergetism was part of a structure of repressive tolerance. However, the same language of euergetism also represented public commitments, to specific actions and to general norms, on the ruler's part, and hence a restriction on his liberty of action: hence the collaborative effort by the community of cities to broadcast and acknowledge, in terms drawn from the language of

---

[168] Contract clause: Ch. 2 § 5. Document **38** is a special case, representing a Roman attempt to exploit the ambivalence of the form: formally free of power, yet indirectly expressing it; another exception is *RC* 52, lines 32–7, where the Ionians promise that Eumenes II will receive 'all things pertaining to honour and repute' if he responds to the *eucharistia* of the Ionians, but the perceived weakness of Eumenes II, after rebuff at Rome, might have influenced the language of the Ionian decree. Hortative clauses and emulation: Habicht 1970: 165 n. 1; Gauthier 1985: 11–12, 129–30. *Inschr. Didyma* 479, lines 27–30, a Milesian decree for Antiochos I, contains a hortative clause, but Antiochos I was not the master of Miletos at the time.

euergetism, norms of royal behaviour, and royal commitments to such norms. The euergetical register also provided the subjects with an effective means to socialize royal officials, and hence weaken the king's means of direct administration. Both parties collaborated in dialogue, but each seeking its own aims and achieving different effects—sometimes simultaneously—from the same language; the open-ended nature of dialogue resulted in this diverse and imbricated situation.

The other phenomenon studied above is less dialectical, but equally complex: the ambiguity of the *polis*' discourse. Some of the evidence can be interpreted as local narratives, expressed in the considerations of civic decrees, or embedded in social memory by deliberate and systematic measures, as at Teos (particularly well documented, but not unusual). Local narratives allowed the cities to describe their world and their relation to the ruler, and to precipitate a potentially traumatic present of royal conquest into a remembered past of euergetical cordiality. By enabling forms of local ideological power, and control over the past, local narratives insulated civic pride and civic identity—which could provide the impetus for political conduct such as opportunism in time of superpower conflict, dissidence, and resistance (as in the case of the former Seleukid cities, Smyrna and Lampsakos). At the same time, the contents of the local narratives were disturbingly consonant with royal ideology and its images of power-as-beneficence or euergetical dialogue without (or overshadowing) any power relation; images which it introduced deep within the institutions of collective life. The evidence for local narratives intersects with the evidence for another phenomenon, the assimilation of royal discourse and the values of the 'patrimonial' empire into civic forms, such as cult, but also the civic decrees, which could praise a royal official or a citizen for services not to the city, but towards the king and his 'affairs'. The Hellenistic kingdoms created, or favoured, a cultural *koine* which mirrored forms of political integration of local communities within a supra-poliad state (even if both cultural *koine* and political forms were not as developed as under the Roman empire). The ideological autarky and local identity of the *polis* were strongly affirmed in the Hellenistic age, even under political subordination; yet the Hellenistic *polis* under royal rule, 'autonomous' or subject, old or new, was open to forms of imperial ideology which went against local autarky.

A preliminary conclusion should bear on the fluidity of the situation, resulting not simply from the fluidity of all dialogue, but from the mediation of power through a language precisely designed to avoid overtly talking about power. The contract clause could express collaboration and exchange, or it could express power and dependency; so that, ambiguously, it spoke in both registers at the same time. The language of euergetism, with its stereotypes and its generalizing vocabularies, performed a stabilizing role in the inter-action between rulers and ruled, important in a period of dramatic change in international politics (Ch. 1):[169] it provided the forms and the substance for exchange in the aftermath of warfare, as in the case of Antiochos III, 'reconquering' what he claimed were ancestral Seleukid possessions. At the same time, it allowed a multiplicity of meanings and functions.

In some cases, the diversity was presumably due to local factors, which are now unclear. Antiochos III, the descendant of Apollo, mentioned this god first whenever associated with other deities: he wrote to his army to respect the shrine of Apollo and Artemis at Amyzon—a shrine we call the Artemision, following local usage. Yet the Amyzonians adopted the Seleukid usage, referring to the shrine in the same order as Antiochos rather than the local 'temple of Artemis'. In contrast, the Xanthians, when inscribing on their gate a summary of Antiochos' decision to consecrate the city to the local triad, wrote Βασιλεὺς μέγας Ἀντίοχος | ἀφιέρωσεν τὴν πόλιν | τῆι Λητῶι καὶ τῶι Ἀπόλλωνι | καὶ τῆι Ἀρτέμιδι διὰ τὴν | πρὸς αὐτοὺς συνάπ-τουσαν | συγγένειαν, 'The Great King Antiochos dedicated the city to Leto, Apollo, and Artemis, on account of the kinship uniting him to them'—restating the traditional order of precedence in a city whose main shrine was dedicated to Leto.[170] Why one subject city adopted a Seleukid form into its decrees, while the other rephrased a royal utterance to fit traditional cultic precedence is baffling; in the case of Amyzon, was it a case of local initiative and loyalism, or did the presence of Menestratos of Phokaia, the Seleukid official in charge of the Artemision, co-opted into the citizen body, influence the behaviour of the assembly and the language of its decrees (above)? At any rate, the example of these two cities invites us to exercise caution over broad statements about the 'internal surrender' or the resilience of the Hellenistic poleis.

Nonetheless, the very fact that the interaction between ruler and ruled was largely conducted in this elaborate, stereotypical, and ambiguous language is highly significant. The king could commu-nicate in short administrative notes to his subordinates, conveying orders (as in the prostagma of 209 appointing Nikanor to his function) or agreeing to requests (such as Ptolemaios' requests con-

---

[169] The notion of 'stabilizing' stereotypes from Orrieux 1983: 123.
[170] Document 6; J. and L. Robert 1983: 202 no. 21; document 22.

cerning his estates at Skythopolis):[171] σύνταξον οὖν, or γενέσθω ὥσπερ
ἀξιοῖ. It thus becomes the more noticeable and significant that this
register was not employed in dealing with the cities: the administrative tone of the king's replies concerning Ptolemaios' Skythopolis
estates contrasts with the courtesy and elaboration of Zeuxis', then
Antiochos' dealings with Herakleia, along set diplomatic forms and
couched in a conventional language of benefaction and reciprocity.
Unlike the brisk dialect of administration, this language was not the
king's own thing, but a pre-existing, institutionalized idiom used in
diplomacy and in relations between cities and individuals. This
style of interaction is removed from the picture of harsh, oppressive,
overwhelming royal power sometimes offered (Orth 1977; Green
1990)—a picture which rather suits the situation of the cities of the
North Pontic shore, at the mercy of the predatory local kings.[172] The
difficulties which Lysimachos or Philip V experienced,[173] when they
behaved in ways perceived as unrestrainedly brutal, demonstrate
the practical importance of the norms, expectancies, and the general
political culture.

Rather than wonder why the kings and cities resorted to the
language of euergetism and the attendant style of politics, and
search for simple functionalist explanations ('the kings needed the
cities' collaboration', 'the cities wished to manipulate the kings'), we
might reflect on the effect of this language on the nature of the relation. It prevented benefaction from becoming a solitary celebration
of royal splendour (as in Theocritus 17) or a pure expression of
asymmetry and royal power: it did so by creating a process of dialogue, and hence an interaction where language was polity, where
both parties had a right to speak back to each other, on the basis of
shared assumptions and values[174] implying some form of parity.

The standardized nature of the euergetical language meant that,
far from being monopolizable, it could be used indefinitely by both
parties. A king could promise to increase τὰ εἰς τιμὴν καὶ δόξαν
ἀνήκοντα of a city; conversely, a city could make the same promise to
a king. The abstract terms minimize the fact that the possibilities of
a king and a subordinate city are rather different—the king could
offer material benefactions; the city, honours. This is precisely the
function of the abstract terminology: the language establishes
parity and asserts the city's belief that the honours it decrees have

---

[171] Above, introduction; Ch. 3; Bertrand 1990: 114–15 on papyrological parallels.
[172] Gauthier 1985: 33–6, with references.
[173] Lysimachos: Bresson 1995, on Lysimachos' difficulties with various cities, partly
stemming from his unacceptable image; Philip V: Ch. 2 § 3.
[174] Pocock 1984; Gauthier 1985: 11, 41.

real (if symbolical) value. A king could praise a city, and the city could praise him. Strikingly, a city could represent itself as the *euergetes* of the king, and speak of royal *eucharistia*, instead of the (more familiar) reverse situation.[175] When Laodike wrote to the Iasians τῶν ἀπαντω[μ]ένων εὐεργεσιῶν μεμνημένοις [εὐ]χαρίστως πειράσομαι καὶ ἄλλα ἃ ἂν ἐπινοῶ συν[κατ]ασκευάζειν,[176] the adverb, εὐχαρίστως, might describe either the Iasians' remembering of past benefactions, or Laodike's euergetical reaction to such remembrance, or perhaps both, ἀπὸ κοινοῦ. This is the final impression we can draw from the eloquent, guarded, stylized sentences on the inscribed stones: no matter what the detailed effects of the application—and I have tried to show how they could work to the advantage of either party, rulers or ruled—the institutionalized nature of the shared, reversible language entailed parity between the two parties, and hence the conversion of the straightforward 'power-as-conquest' of empire into the far less straightforward 'power-as-battlefield' of interaction and negotiation.[177]

---

[175] Τὰ εἰς τιμὴν καὶ δόξαν ἀνήκοντα: documents **5**; **31** B, III 16, IV 11–12; **34**; *OGIS* 219, lines 32–3. Praise: **19** A, 10; **31** A, I 8; **26** B, II 4–5, 14–15; *I. Stratonikeia* 3, 4. Εὐχαριστία: **17**, 25–7; **18**, 74.

[176] Document **26** A, I 27–9. **45**, 15, for the Scipios promising 'return of gratitude' to the Herakleians in exchange for honours.

[177] Foucault 1975: 35: power not as property or privilege, but as 'un réseau de relations toujours tendues', as battlefield. A parallel: G. Algazi, on the negotiations between lord and peasant through constantly reinvented tradition, in late medieval Germany (*Actes de la Recherche en Sciences Sociales* 105 (1994), 26–8).

'Once there was a king, Antiochos the Great . . .'

Antiochos III and the cities: exploring the background to the confrontation of winter 197/6 BC (Liv. 33.38) has initially meant evoking the earlier history of Asia Minor, the Seleukids' presence, the narrative of their power, and of the challenges to their power, in the region; it further entailed reconstructing the political and military narrative of the years 226 to 193 BC, when Antiochos III took over, or took back, what he considered to be ancestral possessions in Seleukid Asia Minor, until diplomatic clashes and geopolitical misunderstandings with Rome led to war. More broadly, the same Livian passage offered the opportunity to explore its ramifications, especially by interpreting the primary evidence which relates to this particular moment in history, or illustrate the issues involved in it. Once the background and the narrative context were established, the implications of the Livian passage led to a characterization of empire and *polis*, and to conclusions about their relation.

I tried to describe and think about the purposes and means of empire—the initial violence of conquest, followed by 'organized violence' in the long term, which enabled the mutually supporting activities of control and exploitation. From this study of 'empire at work' emerges the picture of an impressively extensive, centralized and active administration, in spite of the limitations of the evidence: this picture can be reached by pursuing the richly evocative implications of our documents for the functions and capacities of Seleukid 'institutions', since we cannot collate the evidence to produce a systematic tableau of structures. But this implied picture might be an illusion produced by the inclusive, integrating ideology of empire, to dissimulate material limitations (which our evidence for institutions of power precisely will not tell us about, but which can be detected in other ways, by looking at the implication of other pieces of evidence). Among the ideological resources at the disposal of the Hellenistic imperial states, we must count the very structures of imperial power, which not only carried out concrete duties, but also made visible the empire's ubiquity, effectiveness, and 'natural-ness'. Another set of important ideological functions were per-formed by the legal statuses which were granted to the cities by the ruler, from subjection to full liberty on the ruler's consent. Admittedly, legal statuses and privileges gave material advantages to the local communities, and represented public commitments on the part of the ruler and formal, legal constraints on his power, so that they should not be minimized as mere hypocritical sham, as has been done by some scholars. But I have tried to show that the typology of statuses and privileges, culminating in 'freedom' dependent on the ruler's grant, served to impose the assumption of the ruler's authority over local statuses, his control over definitions, his right to take back as well as to give away: these were meant to form the limit of the local communities' horizon, whatever their status.

Yet faced with the material resources and the ideological force of a Hellenistic empire, the cities were not powerless and abject, as is sometimes claimed on the basis of reductive, insensitive, or super-ficial readings of our documents. To varying degrees (and this diversity in itself is a warning against facile generalizations on the power relationship between ruler and city) the cities were capable of resistance or opportunism, especially because the ideology of empire was expressed through language and interaction between ruler and ruled, and hence through an exchange where both parties could attempt to shape the world and each other. In subordination, the cities drew on the empire's need for collaboration to negotiate privileges; they interacted with their master and mediated power through a stereotypical, ambiguous language designed to talk not about power but about reciprocity and exchange, in an open-ended dialogue. In this dialogue, the cities were acknowledged as inter-locutors of the central power, thus converting what might have been a straight relation of domination into a complicated reality of negotiation and mutual accommodation—even if all the exact details of this reality are, for the moment, all but irrecoverable because we do not have the evidence for a meaningful study of local factors and the complicated flux of power-as-interaction. The 'catalogue-and-speculation' presentation, city by city, sometimes favoured by scholars of the Hellenistic world, does not attain this goal. Nonethe-less, the conclusion remains: the final result of this interaction was not predetermined, and the rewriting of power into the language of beneficence could work to the ruler's profit, or the subjects' profit, or do both at the same time. This conclusion in itself shows the fluidity of the relations between city and ruler in the period, and this is one of the impressions that emerges from this study: the existence of a fluid, open-ended interaction between ruler and ruled, where unspoken power structures, euergetical assumptions, and mutual role assignment along moralizing norms combined in a complex game. Finally, the cities resorted to various strategies (local narratives, selective memory, the practical exercise and the monumental celebration of civic discourse) to preserve their sense of identity and civic pride. The exercise was self-fulfilling, since the very production of these local narratives proved a persistence of local identity: a finding which substantiates L. Robert's dictum on the persistence of the *polis* in the Hellenistic age, and helps to explore it, by focusing on the crucial area of civic pride and identity.

The analyses I have proposed in the preceding chapters are functions of two different, yet complementary perspectives on the Hellenistic world: from above, as the military narrative of conquest and its concomitant history of empire; from below, as a history of local communities, whose diversity influenced the vicissitudes of high political history, but also the shape of empires on the ground, embodying the texture and experience of empire as lived by Hellenistic men and women. Neither perspective is the exclusively 'correct' one, and both must be integrated into any satisfying account of the Hellenistic world, as its greatest historians were aware, from Polybios down to M. Rostovtzeff and L. Robert. The study of Antiochos III and his relation to the cities of Western Asia Minor is thus also an exercise in, and a reflection on, the issues involved in writing the history of the Hellenistic period.

It is this final picture of a complex and shifting reality which matters, beyond the specifically Seleukid aspects of the story (even though I have been at some pains to establish a Seleukid narrative earlier on). The Seleukid aspects were soon dismantled in the Roman–Seleukid War and its aftermath, illustrated by ironical juxtapositions which highlight the typicality, and hence the dispensability, of the Seleukid experience.

The Roman–Seleukid War, conducted, after Antiochos' defeat at Thermopylai (191 BC), in the eastern Aegean and Asia Minor (191–190), presents a military narrative, well documented (through Livy and Appian, reproducing Polybios), and dramatic—the strategic manoeuvring with great naval clashes, Antiochos' ill-advised evacuation of Thrace and Lysimacheia, the land marches leading to the final battle at Magnesia in winter 190/189, in the Lydian plain: Antiochos III lost the cis-Tauric dominions on the same field where Seleukos I had won them, almost a century earlier. Afterwards, the cities surrendered *en masse* to the victor (just as they had surrendered to Seleukos I in 281 BC), starting with several 'Seleukid' cities: Thyateira, where Seleukos I had settled military colonists who offered cultic honours to the king; Magnesia under Sipylos, also a focus of Seleukid military settlement; and Sardeis, the administrative centre for 'the regions on the other side of the Taurus'.[1] At Sardeis, the citizens and the garrison ignored the city-commander and the governor of Lydia, both just appointed by Antiochos: even in Sardeis, the provincial capital, Seleukid authority no longer held (Liv. 37.45.3–7).

As suggested by these cities, there is another, fragmented, narrative, for the local communities caught in 'the changes in circumstances', as an Amyzonian decree puts it, αἱ τῶν καιρῶν μεταβολαί (J. and L. Robert 1983: no. 36, line 11). Many cities rallied to the Romans. Kolophon (probably a Seleukid city till then), revolted from the king: the lower town (Notion, or Kolophon-by-sea) was besieged by Antiochos, but resisted until the king lifted the siege[2] and marched to meet the Roman army in the field, at Magnesia; the city was rewarded with privileges by the Scipios after the war. A sign of this history is recorded in the festivals of Kolophon. In the third century BC, the Kolophonians, under the Seleukids, had celebrated a festival called the Antiocheia, whose importance is conveyed by the fact that public honours at Kolophon were proclaimed at three occasions: the Dionysia, the Great Klaria, and the Antiocheia. In the second century BC, honours were proclaimed only in the two former festivals, suggesting that the Kolophonians ceased to celebrate the Antiocheia, presumably as a result of their rallying to Rome, and their successful resistance against Antiochos III.[3] Other Seleukid cities passed over to the Romans, in different conditions and with different results. Herakleia under Latmos took the step of sending an embassy to the Scipios before the battle of Magnesia, thus securing the city's position after the Roman victory;

---

[1] For a narrative of the Roman–Seleukid War, Will 1982: 204–16. Thyateira: *OGIS* 211 (same document *TAM* 5.901, with commentary by Herrmann on cultic honours). Magnesia under Sipylos: *OGIS* 229. Sardeis: see Ch. 3 § 2.

[2] The Hellenistic walls which enabled Notion to resist Antiochos III are not treated in McNicoll 1997.

[3] Document 42, Liv. 37.26.5–13, document 46. Apollo Klarios is 'leader and saviour [of the city]', τοῦ καθηγέμονος καὶ σωτῆρος [τῆς πόλεως] in a Kolophonian decree of the early second century (*SEG* 42.1065): the title might refer to the city's successful resistance to Antiochos III in 190. Antiocheia: *I. Lampsakos* 33, *Inschr. Priene* 57, *I. Iasos* 80, with P. Frisch, *ZPE* 15 (1974), 98 and *BE* 74. 457; but the festival is absent from *SEG* 42.1065. Unpublished material, discovered in the recent excavations at Klaros, may clarify the situation.

the embassy included three men who once had gone to Zeuxis about the city's privileges. Teos surrendered after a meeting of the assembly, perhaps held in the same *bouleuterion* where Antiochos had once declared the city and its territory free, *asylos* and tax-exempt (privileges which the Romans had acknowledged in 193). If so, the meeting where the Teians renounced their adhesion to the Seleukid king's *pragmata* took place before the bronze king's cult-statue, crowned with seasonal vegetation and earlier made into the focus of carefully recentred civic rituals.[4] Other cities resisted the Romans, such as Patara (Liv. 37.16), or Abydos, held by Seleukid forces—while Sestos, across the Straits, sent two priests of Kybele, in full regalia, to meet the Roman soldiers, before surrendering formally (Pol. 21.6.7; Liv. 37.9.8–11; 37.12.1–3). Iasos, occupied by a Seleukid *phylake*, saw its territory ravaged by Roman troops, but was spared on the intercession of the Rhodians, who intervened in favour of their συγγενεῖς, after being approached by Iasians expelled by the Seleukid garrison; these Iasians claimed that their city was unanimous in wishing to escape *regia servitus*—using the same metaphor as an Iasian decree had done in 197, to castigate the Antigonid dominion from which Antiochos had freed the city.[5] The Rhodians' intervention in favour of the Iasians recalls their earlier intervention, *c*.215, when they interceded with Philip V to protect the Iasians against Olympichos (Ch. 1 § 4). The case of another city, Phokaia, is exceptional only because, divided on which course to chose, it adopted all of them in succession: adhesion to the Romans in 191, 'out of fear' (Liv. 36.43.8; App. *Syr.* 22); after an attempt at neutrality (Pol. 21.6.2–6), rallying to the Seleukids, when the presence of the Roman fleet proved too burdensome, (Liv. 37.9.1–5); military resistance to the Romans, aided by Seleukid troops (Liv. 37.21.8–9). The end came in a Roman siege, the ancient walls breached by the battering-ram: nonetheless, the citizenry repelled the assault by stubborn resistance, 'showing that arms and courage were of greater help than walls' (Liv. 37.32.5, a perplexing echo of 33.38.2). The city finally surrendered, only to be sacked and plundered by the Roman soldiers (Liv. 37.32.10–14)—an incident which recalls the economic motive for empire and warfare (Ch. 3 § 1; Austin 1986)—activities conducted at the expense of the local communities.

After Magnesia and the Peace of Apameia, business carried on, as emphasized by ironical similarities with the now extinct Seleukid

---

[4] Herakleia: document **45**. Teos: Liv. 37.27.3–28.9, with Herrmann 1965*a*: 156–7 (surrender perhaps decided in the *bouleuterion*).

[5] Liv. 37.17.3–7.

dominion. The Romans, at Apameia, exercised the victor's monopoly of performative utterances, and hence the right to define statuses (freedom or subordination), distribute territory, and even give away cities by *fiat*[6]—just as Antiochos III had done. Most of the Seleukid province was divided up (like dishes at a rich feast: Pol. 21.22.13), between Eumenes II (who received Aiolis, the Troas, Ionia, and the inland swathe, down to the Maeander, and to the Kilikian Gates) and the Rhodians (who received Karia and Lykia). For both, the same activities can be traced as for the Seleukids: for the Rhodians, control and administration; for the Attalids, colonization in Lydia (both 'military colonies' and cities), euergetism for the cities, military activity in the inland, notably in Pisidia:[7] the landscape of Asia Minor would bear Attalid traces exactly similar in nature to the traces of Seleukid power. In many cases, the new power continued earlier practice: at Gördes, where a Seleukid officer had made a dedication to Zeus Porottenos for the safety of Apollophanes, physician to Antiochos III, the commander of Attalid troops erected a similar stele for the safety of Eumenes II, 'King Eumenes, Saviour and Benefactor, and his brothers, and Queen Apollonis'; a ruling concerning the shrine of Apollo of Pleura, near Sardeis, issued (probably on the eve of Magnesia) by Nikanor, the 'high-priest of all the shrines' in Anatolia, was confirmed by his Attalid successor, Euthydemos. When granting the status of *polis* to a settlement at Tyriaion, Eumenes II, visiting Phrygia shortly after the peace of Apameia, affirmed the validity of his grant, 'given by me, who have authority from the Romans victorious both in war and in treaties, unlike (a letter) written by those who do not hold power; for the latter favour (χάρις) would be rightly considered empty and deceitful'. In making this allusion to the Seleukids, Eumenes II, though eager to deny their authority and affirm the stability of his Roman-supported rule, also shows how Attalid power has taken precisely the place once assumed by the Seleukids.[8] (There are of course new developments, such as the

---

[6] Pol. 21.45; Liv. 38.39.7–17 (note Rhoiteion and Gergithos, given to Ilion); Appendix 7; Robert 1987: 211.

[7] Lydia: Debord 1985, analysing *TAM* 5; Cohen 1995: 201–4 on Apollonis. Euergetism: e.g. Robert 1937: 74–89, for Aigai. Pisidia: *RC* 54, Kearsley 1994.

[8] Gördes: document **39**; *TAM* 5.690 (Attalid). Pleura: document **49**; the Attalids also kept the office of ὁ ἐπὶ τῶν ἱερῶν (Malay and Nalbantoğlu 1996; Allen 1983: 96–7). Tyriaion: Jonnes and Ricl 1997: 3, lines 20–4. Generally, on the Attalid kingdom after 188, Rostovtzeff 1941: 637–49; Allen 1983: 76–135; new evidence has appeared: Kearsley 1994 and especially Malay 1996, publishing an *ostotheke* found near ancient Tralleis, recording names and titles of Attalid officials (a governor of Tralleis and of active troops (στρατηγὸς τοῦ ὑπαίθρου), a governor of the *topoi* around Ephesos) and discussing previously known evidence (see also the remarks by Ph. Gauthier, *BE* 97. 526).

Attalid introduction of a restricted monetary system, the cistophoric coinage: Will 1982: 229–30; Mørkholm 1991: 171–3).

Local reactions were the same as under the Seleukids, and the similarity of issues and behaviour again produced ironical echoes of the Seleukid period. Apollonia under Salbake sent an embassy before the ten Roman commissioners at Apameia, then to the Rhodians, to negotiate a settlement and oppose the claims of local villagers (probably the Saleioi concerning whom the Apollonians had opposed the Seleukid financial administration); the event, naturally, is recorded in an honorific decree for a citizen who distinguished himself on the mission. The decree was inscribed on the *anta* of a public building, which, in all probability, bore the honorific decree for a Seleukid hipparch who had helped the city in its dealings with the Seleukid administration: high-politics changed, and the political masters that had to be dealt with, but the local community (and its public records, published in stone on a monumental building) remained the same. Amyzon praised a citizen, Dionysios, for going on embassy to Zeuxis, and 'likewise', ὁμοίως, to the Roman consuls in 188, to safeguard the city's privileges. The adverb gives the city's perspective: changes in international politics did not affect the structural need to defend local interests nor the techniques for doing so: sending out embassies of articulate citizens bearing decrees and holding forth before representatives of whatever power held sway in Asia Minor. Thus, the same man, the same city, dealt matter-of-factly with Seleukids and Romans in succession.[9] The Karian cities offered honorific decrees to their Rhodian governors (e.g. *I. Stratonikeia* 9), along the same lines, and no doubt to achieve the same socializing effects, as in their decrees for Seleukid (and, indeed, Ptolemaic) officials. The Trallians, once a Seleukid city named Seleukeia, offered cultic honours to Eumenes II and served as a royal residence for Attalid kings. What happened in Teos to the elaborate cultic arrangements honouring Antiochos III is unknown. At least some form of Seleukid dynastic cult survived, documented in an altar which lists Seleukid kings down to the middle of the second century, long after Antiochos III had lost Asia Minor (*OGIS* 246; new text in *SEG* 35.1521). All the same, we are entitled to wonder if it was soon after 190 that the Teians discarded the pilasters bearing the decrees inaugurating monuments and honours for Antiochos III and Laodike III: the stone blocks

---

[9] Apollonia: documents **48**, **44** and J. and L. Robert 1954: 286. Amyzon: **47**, cf. Wörrle 1988: 455: several Herakleians went both on the crucial embassy to Zeuxis *c*.196 (document **31**) and on the no less crucial embassy to the Scipios in late 190, before the battle of Magnesia (**45**).

were found, broken and not *in situ*, behind the temple of Dionysos. Furthermore, the Teians developed cultic forms directed to, or about, the new dominant power, the Attalids. For the Attalid queen Apollonis, they decreed honours similar to, and perhaps imitated from, those for Laodike III: the agora, where the Teians had wished to set a monument of their *eucharistia* towards Laodike, received an altar commemorating the landing of Apollonis in the city.[10] Apameia in Phrygia, named after a Seleukid queen, and a base for the Pisidian forays of Antiochos III, honoured a citizen for erecting statues of Eumenes II and his brother Attalos, and for providing money for the Attalid army (*MAMA* 6.173 with *BE* 39, 400); Sardeis, the former Seleukid provincial capital, continued as a 'subject' Attalid city.

   Sardeis, though an Attalid city, also illustrates the continuing life of the *polis*. Croesus' palace on the acropolis, which had probably been the residence of the Seleukid king and his governor, was transformed into a *gerousia*, the meeting-place for the council (or perhaps a special council of elders) of Sardeis. The former Seleukid administrative centre honoured a citizen, Heliodoros, for successful embassies and excellence 'in the judge-panels sent out by the people to the other cities': Sardeis now sent 'foreign judges' to help other communities, as a full participant in the concert of *poleis*.[11] The decree, strikingly, is inscribed on the same block as a royal letter, almost certainly by Antiochos III or Laodike III; the juxtaposition in itself contains a small narrative of the new existence of Sardeis as *polis* among *poleis*, and one may wonder if the effect was intended. Even more striking is the continuing evidence for a significant number of cities behaving as military and political actors. Without going into a detailed history of the second century as experienced by the cities, I may mention some of the better known or more evocative events. During the year 189, between the battle of Magnesia and the peace of Apameia, Manlius Vulso marched through Anatolia, to fight the Galatians: his march revealed a world of local rancours and conflicts, carried out with local military forces, a world which Vulso exploited to his financial profit (levying ransom from the cities) but on which he did not impose order. After the settlement of 188, many cities remained free, and pursued their

----

[10] Tralleis: Robert, *OMS* ii. 1178–90 (on a decree republished as *I. Tralleis* 23). Teos: Herrmann 1965a: 149–54, on *OGIS* 246; 31–2, on findspot of Teian decrees (admittedly, Herrmann speaks of the blocks being found *in Sturzlage*, implying collapse rather than deliberate discarding). For the remote possibility that a Roman graffito found near Teos alludes to Antiochos III, Appendix 3. Apollonis: Herrmann 1965a: 61–2 and Robert 1937: 9–20.

[11] *Gerousia*: Vitruv. 2.8.9–10, Plin. *NH* 35.172. Heliodoros: Gauthier 1989: no. 4 B.

interests (Will 1982: 238), especially in Southern Ionia and Western Karia, where Magnesia on Maeander, Priene, Miletos, Herakleia, Euromos, Mylasa, and Alabanda, free cities in or near the Rhodian province, conducted a complicated and protracted game of war and diplomacy. The object of competition seems to have been territory, in a process initiated or aggravated by Philip V, when he redistributed the mosaic of civic territories in the area (Ch. 2 § 3); in the second century, the cities fought wars over disputed territory, finally coming to elaborate peace treaties. Miletos expanded by absorbing its smaller neighbour, the city of Pedasa (which once had figured among the list of Roman demands to Philip V: Pol. 18.44 and Ch. 2 § 5); the adjoining cities of Euromos and Mylasa united in *sympoliteia*, to the alarm (and violent reaction) of their neighbour, Herakleia. Some communities (the Kibyratans, Mylasa, Alabanda) would even fight against Rhodes, in 167, to aid or profit from the revolt of Rhodian subjects.[12] In this world, the Seleukid ruler, Antiochos IV, would only appear as a far-away figure, at whose court Milesians served as royal Friends, and whose benefactions, mediated by these Milesian Friends were gratefully acknowledged by Miletos (Herrmann 1987): the reality and the threat of Seleukid power having disappeared, all that was left was the euergetical cordiality which had once served to mask or make palatable the prospect of Seleukid rule. After 167 BC, the communities of Karia and Lykia were freed from Rhodian domination, becoming actors in their own histories. Lykia, organized in a league of cities, engaged in frequent military activity: Lykian inscriptions honour the services of citizen commanders, such as the military services of Orthagoras of Araxa, who fought, for his city and for the Lykian League, against the Kibyratans, 'tyrants' in the Xanthos valley, and the Termessians, probably in the latter second century.[13] The independence of Lykia would formally last until Claudius provincialized the region in AD 43. This story is given a vivid and monumental representation in the southern gate of the great Lykian city, Xanthos. The right-hand gatepost recorded, in a monumental inscription, the consecration of the city by the 'great king'

[12] Generally, Robert 1987: 210–14. Peace treaties: *Syll.* 633, 588 (with Errington 1989a for date). Miletos and Pedasa: *Inschr. Delphinion* 149. Euromos, Mylasa, and Herakleia: *I. Mylasa* 102. The *sympoliteia* in the latter document might be the 'occupation of the cities in Euromos' of Pol. 30.5.11, which led to the Rhodians fighting against, and defeating, the Mylasans and the Alabandans in 167, at the time when the Kibyratans aided the Kaunians in revolt from Rhodes.

[13] Araxa decree: *SEG* 18.570, with Errington 1987: 114–18 (date must be after 167, when the Lykians gained their freedom from the Rhodians); Zimmermann 1993 would date some of the events in the decree before 167, as describing the struggle of the Lykians against the Rhodians.

Antiochos III, after Seleukid conquest in 197, an event which presumably appeared definitive at the time to the Xanthians (who put up the inscription on their own initiative). Yet the Seleukid dominion was not permanent, and the inscription was erased, perhaps under the Rhodians, when they dominated Lykia. Yet Rhodian rule also came to pass away: constantly challenged, it was finally dissolved by Roman *fiat* in 167. After Lykia was freed, the left-hand post was inscribed with dedications by a local citizen, victorious general and successful admiral of the Lykian fleet, active in the Lykians' own history as manifested by military activity.[14]

The Roman settlement of Asia Minor in 188 BC did more than just debar Seleukid power from the region, using the Taurus, which had once been a feature of Seleukid administrative geography, as an international frontier. It was also an exercise in history-writing: it undid Seleukid Asia Minor, by referring not to the Seleukid past as the *status quo* for local rights, but to the situation which had pertained under the Attalids (in *c*.226, then 218)—an 'Attalid past' (see Appendix 7).[15] The settlement of 188 consigned the Seleukid project to history—no longer a live reality in its manifestations and its ideology, but of interest only to the historian, recorded in the local epigraphical narratives such as the *antas* of the temple of Athena at Herakleia, where Seleukid letters were succeeded by the letter of the Scipios, or the 'epigraphical museum' of the Amyzonian Artemision, recording the life of the city under Ptolemies, Seleukids, Rhodians, and as a free community.[16]

A sense of this evolution can be gained from a rather Cavafian interlude in Polybios (21.41.1–5). Manlius Vulso was surprised to discover, in winter 189/8—just before the peace of Apameia was finalized—that a garrison-commander appointed by Antiochos III over Perge had not evacuated that city; this Seleukid officer had no doubt been overlooked during the more exciting, or depressing, events of the years 190–189. When challenged, the hapless phrourarch invoked his royal orders, and the absence of any sub-

---

[14] Document **21**; *TAM* 2.264, 265. Similar is *Syll.* 1226, Alabandan public epitaphs for citizen commanders fallen in battle ὑπὲρ τῆς πατριδός; also the square basis, of unknown origin, now kept in Smyrna, which the inscription describes as the *heroon* of one Dion, who died for his fatherland in battle (ἐμ παρατάξει): Robert 1937: 98 n. 2.

[15] Bikerman 1937 is aware of this aspect, but attributes it to an Attalid source of Polybios' account, which he rejects as erroneous, compared with the Livian version. I believe both can be reconciled, and reflect two different, but compatible aims of the Romans: restore the *status quo* under Attalos I and also reward defections from the Seleukids in 190. In the settlement of 188, Mysia was considered the Attalids' ancestral possession, which Prousias had seized from them (Baronowski 1991: 452 n. 4; Pol. 21.46.10; Liv. 38.39.15).

[16] Boffo 1988 analyses the function of epigraphy as local historiography.

sequent instructions: παραλαβὼν γὰρ ἐν πίστει παρ' Ἀντιόχου τὴν πόλιν τηρεῖν ταύτην, ἕως ἂν διασαφηθῇ πάλιν παρὰ τοῦ πιστεύσαντος τί δεῖ ποιεῖν· μέχρι δὲ τοῦ νῦν ἁπλῶς οὐδὲν αὐτῶι παρ' οὐδενὸς ἀποδεδηλῶσθαι, 'since he had received the city from Antiochos, as an object of trust, he was holding it, until the further course of action was made clear by him who had entrusted the city; but up to now, he quite simply had heard nothing from anyone'. The phrourarch asked for, and was granted, thirty days to await instructions; unsurprisingly, he was ordered out 'after a few days'. The phrourarch's subsequent fate is not recorded, and we can only speculate about what reward he expected, or what punishment he received. What is striking is his adhesion to Seleukid administrative practice (a garrison-commander under direct oath to the king obeyed orders from no other source, since powers were formally separated, in accordance with an old rule for imperial stability: Ch. 3 §§ 1–2)—and especially the fact that he acted thus even while the Roman settlement was undoing the Seleukid cis-Tauric province, a world of which the phrourarch's behaviour was a last, unwittingly ironical, active remnant. More succinctly, the historicization of Seleukid Asia Minor is embodied by a tag which, Appian notes, gained currency in Rome after Magnesia (*Syr.* 37)—ἦν βασιλεὺς Ἀντίοχος ὁ μέγας, 'once there was a king, Antiochos the Great'.

The Date of *OGIS* 219

Select bibliography: Robert 1966*b*: 11–12, and *OMS* vii. 599–635; Frisch's lemma to *I. Ilion* 32, also including earlier bibliography; Orth 1977: 61–72 (examines the case for Antiochos III but favours Antiochos I; the best, fairest, treatment); Piejko 1991*b* (characteristically depressing; Antiochos III); Jones 1993 (Antiochos I); Mastrocinque 1993 (against the 'war of Syrian succession'; Antiochos III); Strobel 1996: 208, 245–6 (early date: immediately after 278).

OGIS 219 (same document now in *I. Ilion* 32) is a well-known decree of Ilion, honouring a Seleukid king with cultic activity and an equestrian statue. Because the motivating clauses give a short narrative of the king's actions and movements, it has drawn the attention of scholars working on the Hellenistic period. Unfortunately, the date of the inscription is controversial. The king honoured is 'Antiochos, son of Seleukos'—Antiochos I or Antiochos III. In the former case, the date would be some time after 281 BC, when Antiochos I succeeded Seleukos I; in the latter case, the date could be *c*.216, when Antiochos crossed the Taurus to reduce Achaios, or *c*.203, during activity in Anatolia on his return from the East, or 197/6, in the campaign from Kilikia to the Straits. The evidence is familiar, but inconclusive. In my opinion, the question is not settled (in spite of determined cases made for either dating), but on balance, I lean towards the earlier dating, under Antiochos I.

Three main arguments can be offered in support of a low dating (Antiochos III): 1. verbal parallels with the Teian decrees for Antiochos III; 2. the similarity to the early years of Antiochos III as described in Polybios; 3. palaeography. However, each of these arguments is open to challenge.

1. *Verbal Parallels*

The texts from Teos and from Iasos offer parallels to the text from Ilion. Orth 1977: 66–7, listed these, as did Piejko (1991*b*: 18–20) and Mastrocinque (along no less than eight 'temi' he believes he can discern: Mastrocinque 1993: 28–9; also Mastrocinque 1983: 67–8). Both in Teos and Ilion, the king crosses over to the region on 'this side of the Taurus', sets aright a troubled situation and brings peace to the cities.[1] However, parallels in themselves are not compelling, in the present state of the evidence, since it is not clear that 'crossing the Taurus, setting things aright, bringing peace' were ever only said of Antiochos III, and that only he had been honoured by the cities after such actions. All of his predecessors crossed the Taurus at some point of their reign, to reinforce or re-establish Seleukid authority. *OGIS* 229 mentions Seleukos II crossing the Taurus, into the Seleukis: both concepts were operative in the language of the cities before Antiochos III (admitted by Piejko 1991*b*: 32), and the tone of the description of royal fortitude and success recalls *OGIS* 219. Therefore, the presence of these themes in *OGIS* 219 does not make a dating in the time of Antiochos III necessary. Furthermore, there is one major difference between *OGIS* 219 and the documents of Teos and Iasos. These insist on the change brought about by Seleukid takeover: the Teians referred to Antiochos' decision on their status, particularly the abolition of the Attalid tribute (document **17**, 18–20, 47–8), the Iasians spoke of Antiochos III making them free instead of slaves (document **26** B, col. I). In contrast, *OGIS* 219 presents a picture of continuous Seleukid power, more suited to Antiochos I than Antiochos III.

Other parallels: the (unnamed) queen in *OGIS* 219 is called 'sister' (lines 22, 44). That Laodike III was sometimes referred to as Antiochos' 'sister' is well documented (Orth 1977: 64–6; Piejko 1991*b*: 35–7). This argues in favour of the low dating. However, Jones (1993: 81–6) pointed out that 'sister' was not an official title, but used in certain contexts, emphasising the good relations between king and queen. It is possible that this semi-formal usage existed before Antiochos III: there is not enough evidence for a compelling argument *ex silentio*. Orth notes that Apame is called the sister of Seleukos I in Liv. 38.12.5: mistake, or echo of the court title used early on?

Finally, *OGIS* 219, lines 26–7, mentions public prayers by the priests to Apollo, τῶι ἀρχηγῶι τοῦ γένους αὐτοῦ (namely, of the king). Apollo appears under Antiochos III as founder of the Seleukid dynasty.[2] But the parallel merely proves a compatibility with the reign of Antiochos III and not the necessity of attributing *OGIS* 219 to that king. A reference to Apollo as dynastic god is possible under Antiochos I.[3]

2. Parallels between the Reign of Antiochos III and the Events in OGIS 219

The account of Antiochos' first years in Polybios seems to match the events in *OGIS* 219. The troubles in *OGIS* 219 recall the difficult beginnings of

---

[1] Crossing the Taurus: document **17**, 10; Ilion, line 12. Settling the situation: document **17**, 10–11; Ilion, lines 13–14. Peace: document **18**, 50; Ilion, line 13; cf. document **26** B, I 11.

[2] *OGIS* 237; Kraeling 1964; *BE* 55, 122; document **22**.

[3] The coinage of Antiochos I starts representing Apollo on the obverse (Mørkholm 1991: 113), perhaps implying early currency for the myth of Apollinian origins (Sherwin-White and Kuhrt 1993: 27–8).

Antiochos III (on these, Schmitt 1964: 108–88). This similarity has often been noted (Piejko 1991b: 24–9; Mastrocinque 1993: 29, 1983: 65–8). The king of *OGIS* 219 faces rebels in the Seleukis (not revolts by the cities as sometimes said), attacks on the *pragmata*, the necessity of recovering the 'paternal empire'; success is followed by a campaign across the Taurus, bringing peace to the cities and increasing the *pragmata*. It is unclear whether the 'people who attack the *pragmata*' (οἱ ἐπιθέμενοι τοῖς πράγμασιν, line 7), are the same as the rebels, or external aggressors.[4] In the first case, the situation would recall the time of Antiochos III;[5] in the latter case, the situation would fit Antiochos I better than Antiochos III who started his reign by attacking the Ptolemaic possessions of Koile-Syria).[6] The campaigns across the Taurus might apply to Antiochos III recovering Asia Minor from Achaios in 216 (Orth 1977: 68–9).

I have difficulties with dating *OGIS* 219 later than 216 BC, because the narrative, as proposed in the considerations, would be a strange representation of the activity of Antiochos III after those years: if dated in 197, lines 2–12 would have to cover the eventful years 223–197, a *raccourci saisissant* over 26 years. This is unlikely, because the detail of the sufferings of the Syrian cities implies a single event: the war against the Baktrian king Euthydemos might be represented as war against a rebel, ἀποστάτης (Pol. 11.34), but it is improbable that the Ilians imagined that the cities of the Seleukis suffered because of him. It is also difficult to fit the expedition to Atropatene, the Fourth and Fifth Syrian Wars, and the Anatolian campaign of 203 into lines 2–12, which describe the return of the *status quo* as a unified action. Likewise, the chronological scheme of document 17, 8–11 (Teos) involves a first stage 'on the other side of the Taurus', then the king's presence in cis-Tauric Asia: as in *OGIS* 219, both actions are represented as fairly close in time. On the other hand, the local Ilian narrative was under no obligation to accurate or consistent representation of royal campaigns.

Another argument against a dating to 197–196 is that *OGIS* 219 fails to mention by name Antiochos Megas' sons, active and visible in those years (Jones 1993: 88). The Herakleian decree, summarized by Antiochos III in his letter to Herakleia under Latmos, honours each member of the royal family: Laodike, Antiochos the son, Seleukos, and Mithridates (the future Antiochos IV). Admittedly, the documents from Iasos forgo such detail,

---

[4] Jones 1993: 77–8. But Jones does not show that the verb only means external attack (cf. already Orth 1977: 70). To Jones's parallels, one might add *P. Haun.* 6, fr. 1, lines 28–34: Ptolemy III sends his son Magas εἰς Ἀσίαν ἐπιθησόμενον, with Huss 1977 and Habicht 1980: 3); *BE* 61, 419, p. 199 (I thank P. Herrmann for these references).

[5] Molon's royal pretensions, the alleged plot of Epigenes, the murder of Hermeias, Achaios' march on Syria would fit; the ἀποστάται τῶν πραγμάτων of lines 5–6 would then designate the Kyrrhestian rebels, who caused considerable trouble for some time, before being subdued by Seleukid forces (Pol. 5.50.8; in 220, the mutineers were still active: Pol. 5.57.4). In this case, the Kyrrhestian rebels would be the cause for the misfortunes suffered by the cities of the Seleukis (*OGIS* 219, lines 5–6): Piejko 1991b: 29–30.

[6] Jones 1993: 77–8, assumes two distinct threats, but the text might refer to the same event with stylistic *variatio*.

but they were produced after the campaign of 197, when the sons were dispersed. The fact that the queen in *OGIS* 219 is not named[7] also argues against a low dating, since Laodike III was often named in contemporary inscriptions.[8]

Furthermore, *OGIS* 219 does not refer to 'the great king Antiochos', unlike other documents of 197[9] (Jones 1993: 87). *OGIS* 219 refers twice to 'king Antiochos, son of king Seleukos' (lines 2–3, 36–7) and once to the priest of king Antiochos (line 26). This usage would be anomalous for Antiochos III,[10] as far as we can reconstruct practice in 197 and after (Appendix 4). Divergence is possible, but unlikely because of widespread consistency and sufficient documentation. Conversely, 'King Antiochos, son of King Seleukos' fits Antiochos I, the son of the recently deceased Seleukos I.

Finally, the historical situation of Ilion argues against the low dating. In *OGIS* 219, lines 16–18, the Ilians mention that at the time of the accession of the king they continuously performed public prayers and sacrifices on his behalf (εὐχὰς καὶ θυσίας ὑπὲρ αὐτοῦ πᾶσι τοῖς θεοῖς διετέλει ποιούμενος). Piejko (1991*b*: 33) believes that the news of the accession was brought by Achaios when he reconquered the city. However, Ilion probably held out against Achaios,[11] and could not have performed sacrifices at the accession of Antiochos III. In contrast, Ilion was Seleukid at the accession of Antiochos I, taken over after Kouroupedion. In addition, *OGIS* 219, line 26 mentions a priest of King Antiochos, without further details; the office already existed when the decree (the first of its kind for the king in question) was passed.[12] It is unlikely that Ilion had a priest of Antiochos III when the latter took it, since the city had been under Attalos I. The situation would fit Antiochos I better: Ilion could have created a priesthood for the king after Kouroupedion, since Seleukos I and Antiochos I ruled jointly (Phylarchos *FGrHist* 81 F 29, Habicht 1970: 89–90, on joint cultic honours for Seleukos I and Antiochos I in 281).[13] Strobel 1996:

---

[7] Piejko 1991*b*: 43 unacceptably restores Laodike in line 44, on the argument that the royal children (the usual restoration for the line) are not attested in the two other passages where the queen is mentioned (line 22, lines 23–24): but neither is the queen's name.

[8] Documents **17**, **18**, **26** B, **27**, **28**, **30**

[9] The exceptions are Antiochos' own usage in letters, dating formulas in the headings of decrees, and the opening lines of the alliance between Antiochos and Euromos. The latter case can be explained: at the moment of the treaty, the Philippeis were not yet a 'Seleukid' city (though on the point of becoming one).

[10] The filiation of Antiochos III is mentioned once, in a statue set up on Delos by Menippos, the Seleukid ambassador, alongside the title 'great king', as well as a reference to the king's Macedonian origins (*OGIS* 239); but this private dedication, in a pan-Hellenic context, is different in nature from the inscriptions in 'Seleukid' cities.

[11] Ch. 2 § 1. Pol. 5.78.6 does not describe the reconquest (Piejko 1991*b*: 33–4) of the Troad by Attalos in 218, but friendly dealings with cities which had stayed loyal. The movement of Attalos I westwards was occasioned by the mutiny of the Aigosages (Pol. 5.78.1–4), not by the need to reassert authority over the Troad.

[12] Contrast the Iasian decree honouring Laodike (foundation of a priesthood of Laodike, with details about election and responsibilities): document **26** B.

[13] Piejko 1991*b*: 32 and n. 75, thinks that the ambassadors of *OGIS* 219, line 29, are

245–6, dates *OGIS* 219 to 278: on this view, the benefactions for which King Antiochos is praised and honoured as saviour would be the defence of Ilion, by Seleukid forces, against the Galatians, immediately after they crossed the Hellespont. This view is supported by circumstantial evidence (the crossing of the Galatians and their passage by Ilion, the presence of the Seleukid commander Antipatros: Memnon *FGrHist* 434 F 11.2.3, Strabo 13.1.27), but would be stronger if the decree actually mentioned Galatians, as other documents squarely do.

3. *Palaeography*

Arguments from letter-shapes and general presentation of the document have been adduced for both high and low dating.[14] The approach is hampered by the lack of secure local parallels.[15] The letter-forms in *OGIS* 219 vary.[16] Certain features favour a high dating: the airy layout, or the divergent bars of some sigmas. But other features point to a low date. Alpha occurs in a broken-barred version (along straight-barred and curved-barred alphas). Curved-bar alphas appear in *RC* 10–13 (*I. Ilion* 33),[17] but no broken bars (however, the six-line sample which I examined is not sufficient to establish if *RC* 10–13 did not exhibit the same variation in forms as *OGIS* 219, or some of the same shapes). The earliest examples for broken-barred alphas are found before 250, but certainly not as early as the 270s.[18] Therefore, the palaeography appears to favour a date in the late third century or early second century. However, this dating bears only on the actual carving of the document: I suggest that a document from the 270s, under Antiochos I, was recarved under Antiochos III, in the last years of the third or the very early years of the second century. The copying of an earlier document might explain the extremely divergent character of the lettering, which mingles early Hellenistic and later Hellenistic forms. The actual sight of the stone at the Fitzwilliam Museum in Cambridge reinforces this impression of a divergent, almost 'schizo-phrenic' lettering, and hence of probable recarving.

Seleukid envoys sent ahead of the expedition of 197. However, all of his 'parallels' con-cern the normal exchange of correspondence and ambassadors, not diplomatic contact as a forerunner of conquest. The expression would also be remarkably discreet for royal envoys.

[14] Robert 1966b: 11–12, and *OMS* vii. 605, pronounced the letter-forms early (but quoted contrary opinions); Orth 1977: 62, notes that the alphas with broken bar have no match in *RC* 10–13 (using the 'table of alphabets' of *RC*).

[15] The Aristodikides stele (*RC* 10–13; cf. *I. Ilion* 33) is dated to Antiochos I; unfortunately, the stone is now lost, and the photograph in *RC* is too small to be useful. *I. Ilion* 31 (cf. *OGIS* 212) long attributed to Seleukos I, probably honours Seleukos II (Orth 1977: 72–3). *RC* 42 (cf. *I. Ilion* 37) is very possibly from Antiochos III, but might also be (for instance) Attalid.

[16] I am grateful to the Fitzwilliam Museum for a splendid squeeze.

[17] I inspected a squeeze of six lines at the *Inscriptiones Graecae* of Berlin, courtesy of Dr K. Hallof.

[18] In the Laodike land-sale (*RC* 18–20, same document published as *Inschr. Didyma* 492), as pointed out by Piejko.

There are other, even less conclusive, arguments (about a Ptolemaic aggression against Antiochos I,[19] or the expression 'the paternal kingdom', reminiscent of, yet not equivalent to, the 'ancestors' in documents of Antiochos III).[20] I incline to the view that Ilion had not been taken by Achaios, and hence that the situation in *OGIS* 219 cannot apply to the time of Antiochos III; new evidence may confirm or challenge this view. The narrative of *OGIS* 219 might echo the account of the early struggles of Antiochos I, as preserved in Memnon of Herakleia.[21] If the document were to date to Antiochos III, I would favour as the most likely *c*.216 or *c*.203 (for the latter, Mastrocinque 1983: 68–9).

[19] Mastrocinque 1993: 27–39, argues against the 'war of Syrian succession'.

[20] *OGIS* 219, line 8 speaks of recovering 'the paternal empire', ἀνακτήσασθαι τὴμ πατρώιαν ἀρχήν. The verb can be paralleled in the letter of Laodike to Iasos, as well as in the reply of Antiochos III to the Roman commissioners at Lysimacheia in 196 (Pol. 18.51.6, concerning Chersonesos, Thrace, and specifically Lysimacheia). Likewise, the adjective is analogous to the reference to the ancestors, which are so prominent in the literary and the epigraphical evidence (Piejko 1991*b*: 21–4).On the other hand, Memnon does use the expression for Antiochos I: ὁ δὲ Σελεύκου Ἀντίοχος πολλοῖς πολέμοις, εἰ καὶ μόλις καὶ οὐδὲ πᾶσαν, ὅμως ἀνασωσάμενος τὴν πατρώιαν ἀρχήν (*FGrHist* 434 F 9).

[21] Preceding note. It has been claimed that Memnon describes the whole of the reign of Antiochos I (Orth 1977: 63 n. 69; Piejko 1991*b*: 23; Mastrocinque 1993: 30, with examples); such short initial assessments were widespread in Hellenistic historiography (Pol. 10.26.9, disparaging them). But Memnon explicitly locates the recovery of the 'paternal empire' before the dispatch of Patrokles, and the alleged examples of 'caraterizzazione iniziale' gathered by Mastrocinque are simply circumstantial aorist participles. Jones 1993: 90–1, observes that troubles in the Seleukis might explain why Antiochos I stayed in Syria, and sent Patrokles over the Taurus. Jones (1993: 91) points out that a Babylonian document attests the presence of Antiochos I in cis-Tauric Asia, at Sardis, in the years 275 to 274 BC, with his queen. This does not prove that *OGIS* 219 is to be attributed to Antiochos I, but shows that the events described in the inscription are compatible with the record for that king.

APPENDIX 2

The Date of the Teos Documents

Teos has produced a series of important documents relative to Antiochos III (Herrmann 1965*a*, documents **17, 18, 19** in the present volume), especially two decrees honouring the king shortly after he took over Teos. Herrmann dated these two decrees to *c*.203 BC: hence they attested Antiochos' presence in Asia Minor on his return from his eastern expedition. A more recent view holds that the decrees date to Antiochos' campaign of 197/6 BC.

1. *High or Low Dating?*

1.1 The main argument for dating the Teian decrees to *c*.203 (Herrmann 1965*a*: 93–100) is that the declaration of Teian *asylia* by Antiochos should precede all other similar documents (abundantly preserved and published in *LBW* 3.60–85 (see now Rigsby 1996): an 'early series' from the late third century, and a 'late series' from the second century). A. Wilhelm showed that three documents from central Greece (issued by the Aitolians, the Amphiktions, and the Delphians) date between 205 and 201, a view based on the datings for the Delphian archon Megartas and the Aitolian strategos Alexandros of Kalydon;[1] hence a *terminus ante quem* for the Teian documents. The context would thus be Antiochos' passage in Asia Minor on his return from the East: *c*.203.

    1.2. Piejko argues that the Teian documents should be dated to the campaign of 197 (Piejko 1991*a*: 14–27):[2] the early *asylia* documents should

---

[1] Holleaux 1952: 178–9 (quoting earlier conclusions by A. Wilhelm, in *Göttingen Gelehrte Anzeiger* 160 (1898), 219–20); Herrmann 1965*a*: 94. Piejko 1991*a*: 20–1, tries to downdate the Aitolian and Delphian decrees to 196, the second *strategia* of Alexandros of Kalydon; he mistakenly believes that the date of the archonship depends on 'the date already established for Alexander', and that 'the year for Megartas has not been determined by completely independent criteria'. In fact, it is the Delphian archonship which provides the chronological peg for the Aitolian strategos Alexandros: there is no place for Megartas in the Delphian archons of the 190s (Wilhelm) and the five-strong, trimestrial *boule* points to a date before 201 (Colin, *FD*, fasc. 2, no. 135). The Delphian decree falls slightly before 200; the Aitolian document and the Athamanian letter are contemporary, since they name the same Teian ambassadors: see further Lefèvre 1995: 204–5 and n. 166.

[2] Livy 33.38.1 does not speak of '*eodem anno* 197' (Piejko 1991*a*: 14): the year referred to is actually 196.

be dissociated from Antiochos' proclamation of the city as inviolate, since they do not refer to a royal 'grant' of inviolate status, and thus were solely a Teian initiative. Without Herrmann's *terminus ante quem*, the Seleukid takeover of Teos is free to be located in 197/6.

1.3. The literary sources are deficient: Polybios is not extant to confirm or disprove the high dating; Livy is sketchy (33.20.13; 33.38.1). I favour a high dating, but only new documentation will establish the chronological context.

2. *The* Asylia *of Teos*

2.1. To enjoy *asylia*, a city (with its territory) had to be declared 'holy' (ἱερά) to a deity—often a local decision, prompted by an oracle or an apparition.[3] The city then asked for recognition as 'holy and inviolate', which could only be granted piecemeal, by the members of the international community, each in a specific decree; a collection of such decrees could be referred to as 'the *asylias*' (τὰς ἀσυλίας: *I. Stratonikeia* 7, lines 4–5). The procedure combined acknowledgement of the city's consecrated status and an agreement to refrain from spoliation against the city or on its territory.[4] This is how Piejko (1991a: 18–20) classifies the Teians' efforts; Antiochos III simply recognized the Teian claim, but, on this view, did not initiate it, just as the *asylia* of Smyrna was a local initiative acknowledged and supported by Seleukos II, indeed first broadcast by the king on the international scene, but not initiated by him (*OGIS* 228, cf. Tac. *Ann.* 3.63.4; Rigsby 1996: 95–8, somewhat differently).[5]

2.2. However, the *asylia* of a city could also result from a royal grant. In *RC* 70 (same document Rigsby 1996: no. 218), a Seleukid king grants *asylia* to the shrine of Zeus at Baitokaike; under Tiberius, the Sardians described their *asylia* as 'Alexandri victoris donum' (Tac. *Ann.* 3.63.5–6). This might be the case of Antiocheia/Alabanda (document **16** is

---

[3] Herrmann 1965a: 122–4 ('motiviert durch eine göttliche Willenserklärung'), for oracles (e.g. Smyrna, *OGIS* 228, line 5; Antiocheia of the Chrysaorians/Alabanda: document **16**, 16); and for divine apparitions (at Magnesia, the decision was prompted by an apparition of Artemis Leukophryene herself: *Inschr. Magnesia* 16, lines 2–10). All these documents are republished and treated in Rigsby 1996, by city. The Milesian decree *Syll.* 590, at lines 9–10, speaks of the city and territory being consecrated, 'because of Zeus' and Leto's union in this place, and because of the oracles'; this consecration preceded the acknowledgement by *ethne*, cities, kings.

[4] On *asylia* in general, Rigsby 1996; earlier works are Schlesinger 1933; Herrmann 1965a: 118–38; Gauthier 1972: 209–84 modifies Schlesinger; 226–30 on 'l'asylie des sanctuaires et des villes consacrées à une divinité'.

[5] The example of Magnesia on Maeander and its dealings with Antiochos III (*RC* 31–2), which Piejko 1991a: 18, also alleges, is inappropriate, since Magnesia on Maeander was probably not a Seleukid city at this point, and since Antiochos III actually does not acknowledge the *asylia* of the city. Piejko 1991a: 19 nn. 21, 20, further believes that in the case of Antiocheia/Alabanda, 'the new status was also credited to the god's oracle'. This is not the case: the Alabandan ambassador consulted the oracle only after he had started asking the Greek cities for acknowledgement of his city's *asylia* (document **16**, 14–18)—it is possible that Antiochos III had initiated the process.

ambiguous). Stratonikeia received a grant of *asylia* from Sulla, which did not dispense the city from its own subsequent efforts at international recognition (*OGIS* 441, cf. *RDGE* 18). The decrees from Teos give the impression that they belong to this group (Herrmann 1965*a*: 125–6). Antiochos III 'consecrated our city and our territory' to Dionysos (document **17**, 15–16: καθιέρωσεν ἡμῶν τὴν πόλιν καὶ τὴν χώραν), and 'let free our city and our territory as holy and inviolate and free from tribute' (document **17**, 19–20: ἀνῆκε τὴ[ν] πόλιν καὶ τὴν χώραν ἡμῶν ἱερὰν καὶ ἄσυλον καὶ ἀφορολόγητον; document **17**, 47–8: ἀφέντες τὴμ πόλιν καὶ τὴν χώραν ἱερὰν καὶ ἄσυλον). The verbs used are striking. It is unhelpful to write (Piejko 1991*a*: 62) that *asylia* could be indifferently expressed through a plethora of phrases. The usual formulas are δέχεσθαι compounds, an infinitive construction (εἶναι, ὑπάρχειν) dependent on a verb of decision, or the verb ἀναδείκνυναι.[6] In the case of Teos, Antiochos' action is described as ἀνιέναι or ἀφιέναι, a unitary grant of holy status, *asylia*, and ἀφορολογησία. The same expression describes the grant of autonomy to Mylasa by Seleukos II: Σέλευκον δὲ ἀφιέντα τὴν πόλιν ἐλεύθεραν (Crampa 1969: no. 5, line 34); the action in both cases is the royal grant of a privilege. Antiochos III at Teos grants *asylia* and exemption from tribute as part of the same gesture: this is paralleled in the case of the shrine of Zeus at Baitokaike, which received acknowledgement of *asylia* and the grant of a royal prerogative (ἀνεπι-σταθμεία) in the same royal pronouncement (*RC* 70, line 13). Antiochos III seems to have taken the initiative, and 'consecrated' Teos to Dionysos.[7] There are two parallels: Amyzon,[8] where Antiochos 'gave back the shrine inviolate' (document **8** B), and where the verb recalls ἀνιέναι, ἀφιέναι used at Teos; and Xanthos, where 'the Great King, Antiochos, consecrated the city to Leto and Apollo and Artemis, on account of the kinship that unites him to them' (document **22**).

    2.3.1 This interpretation was rejected by Giovannini (1983: 181–2), then Piejko (1991*a*: 17–20) because of the failure of other cities to attribute the

[6] For a list of documents, see Schlesinger 1933: 71–84, and Rigsby 1996, collecting texts, illustrating usage, and analysing the practice.

[7] However, it is possible that Antiochos acknowledged (παραδέχεσθαι) Teian *asylia* upon the Teians' initiative, and then granted (ἀνιέναι) freedom from tribute, and that both actions were condensed into a misleading formulation by the Teian decree (document **17**, 47–48 mentions the actions separately). Another possibility is that Antiochos represented himself as granting *asylia* to Teos, without taking into account the Teians' earlier efforts at winning acknowledgement for *asylia*, the act of royal takeover superseding previous diplomatic activities. Both possibilities would open the way for the low dating. Furthermore, *Inscr. Cret.* 2.3 (Aptera: same document Rigsby 1996, no. 154), no. 2, lines 19–21, in the 2nd cent., refers to earlier recognition of *asylia* by the expression καθιερώσαμεν τὰν χώραν καὶ τὰν πόλιν; likewise, in *Inscr. Cret.* 1.6 (Biannos; Rigsby 1996: no. 156), no. 2, lines 10–13, Teian envoys speak of τὰν πόλιν ὑπὸ τῶν προγόνων καθιερωμέναν τὰν πόλιν καὶ τάν χώραν. These examples suggest that the verb καθιερόω might be used simply to acknowledge *asylia* (but a glance at Rigsby's index will show that they are the only examples in the whole corpus to use the verb this way). The word καθιέρωσεν occurs at Teos in *LBW* 94, probably part of the *asylia* dossier: could it be part of an inscription like the Xanthian record that Antiochos 'dedicated the city and the territory' to a god (document **22**)?

[8] Already Herrmann 1965*a*: 128.

asylia of Teos to royal initiative. In contrast, Smyrna (*OGIS* 228, cf. Rigsby 1996, no. 7), even though that city did not directly receive a grant of *asylia* from Seleukos II, and Antiocheia/Alabanda (document **16**) drew attention to royal support.

2.3.2. In the Cretan decrees concerning the *asylia* of Teos (*c*.201 BC), an envoy of Antiochos III appears three times (in the decrees from Rhaukos, Lappa, and Eleutherna)—in fact, a Rhodian sent to broker a peace between the Cretan cities. In contrast, no less than eight Cretan decrees mention Perdikkas, the envoy of Philip V, as supporting the Teian embassies.[9] This led Holleaux to postulate that Teos, around 201, was taken by Philip V (Holleaux 1952: 184–6). None of the Cretan decrees calls Antiochos III the initiator of the Teian *asylia* campaign, and the Seleukid presence is less prominent than the Antigonid support for the Teians. This is not incompatible with an initial grant of *asylia* by Antiochos III: Philip's standing as προστάτης of many Cretan cities (Pol. 7.11.9), and his *entente* with Antiochos would explain why Teian *asylia* was promoted in Crete mostly by an Antigonid envoy, perhaps upon Antiochos' request; the Antigonid envoy would not insist on the Seleukid origin of the campaign for Teian *asylia*.

2.3.3. The verb ἀνίημι also appears in four of the Cretan decrees acknowledging Teian *asylia* (Polyrrhenia, Kydonia, Aptera, Allaria)[10]—the same verb used to describe the action taken by Antiochos III in the assembly at Teos (see above). It is likely that these Cretan decrees are echoing the terminology used by Antiochos III to grant *asylia* to the Teians, and recycled by the Teians in their speech to these four Cretan cities (Rigsby 1996: 287). However, the converse is also possible: that Antiochos III acknowledged an already pre-existing status of *asylia* at Teos by using a verb supplied to him by the Teians themselves (ἀνιέναι), as had happened with the Cretan cities. The cities which use the peculiar verb ἀνιέναι are also not the same as those three which say that they are acting upon the urging of a Seleukid envoy; indeed, ἀνιέναι turns up at Allaria, which received Perdikkas, the envoy of Philip V.

2.3.4. It is also difficult to explain the absence of any reference to Antiochos III in the documents from Central Greece, especially in the Delphian decree (*Syll.* 565, cf. Rigsby 1996: no. 134), in contrast with *OGIS* 228 (Delphian decree for Smyrna under Seleukos II), and document **16**, which notes the Alabandans' praise for Antiochos III and honours the latter. If both involved royal initiative, why would Antiochos III be so visible in the transaction involving Antiocheia/Alabanda, and yet absent in the contemporary Delphian decree for Teian *asylia*?

---

[9] See Holleaux 1952: 182–94 in general and for the date; Herrmann 1965a: 134–7 (placing the decrees earlier, *c*.203 or 202). The decrees are republished as Rigsby 1996: nos. 136–52.

[10] Polyrrhenia (*Inscr. Cret.* 2.23, no. 3, lines 9–11, same document Rigsby 1996: no. 137); Kydonia (*Inscr. Cret.* 2.10, no. 2, lines 21–2, same document Rigsby 1996: no. 139); Aptera (*Inscr. Cret.* 2.3, no. 1, lines 4–6, same document Rigsby 1996: no. 145); Allaria (*Inscr. Cret.* 2.1, no. 1, lines 24–5, same document Rigsby 1996: no. 151).

2.3.5. However, the procedure is still mysterious. The Alabandan embassy praised Antiochos III before the Amphiktions (document **16**) but failed to mention him at Athens:[11] there may have been diplomatic–political reasons; or the Athenians in their decree refused to echo Alabandan praise for Antiochos III. The decision to talk about royal initiative operated at several levels, that of the community which made the request, and the community which rephrased it in its decree. For instance, the decree of Antiocheia in Persis (*OGIS* 233, cf. Rigsby 1996: no. 111) in response to an embassy from Magnesia on Maeander was issued in response to a direct order of Antiochos III (*RC* 31, lines 25–8; cf. Rigsby 1996: no. 70), and follows the king's will by omitting the *asylia* which the Magnesians requested; however, the Antiocheians mention Antiochos III only obliquely (line 50), motivating their decision through past relations with Magnesia. Thus the absence of any reference to royal patronage or royal initiative in the matter of the consecration and the *asylia* of Teos cannot constitute decisive argument—because the documents only speak in the terms they find acceptable, through diplomatic veiling.

2.4. On balance, it is still likely that the *asylia* of Teos was initiated by a royal grant from Antiochos III, predating and giving the impetus to the (well dated) Teian requests for the acknowledgement of this status in the Greek world; Herrmann's interpretation is followed by Rigsby 1996: 280–3. At any rate, even if Piejko's argument were right, it would simply establish that a low dating were possible, not necessary. Other arguments weaken the case for a low dating.

3. *Against a Low Dating*

3.1. A point against the attribution of the Teian documents to the aftermath of 197–196 BC is the absence of Antiochos' sons, whereas Livy tells us that two of them were part of the expedition of 197, with the land forces (Liv. 33.19.10), and they figure as recipients of honours in the documents from Herakleia under Latmos, issued around that time (document **31** A), which indicates their visibility in the immediate aftermath of the campaign of 197–196; in contrast, the Teian documents only honour Laodike (further, Appendix 1).

3.2. The Teian inscriptions nowhere refer to Antiochos as 'the Great King'; this may support the high dating (Appendix 4), though this argument cannot be pressed without risk of circularity.

3.3. Along with *asylia*, Antiochos III granted ἀφορολογησία, a new status, since the Teians were previously oppressed by heavy Attalid taxation (document **17**, 14; **18**, 51–2). In their letter (*RC* 35, Rigsby 1996: no. 135), the Athamanian rulers, Theodoros and Amynandros, acknowledge the Teian request [π]ε[ρὶ] τοῦ συγχωρηθῆναι παρ' ἡμῶν τήν τε πόλιν καὶ τὴν χώραν ἱε[ρ]ὰν τῶι Διονύσωι καὶ ἄσυλον καὶ ἀφορολόγητον and comply—σ[υ]γχωροῦμεν εἶναι καὶ τὴν πόλιν ὑμῶν καὶ τὴν χώραν ἱερὰν καὶ ἄσυλον καὶ ἀφορολόγητον. The

---

[11] Pounder 1978 (Rigsby 1996: no. 162), Habicht 1987.

formula is anomalous[12] (the obvious parallel is the letter of the praetor M. Valerius Messalla to the Teians, document **38** (same document *RDGE* 34), lines 19–21, another odd phrase: ἀφορολόγητον ἀπὸ τοῦ δήμου τοῦ Ῥωμαίων); it must echo Antiochos' grant (already Welles (*RC*, p. 155), quoting C. Scheffer: 'a recognition of the actual situation of the city under Antiochus III'). The Teian request probably mentioned Antiochos' grant of *aphorologesia*, which was included in the reply of the Athamanian kings, conflated with *asylia*. A parallel, without the conflation, is the Delphian decree *OGIS* 228: Seleukos II, writing to obtain recognition of the Smyrnian *asylia*, is said to have acknowledged the *asylia* himself and granted liberty and exemption from tribute to the Smyrnians (lines 5–8). Besides, *RC* 35, line II 6, shows letters compatible with [βασ]ιλεῖ or perhaps [βασ]ιλεῖ[ς]: Antiochos III sponsoring the Teian demand? This would be anomalous; but much is strange about this document. If *RC* 35 (written *c*.205–201) contains an echo of the various privileges given by Antiochos III, then it establishes a high dating for the Teian decrees.

3.4. Document **17** implies that Attalos I is still alive, since the Teians were paying taxes to him up to the moment of exemption by Antiochos III. It has sometimes been argued that Attalos I, who suffered a stroke in Boiotia in early 197, was still alive late in that year, because a Delphian inscription from that date mentions a works-commissioner sent by king Attalos; but the title only shows that Attalos I was alive when he sent the architect (Allen 1983: 10 n. 6). The position of the relevant Livian passage (33.21.1–5) might suggest that the king died in summer 197, when Antiochos III was still held up by the Rhodians; if this date were secure, it would argue against a low dating of the Teian decrees.

---

[12] The claim by Piejko 1991*a*: 24, that ἀφορολογησία means 'freedom from plunder' (already Giovannini 1983: 184), is unacceptable. To stay within the context of the Teian documents, this view is disproved, in document **17**, by lines 33–4 as παραλέλυκε τὴμ πόλιν . . . ὧν συνετάξαμεν φόρων and at line 48 as παραλύσαντες ἡμᾶς τῶμ φόρων. There is a related series of very fragmentary Cretan decrees, where the Mylasans are mentioned as sending embassies ὅπως . . . ἀφορολόγητοι ἔωντι, τάν τε πόλιν καὶ τὰν χώραν αὐτῶν ἱαρὰν ἐξ ἀρχᾶς . . . (*I. Mylasa* 643, lines 8–13; 644, 7–10; 660, 2–3; 661, 5–7—the last two published in *EA* 19 (1992), 12–13, now *SEG* 42.1003, 1004; the whole series of Cretan documents from Mylasa is republished as Rigsby 1996: nos. 187–209). The date is unknown, but might be contemporary to the Cretan decrees preserved at Teos, since a generalized war in Crete is mentioned in both cases (*I. Mylasa* 643, lines 3–4; 644, lines 6–7). I would suggest interpreting these as reflecting another grant (or acknowledgment?) of *asylia* and *aphorologesia* by Antiochos III, *c*.203, this time for Mylasa.

APPENDIX 3

Dubia

A number of documents might belong to the time of Antiochos III, and reflect his activities; however, their attribution is problematic. In most cases, certitude is impossible to reach without new evidence. The documents are listed below in geographical order.

I. Ilion *45: alliance between Lysimacheia and a king Antiochos*

Frisch and Taşlıklıoğlu edited an inscription from Ilion containing oaths exchanged by the Lysimacheians and a king Antiochos in alliance, associating it with a fragment published by Brückner in 1902: both fragments are published together as *I. Ilion* 45, and dated to Antiochos III.

Ferrary and Gauthier 1981 have interpreted the Frisch–Taşlıklıoğlu fragment as an alliance between Antiochos I and Lysimacheia (distinct from the Brückner fragment). They hold that the text cannot be attributed to Antiochos III, because it stipulates that Lysimacheia will be free and exempt from taxes and garrison; these are precisely not applicable to Lysimacheia under Antiochos III, who repopulated the ruined city, used it as a military base and a regional capital (complete with Seleukid mint),[1] and deported the population in 190: 'la domination séleucide n'avait subi aucune limitation depuis la refondation de 196'. Piejko 1988*b* re-edits the texts with restorations, attributing the text to Antiochos III and arguing (unconvincingly, to my mind) against Ferrary and Gauthier: for Piejko, the status of autonomy in *I. Ilion* 45 squares with his view that Antiochos III presented himself as a liberator to the Greek cities, and the guarantees of autonomy, tax-exemption, and garrison-exemption are mere formalities, which the king disregarded. On the first point, I would argue that Antiochos III did not present himself as a 'liberator', but made occasional grants of liberty in the aftermath of a conquest presented under the heading of dynastic legitimacy (Ch. 2 § 4); on the second point, I believe that legal guarantees such as those given to Lysimacheia in *I. Ilion* 45 represented real commitments (Ch. 3 § 3), incompatible with the behaviour of Antiochos III in 196–190 BC (also Gauthier 1989: 176–7 and n. 11). The arguments adduced by Ferrary and Gauthier are compelling; in the absence of independent evidence, I would consider a treaty between

[1] *WSM* 1615–21.

Antiochos III and Lysimacheia as anomalous as a treaty between Antiochos III and Sardeis, the subject city, his regional capital.

I do not believe the alliance between Antiochos III and Perinthos, soon to be published by M. Sayar (here provisionally reproduced as document **35**), attenuates the force of the arguments presented by Ferrary and Gauthier, since the status of Perinthos (free city, on the outskirts of the Seleukid realm) is different from that of Lysimacheia, the Seleukid 'provincial capital'. In addition, the Perinthos alliance refers to 'kings Antiochos and [Antiochos]', but the alliance which the Euromians (Philippeis) contracted with Zeuxis speaks only of Antiochos III, without Antiochos the son (document **29**). The alliance with Lysimacheia simply mentions a king Antiochos: because of proximity to Perinthos, if this alliance had been concluded in 196, one would expect the formula with both kings, as in Perinthos, so that the formulation (weakly) supports the view that the Lysimacheia alliance dates not to Antiochos III, but to an earlier Antiochos. (Admittedly, this argument could be bypassed by supposing that the alliance between Perinthos and Antiochos III took place at another time than 196 BC).

AJ *12.147–53*: Letter of Antiochos III to Zeuxis

Josephus quotes this letter, purportedly by Antiochos III to Zeuxis, concerning the dispatch of Jewish colonists to Asia Minor. Gauger 1977: 23–151, argued against authenticity, though his arguments have been contested (e.g. J. and L. Robert 1983: 178 n. 119, assertive rather than argumentative; and especially Gauthier 1989: 41–2, including further references). Gauger 1993 reiterates his position, comparing Josephus and the Pamukçu stele (document **4**): in the Pamukçu letter, the king uses the first person plural and simply writes 'to Zeuxis, greetings', whereas in Josephus, the author uses the first person singular, addresses Zeuxis as his 'father' (Ζεύξιδι πατρὶ χαίρειν), and mentions consulting the *philoi* before his decision. These arguments establish that the text cannot be an unadulterated letter of Antiochos III. They might be answered if the letter were written by Antiochos the son, during his father's absence in the east, thus accounting for the first person singular, as in *RC* 32, the address to the senior officer, Zeuxis, as 'father', even the consultation of the Friends before the decision (considered unlikely by Gauger 1977: 139–43, on the uneasily co-existing grounds that Antiochos the son was too young to write this letter, and that the revolts in Anatolia were not serious enough to warrant intervention by the young king).

RC *15*: Letter of a King Antiochos to Erythrai

Piejko attributed this document, *RC* 15 (same document, *I. Erythrai* 31) a complete letter to Erythrai, to Antiochos III, without arguments (for instance, in Piejko 1991*a*: 22 n. 28, the claim that the *galatika* were a civic tax taken over by the Attalids, not a Seleukid tax, is a bald assertion). But there is no trace of a change of *régime*, unlike the documents from Teos, which insist on the passage from Attalid to Seleukid sphere. The *galatika*, a levy linked with war against the Galatians, points to an early Seleukid; the document is followed by a decree, whose considerations start [ἐπειδὴ β]ασιλεὺς Ἀν ι [τίοχος]: the absence of the title βασιλεὺς μέγας argues against the date 197 BC or later (contrast the Iasian decree of *c*.196, document **26** B).

SEG *27.834: Graffito near Teos*

M. Baran and G. Petzl (*Ist. Mitt.* 27/28 (1977–8), 305–6) published a set of graffiti from a cave (the Kaplan Mağarası, 'panther cave'), obviously a sacred place, near the village of Benler, located 22 km. north-east of ancient Teos. The graffito closest to the mouth of the cave reads

Ἀντίοχος
βασιλεὺς
ἐπέγραψε

The letters are *c*.10 cm. high. The lettering implies a late-Roman date: the sigma in the first line is lunate, but in the following line, twice shaped like a Latin S; the upsilon, in the same line, is formed like a Latin V. The meaning of the graffito is obscure; the editors exclude as unlikely any relation with Antiochos III, and also discount the possibility of a (presumably modern) forgery. But an intriguing possibility would be to see this graffito as a Roman fake, or perhaps a piece of whimsy carved in the Roman period (purporting to be an autograph of the Seleukid king?). This would document memory of Antiochos III in Teos centuries after his dealings with the city (could cultic practice or some of the cult statues for that king have survived, to keep at least the name of 'Antiochos, king' alive?). But the last word is best left to the Roberts, who found this inscription rather disquieting ('fait à tous égards une impression un peu inquiétante': *BE* 80, 443).

BCH *10 (1886), 299–314: Alabanda Decree*

Earlier bibliography on this inscription (first published by Ch. Diel and G. Cousin, *BCH* 10 (1886), 299–314) can be found in Holleaux 1968: 21, no. 52 (established by L. Robert). Bikerman 1937 dated this decree, which mentions an embassy to renew the city's friendship with Rome and conduct negotiations concerning *phoroi*, and another embassy to 'the king' to the Roman settlement of Asia Minor in 188, but the date is later, as argued for convincingly by Gruen 1986: 733–5. The most likely date is the aftermath of the First Mithradatic War (established by Marek 1988: 294–302).

Robert 1945, p. 12: Letter of a king Antiochos, Found at Sinuri

This fragmentary letter by an Antiochos, found in Sinuri (the stone, left on the site, appears now lost), was attributed by J. and L. Robert 1983: 140, 187, to Antiochos III, because of the latter's interest in Karian shrines where his letters were often carved. But Antiochos II, or even Antiochos Hierax remain possible. The absence of published photographs precludes palaeographical argument. (The reconstruction offered by Piejko in *OAth* 18 (1990), 153 no. 2, cf. *SEG* 39.1122, is not convincing).

I. Mylasa *126: Mylasan Decree*

This Mylasan decree for a Rhodian, 'friend of the king' and ἀρχιδικαστής of the δικαστήριον ἐγ Καρίαι has been referred to the time of Antiochos III or at least to the Seleukids (Bikerman 1938: 207 n. 2). However, the ἀρχιδικαστής is unknown among Seleukid institutions, whereas it is attested for the Ptolemies (*OGIS* 136), so this document is more likely a Ptolemaic document (I owe this remark to C. Crowther).

RC *41: Letter to Tralleis*

This fragmentary letter, *RC* 41 (also *I. Tralleis* 17), found at Tralleis, is attributed to Antiochos III on palaeographical grounds. Piejko 1988a contested the attribution (58–60), arguing that Antiochos III would have referred to his 'ancestors' rather than the king [Ἀντιό]χου of line 4. The conclusion is correct, though the argument must be adjusted: Antiochos III, if referring to a specific decision by one of his predecessors, would have spoken of 'my grandfather' (cf. document **4**, or 'my father and my brother' in *SEG* 33.673). Piejko attributes the letter to Eumenes II, who received Tralleis in 188, and believes it concerns *asylia*. Neither point is compelling. Piejko also believes the Themistokles of *RC* 41 to be Achaios' subordinate, who defected to Attalos I in 218 and (on this view) served under Eumenes II after 188; alternative scenarios are possible, and it is not assured that the Themistokles in question is the same man (the name is not unique: document **23** for another example). The exact content of the letter (fiscal privileges) is irrecoverable; as for authorship, Zeuxis in 213 (Pleket, *SEG* 38.1170, proposes Antiochos III at this time), a Seleukid official between 213 and 188, or even Achaios himself, as governor or as king, are possibilities.

RC *9: Royal Letter Concerning the Athymbrianoi*

This fragmentary letter by a Seleukos and an Antiochos to an official, concerning the privileges of the Athymbrianoi, has been attributed to Seleukos I and Antiochos I, his co-regent, in 281. Piejko (e.g. *Historia* 38 (1989), 399) dates the document to Antiochos III, without argument (perhaps because Antiochos I was in the east in 281?).[2] This is unconvincing: the Athymbrianoi were synoikized into the Seleukid foundation of Nysa (Cohen 1995: 256–9); there is no reason why the sons of Antiochos III, Seleukos (the future Seleukos IV) and Antiochos (the future Antiochos IV, probably named Mithridates until the death of Antiochos the son in 193) should have written such a letter (Mastrocinque 1983: 64 n. 24). Finally, the squeeze published in *RC* can be read [Βασιλεῦ]ς Σέλευκος καὶ Ἀντίοχος or perhaps [Βασιλεῖ]ς Σέλευκος καὶ Ἀντίοχος, i.e. Seleukos I and Antiochos I (for other examples of the expression, *RC*, p. 36; *SEG* 35.1170).[3]

RC *64: Royal Letter Concerning Nysa*

J. and L. Robert 1983: 144, attributed this fragmentary letter to Antiochos III, because of the prominence of *asylia* in his reign (Piejko, e.g. 1988: 60–1, and *Historia* 38 (1989), 402, proposes Eumenes II). K. Rigsby, *TAPhA* 118 (1988), 149–53 proposes Mithradates as the author, because of the style and the vague reference to 'earlier kings' (Gauthier, *BE* 89, 279, doubts the Nysaians would have inscribed a letter of Mithradates on an archive wall of 1 BC). The first person singular does not suggest Antiochos III.

Tit. Cal. *65: Kalymnian Decree for a Rhodian*

Segre attributed this decree of Kalymna (also published as *OGIS* 243) for a Rhodian friend of 'King Antiochos' to the time of Antiochos III. But Kalymna as *polis* had probably been absorbed by Kos by that time (Sherwin-White 1978; Klaffenbach, *Gnomon* 25 (1953), 457–8, who also inclines to date the lettering to the third rather than the early second century), apart from a short period under Philip V (should we date this decree to those years?).

MAMA *4.75: Boundary Stone in Phrygia*

A 'rough boulder, planted in the ground', close to 'Gazuk Köy' (about 20 km. south-east of ancient Synnada), and bearing the inscription EOPΔ | PAς, was interpreted by its editors, W. H. Buckler, W. M. Calder, and W. K. C. Guthrie, as relating to a donation of land to a colony of Ἐορδαῖοι, members of the Macedonian tribe, in the year 101 SE (212/11); they further wrote that the palaeography, notably the shape of the alpha with its broken cross-bar, suited the date better than a date by the Sullan era (AD 16). However, this interpretation is certainly incorrect. First, L. Robert, *Ant.*

---

[2] Will 1979: 88. If this argument were pressed, Seleukos II and Antiochos Hierax could be considered as the authors.

[3] But G. Rehrenböck, who kindly checked the matter, can find no traces of an iota's vertical stroke to the left of the surviving sigma on the squeeze (kept by the *Kleinasiatische Kommission* of the Austrian Academy).

Class. 4 (1935), 461 (*OMS* 3. 1616), proposed to read *E· ὅρ(ος)· Δ*, interpreting the stone as a boundary marker between two communities, whose initials frame the abbreviation of ὅρος. Second, there are no secure arguments for the editors' dating. The absence of any Seleukid regnal formula (*Βασιλευόντων Ἀντιόχου καὶ Ἀντιόχου τοῦ υἱοῦ*) casts doubt on a date in the Seleukid period (contrast the Seleukid markers in the Aigai boundary stone, published in Herrmann 1959). The broken-bar alpha also inclines to date the stone later rather than earlier.

Th. Drew-Bear has rediscovered and examined the stone, and points out (in an unpublished paper) that the letter ς as an abbreviation for (ἔτους) is Byzantine: this 'rough boulder' is not a Hellenistic inscription, but probably dates to the sixth century AD, when numerous similar boundary-stones were erected. (I am grateful to Th. Drew-Bear for communication on this topic.)[4]

RC 30: Royal Letter Concerning Soloi

Welles summarizes the arguments for the attribution of this letter (found at Soloi) to a Ptolemy: the first person singular, and complaints against the behaviour of οἱ ἔξω τάξεων, a Ptolemaic expression for auxiliary non-combatants (Welles). Piejko (e.g. 1985: 612) has attributed the letter to a Seleukid official, after the conquest of Soloi in 197 BC. However, Seleukid officials usually use the first person plural: document **4**, *RC* 13 and 19; furthermore, Antiochos III does not use a fixed formula for non-combatants, but simply 'the others': *βασιλεὺς Ἀντίοχος στρατηγοῖς, ἱππάρχαις, πεζῶν ἡγέμοσι, στρα{στρα}τιώταις καὶ τοῖς ἄλλοις χαίρειν* (document **6**); the expression οἱ ἔξω τάξεων is nowhere found in a Seleukid document. The document was written by a Ptolemy or a Ptolemaic official.

RC 279: fragment from Hierapolis (Karia)

On the same stone as *RC* 69, a few lines were carved 'of which the character does not appear' (Welles). Because there is a mention of *τὴν πάτριον βα[σιλείαν]* and the letters *XON* appear, F. Piejko has reconstructed a decree for Antiochos III (e.g. Piejko 1991*b*, 33; also *Class and Med.* 42 (1991), 126; see comments in *SEG* 41.927).

---

[4] I had wondered if one could emend the reading to propose *Σ· ὅρ(ος)· Δ*, and interpret the document as marking the boundary between Synnada and Dokimeion, but the editors in *MAMA* claim their reading is secure (confirmed by Drew-Bear, who further notes that the stone looks like a boundary stone between villages).

APPENDIX 4

Μέγας and *βασιλεὺς μέγας*

Antiochos III is conventionally called 'Megas', 'the Great', in both ancient and modern works of history. In his own lifetime, he assumed, or was attributed, this surname, as well as the title *βασιλεὺς μέγας*, 'Great King' (far less frequent than 'Antiochos the Great' in modern usage, though Holleaux used it in his narrative chapters in *CAH*[1] viii). New documents make it worthwhile to recapitulate our knowledge, in order to examine chronology and usage.[1] One important upshot is that the titulature helps to date documents (though this could be overturned by new discoveries). Sensitivity to context is crucial: in Robert's words (1966*b*: 91 and n. 3), 'l'examen des documents et des formules au point de vue de la diplomatique, . . . sous peine des plus graves confusions et de reconstructions les plus fallacieuses'—the title 'Megas' of Antiochos III being quoted as an example (see also Aymard 1948, for an analysis of the historical implications of royal titles and their forms).

1. *Antiochos Megas*

(*a*) At Amyzon, two civic decrees of 202 and 201 (documents **9–10**) start *Βασιλευόντων Ἀντιόχου Μεγάλου καὶ Ἀντιόχου τοῦ υἱοῦ.*

(*b*) At Teos, the epithet appears as *βασιλεὺς Ἀντίοχος Μέγας* in cultic context (document **18**, 11: altar; 30, consecration of the *bouleuterion*). The date is probably around 203 (Appendix 2).

(*c*) *OGIS* 245 (Seleukeia in Pieria) and 246 (Teos) were produced after Antiochos III; the context is cultic: a list of deified Seleukids (Herrmann 1965*a*: 149–54).

(*d*) The blocks bearing *RC* 64, a letter (author unknown) to the Nysaians, also preserve four lines of text, including the words *[Ἀντι]όχου δὲ τοῦ μεγάλου.*[2] Welles assigns these fragments to the end of another letter to the Nysaians, because of the date at the end of the document, an epistolary feature—for Welles, a letter by a later Seleukid. Piejko

---

[1] Most recently Brodersen 1991: 75–7; Jones 1993: 86–7; earlier, Holleaux 1942: 159–63.
[2] Should we add *[βασιλέως]*? This was proposed by Aymard 1948: 262 n. 4; the Roberts expressed doubt (*BE* 50, 28, p. 132), because 'nous ne voyons pas la nécessité de l'addition du titre', and because the line seems to show a *vacat* after *Μεγάλου*.

1988*a*: 60 proposes a covering letter for *RC* 64, which he sees as a letter of Eumenes II.[3]

1.1. The evidence from Amyzon confirms Appian (*Syr.* 1): Antiochos was called *μέγας* after the eastern expedition (see Ch. 2 § 2). The information, probably derived from a Seleukid king-list with biographies,[4] accurately ascribes to this time the assumption, not of the title 'Great King', but of the epithet 'Great'. A decree from Antiocheia in Persis (*OGIS* 233), issued *c*.205 BC mentions a priest of the Seleukid kings, including *βασιλεὺς Ἀντίοχος*—not 'Antiochos the Great': the epithet was probably adopted afterwards (Holleaux 1942: 162). However, the preamble of inscriptions dating to 197 (Euromos) and 196 (Xanthos) simply reads *Βασιλευόντων Ἀντιόχου καὶ Ἀντιόχου τοῦ υἱοῦ* (document **29**, 1–2; **23**, 1–2; **24**, 1); an inscription from Telmessos is dated to the year 193, in the reign of 'Antiochos', without the title (Segre 1938: 190). Therefore, the epithet *μέγας* in the regnal formula was dropped between 201 and 197—probably when the title 'Great King' was adopted.

1.2. The epithet adopted *c*.204 belongs to the category of royal 'nicknames' (Bikerman 1938: 236–42). It may have originated in court usage, or in an acclamation by the army; it was also a cultic epithet used in the ruler cult, in Antiochos' lifetime already.[5] Spranger argued that this epithet could not be a manifestation of *imitatio Alexandri*, because Alexander was not 'the Great' until after Antiochos III (the earliest evidence being Plautus, *Most.* 755).[6] However, indirect evidence suggests that the expression 'Alexander the Great' started early in the Hellenistic period, implying that Antiochos' epithet echoed Alexander's title, just as the eastern expedition imitated Alexander's campaigns (S. Hornblower in *CAH*[2] vi. 877 and n. 3). In spite of the epithet's disappearance from the official regnal formula, it probably endured in common usage, and in ancient historiography written after the time of Antiochos III (Pol. 4.2.7). The occurrence in the Nysaian document (*d*) is historical or chronological, in that the epithet is used as a marker for a past king.

2. *Basileus megas Antiochos*

(*a*) The 'governor and high-priest' of Koile-Syria, Ptolemaios son of Thraseas, sent a petition to [*Βασ*]*ιλεῖ μεγάλω*[*ι*] *Ἀντιόχωι ὑπόμνημα* [*παρὰ*

---

[3] But it is unlikely that an official Attalid document referred to 'Antiochos the Great' (Piejko 1988*a*: 60 n. 14, is muddled); in document **49**, a priest under the Attalids simply says 'Antiochos the king'. Piejko's syntax for these four lines (*Historia* 38 (1989), 402) is incomprehensible. Further, Appendix 3.

[4] Brodersen 1991: 78.

[5] Court: Spranger 1958: 30. Army: cf. Lucian, *Zeuxis* 11. Ruler cult: suggested by Schmitt 1964: 95 and n. 3, on the basis of inscriptions later than Antiochos' lifetime, *OGIS* 245, 246; confirmed by the usage in the civic cult for Antiochos III, preserved in the second Teian decree (*b*), with Herrmann 1965*a*: 147–56 on the Teian imitation of practice in the official state cult and in the cities of the Seleukis.

[6] Spranger 1958: 31–2, with Schmitt 1964: 95 n. 5.

Πτολ]εμ[αίου] στρατηγοῦ | καὶ ἀρχιερέως. The date of this document, part of the Skythopolis dossier, is probably 199/8 BC, preceding a letter by Antiochos III to a Seleukid official, written the fourth of Audnaios, year 114 (rather than 112 as read by the original editor).[7]

(b) At Antioch on the Orontes, an inscription honouring a Seleukeian for his goodwill εἰς βασιλέα μέγαν Ἀντίοχον was put up in year 115, 198/7 (Kraeling 1964, with BE 65, 436).

(c) Ptolemaios son of Thraseas made a dedication to Hermes, Herakles, and βασιλεῖ μεγάλωι Ἀντιόχωι (document 21) at Soloi, which Antiochos III took in 197 (Ch. 2 § 4).

(d) At Xanthos (also taken in 197), an inscription records how the 'Great King' dedicated the city to Leto, Artemis, and Apollo—a local paraphrase of a royal enactment (document 22). See also Addenda.

(e) Zeuxis' letter to Kildara (document 25: probably 197) mentions grants ὑπὸ τοῦ βασιλέως | [μεγάλου] Ἀντιόχου.

(f) Iasos produced three relevant documents after the Seleukid takeover in 197: (f₁) The Iasian decree on cultic honours for Laodike (document 26 B), where the title appears three times: I 9; II 5 ; II 9–11. (f₂) An Iasian decree (document 28) expresses the desire to make clear the people's thoughts ὑπὲρ βασιλέως μεγάλου Ἀντιόχου καὶ | βασιλίσσης Λαοδίκης καὶ τῶν τέκνων αὐτῶν (lines 11–12). (f₃) A decree from an Iasian tribe stipulates public prayers for βασιλεῖ μεγάλωι Ἀ[ντιόχωι] | καὶ βασιλίσσηι Λαοδίκηι καὶ τοῖς τέκνοις (document 27, 3–4).

(g) The alliance between Antiochos III and the Euromians was referred to as τῆς συμμαχίας τῆς συντεθειμένης | πρὸς βασιλέα μέγαν Ἀντίοχον διὰ Ζεύξιδος on an inscription issued after 197 (document 30, 7–8). But the title 'Great King' does not appear in the few lines that are preserved of the alliance itself (document 28).

(h) On Delos, the Seleukid ambassador Menippos dedicated a statue of Antiochos III: [Β]ασιλέα [μέγαν] | Ἀντίοχο[ν] | [β]ασιλέως Σελεύκο[υ] | [Κ]αλλινίκου | [Μ]ακεδόνα (OGIS 239, lines 1–5). The date is either of Menippos' missions to Rome, in 193 and 192 (Holleaux 1942: 159–63).[8]

(i) At Klaros, a statue base for Antiochos the son reads Βασιλέα Ἀντίοχον | βασιλέως μεγάλου Ἀντιόχου (document 42). The inscription was put up before 193 (death of Antiochos the son).

(j) A Pergamene magistrate, [Pro]tas son of Menippos, erected a statue of Antiochos III: Βασιλέ[α μέγαν Ἀντίοχ]ον | [β]ασιλέως Σ[ελεύκου Καλλι]νίκου. (OGIS 240). The date and the context are mysterious.

(k) An Amyzonian decree, issued after 188 in honour of two brothers mentions [β]ασιλεῖ μεγάλωι (Robert 1983: no. 23, line 15)—perhaps to distinguish Antiochos III from the king mentioned earlier at line 6, as a historical marker referring back to a specific king in the past.

---

[7] SEG 29.1613, lines 21–2; date of the letter by Antiochos III: line 20 (Fischer's reading). 199/8 is preferable to 201/0, when Koile-Syria was still contested between Antiochos III and Skopas, the general of Ptolemy V.

[8] Baslez and Vial 1987: 303–4, date this inscription to late 194, when Menippos must have stopped on Delos on his way to Rome.

(*l*) Two statues at Delos dedicated privately by individual Athenians, honour Antiochos IV, son of 'the great king Antiochos' (*OGIS* 249, line 2; *OGIS* 250, line 2).

2.1.1. The evidence suggests that Antiochos III took on the title 'Great King' only after the conquest of Koile-Syria in 200.

2.1.2. The non-dated examples do not disprove this thesis. The Klarian statue-base (i) might date to an earlier period, assuming Kolophon was taken over by Antiochos III in *c*.203, along with Teos (which I suspect was the case); nonetheless, the document probably dates to 197–193 (since Antiochos the son was present in Asia Minor only after 197). The inscription from Pergamon (*j*) cannot date to the *entente* of 216 (when Antiochos had no reason to be called 'Great King'); the 190s provide a possible context, when Antiochos offered his daughter to Eumenes II.[9]

2.2.1 The title 'Great King' marked solemnity. Ptolemaios, son of Thraseas used it in the heading of his memorandum to the king (*c*), perhaps to formalize his petition;[10] the Euromians, in the decree (*g*), gave Antiochos his full title when referring to their alliance with him. In an Iasian decree (*f₂*), Antiochos is referred to simply as 'the king' several times, before being called 'the Great King Antiochos' in the context of loyalty to the dynasty; in an Iasian decree (*f₁*) pertaining to the cult of Laodike, Antiochos is 'the Great King' in an ornate clause praising him as a boon for all men, and in the mention of an altar erected to him. All the other examples quoted above likewise occur in a context that is emphatic, ceremonial, or solemn; in examples (*a*)–(*i*), the author of the inscription is under Seleukid authority.

2.2.2 Context and usage explain the omission of the title, for instance in routine communication between Seleukid officials.[11] In his letter to the Herakleians, Zeuxis refers to Antiochos III as 'the king'[12] rather than the 'Great King', but the letter is business-like rather than solemn. 'Great King' was not used systematically, to refer to Antiochos III whenever he was mentioned.

2.2.3. The text of the alliance between Antiochos III and the Euromians/Philippeis (document **29**) in 197, nowhere uses the title 'Great King'. The title may have appeared in the lost portion of the text. Another possibility is when the alliance was struck, the Philippeis did not observe Seleukid usage yet, since they were not a 'Seleukid' city (though being

[9] Pol. 21.20.8; Liv. 37.53.13; App. *Syr.* 5; Leuze 1923: 211–13 improbably proposes 192 or later, just before the outbreak of war or during the war; see now Tracy 1992. M. Fränkel, in his commentary on this document (his *Inschr. Pergamon* 182), suggests that the dedicant was the son of the Seleukid envoy Menippos, established in Pergamon after the Roman–Seleukid War, making a private dedication reflecting Seleukid usage.

[10] As for the Samaritan petition to Antiochos IV: Βασιλεῖ Ἀντιόχῳ Θεῷ Ἐπιφανεῖ χαίρειν (*AJ* 12.258).

[11] Document **4**, 1–2; Robert 1949, Robert 1967.

[12] Document **31** B, II 9 (Zeuxis recovering the city for the king), III 8 (exports from the land of the king), III 14 (grants by the ancestors of the king), IV 3. On the other hand, Zeuxis' letter to the Kildarians (*e*) discusses grants made 'by the Great King Antiochos'—to impress the community being conquered with the king's majesty?

taken over); they later used the title in a decree passed when they were already under Seleukid influence (g).

2.3. The title is the Greek one for the Achaimenid king; it embodies lordship over Asia (whereas Μέγας may have referred to Alexander-like exploits), as pointed out by E. Bevan (*JHS* 22 (1902), 241–4, otherwise superseded). Antiochos III considered himself as master of Asia not after his expedition to the Upper Regions, but after the conquest of Koile-Syria. The title belongs to an ideological debate with the Ptolemies. Ptolemy III assumed the title 'Great King' after his eastern conquests in the Laodikeian War (*OGIS* 54; exaggerated in Polyainos (8.50), perhaps reflecting Ptolemaic claims over Asia). Ptolemy II also laid claims to authority over Asia, as part of Alexander's heritage and of the Achaimenid dominion: his Alexandrian procession included personifications of 'the cities of Ionia and the other Greek cities which occupied Asia and the islands and had been subjected to the Persians' (Athen. 5.201 E; Rice 1983: 82–6; 105–7; 190–2). Antiochos III as 'Great King' answered these claims. It was also as 'king of Asia' that he claimed cis-Tauric Asia Minor (App. *Syr.* 1 and 12).

3. Consequences

3.1. Spranger proposed that Antiochos III called himself 'Great King' on returning from the east, and that the epithet Μέγας was a derivative, informal usage;[13] Schmitt believed that Antiochos encouraged the surname in the Greek communities as more acceptable (Schmitt 1964: 92–5). The available evidence suggests the contrary: the surname came first, in the context of regnal formulas (Amyzonian decrees) and of cult (Teos); Antiochos became the 'Great King' only after Panion.

3.2.1. The fact that at Teos, in the ceremonial, cultic context of the decree listed above under 2 (b), Antiochos III is βασιλεὺς Ἀντίοχος Μέγας (as in Amyzon in 202 and 201) but not βασιλεὺς μέγας Ἀντίοχος (as in many examples dating to 197, in the same ceremonial context) suggests a date c.203 rather than 197, especially in combination with other arguments (further, Appendix 2).

3.2.2. An Ilian decree for a king Antiochos mentions a statue base inscribed ὁ δῆμος ὁ [Ἰλιέων βασιλέα Ἀντί] l οχον βασιλέως Σελεύκου κτλ. (*OGIS* 219, cf. *I. Ilion* 32, lines 36–8).[14] The statue bases quoted in § 3, as (c), (h), (i), (j), as well as the prevalence of the title 'Great King' after 197 in honorific contexts, make it likely that the title would have been used in Ilion had the decision been taken in 197. In conjunction with other, more decisive arguments, this leads to the conclusion that *OGIS* 219 should then be attributed to Antiochos I, or possibly to the earlier years of Antiochos III (Appendix 1).

---

[13] Spranger 1958: 30–1, followed by e.g. Schmitt 1964: 93–4 and Will 1982: 66 (Antiochos as 'king of kings'); Brodersen 1991: 76–7.

[14] The squeeze shows there is no space for *ὁ δῆμος ὁ [Ἰλιέων βασιλέα μέγαν Ἀντί] l οχον.

APPENDIX 5

Stratonikeia

Two questions occur concerning Stratonikeia, the Seleukid foundation located at a strategically important site in south-west Karia: first, the date and circumstances of its creation, and second, the date of its acquisition by Rhodes. The evidence is not completely straightforward, and is worth laying out, to attempt to find a solution, both for what the events around Stratonikeia tell us about the years 201–197 BC, and for their implications about earlier Seleukid history in the region.

On the first question, Antiochos I has often been favoured as the founder of the city: see now Cohen 1995: 168–73. However, in the present state of our knowledge, it is likely that western Karia fell under Seleukid control only under Antiochos II (Ch. 1 § 2), and that is a more likely chronological context for the foundation of Stratonikeia.

There is a relevant piece of documentary evidence, *I. Stratonikeia* 1030, which was found in the region and dated to 268 by clear markers of Seleukid rule (Seleukid era, kings). But this inscription does not prove that Stratonikeia was founded at that time: the decree indicates that Koliorga (a future deme of Stratonikeia), was then still an independent community, and hence that Stratonikeia was founded later (Debord 1994: 107, 111). I think it more probable that the inscription is a *pierre errante* from eastern Karia, and would maintain the date of foundation under Antiochos II.

The second question is better documented, and falls within the complicated political history of the period and the region. Stratonikeia is prominent in the military narrative of 197; Philip V had taken the city in 201. In 197, the Rhodians unsuccessfully tried to capture the city from Antigonid troops; they finally took possession of the city later, through Antiochos (Liv. 33.18.22). Polybios has the Rhodians mention before the Senate, in 166, that they received the city 'from Antiochos and Seleukos': Στρατονικείαν ἐλάβομεν ἐν μεγάλῃ χάριτι παρ' Ἀντιόχου καὶ Σελεύκου (Pol. 30.31.6). Seleukid forces captured the city in 197, and handed it over to the Rhodians.

This was not the first conveyance of Stratonikeia to the Rhodians. The attempt of 197 was part of a campaign to recover (*vindicare*) their 'ancestral possession' taken by Philip V (Liv. 33.18.1–2). The verb *recipi* (Liv.

33.18.22) designates the Rhodians' recovering of Stratonikeia, recalling ἀνακτάομαι in Polybios: they were not capturing the city, but recapturing it. Stratonikeia was a Rhodian possession in 201, and no longer Seleukid in 201, when Philip V took the city. This is confirmed by the fact that Philip V mostly kept away from Seleukid possessions (Ch. 2 § 3).

Stratonikeia became a Rhodian possession, at some time between its foundation, probably by Antiochos II, and 201. This possibly happened under Seleukos II (as a move to weaken Hierax, or to reward assistance against Hierax?). In which case, the expression παρ' Ἀντιόχου καὶ Σελεύκου in Polybios described the double conveyance, by Antiochos III and, earlier, Seleukos II (the *proteron husteron* order can be explained by the desire to avoid hiatus (Aymard, *REG* 58 (1945), p. xiv, approved by Robert, *OMS* v. 461. For further bibliography, Cohen (above); Robert, *OMS* v. 449–64.).

A Seleukid Invasion of the Attalid Kingdom in 198 BC?

Livy indicates that Antiochos III invaded the realm of Attalos I in 198, but retired on the intervention of the Roman Senate. This incident is problematic as it stands; various efforts have been made to correct Livy's account, to preserve the 'fact' of a Seleukid invasion in 198, on the grounds that the subsequent military operations in 197 make it historically necessary. However, recent evidence challenges this view.

1. *The Account in Livy*

1.1. Livy (32.8.9–16), using an annalistic source, describes an Attalid embassy, introduced by the consuls (including T. Quinctius Flamininus) before the Senate at the first meeting of 198, and claiming that Attalos I could no longer assist the Romans against Philip V, since Antiochos had invaded the Attalid kingdom, when it was defenceless; it requested that the Senate either send troops to Pergamon, or allow Attalos to defend his kingdom. The Senate declined to send military forces against Antiochos, 'an ally and a friend of the Roman people' (*socium et amicum populi Romani*), and allowed Attalos to defend himself. Furthermore, the Senate undertook to send an embassy to Antiochos, promising its gratitude if he kept away from the kingdom of Attalos (32.8.16). Later, 'in the same year, envoys from king Attalos laid a golden crown weighing 246 pounds in the Capitol, and thanked the Senate, because Antiochos, influenced by the authority of the Roman envoys, had withdrawn his army from the kingdom of Attalos' (Liv. 32.27.1).

1.2. There are obvious problems with this account. Antiochos himself cannot have returned from Koile-Syria to attack the Attalid kingdom; if something did take place, Zeuxis was responsible (Leuze 1923: 197). Many details are suspect: the fact that Antiochos should be 'ally and friendly' (in view of the Seleukid request for friendship and alliance in 194/3, at Liv. 34.57.6, which would have been unnecessary had such a relationship already existed in 198); the early intervention of Rome in Asia Minor; the fact that the Romans sent an embassy to Antiochos III in 198, and that this was followed (presumably) by the embassy referred to in Liv. 33.20.8.

2. *Arguments against and for an Invasion in 198*

2.1. Holleaux was dubious about the chronology (Holleaux 1942: 331–5). The attack on Pergamene territories would have taken place in winter 199/8, since the Attalid embassy appeared before the Senate at the first meeting of 198. However, Attalos I was in Pergamon in the winter of 199/8 (Liv. 31.47.2), and only left in the spring of 198 (by which time, Flamininus was already in Epeiros: Liv. 32.16.1–6); therefore, the Attalid kingdom was not devoid of defences when the Seleukid invasion is supposed to have happened. Holleaux suggested that this item might have been misplaced, perhaps from summer 199 or summer 198, or even 197 (Holleaux 1952: 334–5); later, he expressed doubts about the incident (Holleaux 1957: 159 n. 4 and 175 n. 3).

2.2.1. Some have tried to salvage the main items (Seleukid invasion, Attalos' appeal, the Senate's intervention), by rearranging the chronology or disregarding the details of Livy. Leuze placed the invasion in spring 198, and put Flamininus' departure from Rome to the summer of the same year (Leuze 1923: 190–201); but Flamininus is proved to have left in spring (Walbank 1940: 321–2; Magie 1950: 753–4). Badian offers alternative scenarios: Attalos could have left Pergamon, then heard of an invasion of his kingdom, and headed back, before setting out again in the spring, once the Seleukid invasion had been contained or warned off (Badian 1964: 114–15, also Briscoe 1973 *ad.* Liv. 32.8); or Attalos stayed in Pergamon in winter 199/8 without all his troops; or, *pace* Livy, he stayed with his army without deterring Zeuxis. Badian also finds verisimilitude in the tone of the Senate's intervention, which he interprets as moderate. (This judgement is subjective; the tone of the senatorial injunction could well be considered the least likely feature of the incident, and the most obvious sign of annalistic invention emphasizing the Senate's authority and moderation.)

2.2.2. For Schmitt, the invasion of 198 is historically necessary (Schmitt 1964: 271–6, followed by Will 1982: 179–81). In 196, Antiochos' land army was at Abydos (Liv. 33.38.8); to reach the Straits it must have marched through Mysia, which, in Schmitt's view, had been granted by Antiochos III to Attalos I in 216, along with a vast portion of north-western Asia Minor. The campaign of 198 supposedly blazed a trail for the Seleukid advance of 197 (Schmitt 1964: 274).

3. *An Annalistic Invention?*

3.1.1. One problem is that, in Livy's account, the Seleukid forces evacuated what they had invaded (Liv. 32.27.1). Schmitt argues that the evacuation concerned only territory which Antiochos III had once surrendered to Attalos I in the κοινοπραγία of 216 (Schmitt 1964: 275–6). The Roman intervention, in this reconstruction, was not very effective, and Schmitt is forced to suggest that the thankful Attalid envoys and the dedication of a golden crown were annalistic inventions (Schmitt 1964: 276 n. 1). Rawlings 1976: 4–5, argues convincingly against this elaborate and unnecessary scenario. Will (1982: 179–80) proposed another solution: the Seleukid forces may have occupied north-western Asia Minor, but evacuated a different region, probably on the coast; however, this is not at all how Livy describes the events.

3.1.2. In fact, an advance in 198 is not necessary to explain the presence of Seleukid land-forces at Abydos in 196. It is now clear that Mysia was back in Seleukid hands after the defeat of Achaios (see document **4** and Ch. 2 § 1), and that Antiochos III did not allow Attalos I to keep a vast tract of north-western Asia Minor in 216. Seleukid troops operating from Seleukid-held Mysia reached the Straits in 197, without needing a trail-blazing campaign in 198.

3.2. The conclusion must be that if anything did happen, it was a local incursion, led by Zeuxis, against (for instance) Attalid-held Thyateira, followed by evacuation on Roman intervention. However, even this solution entails drastically rearranging Livy. It is simpler to see the Seleukid embassy returning from Rome in spring 197 (Liv. 33.20.8) as a belated response to the Roman embassy of 200 (see Ch. 2 § 2), and reject the 'invasion of 198' as annalistic invention (for a parallel, see Liv. 33.30.11, recording the annalistic invention that Athens was awarded Lemnos, Imbros, Delos, and Skyros, with Habicht 1997: 195–6).

The settlement of Asia Minor in 189/8

In 189, the Senate divided the former dominions of Antiochos III between the Rhodians and Eumenes II: both received territories as 'gifts' (Pol. 21.24.7–8; 22.5, where Lykia is described as ἐν δωρεᾷ). As for 'the Greek cities' (Pol. 21.24.8): those which had paid tribute to Attalos I were to pay tribute to Eumenes II; those which had paid tribute to Antiochos III only (and not to Attalos I) were not to pay tribute to Eumenes II (ὅσαι δ' Ἀντιόχῳ μόνον, ταύταις ἀφεῖσθαι τὸν φόρον, repunctuated with a comma after Ἀντιόχῳ by Baronowski 1991: 455 n. 9). The settlement thus restores the *status quo* under Attalos I.

What Polybios leaves implicit is spelled out by Livy (both versions can be reconciled, *pace* Bikerman 1937): cities which were formerly 'free' are not included in the territories given to Eumenes II and the Rhodians (Liv. 37.56.2: *extra ea oppida quae libera fuissent quo die cum rege Antiocho pugnatum est*; 37.56.4: *oppida nisi quae libera ante bellum fuissent*; 37.56.6: *nisi quae eorum oppida in libertate fuissent pridie, quam cum Antiocho rege in Asia pugnatum est*). Despite differences in detail, the general implications are clear. This category included genuinely independent cities, such as Smyrna, Lampsakos, or Chios; cities which had rallied to the Romans and been declared free by them, such as Herakleia under Latmos (document **45**); and finally, cities which had been granted autonomy by the Seleukids themselves, such as Mylasa, Alabanda, Iasos.

In 188, implementation of these guidelines was nuanced (Pol. 21.45.2–3). The fact that some 'autonomous' cities had once paid tribute to Antiochos III (such as—almost certainly—Herakleia under Latmos), before rallying to the Romans and being declared free, was considered irrelevant (Pol. 21.45.2), as long as these cities had remained faithful to the Romans. If they had not, they were to pay tribute to Eumenes II (Pol. 21.45.3): a punitive measure overriding the Roman grant of freedom during the war. Phokaia falls in this category, since it first surrendered to the Romans, then fought vigorously against them (Liv. 37.32): the restoration of the city's constitution and territory (Liv. 37.32.14, 38.39.12; Pol. 21.45.7) merely expresses consent to the city's political existence, without implying autonomy.[1] Finally, if any 'autonomous' city (of whichever of the three categories above) had once paid tribute to Attalos I, then it would fall

---

[1] Mastrocinque 1994: 452.

under the rule recreating the fiscal *status quo* under Attalos I, and pay tribute to Eumenes II (Pol. 21.45.2). Skepsis, which struck its own tetradrachms under Antiochos III,[2] but was given to Eumenes II, probably falls in this category. In sum, under certain conditions, the Roman settlement deprived autonomous communities of their freedom and subjected them to Eumenes II;[3] the recreation of the Attalid *status quo* was given the precedence over autonomy.

I assume that the Kolophonians, the Kymaians, and the Mylasans, pronounced 'free from tribute' by the Romans (Pol. 21.45.4) were in fact autonomous, rather than somehow subject to the Attalids but tribute-free; genuine freedom was certainly the status of Mylasa after Apameia. It is bothersome that Kolophon and Kyme were once Attalid cities (Pol. 5.77.4–6): since they were left autonomous in 188 and not reduced to paying tribute to Eumenes II, they must have been pronounced tribute-free or even autonomous by Attalos I himself, presumably at some time after 218 (when he recovered the cities from Achaios); another possibility is that these two cities were explicitly excused the burden by Roman intervention, as an exception to the rule, in reward for assistance during the Roman–Seleukid War or in answer to particularly successful petition. A similar explanation is likely for the fact that Aigai, an Attalid city in 218 (Pol. 5.77.4), became independent in the second century (Pol. 33.13.8: the city is named alongside independent communities as a recipient of war indemnities from Prousias II; it also struck its own coinage).[4] It is conceivable that Eumenes agreed to the autonomy of many cities in western Asia Minor in 188, to attract goodwill and because the increase of the Attalid realm had lessened the need for tribute from the cities.

[2] Kagan 1984; Strabo 13.1.54: the city was 'under the Attalic kings'.
[3] But I do not agree with Baronowski 1991 that 'all the cities which had defected from Antiochus during the Roman–Seleucid war' were subjected to the Rhodians or Eumenes II.
[4] Allen 1983: 98–9.

Epigraphical Dossier

INTRODUCTORY NOTE

The present dossier includes forty-nine inscriptions relevant to the relation between Antiochos III and the cities of Western Asia Minor, first the dated documents, then documents of indeterminate date (though certainly produced under Antiochos III), and finally a few of the documents pertaining to the period when Seleukid rule in Asia Minor was being dismantled. Within these sections, the order followed is mainly geographical.

I have not attempted a critical edition of every text anew (though I have made an effort to look at photographs, squeezes and, when possible, stones), but presented the documents, and some thoughts on them, along the following principles. The Leyden conventions rather than Robert's old Continental style are followed; nonetheless, the lemmata follow the 'lemme génétique' model developed in Continental European epigraphy, and vigorously promoted by Robert. I have chosen to restore sparingly in the main text, and to propose restorations and suggestions in the apparatus. Each text is translated, with footnotes mentioning variant possibilities. The commentary gives details on context when known, some short notes on dating or content when necessary, and directions to discussion in the main text of the book.

I   216–209 BC

1. *End of Letter from Antiochos III to the Sardians (March 213 BC)*

Gauthier 1989: no. 1, with very good photographs (plate 1), *editio princeps*, with textual notes (*SEG* 39.1283; Bringmann and von Steuben 1995: no. 260 I). (A preliminary publication by R. Merkelbach appeared in *EA* 7 (1986), 74, literally as a stop-gap to fill in a vacant page.)

Cf. Knoepfler 1993 (review of Gauthier 1989; especially 31–4, 37–8 for a reconstruction of the presentation of the documents). Gauthier 1989 provides a translation (14) and an extensive historical study of the text (15–45).

. *ΑΤΑΛ* . . . *ΚΕΙΑΝΤ* . *Ι* [22–24] *ΙΩΙ*
διορθώσεσθε ἐν ἔτεσιν τρισίν, ε[ὐ]θέ[ω]ς δὲ καὶ ξυλὴν
εἰς τὸν συνοικισμὸν τῆς πόλεως κόψαι καὶ ἐξαγαγέσθαι
ἐκ τῶν ἐν Ταρανζοις ὑλῶν καθ᾽ ἂν συνκρίνῃ Ζεῦξις· vac.   4
παραλύομεν δὲ καὶ τῆς προσεπιβληθείσης εἰκοστῆς
ἐπὶ τὴν πολιτικὴν καὶ τὸ γυμνάσιον ὧι πρότερον ἐχρῆσθε
συντετάχαμεν ἀποκαταστῆσαι ὑμῖν καὶ γεγράφαμεν
περὶ πάντων πρὸς Ζεῦξιν καὶ Κτησικλῆν· ὑπὲρ αὐτῶν δὲ   8
τούτων ἀπαγγελοῦ[ο]σιν ὑμῖν καὶ οἱ περὶ Μητρόδωρον. vac.
        Ἔρρωσθε.   θϘ᾽, Ξανδικοῦ ε᾽.

1 Letters with sublinear dot supplied from Gauthier's apparatus. [κα]ταλ[ελυκ]εῖαν το[
] suggested in Gauthier 1989: 21 n. 16 (tentative).   4 Herrmann, in *SEG*, suggests
that the stone cutter first wrote καθ᾽ ἅ, before adding the *nu* to produce the present text;
the correct Greek would be καθ᾽ ἃ ἄν.   9 An erased round letter ἀπαγγελοῦ[ο]σιν or
ἀπαγγελοῦ[θ]σιν.

. . . (which) you will settle in three years; (we have given orders)[1] also to cut
wood for the rebuilding of the city and to bring it out from the forests in
Taranza, in accordance with whatever Zeuxis may decide; we also exempt
(you) from the tax of one-twentieth, which had been added to the civic
tax,[2] and we have ordered that the gymnasion which you used formerly be
restored to you, and we have written about all things to Zeuxis and
Ktesikles; Metrodoros will also report to you about these very matters.
Farewell. (Year) 99, 5 Xandikos.

Commentary. The text is carved on a block from a *Wandpilaster*, originally
in the entrance to the Metroon of Sardeis (document **2** A and Knoepfler
1993); the blocks were later reused in the Roman synagogue installed in
part of the bath/gymnasion complex at Sardeis.
    See Ch. 2 § 1, on context; Ch. 3 § 2, on Seleukid administration in this
document.

2. *Sardian Decree, Letter of Laodike, Beginning of Letter of Antiochos III*
(June 213)

Gauthier 1989: no. 2, with plates 2, 3, *editio princeps*, with textual notes
(*SEG* 39.1284; Bringmann and von Steuben 1995: no. 260 II).
    Knoepfler (1993: 33–4) argues that the letter of Antiochos III (C below)
is continued in document **3**, because the blocks on which both documents
are carved have exactly the same dimensions (whereas the whole pilaster
tapered upwards slightly); Gauthier (1989: 79) is more cautious. Gauthier
provides translation (48–9) and extensive commentary (49–79).

---

[1] Or perhaps 'we have agreed to let you cut wood': Gauthier 1989: 19–20 (either a
royal order or a royal grant in the earlier lost lines of the royal letter).
[2] This is Gauthier's translation, rather than 'the tax of one-twentieth which had been
added on to the civic territory'.

A.

Ἡρακλείδης Σωκράτου εἶπεν· ἐπε[ιδὴ   c.15   τ]ὴν ἐπι-
στολ[ὴν τ]ὴν γραφεῖσαν παρὰ τῆς βασιλίσσῃ[s πρός τε τὴ]ν βουλὴν
καὶ τὸν δῆμον ὑπὲρ τῶν τιμῶν τῶν ἐψηφισμένων ὑπὸ τοῦ δήμου τῶι τ[ε]
βασιλεῖ καὶ τῆι βασιλίσσηι καὶ τοῖς τέκνοις αὐτῶν ἀναγράψαι εἰς τὴν   4
παραστάδα τοῦ ναοῦ τοῦ ἐν τῶι Μητρώιωι· δεδόχθαι τῆι βουλῆι καὶ τ[ῶι]
δήμωι ἀναγράψαι τὸν ταμίαν· τὸ δὲ ἐσόμενον ἀνήλωμα εἰς ταῦτα δοῦνα[ι]
ἀφ' ὧν χειρίζει προσόδων.   Ὀλωίου.

B.

Βασίλισσα Λαοδίκη Σαρδιανῶν τῆι βουλῆι καὶ τῶι δήμωι χαίρειν·   8
Μητρόδωρος καὶ Μητροφάνης καὶ Σοκράτης καὶ Ἡρακλείδης οἱ παρ' ὑμῶν
πρεσβευταὶ ἀπέδωκαν τὸ ψήφισμα καθ' ὃ τέμενός τε Λαοδίκειον ἀνεῖναι
ψηφίσαισθε καὶ βωμὸν ἱδρύσασθαι, ἄγειν δὲ καὶ πανήγυριν Λαοδίκεια
καθ' ἕκαστον ἔτος ἐν τῶι Ὑπερβερεταίωι μηνὶ τῆι πεντεκαιδεκάτηι   12
καὶ πονπὴν καὶ θυσίαν συντελεῖν Διὶ Γενεθλίωι ὑπὲρ τῆς τοῦ ἀδελφοῦ
ἡμῶν βασιλέως Ἀντιόχου καὶ τῆς ἡμετέρας καὶ τῶν παιδίων vac.
σωτηρίας, καὶ οἱ πρεσβευταὶ δὲ παρεκάλουν ἀκολούθως τοῖς ἐν
τῶι ψηφίσματι κατακεχωρισμένοις, τάς τε δὴ τιμὰς ἀποδε-   16
[δ]έγμεθα ἡδέως καὶ τὴν τοῦ δήμου προθυμίαν ἐπαινοῦμεν
[καὶ πειρασό]μεθα ἀεί τι ἀγαθὸν συνκατασκευάζειν τῆι πό-
[λει· ἀπαγγελ]οῦσιν δὲ περὶ τούτων καὶ οἱ πρεσβευταί. vac.
                              θρʹ ἔτους, Πανήμου ιʹ.   20

C.

[Βασιλεὺς Ἀντίο]χος Σαρδιανῶν τῆι βουλῆι καὶ τῶι δήμωι χα[ί]-
[ρειν· οἱ παρ' ὑμῶν πρεσ]βευταὶ Μητροφάνης, Μητρόδωρος, Μοσ[. . . .]
[Ἀρ]τεμιδ[ω]ρ . . . . . c.9 . . . . NT[   ]

    1 Gauthier 1989: 52 and n. 9 discusses possible restorations for the lacuna; as he
observes, the meaning is clear: 'since it is good/fitting to put up the letter . . .' (ἐπειδή
. . . e.g. καθήκει / προσήκει / προσῆκόν ἐστιν κτλ).   9 Σοκράτης on the stone: see
Gauthier 1989: 59–60 (not a carver's mistake, but a case of divergent spellings within the
same document; Gauthier gives parallels).   18 [καὶ πειρασό]μεθα Gauthier 1989:
60, gives arguments and parallels, e.g. I. Iasos 4, 25–30 (the same document in present
dossier, 26 A, I 25–30).   22 For the third name, Gauthier, 1989: 78, proposes
Μοσχίων, well attested at Sardis.   23 Gauthier, 1989: 78 n. 102, suggests
[ἀπέδωκα]ν τὸ [ψήφισμα], the expected formula

A. Herakleides, son of Sokrates, proposed: since [it is fitting] to put up, on
the *parastas* of the temple in the Metroon, the letter written by the queen
to the council and the people concerning the honours voted by the people
for the king and the queen and their children—let it seem good to the
people to have the treasurer do the putting up, and to have him cover the
subsequent expenditure from the monies he handles.

                                                             Oloos.

B. Queen Laodike to the council and the people of the Sardians, greetings.
Metrodoros, Metrophanes, Sokrates, and Herakleides, your **10** ambassadors, have handed over the decree, according to which you have decreed to
consecrate a sacred enclosure called Laodikeion and to establish an altar,

and to organize a *panegyris* called Laodikeia, each year, on the fifteenth of Hyperberetaios, and to carry out a procession and a sacrifice to Zeus Genethlios for the safety of our brother, king Antiochos, of us, and of our children; your ambassadors also exhorted us in accordance with the content of the decree; we accepted the honours with pleasure, and we praise the eagerness of the people and we will always try to produce some favour for the city; your ambassadors will report on these matters.

20 Year 99, Panemos 10

C. [King Antio]chos to the boule and the people of the Sardians, gree[tings. Your am]bassadors Metrophanes, Metrodoros, Mos[chion? . . . Ar]temidoros . . . (handed over your decree . . .)

Commentary. See notes to document **1** for the material disposition of the text. The decree specifies carving on the *parastas* of the Metroon. The expression can designate the *anta* of a temple; Gauthier 1989: 54, took it to mean a pillar against a wall (German *Wandpilaster*); Knoepfler 1993: 31–4 argues that the word designated the 'entrance' of the temple, framed on both sides by *Wandpilaster*.

At line B 14, Laodike speaks of her children as παιδία, the affective term rather than the more neutral τέκνα: Gauthier 1989: 72–3, to which add document **20** (dedication by Themison for the Seleukid royal family) and Kraeling 1964 (honorific inscription set up by *theoroi* at a Seleukid festival for the agonothete Theophilos, on account of his behaviour towards the royal family). These examples help define Seleukid court usage, and style, insisting on familial tenderness between members of the royal family; Antiochos III would proclaim the φιλοστοργία between him and Laodike as one of the motives for founding a cult of her in 193 (document **37**).

See Ch. 2 § 1; Ch. 4 § 2*b*, on the role of honours in interacting with rulers.

3. *Letter of Antiochos III to the Sardians (Summer 213)*

Gauthier 1989: no. 3, with plate 4, *editio princeps*, with textual notes (*SEG* 39.1285; Bringmann and von Steuben 1995: no. 260 III and IV).

See lemma of previous inscription for bibliography (and the possibility that the beginning of this letter is preserved on another block). Gauthier 1989 provides translation (82) and extensive commentary (83–111).

[συν]-
χωρήσαντες πάντα ἃ διέτε[ιν]εν πρὸς ἐπανόρθωσιν καὶ νῦν 1
προαιρούμενοι γενέσθαι ὑμᾶς ἐμ βελτίονι διαθέσει πεποήκαμεν τὰ
ἐνδεχόμενα· τοῖς τε γὰρ νέοις ἀποτετάχαμεν εἰς ἐλαιοχρίστιον
ἀνθ' ὧν πρότερον ἐλαμβάνετε κατ' ἐνιαυτὸν ἐλαίου μετρητὰς 4
διακοσίους καὶ εἰς τοῦτο τὸ πλῆθος συνετάξαμεν ἀποτάξαι vac.
προσόδους ἀφ' ὧν ἐξ ὑποκειμένου λήψεσθε εὐτάκτως, καὶ εἰς
τοὺς κατασταθμευομένους δὲ παρ' ὑμῖν συνχωροῦμεν λαμβάνεσθαι ὧν ἔχετε οἰκιῶν ἀντὶ τῶν ἡμισέων τὰ τρίτα μέρη· ἀπο- 8

λύομεν δὲ ὑμᾶς καὶ τοῦ ἐνοικίου οὗ τελεῖτε ἀπὸ τῶν ἐργαστηρίων, εἴπερ καὶ αἱ ἄλλαι πόλεις μὴ πράσσονται· οἰόμεθα δὲ δεῖν καὶ ἐν τοῖς
ἀγομέ{με}νοις Λαοδικείοις ὑπὸ τῆς πόλεως ὑπάρχειν ὑμῖν ἀτέλειαν ἐφ' ἡμέρας τρεῖς καὶ περὶ πάντων γεγράφαμεν π[ρὸς] Ζεῦξ[ιν]   12
[καὶ Κτησικλῆν?]

12 As Gauthier observes, all the readings are secure, even though the top half or third
of the letters is all that remains.   13 It is tempting to restore [καὶ Κτησικλῆν], as in
document 1, line 8.

having granted all the things that concerned the recovery (of the city) and
now making it our intention that you should be in a better situation, we
have taken the possible measures; for we have given to the young men, as
replacement for what you received previously, two hundred *metretai* of oil
a year for the oil-anointment, and we have given orders to set aside, up to
this amount, monies from which you will receive (the oil) regularly, out of
specially designated funds; and regarding those among you who have men
billeted upon them, we agree that there should be taken a third instead of
a half of the houses you have, and we exempt you from the rent which you
pay on the workshops, **10** inasmuch as the other cities are not liable to it;
we also think it necessary that in the Laodikeia conducted by the city, you
should have *ateleia* for three days; and we have written concerning all
matters to Zeuxis [and Ktesikles? . . .]

Commentary. See notes to document **1** for the material disposition of the
text.

In translating this document, I have followed the interpretation offered
by Knoepfler 1993: 34–5, for lines 6–8 (concerning billeting), and
approved by Gauthier in *BE* 93, 493 (Gauthier 1989: 97–101, had argued
for translating this difficult sentence as follows: 'regarding the men billeted
upon you, we agree that they should take a third instead of a half of the
houses you have').

See Ch. 2 § 1; Ch. 3 § 2, for Seleukid administration.

4. *Dossier Concerning the High-Priesthood of Nikanor: Correspondence of
Philotas to Bithys, Zeuxis to Philotas, Antiochos III to Zeuxis (209)*

Malay 1987, *editio princeps* with photographs (*SEG* 37.1010). Thanks to
the courteous help of H. Malay and C. Tanıver, I examined the stone in
the Manisa Museum, in 1995 and 1997.

Cf. Ph. Gauthier, *BE* 89, 276 (p. 402, date; p. 403, improved readings
from photographic enlargements); Schwertheim 1988 (historical implications); Sherwin-White and Kuhrt 1993: 198 (date and function of
Nikanor); Malay and Nalbantoğlu 1996 (on both the office of 'high-priest'
and the office of 'official in charge of the sacred finances', continued under
the Attalids).

The stele is topped by a large, semi-circular pediment, with the numerals αβγ′ carved discreetly, perhaps as a reminder for the stonemason of the order in which to carve the letters (Malay 1987: 7 n. 5).

Φιλώτας Βίθυ[ι χ]αίρειν· τῆς παρὰ Ζεύξιδος
γραφείσης πρὸς ἡμᾶς ἐπιστολῆς ὑπὲρ τῶν
κατὰ Νικάνορα κατακεχόρισθαί σοι τὸ ἀν-
τίγραφον· σύνταξον οὖν συντελεῖν   4
καθότι ἐπέσταλται.
            Ἔρρωσο. γρ′, Ἀρτεμισίου κ′.
vacat
Ζεῦξις Φιλώται χαίρειν·
εἰ ἔρρωσαι, τὸ δέον ἂν εἴη· καὶ α[ὐ]τοὶ δὲ   8
ὑγιαίνομεν· τοῦ γραφέντος πρὸς
ἡμᾶς προστάγματος παρὰ τοῦ βασιλέως ὑπὲρ Νικάνορος τοῦ ἐπὶ τοῦ
κ[ο]ιτ[ῶ]νος ὑπογέγραπται σοι τὸ ἀντί-   12
γρ[αφο]ν· κα[λῶς] ἂν οὖν ποιήσαις συν-
[τά]ξας [ἐπακ]ολου[θ]ήσαντας τοῖς
[ἐπισταλ]εῖσ[ι]ν συντελεῖν ὥσπερ οἴ-
[ε]ται δεῖν.   [γ]ρ′, Ἀρτεμισίου γ′   16
vacat
Βασιλεὺς Ἀντίοχος vac.
Ζεύξιδι χ[αίρειν]· Νικάνορα
τὸν ἐπὶ τοῦ κοιτ[ῶνος] ὄντα τῶν
φί[λων δ]ιὰ τὸ [. .]ν [. . .]ΡΙ νειν ἐν τιμῆι   20
[καὶ πιστε]ι Τ . Ν[c. 10   ] συντε-
[θρα]μμένον ἡμῖν [πεποι]ῆσθαι ἀποδεί-
[ξ]εις ἐκτενεῖς [τ]ῆς αὐτοῦ πίστε-
[ω]ς καὶ εὐνοίας, [ἠβουλό]μεθα μὲν   24
ἀπολῦσαι [. .]ν . μ[. . . .]να ἀξίως
τῶν προγεγραμμ[έν]ων [. . .]ΤΕΥΧΑ[4–5]
[τ]ων παρ᾽ ἡμῶν φιλανθρώπων· οὐχ ὑ[πο]-
μένοντος δὲ α[ὐ]τ[ο]ῦ ἐφ᾽ ἕτερα προχει-   28
ρισθῆναι, ἀποδεδ[είχα]μεν ἐν τῆι ἐ[πέ]-
κεινα τοῦ Ταύρου ὥσπερ αὐτὸς ἠ-
ξίωσεν ἀρχιερέα τῶν ἱερῶν πάν-
των, πεπεισμένοι καὶ διὰ τὸ ἦθος   32
ἐξάξειν τά τε κατὰ τὰς θυσίας καὶ
τὰ λοιπὰ ἀξίως τῆς ἡμετέρας
σπουδῆς ἣν ἔχομεν περὶ ταῦτα,
προαιρούμενοι αὔξειν ὥσπερ προσ-   36
ῆκόν ἐστιν· ὠιόμεθα δὲ δεῖν εἶναι αὐ-
τὸν καὶ ἐπὶ τῶν ἱερῶν, καὶ τὰς προσόδους τούτων καὶ τἆλλα διεξάγεσ-
θαι ὑπ᾽ αὐτοῦ καθὰ καὶ ἐπὶ τοῦ πάπ-   40
που ἡμῶν ὑπὸ Δίωνος· σύνταξον
οὖν συνεργεῖν αὐτῶι εἰς τὰ προσ-

ἥκοντα τοῖς προδεδηλωμένοις·
καταχωρίζειν δὲ αὐτὸν καὶ ἐν ταῖς   44
συγγραφαῖς καὶ ἐν τοῖς ἄλλοις
χρηματισμοῖς οἷς εἴθισται· καὶ τῆς
ἐπιστολῆς τὸ ἀντίγραφον ἀναγράψαντας εἰς στήλας λιθίνας   48
ἐχθεῖναι ἐν τοῖς ἐπιφανεστά-vac.
τοις ἱεροῖς.
        γρ', Δ[ύσ]τ[ρ]ου κγ'.

3 κατακεχόρισθαι on the stone.   8 τόδε [εὖ] ἂν εἴη Malay; the present restoration proposed by Gauthier.   12 The restoration κ[ο]ιτ[ῶ]νος proposed by P. Herrmann to Malay.   18–29 Pleket attempts a reconstruction of the meaning in *SEG* 37.1010; see below Pleket's suggestions for lines 26–27.   20 [κ]ρίνειν suggested by Malay, who prints the surviving letters without sublinear dots. One might expect an expression such as διὰ τὸ [συ]ν[εχῶς] μένειν ἐν τιμῆι | καὶ πίστει (though the photograph does not confirm this reading).   25–7 It is tempting to write [ἵ]να at line 25, as in *RC* 44, 18–20: ἵνα μὲν οὖν καὶ εἰς τὸ λο[ιπ]ὸν τυγχάνηι πάντων τῶν εἰς τιμὴν κα[ὶ δ]όξαν ἀνηκόντων, in a similar situation (Antiochos III appoints the high-priest of a temple at Daphne); unfortunately, the letters *TEYX* cannot fit a suitable (active or middle voice) form of τυγχάνειν. Pleket, *SEG* 37.1010 suggests [καὶ] τευχ[θέν|τ]ων or [καὶ ἐν]τευχ[θέν|τ]ῶν. The lacuna is clearly too small for [καὶ ἐν]τευχ[θέντων]. After examining the stone, I believe I can make out the traces of an *alpha* following the preserved letters *TEYX* (autopsy May 1997), and this reading has been reproduced in the text above. The stone certainly contained more space after *TEYX* (line 26) than one or two letters (Malay), as can be seen from Malay's photograph.   27–9 Readings and restorations by Gauthier.   38 Repunctuated by Gauthier.   49 *Vacat* added on basis of autopsy (can be confirmed on Malay's photograph).   50 I believe that the numeral γ' can still be made out on the stone (autopsy September 1995 and photograph).

Philotas to Bithys, greetings. The copy of the letter written to us by Zeuxis about the measures concerning Nikanor is attached; therefore give out orders to carry them out as it is ordered. Farewell. (Year) 103, Artemisios 20.

Zeuxis to Philotas, greetings; if you are well, that would be as is right; we ourselves are in good health. The **10** ordnance written to us by the king concerning Nikanor, the chamberlain, has been copied out for you below; you would do well, therefore, by giving orders for your subordinates[1] to obey the orders and carry out things as he thinks fit. (Year) 10[3], Artemisios 3.

King Antiochos to Zeuxis, greetings. Concerning Nikanor, the chamberlain, one of the **20** Friends, because he . . . in honour [and trust . . .], and, having been raised with us, has given devoted demonstrations of his faithfulness and his goodwill—we wished to free him from . . . so that, in a manner worthy of what is written above, he should obtain all privileges

[1] This translates the plural participle, which agrees with the implicit subject of the infinitive clause. This construction in itself reflects the assumption that Antiochos' orders will be executed not only by Zeuxis, but a host of subordinates (cf. Hdt 6.30.2, Δαρεῖος . . . τὴν κεφαλὴν τὴν Ἱστιάιου λούσαντάς τε καὶ περιστείλαντας εὖ ἐνετείλατο θάψαι κτλ., 'Darius . . . ordered his attendants to wash and wrap up well the head of Histiaios and to bury it . . .').

from us; but since he did not accept to be assigned to other functions, we have appointed him high-priest of the sanctuaries **30** in the region beyond the Taurus, as he has asked himself, being convinced that because of his character, he will carry out both the business concerning the sacrifices and the rest in a manner worthy of the zeal which we have concerning these matters, making it our intention to increase them, as is appropriate. We thought necessary that he should also be in charge of the sanctuaries, and that their revenues and the other matters should be administered **40** by him, just as was done under our grandfather by Dion. Do therefore give orders for your subordinates[2] to collaborate with him in the matters that are appropriate to what has been previously explained, and to mention him in the contracts for which it is usual, and to write up the copy of the letter on stone stelai and expose them in the most conspicuous **50** sanctuaries. (Year) 103, Dystros 23.

Commentary. The three letters are carved on a large marble stele, topped by a heavy semi-circular pediment; though its exact place of discovery is unknown (if *in situ* originally, it would provide us with the location of a local shrine), it was brought to the attention of H. Malay in the vicinity of Pamukçu (formerly Eftele).The plain of Pamukçu is distinguished by hot springs (Cuinet 1894: 42); it plays an important role in communications between Mysia and Lydia, is dominated by a crest (occupied by a Byzantine castle), and (in the time of Robert's travels there) boasted of a pool with sacred fish (Robert 1962: 385–6, 381 n. 3: 'un curieux example d'un bassin avec des poissons sacrés'). Any of these features might have provided the site for a local shrine. This context, along with the size and weight of the stele, make it very likely that the document comes from this part of Mysia.

The documents are dated to early 209. Sherwin-White and Kuhrt 1993: 198, would date Antiochos' letter a year earlier than the others. In their view, it was produced in Dystros, 'the penultimate month of the year', and Zeuxis' letter in Artemisios, 'the first month' of SE 103—hence their position that the king's letter was produced in the preceding year, 102 (even in the year before that, 101). However, this assumes that the order of months observed in this transaction is the Babylonian one; it is much more probable that the order of months is the Macedonian one, which begins in Dios and where Dystros can be followed by Artemisios without crossing the threshold of a new year (Samuel 1972: 142).

The official Philotas might be the commander of the Seleukid garrison at Abydos in 190 (Liv. 37.12.2), even though the latter position seems lowly for the administrator of the Pamukçu inscriptions: the demands of the incipient Asian phase of the war could have dictated his movements, just as Seleukos was moved from his residence of Lysimacheia to Aiolis, for his armed presence to keep the cities of the coast on the Seleukid side.

Nikanor is not linked to the state-organised cult for Antiochos III and

---

[2] See note 1.

his ancestors (an institution created after the king's return from the East, *c*.204): Ch. 1 § 1.

See Ch. 1 § 1 on the implications for the Seleukid view of the past; Ch. 3 § 2, on administrative processes and rhetoric as revealed in this document.

II   203–201 BC

5. *Letter of Zeuxis to the Amyzonians (May 203)*

GIBM 1035, *editio princeps* by F. Marshall, with facsimile and transcription of *CIG* 2899 (= *RC* 40; J. and L. Robert 1983: 141–2, no. 11; in the present collection, document **8** A) which Marshall believed to be part of the left hand portion of the present text (*contra*, Wilhelm, *Akademieschriften* 2, 39–56, esp. 39–50: extensive reconstruction of the text; dissociates *CIG* 2899 and the present text); *RC* 38, with photograph; J. and L. Robert 1983: 132–6, no. 9, basically Wilhelm's text with a few different readings or restorations. All these editions attribute the authorship of the letter to Antiochos; but the letter must be by a Seleukid official, probably Zeuxis. I examined the stone in the British Museum, which also kindly supplied a squeeze.

Cf. Marshall's commentary; Ad. Wilhelm (above), for historical context; J. and L. Robert 1983: 136–7 (against the 'interprétation idyllique' of this document, cf. Sherwin-White and Kuhrt 1993: 58); Ma, Derow, and Meadows 1995 for identification of author, text and historical commentary.

[Ζεῦξις Ἀμυζονέων τῶι δή]μωι χαίρειν. Ἡμεῖς καὶ τοὺς ἄλλους μὲν πάντας
[c.18   a]ὐτοὺς πιστεύσαντες ἡμῖν ἐνεχείρισαν, τὴν πᾶσαν αὐ-
[τῶν   c.14   τ]ὸ μένοντας ἐπὶ τῶν ἰδίων ἐν τῆι πάσηι ENAN
[c.17   ] δὲ πρόκειται ἡμῖν καὶ ὑπὲρ ὑμῶν φροντίζειν   4
[c.11   ὑπάρχο]ντα ὑμῖν τά τε ἄλλα ἃ καὶ ἐν τῆι Πτολεμαίου
[c.15   ] ποήσετε ὄντες εὔθυμοι καὶ γινόμενοι πρὸς τῶι
[c.16   ] τῶν ἰδίων· διαφυλάσσουσι γὰρ ὑμῖν τὴν εἰς τ⟨οὺ⟩ς
[βασιλεῖς εὔνοιαν? π]αρ' ἐκείνων καὶ παρ' ἡμῶν πάντα συγκατασκευ-   8
[c.17   κ]αὶ πολυωρίαν ἀνήκοτα· γεγράφαμεν δὲ καὶ
[c.18   ὅπ]ως ἀντιλαμβάνωνταί τε ὑμῶν
[καὶ μηθενὶ ἐπιτρέπωσιν ἐ]νοχλεῖν ὑμᾶς. vac. Ἔρρωσθε. θρ' Δα⟨ι⟩σίου ιε'

2 J. and L. Robert 1983: 134, propose [Ἕλληνας], though it is impossible to be sure. There are traces of an earlier, erased line, as Welles observed, though it is impossible to make out the earlier text. The line is also much longer than the others: perhaps the words πᾶσαν αὐ- were added later?   3 Marshall in *GIBM* read δομενον τὰς ἐπὶ κτλ.; the present reading is by Wilhelm and accepted by Welles and Robert. The stone only shows traces of an apex.   3–4 Wilhelm proposed Ἐνα{ν} | [ναστρέφεσθαι], assuming a mistaken duplication of the *nu*; unconvincing considering the syllabic division in the rest of the text.   4 [οὐχ ἥκιστα] δὲ Welles, followed by J. and L. Robert 1983: 134 ('nous paraît excellent'); Piejko 1988a: 63 n. 22, [ὁμοίως] δὲ seems equally acceptable. 6 [συμμαχίαι] restored by Wilhelm; though it is legitimate to wonder how a Seleukid

official would have referred to the power of another Hellenistic super-power; συμμαχία is also an unlikely word for a city as subordinate as Amyzon (though this argument perhaps takes the modern categories, invented by Bickerman and Robert, of 'free city' versus 'subordinate city' too seriously and legalistically). More likely, perhaps, is a concrete word, such as 'ordnance' or 'enactment', a specific legal document (ἐπιστολῆι? ἐντολῆι?), issued by 'Ptolemaios': a Ptolemy, or an imperial official? The reading τῶι at the end of the line is a 'lecture de G. Hirschfeld, préférée à celle de Marshall τοὺ⟨s⟩' (Robert 1983: 133 n. 7). The correct reading can be read on Welles' photograph, and, indeed, on the stone (though it is easy to understand how Marshall came to his reading, since there are traces above the iota which make it look like an upsilon); from a methodological point of view, it is interesting to note how *GIBM* misleadingly reproduces Marshall's reading in the authoritative form of the facsimile). 6–7 A possible restoration is πρὸς τῶι | [μένειν ἀδεῶς ἐπὶ] τῶν ἰδίων κτλ, 'directing yourselves towards [staying without fear on] your property', repeating the terms of line 3. 7 The stone has ΤΥΟΣ at the end. 7–8 [τὴν εἰς τοὺς θεοὺς καὶ εἰς ἡμᾶς πίστιν] Wilhelm: Welles, in *RC*, noted that 'the stock reference to the gods has here an unusual form'; indeed, it probably is not justified here (below). 8 For the restoration see below; the supplement εὔνοιαν? could be replaced by near-synonyms, for instance αἵρεσιν. Another possibility might be τὴν εἰς τοὺς βασιλεῖς καὶ τὰ πράγματα εὔνοιαν, a combination which occurs in the inscription honouring the Seleukid high-official Menedemos (Robert 1950: 73)—though the date of the latter document is not at all clear (Schmitt 1964: 19 n. 5). A near-parallel comes from Zeuxis' letter to Herakleia, (document **31** B, IV 9–10): Διὸ καὶ εὖ ποήσετε καὶ αὐτοὶ διαφυλάσ[σοντες τὴν εἰς] τὰ πράγματα εὔνοιαν. Or perhaps even τὴν εἰς τοὺς βασιλεῖς καὶ ἡμᾶς εὔνοιαν, an expression of self-importance from Zeuxis? (The Amyzonians thanked a Seleukid official for writing ὑπὲρ τῆς εὐνοίας ἥν ἔχων διατελεῖ εἴς τε τοὺς βασιλεῖς καὶ εἰς {ι} τὸν Ζεῦξιν: document **10**, 9–10). 9 Welles and Wilhelm wrote ἀνήκο⟨ν⟩τα, but the Roberts (1983: 135 and n. 22) observed that ἀνήκοτα is 'un vulgarisme dans la rédaction', a contemporary spelling which should be respected in edition.

[Zeuxis (?) to the people of the Amyzonians] greetings. As for the others [who] have . . . entrusted themselves to us, we have . . . them, . . . in regard to their staying upon their own property in all . . . we intend to take care of you as well . . . the other things which were yours in the [. . .] of Ptolemy also . . . you will do well, therefore, to be of good cheer and to direct yourselves towards the . . . of your own property; if you preserve your [goodwill? towards the kings, (it is likely that)] from them and from us, all measures will be taken regarding your . . . and your care. We have also written to . . . **10** so that they should be of present assistance to you, and [not to allow anyone to] trouble you. Farewell. Year 109, 15 Daisios.

Commentary. The letter originally figured on a marble block from a building (temple or monumental gate) of the Artemision; J. T. Wood sawed off the inscribed surface, to enable the resulting 14 cm thick plaque to be transported to England (J. and L. Robert 1983: 132–3).

This document is almost certainly a letter from Zeuxis to Amyzon (Ma, Derow, and Meadows 1995). The attribution to Antiochos III was based on Wilhelm's restoration of line 8: the author promised the Amyzonians advantages from the gods and himself, if they kept their trust towards both, a highly anomalous expression. Wilhelm's justification for this restoration is very weak: he refers to *OGIS* 224, where the published text has a Seleukid king mentioning a high-priest 'of the gods and of us'—in fact, the inscription is an edict of Antiochos III concerning the centrally organized ruler-cult; as is now known with certitude, the text should read τῶν προγόνων καὶ ἡμῶν, in relation to a high priest of Antiochos III and his ancestors (document **37**; Robert 1949, Robert 1967). Without this parallel, the necessity to attribute the letter to Antiochos disappears; better an attribution to a royal official, speaking in the first person plural about benefactions from the kings (Antiochos III and Antiochos the son) and himself.

It is possible that the fragmentary letter published as J. and L. Robert 1983: no. 13, records the confirmation and elaboration of Zeuxis' measures by Antiochos III.

See Ch. 2 § 2, on context; Ch. 3 § 2*a*, on Zeuxis.

6. Letter of Antiochos III to his Army at Amyzon (203)

E. Hula, E. Szanto, *Sitzungsberichte der kaiserlichen Akademie der Wissenschaften in Wien, phil. hist. Klasse* 132 (1895), Abh. 2, p. 2 (initial publication); a better text, from the stone, in W. R. Paton and J. L. Myres, *JHS* 16 (1896), 231, no. 34, (*OGIS* 217); *RC* 39, with commentary, translation, and near illegible photograph of squeeze; J. and L. Robert 1983: 138–41, no. 10, with commentary and slightly more legible photograph, but truncated to the left.

Βασιλεὺς Ἀντίοχος στρατηγοῖς,
ἱππάρχαις, πεζῶν ἡγεμόσι, στρα-
{στρα}τιώταις καὶ τοῖς ἄλλοις
[χ]αίρ[ε]ιν. Τὸ ἱερὸν τοῦ Ἀπόλλω-   4
[νος καὶ τῆς Ἀρτ]έμιδος τὸ ἐν
[Ἀμυζῶνι   ]

   5 *ΜΑΟΣΤΟΕΝ* Hula and Szanto.   6 Ἀμυζῶνι Robert.

King Antiochos, to the generals, hipparchs, infantry commanders, soldiers, and to the others, greetings. Concerning the sanctuary of Apollo and Artemis in [Amyzon] . . .

Commentary. The text is carved on an architectural block, probably 'le morceau d'une ante' (J. and L. Robert 1983: 138), from the Artemision at Amyzon, and was found, like almost all of the epigraphical material from that site, reused in the walls of a Byzantine *castro*.

See J. and L. Robert 1983: 140–1, for the typically 'Seleukid' way in which Apollo is named before Artemis, against the local usage. On the basis of document **8**, we could imagine Antiochos III writing to the army to announce that he has 'given back the shrine inviolate', Τὸ ἱερὸν τοῦ Ἀπόλλω[νος καὶ τῆς Ἀρτ]έμιδος τὸ ἐν [Ἀμυζῶνι ἀπεδώκαμεν ἄσυλον]; the initial statement of a royal enactment would then have been followed by a series of direct orders and prohibitions addressed to the army, [ὑμεῖς οὖν εὐτακτεῖτε], as at Labraunda (document **15**). The document perhaps ended with a short remark such as 'we have also written to Zeuxis in this matter'. This organization of the material can be observed in the appointment of

Nikanor (document 4) and (probably) in the letter of Antiochos III to the Koans (*SEG* 33.673): the initial sentence baldly states the tenor of a royal decision, with the object of the decision located at the front of the sentence (e.g. Νικάνορα τὸν ἐπὶ τοῦ κριτ[ῶνος] ὄντα κτλ: document 4, 18–19 and following)—the 'Stichwort' construction analysed by Schubart as a typical feature of business-like administrative notes, probably dictated by the king (Schubart 1920: 334)

On 'the others' (camp-followers), Bikerman 1938: 91.

See Ch. 2 § 2; Ch. 3 § 1, on Seleukid violence.

7. Dedication of Zeuxis at Amyzon (203)

E. Fabricius, *Sitzungsberichte der königlich Preussischen Akademie der Wissenschaften zu Berlin* 1894: 915–17, with drawing of lintel block and tentative commentary (*OGIS* 235); Robert 1983: 93–6, no. 1, from autopsy of the text in 1949, worn but still legible; facsimile, and photograph of squeeze. I did not see the stone when I visited the site in April 1997.

Cf. Robert 1983: 95–6: arguments for size of lacuna, based on size of blocks and the principle that these monumental dedications were symmetrically disposed (*SEG* 33.853).

Ἰδριεὺς Ἑκατό[μνω   ἀνέθηκεν]

Ζεῦξις Κυνάγου Μακέδων τοὺς ἀγροὺς τω[c.78   ]

1 Ἰδριεὺς Ἑκατό[μνω Μυλασεὺς ἀνέθηκε τὸν πυλῶνα Ἀρτεμίδι] Robert.   2 Ζεῦξις Κυνάγου Μακέδων τοὺς ἀγροὺς τῶ[ι θεῶι   ἀποκατέστησεν] Fabricius; Ζεῦξις Κυνάγου Μακέδων τοὺς ἀγροὺς τῶ[ν θεῶν   ] Robert. The restoration proposed by Piejko 1985: 609, τῶ[ν βασιλέων κελευόντων] is not compelling: apart from the oddity of the Greek, his argument, that Zeuxis could only have acted on the orders of the king(s), is disproved by the documents from Euromos and Herakleia under Latmos, where Zeuxis is seen to enjoy considerable authority. Robert 1983: 96, rejects the possibility of restoring τῶ[ι Ἀπόλλωνι καὶ τῆι Ἀρτέμιδι], claiming that the definite article would be anomalous in a dedication. But at Xanthos, a slightly later inscription (197 or later) reads Βασιλεὺς μέγας Ἀντίοχος ἀφιέρωσεν τὴν πόλιν τῆι Λητῶι καὶ τῶι Ἀπόλλωνι καὶ τῆι Ἀρτέμιδι διὰ τὴν πρὸς αὐτοὺς συνάπτουσαν συνγένειαν. The practice of naming Apollo before Artemis, even though the latter was the more important deity in the local shrine, would reflect Seleukid priorities, as in document 6 (where the gods both receive the definite article). I would propose Ζεῦξις Κυνάγου Μακέδων τοὺς ἀγροὺς τῶ[ι Ἀπόλλωνι καὶ τῆι Ἀρτέμιδι c.50 ἀνέθηκεν or ἀπεκατέστησεν].

Idrieus, son of Hekatomnos, dedicated . . .

Zeuxis, son of Kynagos, Macedonian, . . . the fields . . .

Commentary. The support of the texts is 'l'angle gauche d'une architrave dont manque la partie droite', probably from the monumental entrance, ἱερὸς πυλών, of the Artemision (Robert 1983, 93, quoting R. Martin).

The second dedication, by Zeuxis, was carved, some time after the Seleukid takeover in 203, in a script imitating an earlier inscription by the fourth-century satrap, Idrieus. The object and circumstances of Zeuxis' dedication were detailed in the 78-letter gap after τω (J. and L. Robert 1983: 96).

Fabricius' supplement implies the restoration of property (probably a Hekatomnid endowment) to the shrine; the problem is that the great deity of Amyzon was Artemis, and one would rather expect 'the goddess' (though Zeuxis could have mentioned Apollo, then Artemis, following Seleukid usage, as in 9). Robert suggests that Zeuxis handed over to the Artemision land whose owners had fled or died during the Seleukid conquest. This is possible, but hardly squares with the restoration he proposes for line 2: the phrase 'the lands of the gods', with the definite article τοὺς, would indicate that these pieces of property are already in the gods' possession, not that they are being designated as such. Perhaps Zeuxis restored to the shrine land which it had once owned, or which the Amyzonians claimed it had once owned; the land was presumably close enough to the shrine for a definite article to be used without further precisions. At any rate, the content of lacuna gave precise details which we have no other evidence to supply.

See Ch. 3 § 2a, on Zeuxis.

8. *Two Documents Pertaining to the* asylia *of the Artemision at Amyzon* *(203 or later)*

Text A: Leake 1824: 238, from a transcription by W. R. Hamilton (*CIG* 2899; *GIBM* 1035, trying to incorporate the fragments into document 5; *RC* 40; J. and L. Robert 1983: 141–2, no. 11; Rigsby 1996: 336–7).

Cf. Wilhelm, *Akademieschriften* 2: 49–50; J. and L. Robert 1983: 44–6 (W. R. Hamilton at Amyzon); 141–4 (*asylia* of Amyzon).

Readings by Leake in a copy of an Amyzonian inscription—the first to be so identified—found by Hamilton on the site 'in a very defective state of preservation'; unfortunately, Leake does not bother to give a transcription of what he does not understand, and gives no indication of the length of the document or the order of occurrence of the fragments he reads. (Piejko 1985: 613, is unaware of this fact: on the grounds of the layout in *RC*, he believes that the fragments are 'all from the left upper corner' and gives an unacceptable restoration; he also criticizes Welles for not including τὸ before καὶ μηθενὶ κτλ; but Piejko is unaware that the 'earlier tradition' he refers to is a mistake of Böckh (*CIG* 2899), who omitted καὶ and invented the τὸ; silently corrected by Welles, and pointed out by J. and L. Robert 1983: 142 n. 4. The presentation adopted here might make the random nature of the selection by Leake clear to the literal-minded or the careless.)

Enough survives to identify a letter by a royal official, probably Zeuxis, mentioning the asylia of the Artemision. Could this fragment be part of another, fairly well-preserved letter to the Amyzonians, as Marshall suggested? (See lemma above and document 5). J. and L. Robert (1983) precluded this possibility, on the grounds that document 5 was written by Antiochos III. However, if document 5 is from Zeuxis, as I argue (commentary to **5**), this obstacle disappears. How would the preserved fragments fit? Perhaps the phrase βασιλέως εὔνοιαν could be emended to βασιλεῖς εὔνοιαν, and be inserted at the beginning of line 8; lines 7–8 would then read διαφυλάσσουσιν γὰρ ὑμῖν τὴν εἰς τοὺς | βασιλε⟨ῖ⟩ς εὔνοιαν κτλ. But the correction supposes a serious misreading on the part of Leake in Hamilton's copy, or Hamilton on a rather legible stone. Furthermore, it would still be difficult to fit τὸ ἱερὸν ἄσυλον into document **5**.

Ἀμυζονέων—χαίρειν—τὸ ἱερὸν ἄσυλον—[τὴν τοῦ] βασιλέως εὔνοιαν—καὶ μηθενὶ ἐνοχλεῖν ὑμᾶς—ἔρρωσθε

Leake writes 'Towards the beginning [of Hamilton's copy] I observe *AMYTONEWN* and *XAIPEIN*'; unproblematically, Leake amends the first word to Ἀμυζονέων. Welles published these words in close sequence, as Ἀμυζονέων χαίρειν (his line 1). But document **5**, 1, reads [Ζεῦξις Ἀμυζονέων τῶι δή]μωι χαίρειν, the usual construction, so that the two words read by Leake were not contiguous. The expression should probably be restored here.

[Zeuxis? to the people] of the Amyzonians, greetings . . . the shrine as inviolate . . . the goodwill of the king . . . and (to allow) no one to trouble you . . . farewell.

Text B: J. and L. Robert 1983: 142–3, no. 12, with photographs on facing page (Rigsby 1996: 337).

[Ο]ἱ βασιλεῖς
[ἀ]πέδωκαν
[τὸ ἱερ]ὸν ἄσυ-
[λον   ] . ΗΛ   4
[   ] . .

4–5 [ὡς ἡ σ]τήλ[η | περιορίζ]ει Piejko 1985: 613. The photograph of the stone does seem to show a trace of a Τ, but not the squeeze. Rigsby 1996: 337, observes that the singular in Piejko's restoration is difficult to justify (a series of *stelai* rather than a sole pillar would be expected for a delimitation, περιορισμός).

The kings gave back the sanctuary inviolate, . . .

Commentary. B was found by the Roberts on the site of Amyzon, an inscribed column drum.

9. *Decree of the Amyzonians for Chionis, the Governor of Alinda (October–November 202)*

J. and L. Robert 1983: 146–51, no. 14, with photograph of squeeze. I examined the squeeze at the Institute for Advanced Study, Princeton, with the kind permission of G. Bowersock and Chr. Habicht.

Βασιλευόντων Ἀντιόχου Μεγάλου καὶ Ἀντιόχ[ου τοῦ υἱοῦ, ἔτους]
ἐν[δ]εκάτου καὶ ἑκατο[σ]τοῦ, μηνὸς Δίου, ἐπὶ ἀρχιε[ρέως Νικάνορος, τοῦ]
δὲ Διὸς τοῦ Κρηταγενέτα καὶ Δικτύννης Τιμαί[ου], ὡς [δὲ ὁ δῆμος ἄ]-
γει ἐπὶ στεφανηφόρου Ἀπόλλωνος, μηνὸς [Θεσ]μοφοριῶνος· ἔ[δο]ξε   4

τῶι δήμωι· γνώμη πρυτάνεων· ἐπειδὴ Χί[ονις. . c.5 . . .]ΖΗΦ [. . c.5 . . .] φί-
λος ὢν τῶν βασιλέων καὶ τεταγμένος ἐπ᾽ Ἀλίνδων [π]άσ[αις ταῖς ἀπο]-
στελλομέναις ὑπὸ τοῦ δήμου πρεσβείαις πρὸς Ζεῦξιν τ[ὸν ἐπὶ]
[τῶ]ν πραγμάτων καθεσταμένο[ν πά]ντα τὰ συμφέροντα [καὶ κα]- 8
[λῶς ἔ]χοντα συνπράσσων διατελεῖ προθ[ύμως . . .] ΠΑΝΥΠ . . . . .
. . . . . ΟΙΣ κατ᾽ ἰδίαν δὲ τῶν πολιτῶν ἐντυγχάνουσιν αὐτῶι [. . c.4 . .]
[μετὰ πά]σης {ἅπαντα} φιλανθρωπίας ἅπαντα συνκατασκε[νά]-
[ζει αὐ]τοῖς τὰ διατείνοντα πρὸς σωτηρίαν, τῶν τε . .Ο . ΓΥ vac. 12
[. . οἱ πο]λῖται πεποίηνται διὰ τὸν περιεστηκότα π[όλεμον ..c.3..]
[   ] . ΕΤΑΙΦΡΟ . Ε

The stone crumbled on the right hand side when turned over, so that the squeeze is less
complete than the Roberts' text.   2 Nikanor can safely be restored (as suggested
in Robert 1983: 165), now that document 4 has given us the date of the appointment of
the 'high-priest' (209), and documents 23 and 24 show that Nikanor was still in office in
196.   10 The stone reads ἐντυνγχάνουσιν rather than the ἐντυγχάνουσιν printed in J.
and L. Robert 1983.   11 [μετὰ πά]σης φιλανθρωπίας Robert.   12–13 Piejko
1985: 614, would reconstruct τῶν τε [θε]ω[ριῶν] λῦ[σιν οἱ πο]λῖται.   13–14 [ὢν οἱ
πο]λῖται πεποίηνται . . . φρον[τίζει] Robert.   14 The Roberts print Ο . . ΑΙΦΡΟΝ.
The present reading is what I saw on the squeeze ([   ]εται φρο[ν]ε[ῖν]?). Note Piejko
1985: 614, where he would restore [ἐπαγγέλλετ]αι φρον[τίζειν].

When Antiochos the Great and Antiochos the son were kings, in the
hundred and eleventh year, in the month of Dios, in the high-priesthood
of Nikanor and in the tenure of Timaios as priest of Zeus Kretagenetas and
Diktynna, and within the city in the tenure of Apollo as *stephanephoros*, in
the month of Thesmophorion; it seemed good to the people; proposal of
the *prytaneis*; since Chionis [son of . . ., of the city . . .,] being a friend of
the kings and appointed over Alinda, continuously assists with great eagerness, in regard to all the interests of the people and all the things that are
fine, all the embassies sent out by the people to Zeuxis, the official established in charge of affairs . . . and to those of the citizens who go to see him
on their own, 10 he provides all the things which pertain to their safety,
with all generosity, . . . the citizens have made . . . because of the w[ar]
which has broken out all around . . .he takes care (?) . . .

Commentary. The document is carved on the long side of an *anta* block
from the Artemision, beneath document 12 (the block also bears a fragmentary royal letter on the short side): J. and L. Robert 1983: 144 and 281;
the block was found, like almost all of the epigraphical material from that
site, reused in the walls of a Byzantine *castro*.

See Ch. 3 § 2a on the organization of Seleukid officials; Ch. 4 § 2c, on the
socialization of royal officials.

10. *Decree of the Amyzonians for Menestratos of Phokaia, the Epistates of
the Artemision (November–December 201)*

J. and L. Robert 1983: 151–4, no. 15 with photographs of stone and
squeeze.

[Βασιλε]υόντων Ἀντιόχου Μεγάλου κ[αὶ Ἀντιόχου τοῦ υἱοῦ, ἔτους]
[δω]δεκάτου καὶ ἑκατοστοῦ, μηνὸς Ἀπελλαίο[υ, ἐπὶ ἀρχιερέως Νικά]-
[ν]ορος, τοῦ δὲ Διὸς τοῦ Κρηταγενέτα καὶ Δικτύννης [. . . c.7 . . . ., ὡς δὲ]
[ὁ δ]ῆμος ἄγει ἐπὶ στεφανηφόρου θεοῦ δευτέρου καὶ ἱερέως τ[ῶν βασι]-   4
[λ]έων Ἰάσονος τοῦ Βαλά⟨γ⟩ρου· ἔ[δο]ξε τῶι δήμωι· γνώμη πρυτάνε[ων]·
ἐπειδὴ Μενέστρατος Ἀγαθοκ⟨λ⟩είους Φωκαιεὺς κατασταθεὶς ἐπὶ
τοῦ Ἀρτεμισίου ἐπιστάτης ἀποδείξεις πολλὰς πεποίηται τῆς αὐτοῦ
καλοκαγαθίας εἰς πάντα τὰ τῶι δήμωι συμφέροντα, γράφων πρὸς Ζεῦ-   8
ξιν τὸν ἐπὶ τῶν πραγμάτων ὑπὲρ τῆς εὐνοίας ἣν ἔχων διατελεῖ
εἴς τε τοὺς βασιλεῖς καὶ εἰς {ι} τὸν Ζεῦξιν, πολλάκι δὲ γράφων καὶ
πρὸς Νικομήδην καὶ Χίονιν τὸν ἐπ' Ἀλίνδων τεταγμένον ὁμοίως
ἐγμαρτυρῶν ὑπὲρ τῆς εὐνοίας τῶν πολιτῶν· ἐσπούδασεν δὲ   12
καὶ ὑπὲρ τῆς ἀποσκευῆς τῆς κατασχεθείσης ἡμῶν ἐν Ἀλίνδοις ὅπως
κομισώμεθα· φροντίζει δὲ διὰ τέλους καὶ ὑπὲρ τῶν ἄλλων ἡμῶν πολιτῶν τῶν κατοικούντων τὰς αὐτονόμους, προσκαλούμενος εἰς τὸν
συνοικισμὸν τοῦ Ἀρτεμισίου, ἰδίαι τε τοῖς ἐντυγχάνουσι τῶν πολι-   16
τῶν συμπεριφερόμενος διατελεῖ· ἵνα οὖν καὶ ὁ δῆμος φαίνηται
τοῖς ἀξίοις τῶν ἀνδρῶν χάριτας ἀποδιδούς· τύχηι ἀγαθῆι· δεδόχθαι Ἀμυζονέων τῶι δήμωι· ἐπηινῆσθαι Μενέστρατον ἐπὶ τῆι αἱρέσει ἧι ἔχει εἰς τὸν δῆμον· εἶναι δὲ αὐτὸν καὶ εὐεργέτην τοῦ δήμου·   20
δεδόσθαι δὲ αὐτῶι καὶ πολι{ρ}τείαν καὶ ἔνκτησιν καὶ μετουσίαν ἱε-
[ρ]ῶν καὶ ἀρχε⟨ί⟩ων καὶ τῶν ἄλλων ἁπάντων ὧν καὶ Ἀμυζονεῖς με-
[τέ]χουσιν πάντηι· τὰ δὲ αὐτὰ ταῦτα ὑπάρχειν αὐτῶι καὶ ἐκγόνοις· πέμπε[σ]-
[θαι δὲ] αὐτῶι καὶ γέρας ἀπὸ τῶν δημοτελῶν θυσιῶν καθότι καὶ τοῖς   24
[ἄλλοις εὐεργέταις   ]

2–3 As in the case of the decree for Chionis, the 'high-priest' is certainly Nikanor (suggested in J. and L. Robert 1983: 165), appointed in 209 and still in office in 196 (Malay 1987; documents **4, 23, 24**).   3 The Roberts reconstructed an 11–12 letter gap for the name of the priest of Zeus Kretagenetas and Diktynna, but the squeeze and the overall letter count (*c*.45–50 per line) suggest a shorter gap, *c*.7 letters, so that *Τιμαίου*, as in document **9**, is possible.   5 *ΒΑΛΑΠΡΟΥ* on the stone.   6 *ΑΓΑΘΟΚΑΕΙΟΥΣ* on the stone.   15 Piejko 1985, 614, would supply τὰς αὐτονόμους ⟨πόλεις⟩; but the expression might be a fixed, administrative usage   22 *ΑΡΧΕΓΩΝ* on the stone.   25 The restoration from a parallel document, Robert 1983: 239–40, no. 37, line 14.

When Antiochos the Great and [Antiochos the son] were kings, in the hundred and twelfth [year], in the month of Apellai[os, in the high-priesthood of Nikan]or and in the tenure of . . . as priest of Zeus Kretagenetas and Diktynna, and within the city in the tenure of the god as *stephanephoros* for the second time and in the tenure of Iason son of Balagros as priest of [the kings]; it seemed good to the people; proposal of the *prytaneis*; since Menestratos, son of Agathokles, of Phokaia, appointed *epistates* over the Artemision, has given many demonstrations of his excellence in favour of all the interests of the people, by writing to Zeuxis, the official in charge of affairs, concerning the goodwill which the people continuously has **10** towards the kings and towards Zeuxis, and by writing to Nikomedes and to Chionis, the official appointed over Alinda, to give likewise testimony of the goodwill of the people; he zealously took care of our movable property that was held in Alinda, so that we should recover it; he also takes full care concerning the remainder of our citizens, who reside in the autonomous (cities), and summons them to the repeopling of the Artemision, and is kind towards those of the citizens who meet him on their own;—so that the people be seen to return gratitude to those among men who are worthy of it;—with good fortune, let it seem good to the people of the Amyzonians:—to let Menestratos be praised for the disposition **20** which he has towards the people; to let him be a benefactor of the people; to give him citizenship, the right to landownership, and participation, to full extent, in the rites, the offices, and all the other things in which the Amyzonians participate; to extend the same privileges to him and to his descendants; to send to him a share of the public sacrifices, as is done for the (other benefactors) . . .

Commentary. The document is carved on the short side of an *anta* block from the Artemision (document **11**, the decree for Nikomedes, is carved on one of the long sides): J. and L. Robert 1983: 151 and 281.

On the suggestion of C. Crowther, I have taken πάντηι to describe Menestratos' full enjoyment of Amyzonian privileges, rather than translate (with the Roberts) 'all the other things in which the Amyzonians participate fully'.

See Ch. 3 § 2, on the organization of Seleukid officials; Ch. 4 § 2c, on the socialization of royal officials.

11. *Decree of the Amyzonians for Nikomedes (c.200?)*

J. and L. Robert 1983: 192–3, no. 16, with photograph of squeeze.

                    traces of 1 line
[καὶ τῶν ἄλλων ἁπ]άντων ὧν καὶ Ἀ[μυζο]-
[νεῖς μετέχουσιν ἐν τ]αῖς Χρυσαορέωμ πόλ[εσιν]·
[ἑλέσθαι δὲ ἄνδρ]ας οἳ ἀφικόμενοι πρὸς Νικομήδ[ην]   4
[τό τε] ψήφισμα ἀποδώσουσιν καὶ ἀσπασάμενοι αὐτ[ὸν]
[παρ]ὰ τοῦ δήμου παρακαλέσουσιν ὄντα εὐεργέτην πει-
[ρ]ᾶσθαι ἀεί τινος ἀγαθοῦ παραίτιον γίνεσθαι τῶι δήμωι·
[ἀ]ναγράψαι δὲ τόδε ψήφισμα ἐν τῶι ἐπιφανεστάτωι τό-   8
πωι τοῦ ναοῦ τῆς Ἀρτέμιδος· ἐπιμεληθῆναι δὲ τῆς ἀ-
ναγραφῆς τοὺς προστάτας ὅπως ἦι πᾶσι φανερὸν
ὅτι ὁ δῆμος εὐεργετηθεὶς ἀποδιδῶι χάριτας ἀξία[ς]
τοῖς εὐεργετοῦσιν αὐτόν· τὸ δὲ ἀνήλωμα εἰς ταῦτα   12
δότω ὁ καθεσταμένος ταμίας ἀπὸ τῶν κοινῶν
προσόδων. Ἡιρέθησαν Μυωνίδης Ἱεροκλείους, Μένιππος Νικασικλείους.

    5 [τό τε] Piejko 1985: 615.

(let it seem good to the people: . . . and to grant him participation) [in all the other things] in which the Amyzonians as well [participate] among the cities of the Chrysaorians; to elect men who will go to Nikomedes and hand over the decree to him, and, after greeting him on the part of the people, invite him to always try to be responsible for some good for the people since he is a benefactor; to write up this decree in the most conspicuous location of the temple of Artemis; to have **10** the *prostatai* take care of the writing up, so that it be clear to all that the people, when it has received a benefaction, returns worthy tokens of gratitude to those who do good to the people; let the *tamias* in office give the monies to be spent towards these measures out of the public revenues. Myonides son of Hierokles, Menippos son of Nikasikles were elected.

Commentary. The decree is carved on the long side of the *anta* block bearing document **10**, the decree for Menestratos: J. and L. Robert 1983: 192 and 281.

This undated decree may have been issued at the same time as the other two dated decrees for royal officials.

See Ch. 3 § 2, on the organization of Seleukid officials; Ch. 4 § 2*c*, on the socialization of royal officials.

12. *Decree of the Amyzonians for a Royal Official* (c.200?)

J. and L. Robert 1983: 193–4, no. 17, with photograph of squeeze.

[*c*.10   ] τὸ [ψ]ήφισμ[α ἀποδώ]-
[σουσ]ιν καὶ παρακαλέ[σουσιν αὐτὸν]
[ἀκό]λουθα πράσοντα τῆι τ[οῦ βασι]-
[λέ]ως αἱρέσει καὶ τῶι αὐτο[ῦ . . *c*.4. .] ἀε[ί]   4
[τι]νος ἀγαθοῦ παραίτιον γίνεσθαι
[τ]ῶι δήμωι. Ἡιρέθησαν Ἀπολλώνιος
Ἰατροκλείους, Μελαινεὺς Ἀπολλω-
νίου, Οὐλιάδης Ἰατροκλείους,   8
Ἑρμίας Παγκράτου, Διονύσι[ος]
Μυωνίδου.

3 πράσοντα on the stone.   4 τῶι αὐτο[ῦ βίωι] proposed in J. and L. Robert 1983, though the Roberts recognize that 'nous n'avons pas d'exemple de la formule'. 6 The squeeze reads ἡιρέθησαν rather than ἠρέθησαν (Robert).

(and to elect ambassadors to go to . . . and) hand over the decree to him and to invite him to behave in accordance with the [king's] policy and his own . . . and always be responsible for some good for the people. Apollonios son of Iatrokles, Melaineus son of Apollonios, Ouliades son of Iatrokles, Hermias son of Pankratos, Dionysios son of **10** Myonides were elected.

Commentary. Lines 3–4, as well as the dispatch of the embassy, paralleled in the decree for Nikomedes, shows that this document honours another local official, as pointed out by J. and L. Robert. The honorand is asked to behave 'in accordance with the king's policy': the singular (rather than the plural, 'kings', so common in Amyzon for the late third century) might indicate that the document dates to 193 or later, after the death of Antiochos the son. It is not entirely clear that the honorand is a Seleukid official, for no unambiguous indications (reigning kings, era, Macedonian calendar, eponymous officials, named individuals) are preserved. Since the inscription was inscribed, on an *anta* block of the Artemision, above (and hence earlier?) than the decree for Chionis, the governor of Alinda, it could conceivably honour (e.g.) a Ptolemaic official. One of the ambassadors named in the present decree is Hermias, son of Pankrates—the same name as the honorand of document **14**, who went on an embassy to Antiochos III; but this does not necessarily imply that the present decree dates to the time of that king: Hermias might have been active under another ruler, or the Hermias in the present decree might be the grandfather of the Hermias in document **14**.

13. *Decree of the Amyzonians for Soldiers and their Officer (c.200?)*

J. and L. Robert 1983: 196–8, no. 19, with photograph of squeeze.

```
[                                    ]ΛΟΥ ἐπὶ στεφα-
[νηφόρου τοῦ δεῖνα              ἔ]δοξε τῶι δήμωι· γνώ-
[μη πρυτάνεων?· ἐπειδὴ        ] ὑπὸ Ὀφέλανδρον τεταγμέ-
[νοι              ὑπὸ Ζεύξιδος] τοῦ ἐπὶ τῶν πραγμάτων          4
[καθεστάμενου?       μετὰ πάσης εὐτ]αξίας καὶ εὐνοίας διατετε-
[λέκασι                      ἐ]μ πᾶσιν ἀνέγκλητοι ὄντες
[              e.g. τῶν δὲ πολεμίων πο]λιορκούντων τὸ χωρίον ὑπο
[                            ]μονος μετὰ πάσης εὐνοί-          8
[ας              ὑπὲρ] τῶν τῶν βασιλέων πραγμά-
[των                    ἔλ]υσαν αὐτῶν τὴν πολιορκί-
[αν              ] σωτηρίας ἀπόδειξιν
[                    ἵνα ο]ὖν καὶ ὁ δῆμος φαίνη-          12
[ται              ὑ]πὲρ τῶν τῶν βασιλέ-
[ων πραγμάτων                              ]
```

1 The preamble of Amyzonian documents in this period lists the Seleukid kings, Nikanor, and the priest of Zeus Kretagenetas and Diktynna, before the city's *stephanephoros* and the local priest of the kings (cf. documents **9, 10**). The first three preserved letters might therefore belong to the name of the priest of Zeus Kretagenetas and Diktynna, perhaps [(ἐπὶ ἱερέως) τοῦ δὲ Διὸς τοῦ Κρηταγενέτα καὶ Δικτύννης Τιμ]αίου, on the parallel of document **9** (the traces on the photograph of the squeeze look compatible). The letters ΛΟΥ do not allow for the formula introducing the civic *stephanephoria* on other Amyzonian decrees, ὡς δὲ ὁ δῆμος ἄγει. 3 The restoration πρυτάνεων proposed by the Roberts, on the basis of the formulary in documents **9, 10**, though I see no reason to be sure that this time also, the *prytaneis* made the proposal. [ἐπειδὴ οἱ στρατιῶται οἱ] ὑπὸ Ὀφέλανδρον κτλ. Robert. 4 [ἀποσταλέντες ὑπὸ Ζεύξιος (sic)] τοῦ ἐπὶ τῶν πραγμάτων Robert. 5 By analogy with the decree for Chionis, document **9**, 8, perhaps τοῦ ἐπὶ τῶν πραγμάτων | [καθεσταμένου]. 7 τῶν δὲ πολεμίων Robert, *exempli gratia*.

. . . in the tenure of . . . as *stephanephoros*, it seemed good to the people:

since [the soldiers] put under Ophelandros [. . . by Zeuxis] the official in charge of affairs, . . . they have continuously [behaved with all] good discipline and goodwill . . . being above reproach in all matters . . . when . . . were besieging the region, . . . with all goodwill, . . . in defence of the affairs of the kings . . . **10** they put an end to the besieging . . . of safety, a demonstration . . .; so that the people be conspicuous [(in honouring those who make efforts)] in defence of the affairs of the kings . . .

Commentary. The document is inscribed on the long side of an *anta* block from the Artemision at Amyzon; this block bore two more decrees on the same long side (one of which may be Seleukid: J. and L. Robert 1983: 202, no. 21), and a possible Seleukid decree on its short side (ibid. 196 and 281).

Piejko 1985: 615, observes that in the light of this document, the authority of Menestratos of Phokaia 'may have been limited to the temple complex' (though the latter amounted to the urban nucleus of the *polis*)—unless Ophelandros took over from Menestratos as *epistates*, or his military command overlapped, on the ground, with the area under Menestratos' 'civil' authority.

See Ch. 3 § 2, on the organization of Seleukid officials; Ch. 4 § 2c, on the socialization of royal officials.

14. *Decree of the Amyzonians for Hermias* (c.200?)

J. and L. Robert 1983: 195–6, no. 18, with photograph (Bielman 1994: 154–6, no. 42: edition, translation, commentary).

traces of 1 line

. . ΑΝѠΝΑ[   ]

traces of 1 line

κ[αὶ] μεγά[λ]ας χρείας παρεσχημένος τῶι δ[ή]-
μωι διατελεῖ, ἀπαχθέντων τε τῶν ἱερῶν   4
σωμάτων κατὰ πόλεμον ἐπρέσβευσεν πρὸς
βασιλῆ Ἀντίοχον τοῖς ἰδίοις ἀναλώμασιν κα[ὶ ἐ]-
πανήγαγεν τὰ σώματα, ἔν τε τοῖς ἄλλοι[ς]
ἐν οἷς ὁ δῆμος χρείαν ἔσχηκεν αὐτοῦ ἐ[μ]   8
παντὶ καιρῶι παρασκευάζων αὐτὸν πρό[θυ]-
μον διατελεῖ· δεδόχθαι τῶι δήμωι· ἐπ[αίνεσαι]
Ἑρμίαν Παγκράτου ἀρετῆς ἕνεκε[ν καὶ εὐ]-
νοίας ἧς ἔχων διατετέλεκεν εἰς [τὸν δῆ]-   12
μον· δίδοσθαι δὲ αὐτῶι καὶ γέρα ἀπ[ὸ τῶν δη]-
μοτελῶν θυσιῶν· τὰ αὐτὰ δὲ ὑπ[άρχειν]
τοῖς ἐκγόνοις αὐτοῦ· ἵνα δὲ τὸ ψήφ[ισμα ἀνα]-
γραφῆι ἐπὶ τῆς παραστάδος τοῦ [ἱεροῦ πυλῶνος]   16
ἐπιμεληθῆναι τὸν ἐνεστῶτα [νεωποίην]
[κ]αὶ Ἀριεράμνην τὸν νεωκό[ρον].

16 The squeeze shows ἀναγραφῆι, rather than ἀναγραφῇ (Robert). The expression τοῦ [ἱεροῦ πυλῶνος] J. and L. Robert 1983: 217, no. 28, line 10.

(since . . .) and (since) he has continuously performed great services for the people; and when the sacred slaves had been carried off in war, he went on an embassy to king Antiochos, at his own expense, and brought back the slaves; and in the other affairs in which the people has a need for him, **10** he continuously presents himself zealously, in every circumstance;—let it seem good to the people:—to praise Hermias, son of Pankratos, on account of his excellence and the goodwill which he continuously has towards the people; to give him shares from the public sacrifices; to extend the same privileges to his descendants; to have the *neopoies* (temple-overseer) in function at the time and Arieramnes the *neokoros* (temple-warden) take care that the decree be written up upon the *parastas* of the sacred portal.

Commentary. The text is carved on an *anta* block from the monumental entrance to the shrine complex at Amyzon.The document implies that Antiochos III is in Asia Minor, since there is no hint of a journey to e.g. Antioch in northern Syria. The date must be be soon after the Seleukid takeover in May 203, since the king soon left to start the Fifth Syrian War *c.*202; the next passage by Antiochos III in Asia Minor was in 197, six years after the 'war' in which the sacred slaves of Amyzon were carried off, and too long afterwards for a petition like Hermias' to succeed or even to be meaningful any longer (I assume the sacred slaves were carried off by Seleukid troops, and that Hermias intervened before they could be sold off).

See Ch. 2 § 2; Ch. 3 § 1, on Seleukid violence and spoliation—not accidental, but essential activities of empire.

15. *Letter of Zeuxis(?) to the Army at Labraunda (203)*

Crampa 1969: 134–5, with plate 6 (preliminary publication of lines 3–8); revised version, Crampa 1972: 61–3, no. 46 (J. and L. Robert 1983: 139–40, though that text is not as rigorous as Crampa's)

Cf. *BE* 70, 553 (correction by the Roberts of preliminary edition by Crampa: the document was not addressed to the *polis* of the Mylasans, but to the army); J. and L. Robert 1983: 139–40 (comparison with letter to the army at Amyzon, document **6**). Piejko offers restorations (none compelling) and justifications in (1985: 612–13, also *OAth* 18 (1990), 145–6, reproduced *SEG* 40.982, with the criticisms of P. Herrmann).

$$\begin{array}{ll}
\qquad\qquad \text{traces of 1 line} \\
[\quad c.8 \quad]\tau\eta\,[\qquad c.17 \qquad\qquad\qquad] \\
[\quad c.8 \quad]\ o\mathfrak{i}\ \theta\acute{v}o\nu\tau[\epsilon\varsigma \qquad c.14 \qquad\quad] \\
[\ c.3\ ]\underline{\sigma}\upsilon\nu\tau\acute{\epsilon}\tau\alpha\chi\epsilon\nu\ \mathring{\eta}\mu[\mathfrak{i}\nu\ \acute{o}]\ \beta\alpha\sigma\iota\lambda\epsilon\grave{v}\varsigma \\
[A]\nu\tau\acute{\iota}o\chi o\varsigma\ \grave{\epsilon}\pi\iota\mu\acute{\epsilon}\lambda\epsilon\iota\underline{\alpha}\nu\ \pi o\iota\epsilon\hat{\iota}\sigma\theta\alpha\iota\ [\tau\hat{\omega}\nu] \\
[\mathfrak{i}\epsilon\rho]\hat{\omega}\nu\ \kappa\alpha\grave{\iota}\ \mathring{\alpha}\pi\alpha\nu\tau\alpha\ \tau\grave{\alpha}\ \mathring{\alpha}\lambda\lambda\alpha.\ \Upsilon\mu\epsilon\hat{\iota}\varsigma\ o\hat{\underline{v}}[\nu] \\
[\kappa]\underline{\alpha}\underline{\tau}\acute{\alpha}\ \tau\epsilon\ \tau\grave{\alpha}\ \lambda o\iota\pi\grave{\alpha}\ \epsilon\mathring{v}\tau\alpha\kappa\tau\epsilon\hat{\iota}\tau\epsilon\ \mathring{\omega}\underline{\sigma}[\pi\epsilon\rho] \\
[\pi\rho]o\sigma\acute{\eta}\kappa\epsilon\iota\ \kappa\alpha\grave{\iota}\ \mu\acute{\eta}\tau\epsilon\ \grave{\epsilon}\pi\iota\sigma\kappa\eta\nu o\hat{v}\tau[\epsilon\ .\ .\ 4\text{--}5\ .\ .\ .] \\
[.\ .]\grave{\epsilon}\nu\ \Lambda\alpha\beta\rho\alpha\acute{v}\nu\delta o\iota\varsigma\ \mu\acute{\eta}\tau\epsilon\ \grave{\epsilon}\nu\ \tau o\mathfrak{i}[\varsigma\ \mathfrak{i}\epsilon\rho o\hat{\iota}\varsigma]
\end{array}$$

4

8

[τόπ]οις καταλύετε μηδὲ κτήνη σ[c.5]
[. . . μ]ήτε ἐν τοῖς πυλῶσι μ[ή]τε ἐν [. . .6–7 . . . .]
[. . . μή]τε ἐν ταῖς στ[οαῖς   c.14   ]
[c.8   ] θεσθ[ε   c.17   ]   12

2 The mention of 'those who offer sacrifice' recalls Le Roy 1986: 279–80 (*SEG* 36.1221), line 14: a set of religious rules pertaining to the Letoon of Xanthos ends with the prohibition for all except οἱ θύοντες to spend the night in the shrine or even enter it. Perhaps the author of the letter is restating or confirming a local cultic rule comparable to the Xanthian one.   2–4 Piejko, *OAth* 18 (1990), 145 proposes [ἐ̣ | πεὶ] συντέταχεν ἡμῖν ὁ βασιλεὺς [γὰρ] | Ἀντίοχος. The position (indeed, the presence) of γάρ is intolerable. Perhaps the clause started with an adverb followed by γάρ, e.g. [πολλάκις (πλεονάκις) | γὰρ] συντέταχεν ἡμῖν κτλ.   4–5 Present restoration by the Roberts (*BE* 70, 553, accepted by Crampa 1972). Piejko 1985: 612, would like [τοῦ | των], but the size of the space to the left of the surviving letters ωΝ really precludes this (though Piejko claims that a tau with a very big cross-bar would fill the gap).   7–8 Crampa proposed ἰδίαι, μήκετι or αὐτοθι after the verb ἐπισκηνοῦ[τε]. Piejko, *OAth* 18 (1990), 145, proposes τὸ Δῖον or τῶι Δίωι (but the former is really precluded for syntactical reasons: the verb ἐπισκηνόω should take a preposition or the dative, as in Polybios: de Foucault 1972: 349 s.v.).   8–9 τοῖ[ς ἱεροῖς | τόποις] J. and L. Robert 1983: 140, quoting Pouilloux (*Ant. Class.* 1973, 547); τοῖ[ς ἱεροῖς οἴκ]οις Crampa 1972, tentatively; τοῖ[ς περιπάτοις], Piejko 1985: 612. Pouilloux's restoration is probably the correct one, because one expects first a general stipulation, before the detailed orders of lines 10–11. Piejko's περίπατοι might be restored as part of these detailed instructions.   9–10 κτήνη σ[υνάγετε] Crampa; the Roberts (1983: 140 n. 12) would expect the verb εἰσάγετε, which the stone might allow, reading the traces as an E rather than Σ. Piejko, *OAth* 18 (1990), 146, tries to justify σ[ταθμεῦτε] or σ[τήσαιτε], 'do not station animals . . .'. The former construction is impossible morphologically (as pointed out by Herrmann in *SEG*) and of all the 'parallels' quoted by Piejko, only Strabo 4.5.2 supports the transitive construction he proposes for the verb σταθμεύω; all the others show (ἐπι)σταθμεύω with accusative object to mean 'to occupy a place as a billet' or 'to impose billeting on people', not 'to station animals/people in a billet'.

King Antiochos has enjoined upon us to take care of the [sanctuaries], among all the other instructions. So, as regards you, be well disciplined in all other matters as is fitting, and do not camp . . . in Labraunda and do not live in the [sacred places] and [bring in] pack animals . . . **10** nor in the gateways nor in [. . .] nor in the porticoes . . .

Commentary. The inscription is borne by an *anta* block from the *propylaia* of the shrine at Labraunda.

See Ch. 2 § 2 (on context); Ch. 3 §s 1 (on violence), *2a* (on Zeuxis).

16. *Amphiktionic Decree for the* Asylia *of Antiocheia/Alabanda (201)*

L. Couve, *BCH* 18 (1894), 235–47, no. 2, *editio princeps*, facsimile, translation, commentary (*OGIS* 234); R. Flacelière, *FD* 3, fasc. 4, nos. 162 and 163 (from the stone, but with some mistakes in the published text); Rigsby 1996: no. 163 (collated from the stone; edited with commentary and photograph, though the latter is nearly useless).

Cf. *OGIS* 234, n. 1, Lefèvre 1995, 205, Rigsby 1996, 328–329, 334 (for dating); Holleaux 1942: 141–57 (Antiocheia = Alabanda); Herrmann

1965*a*: 121–38 and esp. 127–28 (on *asylia* in general and at Antiocheia/
Alabanda). Pounder 1978 (*SEG* 28.75, Rigsby 1996: no. 162), publishes
a decree from Athens recognizing the *asylia* of Antiocheia of the
Chrysaorians and honouring the same ambassador as in the present decree
(Pausimachos), as well as his brother (Aristophanes). Pounder relates both
to Antiochos' Karian campaign of 203. The absence of any mention of
Antiochos is conspicuous in the Athenian document. Habicht 1987, and
Rigsby 1996: 332, on the dating: the present decree cannot have been
issued in 199/8 (as had sometimes been proposed), since the contemporary
Athenian decree mentions a 650-strong *boule*, which puts it before 201
(when the suppression of the tribes Antigonis and Demetrias reduced the
number of Athenian tribes from 13 to 11, soon increased to 12 by the
creation of the tribe Attalis). Habicht 1994: 167 n. 17 (reprinted from
Chiron 19 (1989), 11), further wonders if Antiochos was named in the (lost)
considerations of the Athenian decree—but the dispositions of the decree
make no mention of honours for the king, unlike *OGIS* 234. Lefèvre 1996
explores the broader historical context. See also Hintzen-Bohlen 1992:
104–6, 140 (on the inscribed block—part of a statue base—and its context).

Θεοί.

Ἄρχοντος ἐν Δελφοῖς Φιλαιτώλου, πυλαίας ὀπωρινῆς, ἱερομνα-
μονούντων· Αἰτωλῶν Τελεσάρχου Ἀπιρικοῦ, Λέωνος Ναυπα-
κτίου, Στομίου Μαχετιέος, Θεοδώρου Ἀργείου, Νικοβούλου Θηβαίου,   4
Εὐρυμάχου Θαυμακοῦ, Δορυμένεος Ὑπαταίου, Θεοδώρου Κοττα-
έος, Λαττάμου Βουκατιέος, Εὐδάμου Ἀρσινοέος, Λαμίου Ἀπολλω-
νιέος· Κεφαλλάνων Οἰανθίου· Δελφῶν Ἀριστομάχου, Καλλικρά-
τεος· Ἀθηναίων Ἀριστοκλέος· Βοιωτῶν Φόξου, Καλλικράτεος·   8
Μαγνήτων Πολεμαίου· Χίων Μητροφάνεος· γραμματεύον-
τος τοῖς ἱερομνάμοσιν Μενάνδρου Θαυμακοῦ·
ἀγαθᾶι τύχαι· ἔδοξε τῶι κοινῶι τῶν Ἀμφικτιόνων, ἐπεὶ ἁ πόλις
ἁ τῶν Ἀντιοχέων τῶν ἐκ τοῦ Χρυσαορέων ἔθνεος, συγγενὴς ἐοῦσα   12
τῶν Ἑλλάνων, ἀποστείλασα πρεσβευτὰς ποτὶ πλέονας τέτευχε
πάντων τῶν τιμίων καὶ φιλανθρώπων, καὶ Παυσίμαχος δὲ ὁ πα-
ρ' αὐτῶν πρεσβεύσας ἐν ἐκείναις τε καλῶς καὶ ἀξίως τῶν Ἑλλάνων ἀνέστρεπται, καὶ νῦν ποτειληφὼς χρησμὸν παρὰ τοῦ θεοῦ,   16
κατακολουθέων {του} τούτωι ποτελθὼν ποτὶ τὸ συνέδριον ἁμῶν
περὶ τε τᾶς ἰδίας πατρίδος πολλὰ κατευφάμηκε, ἐμφανίζων τὰν
εὐσέβειαν αὐτᾶς καὶ τὰν ἀρετάν· ὁμοίως δὲ καὶ περὶ βασιλέος
Ἀντιόχου τοῦ εὐεργέτα Ἀντιοχέων εὐλόγηκε εὐχαριστῶν   20
αὐτῶι διότι τὰν δαμοκρατίαν καὶ τὰν εἰράναν {αν} τοῖς Ἀντιοχεῦσιν
διαφυλάσσει κὰτ τὰν τῶν προγόνων ὑφάγησιν· δεδόχθαι ἀποκρίνασ-
θαι αὐτῶι ὅτι τὸ κοινὸν τῶν Ἀμφικτιόνων τὰμ μὲν πόλιν τὰν Ἀντιοχέων καὶ τὰν χώραν ἀναδεικνύει ἄσυλον καὶ ἱερὰν τοῦ Διὸς Χρυσαορέ-   24
ως καὶ Ἀπόλλωνος Ἰσοτίμου, τὸν δὲ δᾶμον αὐτῶν καὶ βασιλῆ Ἀντίοχον
ἐπαινεῖ, καὶ στεφανοῖ ἑκάτερον εἰκόνι χαλκέαι ὀκταπάχει ἐπὶ πᾶσι
τοῖς προγεγραμμένοις· στᾶσαι δὲ τὰς εἰκόνας ἐν τῶι ἱερῶι τοῦ Ἀπόλλωνος τοῦ Πυθίου καὶ καρῦξαι ἐν τοῖς Πυθίοις· ἐπαινεῖ δὲ καί Παυσί-   28

μαχον Ἰατροκλέος, καὶ στεφανοῖ χρυσέωι στεφάνωι ἀρετᾶς ἕνεκεν καὶ φιλοτιμίας τᾶς εἰς τὰν αὐτοῦ πάτρίδα· καὶ καρῦξαι τὸν στέφανον αὐτοῦ ἐν τᾶι πατρίδι, ὅταν εἰσάγηι τὸν τῶν Σωτηρίων στέ-
φανον· ὅπως δὲ καὶ ὑπόμναμα ἦι εἰς ἅπαντα τὸν χρόνον, ἀναγράψαι   32
τόδε τὸ ψάφισμα ἐν τᾶι βάσει τᾶι τοῦ βασιλέως Ἀντιόχου ἐν τῶι
ἱερῶι τοῦ Ἀπόλλωνος τοῦ Πυθίου, καὶ ἀποστεῖλαι ποτ' Ἀντιοχεῖς
σφραγισαμένους τᾶι κοινᾶι τῶν Ἀμφικτιόνων σφραγῖδι.

On the side of the same stone:

Μειδίας ἐπόησε

6 Λατταμίου Couve.   17 κατακολουθέων δὲ Couve.   21 The stone bears
ΕΙΡΑΝΑΝΑΝΤΟΙΣΑΝΤΙΟΧΕΥΣΙΝ. Couve (followed by Flacelière) published εἰράναν
{ἐ}ν τοῖς Ἀντιοχεῦσιν. The present text follows Wilhelm, GGA 1898, 224–5 (whence the
text in OGIS 234).   22–3 Couve read ἀποκρινασ|σθαι. Present reading from
Flacelière, Rigsby.   23 Couve read τὰμ μὲν. Flacelière, Rigsby read τὰν μὲν.
24 Couve read τοῦ Διὸς Χρυσαορέ|ως, whereas Flacelière and Rigsby publish τοῦ
Χρυσαορέ|ως, assuming that the name of Zeus has been omitted by the stonemason. The
photograph seems to confirm Couve's reading.   30 Couve publishes φιλοτιμίας τᾶς
εἰς τὰν αὐτοῦ πατρίδα, whereas Flacelière and Rigsby write φιλοτιμίας τῆς εἰς τὰν αὐτοῦ
πατρίδα. Couve's reading is obviously correct (and can be confirmed, with difficulty, on
Rigsby's photograph).

Gods. When Philaitolos was archon in Delphi, summer meeting, when the
following were *hieromnemons*: of the Aitolians, Telesarchos of Epiros,[1]
Leon of Naupaktos, Stomios of Maketia, Theodoros of (Amphilochian)
Argos, Nikoboulos of Thebes (in Phtiotis), Eurymachos of Thaumakoi,
Dorymenes of Hypata, Theodoros of Kotta, Lattamos of Boukatia,
Eudamos of Arsinoe, Lamias of Apollonia; of the Kephallenians,
Oianthios; of the Delphians, Aristomachos, Kallikrates; of the Athenians,
Aristokles; of the Boiotians, Phoxos, Kallikrates; of the Magnesians,[2]
Polemaios; of the Chians, Metrophanes; when **10** Menandros of
Thaumakos was secretary for the *hieromnemons*;—with good luck, it
seemed good to the assembly of the Amphiktions:—since the city of the
Antiocheians of the Chrysaorian nation, being related to the Greeks,
having sent ambassadors to very many, has received all honours and
advantages; and Pausimachos, their ambassador has conducted himself in
those cities in a fine manner and worthily of the Greeks; and now having
received an oracle from the god, he has, in accordance with this oracle
come before our council, and said many fine things concerning his own
fatherland, making clear the latter's piety and excellence; likewise, he
spoke well about king **20** Antiochos, the benefactor of the Antiocheians,
giving thanks to him, because he preserves the democracy and the peace for
the Antiocheians, in accordance with the example of his ancestors;—let it
seem good:—to answer him by saying that the assembly of the
Amphiktions recognizes the city and the territory of the Antiocheians as

[1] Not the north-western region, but probably an otherwise unknown Aitolian city
(Dittenberger).
[2] Magnesia on Maeander (see comments by Lefèvre 1995: 205).

inviolable and consecrated to Chrysaorian Zeus and Apollon Isotimos, and praises their *demos* and king Antiochos, and crowns both of them with a bronze statue of eight cubits, for all the aforementioned reasons; to erect the statues in the sanctuary of Pythian Apollo, and to proclaim them at the Pythia; (and to say that) the assembly of the Amphiktions also praises Pausimachos son of Iatrokles, and crowns him with a golden crown, on account of his excellence 30 and his zeal towards his fatherland; and to proclaim the crown in his fatherland, whenever he formally brings in the crown won at the Soteria;—and so that there be a memorial for all time, to write up this decree on the base of king Antiochos, in the sanctuary of Pythian Apollo, and to send it to the Antiocheians, sealing it with the common seal of the Amphiktions.

Meidias made (the statue).

Commentary. The decree, and the one-line artist's signature, are carved on the base of the statue for Antiochos III mentioned in the decree. The base was found on the terrace of the temple of Apollo at Delphi (in the western part of the terrace, in front of the opisthodomos), along with four other similar bases, including the base inscribed with *OGIS* 228, the Delphian decree acknowledging the *asylia* of Smyrna. It has been suggested that all these bases supported statues of Seleukid rulers, and that the statue of Antiochos III was placed among statues of his ancestors (evidence and literature gathered by Hintzen-Bohlen). If so, the gesture elegantly echoed a concept developed by Pausimachos before the Amphiktions, Antiochos' adherence to the example of his ancestors.

See Ch. 2 § 2 (on context); Ch. 4 § 2*d* (on the pan-Hellenic diffusion of perceptions of the ruler); Appendix 2 (on *asylia*).

17. First Teian Decree for Antiochos III and Laodike III (probably 203)

Herrmann 1965*a*: 33–6 (text); 51–5 (textual commentary), and plate 1 (*SEG* 41.1003, I, document reedited by Herrmann, with an especially full apparatus).

Cf. J. and L. Robert, *BE* 68, 451 (improvements to the text); *BE* 69, 495 (detailed analysis of the texts); *BE* 69, 496 (royal cults in the Teian context); Giovannini 1983 (interpretation of the political situation); Gauthier 1985: 51–2; Piejko 1991*a*: 13–37 (arguments for low dating in 197; unconvincing restorations for earlier parts of text; brief line-by-line commentary). Translation: Austin 1981: no. 151.

Τιμού[χων καὶ στρατηγῶν γνώμη· ἐπειδὴ βασιλεὺς]
Ἀντίοχ[ος   ]
. στη[   ]
[9–10   π]ροαίρεσιν κ[αὶ δια]φ[υ]λάσσω[ν . . . .]ΑΡΑΠ[. . .]   4
[9–10   ]ν ἑαυτῶι διὰ προ[γόνω]ν ὑπάρχουσα[ν εὔ]νοιαν κα[ὶ]
[8–9   ] . τασθαι προαιρούμενος πολαπλασ[ι .]ν, κοινὸς [εὐ]-
[ἐργέτης πρ]οείρηται γίνεσθαι τῶν τε ἄλλων Ἑλληνίδωμ [πό]-

[λεων καὶ τ]ῆς πόλεως τῆς ἡμετέρας, καὶ πρότερόν τε ὑπάρ- 8
[χων] ἐν τῇ ἐπέκεινα τοῦ Ταύρου πολλῶν ἀγαθῶν ἐγίνετο παραίτιος ἡμῖ[ν] καὶ παραγενόμενος ἐπὶ τοὺς καθ᾽ ἡμᾶς τόπους ἀποκατέστησε τὰ πράγματα εἰς συμφέρουσαν κατάστασιν καὶ ἐ-
πιδημήσας ἐν τῇ πόλει ἡμῶν καὶ θεωρῶν ἐξησθενηκότας 12
ἡμᾶς κα[ὶ] ἐν τοῖς κοινοῖς καὶ ἐν τοῖς ἰδίοις διά τε τοὺς συνεχεῖς
πολέμου[ς] καὶ τὸ μέγεθος ὧν ἐφέρομεν συντάξεων καὶ βουλόμενος
τά τε πρὸς τὸν θεὸν εὐσεβῶς διακεῖσθαι ὧι καθιέρωσεν ἡμῶν τὴν πόλιν
καὶ τὴν χώραν ⟨καὶ⟩ θέλων χαρίζεσθαι τῶι τε δήμωι καὶ τῶι κοινῶι τῶν 16
περὶ τὸν Διόνυσον τεχνιτῶν παρελθὼν εἰς τὴν ἐκκλησίαν αὐτὸς
ἀνῆκε τὴ[ν] πόλιν καὶ τὴν χώραν ἡμῶν ἱερὰν καὶ ἄσυλον καὶ ἀφορολόγητον κ[αὶ] τῶν ἄλλων ὧν ἐφέρομεν συντάξεων βασιλεῖ Ἀττά-
λωι ὑπεδέξατο ἀπολυθήσεσθαι ἡμᾶς δι᾽ αὐτοῦ, ἵνα γενομένης ἐ- 20
παυξήσ[ε]ως τῶν κατὰ τὴν πόλιν μὴ μόνον εὐεργεσίας λάβῃ τὴν
ἐπιγραφ[ὴ]ν τῆς τοῦ δήμου, ἀλλὰ καὶ σωτηρίας· ἐπεδήμησε δὲ καὶ
ἐν τῇ πόλει μετά τε τῶμ φίλων καὶ τῶν ἀκολουθουσῶν αὐτῶι δυνά-
μεων ἀπόδιξιν ποιούμενος μεγίστην τῆς προϋπαρχούσης αὐτῶι πίσ- 24
τεως πρὸς ἅπαντας ἀνθρώπους, καὶ μετὰ ταῦτα πολλῶν ἀγαθῶν πα-
⟨ρ⟩αίτιος δ[ι]ατελεῖ γινόμενος ἡμῖν παράδειγμα πᾶσιν ἐκτιθεὶς τοῖς Ἕλλη[σι]ν ὃν
τρόπον προσφέρεται πρὸς τοὺς εὐεργέτας καὶ εὔνους ὑπάρχοντας αὐτῶι, κα[ὶ τ]ὰ
μὲν συ[ν]τελεῖ τῶν ἀγαθῶν δι᾽ ὧν εἰς εὐδαιμονίαν παραγίνεθ᾽ ἡ πόλις ἡμ[ῶ]ν, 28
τὰ δ᾽ ἐ[πι]τελέσει· ἐπιστείλας δὲ πρὸς τὸν δῆμον ὑπέλαβε δεῖν πέμψαι [πρὸ]ς
[αὐτὸν π]ρεσβείαν ἢ συλλαλήσει περὶ ὧν ἔφη πεπεῖσθαι καὶ τῶι δήμ[ωι] συμ-
[φέρειν], καὶ τοῦ δήμου πρεσβευτὰς ἐξαποστίλαντος Διονύσιον Ἀπολλο-
[. . . . .], Ἑρμαγόραν Ἐπιμένου, Θεόδωρον Ζωπύρου ἐνεφάνισε τούτοις 32
[ὅτι πα]ραλέλυκε τὴμ πόλιν εἰς ἀεὶ καθότι ἐπηγγίλατο ὧν συνετάξα-
[μεν φ]όρων βασιλεῖ Ἀττάλωι· ὑπὲρ ὧν καὶ γράψας ἔφη ἐντετάχθαι τοῖς
[πρεσβευταῖ]ς ἀναγγέλλειν ἡμεῖν καὶ οἱ πρεσβευταὶ ἀνήγγ[ι]λαν ταῦ-
[τα τῶι δήμ]ωι· κατὰ ταῦτὰ δὲ καὶ ἡ ἀδελφὴ αὐτοῦ βασίλισσα Λαοδίκη ἐν 36
[ἅπασι καιρ]οῖς τὴν αὐτὴν ἔχουσα γνώμην διατελεῖ τῶι βασιλεῖ καὶ
[7–8 κ]αὶ ἐν τοῖς πρὸς τὴμ πόλιν φιλανθρώποις ἐκτενῆ καὶ πρό-
[θυ]μον ἑ[αυτ]ὴν παρέχεται πρὸς τὰς εὐεργεσίας, καὶ τὰ μέγιστα
[τῶ]ν ἀγα[θῶ]ν ὁ δῆμος εἴληφε παρ᾽ ἀμφοτέρων· ἵνα οὖν καὶ ἡμῖς ἐμ 40
[πα]ντὶ κα[ιρῶ]ι φαινώμεθα χάριτας ἀξίας ἀποδιδόντες τῶι τε βασι-
[λε]ῖ καὶ τῇ [βα]σιλίσσῃ καὶ ὑπερτιθέμενοι ἑαυτοὺς ἐν ταῖς τ[ιμ]αῖς ταῖς πρὸς
[τ]ούτους κα[τὰ] τὰς εὐεργεσίας καὶ φανερὸς ᾖ πᾶσιν ὁ δῆ[μος] εὐπορίσ-
τως διακίμε[ν]ος πρὸς χάριτος ἀπόδοσιν· τύχῃ ἀγαθῇ· π[α]ραστῆσαι 44
τῶι ἀγάλματ[ι] τοῦ Διονύσου ἀγάλματα μαρμάρινα ὡς κάλλιστ[α καὶ ἱε]-
ροπρεπέστατ[α] τοῦ τε βασιλέως Ἀντιόχου καὶ τῆς ἀδελφῆς αὐ[τ]οῦ [βα]-
σιλίσσης Λαο[δί]κης, ὅπως ἀφέντες τὴμ πόλιν καὶ τὴν χώραν ἱερὰν
καὶ ἄσυλον καὶ [π]αραλύσαντες ἡμᾶς τῶμ φόρων καὶ χαρισ[ά]μενοι ταῦ- 48
τα τῶι τε δήμ[ω]ι καὶ τῶι κοινῶι τῶμ περὶ τὸν Διόνυσον τεχνιτῶν παρὰ πάντων τ[ὰς] τιμὰς κομίζωνται κατὰ τὸ δ[υνατὸν] κ[α]ὶ ναοῦ καὶ τῶν
ἄλλων με[τέχ]οντες τῶι Διονύσωι κοιν[οὶ σωτῆρε]ς ὑπάρχωσι τῆς
[πό]λε[ως ἡ]μῶν καὶ κοινῇ διδῶσιν ἡ[μῖν ἀγ]αθά· ἵνα δὲ καὶ τὰ 52
[ἐψ]ηφισ[μένα συν]τελῆται ἀποδεῖξαι ἐπισ[τάτας δ]ύο ἐξ ἁπάντων

[τῶμ] πο[λιτῶν οἵτιν]ες ἐπιμελήσονται τ[ῆς τε κα]τασκευῆς τῶν ἀγαλ-
[μάτ]ω[ν καὶ τῆς ἀν]αθέσεως· τὸ δὲ ἀργ[ύριον τὸ] εἰς ταῦτα διδόναι

29 τὰ δ' ἐ[πι]τελέσει can be justified by the same verb in the parallel expression document **18**, 31; pointed out by Oliver 1968: 321.   37 [ἄπασι καιρ]οῖς Herrmann
1965a; [τε τοῖς ἄλλ]οις Habicht, noted in *SEG*.   38 [ἀδελφῶι] Merkelbach 1968:
173; [αἵρεσιν] Habicht by letter to Herrmann, noted in *SEG*, which seems better.
52 τἀγαθά is the 'formule rituelle' restored by J. and L. Robert, *BE* 68, 451.

Timou[choi's and strategoi's proposal. Since King] Antiochos . . . intention and, preserving . . . the goodwill which is his from his ancestors and
. . . choosing to . . . manifold . . ., he has resolved to become the common
benefactor of all the Greek cities and especially of ours, and, whilst staying
on the other side of the Taurus, he was responsible for many advantages **10**
towards us, and, having come to our region, he restored the affairs to a
profitable conclusion and, having stayed in our city and seen our weakness
in matters both public and private, on account of the continuous wars and
the size of the contributions which we paid, and wishing to be piously
disposed towards the god to whom he has consecrated our city and our
territory, and wishing to favour the people and the corporation of the
Dionysiac artists, he went into the assembly and personally granted that
the city and the territory be sacred and inviolate and free from tribute, and,
as for the other contributions which we paid to King Attalos, **20** promised
that we would be freed through his agency, so that on account of the
increase of the affairs of the city, he should not only receive the title of
benefactor of the people, but also that of saviour; he stayed in the city with
his friends and the forces that accompanied him, making a very great
display of the trustworthiness, which was his before, towards all men, and
after that, he consistently is responsible for many favours towards us,
giving an example to all the Greeks of the disposition he adopts towards
those who are his benefactors and show goodwill towards him; and some of
the favours through which our city comes to happiness he now brings
about, others he will bring about; in his letter to the people, he was of the
opinion that it was necessary to send **30** an embassy [to him], to discuss the
matters which he was convinced would benefit the people also, and when
the people sent as ambassadors Dionysios son of Apollo[. . .], Hermagoras
son of Epimenes, Theodoros son of Zopyros, he made clear to them that he
had freed the city in perpetuity, as he had announced, from the taxes which
we paid to King Attalos; in his letter he said that he had instructed the
ambassadors to report to us on these matters, and the ambassadors did so;
in the same manner, his sister, queen Laodike consistently adopts the same
disposition as the king and . . . and shows h[erself] eager and zealous in
benefactions towards the city, and the people **40** has received the greatest
of benefits from both;—in order that we too may be seen to return
appropriate tokens of gratitude, in every occasion, to the king and the
queen, and to surpass ourselves in the honours for them in relation to
their benefactions, and in order that the people may show to all that it is
generously disposed towards the returning of gratitude,—with good

fortune, (it seemed good) to set up, by the cult-image of Dionysos, marble cult-images, as beautiful [and] as fitting for sacred matters as possible, of King Antiochos and his sister, Queen Laodike, so that, for having granted that the city and the territory should be sacred and inviolate and having released us from the tribute and having accomplished these actions as favours to the people and the corporation of the Dionysiac artists, 50 they should receive from everyone the honours, as much as possible, and that they should share in the temple and the other rituals of Dionysos and be the comm[on saviours] of the city and in common bestow favours on us; in order that the content of the decree be executed, to choose [two *epis*]*tatai* out of all the ci[tizens], who will see to the making and the dedication of the statues; to provide the money for this purpose . . .

Commentary. The decrees are carved on two blocks from a pilaster in the entrance to the temple of Dionysos at Teos (Herrmann 1965a: 89–93); they were found near the west wall of the *temenos* of the temple, probably deliberately discarded there (Herrmann 1965a: 31–2).

See Ch. 2 § 2 for context; Ch. 4 §§ 2b, 3 for analysis of the document's functions; on date, see Appendix 2.

18. *Second Decree of the Teians for Antiochos III and Laodike III (probably 203)*

Herrmann 1965a: 36–40 (text); 56–85 (line-by-line commentary), 99–100 (for date), and plates 2, 3, 4 (*SEG* 41.1003, II, re-edited with very detailed and fair apparatus, by P. Herrmann.)

Cf. J. and L. Robert, *BE* 68, 451 (improvements to the text); *BE* 69, 495 (detailed analysis of the texts); *BE* 69, 496 (royal cults in the Teian context); Gauthier 1985: 169–75 (on *isopoliteia* for the cities of the Seleukis); Piejko 1991a: 37–48 (for commentary and—mostly unconvincing—restorations)

```
                     traces of two lines
[              ] μετέχων [                              ]
               ]ης διαφυλάσσῃ[                          ]
[              ]το καὶ θυσιῶν καὶ σ[πονδῶν              ]
[              ] πρὸς αὐτὸν ἐπαύξῃ δια[                 ]      4
[              ]σαν εὐχαρίστως ἄγ[ειν                  ]
[              Ἀντιόχ]εια καὶ Λαοδίκεια τ[             ]
[              κα]ὶ συνεῖναι ἐν τῇ ἡμέ[ρᾳ ταύτῃ πάντας]
[τοὺς τῆς πόλεως ἄρχο]ντας καὶ τοὺς περὶ [τὸν Διόνυσον τεχ]-      8
[νίτας 12–14      ]ς· κατασκευάσασθ[αι δὲ βωμὸν ἑκάστην]
[τῶν] συμ[ορι]ῶν ἐν τῶι ἰδίωι τόπωι ἕνα παρὰ [τὸν βωμὸν τῆς συμο]-
[ρίας] τοῦ τε β[ασιλέως] Ἀντιόχου Μεγάλου καὶ [τῆς ἀδελφῆς]
[αὐτ]οῦ βασιλ[ίσσης Λ]αοδίκης καὶ συντελεῖν τὴν [θυσίαν]      12
[ἐπὶ] τούτου καὶ κα[τάρ]χεσθαι τῶν ἱερῶν τὸν ἱερέα το[ῦ βασι]-
[λέ]ως καὶ τῶν σπο[ν]δῶν καὶ τῶν ἄλλων πάντων προ[ΐστασ]-
```

[θαι] αὐτὸν ἐν τῇ ἑορ[τ]ῇ ταύτηι τῶν συντελουμένων ὑπὸ [τῶν]
[συ]μοριῶν καθάπε[ρ] ὁ ἱερεὺς τοῦ Ποσειδῶνος ἐν το[ῖς Λευ]-   16
[καθ]έοις προέστηκεν· τὸ δὲ ἐσόμενον ἀνάλωμ[α καθ' ἕ]-
[καστον] ἄνδρα τάξαι μὲν [τὸ]ν δῆμον [ἅπ]αξ ἐν ταῖς [πρώταις]
[ἀρχα]ιρεσίαις, τοὺς δὲ ταμίας τοὺς ἑκάστοτε γιν[ομένους]
[διδό]ναι τοῖς τῶν συμοριῶν προστάταις τὸ ταγὲν ἐκ τ[ῆς διοι]-   20
[κήσε]ως ἔσχατον τῇ τετράδι τοῦ Λευκαθεῶνος λαβόν[τας τὴν]
[ἀπογ]ραφὴν παρὰ τῶν π[ρ]οστατῶν τοῦ πλήθους τῶν ἐν ταῖς . . . . .
[. . κα]ὶ τῶν ἐν ἡλικίαι κα[ὶ] τῶν ἀπογραψαμένων πρὸς αὐτοὺς . . . . .
. . . . θύειν δὲ καὶ ἑορτάζειν καὶ τοὺς ἄλους πάντας τοὺς ο[ἰκοῦν]-   24
[τας] τὴμ πόλιν ἡμῶν ἐν τοῖς ἰδίοις οἴκοις ἑκάστους κατὰ δύν[αμιν]·
[στε]φανηφορεῖν πάντας τοὺς ἐν τῇ πόλει ἐν τῆμέραι ταύτ[ῃ· παύε]-
[σθαι δ]ὲ καὶ τὰς ἐργασίας πάσας τάς τ' ἐν τῇ πόλει καὶ τῇ χώ[ραι καὶ εἶ]-
[ναι ἐ]χεχιρίας πᾶσι πρὸς πάντας ἐν τῇ ⟨ἡ⟩μέραι ταύτῃ· ἀναγ[ράψαι]
[δὲ τ]αύτην τὴν ἑορτὴν εἰς τὴν ἱερὰν βύβλον· ἵνα δὲ καὶ καθιε[ρωμέ]-   28
[νος] ὁ τόπος ᾖ τῶι βασιλεῖ Ἀντιόχωι Μεγάλωι ἐν ὧι τὰ μὲν ἐ[τέλεσε]
[τῶν ἀ]γαθῶν, τὰ δὲ ὑπέσχετο καὶ μετὰ ταῦτα ἐπετέλεσεν, ἀ[ναθεῖ]-
[ναι ἄ]γαλμα χαλκοῦν ἐν τῶι βουλευτηρίωι ὡς κάλλιστον [τοῦ βα]-   32
[σιλέ]ως καὶ συντελεῖν θυσίαν ἐπὶ τῆς κοινῆς τῆς πόλεως ἑ[στίας]
[ἐν τ]ῶι βουλευτηρίωι τῶι τε βασιλεῖ καὶ Χάρισιν καὶ Μνήμῃ καθ' ἕκ[αστον]
[ἔτο]ς τὰς ἀρχὰς μετὰ τοῦ ἱερέως καὶ τοῦ πρυτάνεως τήν τ[ε τῶν]
[στρ]ατηγῶν καὶ τὴν τῶν τιμούχων καὶ τὴν τῶν ταμιῶν κατὰ το   36
. . . εἰσιτητήρια τῆς ἀρχῆς ἀρχομένας ἀπ' ἀγαθῶν τῆι νουμη[νίαι]
[τοῦ] Λευκαθεῶνος καὶ θύειν ἱερεῖον τέλειον, συντελεῖν δὲ θυσίαν
[τοῦ]ς ἐκ τῶν ἐφήβων μετὰ τοῦ γυμνασιάρχου τῇ αὐτῇ ἡμέραι καθότι γέγ[ρα]-
[πτ]αι, ἵνα μηθὲν πρότερον ἄρξωνται πράσσειν τῶν κοινῶν πρὶν ἢ χάρ[ι]-   40
[τα]ς ἀποδ[ο]ῦναι τοῖς εὐεργέταις καὶ ἐθίζωμεν τοὺς ἐξ ἡαυτῶν πά[ν]-
[τα] ὕστερα καὶ ἐν ἐλάσσονι τίθεσθαι πρὸς ἀποκατάστασιν χάριτος
[καὶ] τὴμ πρώτην αὐτοῖς εἴσοδον εἰς τὴν ἀγορὰν ἐπὶ ταὐτὰ καλλίστην
[ποι]ήσο[μ]εν· τὰ δὲ ἱερεῖα τὰ εἰς τὰς θυσίας παριστάναι τοὺς πριαμέ-   44
[νους] τῷ πρότερον ἔτει τὴν παράσχεσιν τῶν ἱερείων, τοῖς δὲ εἰσιοῦσι
[ἄρχ]ουσιν καὶ τοῖς ἐκ τῶν ἐφήβων τοὺς ταμίας· ὅσοι δ' ἂν νικήσαντες
[τοὺ]ς στεφανίτας ἀγῶνας εἰσελαύνωσιν εἰς τὴμ πόλιν, παραγίνεσθα[ι]
. . . . ους ἀπὸ τῆς {ἀπὸ τῆς} πύλης πρῶτον εἰς τὸ βουλευτήριον καὶ στεφ[α]-   48
[νοῦν] τὸ ἄγαλμα τοῦ βασιλέως καὶ συντελεῖν θυσίαν καθότι ἐπάνω γέ-
[γραπ]ται· ἐπειδὴ οὐ μόνον εἰρήνην ἡμῖν ὁ βασιλεὺς παρέσχεν, ἀλλὰ καὶ
[τῶν] βαρέων καὶ σκληρῶν ἐκ⟨κ⟩ούφισιν εἰς τὸ μετὰ ταῦτα τελῶν παραλύ-
[σας] τῶν συντάξεων καὶ λυσιτελεῖς τὰς ἐν τῇ χώραι μετ' ἀσφαλεί-   52
[ας π]εποίηκεν ἐργασίας καὶ τὰς καρπείας, τιθέναι πρὸς τὸ ἄγαλμα
[τοῦ] βασιλέως ἀπαρχὰς καθ' ἕκαστον ἔτος τοὺς πρώτους ἐν τῇ
[χώρ]αι ξυλίνους φανέντας καρπούς· ὅπως δὲ καὶ διὰ παντὸς ᾖ τὸ ἄγαλ-
[μα τ]οῦ βασιλέως ἐστεφανωμένον στεφάνωι τῶι κατὰ τὰς ὥρας γινο-   56
[μέν]ωι ἐπιμελεῖσθαι τὸν ἱερέα τοῦ βασιλέως· προσπωλεῖν δὲ τῇ ὠνῇ
[τῆς] στεφανοπωλίας τοὺς ἑκάστοτε γινομένους ταμίας τὴν
[παρ]άσχεισιν τῶν στεφάνων τούτων· ἀποδεῖξαι δὲ καὶ ἐπιστάτας δύο
[ἐξ ἁ]πάντων τῶμ πολιτῶν οἵτινες ἐπιμελήσονται τῆς τε κατασκευ-   60

[ἧς τ]οῦ ἀγάλματος καὶ τῆς ἀναθέσεως καθότι ἂν οἱ τιμοῦχοι καὶ οἱ
στ[ρ]ατηγοὶ παραγγέλλωσιν· τὸ δὲ ἀργύριον τὸ εἰς ταῦτα διδόναι
τοὺς ταμίας ἐκ τῶν τιμῶν τῶμ βασιλέων ἢ ἐκ τῆς διοικήσεω[ς]·
ἵνα δὲ καὶ τῇ ἀδελφῇ τοῦ βασιλέως βασιλίσσῃ Λαοδίκῃ πρὸς [ταῖς]   64
ἄλλαις ταῖς δεδομέναις τιμαῖς ὑπάρχωσιν ἄλλαι μὴ μόνον χ[άριν]
ἔχουσαι τὴμ παραυτίκα ἀλλὰ καὶ μνήμην ποιοῦσαι τὴν εἰς τὸ[ν ἅ]-
παντα χρόνον καὶ τοῖς εἰς τὴμ πόλιν ἀφικνουμένοις τῶν ξένων [παρά]-
δειγμα πᾶσιν ὑπάρχον ἐμ μέσωι φαίνηται τῆς εὐχαριστίας το[ῦ δή]-   68
μου καὶ προσηκούσας ἑκάστοις φαινώμεθα τὰς τιμὰς ψηφιζόμ[ενοι],
κατασκευάσαι τὴγ κρήνην τὴν ἐν τῇ ἀγορᾷ καὶ ἐπιμεληθῆνα[ι ὅ]-
πως εἰς αὐτὴν τὸ ὕδωρ ἀχθῇ καὶ ἀναθεῖναι τὴν κρήνην τῇ ἀδελ[φῇ]
τοῦ βασιλέως Ἀντιόχου βασιλίσσῃ Λαοδίκῃ καὶ εἶναι αὐτὴν ἐπώνυμ[ον]   72
Λαοδίκης, καὶ ἐπειδὴ ἡ βασίλισσα τά τε πρὸς τοὺς θεοὺς εὐσεβ[ῶς]
διακεῖται καὶ τὰ πρὸς ἀνθρώπους εὐχαρίστως καὶ διὰ ταῦτα κ[α]-
λῶς ἔχον ἐστὶν ἐκ τῆς ταύτης ἐπωμύμου κρήνης πάντας κα-
τάρχεσθαι τιμῶντας τοὺς θεοὺς καὶ ἁγνεύοντας· τύχῃ ἀγαθ[ῇ]·   76
ὅσοι ἂν ἱερεῖς ἢ ὅσαι ἱέρειαι πρὸ πόλεως θυσίαν συντελῶσιν, χ[ρῆσ]-
θαι πρὸς τὰς θυσίας ἐν οἷς δεῖ ὕδατι τούτωι, λαμβάνιν δὲ [καὶ τοὺς]
συντελοῦντας τὰ λουτρὰ ἐντεῦθεν, ὑδρεύεσθαι δὲ κα[ὶ ταῖς νύμ]-
φαις τὰ λο[υ]τρὰ ἀπὸ τῆς κρήνης ταύτης· ὅσοι δ' ἂν λαμ[βάνωσιν τὸ]   80
ὕδωρ εἰς τ[ὰς] χρείας τὰς προγεγραμένας παραγίνεσ[θαι ἐπὶ τὴγ]
κρήνην [καὶ ἀ]ποπορεύεσθαι ἐν ἐσθῆτι λαμπρᾶι ἐσ[τεφανω]μ[έ]-
νους, τὰ[ς δὲ ὑδρ]ευομένας τὰ λουτρὰ ταῖς νύμφαις [6–8]ΤΡΙΔ . Σ· [ἵ]-
να δὲ σ[υντελῆται] ἡ κρήνη καθότι γέγραπται ἀ[ποδεῖξαι ἐπι]στάτας δύο   84
ἐξ ἁπ[άντων τῶμ] πολιτῶν οἵτινες [ἐπιμελήσον]ται τῆς κατασκευῆς
τῆς κ[ρήνης καὶ τῆς ἀναθέσεως   c.10   ]νην ὕδατος παρεσομε-
[ν . . τὸ δὲ ἐ]σόμενον ἀνάλω[μα τὸ εἰς ταῦτα δι]δόναι τοὺς ταμίας ἐ[κ]
[τῆς διοι]κήσεως καθότι ἂν οἱ ἐπὶ τῶ[ν] ἔργων τεταγμένοι παραγγέ[λ]-   88
[λωσιν, ὑ]πὲρ δὲ τῶν ἔργων τῆς συντελείας τούτων εἶναι κατὰ τὸν νό-
[μον τὸ]ν γεγραμμένον ὑπὲρ τῆς κατασκευῆς τῶν τιμῶν· ἐπεὶ δὲ κ[α]-
[λῶς ἔ]χον ἐστὶν ἅμα ταῖς ἄλλαις ταῖς δεδομέναις παρὰ τῆς πόλε-
[ως τῶι β]ασιλεῖ τιμαῖς καὶ ἀκόλουθον τῇ τε τοῦ βασιλέως καὶ τῶν   92
[φίλων] εὐνοίαι πρὸς τὸν δῆμον καὶ τῇ παρ' ἡμῶν πρός τε τὸν βασι-
[λέα καὶ] τους φίλους αὐ[τ]οῦ ἐκτενείαι καθάπερ εἰς κοινὸν τεθῆναι τὸ
[τῶν ἐ]πωνύμων πόλεων τῶν τοῦ βασιλέως προγόνων τὰ δε[δο]-
[μένα κ]αὶ δοθησόμενα παρὰ τοῦ βασιλέως ἀγαθὰ τῶι δήμωι ⟨ἵνα⟩ ψη[φισ]-   96
[θείσης] αὐτοῖς πᾶσιν παρ' ἡμῖν τῆς πολιτείας καὶ ἑτοιμότεροι π[ρὸς]
[τὰς εὐ]εργεσίας ὑπάρχωσι σπεύδοντες διὰ παντὸς καθά[π]ερ
[καλό]ν ἐστιν, ὑπὲρ τῆς ἰδίας πατρίδος [κ]αὶ [τὴ]ν προϋπάρχουσαν τοῖς
[. . .]οις πρὸς αὐτοὺς ἀνανεωσόμεθα φιλίαν· τύχῃ ἀγαθῇ· τοὺ[ς] στρα-   100
[τηγο]ὺς καὶ τοὺς τιμούχους εἰσενεγκεῖν εἰς τὰς ἐπιούσας ἀρχαι-
[ρεσία]ς καθότι δοθήσεται πολιτεία τῶι δήμωι τῶι Ἀντιοχέων τῶμ
[πρὸς] Δάφνηι καὶ τῶι δήμωι τῶι Σελευκέων τῶν ἐμ Πιερίαι [κα]ὶ τῶι δή-
[μωι τ]ῶι Λαοδικέων τῶμ πρὸς θαλάσσῃ· ἀναγράψαι δὲ [κ]αὶ τὸ ψή-   104
[φισμα τ]όδε εἰς τὴν παραστάδα τοῦ νεὼ τοῦ Διονύσου κα[ὶ κ]αθιερῶ-
[σαι, τῆ]ς δὲ ἀναγραφῆς τοῦ ψηφίσματος ἐπιμεληθῆνα[ι τ]οὺς ἐνεσ-

[τηκότ]ας τα[μί]ας· ἵνα δὲ ὁ βασιλεὺς Ἀντίοχος καὶ ἡ ἀ[δ]ελφὴ αὐτοῦ
[βασί]λισσα [Λ]αοδίκη εἰδήσωσι τὴν εὐχαριστίαν τοῦ [δ]ήμου, ἀποδεῖ-   108
[ξαι π]ρεσβευτὰς τρὶς ἤδη οἵτινες παραγενόμενοι πρὸς αὐτοὺς τὸ
[μὲν ψ]ήφισμα τόδε ἀποδώσουσι καὶ ἀσπασάμεν[ο]ι ὑπὲρ τοῦ δήμου
[καὶ] συνησθέντες ἐπὶ τῶι ὑγιαίνειν αὐτοὺς [καὶ] πράσσειν ὃν τρόπον
[αὐτ]οί τε βούλονται καὶ ἡμεῖς τοῖς θεοῖς εὐχόμεθα καὶ ἐμφανίσαν-   112
[τες] τὰς [τι]μὰς τὰς ἐψ[η]φισμ[έ]νας καὶ δ[η]λώσαντες αὐτοῖς [ ]

2 Perhaps διαφυλάσσῃ, in which case this verb and at least lines 2–4 belong to a ἵνα-
clause comparable to those at lines 29–31, 64–69, (restored) 96–100; the participle
μετέχων might qualify the subject of the clause (King Antiochos or rather the *demos* of
Teos?).   7–8 πάντας τοὺς τῆς πόλεως ἄρχοντας or τοὺς ἄρχοντας τῆς πόλεως πάντας
proposed by J. and L. Robert, *BE* 77, 405: the first banquet named is not organized for
all the inhabitants of the city (the editor's restoration: τοὺς . . . οἰκοῦντας), but only for
the magistrates and their choice guests, the Dionysiac artists (cf. Robert 1937, 184).
16–17 J. and L. Robert, *BE* 68, 451 propose ἐν το[ῖς Λε|υκαθέοις].   24 τοὺς ἄλους
on the stone.   26–7 [παύ|εσθαι] Dunst 1968: 171.   28 τήμέραι with crasis,
Dunst 1968: 171.   36 κατὰ τὸ[ν νόμον] Piejko 1991a: 43.   48 [αὐτ]οὺς
Piejko 1991a: 44, [τούτ]ους fits the four-letter gap published by Herrmann.
52–3 μετ' ἀσφαλεί[ας] J. and L. Robert, *BE* 68, 451.   72 χ[ρῆσθαι] Daux 1973: 235.
83 τὰ[ς δὲ ὑδρ]ευομένας Dunst 1968: 171. Towards the end, J. and L. Robert, *BE* 69, 499
propose [μετὰ στλεγγ]ίδος, 'wearing a headband'.   86 [καὶ τῆς ἀναθέσεως] Piejko
1991a: 47, by analogy with line 55 of the previous Teian inscription and line 61 of the
present inscription.   92 On the grounds of usage in the rest of the document (e.g.
lines 30, 32) [τῶι β]ασιλεῖ seems better than [τῷ β]ασιλεῖ (though see line 102 for τῶι δήμωι
τῷ Ἀντιοχέων)   99–100 The three-letter gap at the beginning of the line is difficult
to fill, though the meaning is clear (renewing the Teians' friendship for the cities named
after the king's ancestors) Herrmann 1965a proposed [πρόγ⟨ον⟩]οις, meaning the Teians'
ancestors. Piejko 1991a: 47–8, would see [δήμ]οις (without any justification; perhaps
unlikely), and prints τὴν προϋπάρχουσαν τοῖς [. . .]οις πρὸς αὐτούς: 'so that we should renew
the friendship which the peoples had for us'. But the meaning is not the expected one,
and the Teian documents use the form ἡαυτούς or ἑαυτούς: document **17**, 42; present
document, line 41; document **19** A, 6. Dunst 1968: 172, proposes [Τηί]οις, but in these
decrees, the Teians refer to themselves in the first person singular or as 'our city'
(document **17**, 8, 12, 15, etc.). It might be tempting to write τὴν προϋπάρχουσαν {τοῖς}
[ἡαυτ]οῖς πρὸς αὐτοὺς . . . φιλίαν, 'our previous friendship for them' (though the
expression is infelicitous, and the correction harsh).

. . . sharing in . . . preserving . . . of sacrifices and l[ibations] . . . should
increase towards him through (?) . . . with gratitude to conduct [. . .
Antioch]eia and Laodikeia . . . to have on this day [all the magistrates of the
city] and the [Dionysiac artists] assemble for a feast . . .; and to have **10**
[each of the *symmoriai*] build on its own place next to [the altar of the *symmoria*] one [altar] of King Antiochos and [his sister] Queen Laodike, and to
perform the sacrifice on it and to have the priest of the king inaugurate the
rituals and to have him preside in this festival over the libations and all the
other rites which are performed by the *symmoriai* just as the priest of
Poseidon presides at the [Leukath]ea; and to have the people determine
once and for all at the future elections the future expenditure per head, and
to have the successive *tamiai* **20** give the fixed amount to the *prostatai*
of the *symmoriai*, out of the state budget, at the latest on the fourth of
Leukatheon, after having received from the *prostatai* the return of
numbers of those in . . ., those in the age-classes and those registered with

them . . .; and to have all the others who live in our city sacrifice and celebrate the festival in their own houses, each according to his means; and to
have all wear crowns in the city on that day; and [to suspend] all working
activities in the city and in the countryside, and to have on that day court
holidays for all towards all; and to inscribe this festival in the sacred book;
and in order that **30** the place be consecrated to King Antiochos Megas
where he accomplished some of his favours, and promised the others,
which he accomplished later, to dedicate in the *bouleuterion* a bronze
cult-image of the king, as fine as possible, and to have the colleges of the
strategoi and the *timouchoi* and the *tamiai* and . . . along with the priest and
the *prytanis* perform in the *bouleuterion* a sacrifice upon the common hearth
of the city to the king and the Charites and to Memory, as *eisiteteria*
(entrance-ritual) each year when these colleges enter office, for good result,
upon the first of Leukatheon, and to have them offer a full-grown victim;
and to have those who leave the ephebes offer a sacrifice with the gymnasiarch on the same day, as it is written, **40** so that they do not start to
handle anything among the common affairs before returning gratitude to
the benefactors and so that we should accustom our progeny to value everything less than the returning of gratitude and so that we should make their
first entrance into the agora as fine as possible, in the same spirit (?);[1] and to
have those who in the previous year have bought the right to supply the
sacrificial victims make available the victims for the sacrifices, and to have
the *tamiai* supply the victims to the magistrates entering office and those
who leave the ephebes; and to have those who after a victory in the crown-
games make a solemn entrance into the city go from the gate to the
bouleuterion first, and crown the cult-image of the king and offer a sacrifice
as is written above; and **50** since the king brought us not only peace, but
also an alleviation of the heavy and harsh taxes for the future, by releasing
us from the *syntaxeis*, and made the working and harvesting in the land
profitable and safe, (it seemed good) to place before the cult-image of the
king the first produce from trees that appear each year in the land, as first-
fruit offerings; and to have the priest make sure that the cult-image of the
king should be crowned at all times with the crown that fits the season; and
to have the successive *tamiai* add the right to supply these crowns to the
auction (of the contract) of the crown-supplying and to appoint two
epistatai **60** out of all the citizens who should see to the work on the cult-
image and the dedication, following the orders of the *timouchoi* and the
strategoi; to have the *tamiai* give the money for this purpose out of the honours for the kings or out of the state budget;—and in order that Queen
Laodike should have, in addition to the honours given to her, other
honours which not only contain gratitude in the present but also create
memory for the rest of time and so that an example of the gratitude of the
people should be seen in the middle before all the foreigners who come to
the city and so that we should be seen to decree the honours that suit each
and all,[2] to build **70** the fountain in the agora and to see that water should

---

[1] Ἐπὶ ταὐτὰ: 'ebenso' Herrmann, tentatively.
[2] Or 'so that we may be seen by each and all . . .'?

be adducted to it and to dedicate the fountain to the sister of King
Antiochos, Queen Laodike, and that it should take its name from
Laodike;—and since the queen is piously disposed towards the gods and
gratefully towards mankind, and since it is good, for the above reasons, that
all those who honour the gods and are pure should offer libations from this
water named after her—with good fortune, (it seemed good) to have all the
priests and the priestesses who offer sacrifice in favour of the city draw
water from this fountain for the sacrifices where it is appropriate, and to
have those who make offerings of water take it from there, and to draw the
baths for the brides **80** from this fountain; and to have all those who take
the water for the purposes mentioned above go to the fountain and retire
from it in white clothing and wearing crowns, and to have the women who
draw the vessels of water for the brides . . .; and in order that the fountain
be built, as it is written, to appoint two *epistatai* out of all the citizens, who
should see to the work on the f[ountain and the dedication . . .] of water
. . . and to have the *tamiai* cover the future expenditure out of the budget,
according to the instructions of those appointed to the works, and concerning the execution of the works, to follow the written law **90** concerning the
work on honours;—and since, in addition to the honours given to the king
by the city, it is a fine thing and fitting with the goodwill of the king and his
friends towards the people and our eager character towards the king and his
friends, to put in common, so to speak, with the cities named after the
ancestors of the king the favours which were given and those which will be
given by the king to the people, so that, after a grant of our citizenship to
them, they should be the readier to benefactions and show eagerness in all
matters, just as it is a fine thing to do with one's own fatherland, and so that
100 we should renew our pre-existing friendship with them,—with good
fortune, (it seemed good) to have the *strategoi* and the *timouchoi* propose
at the next elections that citizenship be granted to the people of the
Antiocheians by Daphne and the people of the Seleukeians in Pieria and
the people of the Laodikeians by the sea; and to write up this decree on the
parastas of the temple of Dionysos and to consecrate it, and to have the
tamiai in office take care of the writing-up of the decree; and in order that
King Antiochos and his sister, Queen Laodike, should know of the gratitude of the people, to appoint three ambassadors who should go to them
and **110** hand over this decree, and, after bringing greetings from the
people, and after rejoicing that they be in good health and in the situation
which they wish and which we pray the gods for them to be in, and after
informing them of the honours decreed and after telling them . . .

Commentary. As in the case of the previous decree, the present text is
carved on two blocks from a pilaster in the entrance to the temple of
Dionysos; the archaeological context is also the same. The present text is
certainly later than the previous document (Herrmann 1965a: 89–93),
because of the greater elaboration of the honours, and because the
promised benefactions of document **17**, 27–9, are now described as realized
(lines 30–1).

See Ch. 2 § 2 for context; Ch. 4 §§ 2*b*, 3 for analysis of the document's functions; on date, see Appendix 2.

19. *Royal Correspondence Addressed to the the Teians (between 203 and 190)*

Text A: Herrmann 1965*a*: 41–2 (text of letter), 85–9 (textual notes), and plate 5.

Texts B and C: Herrmann 1965*a*: 157–8 (two further letters, both on the same stone, discovered in 1966 and presented 'provisorisch' as an addendum).

Texts D and E: Herrmann 1965*a*: 158–9, letter of Laodike, and a further fragment on the same stone which could be a letter of Antiochos III or Laodike; Piejko 1991*a*: 69, suggests Antiochos the son (but his restoration Βασιλεὺς Ἀντίοχος ὁ νεώτερος? is unlikely, since Antiochos the son is simply βασιλεὺς Ἀντίοχος in *RC* 32, line 1).

The lines on texts B and C, D and E, though both pairs are on the same stone, have been numbered separately.

SEG 41.1003, III–IV, 1004–5, for all four letters re-edited by P. Herrmann with a generous apparatus.

Cf. Piejko 1991*a*: 50–69: attempts at reconstructing complete reading texts of texts B and C, as well as a speculative reconstruction of the fragmentary letter of Laodike *exempli gratia*.

Text A is inscribed in a different hand from documents **16** and **17** (Herrmann 1965*a*: 49–50); the same is true for texts B and C (Herrmann 1965*a*: 159) and presumably D and E (though Herrmann does not comment on the letter-forms).

A.

traces of 2 lines

[Ἀν]τιόχωι[   ]
[   ] καὶ παρη[   ]

vacat

[Βασιλεὺ]ς [Ἀ]ντίοχος Τηίων τῆι βουλῆι κα[ὶ τῶι δήμωι χαίρειν· οἱ παρ' ὑμῶν]
[πρεσβ]ευταὶ Πυθόδοτος καὶ Πολύθρους καὶ [*c*.8   τὸ ψήφισμα ἀπέδωκαν]   4
[ἐν] ὧι ἐγεγράφειτε εὐχαριστοῦντες ἐπὶ τ[οῖς δεδομένοις ὑμῖν ὑφ' ἡμῶν]
[φιλ]ανθρώποις καὶ ὅτι βουλόμενοι τὴν ἑαυτῶν α[ἵρεσιν τὴν πρὸς ἡμᾶς ἀπο]-
δείκνυσθαι στεφανώσαιτε ἡμᾶς χρυσῶι στεφάν[ωι καθ' ἕκαστον ἐνιαυ]-
τὸν καὶ εἰκόνι χρυσῆι· διελέχθησαν δὲ καὶ οἱ πρεσβευταὶ [μετὰ σπουδῆς ἐμφα]-   8
νίζοντες τὴν τοῦ δήμου ἐκτένειαν· θεωροῦντες οὖν ὑμ[ᾶς εὐχαρίστως καὶ γνη?]-
σίως διακειμένους πρὸς τὴν οἰκίαν ἡμῶν ἐπαινοῦμεν ὡς ἐνδ[έχ]ε[ται μάλιστα·]
ἀποδεδέγμεθα δὲ καὶ τὸν στέφανον καὶ τὰς τιμὰς φιλοφρόνως κα . . . ισ[*c*.8   ]
τας ἡμᾶς καὶ τὴν ἀρχὴν ὁμοίως πολλῶι προθυμοτέρους παρασκ[ευά]ζε[ιν εἰς τὸ]   12
πᾶν τὸ συμφέρον συνκατασκευάζειν τῆι πόλει καὶ μὴ μόνον συντηρε[ῖν τὰ ὑπο]-
κείμενα ἀλλὰ καὶ ὅσ' ἂν ἀνήκῃ πρὸς τιμὴν καὶ δόξαν σ[υναύξε]ιν ὑμῖν κα[ὶ κοινῆι]
καὶ ἰδίαι ἑκάστου ποιεῖσθαι τὴμ προσήκουσαν πολυ[ωρίαν· καὶ] νῦν ὑ[πομνη]-
σάντων τῶν πρεσβευτῶν ἐντετάλθαι ὑμᾶς [αὐτοῖς] . . . . Λ . [*c*.10   ]   16

[. . . ὁ]ρῶντες ἐμ πᾶσ[ι]ν ὄντας ὑμᾶς ἐκτενεῖς κ[αὶ   c.20   ]
[c.6] ἀπόδειξ[ιν οἰό]μεθα δεῖν τὴμ πόλιν [ὑμῶν   c.20   ]
[c.12 ἀναγγ]ελοῦσιν ὑμῖν καὶ οἱ π[ρεσβευταὶ   c.15   ]
               traces of 1 line

1–2 Herrmann 1965a: 85–6 suggests these might be the last lines of a Teian decree for Antiochos; another possibility is a short decree recording the decision to inscribe the letter of Antiochos of lines 3–20, as in document **2**.   5 ἐπὶ τ[οῖς πρότερον γεγενημένοις ὑμῖν] Piejko 1991a: 48.   7–8 Herrmann 1965a: 87, justified his restoration καθ' ἕκαστον ἐνιαυτόν with a passage from the Teian decree *Inschr. Magnesia* 97, line 44.   11–15 The construction and the meaning are still unclear (possibilities examined by Herrmann 1965a: 87–8; further suggestions by Dunst 1968 or Piejko 1991a noted by Herrmann in *SEG*, neither convincing).

[. . . to An]tiochos . . .

King Antiochos to the council and [the people of the Teians, greetings; your ambassadors], Pythodotos and Polythrous and [. . . handed over the decree in] which you had written to express your gratitude over the fav[ours given to you by us] and to say that in your wish to make clear your [disposition towards us] you had crowned us with a gold crown [each year] and a golden statue; the ambassadors also spoke [with zeal] to point to the eager character of the people; so seeing that you are [gratefully and honestly] **10** disposed towards our house, we praise you as much as possible; we have accepted the crown and the honours with pleasure, . . . to make ourselves and likewise in the beginning (or: 'our empire'?) more eager to help with all that benefits the city and not only to preserve your present advantages, but also to increase all things that relate to your honour and your standing, and to take all the appropriate attention for each thing, in your favour as a community and as individuals; [and] after the ambassadors [reported] that you had told [them to . . .], seeing that you are eagerly disposed in all matters and . . . demonstration . . . we think it is necessary that [your] city . . . the ambassadors will also [report] to you [(concerning all these matters. Farewell.)]

B.

[Βασιλεὺς Ἀντίοχος Τηίων] τῆι βουλῆι καὶ [τῶι]
[δήμωι χαίρειν· οἱ παρ' ὑμῶν] πρεσβευταὶ Διονύ-
[σιος   τὸ ψή]φισμα ἀπέδωκαν
[   ] ἔχετε διὰ παντὸς   4
[διελέχθησαν δὲ κα]ὶ περὶ τῶν τιμῶν
[τοῖς προγ]όνοις καὶ ὧν ἐμοὶ
[προσδέδεγμα]ι δὲ καὶ τὸν στέφανον
[   ] αἵρεσιν καὶ ἐπὶ ταῖς   8
[τὴν] δημοκρατίαν ὑμῖν
[καὶ τὴν πόλιν καὶ] τὴν χώραν ἱερὰν καὶ
[ἄσυλον   καθά]περ καὶ οἱ πατέρες καὶ
[αὐτός   ]ν εὐνοίας ἀεί τινος   12
[ἀγαθοῦ παραίτιος   ]ι vac. ἔρρωσθε.
               vacat

7 [προσδέδεγμα]ι Herrmann; the present verb on analogy with letter A, line 11.
12 [ἐγώ] Herrmann; [αὐτός] Piejko 1991a: 54.

[King Antiochos to] the council and [the people of the Teians, greetings; your] ambassadors Diony[sios and . . . handed over the decree [. . .] you are always [. . . they also spoke] concerning the honours [. . . the anc]estors and of those which to me [. . . I have also accepted] the crown [. . .] intention and [. . . the] democracy for your [. . . and the city and] **10** the territory to be sacred and [inviolate . . . just] as my fathers and [myself . . .] of good-will, always [responsible for some favour.] Farewell.

C.

[Βασιλεὺς Ἀντίοχος Τηίων τ]ῆι βουλῆι καὶ τῶι δή-
[μωι χαίρειν·   οἱ π]αρ' ὑμῶν πρεσβευταὶ
[   ]οις καὶ ἐμὲ καὶ τὴν ἀ-
[δελφὴν   τὰ ψ]ηφίσματα καθ' ἃ ἐτετι-   4
[μήκειτε ἡμᾶς διότι τὴν] ἐλευθερίαν καὶ τὴν
[καὶ τἄλλα φιλ]άνθρωπα τῆι πόλει
[ὑμῶν διατηροῦμεν?   κ]αὶ τῶν χρησίμων ἀεί
[τι   τῶν] ἄλλων τῶν ἐν τοῖς   8
[ψηφίσμασι?   μετὰ] πάσης [σπ]ουδῆς
[τοὺς στε]φάνους καὶ τὰς ἄλλας
[τιμὰς   ο]ἰκείως προσδεδέγμε-
[θα   τὸν δῆμον? ἐπαινο]ῦμεν διατηροῦντα   12
[τὴν αἵ]ρεσιν ὡς προσῆκόν
[ἐστιν καὶ πειρασόμεθα εἰς τὸ λοιπὸν? κ]αθάπερ ἀξιοῦτε τῆι
[τῶν προγόνων   ὑφηγ]ήσει? κατακολου-
[θοῦντες   συ]νπράσσειν καὶ τὴν   16
[   ] καὶ τὰ ἄλλα τὰ δεδομέ-
[να   φιλάνθρ]ωπα συνδιαφυλάσ-
[σειν   ἐ]ν τῆι αὐτῆι διαθέσει καὶ
[περὶ το]ύτων καὶ οἱ πρεσβευ-   20
[ται   ἀναγγελοῦσιν] ὑμῖν· vacat ἔρρωσθ[ε.]

7–8 τῶν χρησίμων ἀεί [τι] Piejko 1991a: 62, to be completed with a verb meaning 'to provide'; or perhaps τῶν χρησίμων ἀεί [τινος παραίτιοι], as in the expression 'we will always try to be responsible for some good towards you'.   9 [μετὰ] πάσης [σπ]ουδῆς must represent the king's approving description of the ambassadors' speech and conduct. Piejko 1991a: 55: διελέγησαν; above, document A, line 8: διελέχθησαν δὲ καὶ οἱ πρεσβευταί [μετὰ σπουδῆς πάσης]   11–12 On the parallel of RC 32, line 17, perhaps one could restore a singular participle προσδεδεγμένου in the genitive absolute, agreeing with a clause describing an action of Antiochos III (if this letter is a document of Antiochos the son). Another possibility is προσδεδεγμένος, agreeing with the author of the letter, who in line 3 writes in the first person singular.   15–16 If this were a letter of Antiochos the son, τῆι [τοῦ πατρὸς . . . ὑφηγ]ήσει would be possible.

King Antiochos to the council and the people of Teos, greetings. Your ambassadors . . . me and my sister . . . the decrees, according to which you honoured [us because we] . . . the liberty and the . . . [and the other] privileges . . . for the city . . . and always [some] advantage . . . the other things in the . . . with all zeal . . . **10** the crowns and the other [honours]

. . . we gladly accept . . . we praise [the city? (for keeping the same)] policy, as it is fitting and . . . as you ask, following the [ex]ample [of the ancestors] . . . to assist in the . . . the other things which were given . . . preserve the privileges . . . in the same situation and . . . [concerning] these matters, your ambassadors [will report] to you. Farewell.

D.

[   ]ν διει[   ]
[   ] καὶ αὖ[   ]
[κ]αὶ εἰς το[   ]
[   ]ς ἄφιστα[   ]   4
[   ]τοῖς Ἑλλη[σιν   ]
[   ]μένοις α[   ]
[   ] τὴν αὐτὴ[ν   ]
[εὖν]οιαν τὴμ π[ρὸς]   8
[   ] ἐγὼ καὶ ὁ ἀδ[ελφὸς]
                                            ἔρρ[ωσθε]

                    vacat

E.

[τῶι κοινῶι τῶν περὶ τὸν Διόνυσον] τεχνιτῶν [χαίρειν.]
[ψ]ήφισμα το[   ]
[φιλ]ανθρωπ]
[   ]έχετ[ε   ]   4
[   ]ηξ[   ]

(fragments) . . .to the Greeks . . . the same . . . goodwill towards . . . I and my brother . . .
Farewell.

(next letter) . . .to the corporation of the Dionysiac Artists, [greetings]. Decree . . . generous . . . you have . . .

Commentary. Document A comes from a pilaster on the entrance of the temple of Dionysos at Teos. This is probably also the case of B and C, since the depth of the block on which they are inscribed is the same as the *parastas* bearing the other texts (Herrmann 1965*a*: 157); the letter-shapes are also different from those of the preceding Teian documents (Herrmann 1965*a*: 159): larger and coarser, as I noticed when I examined the stone (in 1995, in the new archaeological museum in Izmir). The archaeological context for this block, found in 1966, is similar to that of the material discovered earlier: near the western wall of the sanctuary's *temenos*.

Documents B and C are written (mostly) in the first person singular, which opens the possibility that the author is Antiochos the son rather than Antiochos III (cf. *RC* 32), perhaps acknowledging the new status of Teos granted by his father. It would be appropriate for Antiochos the son to speak of the Seleukid ancestors as οἱ πατέρες (B 11), in addition to the more usual πρόγονοι (though the Iasians refer to the king's πατέρες: document **28**, 4); he could also have referred to his queen as his sister (C 3–4), since he married his sister Laodike, in winter 196/5. The verb συμπράσσειν (C 16) might also designate collaboration with the more powerful figure of Antiochos III (just as it does in *RC* 44, lines 9–10, on the part of a royal Friend).

III 197–190 BC

20. Dedication at Aigeai by Themison, Nephew of the King, for Antiochos III, Antiochos the Son, Laodike III, and the Royal Children (probably 197)

I owe knowledge of this document to the generosity of M. Sayar, who kindly showed his text, due to appear in *Asia Minor Studien* (Münster, forthcoming); the present text is taken from a paper delivered in a conference in Bordeaux (12–13 December 1997), on 'Les cités d'Asie Mineure occidentale au IIe siècle a. C.', now Sayar (2001).

Ὑπὲρ βασιλέως μεγάλου
Ἀντιόχου καὶ Ἀντιόχου
τοῦ υἱοῦ καὶ βασιλίσσης
Λαοδίκης καὶ τῶν παιδίων   4
Θεμίσων ὁ ἀδελφιδοῦς
τοῦ βασιλέως
  Διὶ Κασίωι

For the safety of the Great King Antiochos and Antiochos the son and queen Laodike and the children, Themison, the nephew of the king, to Zeus Kasios.

Commentary. The stele was found near ancient Aigeai. Themison, 'nephew of the king', and author of the dedication, must be the commander on Pol. 5.79.12 and 5.82.11. The inscription dates between *c.*199 (when Antiochos took the title 'great king') and 193 (when Antiochos the son died). It is probably connected to the expedition of 197.

The expression τῶν παιδίων, 'little children' (line 4), rather than the more usual and neutral τέκνων, is paralleled in Laodike's letter to the Sardians, document 2 B, 14. The emotive word, used by the queen and a relative of the king, may be part of court style; it also turns up in the honorific inscription from Antioch for Theophilos of Seleukeia in Pieria, honoured for his attitude towards the royal family (Kraeling 1964). See commentary to document 2.

21. Dedication at Soloi by Ptolemaios, Son of Thraseas, to Hermes, Herakles and Antiochos III (probably 197)

G. Radet and P. Paris, *BCH* 14 (1890), 587–9 (*OGIS* 230). Photograph of the stone, which has now lost its upper right hand corner, in *BCH* 96 (1972), 110. You can still see it in the French School at Athens.

The editors dated the document to 218 (adopted in *OGIS*); for the correct date, Holleaux 1942: 161 and n. 6.

Πτολεμαῖος Θρασέα
στραταγὸς καὶ ἀρχιερεὺς
Συρίας Κοίλας καὶ Φοινίκας
Ἑρμᾶι vac. καὶ vac. Ἡρακλεῖ vac. καὶ   4
βασιλεῖ μεγάλωι Ἀντιόχωι

3 The presence of one-letter spaces between the words can be seen on the photograph. Presumably the intention was to regularize the layout of the whole text by 'justifying' this line on both margins.

Ptolemaios, son of Thraseas, *strategos* and high-priest of Koile-Syria and Phoenicia, to Hermes and Herakles and the Great King Antiochos.

Commentary. The text is preserved on a smallish marble plaque; the modest thickness (5 cm.) suggests that the present stone was sawn off a larger block (architectural? statue base?): though the editors do not mention such an action, this would have allowed transport from Mersin (where it was found and bought) to the French School in Athens (where it is now kept).

Ptolemaios is well known from Polybios and from the Hefzibah inscription; for new information from Kilikia on his Aspendian family, which produced several Ptolemaic officers, see Jones and Habicht 1989, especially Habicht at 338–41.

The dedication, intriguingly, is in Doric. The editors believed this reflected the local dialect at Soloi, which was considered a Rhodian or an Argive foundation.[1] Dittenberger disagreed ('certe non recte'), because, in his view, the dedication must reflect the dialect of the dedicator, not the locality; he proposed that Doric was used in this inscription because Ptolemaios came from a Dorian city. We now know that his family originated from Aspendos, a city which could in fact be viewed as Dorian through its claimed kinship with Argos[2] (Jones and Habicht 1989: 338 and n. 62). Most of the Hellenistic epigraphy of Aspendos is written in the local Hellenized dialect, which exhibits several points of contact with Doric.[3] However, the context for dialect inscriptions is almost entirely funerary.[4]

[1] Pol. 21.24.10 (Soloi, as Argive foundation, was considered by Rhodes as related by kinship, in 188); Strabo 14.5.8 (Soloi was founded by Lindian colonists). Whether these assertions, not documented before the Hellenistic period, reflect a genuine foundation in the Archaic period is unclear (but likely).

[2] *SEG* 34.282 (late 4th-cent. Argive decree granting *isopoliteia* to the Aspendians, their kinsmen); Jones and Habicht 1989: 338 and n. 62; Curty 1995: no. 3, republishing the text with commentary and bibliography.

[3] Brixhe 1976: 146 and n. 1; 191. For 'Doric-like' proper names, see Brixhe, *Etudes d'archéologie classique* 5 (Nancy, 1976), 11 no. 183, 13 no. 189, 14 no. 190; Brixhe and Hodot 1988: 168 no. 193, 175 no. 175, 176–7 no. 198, 192 no. 207, 202 no. 213, 222 no. 224.

[4] *BE* 1991, 601 (Brixhe and Panayotou); the exceptions are the two inscriptions recording a donation for the city walls from women who had filled the office of δαμιοργός (Brixhe 1976: 200–1, no. 17 and 204, no. 18; both from the second century).

In contrast, the language for official affairs was probably *koine*,[5] as shown by the sole surviving Aspendian decree (*SEG* 17.639).

Did Ptolemaios use the 'private', dialectal register of Aspendian dialect for his dedication at Soloi? In a similar situation (dedication by a royal official to the ruling dynasty and the gods of the gymnasion), the Aspendian Meas used *koine* (*SEG* 31.1321): his dedication to Hermes at Meydancık Kale reads Ἑρμεῖ, not the Doric form Ἑρμᾶι which appears at Soloi. The dedication of Meas, exactly parallel to Ptolemaios' except for the dialect, makes Ptolemaios' use of Doric even more peculiar. Was Ptolemaios influenced by the usage at Soloi, as the editors believed? This assumes that Doric was indeed spoken in that city in the Hellenistic period, as a result of its (claimed) Argive/Rhodian ancestry.[6] It is difficult to understand why Ptolemaios would have decided to observe the local dialect ('courtesy' to the local community seems unlikely). Another, perhaps neater, possibility is that Ptolemaios left funds and instructions concerning the gymnasion, and that the city of Soloi put up the dedication in Ptolemaios' name—in local dialect.

22. *Inscription Recording the Consecration of Xanthos by Antiochos III* (*197*)

O. Benndorf, *Beiträge zur alten Geschichte. Festschrift für O. Hirschfeld* (1903), 77–8, with facsimile of squeeze taken by Heberdey (= *OGIS* 746 = *TAM* 2.266, with Benndorf's facsimile). The text was erased at some time after its inscription, but every word can be made out.

Cf. Schmitt 1964: 287 and Herrmann 1965a: 119–20 (both against Benndorf's interpretation that the consecration of the city on the part of Antiochos was only a *Scheingewinn*, a compromise in the face of Xanthian resistance—there is no evidence for this scenario, and other Xanthian documents show that the city adopted formal markers of subjection, namely the complex Seleukid dating system for civic documents); J. and L. Robert 1983: 161, 164 (the inscription was put up by the Xanthians). Boffo 1985: 131–42 for a study of the inscription in its ideological and political context (believes in some form of compromise reached by king and city).

---

[5] Brixhe and Hodot 1988: 217 ('langue de la vie publique', in Aspendos and Pamphylia generally).

[6] Among all the inscriptions listed in G. Dagron, D. Feissel, *Inscriptions de Cilicie* (Paris, 1987), 57–63, the only testimony for Doric is onomastic: a 4th-cent. metrical epitaph for the family of Athanadotos (A. von Gladiss, *Ist. Mitt.* 23–24 (1973–1974), 175–81) and a Hellenistic metrical epitaph for Athanadoros and Athanaios (*GVI* 502). The epitaphs themselves are not in Doric, but this is presumably a factor of the poetical form. The presence of theophoric names derived from Athena may support the tradition of colonists from Lindos, where the main deity was Athena Lindia, and hence make it possible that Doric was spoken (down to the Hellenistic period?) at Soloi.

Βασιλεὺς μέγας Ἀντίοχος
ἀφιέρωσεν τὴν πόλιν
τῆι Λητῶι καὶ τῶι Ἀπόλλωνι
καὶ τῆι Ἀρτέμιδι διὰ τὴν   4
πρὸς αὐτοὺς συνάπτουσαν
συνγένειαν.

The Great King, Antiochos, consecrated the city to Leto and Apollo and Artemis, on account of the kinship uniting him to them.

Commentary. The inscription was carved in monumental letters on a privileged emplacement of the main, southern, gate of Hellenistic Xanthos (inward-facing side of the right hand post when entering the city); the text was later deliberately erased (Benndorf, quoted above; also lemma to *TAM* edition).

Since the inscription gives the full title of Antiochos (which never happens in royal letters), it was probably put up by the Xanthians themselves, acting upon the royal consecration (J. and L. Robert 1983: 164). Furthermore, the inscription mentions the Lykian triad in its traditional order, with Leto named first, as is fitting for the great goddess of Xanthos, and hence ahead of the Seleukid god Apollo; in contrast, Antiochos' letter to the army at Amyzon (document 6), mentions Apollo before Artemis, the main goddess in that city. The respect for the traditional precedence of gods in the present document supports the Roberts' suggestion.

23. Decree of the Xanthians for Themistokles Son of Aischylos, an Ilian Rhetor (September or October 196)

J. and L. Robert 1983: 154–63, no. 15 B (with photograph of squeeze), with commentary at 163–76 (*SEG* 33.1184; Curty 1995: no. 76).
Cf. Malay 1987 on the high-priest Nikanor.

Βασιλευόντων Ἀντιόχου καὶ Ἀντιό[χου]
τοῦ υἱοῦ, σιρ΄, μηνὸς Ὑπερβερεταίου·
ἐπ᾽ ἀρχιερέως Νικάνορος, ἐν δὲ Ξάνθ[ωι]
ἐφ᾽ ἱερέως τῶμ μὲν βασιλέων ⟨Π⟩ρασί-   4
[δ]ου τοῦ Νικοστράτου, πρὸ πόλεως δὲ
Τληπολέμου τοῦ Ἀρταπάτου· ἐκκλησίας οὔσης κυρίας, ἔδοξεν Ξανθίων
τῆι πόλει καὶ τοῖς ἄρχουσιν· ἐπειδὴ   8
Θεμιστοκλῆς Αἰσχύλου Ἰλιεὺς παραγενόμενος εἰς τὴν πόλιν ἡμῶν ἀποδείξεις πεπόηται τῶν ῥητορικῶν λόγων
ἐν αἷς εὐδοκίμηκεν ἐπὶ πλέον· παρεπι-   12
δεδήμηκέν τε χρόνον οὐκ ὀλίον, ἀνέγ-
κλητος γεγονὼς καὶ τῆς ὑπαρχούσης
ἡμῖν πρὸς Ἰλιεῖς συγγενείας ἄξιος·
δεδόχθαι· ἐπαίνεσαι Θεμιστοκλῆν   16

Αἰσχύλου Ἰλιέα, ἄνδρα καλὸν καὶ ἀγαθὸν
γεγονότα ἐν τῆι παρεπιδημίαι
καὶ πρὸς ἡμᾶς εὐνοικῶς διακείμενον·
τιμῆσαι δὲ αὐτὸν καὶ δραχμαῖς   20
τετρακοσίαις· ἵνα δὲ καὶ τοῖς τιμωμένοις
ἰλικρινῆ καὶ βέβαιαν τὴν χάριν ἀπο-
νέμοντες φαινώμεθα, ἀναγραψάτωσαν
οἱ ἄρχοντες τὸ ψήφισμα τόδε   24
[εἰς] στήλας λιθίνας δύο καὶ τέθωσαν
[τὴμ μὲ]ν μίαν εἰς τὸν ἐπιφανέστα-
[τον τό]πον ἐν τῶι τῆς Λητοῦς ἱερῶι
[τὴν δὲ ἄλ]λην ἀποστειλάτωσαν   28
[εἰς Ἴλιον ἵνα] τεθῆι ἐν τῶι τῆς Ἰλιάδος
[Ἀθηνᾶς ἱερῶι] παρὰ τὰς εἰκόνας
[τοῦ Θεμιστοκλ]είους πατρὸς Αἰσχύλου.

4–5 Γρασί[ω|ν]ος Robert (squeeze); rectified Bousquet 1988: 25 n. 13 (stone: Γρασί|[δ]ου), and confirmed by the decree of the Xanthian *neoi* (document **24** with Gauthier 1996: 6).

When Antiochos and Antiochos the son were kings, in the one hundred and sixteenth (year), in the month of Hyperberetaios, in the high-priesthood of Nikanor, and in Xanthos, in the tenure of Prasidas son of Nikostratos as priest of the kings, and of Tlepolemos son of Artapates as priest *pro poleos*; in plenary assembly, it seemed good to the city and magistrates of the Xanthians:—since Themistokles son of Aischylos, of Ilion, after arriving in our city **10** gave demonstrations of rhetorical speeches, in which he won great repute; he stayed for no little time, proving himself blameless and worthy of our kinship with the Ilians; let it seem good:—to praise Themistokles, son of Aischylos, of Ilion, who proved an excellent man during his stay, and well disposed towards us; **20** to honour him with four hundred drachmai; and so that we should be seen to return sincere and firm gratitude to those we honour, let the magistrates write up this decree on two stone stelai, and place one in the most conspicuous place in the shrine of Leto, and let them send the other to Ilion so that it be placed in the shrine of Athena Ilias, **30** next to the statues of Themistokles' father, Aischylos.

Commentary. The document is preserved on a 'petite stèle' found by H. Metzger in the Letoon at Xanthos.

24. Decree of the Xanthian neoi *for Lyson (August 196)*

Gauthier 1996 (*editio princeps*; *SEG* 46. 1721).

[Βασιλευόν]των Ἀντιόχου καὶ Ἀντιόχου τοῦ υἱοῦ, vac.
[(ἔτους) σιϛ´ vac. μ]ηνὸς Γορπιείου, vac. ἐπ᾽ ἀρχιερέως Νικάνορος,
[ἐν δὲ Ξάνθ]ωι ἐπ᾽ ἱερέως τῶν μὲν βασιλέων Πρασί-
δου [τοῦ Νικ]οστράτου, πρὸ πόλεως δὲ Τληπολέμου   4

τοῦ Ἀρ[ταπ]άτου, vac. ἔδοξεν Ξανθίων τοῖς νέοις· ἐπειδὴ Λύσων Δημοσθένου, πολιτευόμενος ὡς καθήκει τοῖς καλοῖς καὶ ἀγαθοῖς ἀνδράσιν, καὶ πολλὰς
ἀποδείξεις τῆς τε πρὸς τὴν πόλιν εὐνοίας καὶ   8
τοὺς νέους πεποίηται ἐν τοῖς ἀναγκαιοτάτοις καιροῖς ἀξίως αὑτοῦ τε καὶ τῆς τῶν προγόνων ἀνα-
στροφῆς, ὧν ἕνεκεν καὶ ὑπὸ τῆς πόλεως τιμᾶται
ταῖς ἁρμοζούσαις [τ]ιμαῖς, vac. αἱρεθείς τε γυμνασί-   12
αρχος τῆς τε περὶ τὸ γυμνάσιον ἐπιμελείας
καὶ κατασκευῆς προέστη μετὰ πάσης ἐκτενεί-
ας καὶ πολλὰ τῶν ἰδίων εἰσανηλώσας ἐκόσμη-
σεν, προαιρούμενος οὐ μόνον τοῖς ἐν τῶι πολιτεύ-   16
ματι πεπραγμένοις αὐτῶι καλοῖς καὶ ἐνδόξοις ἀκό-
λουθος φαίνεσθα[ι], ἀλλὰ καὶ τοῖς ἐξ ἡμῶν ἐπιγινο-
μένοις ὑπόμνημα καταλιπεῖν ἧς ἔσχεν αἱρέσε-
ως πρὸς τὰ τῆι πατρίδι συμφέροντα καὶ τοὺς νέ-   20
ους, ὅθεν καὶ ἡμεῖ[ς, ἐ]πιγνόντες τήν τε ἐν τοῖς [ἐ]-
πάνω χρόνοις περ[ὶ α]ὐτὸν καλοκἀγαθίαν καὶ τὸν [ἐ]-
νεστῶτα καιρὸν θε[ωρο]ῦντες προσδε[ό]μενον ἀν-
δρὸς ἀξίου καὶ δυνα[μέν]ου [δι]εξαγαγεῖν ἀνεγκλή-   24
τως τὴν κατὰ τὸ γυ[μνάσιο]ν ἀρχήν, παρεκαλέσαμε[ν]
αὐτὸν καὶ εἰς τ[ὸν ἐ]χόμενον ἐνιαυτὸν παρασχεῖσ-
θαι τὴν χρεία[ν, κ]αὶ ἐπιδόντος αὐτοῦ προθύμως εἱ-
[λόμεθα αὐτὸν γ]υμνασίαρχον· ἐπεὶ οὖν ἐμ πᾶσιν   28
[τοῖς συμφέρου]σιν τῆι τε πόλει καὶ τοῖς νέοις ὁμοί-
[ως τὴν αὐτὴν] προθυμίαν ἔχων οὐθενὸς ἀφίστα-
[ται τῶν χρησί]μων, vac. ἀγαθῆι τύχηι· δεδόχθαι ἐπαινέ-
[σαι Λύσωνα Δη]μοσθένου ἀρετῆς ἕνεκεν καὶ εὐνοί-   32
[ας ἧς ἔχων διατ]ελεῖ πρός τε τὴν πατρίδα καὶ τοὺς
[νέους καὶ τὰ τῶ]ν βασιλέων πράγματα· vac. τιμῆσαι δὲ
[αὐτὸν καὶ εἰκ]όνι χαλκῆι καὶ ἀναθεῖναι αὐτὴν ἐν τῶι
[γυμνασίωι] ἐν τῶι ἐπιφανεστάτωι τόπωι, ἐπιγρά-vac.   36
[ψαι δὲ καὶ τὴν] ἐπιγραφὴν τήνδε· vac. Ξανθίων οἱ νέοι υυυ
[Λύσωνα Δη]μοσθένου γυμνασιαρχήσαντα ἐφ’ ἔτη
[δύο ἀρετῆ]ς ἕνεκεν καὶ εὐνοίας τῆς εἰς αὐτοὺς
[καὶ τὴν πό]λιν· vac. ἱδρύσασθαι δὲ καὶ βωμοὺς δύο ἐν   40
[τῶι ἐπιφανε]στάτωι τόπωι τοῦ γυμνασίου, τὸμ μὲν
[τοῦ Διὸς τοῦ Σ]ωτῆρος, τὸν δὲ ἄλλον τοῦ Λύσωνος vac.
[c.11   ], ἐφ’ ὧν θύσει Λύσων τε ἕως ἂν ζῆι ἢ ἄλ-vac.
[λος ἀντ’ αὐτ]οῦ τῶι Διί, τὸν δὲ ἕτερον ὁ κατ’ ἐνιαυτὸν   44
[αἱρούμενο]ς γυμνασίαρχος, παριστάντων τοῦ τε
[κοινοῦ τῶν ν]έων καὶ τοῦ γυμνασιάρχου ἀπὸ τῆς
[c.15   ] Τⲱ . [β]οῦς τριετ[εῖ]ς [δύο?]
              traces of one line

38–9 ἐφ’ ἔτη [δύο] carved later, in a different hand, after Lyson's tenure of office.
43 The lacuna was probably taken up by a cultic epithet qualifying Lyson (Gauthier
1996: 18, suggesting [τοῦ Εὐεργετοῦ]).

When Antiochos and Antiochos the son were [kings], [in the one hundred
and sixteenth (year)], in the month Gorpiaios, in the high-priesthood of
Nikanor, and in Xanthos, in the tenure of Prasidas, son of Nikostratos, as
priest of the kings, and of Tlepolemos, son of Artapates, as priest *pro
poleos*, it seemed good to the *neoi* of Xanthos:—since Lyson, son of
Demosthenes, acting as a citizen as is fitting for excellent men, has given
many demonstrations of his goodwill towards the city and the *neoi*, in the
most difficult circumstances, **10** in a fashion worthy of himself and of his
ancestors' behaviour, for which reason he is also honoured by the city with
appropriate honours; and, when elected gymnasiarch, he oversaw the care
and the construction work (or: repair work) of the gymnasion, with all zeal,
and spending much out of his own fortune he adorned it, making it his
intention not only to be seen as consistent with his fine and glorious deeds
in the political sphere, but also to leave to our successors a memorial of the
disposition he had **20** towards the advantages of the fatherland and towards
the *neoi*; for which reason, we too, taking notice of the earlier excellence
about his person and seeing that the circumstances required a worthy man
and one capable of filling the office over the gymnasion in a manner above
reproach, we have invited him to meet this need for next year, and since he
offered himself with enthusiasm, we elected him gymnasiarch; and since in
all the interests of the city and of the *neoi* he shows **30** the same enthusiasm
and refrains from nothing that is advantageous;—with good fortune, let
it seem good to praise [Lyson son of De]mosthenes, on account of his
quality and the goodwill which he [cont]inually [shows] towards the
fatherland and the [*neoi* and the] affairs of the kings; to honour [him also
with a stat]ue of bronze, and to set it up in the most conspicuous place in
the [gymnasion], and to inscribe this inscription: 'The *neoi* of the
Xanthians (dedicated a statue of) [Lyson, son of De]mosthenes, who was
gymnasiarch *for [two] years*, on account of his [quality] and his goodwill
towards them **40** [and the ci]ty'; and to erect two altars in the [most con-
spicu]ous place of the gymnasion, one of [Zeus S]aviour, the other of
Lyson [. . .], on which Lyson for as long as he lives, or another in his stead,
will sacrifice to Zeus, and, as concerns the other altar, the yearly elected
gymnasiarch, with the attendant condition that the [corporation of the
n]*eoi* and the gymnasiarch will supply out of the . . . [two?] oxen three years
in age . . .

Commentary. The decree is carved on a small limestone stele found in the
Letoon near Xanthos. Though the date was inscribed in the part now lost,
the eponymous priest of the kings is the same as in document **23**, issued in
196 (Gauthier).

25. Letter of Zeuxis to Kildarians (probably 197)

J. and L. Robert 1983: 181–7, with photographs of stone and squeeze
(*SEG* 33.867; *I. Mylasa* 962).

μηθενὶ μήτε τῶμ πολιτῶν μή[τε]
[τ]ῶν παροίκ[ω]ν· τοῖς τε ἄλλοις
{ἀλλ}οῖς πᾶσιν ὑπὸ τοῦ βασιλέως
[μεγάλου] [Ἀ]ν[τι]ό[χ]ου [σ]υνκεχώρ-   4
[η]ται καὶ ὑμεῖν τὰ αὐτὰ·[c.6]
. ὑπάρχει καὶ τὰ λοιπὰ . . . Δ
. . τὴμ πᾶσαν πολυωρίαν ποησόμεθα ὑμῶν ὅσωιπερ ἂν εὐ-   8
ν[ο]έστεροι καὶ προθυμότερο[ι]
φαίνησθε εἰς τὰ τῶι βασιλεῖ
Ἀντιόχωι συμφέροντα.

2 The photograph of the squeeze shows that there is not enough space at the beginning of line 2 for the Roberts' [τε τῶμ], but rather simply for [τωμ] or rather [τ]ων. 2–3 Blümel in *I. Mylasa* reads τοῖς τε ἄλλοις {αλλ}οῖς (for ἅ), as antecedent of [νῦν] ὑπάρχει: 'the things which were granted by the Great King Antiochos to the others, are now, these very same things (τὰ αὐτά), at your disposal'. The Roberts' ΑΛΛΟΙΣ is difficult to confirm on the squeeze.   4 It is difficult to substantiate the Roberts' reading Ἀντιό[χ]ου from the photograph of the squeeze. The present reading suggested by C. Crowther. The *rho* at the end of the line can be made out on the photograph (rather than at the beginning of the following line).   6 The squeeze clearly shows that there is not enough space for Robert's [ὅσα], but rather enough for one letter (perhaps [ἅ]) or a *vacat*. Blümel restores [νῦν].   8 The stone reads ὅσωιπερ rather than ὅσωπερ (Robert).   9 εὐ|ν[ο]έστεροι Blümel, rather than the Roberts' εὐ|νωέστεροι which at any rate cannot be read on the photograph of the squeeze.

(I have written to . . . to prevent any harm to be done) to any of the citizens and of the *paroikoi*; the same privileges have been granted to you by the [Great] King Antiochos as to the others, and the other things are at the disposal of . . . we will show all consideration for you, inasmuch as you **10** show yourselves to be the better disposed and the more eager towards the interests of King Antiochos.

Commentary. The marble block bearing this text (built into a well when Robert saw it in 1934, at Kuzyaka, near the site of ancient Kildara) probably came from a major civic temple, 'avec des documents hellénistiques sur les antes et les murs, comme partout en Carie' (J. and L. Robert 1983: 186).

The meaning of the first part of the letter (lines 1–6) is far from clear, and the translation offered here is tentative. The mention of Antiochos alone, without Antiochos the son, might mean that the letter was written after the death of Antiochos the son in 193, but not necessarily (the reference to the king alone might depend on the context and on the use of the expression 'the interests of').

I cannot accept the suggestion made by Piejko 1985: 614–15, that this is a complete document: to support his assertion, Piejko must radically supplement and emend the text, and then blames the subsequent oddities on 'the unskilled redactor' rather than on his own emendations and his own assumptions. The method is circular; furthermore, the present document is quite unlike e.g. the royal *prostagma* from Jerusalem (Jos. *AJ* 12.145–6, with Bickerman 1980: 86–104) or *OGIS* 746 which Piejko would presumably compare it to. On Robert's photograph, it looks as if the final line, with the salutation ἔρρωσθε and the Seleukid year, have been chiselled out, confirming that this text was once part of a complete letter. However, the stone, on the photograph, does not show any traces above the surviving inscribed field, which seems to have been surrounded by a smooth margin. The text presumably started on an adjacent block, in a separate column (for an example of this arrangement, see *GIBM* 477).

26. Letter of Laodike III to Iasians, Decree of the Iasians for Laodike (c.196)

G. Pugliese-Carratelli, *ASAA* 29/30 (1967/8), 445–53, no. 2, with photograph—note that J. and L. Robert, *BE* 71, 621, p. 505, integrate a few lines published as fragment 2*bis* a by Pugliese-Carratelli (p. 448), into the text of the lines here reproduced as B II 18–19 (= *I. Iasos* 4, 80–1). Lines 33–50 of the first edition (here B I 1–18) were corrected from autopsy by Y. Garlan (*ZPE* 13 (1974), 197–8). W. Blümel, *I. Iasos* 4 is based on Pugliese-Carratelli's text, except for the portion revised by Garlan; the same principle is followed here. However, Blümel also acted upon the Roberts' suggestion that *OGIS* 237 was part of the same text and incorporated it in his edition; but *OGIS* 237 is a separate document (below), so I have presented it separately (document **28**). See Bringmann and von Steuben 1995: no. 297. The best text now is Nafissi 2001, used here.

Cf. *SEG* 26.1226, registering literature on textual matters; J. and L. Robert, *BE* 71, 621 (detailed analysis, correct dating; attempt to fit in *OGIS* 237); Robert, *OMS* v. 9–11 (summary of lectures on these documents); Crowther 1989 proves that *OGIS* 237 cannot belong to the same document. Mastrocinque 1995: 132, for the beginning of the text (from autopsy of the text, supported by photographs). Translation of lines 1–32: Austin 1981: no. 156.

The stone presents two columns of text, carved in the same hand. The first column fully preserves a letter of Laodike, here entitled text A, and numbered 1–32, as in the *ed. princ.* and *I. Iasos* 4; the first column also preserves the beginning of the decree of the Iasians, which has been called text B, and renumbered as column I. The second, severely damaged column on the stone preserves another part of text B, here entitled B col. II and renumbered on its own (returning to Pugliese-Carratelli's numbering). However, for reference, Blümel's numbering (which integrates *OGIS* 237/document **28**) has been indicated in brackets for text B.

A (Col. I of the stele).

⟦ἐπὶ στεφανηφόρου Κυδίου τοῦ Ἱεροκλείους⟧
ἐπὶ στεφανηφόρου Κυδίου τοῦ Ἱεροκλείους·
⟦ἐπιστολὴ π . ⟧ Ἐλαφηβολιῶνος·

Βασίλισσα Λαοδίκη Ἰασέων τῆι βουλῆι καὶ τῶι δήμωι χαίρειν· ἀκούουσα πλεονάκις τοῦ ἀδελφοῦ ἤν   4
τε ἀντίληψιν τῶν ἑαυτοῦ φίλων καὶ συμμάχων
διατελεῖ ποιούμενος καὶ ὡς τὴν ὑμέτεραν πόλιν συμπτώμασιν περιπεσοῦσαν ἀπροσδοκή-
τοις ἀνακτησάμενος τήν τε ἐλευθερίαν ὑμῖν   8
ἀπέδωκεν καὶ τοὺς νόμους καὶ τὰ λοιπὰ προτέθειται συναύξειν τὸ πολίτευμα καὶ εἰς βελτίονα διάθεσιν ἀγαγεῖν, προαιρουμένη δὴ καὶ ἐγὼ ἀκόλουθα πράσειν τῇ σπουδῇ αὐτοῦ καὶ ἐκτενείαι καὶ διὰ   12
τοῦτο καταθέσθαι τινὰ εὐεργεσίαμ μὲν εἰς τοὺς
ἀσθενοῦντας τῶν πολιτῶν, εὐχρηστίαν δὲ κοινὴν τῶι σύμπαντι δήμωι, γεγράφεικα Στρουθί-
ωνι τῶι διοικητῆι ἐφ' ἔτη δέκα κατ' ἐνιαυτὸν πυρῶν χιλί-   16
ους μεδίμνους Ἀττικοὺς εἰς τὴν πόλιν παρακομί-
ζοντα παραδιδόναι τοῖς παρὰ τοῦ δήμου· εὖ οὖν ποήσετε συντάξαντες τοῖς μὲν ταμίαις παραλαμβά-
νοντας τακτοῦ πλήθους ἐγδιοικεῖν, τοῖς δὲ προστά-   20
ταις καὶ οἷς ἂν ἄλλοις κρίνητε προνοεῖν ὅπως τὸ γινό-
μενον διάφορον ἐκ τούτων κατατιθῶνται εἰς προῖκας
ταῖς τῶν ἀσθενούντων πολιτῶν θυγατράσιν, διδόν-
τες μὴ πλέω Ἀντιοχέων δραχμῶν τριακοσίων ἑκάσ-   24
τηι τῶν συνο⟨ι⟩κιζομένων· γινομένοις θ' ὑμῖν εἴς τε τὸν
ἀδελφὸν καὶ καθόλου τὸν οἶκον ἡμῶν οἵους καθήκει
[κα]ὶ τῶν ἀπαντω[μ]ένων εὐεργεσιῶν μεμνημένοις
[εὐ]χαρίστως πειράσομαι καὶ ἄλλα ἃ ἂν ἐπινοῶ συν-   28
[κα]τασκευάζειν, παντὶ τρόπωι συνεκτρέχειν προ-
[αιρου]μένη τῇ τοῦ ἀδελφοῦ θελήσει· κατανοῶ γὰρ αὐ-
[τὸν λ]ίαν ἐκτενῶς ἔχοντα πρὸς τὴν ἐπανόρθωσιν
[τῆς] πόλεως. vac. ἔρρωσθε. vac.   32

1–3 Originally, three lines stood at the start of the document; traces of the letters make the following text certain: ἐπὶ στεφανηφόρου Κυδίο[υ τοῦ] Ἱεροκλείου[ς]· | Ε[λ]α[φ]ηβ[ολιῶνος]· | ἐπιστολὴ παρὰ βασιλίσσ[ης Λα]οδίκη[ς]. The same stonecutter erased these three lines and recarved the text, omitting line 3, the archival notice that this was a letter from Laodike; the stonecutter started one line lower (line 2 of the original layout). The treatment by Nafissi 2001 supersedes earlier treatment of these lines (ed. pr., Roberts *BE* 71, 621, p. 506; Blümel, Mastrocinque 1995).   24 πλέον *ed. pr.*   27 ἀπαντω[μ]ένων Chr. Habicht, recorded in *BE* 73, 437, for Pugliese-Carratelli's ἀπάντων ἡμῶν. Habicht is now confirmed by Nafissi's reading.   28–9 συν | [κατ]ασκευάζειν Gauthier 1989: 60, paralleled in the letter of Laodike to the Sardians; the restoration is confirmed by Nafissi's reading.

When Kydias son of Hierokles was stephanephoros, (letter . . .)[1] in the month of Elaphebolion.

Queen Laodike to the council and the people of the Iasians, greetings. Having often heard from my brother what urgent help he continually deploys for his friends and allies, and that after recovering your city as it

[1] Erased words.

had fallen into unexpected calamities, he gave back to you your liberty and
your laws, and in the other matters he strives **10** to increase the citizen
body and bring it to a better condition, and making it my own intention to
act in accordance with his zeal and eagerness, and, because of this, to
confer some benefaction on the poor among the citizens, and a general
advantage to the whole people, I have written to Strouthion the *dioiketes*[2]
for him to send along to the city one thousand Attic medimnoi of wheat a
year, for ten years, and hand them over to the representatives of the people;
you will do well, therefore, to order the treasurers to take over the wheat
and sell it **20** in fixed quantities (?),[3] and to order the presidents (*prostatai*),
and all the others whom you think fit, to see that they pay out[4] the income
from the wheat towards the dowries of the daughters of the poor citizens,
giving not more than three hundred Antiocheian drachmai to each of the
women getting married. If you remain as is right in your behaviour
towards my brother and generally towards our house, and if you gratefully
remember the benefactions which you have met with, I shall try to procure
for you the other favours which I can think up, since I make it my
intention in all matters to concur **30** with the will of my brother; for I
notice that he is extremely eagerly disposed towards the reconstruction of
the city. Farewell.

B (Col. I)

[ἐπὶ σ]τεφανηφόρου Κυδίου τοῦ Ἱεροκλείους·
        Ἐλαφηβολιῶνος·
[πρυτ]άνεων ἐκλησίαν συναγαγόντων τριακάδι· ἔδο-   (35)
[ξε] τῶι δήμωι· Μενοίτιος Ἱεροκλείους ἐπεστάτει· πρυ-   4
[τάν]εων γνώμη Ἑρμοκράτου τοῦ Θεοδότου, Ἀστιάδου
[τοῦ] Ἑκατωνύμου, Ἑρμίου τοῦ Ἀρτεμιδώρου, Ἑκαταίου τοῦ Δι-
[οπε]ίθου, Μενοιτίου τοῦ Ἱεροκλείους, Μενοιτίου τοῦ Με-
[νε]δήμου, Πινδάρου τοῦ Σωπάτρου δι' ἐπιτρόπου Διονυ-   8 (40)
[σίο]υ τοῦ Μενεκλείους· ἐπειδὴ βασιλέως μεγάλου Ἀντιό-
[χο]υ προγονικὴν αἵρεσιν διατηροῦντος εἰς πάντας
[το]ὺς Ἕλληνας καὶ τοῖς μὲν τὴν εἰρήνην παρέχοντος,
[πο]λλοῖς δὲ ἐπταικόσιν βοηθοῦντος καὶ ἰδίαι καὶ κοινῆι,   12
[τι]νὰς δὲ ἀντὶ δούλων ἐλευθέρους πεποιηκότες καὶ τὸ   (45)

---

[2] Wörrle (1988: 466 n. 213) points out that this is unlikely to be a private bailiff of
Laodike III (Blümel), since the bailiff of Laodike I is called ὁ οἰκονομῶν τὰ Λαοδίκης (*RC*
18, lines 24–25).
[3] Blümel suggests 'at a fixed price'; in the present translation I follow Wörrle 1988:
467 n. 219. The effect in the first case would be to provide cheap grain; in the second
case, to avoid sudden changes in the price of grain. The first seems in agreement with
the purpose of social aid, the second might be more suited for the general aim of social
harmony.
[4] Or 'deposit' (Austin), to be invested to produce revenue for the future brides; on
this solution, Laodike allowed the Iasians to decide how to invest the revenue, and when
to give out dowries from the return on the investments. The translation given in the
main text is the one I feel is implied by the specification that no individual dowry is to
exceed 300 drachmai: this sounds like a rule applying to the immediate distribution of
the profit from the grain-sale.

[κα]θ' ὅλον τὸ βασιλεύειν νενομικότος πρὸς εὐεργεσία[ν]
[. . .]σθαι ἀνθρώπων, τὴν δὲ ἡμετέραν πόλιν πρότερό[ν]
[τε] ἐγ δουλείας ῥυσάμενος ἐποίησεν ἐλευθέρα[ν   ]
[ ]το[ὺς φ]ρουροῦντας στρατιώτας καὶ τὰς [   ]
κατεστησ[εν] ἡμᾶς κυρίους τ[   ]   (50)

6–7 Διι[οπε]ίθου Blümel.   18. ατεσανσ.. Garlan

B (Col. II)
Ἀριστολοχ[τῶι βασι]-
λεῖ διαλεξο[μένους   ]
μον ἀξίως δὲ . . [   ]   (65)
ως εἰς τὴν πόλιν δ[ἐπῃνῆσθαι]   4
βασιλέα μέγαν Ἀντίο[χον   ]
γέγονεν καὶ φύλαξ καὶ τ.[οἱ δὲ στρατηγοὶ]
οἱ ἐξιόντες ἐκ τῆς ἀρχῆς .[καθ' ἕκασ]-
τον ἐνιαυτὸν τὰς κλεῖδας π[αραδιδότωσαν τοῖς]   8 (70
μεθ' ἑαυτοὺς στρατηγοῖς τ[παρὰ τὸν βω]-
μὸν ὃν ἱδρύσατο ὁ δῆμος βασ[ιλέως μεγάλου Ἀντιό]-
χου, οἱ δὲ εἰσιόντες εἰς τὴν ἀρ[χὴν θυέτωσαν ἐπὶ τοῦ]
βωμοῦ τῶι τε βασιλεῖ καὶ τοῖς α[κοι]-   12
νοῖς τῆς πόλεως θεοῖς ουτ[   ]   (75)
τὰς κλεῖδας· ἐπηνῆσθα[ι] δὲ κ[αὶ τὴν ἀδελφὴν αὐτοῦ βα]-
σίλισσαν Λαοδίκην· καὶ ἵνα εὔ[χαριστοῦσα ἡ πόλις μη]-
θὲν ἐλλείπῃ τιμῆς πρὸς τ[οὺς ἑαυτὴν εὐεργετοῦν]-   16
τας τὰ μέγιστα, αἱρείσθω κα[θ' ἕκαστον ἐ]νια[υτὸν ἱέρειαν]
παρθένον βασιλίσσης Ἀφρο[δίτης Λα]οδίκης· [ἐν δὲ]   (80)
ταῖς ἐξόδοις ἐχέτω στρό[φιον μεσ]όλευκο[ν· καὶ αὐ]-
τῆι μὴ ἐξέστω δὶς ἱερητεῦ[σαι .πεμπ]έτ[ω δὲ πομ]-   20
πὴν ἐν τῶι μηνὶ τῶι Ἀφροδι[σιῶνι τῆι   ]
ἐν ἧι γέγονεν ἡμέραι ἡ βασίλι[σσα Λαοδίκη παρα]-
γινέσθωσαν πάντες εν[ἔτι δὲ οἱ γα]-   (85)
μοῦντες καὶ αἱ γαμούμενα[ι ἅμα μετὰ τὴν τῶν γάμων σύν]-   24
ερξιν θυέτωσαν βασιλίσσ[ηι Ἀφροδίτηι Λαοδίκηι κατὰ δύ]-
ναμιν ἕκαστοι ὃ ἂν π[βα]-
σιλίσσης συνπομπ[ευέτωσαν   ]
αἱ ἱέρειαι πᾶσαι καὶ αἱ [παρθένοι αἱ μέλλουσαι γα]-   28
μεῖσθαι ἐν τῶι [   ]
δὲ καὶ ἀπαρ[χ   ἡμέ]-
ραι στεφ[αν   ]
ποιου[μεν   ]   32
δε[   ]   (95)
ποτ[γη]-
ραιο[   ]
ηι δυ[   ]   36
ου γιν[   ]
ἡμερα[   ]   (100)

τα χρη[   ]
γηναιχ[   ]   40
γαμου[   ]
κηεσ[   ]
γρα[   ]   (105)
θε[   ]   44

and a further fragment, belonging to this decree:

[   ]ἐν δὲ τῆι πομπ[ῆι   ]
[ἱ]εροκῦρυξ κ[   ]
[μ]ηνὸς [   ]
[   ]αυτ[   ]   4

   1–4 At line 1, Pugliese-Carratelli identifies Aristolochos as a Seleukid official (attested in *RC* 45); he is more likely one of several Iasian ambassadors sent to the king. The parallel can be found in the first Teian decree, lines 31–2, καὶ τοῦ δήμου ἀποστίλαν-τος πρεσβευτὰς Διονύσιον Ἀπολλο[. . .] κτλ. It is then likely that this line still belongs to the considerations of the decree, with the mention of an embassy sent to the king. The lost lines might have described Antiochos' favourable answer to this embassy, or perhaps Laodike's assistance to the envoys. Somewhere in line 3, there must have started a short hortative clause,—ἵνα οὖν ὁ δῆμος . . .—immediately before the first decision, to praise Antiochos, [ἐπηνῆσθαι] βασιλέα μέγαν Ἀντίοχον.   3 διεδε[   ] Pugliese-Carratelli, but the photograph rather countenances ΔΕ followed by two uncertain letters, the first of which possibly a triangular letter. (I owe this observation to C. Crowther.)   4 I have inserted [ἐπηνῆσθαι] on the basis of the parallel with line 14.   5–6 One might restore a διότι in line 5 to govern the γέγονε of line 6, '[because] he has proved himself the . . . and the guardian . . .'   6 [οἱ στρατηγοί] Blümel, to which I have added the δέ, to distinguish this series of resolutions from the previous section.   12–13 τοῖς α[ὐτοῦ προγόνοις ὡς κοι]νοῖς τῆς πόλεως θεοῖς *BE* 71, 621, p. 504; Blümel suggests [καὶ τοῖς κοι]νοῖς θεοῖς; convincing arguments against by Ph. Gauthier and G. Rougemont in *BE* 87, 18 (line length). But Nafissi 2001, 123–7, writes that the space next to the *alpha* is not compatible with this restoration. He proposes τοῖς ἄ[λλοις πᾶσιν κοι]νοῖς τῆς πόλεως θεοῖς.   14–23 Text, restorations from Nafissi 2001. At lines 15–16, the meaning must be right; one could imagine ὁ δῆμος instead of ἡ πόλις, differences which matter but cannot be resolved.   20 ἱερετεῦ[σαι] D. Feissel, recorded *BE* 72, 423.   21 *MHN* Pugliese-Carratelli.   23 ἐν [ἐσθῆσι λαμπραῖς ?] Nafissi   25 I have added 'Aphrodite' in the title of the queen, though this might not leave enough space for indications about the sacrificial victim.   29–31 Nafissi 2001 restores, tentatively, [αἱ] δὲ καί ἀπαρ[χέσθωσαν αὐτῆι τῆς κόμης· ταύτηι δὲ τῆι ἡμέ]ραι στεφα[νεφορείτωσαν πάντες οἱ πολῖται].

B (Col. I)
When Kydias, son of Hierokles was *stephanephoros*, in the month of Elaphebolion. The *prytaneis* having summoned the assembly on the thirtieth, it seemed good to the people;—Menoitios son of Hierokles was president of the *prytaneis* (*epistates*); proposal of the *prytaneis*, Hermokrates, son of Theodotos, Astiades son of Hekatomnos, Hermias son of Artemidoros, Hekataios son of Di[ope]ithes, Menoitios son of Hierokles, Menoitios son of Menedemos, Pindaros son of Sopatros, through his guardian Dionysios son of Menekles;—since, the Great King Antiochos **10**—maintaining his ancestral disposition towards all the Greeks, and bringing peace to some, helping individually and in common

many others who have met with troubles, making some men free instead of slaves, and believing that the whole of the exercise of kingship is . . . towards the benefaction of men,—earlier rescued our city out of slavery and made it free . . . the soldiers in garrison . . . he made us masters . . .

B (Col. II)

Aristoloch[. . .] to speak with the king . . . worthily . . . towards the city . . . [(it seemed good) to praise] the Great King Antiochos [. . . because] he has proved the [. . .] and the guardian and . . . let [the *strategoi*] who leave office each year p[ass on] the keys . . . to the *strategoi* who come after them . . . [next to the] **10** altar which the people has built to the Great King Antiochos, and let those who enter office [sacrifice upon the] altar to the king and to [. . . com]mon gods of the city . . . the keys; and to praise . . . queen Laodike;—and so that the [city, being full of gratitude], should not omit anything in regard to honours for those who have [given us benefactions] to the greatest extent,—let [(the people)] elect [each year] a maiden [as priestess] of queen Aphro[dite La]odike; in the formal processions let her wear a headband of mingled white; let it not be **20** possible for the same to be priestess twice . . . make procession on the [. . . day of] Aphrodision, on which day Queen Laodike was born, and let all the . . . be present [and let the men who] are about to wed and the women who are about to wed, [after the completion of the wedding] sacrifice to Queen [Aphrodite Laodike . . . according to] their means, each one . . . of the queen; let . . . all the priestesses and the [maidens about to wed] all take part in the procession . . . first fruits offering . . . **30** crown . . . (the remainder of the text is too fragmentary for significant translation)

(another fragment)

. . . in the procession . . . sacred herald . . . in the month . . .

Commentary. Both texts are preserved on a marble stele and smaller fragments, discovered at Iasos, reused in a late antique building located in the precinct of the temple of Artemis.

Blümel, in *I. Iasos*, 23 and 26 (on his line 79, here B II 16) dates this inscription between 195 and 193, on the basis of two arguments. Firstly, Liv. 34.32.5 (*I. Iasos* T 22), where Flamininus mentions, in the future tense, the withdrawal of Antigonid garrisons from Iasos and Bargylia, in 195; therefore, Iasos was taken over by Antiochos III only after that date. Secondly, line B II 16 (line 79 Blümel) mentions a priestess of Laodike, whereas the royal *prostagma* of 193 creates the office of 'high-priestess' of Laodike; therefore, according to Blümel, the Iasian documents were produced before this date, presumably on the grounds that the high-priestess would have superseded the priestess of Laodike at Iasos.

However, Liv. 34.32.5 is not a statement (as Blümel misleadingly prints the passage), but a rhetorical question addressed by Flamininus to Nabis: *an ut ab Iaso et Bargyliis praesidia Philippi deducantur curae erit nobis, Argos et Lacedaemon, duas clarissimas urbes, lumina quondam Graeciae, sub pedibus tuis relinquemus?* The future tense *erit* occurs by attraction to *relinquemus*, and the whole sentence can be translated 'after having taken care that Iasos and Bargylia be evacuated by the garrisons of Philip, shall we leave Argos and Sparta under your feet?' Bargylia had already been freed by P. Cornelius Lentulus in 196 (Pol. 18.12.1); when Lentulus appears in Lysimacheia in late 196, there is no hint that his mission has not been successful (Pol. 18.50.2), and the matter is heard of no more. That Lentulus was sent to liberate Bargylia only suggests that Iasos had already been taken over by Antiochos, presumably without the knowledge of the Senate, since it included Iasos among the cities which Philip was to evacuate (Pol. 18.44.4), along with Euromos, which we now know for certain contracted an alliance with Antiochos in 197. The correct *terminus post quem* is therefore 197. Once Blümel's late *terminus post quem* of 195 has been removed, the letter of Laodike and the Iasian decree must be dated some time[5] after the Seleukid takeover, perhaps 196 or 195; Crowther proposed (*c.*) 196/5 as most likely.[6] As for the *terminus ante quem*, proposed by Blümel, one should merely observe that the royal *prostagma* creates a high priesthood of Laodike in the context of the central, 'imperial' ruler cult, which has no influence on the 'municipal' ruler cult, administered by the city within its own boundaries; nor does the state cult have any bearing on the matter of dating the Iasian documents. In fact the only applicable indication is the fact that Laodike's letter was written before her disgrace, which preceded Antiochos' marriage to a young woman from Chalkis in 192.[7]

See Ch. 4 §§ 2*a* (for an analysis of the language of benefaction in this document) and 3 (on local Iasian perspectives).

27. Decree of Iasian Tribe Concerning Rituals for Antiochos III and his Family (c.196)

D. Levi and G. Pugliese-Carratelli, *ASAA* 23/24 (1961/2), 578, no. 5 (*I. Iasos* 5). Read once by the editors in poor light, before the stone was lost.

Cf. L. Robert, *OMS* iii. 1503, for commentary and text; J. and L. Robert, *BE* 71, 621, p. 508.

αι τὴν σπονδοφ[ορίαν   c.16   ]
ἐπεύχεσθαι δὲ τοὺς φυλέτας [πάντα γίν]-
εσθαι τἀγαθὰ βασιλεῖ τε μεγάλωι Ἀ[ντιόχωι]
καὶ βασιλίσσηι Λαοδίκηι καὶ τοῖς τ[έκνοις]   4
καὶ τῆι πόλει· ἀναγράψαι δὲ καὶ τὸ [ψήφισμα τό]-

---

[5] As pointed out by the Roberts in *BE* 71, 621, p. 509; L. Migeotte, *Chiron* 23 (1990), 276 confirms this view by drawing attention to the fact that the Iasians already have an altar to Antiochos III by the time of their decree for Laodike (276–7 on the date of the Iasian documents generally).

[6] *BICS* 37 (1990), 144–5; also *Chiron* 25 (1995), 227 (discussing his dating against Migeotte, *Chiron* 23 (1990), 276 and n. 24).

[7] Robert 1949: 25–9; Aymard 1949 (arguing for divorce rather than mere disgrace, as part of a wider dynastic crisis in 193).

δε ἐν τῶι ἐπιφανεστάτωι τόπω[ι c.9   ἵ]-
να ἥ τε τοῦ βασιλέως εὔνοια [c.11   ]
καὶ ἡ τῆς φυλῆς ὑπὲρ τῆς π[όλεως εὐχαριστία]   8
ἀείμνηστος διαμένηι τ[c.15   ]
βωμοῦ ἵνα τῶι τε μεγέ[θει   c.9   κατα]-
σκευασθῆι πρὸς γ[c.19   ]
ληιδος· ὁμοίω[ς δὲ καὶ   c.14   ψηφ]-   12
ίσματος γ[c.22   τὸ δέ]
ἀνάλω[μα δοῦναι   c.20   ]
ονγ[c.29

The line length appears to be 30–33 letters, from lines 3, 4, 8 (taking *iota* as worth half a full letter space).   2 The restoration (Levi, Pugliese-Carratelli) about fills the gap at 29 letters. πάντας is also possible.   4 τοῖς τ[έκνοις αὐτῶν] Levi, Pugliese-Carratelli, on the parallel of document **28**, line 13. But the restoration is too long. 7 τε Robert, for the editors' γε.   10 μεγέ[θει] Levi and Pugliese-Carratelli; με[γάλου βασιλέως] or με[γίστωι Διί] Robert, tentatively, though neither is compelling. 10–11 The verb restored by Robert.   11 Perhaps πρὸς τ[ ], 'towards t[he . . .]'? 11–12 [βασι]ληιδός Levi and Pugliese-Carratelli; rejected by Robert, who suggests a tribe name, e.g. [Ἡρακ]ληίδος.

the offering of libations . . . (it seemed good) also to have the members of the tribe offer public prayers . . . [for all] advantages to happen to the Great King Antiochos and to Queen Laodike and to their children and to their city; to write up this [decree] on the most eminent place . . .;—so that the goodwill of the king . . . and the [gratitude] of the tribe on behalf of the city should remain remembered for ever, [. . . of the] **10** altar; and so that . . . be erected to . . . [of the tribe (?)—]leis . . .; and likewise, . . . [a copy of?] the decree . . . give out the money for the expenditure . . .

Commentary. The stele was discovered at Iasos, out of its original context (probably reused, near a later building by the east gate of the city) and is now lost.

See Ch. 4 §§ 3*b* (on ruler cult), and 4 (on the form of the public prayers)

28. *Decree of the Iasians in Honour of Antiochos III and his Family* (*c.196*)

GIBM 442 (*OGIS* 237)

Cf. *BE* 71, 621, pp. 507–8 (the Roberts suggest that *OGIS* 237 belonged to the Iasian decree, document **26** B); Crowther 1989 (the Roberts' suggestion is physically impossible, and the script is different; the inscription is about the resort to foreign judges, upon the recommendation of Antiochos and Apollo). Photograph: plates volume to *CAH*[2] vii. 1, no. 40, with commentary by S. Sherwin-White (p. 36). I examined the two squeezes on view on the web-site of the Centre for the Study of Ancient Documents, Oxford University (http://www.csad.ox.ac.uk).

[τὴν δημοκρ]α[τ]ίαν καὶ αὐτονομίαν διαφυλάσσειν, γέγ[ρα]-
[φε] πλεονάκις τῶι δήμωι περὶ τούτων, ἀκόλουθα πράσσων
τῆι διὰ πατέρων ὑπαρχούσηι αὐτῶι πρὸς τοὺς Ἕλληνας
εὐεργεσίαι, ὅ τε θεὸς ὁ ἀρχηγέτης τοῦ γένους τῶμ   4
βασιλέων συνεγμεμαρτύρηκεν τῶι βασιλεῖ παρακα-
λῶν μεθ' ὁμονοίας πολιτεύεσθαι, ὁ δὲ δῆμος ἔχων
ταύτην τὴν αἵρεσιν πολύ τι μᾶλλον μεθ' ὁμονοίας πολιτευόμενος τὰ μέγιστα ἀγαθὰ παρειληφὼς παρὰ τοῦ   8
βασιλέως ταῦτα διατηρεῖ· ἵνα δὲ φανερὸν γένηται τῶι τε
βασιλεῖ καὶ τοῖς ἄλλοις πᾶσιν, ἣν ἔχει διάληψιν ὁ δῆμος
πρῶτομ μὲν ὑπὲρ βασιλέως μεγάλου Ἀντιόχου καὶ
βασιλίσσης Λαοδίκης καὶ τῶν τέκνων αὐτῶν, εἶ[τ]εν   12

12 εἶ[τ]εν Dittenberger, partly out of the context (answering the πρῶτομ μέν) and
partly interpreting the remains of the first three letters.

. . . (since) . . . to preserve the [democr]acy and the autonomy, he wrote
often to the people concerning these matters, acting in accordance with the
propensity to benefactions for the Greeks which is his through his fathers,
and the god who is the origin of the race of the kings bore testimony to
support the king, calling upon us to live harmoniously in the city; the
people, now being so disposed to a much greater degree, and hence living
harmoniously in the city, having received the greatest favours from the 10
king, keeps these—so that it should become clear to the king and to all the
others what opinion the people has, firstly, in favour of the Great King
Antiochos, Queen Laodike and their children, secondly . . .

Commentary. The text is borne by an architectural block, with *anathyrosis*
(Crowther 1989: 137, for physical description of the stone), taken from
Iasos ('from the wall of a bath from the Byzantine period', according to
Hicks) and given to the British Museum by the Duke of St Albans.

Lines 1–10 are obviously part of the liminary ἐπειδή clause, 10–13 are
the 'hortative' clause which immediately precedes the now lost decision
formulas (ἀγαθῆι τύχηι, δέδοχθαι κτλ.)

At line 12, the εἶ[τ]εν preceded a second group, also concerned by the
Iasians' display of feeling. The king's Friends, or his δυνάμεις? Another
possibility would be to restore the name of a city which had sent arbitra-
tors to Iasos, under the sponsorship of Antiochos III (Crowther 1995*b*);
the decree would then honour this city, whilst paying sufficient homage to
the royal involvement in the project (a parallel could be found in *Syll.* 426,
a decree of Bargylia for a Teian arbitrator: the Bargylietans nonetheless
take care to praise Antiochos II and his minister, Alexandros, and to let
them know).

See Ch. 4, introduction (on royally-sponsored foreign judges) and § 3
(on local perspectives at Iasos).

29. *Agreement between Zeuxis and the Philippeis/Euromians Concerning their Alliance with Antiochos III (August/September 197)*

Errington 1986, *editio princeps* with textual and historical commentary; photograph (*SEG* 36.973).

Cf. Gauthier, *BE* 87, 294; Descat 1997 (on an Euromian attested at Theangela as a 'Philippeus').

Βασιλευόντων Ἀντιόχου καὶ Ἀντιόχου
τοῦ υἱοῦ ε ι καὶ ρ̄ Γορπιαίου· ἐπὶ τοῖσδε
συνέθεντο Ζεῦξίς τε ὁ ἀπολελειμμένος ὑ-
πὸ τοῦ βασιλέως Ἀντιόχου ἐπὶ τῶν ἐπιτάδε   4
τοῦ Ταύρου πραγμάτων καὶ Φιλιππεῖς διὰ τῶν
ἀποσταλέντωμ πρεσβευτῶμ παρὰ τῆς πόλεως Ἀνδρονόμου, Σωτάδου, Ἀντιόχου, Χένωνος, ἐ-
φ' ὧι ἔσονται Φιλιππεῖς φίλοι καὶ σύμμαχοι Ἀντιό-   8
[χ]ου τε τοῦ βασιλέως καὶ τῶν ἐκγόνων αὐτοῦ
[κ]αὶ συντηρήσουσιν τήν τε φιλίαγ καὶ συμμαχί-
[αν] εἰς ἅπαντα τὸγ χρόνον ἀδόλως καὶ ἀπ[ρο]φ[ασί]-
[στως   ]   12

7 Gauthier, *BE* 87, 294 points out that the text mentions four ambassadors and not two with patronymics (Errington). The name Χένων is puzzling (Gauthier): the closest parallels seem to be Cretan (*Iscr. Cret.* 1, p. 142 no. 31: Chenos, at Lato; *IG* 12.9.839: Chenon, at Dreros), so the name may support the idea of Cretan influence on Euromos, as ventured by Errington 1993 (see next document). I owe thanks to E. Matthews for assistance with this note.   11 is now damaged; the present reading is R. Harper's, reported by Errington.

When Antiochos and Antiochos the son were kings, in the hundred and fifteenth year, in the month of Gorpiaios. These were the terms of the agreement struck by Zeuxis, the official left in charge of affairs on this side of the Taurus, and the Philippeis through the ambassadors sent forth by the city, Andronomos, Sotades, Antiochos, Chenon, upon which terms the Philippeis will be friends and allies of Antiochos the king and his descendants, **10** and will observe friendship and alliance for all times without deception nor pretence . . .

Commentary. The text, found during clearing and restoration operations at the (Hadrianic) temple of Zeus Lepsynos at Euromos, is located at the very top of a pilaster from the corner of a building—probably the older temple of Zeus Lepsynos (Rumscheid 1994: cat. no. 62; also autopsy in September 1995 of the block, now in the garden of the Milâs Müzesi). By the shape of the stone and the pattern of *anathyrosis*, it is possible to determine that the text did not figure on an *anta*, but on a corner block from the rear of the building (the rear right hand corner if standing in front of the temple entrance).

30. *Decree of the Euromians on Constitutional Matters (after 197)*

Errington 1993: 24–7, no. 5 (*SEG* 43.707).

Cf. Gauthier, in *BE* 95, 525, for criticism and textual contributions.

The text (inscribed on the same stone as document **29**) comes in two columns; the first (of which the greater part is broken off) is too mutilated for any extended text to be published, and the editor recognised exactly four phrases: ἡμεῖς, κοσμοῖς, τῆς πόl[λεως], [τοῦ Διὸς] τοῦ Λεψύl[νου].[1] The second column contains the text below.

[   ] ταῖς ἀρχαιρεσίαις πρώτους κόσμους τρεῖς, μετὰ δὲ
[τούτους] προστάτας τοῦ δήμου γ', τὴν δὲ αἵρεσιν εἶναι τῶν ἀρχείων
τούτωμ πρὸς μέρος ἀπὸ τῶμ φυλῶν, ἐπιτετάχθαι δὲ τοῖς μὲγ κόσ-
μοις ὅσα πρὸς τὴν τῆς πόλεως καὶ τῆς χώρας φυλακὴν ἀνήκει καὶ   4
τὰς κλεῖδας παραδίδοσθαι τούτοις, εἶναι δὲ πρὸς τούτους καὶ τὴν
τῶμ φρουρίων ἐπιμέλειαγ καὶ τὰ κατὰ τὰς στρατείας καὶ ὅσα κατὰ
τὴν συνθήκην τὴμ περὶ τῆς συμμαχίας τῆς συντεθειμένης
πρὸς βασιλέα μέγαν Ἀντίοχον διὰ Ζεύξιδος, μὴ εἶναι δὲ ἄλλο ἀρχεῖ-   8
ον μηθὲν κυριώτερον τούτου πλὴν τῆς βουλῆς μηδὲ τετάχθαι
τούτους ὑπ' ἄλλομ μηθένα, τοῖς δὲ προστάταις τὰ κατὰ τοὺς χρημα-
τισμοὺς ἐπιτετάχθαι καὶ εἴ τι ἄλλο ἐν τοῖς νόμοις διατέτακται,
γράμματα δὲ ἄμ που δέηι πέμπεσθαι ὑπὲρ τῆς πόλεως ἢ ὑπὲρ ἄλλου   12
τινὸς διὰ τῶν ἀρχείων τούτων, ἐξαποστελλέσθω γραφόμενα ἐ-
[πί τε] τῶγ κόσμων καὶ τῶμ προστάτωμ, μὴ ἐξουσία δὲ ἔστω μηδὲ ὁ-
[ποτέρωι] τῶν ἀρχείων τούτων καθ' ἰδίαν γράμματα πέμπειν, μὴ
[   ]τα ἀρχεῖα αἱρεῖσθαι πρὸς μέρος ἀπὸ τῶμ φυλῶν   16
[αἱρεῖσθαι δὲ καθ' ἕ]καστον ἐνιαυτὸν ἐν ἀρχαιρεσίαις πρὸς μέρος
[ἀπὸ τῶμ φυλῶν τὸν στ]εφανή[φορον καὶ ἱερέ]α τοῦ Διὸς τοῦ Κρηταγε-
[νέτα (?) καὶ Δικτύννης (?)   ] ὑπὸ [   ]ου καὶ

12–15 Gauthier, for lines 14–15, restores ὁ l[ποτέρωι] τῶν ἀρχείων τούτων, 'let it not be allowed to either of these magistracies to send letters separately'.   13–14 ἔ[κ τού]τωγ κόσμων . . . ο l ὐθενὶ πλὴν] Errington. Present restorations from Gauthier. 15–16 μη l [δὲ δὶς τὰ αὐ]τὰ ἀρχεῖα κτλ. Gauthier.   18–19 I have restored τοῦ Διὸς τοῦ Κρηταγε[νέτα] (Zeus Kretagenetas), as found on the Amyzonian documents, rather than 'Zeus Kretagenes', as found in Mylasa (*I. Mylasa* 102, line 9; 107, line 1; 806, line 8), where the office is different, a priesthood of 'Zeus Kretagenes and the Kouretai'.

[(it seemed good) . . .] to choose, in the elections for office, first three *kosmoi*, and after these, three *prostatai tou demou*, and to elect these magistrates from the tribes in turn; and to entrust to the *kosmoi* all matters concerning the security of the city and the territory, and to hand over the keys to them, and to entrust to them the care for the forts and the business concerning military expeditions and all matters related to the agreement pertaining to the alliance contracted through Zeuxis with the Great King Antiochos; to allow no magistracy to have more authority than this one,

[1] ΤΗΣ ΠΟ- at the end of line 8, ΛΕΨΥ at the end of line 10, as can be read on the photograph, rather than the editor's πό[λεως], Λεψύ[νου]. I am grateful to W. Blümel for a squeeze of this part of the stone. From this squeeze, further phrases which I tentatively suggest are [ἵν]α γίνη l [ται], line 9, and φύλη, line 11.

except the *boule*, and to subordinate **10** these magistrates to no one else; to entrust to the *prostatai* the matters concerning the official documents[2] and whatever else is stipulated in the laws; and if letters must be sent by these magistrates concerning the city or any other matter, let there be sent a letter written in the presence of both the *kosmoi* and the *prostatai,* and let it not be allowed for [either] of these magistrates to send a letter on his own, . . . to elect magistrates from the tribes in turn . . . during the year? in the elections for office, in turn [from the tribes, (to elect)] the *stephanephoros* and priest of Zeus Kretage[netas (?) and Diktynna (?) . . .]

Commentary. The text is on another face of the corner block which bears the previous text (alliance between Antiochos III and Euromos); from the temple of Zeus Lepsynos at Euromos.

31. *Letters of Antiochos III and Zeuxis to the Herakleians (between 196 and 193)*

Wörrle 1988, *editio princeps* with extensive commentary (chronology, context, and content) and photographs (*SEG* 37.859; Bringmann and von Steuben 1995: no. 296, with translation and commentary). (Wörrle's text supersedes S. Şahin in *EA* 9 (1987), 55–60, a preliminary and controversial publication).

Cf. Ph. Gauthier, *BE* 89, 277; Errington 1989*a* (on dating: see commentary).

The inscription stretches over four architectural blocks (from the north *anta* of the temple of Athena), I–IV, each with its own line numbering; it also falls into two documents: A (letter of Antiochos) and B (letter of Zeuxis). I have preserved Wörrle's numbering.

A. Letter of Antiochos.

I

[Λαοδίκ]ην καὶ τὸν υἱὸν Ἀντί[οχον πρὸς τ]αῖς π[αρ']
[ὑμῶν ψηφι]σθείσαις τιμαῖς οἷς διεσαφεῖτε στέφανοις, ὁμοίως δὲ
[στεφανώ]σαιτε καὶ Σέλευκον καὶ Μιθριδάτην τοὺς ἄλλους ἡμῶν υἱ-
[οὺς, οὓ]ς καὶ ἀνενέγκαντες οἱ πρεσβευταὶ ἠσπάσαντό τε ἡμᾶς ὑπὲρ   4
[τοῦ δ]ήμου καὶ τὸ περὶ τῶν τιμῶν ψήφισμα ἀποδόντες διελέχθησαν
[καὶ α]ὐτοὶ περὶ ἑκάστων ἀκολούθως τοῖς κατακεχωρισμένοις. Τάς τε
[δὴ τι]μὰς καὶ τοὺς στεφάνους ἀπεδεξάμεθα φιλανθρώπως καὶ
[ὑμᾶ]ς ἐπαινοῦμεν ἐπὶ τῆι προθυμίαι. Θέλοντες δὲ καὶ κατὰ τὰ λοιπὰ πο-   8
[λυ]ωρεῖν ὑμῶν τά τε ὑπὸ Ζεύξιδος συγχωρηθέντα ὑμῖν κυροῦμεν
[καὶ] πρὸς τῶι ὑποκειμένωι πλήθει εἰς ἐλαιοχρίστιον τοῖς νέοις ἀπο-
[τάσσομεν κα]τ' ἐνιαυτὸν καὶ ἄλλους μετρητὰς τριάκοντα. Τό τε
[ἐσόμενον ἀ]νήλωμα εἰς τὴν ἐπισκευὴν τοῦ ὑδραγωγίου οἰομέ-   12
[θα δεῖν δίδο]σθαι ἐκ βασιλικοῦ ἐφ' ἔτη τρία, καὶ περὶ τούτων γεγράφαμεν
[c.8/9   τ]ῶι διοικητῆι. Ποιουμένους δὲ καὶ εἰς τὸ λοιπὸν διὰ τῶν [ἐρ]-
[γων τὰς προ]σηκούσας ἀποδείξεις τῆς πρὸς τὰ πράγματα ἡμῶ[ν εὐνοίας]

---

[2] Suggested in *BE* 95, 525, p. 525.

14 [Στρουθίωνι τ]ῶι διοικητῆι would fit the lacuna: Strouthion is the *dioiketes* named, around the same period, in Laodike's letter to the Iasians: document **26** A, I 15–16.

II

ΑΒΑΣΙΛΙ

[ὑπ]ὲρ αὐτῶν δὲ τούτων ἀκο[ύσεσθε ἐκ τ]ῶν πρεσβευτῶν. Ἔρρωσ[θε].

I. [(e.g. your ambassadors have handed over the decree, according to which you wished to honour) . . . Laodik]e and our son, Anti[ochos, in addition to] the honours decreed [by you], with the crowns which you have mentioned, and that you also crowned our other sons, Seleukos and Mithridates; your ambassadors, after handing over these crowns, greeted us in the name of the people, and after handing over the decree concerning the honours, and spoke in person concerning each of these matters, in accordance with the content of the decree. We have acknowledged the honours and the crowns with pleasure, and we praise you for your eagerness. Since we wish to show solicitude for you in the future, we confirm the grants made by Zeuxis to you, and, **10** on top of the monies set aside for the oil-anointment of the young men, we assign thirty additional *metretai* a year. As for the expense to be incurred in the repair and maintenance[1] of the water conduits, we think it right that it should be granted from the royal chest, over three years, and we have written about these matters to . . . the *dioiketes*. If in the future too, you make through your [actions] the appropriate displays of your goodwill towards our affairs, . . .
II. Concerning these same things, you will hear from the ambassadors. Farewell.

B. Letter of Zeuxis
II (continued)
vacat
Ἐπὶ στεφανηφόρου θεοῦ τρίτου τοῦ μετὰ Δημήτριον Δημητρίου, Ἡραιῶνο[ς].
Ζεῦξις Ἡρακλεωτῶν τῆι βούληι καὶ τῶι δήμωι χαίρειν. Οἱ παρ' ὑμῶν πρεσβευταὶ 4
Φανίας, Ἑρμίας, Αἰσχρίων, Ἀπολλώνιος, Ἑρμογένης, Ἰάσων, Αἰνέας, Παρ-
μενείδης, Παγκράτης, Διᾶς, Εὔανδρος, Θαργήλιος, Ἑρμίας, Ἀριστέας, Μενεκράτης, Ἡρακλεόδωρος, Διονύσιος, Πρωτέας, Διονυσικλῆς, Ἀντιλέων, Ἱερο-
κλῆς, Μένης, ἀνήνεγκαν τὸ ψήφισμα καθ' ὃ ὤιεσθε δεῖν, ἀνακεκομισμέ- 8
νων ἡμῶν τῶι βασιλεῖ τὴν πόλιν ἐξ ἀρχῆς ὑπάρχουσαν τοῖς προγόνοις αὐτοῦ,
θυσίας τε συντελεσθῆναι τοῖς θεοῖς καὶ τοῖς βασιλεῦσιν καὶ τοῖς τέκνοις αὐτῶν
καὶ εἰς τὸ λοιπὸν ὁμοίως γίνεσθαι κατὰ μῆνα τῆι ἕκτηι ἀπιόντος, αἱρεθῆναι
δὲ καὶ πρεσβευτὰς τοὺς ἐμφανιοῦντας ὑπὲρ τῆς γεγενημένης στενοχω- 12
[ρία]ς περὶ τὴν πόλιν ἐκ τῶν ἐπάνω χρόνων διὰ τοὺς πολέμους καὶ τὰς κα-
[ταφθ]ορὰς καὶ παρακαλέσοντας τά τε ὑπὸ τῶν βασιλέων συγκεχωρημένα
[συνδιατηρηθῆν]αι, ὅπως ὑπάρχῃ καὶ μετὰ ταῦτα ἥ τε ἀνεπισταθμεία καὶ τὰ
[c.16/17   κ]αὶ τὰ τέλη καὶ ἔγγαια καὶ τὰ εἰσαγώγια καὶ ἐξαγώγ[ια] 16
traces of one line

---

[1] Wörrle 1988: 466 n. 209 for the meaning of ἐπισκευή.

III

[πρ]ᾶσις, δίδωται δὲ καὶ ἐκ βασ[ιλικοῦ εἰς χρῆ]σιν τῆς πόλεως μάλιστα {μὲν}
μὲν πλέον, εἰ δὲ μή γε τάλαντα [c.5 ὥ]s πρότερον καὶ τὸ ἐλαιοχρίστιον δ[ι]-
αμένηι τὸ ἀποτεταγμένον τοῖς ν[έοις, ὃ] ἐπεκηρύσσετο τῆι ὠνῆι τοῦ λιμέ-
νος, ἀξιώσοντας δὲ καὶ ἀτέλειαν συγχωρῆσαι τῶν τε ἐκ τῆς γῆς καρπῶν πάν-   4
των καὶ τοῦ ἐννομίου τῶν τε κτηνῶν καὶ τῶν σμηνῶν ἐφ᾽ ἔτη ὅσ᾽ ἂν φαίνηται καὶ ζεύγη τοῖς πολίταις, μνησθησομένους δὲ καὶ ὅπως σῖτος δοθῆ τῆι πό-
[λ]ει δωρεὰν καὶ ἀτέλεια{ν} τοῦ τε εἰσαγομένου εἰς τὴν πόλιν καὶ τοῦ πωλουμένου καὶ ἵνα οἱ ἐξάγοντες ἐκ τῆς τοῦ βασιλέως εἰς τὴν πόλιν ἐπὶ τὰς   8
ἰδίας χρείας καὶ εἰς πρᾶσιν ἀτελεῖς ὦσιν, ἀποκατασταθῆι δὲ ὑμῖν καὶ ἡ χώρα
καὶ οἱ δῆμοι καὶ οἱ οἰκηταὶ συναχθῶσιν καθότι καὶ πρότερον ὑπῆρχον. Καὶ οἱ πρεσβευταὶ περί τε τῶν δεδηλωμένων διελέγησαν ἡμῖν μετὰ σπουδῆς ἀκολούθως
τοῖς ἐν τῶι ψηφίσματι κατακεχωρισμένοις, εὐθέως δὲ καὶ ὑπὲρ τῶν συντεθε[ιμέ]-   12
[ν]ων αὐτοῖς ὑπομνημάτων. Σπεύδοντες οὖν καὶ αὐτοὶ τὸν δῆμον εἰς τὴν ἐξ ἀ[ρ]-
[χῆ]s διάθεσιν ἀποκατασταθῆναι καὶ τά τε ἐπὶ τῶν προγόνων τοῦ βασιλέως
[συγκεχ]ωρημένα συντηρηθῆναι αὐτῶι καὶ ἐν τοῖς ἄλλοις ἐπαύξεσθαι τὴν π[ό]-
[λιν μετέχ]ουσαν πάντων τῶν εἰς πόλεως ἀνηκόντων . . ΟΣ . . ΠΑΝ[   ] 16

IV

    (4 lines of text missing
[εἰ]σαγωγη[   ]
. . . . . . c.11 . . . . . σθε· ἔσται δὲ ἡμῖν ἐπιμελ[ὲς   ]
[c.13   ἀπ]ολύομεν δὲ καὶ το[ῦ [c.11   ]ΝΩΝ . . . ΙΙΩΝ τοὺς [   ] 4
[c.13   κα]θῆκον ἦν λαμβάνεσθαι αὐτὸ, βουλόμενοι καὶ ἐν τούτο[ις
[c.15   ] ἐπιχωροῦμεν δὲ ὑμῖν καὶ τὴν πανήγυριν ἀτελῆ συντελεῖν ὁ[ὕ]-
[τως ὥσπερ] καὶ πρότερον εἰώθειτε ἄγειν, καὶ καθόλου καὶ ἐν τοῖς ἄλλοις φρον-
[τιοῦμεν ἵνα ἐ]μ μηθενὶ τῶν δυνατῶν καὶ καλῶς ἐχόντων ὑστερῆτε, ἀλλὰ τύ-   8
[χητε τῆς προ]σηκούσης ἐπιμελείας. Διὸ καὶ εὖ ποήσετε καὶ αὐτοὶ διαφυλάσ-
[σοντες τὴν εἰς] τὰ πράγματα εὔνοιαν· οὕτω γὰρ πολλῶι μᾶλλον καὶ ἡμεῖς
[οὐδὲν ἐλλείψομε]ν πρ(ο)θυμίας εἰς τὸ συγκατασκευάζειν τ[ὰ πρὸς δ]ό[ξαν]
[καὶ τιμὴν ἀνήκοντα   ]ΤΑ . . φιλανθ[ρωπ   ] 12
[   ]Ο[   ]
                  traces of one line

11 Wörrle's text suggests τ[ὰ πρὸς δ]ό[ξαν καὶ τιμὴν ἀνήκοντα] as in document 34, 6.

When the god was *stephanephoros* for the third time after Demetrios,
son of Demetrios, in the month of Heraion. Zeuxis to the council and
the people of the Herakleians. Your ambassadors, Phanias, Hermias,
Aischrion, Apollonios, Hermogenes, Iason, Aineas, Parmenides,
Pankrates, Dias, Euandros, Thargelios, Hermias, Aristeas, Menekrates,
Herakleodoros, Dionysios, Proteas, Dionysikles, Antileon, Hierokles,
Menes, have handed over the decree according to which you thought it
necessary, after we recovered for the king the city that had originally
belonged to his ancestors, 10 to perform sacrifices the gods and the kings
and their children, and to observe this practice in the future, on the sixth
day before the end of every month; to elect ambassadors who should speak

concerning the poverty[2] which has befallen the city from preceding times, on account of the wars and the destructions, and who should ask that the measures granted by the kings be preserved; namely, that the city should enjoy freedom from billeting and . . . and the taxes and property,[3] and the tolls on imports and exports . . . **III.** farming out, and that out of the royal chest, preferably more, but at least . . . talents be given, as before, and that the sum proclaimed for the farming contract for the harbour tax[4] for the oil-anointment of the young men, stay the same; the ambassadors should also ask for the grant to the citizens of exemption from taxes on all produce of the land and from pasturage dues (*ennomion*) on herds and bees, for as many years and yokes[5] (*zeuge*) as seems appropriate[6]; the ambassadors should also request that grain be given to the city as a gift, and that exemption from taxes be granted to grain[7] imported into the city and sold there, and that those who import from the land of the king into the city, for their own use or for sale, be exempt from taxes, and that the territory be restored to you **10** and that the villages and the dwellers (*oiketai*) be gathered,[8] as they used to be before. The ambassadors spoke to us with zeal concerning the above, in accordance with the content of the decree, and, specifically, concerning the dossiers which had been entrusted to them. Since we too are eager that the people be restored to its original situation, and that the concessions made by the ancestors of the king be preserved for the people, and that the city be increased and partake in all the things which are fitting for the city's . . . **IV.** import . . . we will take care that . . ., of the king, and the territory and . . . we also free you from . . . it was fitting that it be taken, wishing in these matters also . . . we grant you the right to conduct the festival exempt from taxes, as you were accustomed to before, and in all other matters too, we will take complete care that you should not be deprived in any matter of the possible measures that would benefit you, but that you should receive the appropriate attention. Therefore, you will do well, on your part, to preserve your goodwill towards the (king's) affairs, for thus we will all the less leave out anything pertaining to eagerness to

---

[2] Gauthier gives parallels for this widespread meaning of στενοχωρία, preferable here to the strictly etymological 'Landnot' (Wörrle).

[3] Τὰ τέλη καὶ ἔγγαια seems like a fixed expression, 'taxes and unmovable property'.

[4] Wörrle 1988: 461–2 for the explanation of this phrase: the money for oil-anointment was formerly paid for by the tax-farmer who took on the harbour tax.

[5] Wörrle 1988: 464–5, assumes that these 'yokes' are a local measure of land surface. Another possibility is to take the 'yokes' as units of measurement for the herds subject to the *ennomion* (the expression 'yokes' would be appropriate for oxen: Robert 1987: 182–4 for pastures—and hives—in the territory of the city, in the twentieth century as in antiquity).

[6] I have supposed that τοῖς πολίταις is the indirect object of ἀτέλειαν συγχωρῆσαι. The same use of φαίνεσθαι in document **49**.

[7] Wörrle's translation of τοῦ εἰσαγομένου εἰς τὴν πόλιν καὶ τοῦ πωλουμένου, supplying (σίτου). Another possibility is to take the expression as designating all imports and sales in the city, τὸ εἰσαγόμενον καὶ τὸ πωλούμενον.

[8] The verb might designate some form of (re)incorporation into the *polis* of Herakleia, as C. Crowther points out to me.

carry out measures which [have to do with the honour and the repute of the city] . . . privileges (?) . . .

Commentary. The letters come from *anta* blocks of the temple of Athena, near which they were found by A. Peschlow-Bindokat (Wörrle 1988: 421). (They still lie in their findspot, where I saw them in April 1997, close to the edge of the rock on which the temple stands).

The inscription bears a local dating, the third stephanephorate of the god after Demetrios Demetriou. Both letters were issued before the death of Antiochos the son in autumn 193. Wörrle further refines the dating: since Herakleia under Latmos fought on the side of Miletos in the war that opposed the latter to Magnesia on Maeander, and was included in the peace treaty that followed that war, supposedly around 196,[9] Herakleia must have been independent until then, and submission to the Seleukids, and the diplomatic transactions reflected in the two letters, took place after that date.

Wörrle 1988: 431–7, adduces three documents to support this dating (between 196 and 193): (*a*) the treaty between Miletos and Herakleia (*Inschr. Delphinion* 150), dated to 'the fourteenth stephanephorate of the god after Demetrios [in Herakleia]', presumably the same Demetrios Demetriou as the one named in the preamble to the publication of Zeuxis' letter, and to the stephanophorate of Menandros in Miletos; (*b*) the list of Milesian *stephanephoroi, Inschr. Delphinion* 124; (*c*) the treaty between Miletos and Magnesia, dated to 'the stephanephorate of the god after . . . [in Miletos]' (*Inschr. Delphinion* 148, *cf. Syll.* 588). As mentioned, item (*c*) has conventionally been dated to 196; the treaty between Miletos and Herakleia (*a*) dates to at least three years after the end of (*b*) the Milesian *stephanephoroi* list (Wörrle 1988: 432 n. 28). Wörrle identifies the stephanephorate in the treaty between Miletos and Magnesia (*c*) as Apollo after Menalkes, which provides a fixed point within the Milesian stephanephorate list (*b*) and puts its end in 190/89; the earliest date for the treaty between Miletos and Herakleia (*a*) is therefore 186/5. If 186/5 (or after) is the date of 'the fourteenth stephanephorate of the god after Demetrios [presumably Demetrios Demetriou, in Herakleia]', the 'third stephanephorate of the god after Demetrios Demetriou' should fall in 197/6[10] or after.

However, Errington 1989*a* convincingly attributes (*c*) to the late 180s. He still accepts Wörrle's dating scheme, on grounds of general plausibility; but his arguments remove one firm foundation for dating. However, as Errington observes, Wörrle has shown that Rehm's datings for the *stephanephoroi* list (*b*) are too low, and must be moved upwards in time.

---

[9] *Inschr. Delphinion* 148 (cf. *Syll.* 588), with secondary literature noted in Wörrle 1988: 431 n. 25.

[10] Rather than 198/7, as Wörrle 1988: 432 writes ? I assume non-inclusive counting, since these are not regnal years, or years counted from a fixed point: it does not make sense to call the first time the god served as *stephanephoros* 'the second stephanephorate of the god'. If 186/5 is the fourteenth stephanephorate of the god after Demetrios, Demetrios served in 200/199, and the god's third stephanephorate falls in 197/6.

Errington further offers a corroborating argument for Wörrle's datings for the *stephanephoroi* list. We know that Menandros, the Milesian *stephanephoros* in the alliance between Miletos and Herakleia (*a*), was preceded by at least three other *stephanephoroi*, none of which appears in the *stephanephoroi* list (*b*): Pasikles, Philidas, and the god Apollo (*Inschr. Delphinion* 248). Under Pasikles, a treaty between Miletos and Pidasa was contracted (*Inschr. Delphinion* 149). Since this document does not mention the Roman legates who presided over Asian affairs in 188, it should be dated at the earliest to 188/7:

Pasikles	at the earliest 188/7
Philidas	at the earliest 187/6
Apollo	at the earliest 186/5
Menandros	at the earliest 185/4

If the stephanephorate of Menandros at Miletos, and with it the fourteenth stephanephorate of the god after Demetrios at Herakleia, are dated to 185/4 at the earliest, then the letter of Zeuxis to the Herakleians, issued in the third stephanephorate of the god after Demetrios should be dated to the Milesian stephanephorate year (spring) 196–(spring) 195 at the earliest.[11] (Demetrios was *stephanephoros* in 199/8, hence the god's third stephanephorate fell in 196/5).

The majority of Zeuxis' response to the Herakleians' petition is lost, but the fragments seem to correspond to the order of the demands: IV 1 seems to pick up the mention of imported grain in III 7, the phrase 'of the king' could correspond to the request for tax-exemption on imports from the royal territory (III 8), and mention of 'the territory ' (IV 3) can be plausibly linked with the Herakleian petition for 'the restoration of the territory' (III 9–10). In this case, the exemption preserved in IV 4 is an initiative of Zeuxis, in addition to the Herakleian schedule of petitions, as is the grant of *ateleia* for the festival (IV 6–7).

See Ch. 3 §§ 2*b* (on the royal economy) and 3 (on 'repressive tolerance'); Ch. 4 §§ 2*a* (on Zeuxis' answer), 2*b* (on the petition).

32. Decree of the Citizens of Laodikeia on Lykos for Foreign Judges from Priene (between 196 and 190)

GIBM 421 (*Inschr. Priene* no. 59). Crowther 1993: 40–55 (extensive discussion and revision of text, with full justification of all new readings, translation), Gauthier 1994: 179–94 (*SEG* 43.850; *I. Laodikeia am Lykos* 5, drawing on both Crowther and Gauthier, and with very full apparatus).

---

[11] Wörrle 1988: 429–30 and n. 20, suggests that the Herakleian stephanephorate year began in summer, probably at the summer solstice; but I do not see how the document adduced, *Syll.* 633, and specifically lines 74–7, prove this. Contrary to what Wörrle says, the Herakleian *stephanephoros* has not changed between the first month of the Milesian year, Taureon (lines 25–27) and the fifth month of the Milesian year, Metageitnion (lines 74–77): in both passages, the Herakleian *stephanephoros* is the god for the fourteenth time after Demetrios.

Crowther and Gauthier both reached the same revisions of the text with some very minor differences, and their version is taken as the basis here.

Cf. Crowther 1993, who gives a complete archaeology of the text, summarizing the criticisms and improvements of Ad. Wilhelm, *GGA* 162 (1900), 96–7 and U. v. Wilamowitz's important textual notes in E. Sonne, *De arbitris externis quos Graeci adhibuerunt ad lites et intestinas et peregrinas componendas* (Diss. Göttingen 1888), 55 n. 29; Holleaux 1938a: 301–2 (*REA* 1899, 14–15).

$$Τ[ὸ\ παρ]ὰ\ Λαοδικέων$$
traces of four crowns

Κύδωρος Διονυσίου εἶπεν· ἐπειδὴ ἐκ πλ[ε]ίονος [χρόν]ου δικῶν οὐ-
[σ]ῶν ἀδικάστων παρ' ἡμῖν ὁ δῆμος ἔπε[μ]ψε πρεσβείαν πρὸ[s]
Ζεῦξιν περὶ ξενικοῦ δικαστηρίου, Ζεῦξις [δ]ὲ ὑπολαμβ[ά]-   4
[ν]ων μάλιστα προστήσεσθαι τῶγ κατὰ τὰς δίκας [δε]όντως τοὺς πα[ρὰ]
Πριηνέων ἀποσταλησομένους δικαστάς, ἔγρ[αψ]εν αὐτῶν τῆι βο[υ]-
[λ]ῆι καὶ τῶι δήμωι, ὅπως προχειρίσ[ων]ται δικαστὰς τρεῖς ὡς ἐπιει-
κεστάτους καὶ πέμψωσι πρὸς ἡμᾶς· ἀποστείλαντός τε καὶ τοῦ δ[ή]-   8
μου πρὸς αὐτοὺς πρεσβείαν, Πριηνεῖς ὄντες ἡμῶν φίλοι ἔπεμ-
ψαν δικαστὰς Μενίσκον Μητροδώρου, Ἀγίαν Σίμου, Μόλωνα Διαγ[ό]-
ρου, οἳ παραγενόμενοι εἰς τὴμ πόλιν ἐδίκασαν τὰς δίκας δικαί[ως]
κατὰ τοὺς ὑπάρχοντας ἡμῖν νόμους· ἐπεὶ δὲ καλῶς ἔχον ἐσ[τὶ]   12
τιμᾶσθαι τοὺς εὔνους ἄνδρας, τύχηι ἀγαθῆι καὶ ἐπὶ σωτηρίαι· δεδ[ό]-
[χ]θαι τῆι βουλῆι καὶ τῶι δήμωι· Ζεῦξιν μὲν ἐπηνῆσθαι ἐπὶ τῶι γ[ρ]άψα[ι]
[Π]ριηνεῦσιν, Πριηνεῖς δὲ ἐπὶ τῶι πέμψα[ι ἄνδρας κα]λοὺς καὶ ἀγαθούς, τοὺ[s]
δὲ δικαστὰς Μενίσκον Μητροδώρου, Ἀγίαν Σίμου, Μόλωνα Διαγόρου   16
ἐπηνῆσθαί τε καὶ καλεῖσθαι ὑπὸ τοῦ δήμου εἰς τὸ θέατ[ρ]ον καὶ στεφ[α]-
νοῦσθαι ἕκαστον αὐτῶν χρυσῶι στεφάνωι καθ' ἕκαστον ἔτος δι[ὰ]
[β]ίου ἐν τῶι ἀγῶνι τῶι γυμνικῶι τῶι συντελουμένωι ἐν τοῖς Ἀντ⟨ι⟩οχ[εί]-
οις, ἐπηνῆσθαι δὲ καὶ τὸν συναποσταλέντα αὐτοῖς γραμματέα Ἡγ[έ]-   20
πολιν Ἡγίου καὶ στεφανωθῆναι ἐν τοῖς Ἀντιοχείοις ἐλαίας στεφά-
νωι· περὶ δὲ τοῦ καλεῖσθαι εἰς τὴν προεδρίαν τοὺς δικαστὰς ⟨καὶ⟩ τῆς
ἀναγγελίας τῶν στεφάνων ἐπιμέλειαν ποιήσασθαι τόν τε
ἀγωνοθέτην καὶ τοὺς πρυτάνεις τοὺς ἑκάστοτε γινομένους·   24
ὑπάρχειν δὲ τοῖς δικασταῖς καὶ ἐμ πρυτανείωι σίτησιν καὶ ἔφοδον
ἐπὶ τὴν βουλὴν καὶ τὸν δῆμον πρώτοις μετὰ τὰ ἱερά· ἵνα δὲ καὶ ὁ δῆμο[s]
ὁ Πριηνέων εἰδήσηι τὰ ἐψηφισμένα, ἑλέσθαι πρεσβευτήν, ὃς ἀφ[ι]-
κόμενος εἰς Πριήνην τό τε ψήφισμα ἀποδώσει καὶ τὴν τοῦ δήμο[υ]   28
εὔνοιαν ἐμφανίσει, ἣν ἔχει πρὸς Πριηνεῖς, παρακαλέσει τ[ε]
αὐτοὺς ποιήσασθαι τὴν ἀν{αν}αγγελίαν τῶν ἐψηφισμένων στεφάνων τοῖς τε δικασταῖς καὶ τῶι γραμματεῖ
ἐν τῶι ἀγῶνι τῶν Διονυσίων, ὅταν [σ]υν⟨τελῶσιν⟩ τὰς πρώτας υυ   32
σπονδάς, καὶ ἵνα ἀναγραφῆι τὸ ψήφισμα εἰστήλην καὶ σταθῆι
ἐν τῶι ἱερῶι τῆς Ἀθηνᾶς· εἶναι δὲ τὸ ψήφισμα τοῦτο ἐπὶ σω-
τηρίαι τῆς πόλεως· τοὺς δὲ ἐξεταστὰ[s ἀνα]γράψαντας
αὐτὸ εἰς λεύκωμα θεῖναι ἐν τῶι Ἀρ[τέμιδο]ς θησαυρῶ[ι].   36
πρεσβευτὴς Κύδωρος Διονυσίου.

3–4 Hicks read πρό | σευξιν; Hiller von Gaertringer restored προ[έν]τευξις. Crowther and Gauthier for the correct reading. 4 For Ζεῦξις δέ, Hicks in *GIBM* read ποιούμενος. 22 καί at the end of the line added by Crowther; omitted on the stone. 32 Hicks in *GIBM* reads ὅταν συνθυῆται πρὸ πάσης; Crowther 1993: 52–3, reads [.]Υ[.] ΤΑΣΠΡѠΤΑΣ vv; he argues that the first three letters can be restored as [σ]υ[ν], and that the stonecutter omitted the rest of the verb συντελῶσιν. The formula is paralleled in another Prienian inscription, *Inschr. Priene* 83, line 7 (with Crowther 1993: 53 n. 39).

[Decree fro]m the Laodikeians.

Kydoros son of Dionysios proposed:—since, there being over a long period unresolved lawsuits among us, the people sent an embassy to Zeuxis concerning a foreign court, and Zeuxis, believing that the judges who would be sent from the Prienians would take care of the matters concerning the lawsuits most [satisfacto]rily, wrote to their council and their people, so that they should select three judges as fair-minded as possible and send them to us; after the people had also sent an 10 embassy to them, the Prienians, being our friends, sent as judges Meniskos, son of Metrodoros, Agias son of Simos, Molon son of Diagoras, who, after arriving in the city judged the suits justly, according to our laws;—and since it is a finc thing to honour well disposed men—with good luck and for the safety (of the city), let it seem good to the council and the people:— to let Zeu[xis] be praised for writing to the Prienians, and the Prienians for sending [good] and noble men, and to let the judges, Meniskos son of Metrodoros, Agias son of Simos, Molon son of Diagoras, be praised, and invited by the people to the theatre and to let each one of them be crowned with a golden crown, each year, for life, in the gymnic contest organized at the Antiocheia, 20 and to let the secretary sent along with them, Hegepolis son of Hegias, be praised and crowned at the Antiocheia with a crown of olive; to have the agonothete and the *prytaneis* in office on each occasion take care of the invitation of the judges to front seats and the proclamation of the crowns; to provide free dining in the *prytaneion* for the judges and right of access to the council and people in priority after the sacred matters; and so that the people of the Prienians should also know what has been decreed, to choose an ambassador who, after going to Priene, will hand over the decree and make clear the goodwill which the people has towards the Prienians, and invite 30 them to make a proclamation of the crowns decreed for the judges and the secretary, in the Dionysia whenever they per(form) the first libations, and request that the decree be written up on a stele and erected in the sanctuary of Athena; and to let this decree be for the safety of the city; to have the *exetastai*, after writing it up on a whitened board, put it in the treasury of Ar[temis]. Ambassador: Kydoros, son of Dionysios.

Commentary. The decree is preserved on a 'stele of blue marble, from the temple of Athenè Polias, Prienè' (Hicks in *GIBM*).

It is likely that Priene, the recipient of a letter of instructions from Zeuxis, was under Seleukid control; the date for this document would then fall after 197, the most probable date for a Seleukid takeover. However, it is still possible that Zeuxis wrote to Priene when the city was independent:

in that case, the document would date between his appointment over the cis-Tauric province (214) and Magnesia (190).

See Ch. 3 § 3 (on subject cities and the limitations on their external life).

33. Decree of the Prienians for Ameinias (between 196 and 190)

Inschr. Priene 82; but lines 1–5 are taken from Ph. Gauthier (below), 11–25 from Ad. Wilhelm (below). I am grateful to C. Crowther for photographs of a squeeze and for discussion of the text.

Cf. Ad. Wilhelm, *Wiener Studien* 29 (1907), 11–13, for lines 15–25 (used as basis here); Ph. Gauthier, *Chiron* 21 (1991), 51, nn. 11, 12, 13, for the text of lines 1–6, restored in line with other Prienian documents (used as a basis here); S. Dmitriev, *EA* 21 (1993), 43–4 (=*ZPE* 103 (1994), 115–16) for restorations (reviewed by Gauthier in *BE* 95, 494; also *SEG* 43.849).

We have the left-hand edge of the text; the squeeze shows that the text was flanked by engraved crowns (at least six can be made out) on the left hand side, and perhaps also on the (now lost) right hand margin. The squeeze also shows that the heading (lines 1–6 in the restoration of Gauthier) was written in much larger letters than the rest of the decree, so that the text must have shown a considerable overhang on the right hand side (the letters of the heading are not large enough to suggest that the heading actually took up a width sufficient for a text in two columns underneath; the line-length of the decree proper can be determined by the secure restorations at lines 7–8). The lettering, with its great serifs and its long-stemmed phi and rho, is closely related to e.g. *Inschr. Priene* 49 or 64.

[Ἐπὶ σ]τεφανηφόρου [c.20   , μηνὸς]
[Μετ]αγειτνιῶνος [πεμπτῆι?], ἐτίμησεν ἡ βουλὴ καὶ ὁ δῆμος
[Διοκ]λῆν Ἀμεινίου [σιτήσει ἐμ πρυτανείωι καὶ]
[ἐμ Π]ανιωνίω[ι καὶ στ]ε[φάνωι χρυσέωι ἀριστείωι]   4
[καὶ πρ]οεδρίαι [ἐμ πᾶσιν τοῖς ἀγῶσιν καὶ ἀτελείαι]
[τοῦ σ]ώματος [   ]
ὑπὲ[ρ τι]μῶν Διοκλε[ῖ] ἔδοξε [τῆι βουλῆι καὶ τῶι δήμωι]·
Ἀπο[λ]λοφάνης Ἀκεσάνδ[ρου εἶπεν· ἐπειδὴ Διοκλῆς]   8
Ἀμεινίου ἀνὴρ ὢν καλὸς [καὶ ἀγαθὸς καὶ χρήσιμος],
ἐκτενῆ καὶ πρόθυμον ἐμ π[ᾶσι καιροῖς? παρασκευάζων]
ἑαυτὸν διετέλει καὶ τὴν Δ[   ]
πολιτείαν τὰ βέλτιστα, καὶ [κοινῆι παντὶ τῶι δήμωι]   12
ἰδίαι τε τοῖς ἐντυγχάνου[σιν αὐτῶι τῶν πολιτῶν]
εὔνουν αὐτὸν καὶ πρόθυμ[ον παρείχετο, ἐπιμελού]-
μενος τῶν τῶι δήμωι σ[υμφερόντων·   ὑπὸ τοῦ]
δήμου κατὰ τὴν σιτικ[ὴν παράθεσιν ἀποσταλεὶς]   16
πρὸς Ζεῦξιν τὸν τοῦ βασιλέ[ως στρατηγὸν μετὰ τοῦ]
συναποδειχθέντος οὐκ ἀτ[   ],
ἀ[λ]λ' ἔλαβε τῶι δήμω[ι   ]
μ[.]τα τε ταῦτα ἀπο[   ]   20
[τα] τὴν ἐνεστῶσα[ν   ]

[τ]ῶι δήμωι ἔλαβεν [   ]
ἐξαγωγήν, ἀτελ[   ]
[π]ρὸς τὸν δῆμο[ν   ]   24
. . . . ΤῳΝΓ

1–6 The first lines, with their summary of the decree, restored by Gauthier: since Prienian inscriptions do not mention the patronymic of the *stephanephoros*, line 1 either read ἐπὶ στεφανηφόρου τοῦ δεῖνα τὸ δεύτερον or ἐπὶ στεφανηφόρου τοῦ θεοῦ τοῦ μετὰ τὸν δεῖνα. 7–8 The restorations in these lines are absolutely certain, and determine the line-length for the rest of the inscription.   10 [παρασκευαζόμενος] Hiller von Gaertringen in *Inschr. Priene*; [παρασκευάζων] suggested by C. Crowther, since the active appears in other examples of this formula (e.g. *Inschr. Priene* 108, lines 88–9, 313). 15–16 [θλιβομένου δὲ τοῦ] δήμου Wilhelm. Dmitriev proposed (15) μενος τῶν τῶι δήμωι σ[υμφερόντων· πρεσβευτὴς ὑπὸ τοῦ] | δήμου . . .[ἀποσταλείς], but the restoration is perhaps slightly too long for line 15, since the indications of lines 7 and 8 allow a maximum of *c*.20 letters for the gap. However, the general meaning 'being sent as ambassador by the people' is convincing, and the elements πρεσβευτής and ἀποσταλείς might be restored later in the text.   16 τὴν σιτικ[ὴν οἰκονομίαν] Wilhelm, [παράθεσιν] Dmitriev. 17 Ζεῦξιν τὸν τοῦ βασιλέ[ως στρατηγὸν] Wilhelm. This would be the only epigraphical evidence for such a title, instead of the more usual ὁ ἐπὶ τῶν πραγμάτων. Bengtson 1944: 112 n. 3, for argument against the restoration [σατράπην] (Wilhelm, p. 12, tentatively). Perhaps φίλον or even συγγενῆ?   18 οὐκ ἀτ[ελῆ ἐποιήσατο τὴν ἔντευξιν] Wilhelm. 19–22 At line 20, the traces suggest μ[α]τα rather than μ[ε]τα. Wilhelm proposed to restore: [καὶ τὰ χρή] | [μα]τά τε ταῦτα ἀπο[δέδωκεν καὶ τὰς ἄλλας δωρεὰς ἃς κα-] | (20) [τὰ] τὴν ἐνεστῶσα[ν σιτοδείαν παρὰ τῶν εὐνοικῶς ἐχόντων] | τ]ῶι δήμωι ἔλαβεν. Dmitriev sees in the two similar phrases ἔλαβε τῶι δήμωι (line 19) and τῶι δήμωι ἔλαβεν (line 22) the proof that Diokles went on an embassy twice, and restores line 20 as [με]τὰ δὲ ταῦτα ἀποσταλείς]. The restoration is tempting, but the similarity of recurrence of the phrase might also refer to the reception of two different benefactions from Zeuxis on the same occasion.   25 Wilhelm's readings, from a squeeze.

When . . . was *stephanephoros*, [in the month of Met]ageitnion, [the council and the people honoured Diok]les son of Ameinias, [with free dining in the *prytaneion* and] in the Panionion, with [a gold crown and] front seating [in the contests . . .] and *ateleia tou somatos*. Concerning the honours for Diokles, it seemed good [to the council and to the people], Apol[l]ophanes son of Akesand[ros proposed: since Diokles] son of Ameinias, being a good [and noble and useful man] **10** continuously [puts] himself [forward] as an eager and zealous man and . . . the best towards the community (*politeia*), and [behaved] with goodwill and zeal both [towards the whole people in common] and individually to those of the citizens who deal with him, taking care of the [interests] of the people; and [having been sent by] the people, because of the grain [supply,] to Zeuxis the [governor (*strategos*)] of the king, with his fellow-ambassador, he did not [conclude his mission unsuccessfully?], but received for the people . . . **20** and [after?] this, . . . on account of the [shortage?] which prevailed, . . . he received for the people, and . . . export (of grain?), exem[ption from taxes?] . . .

Commentary. The decree was carved on a unfluted column in the West stoa of the agora at Priene (as several other contemporary Prienian documents). See Ch. 4, introduction (on royal benefactions).

34. Letter of Antiochos III (?) to Ilion (Winter 197/6 or Spring 196?)

A. Brückner, in W. Dörpfeld, *Troia und Ilion* (Athens, 1902), ii. 448–9, no. 4 with plate 59 (*RC* 42); *I. Ilion* 37. I examined a squeeze in the archive of the *Inscriptiones Graecae* in Berlin (summer 1994), courtesy of Dr K. Hallof.

Cf. Piejko 1991*b*: 47–8, for some restorations.

τε πρὸς τὸ σ[υ]γκατασκ[ευάσασθαι ἅπαν]-
τα τὰ πρὸς ἐπιμέλειαν κ[αὶ c.8 ἀνή]-
κοντα· πειρασόμεθα γὰ[ρ οὐ μόνον τὰ δι]-
ὰ προγόνων προϋπηργμ[ένα πρὸς τὸν δῆ]-
μον συντηρεῖν, ἀλλὰ κ[αὶ ἵνα τῶν εἰς]
δόξαν καὶ τιμὴν ἀνηκ[όντων ἐν μηθενὶ]
ὑστερῆτε, ποεῖσθαι τ[   ]
[   ] καὶ κοινῆι καὶ ἰδίαι ἑκ[άστου   ]
[συγχω]ροῦμεν δὲ καὶ τα[   ]

8

1 [ὁμοίως] | τε Piejko 1991*b*: 48. 2 εὔνοιαν Welles, for the editor's καταλογήν. Perhaps πολυωρίαν, as in document **5**, 9, might fit the lacuna. 4 πρὸς Welles, εἰς Brückner. 6 Brückner's ἐν μηθενί is paralleled in Zeuxis' letter to Herakleia under Latmos, document **31** B, IV 8: [ἵνα ἐ]μ μηθενὶ τῶν δυνατῶν καὶ καλῶς ἐχόντων ὑστερῆτε, better than Welles's μηθενός. 7–8 τ[ὴν πᾶσαν πρόνοι|αν] Welles; τ[ὴν προσήκου|σαν] καὶ κοινῆι καὶ ἰδίαι ἑκ[άστου πο|λυωρίαν] Piejko 1991*b*: 48, on the basis of the first letter of Antiochos to Teos, document **19** A, 15. The word order thus obtained is somewhat odd. 9 [συγχω]ροῦμεν Welles. Frisch writes that the squeeze shows a 'schräge Hasta' which would make this impossible. The restoration proposed by Piejko, [ἐπικ]υροῦμεν is not compelling, since the parallel he quotes (Antiochos to Herakleia under Latmos, confirming—κυροῦμεν—the grants made by Zeuxis: document **31** A, I 9) is not obviously relevant to the situation in the present letter, where nothing indicates whether Antiochos is talking about privileges granted by another. In any case the 'schräge Hasta' on the squeeze starts and ends too low to be the right branch of an upsilon, and is probably a few pits on the stone or perhaps the edge of the break, as I believe after inspecting the squeeze. Welles's restoration still seems the best.

. . . and to carry out all measures pertaining to care and [goodwill]; for we will not only try to preserve the things which the people enjoyed through our ancestors, but also, so that you may be deprived of none of the things pertaining to your glory and your honour, to show all solicitude in common and individually to each . . . we also [grant] . . .

Commentary. The text, found in the Troad, is preserved on the fragment of a stele, as the dimensions published by Brückner indicate.

Welles canvasses possibilities for authorship, mentioning a Roman official as a possibility (the context would then be the settlement of Asia Minor in 188, and the ancestral theme might be an allusion to past contacts between Ilion and Rome, real or imagined). Welles excludes the possibility of an Attalid, arguing that the first person plural would be unusual in that case; however, Attalid rulers could write *we* (*RC* 16, 23, 49, 50), and the ancestral theme would be fitting, since Ilion had been close to the Attalids since Attalos I. Welles favoured Antiochos III, whose actions provide a very suitable context, and whose other letters provide close parallels. This is the most appealing solution (though by no means absolutely certain, on account of the ruinous state of the document).

See Ch. 4 § 1 (on the language of euergetism).

35. *Alliance between Antiochos III and Perinthos (196?)*

I owe knowledge of this document to the generosity of M. Sayar, who showed me his text, due to appear imminently in M. Sayar, *Perinthos-Herakleia und Umgebung. Geschichte, Testimonien, Griechische und Lateinische Inschriften* (Vienna, 1998), as nos. 3*a* and 3*b* (*nondum vidi*) ; the present version is taken from a paper delivered in a conference in Bordeaux (12–13 December 1997), on 'Les Cités d'Asie Mineure occidentale au IIe siècle a. C.', for which see now Sayar 2001. In consequence, the following text is provisional.

A.

traces of 4 or 5 lines

```
[      ]ΔΙΕΛ[                              ]
[      ]Σ στρα[τ                           ]
[      ]vac. ὅρκος [Περινθίων? ὀμνύω Δία    ]
[   Ποσ]είδω Ἄρ[εα Ἀθην]ᾶν [Ἄρειαν καὶ θεοὺς πάντας]    4
[καὶ] πάσας καὶ τὴν Τα[υρόπολον    συμμαχήσω? τοῖς]
[βασι]λεῦσιν Ἀντιόχωι καὶ [Ἀντιόχωι τῶι]
[υἱῶι? κ]αὶ τοῖς τούτων ἐκγό[νοις          ]
[      ]σαν οἱ βασιλεῖς οἱ ΤΟ[          ]    8
[      ]ΩΝ καὶ ὁμόσωσιν Περίν[θιοι?     ]
[τὴ]ν συμμαχίαν ἀπὸ ΤΟ[          ]
       traces of 1 line
```

The restorations are tentative.   6–7 seem to indicate a very short line length. Another possibility is to suppose a very long line length, so as to fit the elements of the oath formula, as attested in two parallel documents, the alliance between a king Antiochos and Lysimacheia (*I. Ilion* 45, with Ferrary and Gauthier 1981) and the alliance between Philip V and Lysimacheia (*Staatsvertr.* 549): (*a*) ὀμνύω + list of gods; (*b*) ἐμμενεῖν ἐν τῆι συμμαχίαι ἣν πεπόημαι πρὸς βασιλεῖς Ἀντίοχον καὶ Ἀντίοχον; (*c*) various formulas promising aid, in different circumstances, to the kings Antiochos and Antiochos and their descendants (so that the datives of lines 6–7 would belong to different sub-sections of the oath).   6–7 I am not sure [τῶι υἱῶι] is necessary.   8 [ὀμωσάτω]σαν οἱ βασιλεῖς {οι} τὸ[ν ὅρκον τὸν ὑπογεγραμμένον].

. . .oath [of the Perinthians? I swear by Zeus . . . Pos]eidon, Ar[es, Athen]a [Areia and all the gods and] all the [goddesses] and the Ta[uropolos: I will be an ally?] to kings Antiochos and [Antiochos (the son?)] and their descendants . . . [let?] the kings [swear the oath written below?] . . . the alliance from . . .

B.

traces of several lines

```
[      ]ἐποήσαντο ΤΗ[          ]
[συμμα]χίαν εἰς τὸν ἄπα[ντα χρόνον]
```

[πρὸ]ς βασιλέα Ἀντίοχο[ν   ]
[   ]ΜΟΥ καὶ βασιλέως[   ]   4
[   ] ΤΟΣ Περινθου[   ]
[   ]ΟΥ[   ]
    traces of several lines

1 [ἀδόλως καὶ ἀπροφασίστως] could be added.   3 Ἀντίοχο[ν καὶ Ἀντίοχον]?
Another possibility is that the text here refers to earlier contacts, perhaps bewteen
Perinthos and Antiochos II.

. . . they made the [alliance?] . . . alliance for all time . . . towards King
Antiochos . . . (the rest is too fragmentary for translation).

Commentary. Both fragments were found on the site of ancient Perinthos
(now reused in a garden wall); that they come from the same document is
assured by the identity of script, and the presence of a King Antiochos in
both. The Seleukid rulers mentioned are Antiochos III and Antiochos the
son, and the document must date to the activity of Antiochos III in
Thrace: most likely in 196, though a later campaign cannot be excluded.

36. *Letter of a Royal Official(?) Concerning an Indeterminate City*
(bewteen 209 and 193, probably c.197)

Sardis, 7–9, no. 2, with facsimile of the 'marble slab', found in Sardeis, left
by J. Keil in the Consulate of the United States at Smyrna, and lost in the
destruction of the city in 1922 (Gauthier 1989: 171–8 for new text, incorporating remarks subsequent to the *editio princeps*, and refuting an attempt
by Piejko to attribute this inscription to the events of Sardeis in 214/13,
Piejko 1987, noticed in *SEG* 37.1003 with additions for lines 21–4 from
CM 39 (1988), 111). The text given here is Gauthier's except for a few
sublinear dots added from Buckler and Robinson, and a transcription of
lines 23–7, from the facsimile (readings of J. Keil).
    Cf. Robert 1964: 19–20 (analysis, corrections to the text),

[c.7   ]ΤΑΣΕΛ [c.25   τοῖς βα]-
[σι]λεῦσιν Ἀντιό[χωι καὶ Ἀντιόχωι   c.17   ]
[τ]ὴν ἀρχὴν ἧς ἀνέχον[το   c.22   ]
[. . .]άρχου συνχωρήσαντο[ς   c.19   ]
[.]ωσιν πρὸς αὐτοὺς ὀλβίαν [κ]αὶ A [c.15   ]   4
[. .] A [.], χρήσον[ται? δ]ὲ ἐπ᾽ ἑαυ[τ]οῖς κα[ὶ νόμοις πᾶσιν οἷς]
[κ]αὶ ἐξ ἀρχῆς ἐχρῶντο· καὶ ἐπεὶ ἀπελ[ογίσ]αντ[ο   c.4   ]
[. .]Ι τήν τε πόλιν αὐτῶν ἐνπεπυρ[ῶσθ]αι καὶ [c.7   ]   8
[.]ωσθαι ἐν τῶι πολέμωι καὶ τὰ ἴδια ἀπολωλε[κότας τῶν]
[πολι]τῶν τοὺς πλείστους διαπεφωνηκέ[ναι   c.6   ]
[. . . .] δὲ ὀλίους παντάπασιν καὶ ἠξίωσαν [c.8   ]
. . ΤΩΝ ποιήσ[α]σθαι καὶ τῶν [φ]όρων ἀπολῦ[σαι καὶ]   12
[ἐ]ποικίσαι τὸν τόπο[ν], συνεχώρησεν [α]ὐ[τοῖς   c.6   ]
[δ]ωρος ἕως μὲν ἐτῶν ἑπτα μηθὲν α[ὐτοὺς   διορ]-
[θοῦ]σθαι εἰς τὸ βασιλι[κ]ὸν ἀλλὰ ἀπολε[λύσθαι   c.4   ]

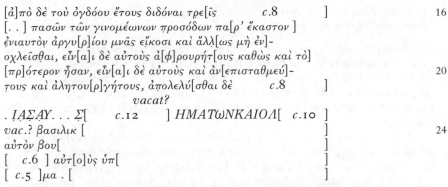

[ἀ]πὸ δὲ τοῦ ὀγδόου ἔτους διδόναι τρε[ῖς   c.8   ]   16
[. .] πασῶν τῶν γινομέωνων προσόδων πα[ρ' ἕκαστον]
ἐνιαυτὸν ἀργυ[ρ]ίου μνᾶς εἴκοσι καὶ ἄλλ[ως μὴ ἐν]-
οχλεῖσθαι, εἶν[α]ι δὲ αὐτοὺς ἀ[φ]ρουρήτ[ους καθὼς καὶ τὸ]
[πρ]ότερον ἦσαν, εἶν[α]ι δὲ αὐτοὺς καὶ ἀν[επισταθμεύ]-   20
τους καὶ ἀλητου[ρ]γήτους, ἀπολελύ[σθαι δὲ   c.8   ]
                                    vacat?
. ΙΑΣΑΥ. . . Σ[c.12   ] ΗΜΑΤѠΝΚΑΙΟΛ[c.10]
vac.? βασιλικ [   ]   24
αὐτὸν βου[   ]
[c.6] αὐτ[ο]ὺς ὑπ[   ]
[c.5]μα . [   ]

7 ἀπέ[δει]ξαν T . . . edd., 'since the T . . . pointed out'; present restoration Robert
1964: 20 n. 1.   20–1 ἀνεπισταθμευτούς Launey 1987: ii. 697–8.   22 'Line 22
is effaced' edd. (attempted reconstruction by Piejko, CM 39 (1988), 111). But Buckler's
drawing suggests a vacat: the space between lines 21 and 23 seems slightly greater than
that of a normal line of text. Could line 23 be the beginning of another document?
23 [κτ]ημά[των]? Piejko's [ἐκ τῶν γεν]ημάτων, for a tax on agricultural produce, is
attractive (CM 39 (1988), 111); [γενν]ημάτων also possible.

to the kings Antiochos and [Antiochos] the beginning (?) the . . . which
they endured (?) . . . [. . .]archos having granted . . . to them prosperity and
. . . and they are to use all the same laws which they did originally; and
since they reported that . . . their city had been burnt and . . . in the war
and that 10 most of the citizens had lost their property and been killed . . .
very few, and they asked . . . to do . . . and to grant exemption from the
tribute and to settle the place, [. . .]doros granted to them . . .that for seven
years, they should pay nothing to the royal treasure, but be released . . .
from the eighth year, that they give three . . . out of all the income produced, 20 mnai of silver, for each year, and not to be troubled in any other
way; that they be free from garrisoning, as 20 they were before, and free
from billeting and from obligations to provide services, and that they be
released from . . . [of the] agricultural produce? . . . royal (or: the treasure?)
. . . (the rest of the document is too fragmentary for translation).

Commentary. The document must date between 209 and 193, because of
the mention of the kings Antiochos III and Antiochos the son; it probably
reflects the activities of the land army's campaign in 197, the most likely
context for the recapture of a city by Seleukid forces within that chronological bracket (see Ch. 2 § 4).

The nature of the document is unclear: this is unlikely to be a city decree
or a royal letter, more probably a letter from a Seleukid official, informing
subordinates of decisions taken by other officials, affecting the status and
the privileges of the city in question (Gauthier 1989: 172–3).

37. Royal Enactment Concerning the State Cult for Laodike (February/March to May 193)

M. Holleaux and P. Paris, *BCH* 9 (1885), 324–30 (*editio princeps*, 'copié au milieu de la crotte de chameau': Robert 1949: 8); improved M. Holleaux, *BCH* 13 (1889), 523–9 (*OGIS* 224); final version M. Holleaux, *BCH* 54 (1930), 245–62, with plates 12–13 (Holleaux 1942: 165–81); *RC* 36–7. I examined the stone in the Louvre (MA 2936) in March 1997, thanks to Ph. Gauthier.

Cf. Robert 1949: 5–31 for parallel document from Nehavend in Iran, which establishes text and date; yet a third version of the same enactment was found in Kermanshah, also in Iran (Robert 1967); Aymard 1949, for dates and speculation on surrounding events. Austin 1981: no. 158, for translation of Nehavend version.

The text presented below is that of Robert 1949: 9–13, combining Holleaux (1930) with secure restorations from the parallel Iranian document: 'le nouvel exemplaire permet de compléter, de façon définitive, toutes les lacunes de l'inscription de Phrygie, à l'exception d'une seule' (line 31). I have nonetheless preserved Welles's sublinear dots and square brackets: the Nehavend copy allows us to restore all the lacunae, but not to read what is not on the stone.

[Ἀναξίμ]βροτος vac. Διονυτᾶι vac. χαίρειν· τοῦ γρα-
[φέντος] παρὰ τοῦ βασιλέως προστάγματος
[περ]ὶ τοῦ ἀποδεδεῖχθαι τῆς βασιλίσσης
[ἀ]ρχιέρειαν τῶν ἐν τῆι σατραπείαι Βερενίκην   4
τὴν Πτολεμαίου τοῦ Λυσιμάχου θυγατέρα
κατακεχώρισται τὸ ἀντίγραφον· ἐπακολουθῶν
οὖν τοῖς ἐπεσταλμένοις συντέλει καθ' ἃ
οἴεται δεῖν, ἵνα δὲ καὶ τὰ ἀντίγραφα ἀναγρα-   8
φέντα εἰς στήλην λιθίνην ἀνατεθῆι ἐν τῶι
ἐπιφανεστάτωι τόπωι προνοήθητι.
          Ἔρρωσο. [Θ]ιρ', Ἀρτεμισίου ιθ'.

[Βασιλε]ὺς Ἀντίοχος Ἀναξιμβρότωι χαίρειν·   12
[βουλόμεν]οι τῆς ἀδελφῆς βασιλίσσης Λαοδίκη[s]
[τὰ]ς τίμας ἐπὶ πλεῖον αὔξειν καὶ τοῦτο ἀναγ-
[καιό]τατον ἑαυτοῖς νομίζοντες εἶναι διὰ τὸ
[μὴ μ]όνον ἡμῖν φιλοστόργως καὶ κηδεμονι-   16
[κῶς] αὐτὴν συμβιοῦν, ἀλλὰ καὶ πρὸς τὸ θε[ῖ]-
[ον ε]ὐσεβῶς δια[κ]εῖσθαι, καὶ τὰ ἄλλα μὲν
[ὅσα πρ]έπει καὶ δίκαιόν ἐστι παρ' ἡμῶν αὐτῆι
[συνα]ντᾶσθαι δια[τ]ελοῦμεν μετὰ φιλοσ-   20
[τ]ο[ρ]γίας ποιοῦντε[ς, κρ]ίνομεν δὲ καθάπερ
[ἡμ]ῶν [ἀπο]δείκ[ν]υν[ται κ]ατὰ τὴν βασιλεί-
[αν ἀ]ρ[χ]ιερεῖς, καὶ ταύτης καθίστασθαι
[ἐν] τοῖς αὐτοῖς τόποις ἀρχιερείας αἳ φο-   24
[ρή]σουσιν στεφάνους χρυσοῦς ἔχοντας

[εἰκόνας αὐ]τῆς, ἐπιγραφήσονται δὲ καὶ ἐν
[τοῖς] συναλλάγμασι μετὰ τοὺς τῶν
[προγόν]ων καὶ ἡμῶν ἀρχιερεῖς· ἐπεὶ οὖν　　　　　28
[ἀποδ]έδεικται ἐν τοῖς ὑπὸ σὲ τόποις
[Βερ]ενίκη ἡ Πτολεμαίου τοῦ Λυσιμάχου
τοῦ [. . .]όντος ἡμῖν κατὰ συγγένειαν θυγάτη[ρ],
συντελείσθω πάντ[α] τοῖς προγεγραμμέ-　　　　　32
νοις ἀ[κο]λούθως, καὶ τὰ ἀντίγραφα τῶν
ἐπιστολῶν ἀναγραφέντα εἰς στήλας
ἀνατεθήτω ἐν τοῖς ἐπιφανεστάτοις
τόποις, ὅπως νῦν τε καὶ εἰς τὸ λοιπὸν　　　　　36
πᾶσιν φανερὰ φαίνηται ἡ ἡμετέρα καὶ ἐν τού-
[τοι]ς π[ρ]ὸς τὴν ἀδελφὴν π[ρ]οαίρεσις.

1 For spaces between the first three words, plates 12–13 in *BCH* 54 (1930) and Holleaux 1942: 171.　　11 For date, Robert 1949: 13–15 (new reading, based on the Nehavend text).　　16 The Nehavend text reads μὴ μόνον, so that expression is to be restored instead of Welles [οὐ μ]όνον.　　20 [ἀπα]ντᾶσθαι Welles; present reading from Nehavend copy.　　20–1 φιλο[στοργί]ας Welles.　　26 [εἰκόνας αὐ]τῆς, proposed by Robert, *BCH* 54 (1930), 262–7, also in Holleaux 1942: 181; Robert's intuition is confirmed by the Iranian text.　　28 [προγόν]ων Welles, also in Nehavend text.　　31 Welles proposed [συν]όντος (*RC*, p. 162); [ἅπτ]οντος might be possible, cf. document 22 (Xanthos) Βασιλεὺς μέγας Ἀντίοχος ἀφιέρωσεν τὴν πόλιν τῆι Λητῶι καὶ τῶι Ἀπόλλωνι καὶ τῆι Ἀρτέμιδι διὰ τὴν πρὸς αὐτοὺς συνάπτουσαν συγγένειαν. When I examined the stone, I read \ I . O V I O Σ, traces which are compatible with the restoration I propose above.　　37 τού | [τοις] Robert 1949.

Anaximbrotos to Dionytas, greetings. The copy of the enactment written by the king concerning the appointment of Berenike, daughter of Ptolemy the son of Lysimachos, as high-priestess of the queen for the rites in the satrapy,[1] is enclosed. Therefore, conform to the instructions and carry them out as he thinks necessary, and take care that the copies are put up on a stone stele in the **10** most prominent place. Farewell. Year 119. Artemisios 19.

King Antiochos to Anaximbrotos, greetings. Wishing to increase the honours of our sister, Queen Laodike, and thinking that this was a most necessary task for us, since she not only is a loving and caring consort, but also is piously disposed towards the divine, **20** we continuously do, with love, the things which it is fitting and just that she should receive from us, and we decree that, just as high-priests of us are appointed throughout the kingdom, so there should be established, in the same places, high-priest-esses of her also, who will wear golden crowns bearing her image, and be inscribed in the contracts after the high-priests of our ancestors and of us. Since **30** Berenike, the daughter of Ptolemaios son of Lysimachos, who is

---

[1] Robert 1949: 18 n. 4, prefers 'high-priestess of the shrines (ἱερά) in the satrapy' to Welles's translation, 'in the satrapy' (the phrase τὰ ἐν τῆι σατραπείαι meaning 'the satrapy': *RC*, p. 164). The phrase is different from the περί or κατά periphrases Welles would compare it to. I have taken the phrase in a vaguer interpretation than Robert's 'shrines'.

[. . .] to us by kinship, has been appointed in the regions under you, let everything be done in accordance to the instructions written above, and let the copies of the letters be written up on stelai and erected in the most prominent places, so that for now and for future times our intentions towards our sister in these matters too may be obvious to all.

Commentary. The text, now very worn, is inscribed on a white marble stele, found at 'Dodurga' (modern Dodurcular), in the Acıpayam plain.[2] See Ch. 3 § 2*d* (on the rhetoric of the hierarchical dossier).

Sherwin-White and Kuhrt 1993: 209–10, suggest that the cult for Antiochos III and his ancestors was created in 193, at the same time as the cult for Laodike. They reach this conclusion by taking the present tense in the present *prostagma*, on cult for Laodike, in the strictest sense: 'we decree that, just as high-priests of us are appointed (in the sense of 'are being appointed right now') throughout the kingdom, so there should be established, in the same places, high-priestesses of her also' (above, lines 21–4). I prefer to interpret the present tense as describing general practice since the foundation of the cult in *c.*204 (the likeliest date), rather than implying that priests of Antiochos III were being appointed at that very moment, even as Antiochos III was writing (193).

38. *Letter of M. Valerius Messalla, the Tribunes, and the Senate of Rome to the Teians (193)*

Chishull 1728: 102–4: *editio princeps*, dating, Latin translation. Hessel 1731: p. 12 (unnumbered), no. 1 (text by C. A. Duker, communicated to him by J. de Hochepied, Dutch consul in Smyrna).[1] (*CIG* 3045 corrects Chishull with readings from Hessel. The *CIG* text is the basis for Rigsby 1996: 314–16, no. 153.) *LBW* 3.60, locating the stone at Hereke (modern Düzce), north of Teos, and giving a facsimile (*Syll.* 601). (P. Viereck, *Sermo Graecus quo senatus populusque Romanus magistratusque populi Romani . . . usi sunt* (Göttingen, 1888), no. 2, combines elements of both

---

[2] The traditional title, 'édit d'Eriza', is misleading: there is no clear evidence as to the provenance of the stone (nor is Eriza securely located near Dodurcular, at 'Ischkian Bazar': Robert 1962: 112 n. 4).

[1] Hessel writes: 'Itaque in antecessum dabo fasciculum inscriptionum, quas mecum benigne communicavit Carolus Andreas Dukerus in Academia Trajectensi historiarum atque eloquentiae professor ordinarius, vir adprime eruditus: cui plerasque omnes miserant Justinus de Hochepied vir nobilis, consul nostras apud Smyrnaeos; & Hermannus vander Horst theologus, vir egregie doctus, & tunc a sacris nostratium, qui Smyrnae negotiantur.' The present text was copied by de Hochepied, as made clear by Duker's comments on p. 22 (unnumbered) of the *praefationis appendix* (Hessel 1731). In the recent epigraphical litterature, this was first clarified by Rigsby 1996: 292 n. 47 (but de Hochepied was not 'Belgian consul', as Rigsby writes: Belgium was not independent in 1731, and *Belgica natio* is the Dutch baroque humanist Duker's expression for Holland). It is worth bearing in mind that the text which Böckh (in *CIG*) uses to correct the readings in *LBW*, came through two intermediaries, Baron de Hochepied and C. A. Duker, before reaching print.

CIG 3045 and *LBW* 3.60 (reproduced as *RDGE* 34). The same principle for the basis of the text given below.)

Rigsby 1996: 292, on the textual history of the *asylia* texts from Teos. Austin 1981, no. 157 gives translation.

vac. Ῥωμαίων. *vac.*
Μάρκος Οὐαλάριος Μάρκου στρατηγὸς καὶ
δήμαρχοι καὶ ἡ σύνκλητος Τηΐων τῆι βουλῆι καὶ τῶι
δήμωι χαίρειν. *vac.* Μένιππος ὅ τε παρ' Ἀντιόχου τοῦ βα-   4
σιλέως ἀποσταλεὶς πρὸς ἡμᾶς πρεσβευτής, προ-
χειρισθεὶς καὶ ὑφ' ὑμῶν πρεσβεῦσαι ὑπὲρ τῆς πόλεως
τό τε ψήφισμα ἀνέδωκεν καὶ αὐτὸς ἀκολούθως τούτωι
διελέχθη μετὰ πάσης προθυμίας· ἡμεῖς δὲ τόν τε ἄν-   8
δρα ἀπεδεξάμεθα φιλοφρόνως καὶ διὰ τὴν προγεγενη-
μένην αὐτῶι δόξαν καὶ διὰ τὴν ὑπάρχουσαν καλοκἀγαθίαν περί τε ὧν ἠξίου διηκούσαμεν εὐνόως· καὶ ὅτι
μὲν διόλου πλεῖστον λόγον ποιούμενοι διατελοῦ-   12
μεν τῆς πρὸς τοὺς θεοὺς εὐσεβείας, μάλιστ' ἄν τις στο-
χάζοιτο ἐκ τῆς συναντωμένης ἡμεῖν εὐμενείας
διὰ ταῦτα παρὰ τοῦ δαιμονίου· οὐ μὴν ἀλλὰ καὶ ἐξ ἄλλων πλειόνων πεπείσμεθα συμφανῆ πᾶσι γεγονέναι   16
τὴν ἡμετέραν εἰς τὸ θεῖον προτιμίαν. διὸ καὶ διά τε ταῦτα καὶ διὰ τὴν πρὸς ἡμᾶς εὔνοιαν καὶ διὰ τὸν ἠξιω[μέν]ον
πρεσβευτὴν κρίνομεν εἶναι τὴν πόλιν καὶ τὴν χώ-
ραν ἱεράν, καθὼς καὶ νῦν ἐστιν, καὶ ἄσυλον καὶ ἀφορο-   20
λόγητον ἀπὸ τοῦ δήμου τοῦ Ῥωμαίων καὶ τά τε εἰς
τὸν θεὸν τίμια καὶ τὰ εἰς ὑμᾶς φιλάνθρωπα πειρασόμεθα συνεπαύξειν, διατηρούντων ὑμῶν καὶ εἰς τὸ
μετὰ ταῦτα τὴν πρὸς ἡμᾶς εὔνοιαν. *vac.* ἔρρωσθε.   24

4 The *vacat* comes from the fac-simile in *LBW*, which however does not give τοῦ found in Duker and Hessel, reproduced in *CIG*. The word order presumably reflects the Latin *ab Antiocho rege*, rather than the usual Greek practice (βασιλεὺς Ἀντίοχος). 6 ὑπὲρ from Duker and Hessel, reproduced in *CIG*. *LBW* gives περί in its facsimile and its text (easy enough a misreading).   16 πᾶσι from Duker and Hessel, reproduced in *CIG* and not in *LBW*.   18 πρὸς ὑμᾶς Duker and Hessel, reproduced in *CIG*. I have preferred Chishull's πρὸς ἡμᾶς, which perhaps makes better sense in this passage.

Of the Romans.
M. Valerius, son of Marcus,[2] praetor, and the tribunes, and the Senate, to the council and the people of the Teians, greetings. Menippos, the ambassador sent by King Antiochos to us, having also been selected by you to represent the city, has handed over your decree and spoke in accordance with its content, with all zeal; as for us, we have received the man with friendly mind, on account of his pre-existing repute 10 and his present good qualities, and we have listened to his request with goodwill. That we continuously take the greatest consideration possible of piety towards the gods, might best be deduced from the favour which we enjoy from the

[2] M. Valerius, M. f., Messalla, *pr. peregrinus* 193: *MRR* i. 347.

superhuman (*daimonion*) on account of our piety. Indeed, we are convinced that our honour for the divine has become manifest to all through very many other signs. For this reason, and on account of your goodwill towards us[3] and on account of the ambassador making the request,[4] we decided that the city and the territory should be sacred, **20** as it is now, and inviolate and free from tribute as concerns the Roman people,[5] and we will try to increase the honours for the god and the privileges for you, if you observe in the future also your goodwill towards us. Farewell.

Commentary. The document was carved on an architectural block from the temple of Dionysos (as were the other documents of the series it belongs to, the early *asylia* texts of Teos).

This document is treated in Ch. 2 § 5 (Roman discursive interference in the Seleukid space).

IV DATE UNDETERMINED BUT CERTAINLY UNDER ANTIOCHOS III

39. *Ex-voto Erected at Gordos for the Safety of Apollophanes, Physician of Antiochos III*

Herrmann 1970: 94–8, no. 1, *editio princeps*, dating (= *TAM* 5.1.689). Photograph of stele, with its wreath encompassing an intricate flower motif, in *Anz. Ak. Wien* 1974, opposite 440, and of the inscription in *TAM* 5.1. The stone is now kept in the collection of antiquities of Ege Universitesi, where I examined it in May 1997, thanks to H. Malay and C. Tanrıver.

Διὶ Ποροττηνῶι
ὑπὲρ [5–6] ἰατροῦ
[. . .] βασιλέως
Ἀπολλοφάνου τοῦ Ἀπολλοφάνου   4
Σελευκέως τῆς ἀπὸ Πιερίας
Ἀρκεσίλα[ο]ς Ἀρκεσιλάου
ἡγεμὼν χαριστήρια

2–3 The word ἰατροῦ is inscribed on an extensive *rasura* which was carried out on the whole of the line after ὑπέρ; this erasure, and that at the beginning of line 3, as well as the failure to recarve a syntactically complete text, are puzzling (Herrmann 1970: 97). When I examined the stone I could read Λ Ε as the last two letters before ἰατροῦ, so that the stone mason may have first inscribed a formula starting ὑπὲρ βασιλέ(ως), as in a

---

[3] It might be possible to read 'on account of our goodwill towards you (ὑμᾶς)', but the present text perhaps reads better and announces the 'contract clause' at the end of the document.

[4] τὸν ἠξιωμένον πρεσβευτήν: the translation given here assumes the participle is in the middle voice.

[5] Literally 'free from tribute from the Roman people', a very problematic expression (Ch. 2 § 5 and Appendix 2).

dedication for the king's safety, rather than the less common dedication on behalf of the royal physician's safety.

To Zeus Porottenos, for (*erasure*) doctor (*erasure*) of king, Apollophanes son of Apollophanes, of Seleukeia in Pieria, Arkesilaos, son of Arkesilaos, officer, in token of gratitude.

Commentary. The stele bearing this ex-voto was found in modern Gördes, in eastern Lydia (photograph of site in *TAM* 5.1, plate 5; also Herrmann 1970).

See chap. 2, introduction (on this document as emblem for Antiochos' movements); Ch. 3 § 1 (on garrisons).

40. *Honorific Decree of the Sardians (between 209 and 193)*

Robert 1964: 9–19, no. 1 (*editio princeps*, commentary), plates 1–2.

[πέμπεσθαι δὲ αὐτῶι ἀ]-
πὸ τῶν δημοτ[ε]λῶν θυσ[ιῶν γέρας· κα]-
λεῖσθαι δὲ καὶ εἰς τὰς θυσίας τ[ὰς δημοτε]-
[λε]ῖς καὶ εἰς τὸ πρυτανεῖον [ὁμ]οίως· κ[αλεῖσθαι δὲ]
[αὐ]τὸν καὶ εἰς προεδρίαν ἐν τοῖς ἀγῶσι π[ᾶσιν]   4
[οἷς ἡ] πόλις συντελεῖ· στῆσαι δὲ αὐτο[ῦ καὶ εἰ]-
[κόνα] χαλκῆν· στεφανῶσαι δὲ αὐτὸν καὶ χρ[υ]-
[σῶι σ]τεφάνωι ἀπὸ χρυσῶν δέκα ἐν τῆι ἐκκλ[η]-
[σίαι ἐ]ν ἧι ἂν ἡ περὶ τούτων ἀπόκρισις γραφεῖσ[α]   8
[ὑπὸ Ζ]εύξιδος ἀναγνωσθῆι, ἵνα πάντε[ς]
[εἰδῶσ]ιν τὴν εὐχαριστίαν τοῦ Σαρδιανῶ[ν]
[δήμου] καὶ τὴν κρίσιν, ὅτι το[ὺ]ς ἀξίους ἐπίσ-
[ταται π]ροσηκόντως τιμᾶν· ἀναγράψαι δὲ   12
[τόδε τὸ ψ]ήφισμα εἰς στή[λη]ν λευκοῦ λίθου καὶ
[παρασ]τῆσαι τῶι ἀνδριάντι· τὴν δὲ ἔγδοσ[ιν]
[τοῦ] στεφάνου καὶ τῆς εἰκόνος κ[αὶ] τῶν ἄλ-
[λων] ποήσασθαι Ἀθήναιον τὸν ταμίαν κ[αὶ]   16
[δοῦν]αι τὰ ἀναλώματα ἀφ' ὧν [χ]ειρί[ζει προσό]-
[δων πλ]ὴν τῶν ἀποτεταγμένων εἰς [τὰς τι]-
[μὰς? τ]ῶν βασιλέων καὶ τῆς βασιλία[σης].

18–19 'Peut-être ε[ἰς τοὺς ἀγῶνας τ]ῶν βασιλέων', Robert 1964, 18 (on grounds of line length, always a shaky criterion), though he notes that the meaning 'funds for honours for the kings' is certain, and suggests τιμάς; the same expression is found in the second Teian decree, document **18**, 63.

[(It seemed good to the council and the people) . . . to send to him a share] from the public sacrifices, and to invite him to public sacrifices, and to the *prytaneion* as well; to invite him to front seating in all the contests which the city celebrates; to erect a bronze statue of him; to crown him with a gold crown worth ten golden (staters) in the meeting of the assembly in which the answer written by Zeuxis on these matters will be read, so that all may **10** know of the gratitude of the people of the Sardians and the decision, namely that the people knows how to honour worthily those who deserve it; to write up this decree on a stele of white stone and to set it up next to the statue; to let Athenaios the treasurer contract out the supplying of the crown and the statue and the other things, and to let him cover the expenditure from the income which he handles, except for those allocated to the honours of the kings and the queen.

Commentary. The text is preserved on a marble stele found in Sardeis. It can be dated after 209, by the mention of 'the kings', Antiochos III and Antiochos the son (who was appointed co-regent in that year: Robert 1964: 18 and n. 2; J. and L. Robert 1983: 163 n. 1; Schmitt 1964: 13 and n. 1, generally 13–20).

The honorand is not a Sardian, and could be a Seleukid official honoured by the city of Sardeis. The κρίσις of line 11 is tentatively interpreted by Robert as 'la décision prise par ce décret' (Robert 1964: 14 n. 1), and expanded by the ὅτι clause.

41. *Royal Documents from Sardeis (213–190)*

Text A: Gauthier 1989: 112–16, no. 4 A, edition, commentary, plate 5 (*SEG* 39.1286 A).
Text B: Gauthier 1989: 125–6, no. 5, edition, commentary, plate 6 (*SEG* 39.1287).
Text C: Gauthier 1989: 127–9, no. 6, edition, commentary, plate 7 (*SEG* 39.1288).
Text D: Gauthier 1989: 129–34, no. 7, edition, commentary, plate 8 (*SEG* 39.1289).

A.

ΚΑΘ . . Α Σ [ἀπ]αγγελο[ῦ]-

[σιν ὑ]μῖν καὶ οἱ πρεσβευταὶ περὶ τῶν αὐτῶν. vac. Ἔρρωσθε

1 Gauthier suggests ἐν τοῖς καθ᾽ [ἡμ]ᾶς or ἐν τοῖς καθ᾽ [ὑμ]ᾶς.

[. . . in matters] concerning you (?). Your ambassadors will also tell you about these same matters. Farewell.

B.

Βασιλεὺς [Ἀντίοχος Σαρδιανῶν τῆι βουλῆι καὶ τῶι]
δήμωι χαίρ[ειν·   three or four names   οἱ παρ᾽ ὑ]-
μῶν πρ[εσβευταὶ ἀπέδωκαν ἡμῖν τὸ ψήφισμα ἐν ὧι]
ἐγεγ[ράφειτε   c.29   ]   4
γη[   ]
τοῖς [   ]
καὶ ἐ[   ]
ὅσοι Μ[   ]   8
ΑΔΙΑ[   ]
χιστ[   ]
μηδ[   ]

Gauthier proposes the following restorations, tentatively: 5 γῆ[ν] or γῆ[ς]   8 ὅσοι
μ[ή]   9 e.g. ἀδια[ίρετος], ἀδιά[λειπτος] or ἀδιά[πτωτος]   9–10 [ὡς τά]χιστ[α] or
[τὴν τα]χίστ[ην]   11 μηδ[έ] or μηδ[έν].

King [Antiochos to the council and the] people [of the Sardians] greetings
(three or four names) your am[bassadors handed over to us the decree in
which you had] written . . . land (?) . . . the . . . and . . . as soon as possible
(?) . . .

C.
These three fragments belong to the same document, but the order of C 2
and C 3 is uncertain

C. 1
[Βασιλεὺς Ἀντίοχος Σ]αρδια[νῶν τῆι βουλῆι καὶ τῶι δήμωι χαίρειν]
[e.g. Ἀπολ]λων[ίδης   ]

   The exact beginning and end of the lines are unknown, and the reconstruction presented above is merely a possibility.   2 Ἀπολλώνιος is another possibility. Both
names, Gauthier observes, are well attested in Sardeis.

C. 2
        ἀτέλειαν ἐ[τῶν numeral]
[διατ]ροφὴν καὶ σπέ[ρμα]

   2 On the parallel of the Korrhagos decree (SEG 2.663), as pointed out by Gauthier,
[σῖτον εἰς διατ]ροφὴν καὶ σπέ[ρμα].

(we grant) exemption from taxes for [. . .] y[ears . . . (grain for) sub]sistence
and so[wing . . .]

C. 3
[   ]ΚΟΜΙ[   ]
[   ]ΑΕ[   ]
[   ] Γ [   ]

   1 A form of κομίζειν or κομιδή, Gauthier.   2 ἀε[ί], Gauthier.

D.
[ἡ] βασίλισσα γέγρα[φεν   ]
[   ]ΕΝΕΙ τῶν περὶ ΗΜΑΣΕΙ[   ]
[   ]ἐν τῆι περὶ Σάρδεις οἰκον[ο]μία[ι   ]
[   ]Πορσουδδα κώμην καὶ ΣΑΝΝ . ΦΕ[   ]   4
[   ]ΤΑΙΣ κατὰ τοὺς προυπάρχοντ[ας περιορισμούς?   ]
[   ]ΣΙΝ ἐν ταῖς κώμ[αι]ς καὶ τοῖ[ς] ἀγ[ροῖς?   ]
[   ]ΤΑΙ αὐτός τε καὶ οἱ ἔγγονοι αὐτοῦ[   ]
[   ]Υ [ ]ΠΛΗ . ωΝΤΟ[   ]   8

   6 ἀγ[ροῖς] seems a reasonable suggestion, especially since on the photograph the
letter after gamma seems to present the 'haste verticale très longue' typical of the rho in
this inscription (Gauthier 1989: 131). However, RC 10–13 and 18–21 use the word χώρα
for land given or sold by a king. Gauthier notes that the last letter preserved in the line
could be pi as well as gamma: perhaps τοῖ[s] ἀπ[ο   ], for instance a noun qualified
by a passive participle of ἀποδείκνυμι?

The queen wrote . . . in the *oikonomia* around Sardeis . . . the village of Porsoudda and . . . according to the pre-existing [surveys?] . . . in the villages and the [fields?] . . . himself and his descendants . . .

Commentary. Text A: these two lines are carved on a marble block, no doubt from the Metroon since it comes from the excavations of the Roman synagogue where blocks from the Metroon were reused. However, the block does not belong to the pilasters on which documents **1**, **2**, **3**, are carved. Below these lines, there is a Sardian decree for Heliodoros, honoured for going on embassies and serving as a foreign judge (Attalid period).

Text B: the text is preserved on three marble fragments from the synagogue excavation; Gauthier associates it with documents from the time of Antiochos III on grounds of appearance and letter-form.

Text C: on material grounds (letter-forms, dimensions, weathering), Gauthier showed that three marble fragments belong to the same document, a royal letter. Unfortunately, there is no join between any of the three pieces.

Text D: this small fragment was found near the synagogue in the bath–gymnasion complex at Sardeis, in a disturbed archaeological context.

Though it is almost certain that these three documents date from the time of Antiochos III, there is no further indication of date, so that they were not necessarily produced at the same time as documents **1–3**, in 213, immediately after the recapture of Sardeis by Antiochos; they could date to later contacts between the king and the city. Documents C and D, the first concerning a gift of grain, the second a land conveyance, could belong to the settlement of affairs in 213. C could concern a gift of grain to the city of Sardeis, to help it through an agricultural year after the sack of the city, and thus would belong to the measures the king took for the city's ἐπανόρθωσις (document **3**). Alternatively, it could concern the initial gift of grain and tax-exemption to a colony near Sardeis, like the Jews Zeuxis settled in Lydia and Phrygia, according to a document preserved in Josephus (*AJ* 12.147–53: on authenticity, see Appendix 3). However, a royal letter concerning the installation of a colony would rather be addressed to Zeuxis (in addition to the letter in Josephus, see Segre 1938 for a parallel: Eumenes II writes to an official, Artemidoros, concerning the settlement of the Καρδάκων κώμη near Telmessos).

42. Statue Base of Antiochos the Son (Klaros, between 197 and 193)

Robert 1964: 18 (with reference to future publication of a photograph of the 'belle base' with its 'inscription honorifique en très belles lettres'). I saw the stone in Klaros, in April 1997.

> Βασιλέα Ἀντίοχον
> βασιλέως μεγάλου Ἀντιόχου
> Διοσκουρίδης Χάρητος

King Antiochos, son of the great king Antiochos, dedicated by Dioskourides son of Chares.

Commentary. The base was found next to the temple of Apollo at Klaros, prolonging its south-east angle. It is still *in situ*: the recent reopening of the excavation at Klaros has made it visible, and the elegant, airy lettering is easily legible. The inscribed surface was much later reused to record a delegation to the oracle at Klaros.

The form of the dedication implies that the now-lost statue of Antiochos the son was put up, not by the Kolophonians, but by an individual—a Seleukid official, or a local friend of the Seleukids?

43. *Letter of Antiochos III to the Nysaians*

W. Judeich, *Ath. Mitt.* 15 (1890), 281–2, no. 32 (*RC* 43).

J. and L. Robert 1954: 291 n. 9, remark that 'rien dans les débris du texte ne permet de soutenir qu'il s'agit des "privilèges du Ploutonion", comme on l'a dit'; the text does not belong to the great archival inscription which recorded the temple privileges, but was carved on an independent stele found in Nysa and not at or near the site of the Ploutonion. The mention of a *dioiketes* does not prove, as Welles claims, that the privileges of the Ploutonion were involved; Antiochos would also have written to the *dioiketes* to give instructions for the implementation of a gift (for instance various subsidies, as at Herakleia: document **31** A; or Laodike's gift of grain to Iasos: document **26** A), a financial privilege or a transaction involving the city (as in the case of Apollonia under Salbake: document **44**). Piejko, *Historia* 38 (1989), 399, proposes various restorations, such as inserting a mention of an *epistates* as an addressee, presumably to fill the gap in line 1 (but the office is not attested elsewhere for Nysa) and naming the *dioiketes* Sopatros, on the basis that *RC* 9 (where one Sopatros does appear) should be dated to Antiochos III (not argued for, and highly unlikely: Appendix 3)

Βασιλεὺς Ἀν[τίοχος	c.20	τοῖς]
ἄρχουσιν καὶ [		]
ἧς γεγράφ[αμεν ἐπιστολῆς πρὸς		τὸν διοι]-
κητὴν [κατακεχώρισται τὸ ἀντίγραφον		] 4

King Antiochos . . . to the magistrates and [(the city) . . ., greetings; a copy of the letter] which we wrote [to . . . the *dioi*]*ketes* [is appended . . .]

Commentary. The inscription is preserved on a stele (see above, in lemma), next to a fragmentary decree, the exact relation of which to the royal letter is unclear (*RC*, p. 179; see p. 271 of this book).

44. *Decree of the Citizens of Apollonia under Salbake Honouring the Seleukid Hipparch, Philo . . . (between 213 and 190)*

J. and L. Robert 1954: 285–302, no. 166 (first edition with photograph of squeeze at plate 46; translation and commentary by sections; historical analysis of information on Seleukid administration).

Cf. Malay 1987: 14 (on the function of ὁ ἐπὶ τῶν ἱερῶν: the Pamukçu stele published by Malay, document **4**, makes explicit the financial nature of the office); Gauthier 1989: 42–5 (confirmation of the dating proposed by J. and L. Robert 1954; Ktesikles, Menandros the *dioiketes*, Demetrios the *eklogistes* all resided at Sardeis, in the light of the documents from this city). Austin 1981: no. 187, translation.

[ἔν τε τοῖς]
[πρότερον] χρόνοις εὔ[νους ὢν διετέλει κοινῆι τῶι]
[δή]μωι καὶ ἰδίαι ἑκάσ[τωι τῶν πολιτῶν· ταχθεὶς?]
[δὲ ἱπ]πάρχης ἐπὶ τῶν παρ' [ἡμῖν στρατιωτῶν?]
[τὴν πᾶ]σαν εὐταξίαν παρέσ[χηται· πρεσβευ]-   4
[τῶν δ]ὲ πεμφθέντων περὶ τῶν [συμφερόντων]
[τῶι δ]ήμωι πρός τε Κτησικλῆν τὸν [c.9   ]
. . . . . καὶ Μένανδρον τὸν διοικητὴ[ν ἐκτενῶς]
[ἑαυτὸ]ν ἐπιδοὺς, ὅτε οἱ πρεσβευταὶ ἀπῆ[λθον, καὶ]   8
[συνε]ισπορευόμενος αὐτοῖς ἔσπευδεν εἰ[ς τὸ πάν]-
[τα πορι]σθῆναι πε[ρὶ] ὧν ἠξιοῦμεν· ἔτι δὲ καὶ Δ[ημη]-
[τρίου] τοῦ ἐγλογιστοῦ εἰσκαλεσαμένου τοὺς
[πρεσ]βευτὰς ὑπὲρ ὧν ἐμπεφανίκει αὐτῶι Δημή-   12
[τριος] ὁ τεταγμένος ἐπὶ τῶν ἱερῶν, καὶ διαμ[φι]σβη[τή]-
[σαντο]ς πρὸς αὐτοὺς ὑπὲρ τῶν ἱερῶν κωμῶν [Σ]αλε[ι]-
[ων τε] τῶν ὀρείνων καὶ Σαλειων τῶν πεδιεινῶ[ν]
. . . .μενος παρεκάλει Δημήτριον μηθὲν τῶν   16
[προυπα]ρχόντων τῶι δήμωι κινεῖν ἐπὶ τῆς αὐτο[ῦ] πρα-
. . . . ιας, ἀλλ' ἐὰν διαμένειν καθάπερ [ἕ]ως
[τοῦ νῦν] καὶ τοῖς μετὰ ταῦτα πεμφθεῖσιν πρε[σ]βε[υ]-
[ταῖς περ]ὶ τῶν προδεδηλωμένων κωμῶν οὐ μ[ό]νο[ν]   20
[ἀκόλο]υθον τοῖς ἐψηφισμένοις προήκατο ἐπι[σ]τ[ο]-
[λὴν π]ρὸς Δημήτριον, ἀλλὰ καὶ ἀπαντήσας
[αὐτῶ]ι διελέγη φιλοτιμότερον καθότι καὶ οἱ [π]ρε[σ]-
[βευτα]ὶ ἀκούσαντες προσεμαρτύρησαν· τὸ δ' ὅ-   24
[λον ο]ὖ διαλείπει ἀεί τινος ἀγαθοῦ παραίτ[ι]ος
[γινό]μενος τοῖς πολίταις· δεδόχθαι Ἀπολλω-
[νιατ]ῶν τῆι βουλῆι καὶ τῶι δήμωι· ἐπηνῆσθα[ι] Φιλο-
. . . . ἀρετῆς ἕνεκεν καὶ εὐνοίας ἣν ἔχων   28
[διατ]ελεῖ εἰς τὸν δῆμον· δεδόσθαι δὲ αὐτ[ῶ]ι τε
[καὶ ἐ]κγόνοις πολιτείαν καὶ ἀτέλειαν πάντω[ν]
[ὧν ἡ] πόλις κύρια· καλεῖσθαι δὲ αὐτὸν κα[ὶ] εἰ[ς]
[προε]δρίαν καθ' ἕκαστον ἐνιαυτὸν καὶ στεφα-   32
[νοῦσ]θαι χρυσῶι στεφάνωι ἐν τῶι γυμνικῶ[ι] ἀγω-
[νι τῶ]ι συντελουμένωι τῶι βασιλ[εῖ] Σ[ελεύκωι]

1 The 'Seleukid' prescript was reconstructed in general terms by Robert 1954: 288. The secure attribution to the time of Antiochos III (see commentary below) allows us to fill in some of the specifics: [Βασιλευόντος Ἀντιόχου or βασιλευόντων Ἀντιόχου (Μεγάλου) καὶ Ἀντιόχου τοῦ υἱοῦ, ἔτους numeral μηνὸς Macedonian month, ἐπ' ἀρχιερέως Νικάνορος, ἐκκλησίας κυρίας γενομένης, ἔδοξεν Ἀπολλωνιατῶν τῆι βουλῆι καὶ τῶι δήμωι· ἐπειδὴ Φιλο— patronymic, ethnikon, κτλ. A mention of Nikanor as high-priest is probable: the official Demetrios, ὁ τεταγμένος ἐπὶ τῶν ἱερῶν, must be a successor or a subordinate of Nikanor (as official in charge of the sanctuaries), who was appointed in 209 (document 4). 2 πεμφθείς is also possible (J. and L. Robert 1954: 288). 3 J. and L. Robert 1954: 289–90 argue for their restoration τῶν παρ' [ἡμῖν στρατιωτῶν?]; though they admit that it is not absolutely certain; in any case, the sense is that Philo . . . commanded the local cavalry garrison (so perhaps ἱππέων should be restored; if that is too short, perhaps the word was something more exotic and specific, such as ἱπποτοξοτῶν or Ταραντίνων). 6 J. and L. Robert 1954: 292 and n. 1, τὸν [ἐπὶ τῶν προσόδων] would suit the lacuna, though the Roberts are cautious in proposing this restoration. 7 The adverb could also be, say, φιλοτίμως. 17–18 πραl[γματε]ίας is tempting, because the word can precisely designate the business of an official: LSJ πραγματεία (2), Preisigke, Wörterbuch πραγματεία (3), but the restoration might be too short for the lacuna (on the other hand, the last letter before IA is compatible with an epsilon). 34 The Roberts are categorical about the restoration Σ[ελεύκωι] ('il est absolument certain que c'est un sigma'), and the top of the sigma can be made out on the photograph of the squeeze.

(When Antiochos was king / Antiochos (the Great?) and Antiochos the son were kings, year . . ., month . . ., when Nikanor was high-priest, in full assembly; it seemed good to the council and the people of the Apollonians:—since Philo . . . son of . . .) earlier was continuously well [inclined in general towards the] people and in particular towards each [one of the citizens]; [having been named hip]parch over the [troops which stay with us], he ensures a complete state of discipline; ambassadors having been sent to Ktesikles the . . . and to Menandros the manager of finances (dioiketes), concerning the interests of the people, he put himself forward with great [zeal] when the ambassadors left, and 10 travelling with them he made efforts so that all the things which we were asking for should be procured; moreover, when Demetrios the controller of finances (eklogistes) summoned the ambassadors concerning the matters which Demetrios the official in charge of the sanctuaries had brought to his attention, and laid claims against the ambassadors concerning the sacred villages of [S]ale[ioi] in the mountains and Saleioi in the plain, . . . he invited Demetrios to change none of the privileges which the people enjoyed under his . . ., but to let them be as they had been until the present time, and he not only delivered to the ambassadors, who were sent at a later time 20 about the matter of the villages mentioned above, a letter addressed to Demetrios and which agreed with the (people's) decree, but he also went to meet him and spoke to him with great zeal, as the ambassadors bore witness, since they had heard him; in general, he does not cease to be always responsible for some good towards the citizens;—let it seem good to the council and the people of the Apollonians:—to praise Philo . . . on account of his quality and his goodwill towards the people; to give him 30 and to his descendants citizenship and exemption from all the taxes which the city has control of; to invite him to front seating every year, and to crown him with a gold crown in the gymnic contest which is celebrated in honour of king S[eleukos].

Commentary. The text is carved on a 'bloc de marbre' (J. and L. Robert 1954: 285; though the thickness (8 cm.) means the block was sawn down for reuse). The width can be reconstructed as 51 cm., the same as on the block bearing document **48**: both texts were inscribed on a same building, on the *antas* (Robert 1954: 286).

Since Ktesikles is also mentioned in the first letter of Antiochos to the Sardians (document **1**, 8), this inscription can be securely dated to that king's reign, between 213 (the date of the Sardian document) and the end of Seleukid rule in Asia Minor in 189/8, thus confirming the Roberts' attribution (J. and L. Robert 1954: 286–8).

Ktesikles' involvement in financial matters concerning Sardeis as well as Apollonia suggests that he wielded authority over the whole of cis-Tauric Asia, as a financial counterpart of the viceroy Zeuxis. Ktesikles, as well as the other officials mentioned in the Apollonian document, probably operated from Sardeis, and the Apollonian embassy presumably travelled there to meet them, and back. It is likely that Demetrios ὁ τεταγμένος ἐπὶ τῶν ἱερῶν (lines 12–13) was appointed to succeed Nikanor as official in charge of the shrines in cis-Tauric Asia Minor (rather than an official operating locally in Karia).

See Ch. 3 § 2 on this document's implications for the workings of Seleukid administration; Ch. 4 § 2c (on the socialization of royal officials).

IV Aftermath

45. *Letter of the Scipios to the Herakleians (late 190)*

CIG 3800 ('ex schedis Pittaci,' i.e. K. Pittakis; misattributing the text to Herakleia Pontike); *LBW* 3.588; W. Judeich, *Ath. Mitt.* 15 (1890), 254–8, no. 7 (*Syll.* 618); *RDGE* 35 (composite text, taking into account the identification of the authors and the improvements by de Sanctis and Holleaux: below). The stone (whose left side is eroded) is in the Louvre (MA 2819), where I examined it in March 1997, with Ph. Gauthier.

M. Holleaux, *REA* 19 (1917), 237–51 (reprinted in ΣΤΡΑΤΗΓΟΣ ΥΠΑΤΟΣ (Paris, 1918), 131–46), arguing against attribution to Manlius Vulso; G. de Sanctis, *Atti Accad. Torino* 5 (1921/2), 242–9 (attribution to the Scipios), accepted and refined by M. Holleaux, *Riv. Fil.* 52 (1924), 29–44 (esp. 39–41). Wörrle 1988: 428 n. 14 for textual notes from autopsy and squeeze; photograph published by Robert 1987: 197 (reproduced from *BCH* 102 (1978), 501). Wörrle 1988: 455 (Dias, Dionysios, and Menes appear in embassies both to Zeuxis and to the Scipios). On date, Gauthier in *BE* 89, 277, p. 406. Austin 1981: no. 159, translation.

[Λεύκιος Κορνήλιος Σκιπίω]ν στρατηγὸς ὕπατος Ῥωμαίων
[καὶ Πόπλιος Σκιπίων ὁ ἀδελ]φὸς Ἡρακλεωτῶν τῆι βούληι καὶ τῶι δή-

[μωι χαίρειν·] ἐνέ[τυχον] ἡμῖν οἱ παρ᾽ ὑμωμ πρέσβεις Διᾶς, Διῆς, Διονύ-
[σιος,   ]άμ[αν]δρος, [Εὔ]δημος, Μόσχος, Ἀριστείδης, Μένης, ἄνδρες κα-   4
[λοὶ κἀγαθοί], οἳ τό τε [ψήφ]ισμα ἀπέδωκαγ καὶ αὐτοὶ διελέγησαν ἀκολού-
[θως τοῖ]ς ἐν τῶ[ι ψη]φίσματι κατακεχωρισμένοις οὐδὲν ἐλλειπόντες
[φιλοτι]μίας· ἡμ[εῖ]ς δὲ πρὸς πάντας τοὺς Ἕλληνας εὐνόως διακείμεν[οι]
[τυγχά]νομεγ καὶ πειρασόμεθα, παραγεγονότων ὑμῶν εἰς τὴν ἡμέτεραμ   8
[πίστιμ], πρόνοιαμ ποιεῖσθαι τὴν ἐνδεχομένην, ἀεί τινος ἀγαθοῦ παρα[ί]
[τιοι γεν]όμενοι· συγχωροῦμεν δὲ ὑμῖν τήν τε ἐλευθερίαγ καθότι καὶ
[ταῖς ἄ]λλαις πόλεσιν, ὅσαι ἡμῖν τὴν ἐπιτροπὴν ἔδωκαν, ἔχουσιν ὑ[φ᾽]
[αὑτοὺς πά]ντα τὰ αὐτῶμ πολιτεύεσθαι κατὰ τοὺς ὑμετέρους νόμους   12
[καὶ ἐν τ]οῖς ἄλλοις πειρασόμεθα εὐχρηστοῦντες ὑμῖν ἀεί τινος ἀγαθοῦ
[παραίτ]ιοι γίνεσθαι· ἀποδεχόμεθα δὲ καὶ τὰ παρ᾽ ὑμῶμ φιλάνθρωπα καὶ τὰς
[τιμάς, κ]αὶ αὐτοὶ δὲ πειρασόμεθα μηδενὸς λείπεσθαι ἐγ χάριτος ἀποδόσει·
[ἀπεστά]λκαμεν δὲ πρὸς ὑμᾶς Λεύκιον Ὄρβιον τὸν ἐπιμελησόμενον τῆς   16
[πόλεως κ]α[ὶ] τῆς χώρας ὅπως μηδεὶς ὑμᾶς παρενοχλῆι. Ἔρρωσθε.

1 Wörrle holds the *nu* in [Σκιπίω]ν for absolutely certain; Haussoullier and, more
tentatively, Rayet had read the same letter (*Rev. Phil.* 23 (1899), 278, though admitting
sigma as a possibility); the photograph published by Robert also suggests a *nu*. After
examining the stone, I also read a *nu* (*sigma* is excluded). This reading compels the
restoration of the name of L. Scipio as given above.   2 The *phi* entails the word
[ἀδελ]φός and hence the authorship by the Scipios; the reading was proposed by
Holleaux, *Riv. Fil.* 52 (1924), 39–41, and reproduced by Sherk in *RDGE*. *Phi* is considered as certain by Wörrle, according to whom the stone bears a long vertical stroke
which can only belong to a *phi* (and not the *rho* of earlier texts). On examining the stone
I could not make out this long vertical stroke, but could see a small ellipse suggesting
the middle part of a *phi*.   15 [πίστεις] from Böckh, and reproduced ever since; but
it is better to restore τιμάς, to obtain ἀποδεχόμεθα δὲ καὶ τὰ παρ᾽ ὑμῶν φιλάνθρωπα καὶ τὰς
[τιμάς]. For a parallel, e.g. document 31 A, I 6–7 (ironically, Antiochos III to Herakleia
under Latmos); *RC* 52, lines 41–42 (Eumenes II to the Ionians), is similar.

[Lucius Cornelius Scipio] consul of the Romans, and [Publius Scipio], his
brother, to the council and the people of the Herakleians, greetings. Your
ambassadors have met us: Dias, Dies, Diony[sios, . . .]am[an]dros,
[Eu]demos, Moschos, Menedemos, Aristeides, Menes, e[xcellent] men,
who handed over the decree and themselves spoke according to the
contents of the decree, leaving out nothing in matters of zeal. As for us, we
happen to be well disposed towards all the Greeks, and we will try, since
you have come over into our [faith], to show solicitude as much as
possible, always trying to be **10** responsible for some advantage. We grant
you your liberty, just as to other cities which have entrusted themselves to
us, with the right to see all your own affairs conducted by yourselves
according to your laws, and in all other matters we will try to assist you and
always be responsible for some advantage. We also acknowledge the
favours and the [honours] from you, and we will try for our part to fall
behind in nothing as concerns the returning of gratitude. We have sent to
you Lucius Orbius who will take care of your city and your territory, so
that no one should trouble you. Farewell.

Commentary. The text is preserved on an *anta* block from the temple of
Athena at Herakleia (now in the Louvre).

46. *Letter of the Scipios to the Kolophonians (189)*

Ch. Picard, *Ephèse et Claros* (Paris, 1922), 144–6, text at 145 n. 5 (*SEG* 1.440); M. Holleaux, *Riv. Fil.* 52 (1924), 29–44, with new supplements and historical commentary (*RDGE* 36 is Holleaux's version); L. Robert, from a squeeze,[1] provided elements for a new text, notably by determining that the text was complete or nearly complete on the right hand side, and by offering a new reading at line 3 (Robert in Holleaux 1968: 34–5). Robert's text is followed below.

Picard (above) describes the lettering as first century BC, and hence suggests that the text was recut.

[*c*.13   Λ]εύκιος [Κορνήλιος Σκι]-
[πίων στρατηγὸ]ς ὕπατος Ῥωμαίων καὶ [Πό]-
[πλιος Σκιπίων ὁ] ἀδελφὸς Κολοφονίων (sic) τῆ[ι]
[βουλῆι καὶ τῶι δήμ]ωι χαίρειν. ἐνέτυχο[ν]   4
[ἡμῖν οἱ παρ' ὑ]μῶν πρέσβεις Ἀγαμήδης καὶ
[*c*.7   ἄνδρε]ς καλοὶ κἀγαθοι, ⟨οἳ⟩ τό τε
[ψήφισμα ἀπέδω]καν καὶ αὐτοὶ διελέγη- vac.
[σαν ἀκολούθ]ως τοῖς ὑφ' ὑμῶν δεδογμέ-   8
[νοις, οὐδὲν ἐλ]λείποντες φιλοτιμίας καὶ
[*c*.17   ]ναι τὸ ἱερὸν ἄσυ-
[λον   ]

1 Robert proposed Παρὰ Ῥωμαίων to fill the lacuna, since the document belonged to a dossier of *asylia* acknowledgements. Another possibility is a local dating formula, ἐπὶ τοῦ δεῖνα.   1–3 The solution for the names adopted here is Holleaux's, with hesitations as to the last form. Robert could not read a *nu* in line 3, and hence proposed [Λ]εύκιος [Κορνήλιος Πο | πλίου] and [Πό | πλιος Κορνήλιος]; but the parallel letter of the Scipios to Herakleia makes Λεύκιος Κορνήλιος Σκιπίων certain.   3 I have added the definite article to read [ὁ] ἀδελφός, favoured by Holleaux but ruled out by the *nu* which Robert subsequently dismissed. Picard's text, reproduced above, is Κολοφονίων, usually corrected to Κολοφ⟨ω⟩νίων; Robert's Κολ⟨ο⟩φωνίων is presumably an oversight. 5 Picard's [οἱ δύο παρ' ὑμῖν πρέσβεις] is not necessary.   6 *Pace* Hondius in *SEG* 4.567, the relative clause is necessary, since it also appears in the letter of the Scipios to Herakleia.   9–10 The general sense is clear: the ambassadors made a request for the *asylia* of the temple of Apollo Klarios to be acknowledged or declared.

[. . . L]ucius [Cornelius Scipio, consul] of the Romans and [Publius Scipio, his] brother, to the council and the people of the Kolophonians, greetings. Your ambassadors Agamedes and . . ., excellent men, met [us], (who) handed over [the decree] and themselves spoke [in accord]ance with the things you had decreed, omitting [nothing] pertaining to zeal and [. . .] to . . . the shrine inviolate . . .

[1] Robert does not give details, but this squeeze presumably figured among the collection of squeezes taken from the stones found by Th. Macridy-bey and Ch. Picard in 1913: this collection was entrusted to L. Robert by Picard (Robert 1989: 2 n. 6). Another possibility is that Robert took this squeeze from the stone (Robert 1989, *ibid*. states that some of the 1913 stones were seen again by the Roberts in their first season at Klaros), in the field or in the old museum in Izmir, in Basmane, which had acted as a depot for the excavations by Picard and Macridy-Bey.

Commentary. The support for the text is an architectural block from the shrine of Apollo at Klaros (Picard, *Ephèse et Claros*, 143–4).

47. Decree of the Amyzonians for Dionysios (after 188)

J. and L. Robert 1983: 202–4, no. 22 with photograph of squeeze.

```
[                                        ἔδοξεν τῆι]
βούληι καὶ τῶι δ[ήμωι· γνώμη πρυτάνεων· ἐπειδὴ Διο]-
[ν]ύσιος {ιος} Ἱεροκλείους τῶν πολι[τῶν            ]
[χρή]σιμον ἑαυτὸν εἰς πάντα τὰ συμφέροντα [τῶι]
[κοινῶι πα]ρέχεται, πρότερόν τε πρεσβεύων πρὸ[ς Ζεῦ]-          4
[ξιν τὸν γε]νόμενον ἐπὶ τῶν πραγμάτων π[ολλὰ καὶ]
[μεγάλα φι]λάνθρωπα περιεποίησεν· ὁμοίω[ς δὲ καὶ]
[νῦν πρὸς τ]οὺς στρατηγοὺς πρεσβεύων [    c.6–7    ]
[     c.8     ] σ[υ]γκατασκευ[άζ]ει τῶι κοινῶ[ι    c.6–7   ]     8
[    c.8–9    συγ]κεχω[ρημένα φιλάνθρωπ[α    c.6–7   ]
[           ]Π[          ] τίμια [                  ]
               traces of 1 line
```

1 In the lacuna, formula for date. 4 κοινῶι on the basis of line 8; the Roberts also suggest δήμωι.

. . . it seemed good to the council and the people; [proposal of the *prytaneis*; since Dio]nysios, son of Hierokles, among the citizens, . . . makes himself useful concerning all the interests of [the commonwealth]; first, by going on embassies to [Zeuxis] the official in charge of affairs, he secured many great favours; likewise, at the present time, by going on embassy to the generals, . . . he obtains for the commonwealth . . . conceded privileges . . . grants of honours . . .

Commentary. The marble fragment which bears this text no doubt came from an *anta* block of the temple or the monumental gateway to the Artemision.

48. Decree of the Citizens of Apollonia under Salbake for Pamphilos (after 188)

Robert 1954: 303–12, no. 167, with plate 47 (edition, translation, commentary by paragraphs).

```
[                     τῶν δέκα πρεσβευτῶν ἀπὸ Ῥώ]-
μης μετὰ Γναί[ο]υ τοῦ στρατηγοῦ τἄλ⟨λ⟩α δι[οι]-          1
κούντων ἐν Ἀπαμείαι, πορευθεὶς πρὸς
αὐτοὺς καλῶς καὶ συμφερόντως
ὑπὲρ τῆς πατρίδος ἐστήσατο καὶ ἐν ἐ-          4
κείνοις τοῖς καιροῖς, οὔτε κίνδυνον ὑφι-
δόμενος τὸν ὄντα πρὸ ὀφθαλμῶν οὔτε
κακοπαθίαν οὐδεμίαν ἐκκλίνων, μετὰ
```

πάσης σπουδῆς καὶ φιλοτιμίας ἕκαστα τού-   8
των διώικησεν· μετὰ δὲ ταῦτα πεμφθεὶς
εἰς Ῥόδον καὶ διαγωνισάμενος μετὰ τῶν
συμπρεσβευτῶν πρὸς τοὺς ἀντικειμέ-
νους τῶν ἐγχωρίων, ὡς ἐνεδέχετο μά-   12
λιστα συμφέρειν, οὕτως ἐποιήσατο τὰς συν-
θήκας πρὸς Ῥοδίους· ἄλλας τε πλείονας
πρεσβείας πρεσβεύσας ὑπὲρ τῶν κοινῶν
καὶ ἐμ πάσαις δεόντως ἀναστραφεὶς καὶ ὀρ-   16
θῶς χρησάμενος τοῖς πράγμασιν πολλῶν ἀγα-
θῶν τῆι πόλει παραίτιος γέγονεν· τῶν δὲ προσόδων
τῶν δημοσίων μὴ ὀρθῶς διοικουμένων, ἀλλὰ διαφ[ω]-
νουσῶν οὐχ ὡς ἔτυχεν, ψήφισμα γράψας καὶ ἐπιδοὺς   20
τῆι βούληι καὶ τῶι δήμωι ἐποίησεν αὐτὰς διασώιζεσ-
θαι, τῶν προχειρζομένων ἀνδρῶν κατ' ἐνιαυτὸν ἕκασ-
[τ]α διοικούντων κατ⟨ὰ τὸ⟩ ψήφισμα ὥστε μηθὲν ἔτι διάπτω-
μα γενέσθαι, καὶ τὸ ὅλον [ἐμ π]αντὶ καιρῶι καὶ λέγων καὶ γρά-   24
φων καὶ πράσσων τὰ βέλτιστα ὑπὲρ τοῦ δήμου διατελεῖ
τηλαυγῆ δεικνύων τὴν σπ[ου]δὴν ἐμ πᾶσιν ἣν ποιεῖται
ὑπὲρ τῆς πόλεως· ἐπ[ε]ὶ οὖν πολλὰς καὶ μεγάλας χρείας
παρείσχηται τῶι δήμωι, δίκαιον δέ ἐστιν τοὺς ἀγαθοὺς   28
τῶν ἀνδρῶν καταξίας χάριτας κομίζεσθαι τῶν εὐε[ρ]-
γετημάτων· δεδόχθαι Ἀπολλωνιατῶν τῆι βουλ[ῆι]
καὶ τῶι δήμωι· ἐπηινῆσθαι Πάμφιλον ἀρετ[ῆς ἕνεκεν]
[κ]αὶ εὐνοίας ἣν ἔχων διατ[ελεῖ   ]   32
[κ]αλεῖσθαι δὲ αὐ[τὸν   εἰς προεδρί]-
αν καθ' ἕκα[στον ἐνιαυτὸν ἐν τῶι συνελουμέ]-
νωι γυ[μικῶι ἀγῶνι   ]

33 Robert proposes [καὶ τοὺς ἐκγόνους].   35 Robert 1954: 312, suggests that the
contest was celebrated for Seleukos (I), here as for the decree in honour of the Seleukid
hipparch (line 34).

[. . . as the ten legates from Ro]me were settling all the other matters, with
Cnaeus the consul, at Apameia, (Pamphilos) travelled to see them and
behaved in a fine and useful manner on behalf of his fatherland, and in
those circumstances, without avoiding the danger that lay before his eyes
nor any hardship, he handled each of these matters with all eagerness and
zeal; after these events, having been sent **10** to Rhodes and having
struggled, with his fellow-ambassadors, against those of the locals who
were our opponents, he concluded agreements with the Rhodians, in the
manner that was the most likely to be useful; having gone on many other
embassies on behalf of the common interests, and having behaved properly
on all of them, and having dealt with affairs rightly, he has been
responsible for many advantages for the city; and as the public finances
were not administered rightly, but **20** were being squandered in a quite
extraordinary way, having written a decree and passed it on to the council
and the people, he brought it about that the public finances be saved, since

the citizens elected year by year were administering everything according
to the decree, so that no losses occurred anymore; and in general, on every
occasion, by speaking, writing, and doing the best on behalf of the people,
he continuously demonstrates the brilliance of the zeal which he has in all
matters on behalf of the city;—since then he has performed many great
services for the people, and since it is just that good men should receive
tokens of gratitude worthy of their benefactions;—**30** let it seem good to
the council and the people of the Apolloniates:—to praise Pamphilos on
account of his excellence and the goodwill which he continuously has
[(towards the city) . . .]; to invite him [and his descendants? . . .] to front
seating, each [year, in the] gymnic [contest celebrated for (king Seleukos?)]

Commentary. The decree is preserved on an architectural block, probably
from the *anta* of a monumental building: 'sans doute une parastade' (J. and
L. Robert 1954: 303), found in Medet, on the site of Apollonia. The width
of the block (51 cm.) is the same as can be restored for the block bearing
the decree for a Seleukid hipparch (document **44**), so that both documents
were probably inscribed on the same building (J. and L. Robert 1954: 286).

49. *Attalid Dossier Concerning the List of* Mystai *of Apollo Pleurenos (after 188)*

Malay and Nalbantoğlu 1996: 75–9, no. 1 (*editio princeps*; *SEG* 46. 1519).
See H. Müller, *Chiron* 30 (2000) 519–42.

Ἐπὶ Εὐθυδήμου ἀρχιερέως καὶ
ἱερέως Καδοου Πληρι· Εὐθυδ-
ήμωι ἀρχιερεῖ ὑπόμνημα πα-
ρὰ Καδοου, ἱερέως τοῦ ἐν Πλευ-   4
ροῖς Ἀπόλλωνος, ἔχοντος τὴν
ἱερητήαν ἐκ πλείονος χρόνου· ἠξ[ί]-
ωσα πρότερον ἐπ' Ἀντιόχου τοῦ
βασιλέως Νικάνορα τὸν ἀρχιερ[έ]-   8
α ἵνα στήσω στήλην ἐν τῶι ἱερῶι
κατατάξαντός μου τὸ ἐκείνου
ὄνομα καὶ τὸ ἐμὸν καὶ τῶν μυ[στ]-
ῶν καὶ νῦν ἀξιῶ σ' εἰ φαίνετα[ι]   12
συντάξαι γράψαι Ἀσκληπιάδ[ηι]
τῶι οἰκονόμωι ἵνα παραδείξῃ μοι
τόπον ἐν ᾧ σ[τ]ήσω τὴν στήλην
ἐν ᾗ κατατάξω τό τε σὸν ὄνομα   16
καὶ τὸ ἐμὸν καὶ τῶν μυστῶν.
Διόφαντος Ἀττινᾷ· τῆς γραφ[εί]-
σης μοι ἐπιστολῆς παρὰ Εὐθυδή-
μου τοῦ ἀρχιερέως ὑποτέταχά   20
σοι τὸ ἀντίγραφον. Εὐθύδημος Ἀ-
σκληπιάδῃ· τοῦ ἀναδοθέντος

μου ὑπομνήματος παρὰ Καδ-
οου ἱερέως τοῦ ἐν Πλευροῖς   24
Ἀπόλλωνος γενέσθω αὐτω-
ι καθάπερ ἠξίωσεν.
Μενεκράτης Ἑρμογένου
Μητρόδωρος Μιθρέους   28
     traces of one line

14 The stone reads ΠΑΡΑΔ^{E}ΙΞΗ, with an epsilon inserted above the line as an after-
thought (eds.).

When Euthydemos was high-priest, and Kadoos son of Pleri was priest.
Memorandum to Euthydemos the high-priest from Kadoos, the long-
standing priest of Apollo in Pleura: I earlier asked Nikanor, under
Antiochos the king, for permission to put up in the shrine a stele on which
10 I should record his name, and mine, and that of the initiates (*mystai*),
and now I ask you, if it seems appropriate to give that order, to write[1] to
Asklepiades the *oikonomos* to give me a place in which I may set up the stele
on which I may record your name and mine and that of the initiates.
Diophantos to Attinas: I have **20** joined a copy of the letter from
Euthydemos the high-priest. Euthydemos to Asklepiades: of the memorandum given to me from Kadoos the priest of Apollo in Pleura, let it be
for him as he asks. (List starts:) Menekrates son of Hermogenes,
Metrodoros son of Mithres . . .

Commentary. The dossier is inscribed on a stele, purchased by the Bergama
Museum and reportedly found north of the lake Koloe (modern Marmar
Gölü).
    Apollo Pleurenos and his *mystai* were already known from an inscription
published and treated by Robert (see Robert 1987: 323–9, reproducing the
original publication in *BCH* 106 (1082), 361–7): the priest Apollonios, son
of Kadoos, and the *mystai* honour one Menandros, the 'official in charge of
the sacred incomes', under the high-priesthood of Hermogenes. Thanks to
the new document, reproduced here, Malay and Nalbantoğlu 1996 reinter-
pret Robert's inscription: rather than dating to the first century BC, it must
be an Attalid document, relating to the same institutions as the present
inscription, and produced slightly later.
    See Ch. 3 § 2c (on the implications of this document for the activity of
Nikanor, and the control of the Seleukid state over the local shrines).

[1] I have preferred to punctuate and translate εἰ φαίνετα[ι] | συντάξαι, γράψαι
Ἀσκληπιάδ[ηι], literally 'if it seems good to you to order, (I ask you) to write to
Asklepiades', rather than the editors' 'If it seems good to you, (I ask you) to order to
write'. Euthydemos did not need to give an order to write: as a royal official, his medium for conveying orders was the writing of letters. To order and to write were coterminous for him: hence the interchangeability of the terms, and Kadoos could as well have
said 'If it seems good to you to write it, please give the order that . . .'.

AFTERTHOUGHTS

The Great King and the cities: I tried to talk about empire, and generally about power; about the *polis*, and generally about freedom; about documents, and generally about language. At least, there are lots of inscriptions. The more general propositions are firstly, that a Hellenistic kingdom such as the Seleukid developed powerful integrative structures, concrete and ideological—indeed, the apparatus of administration is also a body of knowledge and a language that express power; secondly, that empire existed as dialogue in a space where power was not monopolizable, with entities that preserved agency, local purpose and identity, the Hellenistic *poleis*. But to whose advantage the dialogue? There are various places on the dialectical spiral (I get you to allow me, I allow you to get me to allow you, etc.) where one can get off; that very indeterminacy is what matters, as the general context for individual cases.

There are two areas that I regret not treating in this work. The first is art history. It is true that there is little evidence directly concerning the story of Antiochos III and the cities of Asia Minor: we do not have the Teian statues for king and queen (documents **17**, **18**), or the honorific portrait of Antiochos III set up by the Xanthians (see below), or an image-bearing crown from the cult of Laodike (document **37**), or the statue put up privately by one Chares for Antiochos the son as the first monument on the sacred way leading south from the temple of Apollon Klarios, then being built (document **42**), or the statue of Antiochos III set up at Delos by Menippos (*OGIS* 239) or a statue of Zeuxis, either with his king, Antiochos III, or set up by his royal master (no documents yet, though *OGIS* 236 is a statue base for Zeuxis, set up by the people of Pergamon). However, this very list of instances shows how central images were to the relations between rulers and ruled; they served as tokens in the various political transactions, and they did so in a visual language of kingship, which deserves analysis as much as the decrees and letters. Even if there are no actual statues of Antiochos III or Zeuxis surviving (and a head in the Louvre might well be a copy of a portrait of the king), there is enough material to study the visual aspects as a central part of royal ideology. This has been made clear by R. R. R. Smith, *Hellenistic*

Royal Portraits (Oxford: Clarendon Press, 1988), and A. Stewart, *Faces of Power: Alexander's Image and Hellenistic Politics*, Berkeley and London: University of California Press, 1993).

The second area is numismatics, which in this work depends on the teaching of Le Rider dating back to the 1970s (p. 15). More generally, the paradigm is that developed by E. Bickerman, H. Seyrig, and G. Le Rider: silver coinage and autonomy are closely linked. This model has been challenged, for other periods than the Hellenistic; for the Hellenistic period, a paper by A. Meadows should give pause before repeating the orthodox views too easily: 'Money, freedom and empire in the Hellenistic world', in A. Meadows and K. Shipton (eds.), *Money and its Uses in the Ancient Greek World* (Oxford: Oxford University Press, 2001), 53–64. Furthermore, the numismatic evidence is highly relevant to the economy of Asia Minor, both in the third century BC, when the Seleukids levied tribute from the cities and the countryside, and the complicated second century BC, when civic coinage on the Attic standard, the Attalid system and the Rhodian system all co-existed: see essays by G. Le Rider and A. Bresson, in A. Bresson and R. Descat (ed.), *Les cités d'Asie Mineure occidentale au IIᵉ siècle a. C.* (Bordeaux: Ausonius, 2001), with further bibliography.

These two areas are whole fields in themselves, each offering its own possibilities for the study of royal power and civic identity. In the fields to which the present work has restricted itself, political history and epigraphy, enough new work has appeared recently to warrant discussion, or at least mention, for the sake of completeness.

H. Müller, 'Der hellenistische Archiereus', *Chiron* 30 (2000), 519–42, has thoroughly re-examined the problems and issues surrounding the title and function of Nikanor, the *archiereus* appointed over the shrines of Asia Minor in 209, and still in function at the eve of Magnesia (documents **1, 49**). Müller notably draws important parallels with the *prostagma* concerning cult for Laodike and the appointment of an *archiereia* (document **37**). He also points to an unnoticed appearance of the Attalid high-priest, Euthydemos; and suggests that the Attalid high-priest may have had to do with ruler cult for the Attalid kings. All relevant documents are reproduced and commented.

Müller agrees with my suggestion that the high-priest Nikanor was appointed to religious administration of local shrines; he suggests that the office was introduced across the Seleukid empire. However, he also argues that the office of *archiereus* was assigned to the empire-wide cult of Antiochos III and his ancestors. The *prostagma* concerning cult for Laodike (**37**) makes it clear that her eponymy in legal documents is analogous to the eponymy of 'the high-priest of us and our ancestors', in the imperial, centrally organized ruler cult. But the only *archiereus* which turns up as eponymous on documents is Nikanor: he must have turned into a high-priest of the ruler cult, when the latter was introduced, presumably in 204, on Antiochos' return from the Upper Regions. When Nikanor is named as high-priest in the pre-amble to documents from Amyzon in 202 and 201 (**10**, **11**) and from Xanthos in 196 (**23**, **24**), he must already be the high-priest of the ruler cult. Around 190, when Kadoas asked Nikanor for permission to publish a *stele* with the name of Nikanor at the head of it (document **49**), he was applying the rule that the high-priest should be eponym-ous on legal documents—the only high-priest being Nikanor, and hence also the high-priest of the ruler cult.

This argument is very neat and powerful in accounting for the evi-dence. A counter-scenario could be proposed, but would need chan-ging various elements in the data. One could imagine that Nikanor remained 'high-priest' with a general purview over the shrines; that the central ruler cult was introduced in 193 BC, at the same time as, or shortly before, the cult for Laodike (contrary to what I wrote, pp. 64 and n. 47, 356). It is true that the document for Laodike only men-tions the high-priestess of the queen and the high-priest of Antiochos III and his ancestors as eponymous, but this might be because the high-priest of the king is the only one needed for the analogy.

Proof for this counter-hypothesis to Müller's argument is correct would come in the form of a document securely dated by the Seleukid era after the appointment of high-priestesses of Laodike in spring 193 BC (but before the Seleukid collapse of 190 BC) and showing the fol-lowing preamble: King Antiochos (without his son, who died before September 193 BC: above, p, 93), Seleukid era, Macedonian month, (general) high-priesthood of Nikanor, high-priesthood of Antiochos III and his ancestors, high-priesthood of Laodike. (I suggested some-thing similar at p. 145 n. 140). If this counter-hypothesis is wrong, a document of 192 should show Nikanor's high-priesthood of Antiochos III and his ancestors, and Berenike's high-priesthood of Laodike, in parallel. This solution is less cumbersome than the one I propose as a possibility.

In a recent fascicle of *Parola del Passato* devoted to Iasos and Italian work on the site, M. Nafissi has treated the letter of Laodike to Iasos and the Iasian decree for the queen 'L'iscrizione di Laodice (*IvIasos* 4). Revisione del testo e nuove osservazioni', *PP* 54 (2001), 101–46. He offers new readings and restorations, on the basis of autopsy of the stone. This is now the best text. I do not have the space to redo entirely the text and especially my apparatus for my version, document **26**, but I have used Nafissi, notably as the source for corrections at lines A 24 (πλέω for Pugliese Carratelli's πλέον), 25, 29, B I 3 (ἐκλησίαν, sic), 8 (Σωπάτρου for Garlan's Σωστράτου), B II 6 (καὶ τ. for Pugliese-Carratelli's ΑΓΗ), 8 (oblique stroke after ἐκ τῆς ἀρχῆς, thus excluding Blümel's [παραδιδότωσαν], which word is restored by Nafissi at the following line), 14–23.

In the same fascicle, R. Fabiani has published a document from Iasos, dating to the early second century BC: 'Un decreto ateniese riproposto a Iasos (IG II² 3 e Iasos 3926)', Parola del Passato 56 (2001), 69–100. This document records the decision to reinscribe an Athenian decree (known from a stele in Athens!) dating to the Ionian war, probably 412 BC, Fabiani proposes the years after 188 BC as a possible context: the Athenian praise and care for Iasians who had suffered at the hands of the Persians perhaps paralleling the expulsion of anti-Seleukid elements, and 'enslavement' at the hands of the Great King, Antiochos III. This theme can be paralleled in Rhodian propaganda and historiography (the allusion to the Peace of Kallias in dealings with Antiochos III in 197 BC, whether actually voiced then, or invented after 188 BC: p. 111). For further echoes (Antiochos cast in the role of the Persian king in Roman historiography), see J.-M. Bertrand, 'Continent et outre-mer: l'espace vécu des Romains', in P. Cabanes (ed.), L'Illyrie meridionale et l'Épire dans l'antiquité (Clermont-Ferrand: Adosa, 1987), 263–70 at 269.

Antiochos III has turned up, rather surprisingly, on a document from the island of Keos, close to Attika: P. G. Kalligas, 'Ἡ πόλη τῆς Ἰουλίδας στα Ἑλληνιστικὰ χρόνια', in L. Mendone and A. Mazarakis Ainian (eds.), Kea-Kythnos: historia kai archaiologia (Athens: Research Centre for Greek and Roman Antiquity, 1998), 625–30; there are important corrections by Ph. Gauthier, BE 99, 427.

Ἀρχέλας εἶπεν· ἔδοξε τῆι βου[λῆι καὶ τῶι δήμωι·]
ἐπειδὴ ἀναγγέλλει Θεοτελίδης Ἀ[δείμαντον]
καὶ Μένιππον Κρίτωνος τεταγμέ[νου ὑπὸ]
τὸμ βασιλέα Ἀντίοχον, ἄνδρας ἀγα[θοὺς εἶναι]   4
περὶ τὴμ πόλιν καὶ τοῖς ἐντυγχάνου[σιν αὐτοῖς τῶμ]
πολιτῶν χρείας παρέχεσθαι καὶ ποιεῖν [ὅτι δύ]-
νανται ἀγαθόν· ἐπαινέσαι αὐτοὺς καὶ σ[τεφα]-
νῶσαι θαλλοῦ στεφάνωι ἀρετῆς ἕνεκεν   8
καὶ εὐνοίας ἧς ἔχοντες διατελοῦσιν εἰς
τὴμ πόλιν τὴν ἑαυτῶν καὶ ἀνακηρῦξαι τὸν
στέφανον Διονυσίοις τῶι ἀγῶνι τῶν τρα-
γωιδιῶν, ἀναγράψαι δὲ τὸ ψήφισμα εἰς στή-   12
λην λιθίνην καὶ στῆσαι εἰς τὸ ἱερὸν τοῦ
Ἀπόλλωνος· τὸ δὲ ἀνήλωμα δοῦναι τὸν
ταμίαν.
Ἀρχέλας εἶπεν· ἔδοξε τῆι βουλῆι καὶ τῶι δήμωι·   16

ἐπειδὴ ἀναγγέλλει Ἀρχέστρατος Κρίτωνα
Ἀδειμάντου πολίτην ὄντα καὶ τεταγμένον ὑπὸ τὸμ βασιλέα Ἀντίοχον πᾶσαν ἐπιμέλειαν ποειῖσθαι βουλεύοντα καὶ πράτ-   20
τοντα τῆι τε πατρίδι τὰ συμφέροντα καὶ
τοῖς ἐντυγχάνουσι αὐτῶι τῶν πολιτῶν
βουλόμενος ἐνδείκνυσθαι τὴν εὐνοίαν
καὶ τὴν φιλοτιμίαν ἣν ἔχων διατελεῖ· δεδό-   24
χθαι τῆι βουλῆι καὶ τῶι δήμωι· ἐπαινέσαι Κρίτωνα Ἀδειμάντου καὶ στεφανῶσαι θαλλοῦ
στεφάνωι ἀρετῆς ἕνεκεν καὶ εὐνοίας τῆς εἰς
τοὺς πολίτας καὶ ἀνακηρῦξαι τὸν στέφανον   28
Διονυσίοις τῶι ἀγῶνι τῶν τραγωιδιῶν, ἀναγρά-
ψαι δὲ τὸ ψήφισμα ⟨εἰς στήλην λιθίνην καὶ στῆσαι⟩ εἰς τὸ ἱερὸν τοῦ Ἀπόλλωνος·
τὸ δὲ ἀνήλωμα δοῦναι τὸν ταμίαν.

Archelas proposed; it seemed good to the council and the people; since Theotelides reports that A[deimantos] and Menippos, sons of Kriton, set under king Antiochos, [are] good men towards the city and that they perform services for those of their fellow citizens who meet them and that they do what good they can—to praise them and to crown them with a crown of leaf, for their goodness and their goodwill towards their own city, and to announce the crown at the Dionysia, during the contest of the tragedians, and to write up the decree on a stone *stele* and to erect it in the shrine of Apollon; and to have the treasurer give the expense.

Archelas proposed; it seemed good to the council and the people; since Archestratos reports that Kriton, son of Adeimantos, being a fellow citizen, and set under king Antiochos, takes all good care towards deliberating and doing the useful things for his fatherland, and that he demonstrates to those of his fellow citizens that meet him the good will and zeal which he continuously has—let it seem good to the council and the people—to praise Kriton son of Adeimantos and to crown him with a crown of leaf, for his goodness and his goodwill towards his fellow citizens, and to announce the crown at the Dionysia, during the contest of the tragedians, and to write up the decree (on a stone *stele* and to erect it) in the shrine of Apollon; and to have the treasurer give the expense.

Since the script dates to *c*.200, the king must be Antiochos III. Gauthier, on the grounds of formulas and institutions, has attributed this decree to Karthaia, rather than Ioulis (Kalligas). But both Gauthier and Kalligas seem to agree that these decrees reflect Seleukid control over Keos, at some time in the 190s. Gauthier suggests 194–192 BC, during the period of rising tension with Rome—or could 192 BC be possible, during the first year of the Romano-Seleukid war? However, are the honorands Seleukid governors of Keos (as Kalligas seems to imply, and Gauthier certainly states; also A. Bresson, same volume, p. 645). A family of governors is perfectly possible: *SEG*

2.536 shows us a team of brothers governing Herakleia under Latmos, probably for Philip V (Wörrle 1988, 433–4). But the expression here, τεταγμένον ὑπό +accusative, simply designates a royal officer, 'sous les ordres du roi', as Gauthier writes (in contrast with the expression τεταγμένος ἐπί which indicates appointment to local governorship: for instance documents **9, 10**, Amyzon, Alinda; document **19** shows the usage ὑπό +accusative for soldiers under an officer). In these two decrees, there are no specifications of place, especially any indication that these three men are governing their own city.

Two parallel documents are relevant, but inconclusive. First, *IG* 12.5.1061, also from Karthaia, dating to the time of the Chremonidean War (*c*.267): [Ἄ]ρ[ι]στοπείθης εἶπεν· ἔδοξε τῆι βουλῆι καὶ τῶι δήμωι· ἐ[πει]δὴ Ἱέρων Τιμοκράτους Συρακόσιος τεταγμένος ὑπὸ τὸμ βασιλ[έα] Πτολεμαῖον, παραγενόμενος εἰς τὴν νῆσον μετὰ τοῦ στρατηγοῦ Πατρόκλου, καθεστηκὼς ἐπιστάτης ἐν Ἀρσινόηι κτλ. Second, *IG* 11.4.1042 (earlier text *OGIS* 40), a decree of the Islanders of the early third century BC, found on Delos: [ἔδοξε τ]οῖς συνέδροις τῶν [νησι]ωτῶν· ἐπειδὴ Θέων [Φιλ]ίσκου Αἰγαεὺς τεταγμέ[νο]ς ὑπὸ τὸμ βασιλέα Πτολε[μα]ῖον ἐν Ἀλεξανδρείαι κτλ. These parallels might indicate that the Karthaians honoured in the decrees published by Kalligas were Seleukid officers, but not the governors of their city or the whole island of Keos: had they been so, the decrees would have specified the conditions and nature of their appointment, as in *IG* 12.5.1061. (The alternative, that there is no specification precisely because the men are governors, seems to me less likely.) However, if these three Karthaians are simply Seleukid officers, what are the relations between Keos and the Seleukid kingdom, and in what context are Keians meeting these Seleukid officers? Antiochos' presence in central Greece might be the occasion.

Less bafflingly, a new document has been published from Xanthos, thus adding to our picture of the city's history *c*.197: A. Bresson, 'Dédicace des Xanthiens à Antiochos III', in A. Bresson and R. Descat (eds.), *L'Asie Mineure occidentale au IIe siécle a. C.* (Bordeaux: Ausonius, 2001), *editio princeps*, photograph, and full commentary, especially on the implications for the status of Xanthos.

Βασιλέα Μέγαν Ἀντίοχον
ἀρετῆς ἕνεκεν καὶ εὐνοίας
τῆς εἰς αὐτόν, Ξανθίων ὁ δῆμος

The Great King Antiochos, dedicated by the people of the Xanthians on account of his quality and his goodwill towards it.

The document is inscribed on a block which belonged to a statue base. (The monument was not a cult statue dedicated to Antiochos, *qua* god, but an honorific statue representing Antiochos.) In addition to this honorific statue, the Xanthians did honour Antiochos III with a cult, as we know from the priest of the kings, Prasidas (documents 23, 24). The date of this document cannot be fixed precisely within the years 197–190 BC (say), the Seleukid takeover and the Seleukid defeat in the Roman-Seleukid War. It is possible, or even likely, that the Xanthians honoured Antiochos III with a statue early in their dealings with him, in the same negotiations that resulted in Antiochos 'consecrating' the city and in cultic honours for the king (document 22).

Bresson, after reviewing past scholarship, emphasizes the implications of the honorific aspect of the transactions between king and city, to re-examine the status of Xanthos under Antiochos III. It is not clear that Xanthos received privileges, in addition to, or as part of, its status as a 'holy' city. Bresson further argues (on the basis of Arrian 5.1.3–4, Alexander's grant to Nysa in India) that Xanthos was declared free and autonomous, and exempt from tribute. I am doubtful about this claim. The two Xanthian documents from the Seleukid period (23, 24) start with Seleukid regnal formulas (ruling kings, Macedonian month, Nikanor): I argued that these formulas were decided centrally in imperial edicts immediately performative in subject cities. Amyzon was declared *asylos* by Antiochos III (document 8), but used the Seleukid formulae in its decrees, and saw a Seleukid official in charge of the shrine (document 10). The case of Amyzon shows that *asylia* does not necessarily entail independence (see above, p. 157), and also, suggests that the use of Seleukid regnal formulae and other eponymous formulae are related with civic status.

Finally, a recently published document relates to the complicated situation in Western Asia Minor in the very last years of the third century BC and the first years of the second century BC: remarkably, three kings, Antiochos III, Philip V, Ptolemy V, are mentioned within three lines.

W. Blümel, 'Ein rhodisches Dekret in Bargylia', *EA* 32 (2000), 94–6 *editio princeps* with photograph (H.-U. Wiemer, 'Karien am Vorabend des 2. Makedonsichen Krieges. Bemerkungen zu einer neuen Inschrift aus Bargylia', *EA* 33 (2001), 1–14: much improved text, historical analysis). The text given here is Wiemer's, but with additions from a text kindly shown to me by C. Crowther, from a seminar session organized by P. S. Derow and led by A. Meadows in Oxford in 2000 (referred to below as Crowther-Meadows). I have also assumed that a few letters are missing on the left margin, for all lines. Many thanks to C. Crowther for discussing the text and giving me pictures.

[ ]ΝΤΩΝΘΕΑΘ ...6–7... ΝΕΙΛ
[ ]ΣΤΑΤΑΣ .. 4–5.. ΓΓ... ΑΝΕΙ.. 6.–7... Ο
[ ]ΩΡΙΣ.. .ΙΟ.. ΚΑΤΕΣΤΑΕΠΑ.....10–11.....Ν.Σ
[c.10–11 χρ ?]ηματος ΕΚΒΕΚΛ....8–9....ΝΤΑ   4
[ ]ΑΣΚΑ . Σ... ΕΚΒΕΒΛΗ ... [   ]
[π]οιησάμενοι [ὅπ]ως τῶν δικαίων τ ... 6-7...ΡΤΟ
[ ]ΟΙΣΕ.Τ.....10–11.....Υ γινέσθαι Τ. .. 6–7.... ΑΝΥΛ
[εὐ]χρηστήκειν πολλάκις αὐτοῖς καὶ ΕΙΣ.. 4.. Ω... [πο]λιτικω..ΤΩΝ 8
[ ] δεδανείκεαιν καὶ τὰ ψαφίσματα τὰ ὑπὲρ τού[τ]ων παρανε [γν]ώ[σ]θη
[σ]υνστάντος δὲ πολέμου βασιλεῖ Ἀντιόχωι ποτὶ βασιλῆ Π[το]λεμ[αῖον]
[τὸν] νῦν βασιλεύοντα κυριεῦσαι τοὺς παρὰ βασιλέως Ἀντι[ό]χο[υ   ]
[Κιλλα]ρῶν καὶ Θωδασων πρὸ τοῦ παρὰ βασιλέως Φιλίππου παρα[δ]ο[θήμειν] 12
[ ]Ἀντι[ό]χωι Θεάγγελα καὶ συμπολιτεύεσθαι Κιλλαρεῖς καὶ Θ[ωδασεῖς]
. ΕΠ......ΑΣΕΩΝΚΑΓΛ.......ΣΑ.. ΟΥΣ εἰς τὰν αὐτὰν
.....11.....βασιλ ..[παρανα]γινώσκοντας ἐπιστο[λὴν   ]
[   ]ΤΟ Κυλβισσεῦ[σι] 16

1–5 The text given here comes from Crowther-Meadows (reading and restorations), with a few more letters than Wiemer's text. At line 2, perhaps a form of [δ]ανεί[ζω], as in line 9? At 4, [ ]ΝΤ[ ] Wiemer. At line 3, Wiemer prints [ ]ΩΡΙΣ[ἀπο]κατέστα ΕΠ [ ]. The first few letters of the line could be restored [ἀφ]ωρίσ[θη], 'it was delimited', as part of a territorial arbitration. Wiemer sees no alternative to ἀπο]κατέστα, 'it was restored, given back', which would suit the context (a case made before an arbitration panel) very well. But the traces on the photograph are not compatible. Line 4 is printed as ΟΣΕ. ΒΕΒ[ ]ΤΟ by Wiemer.   6 Blümel [βασιλέ]ως γυναῖκα. Present reading by K. Hallof, reproduced in Wiemer.   8 εἰς [χρείας τὰς πο]λιτικ[ὰς αὐ]τῶν Wiemer. But the stone seems clearly to show an omega in the lacuna between ΕΙΣ and [πο]λιτικ[ ]. (Wiemer would like to see this as a mistake.) The reading must be πο]λιτικω[ ], for the left-hand serif of the omega is clearly visible on the photograph. Wiemer restores [ἄ | τοκα] at lines 8–9, '(he/they) lent money without interest'.   12 [ ]σων καὶ Θωδασων Blümel, Wiemer; the restoration printed above on the basis of the appearance of Kildara and Th[odoas/a/]. At the end of the line, Blümel printed πρὸ τοῦ παρὰ βασιλέως Φιλίππου παρα[γεν]ο[μένου], 'before the man arriving from King Philip'. But there is not enough space on the stone for this restoration, as shown by the photograph. The present restoration from Wiemer.   14 The readings from Crowther and Meadows, a few more letters than Blümel, followed by Wiemer.   15 παρανα]γινώσκοντας ἐπιστο[λὴν Wiemer's restoration.

... restored (?) ... expelled (?) ... of the rights ... (they said that e.g. such and such a community) often as useful to them and for political [uses? bodies?] made loans, and decrees concerning these matters were read out; (and they said) that, when war broke out from King Antiochos against King Ptolemy, the one now ruling, King Antiochos' men gained control of [Kilda]ra and Thodasa, before Theangela was handed over to Antiochos by King Philip and before the Kiladrians and Th[odasians] joind in sympolity, ... in the same ... reading out a letter (?) ...

Commentary. The events are placed in a clear order. Which of these events can be dated securely? Ptolemy V, 'the one ruling now', acceded in 203 BC or thereabouts. The handing over of Theangela must date after it was taken over by Philip V, during his campaign in

Asia Minor, in 201 BC. But which is the war between Antiochos III and Ptolemy V? Must this be the Fifth Syrian War (200 BC), as Wiemer believes? Or could the Seleukid advance in Karia in 203 BC been considered as an attack against Ptolemaic possessions, seen from the ground in Karia and hence described as such by local actors? But it is not at all clear whether Amyzon, taken over in that year, was still Ptolemaic: see pp. 69–71. When did the Seleukid takeover of Kildara take place? c.203 BC, as part of Zeuxis' advance? In that case, Zeuxis would have moved southwards from the plain of Mylasa; did his advance affect Iasos and Bargylia already? (If so, were these places evacuated to make way for Philip V in 201 BC? Why? As part of a 'secret agreement'?)

Assuming (for the moment) that the war between Antiochos III and Ptolemy V is the Fifth Syrian War, the Seleukid takeover of Kildara and Thodasa, and the handover of Theangela by Philip V to Antiochos III, could have taken place c.200 BC, in local operations coinciding with the Fifth Syrian War: this is the interpretation of Wiemer. Such movements could be part of broader Seleukid operations in Asia Minor at this time, perhaps at the origin of a recorded Seleukid attack on the Attalid kingdom (Appendix 6).

In the present state of the evidence, I find none of these scenarios necessarily the correct one: it all is a question of what we would find surprising, worthy of comment, or normal (how can we know?), if we knew the full story. Another possibility is the following: the war between Antiochos III and Ptolemy V might be the Fifth Syrian War, but there is no reason for the Seleukid takeover of Kildara and Thodasa to have followed immediately on the outbreak of hostilities in Syria, as Wiemer thinks (after all, peace between the two kings was concluded only in 196 or 195 BC). The narrative in our document is not a matter of a full account of hostilities and military operations, but rather focuses on precedence and order of events, no doubt to prove some legal point (hence the construction, πρὸ τοῦ παρὰ βασιλέως Φιλίππου παρα[δ]ο[θήμειν] κτλ.). So could the takeover of Kildara, and the ensuing handing over of Theangela, be part of the operations of 197 BC and thereafter? This is at least one way of reading the text, but by no means the only way (it is rejected by Wiemer).

The problems surrounding the 'three kings' inscription illustrate the complexity of the political history of the very last years of the third century BC, with their constant clashes between rival superpowers in the imbricated landscape of the Aegean, the rise of one particularly successful king, Antiochos III, and the gradual involvement of Rome, which eventually brought the end of high politics in the Hellenistic world. It is astonishing enough that we know about places

such as Kildara, from dovetailing pieces of evidence, mostly epigraphical; it is equally astonishing that the great kingdoms, and soon
Rome, would make places such as Euromos or Bargylia issues of
superpower politics, which explains why these names appear in
Polybios and Livy. None of this means that we actually know very
much about the period, even though we try (as in this book) to provide
smooth, coherent narratives. The map of Seleukid control and campaigns in Western Asia Minor, even for Antiochos III, is still unclear:
for instance, in the Troad or in Mysia, down to 197 BC. We know next
to nothing for Miletos in the time of Antiochos III (its dealings with
Philip V in 201 BC, and with the Roman commission in 188 BC), as
pointed out by P. Herrmann ('Milet au IIe siècla a. C', in A. Bresson
and R. Descat (ed.), *Les cités d'Asie Mineure occidentale au IIe siècle a.
C.* (Bordeaux: Ausonius, 2001), 109–16. We do know that Miletos (an
independent city?) concluded treaties of *isopoliteia* with Seleukeia-
Tralleis in 218/7 BC (and hence in the time it was controlled by
Achaios), and with Mylasa in 215/4 BC (when it was presumably
under Olympichos' control, and nominally an Antigonid possession)
—but it is difficult to match this set of institutional, city-centred
actions with our conceptualization of empires and boundaries (*Inschr.
Delphinion* 143, 16 with Herrmann, *op. cit.*, 112). We can read an
important decree honouring an Attalid officer, Korrhagos, after the
Attalids took over vast swathes of Asia Minor (*SEG* 2.663, perhaps a
document I should have reproduced in the 'Aftermath' section of the
epigraphical dossier), but we still have as little certitude concerning
the city involved as when the text was found (in 1921, at Bursa, during
another episode of Big War in the area, this time between young,
modern nations, Greece and what was to become the Turkish
Republic).

   Earlier, the decades between 246 and 226 BC, the death of Antiochos II and the Third Syrian War, and the accession of Antiohcos III,
are still obscure: none of the recent crop of Attalid inscriptions has
thrown light on this period of Seleukid weakness and Attalid success.
The maps of empire on the ground are still a matter for much guess-
work: it now turns out that the Ptolemaic dominion in Karia stretched
further east than I suggested in this book: two texts make clear that
the Ptolemies controlled the Harpasos valley (P. Briant, P. Brun
and E. Varinlioğlu, 'Une inscription inédite de Carie et la guerre
d'Aristonicos', in A. Bresson and R. Descat (eds.), *Les cités d'Asie
Mineure occidentale au IIe siècle a. C.* (Bordeaux: Ausonius, 2001),
241–59. Was this the eastern limit of the Ptolemaic dominion? This is
suggested by the Seleukid colonies in the next two valleys, the
Morsynos valley and the Tabai plateau (Antiocheia on the Maeander,

Apollonia under Salbake). What were the inland communications in the Ptolemaic province of Karia?

Why do these details matter? At the simplest level, they represent the density and eventfulness of late third-century BC high political history. More generally, this political history of competition over places and landscape is an essential part of royal style, with its dual insistence on inherited rights and on conquest. But the details also show how constant competition meant that empire, on the ground, had ragged edges: places such as Miletos, periods such as the decades betwen 246 and 226 BC, show the difficulty of drawing neat maps of empire. Skepsis, a community in the Troad, was integrated by Antigonos Monophtalmos into Antigoneia (later Alexandreia Troas), then freed by Lysimachos, favoured by Antiochos I or II, probably with autonomy (I follow L. Robert: *BE* 76, 573), taken over by Attalos I, then free again under Antiochos III (above, p. 163), and taken back by Eumenes II, probably as a tributary city (above, p. 283). What do we mean by the question 'who took over what place and when'? The answer can only be obtained through examining the workings and details of Hellenistic history on the ground, by looking at statuses and interaction.

The political anthropology of empire I tried to elaborate here, on the problems of authority and freedom, between structure and negotiation, depended greatly on P. Briant's collection of essays, *Rois, tributs, paysans* (Briant 1982), and on a seminal essay of J.-M. Bertrand on civic and royal language, in their different relationships to power (Bertrand 1990). But Briant's work has evolved since the collection and republication of earlier work in 1982: his *Histoire de l'empire perse de Cyrus à Alexandre* (Paris: Fayard, 1996), argues for Achaimenid strength, specifically in the face of diversity, local autonomy, and what seems like looseness of control (the problem of local 'dynasts'); my concept of 'imagined empire' is less optimistic about the acutal degree of control the Seleukids wielded.

On honours from cities for kings, the evidence, epigraphical, literary, and archaeological, is comprehensively gathered in H. Kotsidu, *TIMH KAI ΔΟΞΑ. Ehrungen für hellenistische Herrscher im griechischen Mutterland und in Kleinasien unter besonderer Berücksichtigung der archäologischen Denkmäler* (Frankfurt on Main: Akademie Verlag, 2000), which explicitly sets out to complete the collection of material pertaining to royal euergetism, Bringmann and von Steuben 1993. I tried to study the texts as examples of the power of language to create social reality—specifically, a reality of commitment and exchange. But on re-reading the texts, I am struck by the violence involved in the king's gifts: Alexander's grant of privileges to Priene, or the dealings of Antiochos III with Teos and Herakleia under Latmos seem to me to impose their world in the irresistible form of gifts, that create their performativeness by assuming it, and assuming that the audience will accept it. In response to benefactions, a civic language of honours: does this language establish reciprocity and hence parity in the face of the violence of the gift, by carrying out the founding moves for local agency and identity? This is the view I proposed above, in Chapter 4. Or is the practice of civic honours for royal benefaction, *qua* 'misacknowledgement' of the disparity of power, a tool which embodies the domination of the local communities? Reciprocity between civic honours and royal power, is a fiction. Honours claim to acquit any debt and shift attention away from the royal giver to the community's capacity to elicit gifts by exemplary rewards: does this claim in fact establish an unspoken, political debt which precisely cannot be repaid in purely symbolical terms? (This is also a view suggested above, in Chapter 4, though uneasily.) What if the *eleutheria* and *demokratia* the kings were praised for preserving were not genuine local values, tenaciously defended by the cities, but 'local values' invented and shaped by supra-local state formations, to fit the bigger world of the Hellenistic kingdoms? To ask these questions is to confront the problem of the nature of the post-classical *polis*.

At least, it might be worth mentioning the paradigms involved. This book was written within the 'vitality' model: informed by the epigraphical evidence, this model insists on continuities, especially in political institutions and language, but also in political activity and dignity. The view was articulated notably by Ph. Gauthier ('Les cités hellénistiques: épigraphie et histoire des institutions et des régimes politiques', in *Praktika tou E' Diethnous Synedriou Hellenikis kai Latinikis Epigraphikis* (Athens: Hypourgeio Politismou kai Epistemon, 1983), 82–107; 'Grandes et petites cités: hégémonie et autarcie', *Opus* 6–8 (1987–9), 187–97, also his essay on euergetism, Gauthier 1985, much used in this book; on this view, change took place much later, *c*.150 BC). Gauthier developed this view from many pronouncements by L. Robert, whose positions also inform this book; but the 'vitality' model goes far back, and M. Rostovtzeff already wrote in 1941 '[a]s every student of ancient history knows, the old-fashioned conception of this age as a time of decay of Greek civilization and of a pitiful collapse of Greek political life is unfounded or at least one-sided and misleading' (Rostovtzeff 1941, p. v). The giveaway is the normative force of the sentence, and especially that little phrase at the beginning: 'as every student . . .' precisely betrays the existence of the other paradigm, that of radical change in the Hellenistic period. This model compares the Hellenistic period to Classical exemplars, often democratic Athens, more or less explicitly taken if not for the typical, then the achieved form of the *polis*. The Classical viewpoint entails dependency on literary sources rather than the epigraphical; it sees a radical break after Alexander, the end of freedom and existence for the *polis*, socio-economic inequality, subservience to kings and local Big Men, nostalgia, forcedness and irony in cultural and political practice. This view can be founded in recent, sophisticated work on the Archaic and Classical periods, where change in the Hellenistic period is attributed to the 'end of the *polis*' (e.g. I. Morris, *Burial and Ancient Society: the Rise of the Greek City-State* (Cambridge: Cambridge University Press, 1987)). Both models have their own ideology and historiography; and they still exist in opposition nowadays (for instance, the 'decline' model was restated by G. Herman, *Studia Classica Israelica* 18 (2000), 298). The 'vitality' paradigm draws part of its energy from the argument against the Classicizing model, and sometimes has difficulty transcending this adversarial mode ('no, no, look at the harlequins'). This approach has the capacity to irritate and provoke the other side into outbursts of surprising animosity (e.g. V. D. Hanson, *The Other Greeks: The Family Farm and the Agrarian Roots of Western Civilization* (New York: Free Press, 1995), 390–403). Why the passion? What are the various scholars' relations of resentment, investment in the subject, and desire for the *polis* and its forms?

Since I write within the 'vitality' paradigm, the temptation is to spring up and make some points: on the Classical end of the argument, the relationship between *polis* and autonomy has been challenged by M. Hansen, who has shown the existence in the Archaic and Classical periods of entities called *poleis* but subordinate (Hansen 1995), exactly as in the Hellenistic period with its 'cités sujettes'; at the Hellenistic end, the evidence shows clearly not just continuities in language and ideology, but also civic practice: democracy, accountability and even local warfare (P. Fröhlich, *Le contrôle des magistrats dans les cités grecques IVe-Ier s. av. J.-C.* (Diss. Paris-IV, 1997); J. Ma, 'Fighting *poleis* of the Hellenistic world', in H. van Wees (ed.), *War and Violence in Greek Society* (London: Duckworth and The Classical Press of Wales, 2000), 337–76). Beyond any contradiction between these two points, and more generally the reticence of the 'vitality' model to admit change (the 'never-ending *polis*' problem), what remains is the difficulty to overcome the 'vitality'/'decline' dichotomy. The city of Lilaia, in Phokis, was freed from Antigonid domination by its citizenry, led by a citizen, Patron: the event, one of many in the record of warlikeness on the part of Hellenistic *poleis*, is noted in Pausanias (10.33), but also attested by the statue base set up by the

Lilaians for Patron at Delphi (*SEG* 16.328), complete with epigram, commemorating his action—'driving away the garrison and the enemy s[pears], he set it up (Lilaia) to live autonomous, in freedom'. Yet a document from Lilaia also grants *isopoliteia* to the soldiers of a garrison sent by Attalos I (*ISE* 81). How are we to relate these documents? Chronology is one approach (perhaps the exploits of Patron came after the Attalid garrison had left?); the other is institutional to distinguish between the Antigonid garrison (oppressive) and the Attalid garrison (helpful)—did Attalid soldiers in fact do the brunt of the fighting against the Antigonid troops? The *isopoliteia* decree mentions the soldiers protecting the city 'along with divine power (*tou daimoniou*) and with the citizens'. The story of Lilaia in *c.*200 BC does not fit any simple model ('vitality'/subservience). A similar impression is left by a document from Methymna, on Lesbos: the *chellestys* (civic subdivision) of the Proteoi honours one of its own for pious religious conduct in office, by an extra share of sacrificial meat at the common sacrifices; the picture is one of powerful communitarian ideals and ancestral rituals, of sharing and distributing around civic religion—but one of the sacred occasions at which the honour is proclaimed is the Ptolemaea (to use the local spelling), a festival for the cult of Ptolemy III, held in the *polis* of which the Proteoi are part (*OGIS* 78 with *IG* 12 suppl., p. 30). Which element should we focus on, the lovingly detailed local activity, or the incidental mention of the ruler-cult implying imperial presence and political subordination?

Flexibility is needed: E. Will could write to correct Y. Garlan's views on the defenceless, powerless, non-military Hellenistic *polis* ('Le territoire, la ville et la poliorcétique grecque', *Revue Historique* 253 (1975), 297–318), but also to take issue with Gauthier on the impact of ruler-cult, subordination, and the bending of honorific language to talk about power—what effect did this have on the 'soul of the *polis*'? ('Poleis hellénistiques: deux notes', *Echos du Monde Classique/Classical Views* 32, n.s. 7 (1988) 329–352, quoted in this work as Will 1988). The recent collections, M. Wörrle and P. Zanker (eds.), *Stadtbild und Bürgerbild* (Munich: Beck, 1995), and A. Bresson and R. Descat (eds.), *Les cités d'Asie Mineure occidentale au IIe siècle a. C.* (Bordeaux: Ausonius, 2001), are good examples of this, and point the way forward.

Ultimately, this book was written about reading intriguing cases such as those mentioned above. A king, Antiochos III (who has not yet called himself 'the Great') writing to his minister, appointing his own chamberlain over 'the land on the other side of the Taurus', even though his control over that landscape is at best tenuous and recent. The minister, Zeuxis, conquering a small mountain community in

conditions of great violence, and writing about the care that his subordinates will show to this community, Amyzon; the Amyzonians
will later negotiate with the king and his ministers about getting back
their looted property, their shrine's sacred slaves and their dispersed
citizenry. Antiochos III at Teos, taking over the city, appearing
before the assembled citizens to declare the city 'sacred and inviolate
and free from tribute'; when a follow-up embassy comes to see him,
the king says that he already has freed the city from various contributions which it once paid to Attalos I: administrative process as royal
fiat, something which has already been decided, ineluctably and
beneficiently. The city can only respond by a vast array of cultic
honours. Herakleia upon Latmos sends a twenty-two strong panel of
envoys to see Zeuxis, to negotiate the aftermath of takeover. They will
ask for a cash grant, a gift of grain, and, remarkably, an undertaking
from the king that, on taking over the local harbour tax, he will keep
on paying a slice of the revenue to the city as money for gymnasion-
oil, just as the citizen tax-farmers had to do when bidding for this tax.
Surprisingly, or perhaps not surprisingly, the king seems to have
agreed to this collaborative meshing of imperial extraction and civic
budget, and promised even more benefactions. Rather than reproduce clichés about decline, and teleological or retrospective stereotypes (Alexander as rupture, cultural fusion paving the way for
Christianity, etc.), Hellenistic history should be written out of the
richness and vividness of these transactions.

ADDENDA

p. 3 n. 4 'Piginda'. On the site of Çamlıdere (in the Akçay valley, the valley of the ancient Harpasos), P. Briant, P. Brun, and E. Varinlioğlu, 'Une inscription inédite de Carie et la guerre d'Aristonicos', in A. Bresson and R. Descat (eds.), *Les cités d'Asie Mineure occidentale au IIe siècle a. C.* (Bordeaux: Ausonius, 2001), 241–59, especially 249–52. Piginda, mentioned as a Karian δῆμος by Stephanos of Byzantion, must be a civic subdivision or village in a *polis*—probably Bargasa, the only of the *poleis* in this part of the Maeander valley which has not yet been located; local finds of Bargasan bronze coins reinforce the identification. The argument is carefully and cautiously made, and, in the present state of the evidence, convincing.

p. 14 On the Laodikeis of Karia, debate has continued: G. Reger, 'The Koinon of the Laodikeis in Karia', *EA* 30 (1998) 11–17. P. Debord, in A. Bresson and R. Descat (ed.), *Les cités d'Asie Mineure occidentale au IIe siècle a. C.* (Bordeaux: Ausonius, 2001), 167–70, argues for seeing the Laodikeis of the new inscription (*SEG* 44.1356–7) and of Liv. 33.18.2–3 as those of Laodikeia on Lykos. But the upshot, that Laodikeia on Lykos was a Rhodian possession after 188 BC, seems to me unacceptable. That Laodikeia is south of the Maeander does not mean that it was attributed to Rhodes: Hierapolis is also south of the 'boucle du Méandre', the great northwards arc of the Maeander; yet Hierapolis was clearly an Attalid city (see Cohen 1995, 305–8 for the evidence). Laodikeia on Lykos must have been given to Eumenes II, and I assume the tribe Attalis comes from the period of Attalid domination (Cohen 1995, 308–10). The Tabai plateau must therefore have constituted the eastern limit of Karia, at least in the Seleukid geography that was partly taken as a basis for the settlement of 188 BC. See Th. Corsten, *BMCR*, 2002.03.05.

p. 21 n. 34 For R. Osborne on epigraphy, 'Inscribing performance', in S. Goldhill and R. Osborne (eds.), *Performance Culture and Athenian Democracy* (Cambridge: Cambridge University Press, 1999), 341–58; also *Demos: the Discovery of Classical Attika* (Cambridge: Cambridge University Press, 1985), 80.

p. 74 On Philip V, see now H.-U. Wiemer, *Rhodische Traditionen in der hellenistischen Historiographie* (Frankfurt am Main: Marthe Clauss, 2001), chap. 5, on narrative issues and sources.

p. 87 n. 126 Robert (1960), p. 510 n. 2, proposes Miletoupolis as the city mentioned in the 'Korrhagos decree' (*SEG* 2.663); the point about a drive by the land army in Mysia and Hellenspontine Phrygia remains.

p. 123 On Zeuxis, see the entry, with bibliography, in A. B. Tataki, *Macedonians Abroad: A Contribution to the Prosopography of Ancient Macedonia* (Athens: Research Centre for Greek and Roman Antiquity, 1998), 317.

p. 124 Mitchell (1994), p. 91 and n. 120 for further bibliography on hyparchies.

p. 130 On royal land, P. Briant, *Histoire de l'empire perse de Cyrus à Alexandre* (Paris: Fayard, 1996), chap. 10, sec. 7, and chap. 11 (notably on the king's own patrimony—hence supporting the possible existence of such an institution in the Hellenistic period), 467, on tribute in grain (also P. Briant, 'Prélèvements tributaires et échanges en Asie Mineure achéménide et hellénistique', in J. Andreau, P. Briant, R. Descat (eds.), *Economie antique. Les échanges dans l'Antiquité: le rôle de l'Etat* (Saint-Bertrand-de-Comminges: Musée Archéologique Départmental, 1994), 69–81).

p. 143–4 Interpreting Derkyllidas' speech in Xen. *Hellenica* 4.8.5 as proof that Achaimenid authority did not prevail in Aigai and Temnos now seems to me very risky. Apart from the problems with using as a simple piece of evidence a speech, by a famously cunning Spartiate, the whole notion of Persian 'looseness' on the ground is part of the fourth-century BC Greek imagining of Persia as a porous space of weakness. P. Briant has argued that local 'looseness' co-existed with strong control, actual and ideological. On the other hand, I am not sure that the evidence really allows us to say that Mysia was firmly under Antiochos III (p. 144 n. 136).

p. 151 n. 153 On the theorodokoi lists and their relevance to the nature of the *polis*, P. Perlman , 'ΘΕΩΡΟΔΟΚΟΥΝΤΕΣ ΕΝ ΤΑΙΣ ΠΟΛΕΣΙΝ. Panhellenic Epangelia and Political Status,' in M. Hansen (ed.), *Sources for the Greek City-State* (Copenhagen: Munksgaard, 1995), 113–64.

p. 156 n. 172 The Kolophon document on tax-farming is now published: R. Etienne and L. Migeotte, 'Colophon et les abus des fermiers des taxes', *BCH* 122 (1998), 143–57.

p. 151 n. 173 On civic governors, the *epistates* in Seleukeia in Pieria is more likely a 'Macedonian' style *epistates*, as studied by M. Hatzopoulos (1996, vol. 1, 372–429).

On the trilingual *stele* from Xanthos, see now P. Briant, 'Cités et satrapes dans l'empire achéménide: Xanthos et Pixôdaros', *CRAI* 1998, 305–40 (Pixodaros was not 'master' of the whole decision, but only to intervene in case of problems in applying the decision taken by the citizens of Xanthos). Local agency exists, and local decisions do not have to be vetted by the satrap.

p. 163 Side not only minted coinage in the period of Antiochos' control, the city was also free in 188 BC; which supports the relation between silver coinage and formally recognized freedom (be it by an encompassing ruling power, or an international peace treaty). See J. Nollé, in G. Dobesch and G. Rehrenböck (eds.), *Die epigraphische und altertumskundliche Erforschung Kleinasiens: hundert Jahre Kleinasiatische Kommission der Österreichischen Akademie der Wissenschaften* (Vienna: Verlag der Österreichischen Akademie der Wissenschaften, 1993), 306–7.

p. 245 On Antiochos III in the islands, on his way back from Greece in 192 BC, and certain islanders' military resistance to him, G. Reger, 'Athens and Tenos in the Early Hellenistic Age', *CQ* 42 (1992), 365–83.

p. 248–50 On the second century BC, especially in Asia Minor, two collections: M. Wörrle and P. Zanker (eds.), *Stadtbild und Bürgerbild* (Munich: Beck, 1995), and A. Bresson and R. Descat (eds.), *Les cités d'Asie Mineure occidentale au IIe siècle a. C.* (Bordeaux: Ausonius, 2001).

p. 269 Sinuri fragmentary letter. L. Robert, *Hellenica* 7 (Paris: Adrien Maisonneuve, 1949), 67: the Roberts saw the stone again, with no advance in reading.

p. 274 On *OGIS* 240, see I. Savalli-Lestrade, *Les* philoi *royaux dans l'Asie hellénistique* (Geneva: Droz, 1998), 38–9: no real reason to read [Pro]tas, and perhaps not a [νομό]φυλαξ (M. Fränkel in *Inschr.*

Pergamon), but rather a [σωματό]φυλαξ—a royal officer rather than a Pergamene magistrate.

p. 279 Under d (βασιλεὺς μέγας in Xanthos), a new document must be taken into account, the statue base erected by the Xanthians for Βασιλέα μέγαν Ἀντίοχον. The document dates to 197 BC or afterwards (see above, Afterthoughts).

p. 282 On the events of 189/8 BC, see now H. U. Wiemer, *Rhodische Traditionen in der hellenistischen Historiographie* (Frankfurt am Main: Marthe Clauss, 2001), 137–49, where the source problems, but also on the details of the settlement are treated with very great clarity (helpful diagrams and quotation of all relevant sources).

p. 284 Epigraphical dossier. I tried to follow, as much as possible, the principles of the 'genetical lemma'; in reaction against what I perceived to be excessive restoration in documents relating to Antiochos III, especially by F. Piejko, I followed extreme austerity in proposing my own restorations, and even more so in actually printing restorations within the text rather than in the basement of the apparatus. Finally, I also tried to keep the titles of each document as neutral as possible, struck by a remark in conversation by T. Rood on the disparity between the title of an Athenian document in the epigraphical collection of Meiggs and Lewis ('Honours for the assassins of Phrynichos') as the text of the document, where neither assassination nor Phrynichos appear, but only bland mentions of 'doing good to the people' and much debate about honours and procedure (*ML* 89). Though the present titles are short, and simple, they still might avoid being too misleading. I regret not better structuring and extending my commentaries. They could have fallen into three parts: a first section explaining the physical nature of the stone, and its original monumental context; a second part discussing technical issues and problems; a third part thinking about what the document meant and why it mattered. This would not have been difficult or space-consuming, and would have aided reading and engagement considerably. However, it would represent far too extensive a change to the present state of the book.

   Of course, this is a very large amount of Greek text. Should you read these texts first? Last? Alongside the analysis? (However that is possible.) At any rate, try to read them. They make for a good chunk of the formalized, dialogic interaction between the powerful and the not-quite-powerless in the Hellenistic world. In addition, each text is fairly short.

p. 284, document **1** (Sardeis) See P. Briant, 'Prélèvements tributaires et échanges en Asie Mineure ahcéménide et hellénistique', in J.
Andreau, P. Briant, and R. Descat (eds.), *Economie antique. Les
échanges dans l'Antiquité: le rôle de l'Etat* (Saint-Bertrand-de-
Comminges: Musée Archéologique Départmental, 1994), 69–81, for
an important discussion of this document and the economic functioning of the royal land.

p. 305, document **16** This is treated by H. Kotsidu, *TIMH KAI
ΔΟΞΑ. Ehrungen für hellenistische Herrscher im griechischen Mutterland und in Kleinasien unter besonderer Berücksightigung der archäologischen Denkmäler* (Frankfurt on Main: Akademie Verlag, 2000),
149–52, no. 89 (with three rubrics: the epigraphical document from
Delphi [E], the stone on which the decree is carved [A1], and a round
base assigned to Antiochos III by H. Pomtow, mistakenly according
to Kotsidu [A2]). Kotsidu examines the archaeological problem: the
block (apparently part of an equestrian monument) is in an unfinished
state; she claims the basis which the block belonged to would be too
small for the eight-cubit tall statue mentioned in the decree. But what
are we to make of line 33, stipulating that the decree is to to be
inscribed 'on the base of king Antiochos'? Kotsidu dismisses the idea
that this means the block we now have is indeed the base of the statue;
I find this problematic, though have no obvious solution.

p. 366 The story of the sacred villages in the Tabai plain continued
into the Roman period, when there is an imperial rescript concerning
the matter: R. Haensch, 'Heraclea ad Salbacum, die heilige Döfer de
Artemis Sbryallis und der Kaiser', in W. Eck and E. Müller-Luckner
(eds.), *Lokale Autonomie und römische Ordnungsmacht in den kaiser-
zeitlichen Provinzen vom 1. bis 3. Jahrhundert* (Munich: R. Olden-
burg, 1999), 115–39.

BIBLIOGRAPHY

AGER, SH. L. (1996) *Interstate Arbitrations in the Greek World, 337–90 B.C.* (Hellenistic Society and Culture 18). Berkeley, Calif., and London: University of California Press.

AKARCA, A. (1959) *Les Monnaies grecques de Mylasa* (Bibliothèque archéologique et historique de l'Institut français d'archéologie d'Istanbul 1). Paris.

ALLEN, R. E. (1983) *The Attalid Kingdom: A Constitutional History*. Oxford: Clarendon Press.

ANDERSON, B. (1991) *Imagined Communities: Reflections on the Origin and Spread of Nationalism* (rev. edn.). London and New-York: Verso.

ARENDT, H. (1970) *On Violence*. London: Allen Lane.

ATKINSON, K. T. M. (1972) 'A Hellenistic Land-Conveyance: The Estate of Mnesimachus in the Plain of Sardis', *Historia* 21: 45–74.

AUSTIN, J. L. (1975) *How to do Things with Words* (2nd edn., ed. J. O. Urmson and M. Sbisà). Cambridge, Mass.: Harvard University Press.

AUSTIN, M. M. (1981) *The Hellenistic World from Alexander to the Roman Conquest. A Selection of Ancient Sources in Translation*. Cambridge: Cambridge University Press.

——(1986) 'Hellenistic Kings, War and the Economy', *CQ* 36, 450–66.

—— and VIDAL-NAQUET, P. (1972) *Economies et sociétés en Grèce ancienne*. Paris: Armand Colin.

AYMARD, A. (1940) 'La Mort d'Antiochos, fils d'Antiochos III Mégas. Étude de chronologie', *Rev. Phil.* 14: 89–109.

——(1948) 'Le Protocole royal grec et son évolution', *REA* 50: 232–63.

——(1949) 'Du nouveau sur Antiochos III d'après une inscription grecque d'Iran', *REA* 51: 327–45.

BABINGER, Fr. C. H. (1978) *Mehmed the Conqueror and his Time* (Bollingen series 96) (trans. R. Manheim, ed. W. C. Hickman). Princeton: Princeton University Press.

BADIAN, E. (1964) 'Rome and Antiochus the Great: A Study in Cold War', in *Studies in Greek and Roman History*, Oxford: Basil Blackwell, 112–39.

——(1966a) 'Alexander the Great and the Greeks of Asia', in E. Badian (ed.), *Ancient Society and Institutions (Studies presented to Victor Ehrenberg on his 75th birthday)*, Oxford: Basil Blackwell, 37–69.

——(1966b) Review of Schmitt 1964, *Gnomon* 38: 709–16.

BAGNALL, R. S. (1976) *The Administration of the Ptolemaic Possessions outside Egypt* (Columbia studies in the Classical tradition 4). Leiden: E. J. Brill.

BAR-KOCHVA, B. (1976) *The Seleucid Army: Organization and Tactics in the Great Campaigns*. Cambridge: Cambridge University Press.

BARKEY, K. (1994) *Bandits and Bureaucrats: The Ottoman Route to State Centralization*. Ithaca and London: Cornell University Press.

BARNES, B. (1988) *The Nature of Power*. Cambridge: Polity.

BARONOWSKI, D. W. (1991) 'The Status of the Greek Cities of Asia Minor after 190 B.C.', *Hermes* 119: 450–63.

BASLEZ, M.-FR., and VIAL, CL. (1987) 'La Diplomatie de Délos dans le premier tiers du IIe siècle', *BCH* 111: 281–312.

BEAN, G. E. (1971) *Turkey beyond the Maeander: An Archaeological Guide*. London: E. Benn.

——and COOK, J. M. (1955) 'The Halicarnassus Peninsula', *BSA* 50: 85–171.

BELOCH, K. J. (1927) *Griechische Geschichte* (2nd edn.), iv.2. Berlin and Leipzig: de Gruyter.

BENGTSON, H. (1937) *Die Strategie in der hellenistischen Zeit. Ein Beitrag zum antiken Staatsrecht*, i (Münchener Beiträge zur Papyrusforschung und antiken Rechtsgeschichte 26). Munich.

——(1944) *Die Strategie in der hellenistischen Zeit. Ein Beitrag zum antiken Staatsrecht*, ii (Münchener Beiträge zur Papyrusforschung und antiken Rechtsgeschichte 32). Munich: Beck.

——(1952) *Die Strategie in der hellenistischen Zeit. Ein Beitrag zum antiken Staatsrecht* iii (Münchener Beiträge zur Papyrusforschung und antiken Rechtsgeschichte 36). Munich: Beck.

BÉQUIGNON, Y., and LAUMONIER, A. (1925) 'Fouilles de Téos (1924)', *BCH* 49: 288–9.

BERNARD, P., and RAPIN, CL. (1994) 'Un parchemin gréco-bactrien d'une collection privée', *CRAI* 1994: 261–94.

BERTHOLD, R. M. (1975) 'Lade, Pergamum and Chios', *Historia* 24: 150–63.

——(1975–6) 'The Rhodian Appeal to Rome in 201 B.C.', *CJ* 71: 97–107.

BERTRAND, J.-M. (1974) 'Sur les hyparques d'Alexandre', in *Mélanges d'histoire ancienne offerts à William Seston*, Paris: E. de Boccard, 25–34.

——(1990) 'Formes de discours politiques: décrets des cités grecques et correspondance des rois hellénistiques', in Cl. Nicolet (ed.), *Du pouvoir dans l'antiquité: mots et réalités* (Cahiers du Centre Glotz 1), Paris and Geneva: Droz, 101–15.

——(1992) *Cités et royaumes du monde grec: espace et politique*. Paris: Hachette.

BERVE, H. (1926) *Das Alexanderreich auf prosopographischer Grundlage*. 2 vols. Munich: Beck.

BEVAN, E. R. (1902) *The House of Seleucus*. London: E. Arnold.

BICKERMANN, E.† (1932a) 'Bellum Antiochicum', *Hermes* 67: 47–76 (= Bickerman 1985, 38–68).

† This remarkable scholar transcribed his Russian name in three different ways, according to the language each article was written in: Bickermann in German, Bikerman in French, and Bickerman in English (reflecting his own movements from Germany to

BICKERMANN, E. (1932b) 'Rom und Lampsakos', *Philologus* 87: 277–99.
BIKERMAN, E. (1934) 'Alexandre le Grand et les villes d'Asie', *REG* 47: 346–74 (= Bickerman 1985: 71–99).
——(1937) 'Notes sur Polybe. I. Le statut des villes d'Asie après la paix d'Apamée', *REG* 50: 217–39 (= Bickerman 1985: 143–65).
——(1938) *Institutions des Séleucides* (Haut-commissariat de la République française en Syrie et au Liban. Service des antiquités. Bibliothèque archéologique et historique 26). Paris: Geuthner.
——(1939) 'La Cité grecque dans les monarchies hellénistiques', *Rev. Phil.* 13: 335–49 (= Bickerman 1985: 215–29).
BICKERMAN, E. (1943/4) 'Notes on Seleucid and Parthian chronology. 2. Antiochus Hierax and Attalus I', *Berytus* 8: 76–8.
BIKERMAN, E. (1950) 'Remarques sur le droit des gens dans la Grèce classique', *RIDA* 4: 99–127 (= Bickerman 1985: 325–53).
BICKERMAN, E. (1980) *Studies in Jewish and Christian history* (Arbeiten zur Geschichte des Antiken Judentums und des Urchristentums 9), part 2. Leiden: E. J. Brill.
——(1985) *Religion and Politics in the Hellenistic and Roman Periods* (ed. E. Gabba and M. Smith). Como: New Press.
BIELMAN, A. (1994) *Retour à la liberté: Libération et sauvetage des prisonniers en Grèce ancienne. Recueil d'inscriptions honorant des sauveteurs et analyse critique* (Études Epigraphiques 1). Lausanne: École Française d'Athènes, Université de Lausanne.
BILLOWS, R. A. (1990) *Antigonos the One-Eyed and the Creation of the Hellenistic State* (Hellenistic Culture and Society 4). Berkeley, Calif., and London: University of California Press.
——(1995) *Kings and Colonists: Aspects of Macedonian Imperialism* (Columbia Studies in the Classical Tradition 22). Leiden: E. J. Brill.
BLÜMEL, W. (1992) 'Ein Brief des ptolemäischen Ministers Tlepolemos an die Stadt Kildara in Karien', *EA* 20: 127–33.
——(1996) 'Ergänzungen in dem Funktionärbrief aus Euromos', *EA* 27: 61–2.
BOFFO, L. (1985) *I re ellenistici e i centri religiosi dell'Asia Minore* (Pubblicazioni della facoltà di lettere e filosofia dell'Università di Pavia 37). Florence: La Nuova Italia.
——(1988) 'Epigrafi di città greche: un'espressione di storiografia locale', in *Studi di storia e storiografia antiche per Emilio Gabba*. Pavia and Como: New Press, 9–48.
BOSWORTH, A. B. (1988) *Conquest and Empire: The Reign of Alexander the Great*. Cambridge; Cambridge University Press.
BOUSQUET, J. (1986) 'Lettre de Ptolémée Evergète à Xanthos de Lycie', *REG* 99: 22–32.
——(1988) 'La Stèle des Kyténiens au Létôon de Xanthos', *REG* 101: 12–53.

France and finally the USA). The original spellings have been preserved; in this book (written in English), 'Bickerman' is used to refer to him discursively.

BRANDT, H. (1992) *Gesellschaft und Wirtschaft Pamphyliens und Pisidiens im Altertum* (Asia Minor Studien 7). Bonn: R. Habelt.

BRASHEAR, W. M. (1984) 'A New Fragment on Seleucid History (*P. Berol. 21286*)', in *Atti del XVII congresso internazionale di papirologia*, ii. Naples: Centro internazionale per lo studio dei papiri ercolanesi, 345–50.

BRAUDEL, F. (1966) *La Méditerranée et le monde méditerranéen à l'époque de Philippe II* (2nd edn.). 2 vols. Paris: Armand Colin.

BRESSON, A. (1995) 'Un diadoque pas comme les autres', *DHA* 21: 87–8.

BRIANT, P. (1982) *Rois, tributs et paysans. Études sur les formations tributaires du Moyen Orient ancien* (Annales littéraires de l'Université de Besançon 269). Paris: Les Belles Lettres.

——(1994) 'De Sarmarkhand à Sardes et de la ville de Suse au pays des Hanéens', *Topoi* 4: 455–67

BRINGMANN, K. (1993) 'The King as Benefactor: Some Remarks on Ideal Kingship in the Age of Hellenism', in Bulloch *et al.* 1993: 7–24.

——and VON STEUBEN, H. (eds.) (1995) *Schenkungen hellenisticher Herrscher an griechische Städte und Heiligtümer. Teil I. Zeugnisse und Kommentare*. Berlin: Akademie.

BRISCOE, J. (1972) 'Flamininus and Roman politics, 200–189 B.C.' *Latomus* 31: 22–53.

——(1973) *Commentary on Livy Books XXXI–XXXIII*. Oxford: Clarendon Press.

——(1981) *Commentary on Livy Books XXXIV–XXXVII*. Oxford: Clarendon Press.

BRIXHE, CL. (1976) *Le Dialecte grec de Pamphylie. Documents et grammaire* (Bibliothèque de l'Institut Français d'études anatoliennes d'Istanbul 26). Paris: A. Maisonneuve.

——and HODOT, R. (1988) *L'Asie mineure du nord au sud. Inscriptions inédites* (Études d'archéologie classique 6). Nancy: Presses Universitaires de Nancy.

BRODERSEN, K. (1991) *Appians Antiochike (Syriake 1–44, 232). Text und Kommentar. Nebst ein Anhang: Plethons Syriake-Exzerpt* (Münchener Beiträge zur Alten Geschichte 3). Munich: Editio Maris.

BROWN, P. (1992) *Power and Persuasion in late Antiquity: Towards a Christian Empire*. Madison, Wis.: University of Wisconsin Press.

BROWN T. S. (1961) 'Apollophanes and Polybius, Book 5', *Phoenix* 15: 187–95.

BULLOCH, A., GRUEN, E. S., LONG, A. A., and STEWART, A. (eds.) (1993) *Images and Ideologies: Self-Definition in the Hellenistic World* (Hellenistic Culture and Society 12). Berkeley, Calif., and London: University of California Press.

BURSTEIN, S. (1986) 'Lysimachus and the Greek Cities: A Problem in Interpretation', in *Ancient Macedonia* 4, Thessaloniki: Hidryma Meleton Chersonesou tou Haimou, 133–8.

CARSANA, C. (1996) *Le dirigenze cittadine nello stato seleucidico* (Biblioteca di *Athenaeum* 30). Como: New Press.

CARTLEDGE, P., GARNSEY, P., and GRUEN, E. (1997) *Hellenistic Constructs: Essays in Culture, History and Historiography* (Hellenistic Culture and Society 26). Berkeley, Calif., and London: University of California Press.

CHANIOTIS, A. (1988) *Historie und Historiker in den griechischen Inschriften. Epigraphische Beiträge zur griechischen Historiographie* (Heidelberger althistorische Beiträge und epigraphische Studien 4). Stuttgart: F. Steiner.

——(1993) 'Ein diplomatischer Statthalter nimmt Rücksicht auf den verletzten Stolz zweier hellenistischer Kleinpoleis (Nagidos und Arsinoe)', *EA* 21: 31–42

——(1996) *Die Verträge zwischen kretischen Poleis in der hellenistischen Zeit* (Heidelberger althistorische Beiträge und epigraphische Studien 24). Stuttgart: F. Steiner.

CHISHULL, E. (1728) *Antiquitates Asiaticae Christianam aeram antecedentes.* London.

CLAESSEN, H., and SKALNÍK, P. (eds.) (1978) *The Early State* (New Babylon, Studies in the Social Sciences 32). The Hague: Mouton.

COBB, R. (1975) *Paris and its Provinces.* Oxford: Oxford University Press.

COHEN, G. M. (1995) *The Hellenistic Settlements in Europe, the Islands and Asia Minor* (Hellenistic Culture and Society 17). Berkeley, Calif., and London: University of California Press.

COOK, B. F. (1966) *Inscribed Hadra Vases in the Metropolitan Museum* (Metropolitan Museum of Art Papers, no. 12). New York: Metropolitan Museum of Art.

CORSARO, M. (1985) 'Tassazione regia e tassazione cittadina dagli Achemenidi ai re ellenistici', *REA* 87: 73–95.

CRAMPA, J. (1969) *Labraunda. Swedish Excavations and Researches*, iii.1, *The Greek Inscriptions. Part I: 1–12 (Period of Olympichus).* Lund: C. W. K. Gleerup.

——(1972) *Labraunda. Swedish Excavations and Researches*, iii.2, *The Greek Inscriptions. Part II: 13–133.* Lund: C. W. K. Gleerup

CROWTHER, CH. V. (1989) 'Iasos in the Early Second Century B.C.: A Note on OGIS 137', *BICS* 36: 136–8.

——(1993) 'Foreign Judges in Seleucid Cities (*GIBM* 421)', *Journal of Ancient Civilizations* 8: 39–77.

——(1995*a*) 'The Chronology of the Iasian Theatre Lists: Again', *Chiron* 25: 225–34.

——(1995*b*) 'Iasos in the Second Century B.C. III: Foreign Judges from Priene', *BICS* 40: 91–138.

CUINET, V. (1894) *La Turquie d'Asie. Géographie administrative. Statistique descriptive et raisonnée de l'Asie-Mineure*, iv. Paris: E. Leroux.

CURTY, O. (1989) 'L'Historiographie hellénistique et l'inscription "Inschriften von Priene" no. 37', in M. Piérart and O. Curty (eds.), *Historia testis. Mélanges d'épigraphie, d'histoire ancienne et de philologie offerts à Tadeusz Zawadzki*. Fribourg: Éditions Universitaires, 21–35.

CURTY, O. (1995) *Les Parentés légendaires entre cités grecques. Catalogue raisonné des inscriptions contenant le terme ΣΥΓΓΕΝΕΙΑ et analyse critique* (École Pratique des Hautes Études, IVe section. Hautes Études du monde gréco-romain 20). Geneva and Paris: Droz.

DAUX, G. (1973), 'Un passage du décret de Téos pour Antiochos III', *ZPE* 12: 235–6.

DEBORD, P. (1982) *Aspects sociaux et économiques de la vie religieuse dans l'Anatolie gréco-romaine*. Leiden: E. J. Brill.

——(1985) 'La Lydie du Nord-Est', *REA* 87: 345–58.

——(1994) 'Essai sur la géographie historique de la région de Stratonicée', *Mélanges Pierre Lévêque* 8: 107–22.

DE PLANHOL, X. (1958) *De la plaine pamphylienne aux lacs pisidiens. Nomadisme et vie paysane*. Paris: A. Maisonneuve.

DESCAT, R. (1997) 'A propos d'un citoyen de Philippes à Théangela', *REA* 99: 411–13.

DESIDERI, P. (1970/1) 'Studi di storiografia eracleota. II. La guerra con Antioco il grande', *SCO* 19–20: 487–537.

DOYLE, M. W. (1986) *Empires*. Ithaca: Cornell University Press.

DUNST, G. (1968) 'Zu dem neuen epigraphischen Dokument aus Teos. I', *ZPE* 3: 170–3.

ELWYN, S. (1990) 'The Recognition Decrees for the Delphian Soteria and the Date of Smyrna's Inviolability', *JHS* 110: 177–80.

ERRINGTON, R. M. (1971) 'The Alleged Syro-Macedonian Pact and the Origins of the Second Macedonian War', *Athenaeum* 49: 336–54.

——(1980) 'Rom, Antiochos der Grosse und die Asylie von Teos', *ZPE* 39: 279–84.

——(1986) 'Antiochos III, Zeuxis und Euromos', *EA* 8: 1–8.

——(1987) 'Θέα Ρώμη und römischer Einfluss südlich des Mäanders im 2. Jh. v. Chr.', *Chiron* 17: 97–118.

——(1989a) 'The Peace Treaty between Miletus and Magnesia (I. Milet 148)', *Chiron* 19: 279–88

——(1989b) 'Rome against Philip and Antiochus', in A. E. Astin, F. W. Walbank, M. W. Frederiksen, and R. M. Ogilvie (eds.), *CAH²*, viii. 244–89.

——(1993) 'Inschriften von Euromos', *EA* 21: 15–32.

ERSKINE, A. (1994) 'The Romans as Common Benefactors', *Historia* 43: 70–87.

FELLOWS, CH. (1839) *A Journal Written During an Excursion in Asia Minor*. London.

——(1841) *An Account of Discoveries in Lycia, Being a Journal Kept during a Second Excursion in Asia Minor*. London.

FERRARY, J.-L. (1988) *Philhellénisme et impérialisme. Aspects idéologiques de la conquête romaine du monde hellénistique de la seconde guerre de Macédoine à la guerre contre Mithridate* (BEFAR 271). Rome: École française de Rome.

——(1991) 'Le Statut des cités libres dans l'Empire romain à la lumière des inscriptions de Claros', *CRAI* 1991: 557–77.

——and GAUTHIER, PH. (1981) 'Le Traité entre le roi Antichos et Lysimacheia', *Journ. Sav.* 1981: 327–45.

FINLEY, M. I. (1983) *Economy and Society in Ancient Greece.* (ed. B. Shaw and R. P. Saller). Harmondsworth: Penguin.

FLEISCHER, R. (1972–5) 'Marsyas und Achaios' *ÖJh* 50, Beibl., 103–22.

FOGEL, M. (1989) *Les Cérémonies de l'information dans la France du XVIe au milieu du XVIIIe siècle.* Paris: Fayard.

DE FOUCAULT, J.-A. (1972) *Recherches sur la langue et le style de Polybe.* Paris: Les Belles Lettres.

FOUCAULT, M. (1975) *Surveiller et punir. Naissance de la prison.* Paris: Gallimard.

FOWDEN, G. (1993) *Empire to Commonwealth: Consequences of Monotheism in Late Antiquity.* Princeton: Princeton University Press.

FOXHALL, L. and FORBES, H. A. (1982) '*Sitometreia*: The Role of Grains as a Staple Food in Classical Antiquity', *Chiron* 12: 41–90.

FRANCO, C. (1993) *Il regno di Lisimaco. Strutture amministrative e rapporti con le città* (Studi ellenistici 6). Pisa: Giardini.

GALLANT, T. W. (1989). 'Crisis and Response: Risk Buffering Behavior in Hellenistic Greek Communities', *Journal of Interdisciplinary History* 19: 393–413.

GARNSEY, P. (1988) *Famine and Food Supply in the Graeco-Roman World: Responses to Risk and Crisis.* Cambridge: Cambridge University Press.

GAUGER, J.-D. (1977) *Beiträge zur jüdischen Apologetik: Untersuchungen zur Authentizität von Urkunden bei Flavius Josephus und im I. Makkabäerbuch* (Bonner Biblische Beiträge 49), Cologne: P. Hannstein.

——(1993) 'Formalien und Authentizitätsfrage: noch einmal zum Schreiben Antiochos' III. an Zeuxis (Jos. Ant. Jud. 12: 148–53) und zu den Antiochos-Urkunden bei Josephus', *Hermes* 121: 63–9.

GAUTHIER, PH. (1972) *Symbola. Les étrangers et la justice dans les cités grecques* (Annals de l'Est. Mémoires 42). Nancy: Université de Nancy II.

——(1979) '*ΕΞΑΓΩΓΗ ΣΙΤΟΥ*: Samothrace, Hippomédon et les Lagides', *Historia* 28: 76–89.

——(1980) 'Les Honneurs de l'officier séleucide Larichos à Priène', *Journ. Sav.* 1980: 35–50.

——(1985) *Les Cités grecques et leurs bienfaiteurs (IVe–Ier siècle avant J.-C.). Contribution à l'histoire des institutions* (*BCH* supplément 12). Paris: École française d'Athènes.

——(1989) *Nouvelles inscriptions de Sardes* II (Archaeological Exploration of Sardis/École Pratique des Hautes Études, IVe section. Hautes Études du Monde Gréco-Romain 15), Paris and Geneva: Droz.

——(1993a) 'Epigraphica II. 4. *Prostagmata* attalides à Égine (*OGI* 329)', *Rev. Phil.* 67: 41–8.

——(1993b) 'Les Cités hellénistiques', in Hansen 1993: 211–31.

——(1994) 'Les Rois hellénistiques et les juges étrangers: à propos de décrets de Kimôlos et de Laodicée du Lykos', *Journ. Sav.* 1994: 165–95.

GAUTHIER, PH. (1996) ' Bienfaiteurs du gymnase au Létôon de Xanthos', *REG* 109: 1–34.

GAWANTKA, W. (1975) *Isopolitie. Ein Beitrag zur Geschichte der zwischenstaatlichen Beziehungen in der griechischen Antike* (Vestigia 22). Munich: Beck.

GEERTZ, C. (1993) *Local Knowledge: Further Essays in Interpretive Anthropology*. London: Fontana.

GERA, D. (1987) 'Ptolemy son of Thraseas and the Fifth Syrian War', *Anc. Soc.* 18: 63–73.

——(1998) *Judaea and Mediterranean Politics. 219 to 161 B.C.E.* (E. J. Brill's series in Jewish Studies 8). Leiden: E. J. Brill.

GIOVANNINI, A. (1983) 'Téos, Antiochos III et Attale Ier', *Mus. Helv.* 40: 178–84.

GRAINGER, J. D. (1990) *Seleukos Nikator. Constructing a Hellenistic Kingdom*. London: Routledge.

——(1996) 'Antiochos III in Thrace', *Historia* 45: 329–43.

GRANDJEAN, J. (1971) 'Note sur une épigramme de Maronée', *BCH* 95: 283–94

GREEN, P. (1989) *Classical Bearings: Interpreting Ancient History and Culture*. London: Thames and Hudson.

——(1990) *Alexander to Actium. The Historical Evolution of the Hellenistic Age* (Hellenistic Culture and Society 1). Berkeley, Calif., and London: University of California Press.

GRUEN, E. S. (1986) *The Hellenistic World and the Coming of Rome* (reprint of orig. edn., 1984). Berkeley, Calif., and London: University of California Press.

——(1992) *Culture and National Identity in Republican Rome* (Cornell Studies in Classical Philology 52). Ithaca, New York: Cornell University Press.

——(1993). 'The Polis in the Hellenistic World', in R. M. Rosen and J. Farrell (eds.), *Nomodeiktes: Greek Studies in Honor of Martin Ostwald*. Ann Arbor: University of Michigan Press, 339–54

——(1996) *Studies in Greek Culture and Roman Policy* (reprint of orig. edn., 1990). Berkeley, Calif., and London: University of California Press.

GÜNTHER, W. (1988) 'Milesische Bürgerrechts- und Proxenieverleihungen der hellenistischen Zeit', *Chiron* 18: 383–419.

HABICHT, CHR. (1956) 'Über die Kriege zwischen Pergamon und Bithynien', *Hermes* 84: 90–110.

——(1957) 'Samische Volksbeschlüsse der hellenistischen Zeit', *Ath. Mitt.* 72: 152–274.

——(1970) *Gottmenschentum und griechische Städte* (2nd edn.) (Zetemata 14). Munich: Beck.

——(1976) 'Royal Documents in Maccabees, II', *HSCP* 80: 1–18.

——(1980) 'Bemerkungen zum P. Haun. 6', *ZPE* 39: 1–5.

——(1987) 'Der Archon Philaitolos von Delphi', *ZPE* 69: 87–9.
——(1994) *Athen in hellenistischer Zeit. Gesammelte Aufsätze*. Munich: Beck.
——(1996) 'Neue Inschriften aus Kos', *ZPE* 112: 83–94.
——(1997) *Athens from Alexander to Antony* (expanded trans. by D. L. Schneider, of German orig. edn. 1995). Cambridge, Mass., and London: Harvard University Press.
HAHN, I. (1978) 'Königsland und königliche Besteuerung im hellenistischen Osten', *Klio* 60: 11–34.
HALL, A. S. (1986) 'Regional Epigraphical Catalogues of Asia Minor. Notes and Studies IX: the Milyadeis and their Territory', *Anat. Stud.* 36: 137–57.
HAMILTON, W. J. (1842) *Researches in Asia Minor, Pontus and Armenia; with some Account of their Antiquities and Geology.* 2 vols. London.
HANSEN, M. H. (ed.) (1993) *The Ancient Greek City-State. Symposium on the Occasion of the 250th Anniversary of the Danish Academy of Sciences and Letters. 1–4 July 1992* (Det Kongelige Danske Videnskabernes Selskab, Historisk-filosofiske Meddelelser 67). Copenhagen: Munksgaard.
——(1995) 'The "autonomous city-state". Ancient Fact or Modern Fiction?', in M. H. Hansen and K. Raaflaub (eds.), *Studies in the Ancient Greek Polis* (Historia Einzelschrift 95), Stuttgart: F. Steiner, 21–43.
HATZOPOULOS, M. B. (1996) *Macedonian Institutions under the Kings*, 2 vols. (Meletemata 22). Athens: Research Centre for Greek and Roman Antiquity.
HAUSSOULLIER, B. (1902) *Études sur l'histoire de Milet et du Didyméion* (Bibliothèque de l'École des Hautes Études, sciences historiques et philologiques, 138). Paris: E. Bouillon.
HERMAN, G. (1980/1) 'The "Friends" of the Early Hellenistic Rulers: Servants or Officials ?', *Talanta* 12/13: 103–49.
HERRMANN, P. (1959) *Neue Inschriften zur historischen Landeskunde von Lydien und angrenzenden Gebieten* (Denkschriften der Österreichischen Akademie der Wissenschaften, phil.-hist. Klasse, 77.1), 4–6, no. 2.
——(1965a) 'Antiochos der Grosse und Teos', *Anadolu* 9: 29–159.
——(1965b) 'Neue Urkunden zur Geschichte von Milet im 2. Jahrhundert v. Chr.', *Ist. Mitt.* 15: 71–117.
——(1970) 'I. Weihungen an Zeus Pottorenos. 1. Der Hegemon Arkesilaos für Apollophanes, den Leibarzt Antiochos' III', *Anzeiger der Österreichischen Akademie der Wissenschaften, phil.-hist. Klasse* 1970: 94–8.
——(1979) 'Die Stadt Temnos und ihre auswärtigen Beziehungen in hellenistischer Zeit', *Ist. Mitt.* 29: 220–71.
——(1987). 'Milesier am Seleukidenhof. Prosopographische Beiträge zur Geschichte Milets im 2. Jhdt. v. Chr.', *Chiron* 17: 171–92.
HERZOG, R., and KLAFFENBACH, G. (1952) *Asylieurkunden aus Kos*

(Abhandlungen der Deutschen Akademie der Wissenschaften zu Berlin, Klasse für Sprachen, Literatur und Kunst, 1952.1). Berlin: Akademie-Verlag.

HESSEL, F. (1731) *Praefationis appendix* to *Antiquae inscriptiones quum Graecae tum Latinae olim a Marquardo Gudio collectae, nuper a Ioanne Koolio digestae, hortatu consilioque Ioannis Georgii Graevii, nunc a Francisco Hesslio editae cum adnotationibus eorum.* Leeuwarden.

HEUSS, A. (1937) *Stadt und Herrscher des Hellenismus in ihren staats- und völkerrechtlichen Beziehungen* (Klio Beiheft 39, NS 26). Leipzig: Dieterich.

HINTZEN-BOHLEN, B. (1992) *Herrscherrepräsentation im Hellenismus. Untersuchungen zu Weihgeschenken, Stiftungen und Ehrenmonumenten in den mutterländischen Heiligtümern Delphi, Olympia, Delos und Dodona.* Cologne and Weimar: Bühlau.

HOLLEAUX, M. (1935) *Rome, la Grèce et les Monarchies Hellenistiques.* Paris: E. de Boccard.

——(1938*a*) *Études d'épigraphie et d'histoire grecques*, i (ed. L. Robert). Paris: A. Maisonneuve.

——(1938*b*) *Études d'épigraphie et d'histoire grecques*, ii (ed. L. Robert). Paris: A. Maisonneuve.

——(1942) *Études d'épigraphie et d'histoire grecques*, iii, *Lagides et Séleucides* (ed. L. Robert). Paris: A. Maisonneuve.

——(1952) *Études d'épigraphie et d'histoire grecques*, iv, *Rome, la Macédoine et l'Orient grec. Première partie* (ed. L. Robert). Paris: A. Maisonneuve.

——(1957) *Études d'épigraphie et d'histoire grecques*, v, *Rome, la Macédoine et l'Orient grec. Seconde partie* (ed. L. Robert). Paris: A. Maisonneuve.

——(1968) *Études d'épigraphie et d'histoire grecques*, vi, *Bibliographie et index détaillé* (ed. L. Robert). Paris: A. Maisonneuve.

HORNBLOWER, S. (1982) *Mausolus.* Oxford: Clarendon Press.

——(1985) *The Greek World 479–323* (corr. printing of 1st edn., 1983). London: Routledge.

HUSS, W. (1976) *Untersuchungen zur Aussenpolitik Ptolemaios' IV.* (Münchener Beiträge zur Papyrusforschung und Antiken Rechtsgeschichte 69). Munich: Beck.

——(1977) 'Eine ptolemäische Expedition nach Kleinasien', *Anc. Soc.* 8: 187–93.

——(1998) 'Ptolemaios der Sohn', *ZPE* 121: 229–50.

JONES, A. H. M. (1940) *The Greek City from Alexander to Justinian.* Oxford: Clarendon Press.

JONES, CHR. P. (1993) 'The Decree of Ilion in Honor of a King Antiochus', *GRBS* 34: 73–92.

——and HABICHT, CHR. (1989) 'A Hellenistic Inscription from Arsinoe in Cilicia', *Phoenix* 43: 317–46.

——and RUSSELL, J. (1993) 'Two New Inscriptions from Nagidos in Cilicia', *Phoenix* 47: 293–304.

JONNES, L. and RICL, M. (1997) 'A New Royal Inscription from Phrygia

Paroreios: Eumenes II Grants Tyriaion the Status of a Polis', *EA* 29: 1–29.

KAGAN, J. H. (1984) 'Hellenistic Coinage at Scepsis after its Refoundation in the Third Century B.C.', *ANSMusN* 29: 11–24.

KEARSLEY, R. A. (1994) 'The Milyas and the Attalids: A Decree of the City of Olbasa and a New Royal Letter of the Second Century B.C.', *Anatolian Studies* 44: 47–57.

KNOEPFLER, D. (1993) 'Le Temple du Métrôon de Sardes et ses inscriptions', *Mus. Helv.* 50: 26–43.

KOBES, J. (1996) *Kleine Könige. Untersuchungen zu den Lokaldynasten im hellenistischen Kleinasien (323–188 v. Chr.)*. St Katharinen: Scripta Mercaturae.

KRAELING, C. H. (1964) 'A New Inscription from Antioch on the Orontes', *AJA* 68: 178–9.

KREUTER, S. (1992) *Aussenbeziehungen kretischer Gemeinden zu den hellenistischen Staaten im 3. und 2. Jh. v. Chr.* (Münchener Arbeiten zur alten Geschichte 6). Munich: Editio Maris.

KRISCHEN, FR. (1922) *Die Befestigungen von Herakleia am Latmos* (Milet, Ergebnisse der Ausgrabungen und Untersuchungen seit dem Jahre 1899, ed. Th. Wiegand, vol. 3, fasc. 2). Berlin and Leipzig: Vereinigung wissenschaftlicher Verleger.

LAFFI, U. (1971) 'I terreni del tempio di Zeus ad Aizanoi. Le iscrizioni sulla parete interna dell'anta destra del pronaos', *Athenaeum* NS 49: 5–53.

LANDAU, Y, H. (1961) 'A Greek inscription from Acre', *IEJ* 11: 118–26.

LAUNEY, M. (1987) *Recherches sur les armées hellénistiques* (BEFAR 169). 2 vols. (reprint of original edn. (1949–50), with additional comments by Y. Garlan, Ph. Gauthier, and Cl. Orrieux). Paris: E. de Boccard

LE BOHEC, S. (1993) *Antigone Doson, roi de Macedoine* (Travaux et mémoires. Études anciennes 9). Nancy: Presses Universitaires de Nancy.

LE RIDER, G. (1971/2) 'Numismatique grecque', *Annuaire de l'École Pratique des Hautes Études (IVe section)*, 227–42.

—— (1972/3) 'Numismatique grecque', *Annuaire de l'École Pratique des Hautes Études (IVe section)*, 243–59.

—— (1973/4) 'Numismatique grecque', *Annuaire de l'École Pratique des Hautes Études (IVe section)*, 251–60.

—— (1975/6) 'Numismatique grecque', *Annuaire de l'École Pratique des Hautes Études (IVe section)*, 345–58.

—— (1990) 'Antiochos II à Mylasa', *BCH* 114: 543–51.

LE ROY, CHR. (1986) 'Un règlement religieux au Létôon de Xanthos', *RA* 1986: 279–300.

LE ROY LADURIE, E. (1975) *Montaillou, village occitan de 1294 à 1324*. Paris: Gallimard.

LEAKE, W. M. (1824) *Journal of a Tour in Asia Minor, with Comparative Remarks on the Ancient and Modern Geography of that Country*. London.

LEFÈVRE, FR. (1995). 'La Chronologie du IIIe siècle à Delphes, d'après les actes amphictioniques (280–200)', *BCH* 119: 161–208.

LEFÈVRE, FR. (1996) 'Antiochos le Grand et les Etoliens à la fin du IIIe siècle', *BCH* 120: 757–71.

LENGER, M.-TH. (1953) 'La Notion de bienfait (philanthrôpon) royal et les ordonnances des rois lagides', in *Studi in onore di Vincenzo Arangio-Ruiz nel XLV anno del suo insegnamento* (Naples: Jovene), i. 483–99.

LEUZE, O. (1923) 'Die Feldzüge Antiochos des Grossen nach Kleinasien und Thrakien', *Hermes* 58: 187–229, 241–87.

LEWIS, D. M. (1977) *Sparta and Persia* (Cincinnati Classical Studies 1). Leiden: Brill.

LORAUX, N. (1997) *La Cité divisée. L'oubli dans la mémoire d'Athènes*. Paris: Payot.

LUCE, T. J. (1977) *Livy : The Composition of his History*. Princeton: Princeton University Press.

LUKES, ST. (1974) *Power: A Radical View*. London: Macmillan.

LUND, H. S. (1992) *Lysimachus: A Study in Early Hellenistic Kingship*. London: Routledge.

MCNICOLL, A. W. (1997) *Hellenistic Fortifications from the Aegean to the Euphrates* (rev. N. P. Milner) Oxford: Clarendon Press.

MA, J. (1997) 'The *koinon* of the Laodikeis in the Rhodian Peraia', *EA* 27: 9–10.

——DEROW, P., and MEADOWS, A. (1995). '*RC* 38 (Amyzon) reconsidered', *ZPE* 109: 71–80.

MCDONALD, A. H. (1967) 'The Treaty of Apamea (188 B.C.)', *JRS* 57: 1–8.

MAGIE, D. (1939) 'The "Agreement" between Philip V and Antiochus III for the Partition of the Egyptian Empire', *JRS* 29: 32–44.

——(1950) *Roman Rule in Asia Minor to the End of the Third Century after Christ*. 2 vols. Princeton: Princeton University Press.

MALAY, H. (1983) 'A Royal Document from Aigai in Aiolis', *GRBS* 24: 349–53.

——(1987) 'Letter of Antiochos III to Zeuxis with Two Covering Letters (209 B.C.)', *EA* 10: 7–17.

——(1996) 'New Evidence Concerning the Administrative System of the Attalids', *Arkeoloji Dergisi* 4: 83–6.

——and NALBANTOĞLU, C. (1996) 'The Cult of Apollon Pleurenos in Lydia', *Arkeoloji Dergisi* 4: 75–81.

MANN, M. (1986) *The Sources of Social Power. A History of Power from the Beginning to A.D. 1760*, i. Cambridge: Cambridge University Press.

MANVILLE, P. B. (1990) *The Origins of Citizenship in Ancient Athens*. Princeton: Princeton University Press.

MAREK, CHR. (1988) 'Karien im ersten Mithridatischen Krieg', in P. Kneissl, V. Losemann (eds.), *Alte Geschichte und Wissenschaftsgeschichte. Festschrift für Karl Christ zum 65. Geburtstag* (Darmstadt: Wissenschaftliche Buchgesellschaft), 285–308.

MARIN, L. (1978) *Le Récit est un piège*. Paris: Éditions de Minuit.

MASTROCINQUE, A. (1979) *La Caria e la Ionia meridionale in epoca ellenis-*

tica (323–188 a. C.). Rome: L'Erma di Bretschneider.

——(1983) *Manipolazione dell storia in età ellenistica: i Seleucidici e Roma* (Universittà di Venezia—Istituto di studi classici—Pubblicazioni del seminario di storia antica 1). Rome: L'Erma di Bretschneider.

——(1993) ' "Guerra di successione" e prima guerra di Celesiria: un falso moderno e una questione storica', *Anc. Soc.* 24: 27–39.

——(1994). Review of Brodersen 1991, *Gnomon* 66: 451–3.

——(1995) 'Iaso e i Seleucidici', *Athenaeum* 83: 131–42.

MEADOWS, A. (1996) 'Four Rhodian decrees. Rhodes, Iasos and Philip V', *Chiron* 26: 251–66.

MEHL, A. (1980/1) '*ΔΟΡΙΚΤΗΤΟΣ ΧΩΡΑ*. Kritische Bemerkungen zum "Speererwerb" in Politik und Völkerrecht der hellenistischen Epoche', *Anc. Soc.* 11–12: 173–212.

——(1986) *Seleukos Nikator und sein Reich. I. Seleukos' Leben und die Entwicklung seiner Machtposition* (Studia Hellenistica 28). Louvain.

——(1990) 'Zu den diplomatischen Beziehungen zwischen Antiochos III. und Rom, 200–193 v. Chr.' in Chr. Börker and M. Donderer (eds.), *Das antike Rom und der Osten. Festschrift für Klaus Parlasca zum 65. Geburtstag* (Erlanger Forschungen, Reihe A, Geisteswissenschaften, 56), Erlangen: Universitätsbund Erlangen-Nürnberg, 143–55.

MELLOR, R. (1975) *ΘΕΑ ΡΩΜΗ. The Worship of the Goddess Roma in the Greek World* (Hypomnemata 42). Göttingen: Vandenhoeck & Ruprecht.

MELONI, P. (1949) 'L'usurpazione di Acheo sotto Antiochos III di Siria. I. Le circostanze ed i primi atti dell'usurpazione', *Rendiconti della Classe di Scienze Morali, Storiche e Filologiche dell'Accademia dei Lincei* 8.4: 535–53.

——(1950) 'L'usurpazione di Acheo sotto Antiochos III di Siria. II. Le campagne di Acheo in Asia Minore e la sua morte', *Rendiconti della Classe di Scienze Morali, Storiche e Filologiche dell'Accademia dei Lincei* 8.5: 161–83.

MERKELBACH, R. (1968) 'Zu dem neuen epigraphischen Dokument aus Teos. II', *ZPE* 3: 173–4.

MIGEOTTE, L. (1984) *L'Emprunt public dans les cites grecques: recueil des documents et analyse critique*. Quebec: Éditions du Sphinx and Paris: Les Belles Lettres.

——(1992) *Les Souscriptions publiques dans les cités grecques*. Geneva: Droz and Quebec: Éditions du Sphinx.

MILLAR, F. (1967) *The Roman Empire and its Neighbours* (trans. of original German edn., Frankfurt am Main and Hamburg, 1966; with contributions by D. Berciu, R. N. Frye, G. Kossack, and T. T. Rice). London: G. Weidenfeld and Nicholson.

——(1983) 'Empire and City, Augustus to Julian: Obligations, Excuses and Status', *JRS* 73: 76–96.

——(1987). 'Polybius between Greece and Rome', in J. T. A. Koumoulides (ed.), *Greek Connections* (Notre-Dame: University of Notre Dame Press), 1–18.

MILLAR, F. (1992) *The Emperor in the Roman World (31 BC–AD 337)* (reprint of 1st edn., 1977, with afterword). London: Duckworth.
——(1994) *The Roman Near-East. 31 BC–AD 337* (2nd edn.) Cambridge, Mass.: Harvard University Press.
MITCHELL, ST. (1991) 'The Hellenization of Pisidia', *Mediterranean Archaeology* 4: 119–45.
——(1993) *Anatolia. Land, Men, and Gods in Asia Minor*, i, *The Celts and the impact of Roman rule*. Oxford: Clarendon Press.
MØRKHOLM, O. (1969) 'Some Seleucid Coins of the Mint of Sardes', *Nordisk Num. Arsskrift* 1969: 5–20.
——(1991) *Early Hellenistic Coinage from the Accession of Alexander to the Peace of Apameia (336–188 B.C.)* (ed. Ph. Grierson and U. Westermark). Cambridge: Cambridge University Press.
MOURGUES, J.-L. (1995) 'Écrire en deux langues: bilinguisme et pratique de chancellerie sous le Haut-empire romain', *DHA* 21: 105–29.
MURRAY, O. (1970) Περὶ βασιλείας. D.Phil. thesis, Oxford University.
——(1990) 'Cities of Reason', in O. Murray and S. Price (eds.), *The Greek City from Homer to Alexander*, Oxford: Clarendon Press, 1–25.
MUSTI, D. (1965) 'Aspetti dell'organizzazione seleucidica in Asia Minore nel III. sec. a. c.', *PP* 20: 153–60.
——(1966) 'Lo stato dei Seleucidi: dinastia, popoli, città da Seleuco I ad Antioco III', *SCO* 15: 61–197.
NAFISSI, M. 'L'iscrizione di Laodice (Iv Iasos 4). Revisioni del resto e nuove observazioni', 66 (2001), 101–46.
NICOLET, CL. (1990) 'Du pouvoir dans l'antiquité: les mots et les réalités', in Cl. Nicolet (ed.), *Du pouvoir dans l'antiquité: mots et réalités* (Cahiers du Centre Glotz 1), Paris and Geneva: Droz, 3–11.
OBER, J. (1989). *Mass and Elite in Democratic Athens: Rhetoric, Ideology, and the Power of the People*. Princeton: Princeton University Press.
OLIVER, J. H. (1968) 'Notes on the Inscription at Teos in Honor of Antiochus III', *GRBS* 9: 321–2.
OLSHAUSEN, E. (1974) *Prosopographie der hellenistischen Königsgesandten. Teil I: von Triparadeisos bis Pydna* (Studia Hellenistica 19). Louvain: Nauwelaerts.
OPPERMANN, H. (1924) *Zeus Panamaros*. Giessen: A. Topelmann.
ORMEROD, H. A. (1924) *Piracy in the Ancient World: An Essay in Mediterranean History*. Liverpool and London: Hodder and Stoughton.
ORRIEUX, CL. (1983) *Les Papyrus de Zénon. L'horizon d'un grec en Egypte au IIIe siècle avant J. C.* Paris: Macula.
ORTH, W. (1977) *Königlicher Machtanspruch und städtische Freiheit. Untersuchungen zu den politischen Beziehungen zwischen den ersten Seleukidenherrschern (Seleukos I., Antiochos I., Antiochos II.) und den Städten des westlichen Kleinasien* (Münchener Beiträge zur Papyrus-forschung und antiken Rechtsgeschichte 71). Munich: Beck.
OSBORNE, R. (1990) 'The *Demos* and its Divisions in Classical Athens', in

O. Murray and S. Price (eds.), *The Greek City from Homer to Alexander*. Oxford: Clarendon Press, 265–93.

OZOUF, M. (1976) *La Fête révolutionnaire 1789–1799*. Paris: Gallimard.

PETIT, TH. (1990) *Satrapes et satrapies dans l'empire achéménide de Cyrus le Grand à Xerxès Ier*. Liège: Bibliothèque de la faculté de philosophie et lettres de l'Université de Liège (254).

PIEJKO, F. (1985) Review of J. and L. Robert 1983, *Gnomon* 57: 608–21.

——(1987) 'The Settlement of Sardis after the Fall of Achaeus', *AJP* 108: 707–28.

——(1988a) 'Letter of Eumenes II to Tralles concerning Inviolability and Tax Exemption for a Temple. After 188 B.C.', *Chiron* 18: 55–69.

——(1988b) 'The Treaty between Antiochos III and Lysimachia ca. 196 B.C. (with a discussion of the earlier treaty with Philip V)', *Historia* 37: 151–65.

——(1991a) 'Antiochus III and Teos Reconsidered', *Belleten (Türk Tarih Kurumu)*: 13–69.

——(1991b) 'Antiochus III and Ilium', *APF* 37: 9–50.

POCOCK, J. G. A. (1984) 'Verbalizing a Political Act: Toward a Politics of Speech', in Shapiro 1984: 25–43.

——(1987) 'The Concept of a Language and the *métier d'historien*: Some Considerations on Practice', in A. Pagden (ed.), *The Languages of Political Theory in Early-Modern Europe*, Cambridge: Cambridge University Press, 19–38.

POUNDER, R. L. (1978) 'Honours for Antioch of the Chrysaorians', *Hesperia* 47: 49–57

PRICE, S. R. F. (1984) *Rituals and Power: The Roman Imperial Cult in Asia Minor*. Cambridge: Cambridge University Press.

PRICE, M. J. (1991) *The Coinage in the Name of Alexander the Great and Philip Arrhidaeus. A British Museum Catalogue*. Zurich: Swiss Numismatic Society and London: British Museum.

PRITCHETT, W. K. (1982) *Studies in Greek Topography. Part IV (passes)* (University of California publications: Classical Studies 28). Berkeley, Calif., and London: University of California Press.

PUGLIESE-CARRATELLI, G. (1987). 'Epigrafi di Cos relativi al culto di Artemis in Knido e in Bargylia', *PP* 232: 110–23.

RAMSAY, W. M. (1895) *The Cities and Bishoprics of Phrygia, Being an Essay of the Local History of Phrygia from the Earliest Times to the Turkish Conquest*, i, *The Lycos Valley and Southwestern Phrygia*. Oxford: Clarendon Press.

RAWLINGS III, H. (1976) 'Antiochus the Great and Rhodes', *AJAH* 1. 2–28.

REYNOLDS, J. (1982) *Aphrodisias and Rome. Documents from the Excavation of the Theatre at Aphrodisias Conducted by Professor Kenan T. Erim, together with some Related Texts (Journal of Roman Studies* Monographs 1). London: Society for the Promotion of Roman Studies.

RHODES, P. J., with LEWIS, D. M. (1997) *The Decrees of the Greek States*. Oxford: Oxford University Press.

RICE, E. E. (1983) *The Grand Procession of Ptolemy Philadephus*. Oxford: Oxford University Press.

RIGSBY, K. J. (1996) *Asylia. Territorial inviolability in the Hellenistic World* (Hellenistic Culture and Society 22). Berkeley, Calif., and London: University of California Press.

ROBERT, J. and Robert, L. (1948) *Hellenica. Recueil d'épigraphie, de numismatique et d'antiquités grecques*, vi. Paris: Impr. A. Bontemps.

———(1954) *La Carie. Histoire et géographie historique, avec le recueil des inscriptions antiques. Tome II. Le plateau de Tabai et ses environs.* Paris: A. Maisonneuve.

———(1983) *Fouilles d' Amyzon en Carie. Tome I. Exploration, histoire, monnaies et inscriptions.* Paris: Commission des fouilles et missions archéologiques au Ministère des relations extérieures.

———(1989) *Claros. Décrets hellénistiques*, fasc. 1. Paris: Éditions Recherche sur les civilisations.

ROBERT, L. (1936) *Collection Froehner*, i. *Les inscriptions grecques*. Paris: Editions des bibliothèques nationales.

——(1937) *Études Anatoliennes. Recherches sur les inscriptions grecques de l'Asie Mineure.* Paris: E. de Boccard.

——(1945) *Le Sanctuaire de Sinuri près de Mylasa* I. *Les inscriptions grecques* (Mémoires de l' Institut Français d'Archéologie de Stamboul 7). Paris: E. de Boccard.

——(1949) *Hellenica. Recueil d'épigraphie, de numismatique et d'antiquités grecques*, vii. Paris: Impr. A. Bontemps.

——(1950) *Hellenica. Recueil d'épigraphie, de numismatique et d'antiquités grecques*, viii. Paris: Impr. A. Bontemps.

——(1951) *Études de numismatique grecque.* Paris: Collège de France.

——(1955) *Hellenica. Recueil d'épigraphie, de numismatique et d'antiquités grecques*, x. Paris: Impr. A. Bontemps.

——(1960) *Hellenica. Recueil d'épigraphie, de numismatique et d'antiquités grecques*, xi/xii. Paris: Impr. A. Bontemps.

——(1962) *Villes d'Asie Mineure. Études de géographie ancienne* (reprint of 1st edn., 1935, with updates and postface). Paris: E. de Boccard.

——(1964) *Nouvelles inscriptions de Sardes* I. Paris: A. Maisonneuve.

——(1966a) *Documents de l'Asie mineure méridionale.* Paris and Geneva: Droz.

——(1966b) *Monnaies grecques en Troade.* Paris and Geneva: Droz.

——(1967) 'Encore une inscription grecque de l'Iran', *CRAI* 1967: 281–97.

——(1973) 'Sur des inscriptions de Délos. I. Sur un proxène d'Antioche de Carie', in *Études déliennes* (*BCH* supplément 1), Paris, 435–68.

——(1987) *Documents d'Asie Mineure* (BEFAR 239bis). Paris: E. de Boccard.

ROBIN, R. (1973) *Histoire et linguistique.* Paris: Armand Colin.

ROGERS, G. M. (1991) *The Sacred Identity of Ephesos. Foundation Myths of a Roman city.* London and New York: Routledge.

Rostovtzeff, M. (1935) '*ΠΡΟΓΟΝΟΙ*', *JHS* 55: 56–66.

——(1941) *The Social and Economic History of the Hellenistic World*, 3 vols. Oxford: Clarendon Press.

Rumscheid, F. (1994) *Untersuchungen zur kleinasiatischen Bauornamentik des Hellenismus* (Beiträge zur Erschliessung hellenisticher und kaiserzeitlicher Skulptur und Architektur 14). Mainz: Zabern.

Sachs, A. J., and Hunger, H. (1988) *Astronomical Diaries and Related Texts from Babylonia*, i (Denkschriften der Österreichischen Akademie der Wissenschaften, phil.-hist. Klasse 195). Vienna: Verlag der Österreichischen Akademie der Wissenschaften.

——————(1989) *Astronomical Diaries and Related Texts from Babylonia*, ii (Denkschriften der Österreichischen Akademie der Wissenschaften, phil-hist. Klasse 210). Vienna: Verlag der Österreichischen Akademie der Wissenschaften.

Şahin, S. (1985) 'Ein neues Dekret der Symmoria zu Ehren ihrer Prostatai in Teos', *EA* 5: 13–18.

Sakellariou, M. V. (1989) *The Polis-State: Definition and Origins* (Meletemata 4) Athens: Research Centre for Greek and Roman Antiquity.

Samuel, A. E. (1972) *Greek and Roman Chronology: Calendars and Years in Classical Antiquity* (Müllers Handbücher der Altertumswissenschaft 1.7). Munich: Beck.

Sartre, M. (1991) *L'Orient romain. Provinces et sociétés provinciales en Méditerranée orientale d'Auguste aux Sévères (31 avant J.-C.–235 après J.-C.)*. Paris: Seuil.

——(1995) *L'Asie Mineure et l'Anatolie d'Alexandre à Dioclétien (IVe siècle av. J.-C./IIIe siècle ap. J.-C.)*. Paris: Armand Colin.

Savalli-Lestrade, I. (1996) 'Courtisans et citoyens: le case des philoi attalides', *Chiron* 26: 149–80.

Sayar, M. (2001) 'Von Kilikien bis Thrakien: Neuen Erkenntnisse zur Politik Antiochos' III. zwischen 197–195 v. Chr. anhand von zwei neugefundenen Inschriften', in A. Bresson and R. Descat (eds.), *Les Cités d'Asie Mineure occidentale au IIe siècle a. C.*, 227–34.

Schede, M. (1919) 'Aus dem Heraion von Samos', *Ath. Mitt.* 44: 1–46.

Schlesinger, E. (1933) *Die griechische Asylie*. Giessen: W. F. Kaestner.

Schmitt, H. (1964) *Untersuchungen zur Geschichte Antiochos' des Grossen und seiner Zeit* (Historia Einzelschrift 6). Stuttgart: F. Steiner.

Schubart, W. (1920) 'Bemerkungen zum Stile hellenistischer Königsbriefe', *APF* 6: 324–47.

——(1937) 'Das hellenistische Königsideal nach Inschriften und Papyri', *APF* 12: 1–26.

Schürer, E. (1973) *The History of the Jewish People in the Age of Jesus Christ (175 B.C.–A.D. 135)* (eds. G. Vermes and F. Millar), i. Edinburgh: Clark.

Schwertheim, E. (1988) 'Studien zur historischen Geographie Mysiens. 1. Mysia im Vertrag von Apameia', *EA* 11: 65–78.

SEGRE, M. (1938) 'Iscrizioni di Licia. I. Tolomeo di Telmesso', *Clara Rhodos* 9: 181–208.

SEYRIG, H. (1986) *Scripta numismatica* (Institut français d'archéologie au Proche-orient—Bibliothèque archéologique et historique 126). Paris: Geuthner.

SHAPIRO, M. J. (ed.) (1984) *Language and Politics*. Oxford: Basil Blackwell.

SHAW, B. (1984) 'Bandits in the Roman empire', *Past and Present* 105: 3–52.

SHERWIN-WHITE, S. M. (1978) *Ancient Cos: An Historical Study from the Dorian Settlement to the Imperial Period* (Hypomnemata 51). Göttingen: Vandenhoeck und Ruprecht.

——(1985) 'Ancient Archives: The Edict of Alexander to Priene, a Reappraisal', *JHS* 105: 69–89.

——and KUHRT, A. (eds.) (1987) *Hellenism in the East: Interaction of Greek and Non-Greek Civilizations from Syria to Central Asia after Alexander*. London: Duckworth.

————(1993) *From Samarkhand to Sardis: A New Approach to the Seleukid Empire*. London: Duckworth.

SHIPLEY, G. (1987) *A History of Samos, 800–188 B.C.* Oxford: Clarendon Press.

SPRANGER, P. P. (1958) 'Der Grosse. Untersuchungen zur Entstehung des historischen Beinamens in der Antike', *Saeculum* 9: 22–58.

STROBEL, K. (1991) 'Die Galater im hellenistischen Kleinasien: historische Aspekte einer hellenistichen Staatenbildung', in J. Seibert (ed.), *Hellenistische Studien. Gedenkschrift für Herrmann Bengtson* (Münchener Arbeiten zur alten Geschichte 5), Munich: Editio Maris, 101–34.

——(1996) *Die Galater. Geschichte und Eigenart der keltischen Staatenbildung auf dem Boden des hellenistischen Kleinasien*, i (Untersuchungen zur Geschichte und historischen Geographie des hellenistischen und römischen Kleinasien 1). Berlin: Akademie Verlag.

SYME, R. (1995) *Anatolica. Studies in Strabo* (ed. A. Birley). Oxford: Clarendon Press.

TARN, W. W. (1948) *Alexander the Great*. 2 vols. Cambridge: Cambridge University Press.

TAŞLIKLIOĞLU, Z., and FRISCH, P. (1975) 'Inscriptions from the Troad', *ZPE* 19: 219–24.

THOMPSON, W. E. (1971) 'Philip V and the Islanders', *TAPA* 102: 615–20.

TILLY, CH. (1985) 'War Making and State-Making as Organised Crime', in P. B. Evans, D. Rueschemeyer, and T. Skocpol (eds.), *Bringing the State back in*, Cambridge: Cambridge University Press, 169–91.

TRACY, ST. V. (1992) 'Inscriptiones Deliacae. IG XI 713 and IG XI 1056', *Ath. Mitt.* 107: 303–14.

TUPLIN, CHR. (1987) 'Xenophon and the Garrisons of the Achaemenid Empire', *AMI* 20: 167–245.

VAN BERCHEM, D. (1982) *Les Routes et l'histoire. Études sur les Helvètes et leurs voisins dans l'empire romain* (Université de Lausanne. Publications de la Faculté de Lettres 25) (eds. P. Ducrey and D. Paunier, with H. Lichtenthaeler). Geneva: Droz.

VAN PROOSDIJ, B. A. (1934) 'De morte Achaei', *Hermes* 69: 347–50.

VERSNEL, H. S. (1990) *Inconsistencies in Greek and Roman religion*, i. *Ter Unus. Isis, Dionysos, Hermes. Three Studies in Henotheism* (Studies in Greek and Roman Religion 6). Leiden: E. J. Brill.

VEYNE, P. (1976) *Le Pain et le cirque. Sociologie historique d'un pluralisme politique*. Paris: Seuil.

——(1978) *Comment on écrit l'histoire* (abridgement of 1st edn., 1978). Paris: Seuil.

VIRGILIO, B. (1987) 'Strutture templari e potere politico in Asia Minore', *Athenaeum* 65: 227–31.

WAELKENS, M. (ed.) (1993) *Sagalassos*, i. *First General Report on the Survey (1986–1989) and the Excavations (1990–1991)* (Acta Archaeologica Lovaniensia, Monographiae 5). Leuven: Leuven University Press.

——and POBLOME, J. (eds.) (1995) *Sagalassos*, iii. *Report on the Fourth Excavation Campaign of 1993* (Acta Archaeologica Lovaniensia, Monographiae 7). Leuven: Leuven University Press.

WAGGONER, N. M. (1989) 'A New Wrinkle in the Hellenistic Coinage of Antioch/Alabanda', in G. Le Rider, G. K. Jenkins, N. M. Waggoner, and U. Westermark (eds.), *Kraay-Mørkholm Essays. Numismatic Studies in Memory of C. H. Kraay and O. Mørkholm* (Publications d'histoire de l'art et d'archéologie de l'Université catholique de Louvain 59), Louvain: Institut supérieur d'archéologie et d'histoire de l'art, Séminaire de numismatique Marcel Hoc, 283–90.

WALBANK, F. W. (1940) *Philip V of Macedon*. Cambridge: Cambridge University Press.

——(1942) 'Alcaeus of Messene, Philip V and Rome', *CQ* 36: 134–5.

——(1965) Review of SCHMITT 1964, in *JRS* 55: 262–4.

——(1972) *Polybius* (Sather Lectures 42). Berkeley, Calif., and London: University of California Press.

——(1992) *The Hellenistic World* (corr. 3rd edn.). London: Fontana.

WARRIOR, V. (1996) *The Initiation of the Second Macedonian War: An Explication of Livy Book 31*. (Historia Einzelschrift 97). Stuttgart: F. Steiner.

WEBER, M. (1968) *Economy and Society: An Outline of Interpretive Sociology* (ed. G. Roth and Cl. Wittich). 3 vols. New York: Bedminster Press.

WELLES, C. B. (1956) 'The Greek City', in S. Pagani (ed.), *Studi in onore di Aristide Calderini e Roberto Paribeni*, i. Milan: Ceschina, 81–99.

WHITE, H. (1992) *The Content of the Form: Narrative Discourse and Historical Representation*. Baltimore and London: Johns Hopkins University Press.

WHITEHEAD, D. (1993) 'Cardinal Virtues: The Language of Public Approbation in Democratic Athens', *Class. et Mediaev.* 44: 37–75.

WILL, E. (1962) 'Les Premières années du règne d'Antiochos III (223–219 av. J.-C.)', *REG* 75: 72–129.

WILL, E. (1979) *Histoire politique du monde hellénistique* (2nd edn.), i. Nancy: Université de Nancy II.

——(1982) *Histoire politique du monde hellénistique* (2nd edn.), ii. Nancy: Université de Nancy II.

——(1988) 'Poleis hellénistiques: deux notes', *Echos du Monde Classique/Classical Views* 32, NS 7: 329–52.

WÖRRLE, M. (1975) 'Antiochos I., Achaios der Ältere und die Galater. Eine neue Inschrift in Denizli', *Chiron* 5: 59–87.

——(1977) 'Epigraphische Forschungen zur Geschichte Lykiens I', *Chiron* 7: 43–66.

——(1978) 'Epigraphische Forschungen zur Geschichte Lykiens II. Ptolemaios II. und Telmessos', *Chiron* 8: 201–46.

——(1979) 'Epigraphische Forschungen zur Geschichte Lykiens III. Ein hellenistischer Königsbrief aus Telmessos', *Chiron* 9: 83–111.

——(1988) 'Inschriften von Herakleia am Latmos I: Antiochos III., Zeuxis und Herakleia', *Chiron* 18: 421–76.

WURSTER, W. W. (1974) 'Die Burg von Limyra. Ein Vorbericht', *Arch. Anz.* 89: 259–73.

ZIMMERMANN, M. (1993) 'Bemerkungen zur Rhodischen Vorherrschaft in Lykien (189/8–167 v. Chr.)', *Klio* 75: 110–130.

CONCORDANCE

Crampa 1972 (Labraunda), no. 46: **15**

Gauthier 1989 (Sardeis), no. 1: **1**
Gauthier 1989 (Sardeis), no. 2: **2**
Gauthier 1989 (Sardeis), no. 3: **3**
Gauthier 1989 (Sardeis), nos. 4A–7: **41**

Hermann 1965 (Teos): **17**, **18**, **19**

Malay 1987 (Pamukçu): **4**

Rigsby 1996, no. 163 (Alabanda): **16**

Robert 1964, no. 1 (Sardeis): **40**

Robert and Robert 1954, no. 166 (Apollonia under Salbake): **44**
Robert and Robert 1954, no. 167 (Apollonia under Salbake): **48**

Robert and Robert 1983 (Amyzon), no. 1: **7**
Robert and Robert 1983 (Amyzon), no.11: **8**
Robert and Robert 1983 (Amyzon), no.14: **9**
Robert and Robert 1983 (Amyzon), no. 15: **10**
Robert and Robert 1983 (Amyzon), no. 15 B: **23**
Robert and Robert 1983 (Amyzon), no. 16: **11**
Robert and Robert 1983 (Amyzon), no. 17: **12**
Robert and Robert 1983 (Amyzon), no. 19: **13**
Robert and Robert 1983 (Amyzon), no. 18: **14**
Robert and Robert 1983 (Amyzon), no. 22: **47**

Wörrle 1988 (Herakleia under Latmos): **31**

FD 3, fasc. 4, nos. 162 and 163 (Alabanda): **16**

GIBM 421 (Priene): **32**
GIBM 442 (Iasos): **28**
GIBM 1035 (Amyzon): **5**

I. Iasos 4: **26**
I. Iasos 5: **27**
I. Ilion 37: **34**
I. Mylasa 962 (Kildara): **25**

Inschr. Priene 59: **32**
Inschr. Priene 82: **33**

OGIS 217 (Amyzon): **6**
OGIS 230 (Soloi): **20**
OGIS 234 (Alabanda): **16**
OGIS 235 (Amyzon): **7**
OGIS 237 (Iasos): **28**
OGIS 746 (Xanthos): **22**

RC 36-7 (Doducular/Dodurga): **37**
RC 38 (Amyzon): **5**
RC 39 (Amyzon): **6**
RC 42 (Ilion): **34**
RC 43 (Nysa): **43**

RDGE 34 (Teos): **38**
RDGE 35 (Herakleia under Latmos): **45**
RDGE 36 (Kolophon): **46**

Sardis no. 2: **36**

SEG 1.440 (Kolophon): **46**
SEG 33.1184 (Xanthos): **23**
SEG 33.867 (Kildara): **25**
SEG 37.1010 (Pamukçu): **4**
SEG 37.859 (Herakleia under Latmos): **31**
SEG 39.1283 (Sardeis): **1**
SEG 39.1284 (Sardeis): **2**
SEG 39.1285 (Sardeis): **3**
SEG 39.1286 A- 1289 (Sardeis): **41**
SEG 41.1003 I (Teos): **17**
SEG 41.1003 II (Teos): **18**
SEG 41.1003 III-IV (Teos): **19**
SEG 43.707 (Euromos): **30**
SEG 43.850 (Priene): **32**
SEG 46.1721 (Xanthos): **24**
SEG 46.1519 (Pleura): **49**

TAM 5.1.689 ([Julia] Gordos): **39**
TAM 2.266 (Xanthos): **22**

INDEX OF PRIMARY SOURCES

INSCRIPTIONS

PAPYRI

DOCUMENTS REPRODUCED IN THIS VOLUME

LITERARY SOURCES

GENERAL INDEX